History of Sociological Thought

History of Sociological Thought

Jerzy Szacki

Contributions in Sociology, Number 35

GREENWOOD PRESS
WESTPORT, CONNECTICUT

Library of Congress Cataloging in Publication Data

Szacki, Jerzy.
  History of sociological thought.

  (Contributions in sociology ; no. 35)
  Bibliography: p.
  Includes index.
  1. Sociology—History. 2. Historical
sociology. I. Title.
HM19.S98   301'.09   78-67566
ISBN 0-313-20737-2

Library of Congress Catalog Card Number: 78-67566
ISBN: 0-313-20737-2
ISSN: 0084-9278

First published in 1979

Greenwood Press, Inc.
51 Riverside Avenue, Westport, Connecticut 06880

Printed in the United States of America

10 9 8 7 6 5 4 3 2 1

ACKNOWLEDGMENTS

The following publishers have kindly granted me permission to quote passages from their publications:

George Allen and Unwin Ltd, London, for *Elementary Forms of the Religious Life* by Emile Durkheim; *Understanding Social Life: The Method Called Verstehen* by William Outhwaite; and *Politics and Vision* by Sheldon S. Wolin.

Cassel Ltd, London, for *New Directions in Sociological Theory* by Paul Filmer, Michael Phillipson, David Silverman and David Walsh.

Dover Publications, Inc., New York, for *The Mind and Society: A Treatise on General Sociology* by Vilfredo Pareto.

Edinburgh University Press, for permission to reproduce extracts from the edition of Adam Ferguson's *Essay on the History of Civil Society,* edited by Duncan Forbes. This Edinburgh volume is available in paperback, 1978.

Harcourt Brace Jovanovich, Inc., New York, for *Ideology and Utopia: An Introduction to the Sociology of Knowledge* by Karl Mannheim.

George G. Harrap & Company Ltd, London, for *A History of Political Theory* by George H. Sabine.

Michael Joseph Ltd, London, for *Karl Marx: Economy, Class and Social Revolution* edited by Z. A. Jordan.

Lawrence & Wishart Ltd, London, for *The Modern Prince and Other Writings* by Antonio Gramsci, 1957.

Little, Brown and Company, Publishers, Boston, for *Politics and Vision* by Sheldon W. Wolin. © 1960 Little, Brown and Company, Inc.

Macmillan Publishing Co., Inc., New York, for *The Elementary Forms of the Religious Life* by Emile Durkheim; *Social Anthropology* by E. E. Evans-Pritchard; *The Sociology of Georg Simmel* translated and edited by Kurt H. Wolff; Emile Durkheim's *The Rules of Sociological Method* translated by Sarah A. Solovay and John H. Mueller, edited by George E. G. Catlin; Max Weber's *The Methodology of the Social Sciences* translated and edited by Edward A. Shils and Henry A. Finch.

Oxford University Press, New York, for *The Sociological Imagination* by C. Wright Mills.

Ohio State University Press, Columbus, Ohio, for *Georg Simmel, 1858-1918: A Collection of Essays, with Translations and a Bibliography,* edited by Kurt H. Wolff.

Pitman Publishing Limited, London, for *Karl Marx: Selected Writings in Sociology and Social Philosophy* edited by T. B. Bottomore and M. Rubel.

Prentice-Hall, Inc., Englewood Cliffs, N.J., for *Ideology and the Development of Sociological Theory* by Irving M. Zeitlin.

Princeton University Press, Princeton, N.J., for *Dilthey: Philosopher of the Human Studies* by Rudolf A. Makkreel. (Copyright © 1975 by Princeton University Press): pp. 56, 67, and 250. Reprinted by permission of Princeton University Press.

Routledge & Kegan Paul Ltd, London, for *Social Anthropology* by E. E. Evans-Pritchard; and *Ideology and Utopia* by Karl Mannheim.

The University of Chicago Press, Chicago, for *Ferdinand Toennies on Sociology: Pure, Applied and Empirical,* edited by Werner J. Cahnman and Rudolf Heberle, Copyright 1971; and *Georg Simmel on Individuality and Social Forms* edited by Donald N. Levine, copyright 1971.

University of Toronto Press, Toronto, and Routledge and Kegan Paul Ltd, London, for *Collected Works of John Stuart Mill* edited by J. M. Robson.

Every reasonable effort has been made to trace the owners of copyright materials in this book, but in some instances this has proven impossible. The publishers will be glad to receive information leading to more complete acknowledgments in subsequent printings of the book, and in the meantime extend their apologies for any omissions.

CONTENTS

Contents

PREFACE

This book had its origin in my many years of lecturing to students at the University of Warsaw on the history of sociology, which came to fascinate me more and more with each year. My other specialization was the history of ideas. These interests led me to write an extensive handbook, one that goes beyond the needs of undergraduate students.

My studies in 1972-1973 at the University of Minnesota on an American Council of Learned Societies fellowship and in 1976 at All Souls, Oxford, England, have contributed greatly to the final shape of this book.

I should like to express my gratitude to my wife, Professor Barbara Szacka, Professor Olgierd A. Wojtasiewicz, Doktor Joanna Kurczewska, and all other persons who have helped me in preparing this book.

INTRODUCTION

THE USES OF THE HISTORY OF SOCIOLOGY

Unlike philosophers, sociologists do not pay much attention to the history of their discipline. The more certain they feel about the scientific status of sociology, the less importance they attach to the knowledge of "prescientific" doctrines and practices. Even if they reach for their predecessors' works, they judge them just as they judge their colleagues' works: They are interested in the truth or falsehood of the statements therein and not in the context in which those statements were formulated. What use can a sociologist make of a more comprehensive knowledge of the history of sociology if he is not a historian as well? What are the consequences of the fact that the views of Plato, Aristotle, Montesquieu, Hume, Comte, or Marx were such and such and were formed under such and such circumstances?

By writing this book, and by writing it for sociologists, I have taken a definite stand in the controversy over sociology's use of the history of sociology. My position is based on the following considerations.

First, as Jensen wrote, "ideas about the social process are themselves a part of the social process, and unless these ideas are treated sociologically, an important phase of human culture falls outside the field of sociological analysis."[1] Acquiring the knowledge of the social knowledge of a society means simultaneously acquiring the knowledge of that society itself.

Second, the peculiarities of the accumulation of knowledge in the social sciences account for the fact that, as S. Ossowski wrote,

sociological observations made by ancient historians, such as Thucydides, Polybius, and Tacitus, and in Aristotle's *Politics* and ibn-Khaldun's *Prolegomena* and reflections of Machiavelli, Montaigne, Hobbes, and Helvetius seem much less outdated to the present-day reader interested in social problems than their contemporaneous works on natural sciences seem to the present-day natural scientist. Reading sociological studies written centuries ago, not to mention those dating from the nineteenth

century, can be instructive in various ways (not only as the study of the documents
of the period) and even inspiring for the present-day sociologist. . . . The history
of the social sciences is the history of specific knowledge and, at the same time,
the history of social ideas; and "social ideas," if we disregard the technical means
of putting them into effect and the scientific apparatus for substantiating them, are
not ordered in time by the criterion of progress, just as art, literature, and religious
mysticism are not.[2]

The history of social thought provides examples of the permanence of
certain ideas, viewpoints, and systems of values that can be found in today's
sociology, though perhaps worded differently. We are far from believing
that *nihil novi sub sole*, but even the most superficial observations reveal
common motifs and remind us that probably every modern approach has
roots that reach far into the past. In the natural sciences scholars usually
refer to their immediate predecessors, but in the social sciences this practice
is far from the rule. Such being the case, the knowledge of the history of a
discipline is not an extravagance for the social scientist, but a matter of elementary theoretical training: Even if he does not draw inspiration from the
past, history reveals issues that have remained of topical interest, although
it does not, of course, provide any ready-made solutions.

This seems to be true for the "classics" in general. A writer does not read
books by Balzac, Dostoyevsky, and Proust to learn how to write about the
same things and in the same way that they did. He simply cannot afford not
to read them, because he works in the cultural area in which literary ideas
are positively or negatively associated with those authors. The sociologist's
position is analogous: Whatever he says, he inevitably remains within the
sphere of a certain heritage. If he knows nothing about it, he is just ignorant;
he discovers what was discovered long ago, he opposes opinions that have
never been voiced, and he fails to notice those problems that most strongly
attract the researcher's attention and hence, in all probability, are of special
significance in social life.

Third, studying the history of social thought may train the sociologist to
comprehend viewpoints that differ from his own. Ossowski wrote: "Works
of the past preserve for us the ways in which social facts were viewed by
their contemporaries, thus widening the horizon of the student of social
phenomena—not only his historical horizon (the viewpoint of milieus in
past epochs), but his sociological horizon as well (the viewpoint of *different*
milieus)."[3] In this respect the history of social thought seems to play a role
analogous to that of contacts with representatives of other contemporary
trends; it develops enlightened skepticism in the researcher and undermines
the belief, deeply rooted in both everyday thinking and science, that one's
own standpoint is *the* natural one and that its rejection testifies to the
mental incompetence of those who reject it. The sociologist should beware
of such prejudices because they disqualify him as a student of various social

milieus and reduce his social role to that of perpetuating the mental habits of a single milieu. This does not mean that he should be denied the right to have an opinion of his own and to defend it as correct, but such an opinion must result from a comparison of various opinions and a conscious choice of one's standpoint. The history of social thought can help the sociologist in making such a choice.

THREE APPROACHES TO THE HISTORY OF SOCIOLOGY

Obviously, I assign an important educational function to the history of this discipline. Whether or not that function is performed well depends on how the history of sociology is pursued and how the comprehensive set of data (which sometimes seems to be merely a collection of random statements) is ordered. The problem is, then, how to arrange the subject matter of the discipline that tells us how social life was seen in the past. There are apparently three principal approaches.

First, we can trace the development of the cognitive activity labeled by the name of the discipline that we study. Thus, for instance, the historian of philosophy will describe the work of those who styled themselves philosophers over the centuries, even though their interests were sometimes directed to subjects that are no longer the concern of philosophers and are left to physicists, biologists, and representatives of other specialized disciplines. The historian of sociology who adopts this posture would have to begin with Comte and then describe what was done by various "sociologists" (that is, by those thinkers who either designated themselves or were commonly designated "sociologists") without worrying too much that at least some of their works are outside the sphere of sociology today or that thinkers who did not avail themselves of this label quite often (both before and after Comte) took up problems whose consideration was indispensable to the evolution of sociology.

Of course, this approach would not be practical, because it would yield a history of sociology without Marx, Tocqueville, Freud, and dozens of other authors who contributed more to the development of the knowledge of society than did many of their contemporary professional sociologists. The development of that knowledge is too closely connected with practical social activity, on the one hand, and with the various nonsociological disciplines (such as philosophy, history, political economy, psychology, anthropology, geography, and even biology and mathematics), on the other, to allow us to limit consistently the history of sociology to "sociologists" alone. However, such facts as the emergence of the name of that discipline, the changes in its scope, the tentative delineation of its subject matter, its transformation into a distinct academic discipline, the rise of various bodies concerned with sociology, and its increasing popularity are not without significance.[4]

Second, the historian of sociology can study the development of sociological problems—that is, the problems on which present-day sociology
focuses—without bothering about those who took them up. From this point
of view, the sociologists would not be privileged in any way. One can even
imagine a history of sociology in which Auguste Comte would be treated
marginally, because many scholars do not consider him to have been the
real founder of "the science of society," although, of course, no one
denies his authorship of that barbarous neologism, the word *sociology*,
in the 1830s.

So the history of sociology can concern itself with all those thinkers
who took up sociological problems, even if they considered themselves to
be philosophers, politicians, psychologists, or representatives of another
discipline. Yet this replacement of formal criteria by substantial ones does
not make our task easier, primarily because of the notorious divergence of
opinions on what sociological problems really are. Various schools hold
different opinions on the issue, and hence the subject matter of the history
of sociology is the center of endless controversy over who is to be treated as
a "sociologist." Usually this controversy changes imperceptibly into a
discussion of the tasks of that discipline, which makes it unresolvable for
the present (and probably also for the near future). If a person thinks that
sociology began with Montesquieu rather than Aristotle, or with Durkheim
rather than Saint-Simon, he usually does so not because he is unfamiliar
with the works of Aristotle or Saint-Simon or fails to understand them
correctly, but because Montesquieu's or Durkheim's statements and/or
methods seem to come much closer to what he himself considers to be
sociology.

Modern sociology is divided into numerous schools and trends whose
representatives differ from one another not only in their opinions on the
same issues, but also in the issues on which they have opinions. "Sociology,"
R. Aron notes, "seems to be marked by the incessant quest for itself."[5]
For the time being, we may disregard the reason for this state of affairs:
Is it to be ascribed to the relatively young age of sociology as a conscious
discipline, or was Max Weber right in saying that all sciences of culture are
doomed to eternal youth?[6] The fact is that there is no sociology uniform
enough as a science to escape fundamental differences of opinion on its
attainments to date. To use T. S. Kuhn's terminology, one can say that
sociology still is not a "normal science."[7]

If such is the case, the historian of sociology cannot proceed as, for
instance, the historian of mathematics does; the latter starts with the body
of mathematics as it is in his day and age and then moves backward to
the period when it was beginning to take shape. If backward movement
is possible at all in the history of sociology, then it must take place within
the various schools, thus resulting in establishing their respective genealogies.
It is true that nearly all sociological schools claim certain authors to have

been their ancestors. But the list of such unquestionable classics is not a long one, and every school refers to them because of different issues and interprets their works differently.

Therefore, defining the scope of the history of sociology by reference to present-day sociological issues involves a certain risk, especially if one does not realize that one's point of departure is, in fact, not modern sociology in general, but merely a certain trend within that discipline. The danger lies either in having one's historical horizon limited to one's own intellectual patrons or in eclectically bringing together thinkers who have been promoted to the rank of the classics by different schools and on the strength of different criteria. Many years ago, Florian Znaniecki commented that sociology has not yet imposed on its workers a single common definition of its own subject matter, but either consists of general systems based on assumptions made a priori or passively assimilates everything contributed by anyone on any subject whatever; his remark remains valid to this day.[8]

Third, the historian of sociology can focus his attention on the development of the scientific method of investigating social facts. If he adopts that viewpoint, then he will be interested not in all statements on sociological issues, but only on those which comply with his standards of a science or, at least, seem to have anticipated them. There is no doubt that reflection on social facts is much older than the science of such facts. As Emile Durkheim wrote, "Men already had ideas on law, morality, the family, the state, and society itself before the advent of social science, for these ideas were necessary conditions of his life."[9]

We can single out a certain area of social science (whose size depends on the adopted criteria of what is scientific) located within the sphere of social thought, which is interpreted broadly as the totality of statements on sociological issues. We shall then focus attention not on specified problems, but on the ways in which they were posed and solved. As Howard E. Jensen says,

Brilliant intuitions, significant insights, and unsurpassed capacity for sustained reasoning are indeed as universal as mankind and older than history. But they lack the precise formulation which admits of their being brought to the test of empirical fact. They are unsupported by the techniques of documentation, controlled observation, and experimentation that permit the accurate prediction and dependable control of phenomena on which rest both the "truth value" of pure science and the "utility value" of its applications in practice. What is needed is a realistic appreciation of the way in which these generic insights into interpersonal and collective behavior have been winnowed out, extended, and given increasing precision by the work of successive generations who improved upon their predecessors in objective methods of verification so gradually that the most competent of contemporary scholars differ widely in their judgements even as to the century in which social science must be acknowledged to have emerged from the womb of social thought.[10]

Delineating the scope of the history of sociology, as discussed now, is not easy in practice, either. The first serious difficulty is analogous to the difficulty of identifying sociological problems. The heterogeneity of contemporary sociology is revealed no less clearly when we define the requirements of the scientific method than when we define the subject matter of that discipline. The various sociological schools blame one another for being nonscientific; inevitably, this influences their appraisal of their own predecessors and those of the other schools. We must, therefore, choose between limiting the history of sociology to the advocates of our own idea of social science and including in it all of those thinkers who considered themselves advocates of science.

The other difficulty is due to the fact that the development of the scientific method in sociology can rarely be treated independently of extrasociological issues, namely, those in the sphere of philosophy, psychology, and so on. If we confined ourselves to tracing the emergence of scientific methods in sociology, the history of that discipline would be quite incomprehensible. The various advances did not necessarily result from one another, but often took place independently and were integrated into the science of society only ex post facto, with varying degrees of success. I intentionally abstain from all skeptical remarks about that integrated social science, because the assessment of its condition today, whatever that might be, is of little significance for the problem now under consideration. Even if there is a social science, the historian of sociology must reckon with the fact that it exists only from the point of view of certain schools and does not exist as an unquestionable social fact.

I have, thus, singled out three possible scopes of the history of sociology. By freely paraphrasing what Joseph A. Schumpeter has said on the history of political economy, we may label them, respectively, the history of *sociology*, the history of *sociological thought*, and the history of *sociological analysis*.[11] It is worthwhile to recognize the differences among those scopes, for otherwise we can easily engage in pointless controversy over the beginning of the history of sociology. Opinions on the issue may differ greatly. A person may claim that sociology existed all the time, because some sociological problems have been taken up in all epochs. However, one might claim equally well that it still does not exist, because it does not have scientific methods that are as reliable as those used in physics, chemistry, or biology.

Checking the contents of the available handbooks on the history of sociology indicates how many different standpoints are possible. There are authors who date the origins of sociology in antiquity, but there are others (probably much more numerous) who place its origin as late as the twentieth century. Between these two extremes are a gamut of intermediate opinions, the most popular being that which locates the birth of sociology in the nineteenth century. In this book one may find reasonable arguments in favor of each possible standpoint. At this point I want simply to stress that the problem of sociology's origin is in fact undecidable, because every conceivable solution ultimately depends on how sociology is defined.

Since our attention is focused on the history of sociological thought, it seems most reasonable to adopt a broad definition. Such a definition enables us to watch the changes in the interest in social life throughout centuries and also to notice the revolutions that have marked the knowledge of society.

The first revolution consisted of singling out the human order from the order of nature, which was at first experienced in its totality; this fact explains our interest in the work of ancient Greek thinkers. The second great revolution was marked by a clear distinction between society and the state; hence, the need to consider social thought in modern times, especially in the seventeenth and eighteenth centuries. The third revolution manifested itself by making society a subject matter of systematic reflection and also by formulating the concept of the science of society as a science that discovers laws. It took place only under full-fledged capitalism.[12] This is why there are grounds for arguing that sociology originated in the nineteenth century. Finally, the fourth revolution, which seems far from being completed, is making that reflection on society scientific—that is, imposing formal rigors on it, subjecting it to strict control of empirical data, and purifying it of relics of religious thinking and philosophical speculations.

This is merely a rough sketch, and hence it would be easy to find gaps and obscurities in it. But here our concern is merely the general direction in which investigations are to be made. In most general terms, we shall be interested above all in the emergence of those problems which are considered sociological today, in their most typical and still valid solutions, in the development of the requirements for their being treated from the scientific point of view, and in the gradual satisfaction of such requirements.

I shall have relatively less to say about compliance with the requirements of research, and I shall not try to cover all of the issues, because for the last fifty years or so sociological research has been many-directional and scattered over various fields. It could hardly be covered by any single review. Moreover, the relationship between research and theories propounded during a period of time is far from self-evident, so I would have to begin with an immense analytical work to bring out those theoretical assumptions which, implicitly or explicitly, underlie various research projects. This book is, by design, concerned with the development of sociological thought and not with specialized branches of sociology, whose number has been growing in the twentieth century.

The scope of the history of sociology that I have outlined is still extremely broad. Reflecting on the genealogy of present-day sociology, Stanislaw

Ossowski wrote that "we can single out at least six separate spheres of interest that took up problems which we class as sociological."[13] The spheres of interest that he singled out were (1) the science of the state and the art of government; (2) "historiography, which made historians engage in the philosophy of history or in generalizations based on historical data"; (3) the science of economy; (4) "the science of alien peoples"; (5) the science of man, that is, physiology and psychology; (6) "sociology," or the science that already availed itself of that name. The list is, of course, incomplete, a fact that Ossowski himself recognized. We should add to it, first of all, philosophy, which from antiquity to our times has taken up numerous issues that today fall into the field of sociology and social psychology; also theology or, more broadly, religious thought, because we can find in it many sociological statements; theoretical arguments in favor of social reforms, which were often linked with "new science," especially in the nineteenth century (Saint-Simon, Owen, and others); and ideologies of social movements, which usually include certain sociological ideas. The list could be continued: the whole of this book consists of extensions of, and additions to, that register of problems. Here the list is drawn mainly to help the reader realize the wealth of data on which a complete and source-based history of sociology would have to be founded.

The task assigned to this book is a very modest one: It has been conceived as a popular handbook on sociology, as a subject included in university curricula and as a discipline arousing a growing curiosity among the non-academic reading public. I have availed myself amply of studies written by other authors, and only in some chapters have I been able to refer to results of my own research. This is not a complete history of sociology in any sense of the term. Many thinkers have been totally disregarded, and many others have been treated summarily or considered only from the point of view of a certain portion of their work. If we are concerned here with, say, Aristotle, Bodin, Hume, Smith, Hegel, Freud, and Lukács, we cannot be expected to provide exhaustive information about them, because we read their works from a definite point of view, one which no philosopher, jurist, economist, literary historian, psychologist, nor representative of any other discipline will find satisfactory if he is not interested in sociology. Equally one-sided pictures will be given of those thinkers who were active (like Simmel) in other fields, not connected with sociology. In brief, this is a book for sociologists about sociologists and not a universal history of intellectual activity, nor a history of the social sciences in general, nor a fortiori an encyclopedia of the history of ideas.

NOTES

1. Howard E. Jensen, "Developments in Analysis of Social Thought," in Howard Becker and Alvin Boskoff, eds., *Modern Sociological Theory in Continuity and Change* (New York: Dryden Press, 1957), p. 46.

2. Stanislaw Ossowski, *O osobliwościach nauk spolecznych*, in Dziela (Warsaw: PWN, 1967), 4:298, 300.

3. Ibid., p. 299.

4. See Anthony Oberschall, ed., *The Establishment of Empirical Sociology: Studies in Continuity, Discontinuity, and Institutionalization* (New York: Harper and Row, 1972); Terry Nichols Clark, *Prophets and Patrons: The French University and the Emergence of the Social Sciences* (Cambridge, Mass.: Harvard University Press, 1973); Edward Shils, "Tradition, Ecology, and Institution in the History of Sociology," *Daedalus* (Fall 1970), pp. 760-825.

5. Raymond Aron, *Dix-huit leçons sur la société industrielle* (Paris: Gallimard, 1962), p. 13.

6. Max Weber, *The Methodology of the Social Sciences* (New York: Free Press, 1949), p. 104.

7. "In this essay, 'normal science' means research firmly based upon one or more past scientific achievements, achievements that some particular scientific community acknowledges for a time as supplying the foundation for its further practice" (Thomas S. Kuhn, *The Structure of Scientific Revolutions*, 2d ed., enlarged [Chicago: University of Chicago Press, 1970], p. 10).

8. Florian Znaniecki, *Wstep do socjologii* (Poznan: Poznańskie Towarzystwo Przyjaciól Nauk, 1922), p. 207.

9. Emile Durkheim, *The Rules of Sociological Method* (Glencoe, Ill.: Free Press, 1950), p. 17.

10. Jensen, "Developments in Analysis," p. 45.

11. Joseph A. Schumpeter, *History of Economic Analysis* (London: Allen and Unwin, 1954), pp. 38-43.

12. Georg Lukács, *History and Class Consciousness: Studies in Marxist Dialectics* (Cambridge, Mass.: MIT Press, 1971), p. 19.

13. Ossowski, *O osobliwościach*, 4:129-31.

History of Sociological Thought

1

FROM THE CITY-STATE TO MODERN CIVIL SOCIETY

THE SOURCES OF SOCIAL THEORY

There is no doubt that reflection about social life is as old as reflection in general. All the ancient civilizations, whose spirit we are now in a position to reconstruct, have left fairly clear traces of their specifically "sociological" ideas. But the possibility of our performing such reconstruction is limited by the fact that we know very little about those civilizations. The knowledge that an average sociologist has of preliterate societies is not very comprehensive, even though those societies, discovered by travelers and missionaries, have been studied by social anthropologists. Those societies, too, have had and still have a specific "sociology," if by this term, which is cautiously placed between quotation marks, we mean not a specialized sphere of reflection on the world, but any set of views of society.

Historians of social thought did not often penetrate areas so remote from our own civilization and instead focused their attention on the mental tradition that originated in the Greek *polis*. This is easy to understand. The student of other cultures and/or civilizations faces exceptionally great difficulties. If he lacks the special training required in a given case, he always runs the risk of dismissing or ignoring ideas expressed in a manner to which he is not accustomed or, instead, he may succumb to a naive fascination with superficial similarities or analogies. A history of ideas that would cover the whole of mankind, and not only that part which we are inclined to identify with one or another particular viewpoint, is still in the sphere of Utopia.

But if historians of social thought so rarely yield to the temptations of that Utopia—a truly universal history of ideas—they are not necessarily guided by the fear of the difficulties described or by the belief that the difficulties are unsurmountable. Many historians think that it was only in our culture area that the "scientific" way of thinking was developed.

Like all generalizations, this opinion may give rise to widespread objections. Experts in other culture areas—especially China—can offer examples that refute that opinion to some extent. In any field, after all, it is difficult to draw the demarcation line in the past from which rational thinking begins; and hence it is not our intention to make here any categorical and excessively generalized statements. It will suffice if we try to explain, first, why we are inclined to assign to the Greeks a privileged position in the history of social thought and, second, why so many present-day sociologists see Plato or Aristotle as the forerunners or founders of sociological theory.[1] The criteria, it is true, are not always clearly formulated, and among historians of social thought there is probably no complete agreement on the issue. Three points deserve attention.

First, Greek social thought was fairly systematized, and problems of social order were clearly spelled out in it.

Second, there occurred a transition from naive monism to critical dualism. This point, first formulated by Karl R. Popper, requires more comprehensive comment. In Popper's opinion, "the beginning of social science goes back at least to the generation of Protagoras, the first of the great thinkers who called themselves 'Sophists.' It is marked by the realization of the need to distinguish between two different elements in man's environment—his natural environment and his social environment." One of the characteristics of the early views of social life, he continues, was the faith—which he terms "naive monism"—that society "lives in a charmed circle of unchanging taboos, of laws and customs which are felt to be as inevitable as the rising of the sun, or the cycle of the seasons, or similar obvious regularities of nature." Critical dualism means "conscious differentiation between the man-enforced normative laws, based on decisions or conventions, and the natural regularities which are beyond his power."[2]

And third, the Greeks discovered the problems of the autonomy of individual and of his participation and place in society. As Z. Barbu says, "The Greeks were the first to build up a type of civilization which enabled man to become aware of himself as an individual. In Greece, the history of the ancient world passed from a pre-individualistic to an individualistic stage."[3] And it would be difficult to disagree with E. Barker when he claims that "it is the precedent condition of all political thought that the antithesis of the individual and the state should be realized."[4] Man posed the question about his place in society only when it had ceased to be determined once and for all by self-evident tradition.

If we agree on the point that the Greeks were the first to make a breakthrough in those three respects, we have to ask why they were the ones to initiate that memorable "scientific revolution," which opened the prehistory of social science by singling the social order out of the order of the world conceived as a whole and by making relationships among human beings a problem to be solved by human beings themselves, without the assistance of gods and tradition.

At the time when the theory of society was born, Greece was, like Western Europe at the time when sociology was born, in a state of a permanent social *crisis*; this led to a decomposition of the age-old ways of life, the emergence of new institutions, and an intensification of social unrest and antagonisms. Some authors speak about the transition from a closed to an open society, while others mention the transition from a sacred to a secular society. Whichever point of view we adopt, we must take into account the intensifying processes of individualization, cross-cultural contacts, social mobility, social differentiation, and instability of beliefs and political systems. Those who watched these processes had to develop an entirely new world outlook, an integral part of which would be a view of society that would consider the realities of this epoch of crisis.

Greek society of that time was changing too rapidly and taking on so many forms (one need only recall the innumerable political upheavals and political systems of the Greek city-states) to appear to its watchers as part of a constant and uniform order of nature. *Nature* came to be distinguished from *convention*. In the extant fragment of a treatise, *On Truth*, by the Sophist Antiphon, we read:

Justice in the ordinary view consists in not transgressing or, rather, in not being known to transgress any of the legal rules of the State in which one lives as a citizen. . . . the rules of Nature are inevitable and innate; . . . the rules of the laws are created by covenant and not produced by nature, while the rules of nature are exactly the reverse.[5]

Whether or not those new attitudes were very common in Greece at that time is not important here. It is known that in many circles they were received reluctantly and disapprovingly. The essential point is that critical dualism did take root in Greek thought and did bring about a new intellectual climate, with which even thinkers like Plato, who tended to defend the traditional values, had to reckon. Social order became a problem that could not be dismissed merely by a return to naive monism, because this perspective did not correspond to the type of society that took shape in Athens and in other city-states affected by the disintegration of the old conditions. Plato has been termed a "conservative" by many historians because he wrote about the "disease" of his contemporaneous Athenian state and opposed to it the Utopia that Marx labeled "the Athenian idealization of the Egyptian system of castes."[6] The point is, however, that Platonian Utopia, even if it owed much to conservative longings, was a result of the acceptance of politics as an issue of human *ability*, not received as a gift of the ancestors, but acquired through reasoning and observation. Despite the differences among them, all philosophers in classical Greece set themselves to looking for the secrets of that ability and thus laid the foundation of a new kind of social knowledge.

PLATO

Plato (ca. 427-347 B.C.), the great idealistic philosopher, is the author to whom many historians ascribe a particularly vast "sociological" perspective. Popper says that "in an attempt to understand and to interpret the changing social world as he experienced it, Plato was led to develop a systematic historicist sociology in great detail."[7] As a historian of political science, Wolin makes a similar comment and claims that people have learned from Plato to treat "political society" as a functioning system: "Although Plato may have exaggerated the possibilities of a society's achieving systematic unity, the greatness of his achievement was to point out that in order to think in a truly political way, one had to consider society as a systematic whole."[8]

These formulations are sufficient to make the reader realize that Plato's "sociology" was in some respects in opposition to Sophist thought: The author of *Republic*, *Politicus*, and *Laws* was concerned not with the individual freed from the traditional bonds, but with the durable community whose foundations are more solid than the will of the individuals and whose goal is higher than that of making individuals happy:

"You have forgotten again, my friend," I said, "that it is not the law's concern that any one class in a state should live surpassingly well. Rather it contrives a good life for the whole state, harmonizing the citizens by persuasion and compulsion, and making them share with one another the advantage which each class can contribute to the community."[9]

The state is not a festival, intended to ensure a feeling of well-being to every participant, but a permanent organization that as a whole, has definite needs and a definite inner structure. The best state is that which is "nearest the condition of a single individual. . . . For consider, when any one of us hurts his finger, the whole fellowship of body and soul which is bound into a single organization, namely, that of the ruling power within it, feels the hurt, and is all in pain at once, whole and hurt part together."[10]

Such is, according to Plato, a "sound" state, which *Republic* attempted to describe. Hostile toward the Athenian democracy and critical of his own epoch, Plato did not in the least think that all existing states were like that. The state "that is nearest the condition of a single individual" is Utopia. It would even be deceptive to say that the subject is a political program. Rather, Utopia was the pattern by which actual conditions were to be assessed, those actual conditions being, in Plato's opinion, a result of decadence and the distance between the world of things and the world of ideas. Only in the latter is perfection possible. Real states are states that are more or less "diseased"; these entities are called states, but do not conform with the idea of a state. However remote from reality that pattern may seem, Plato's works abound in realistic observations and include elements of a remarkable theory of society. The point is merely that his manner of exposition varies from our own customs. As attractive as they are from the literary point of view, Plato's writings require a lot of interpreting from the sociologist's perspective.

When looking for the Platonic theory of society, we have to pay attention to at least three kinds of statements:
1. Statements directly concerned with what society is, what its present condition is, what changes it is undergoing, and so on;
2. Statements supporting definite practical solutions, which require that certain opinions about society be assumed;
3. Statements on the principles of organization of the ideal state; these statements lack detailed explanations, but enable us to guess what theoretical assumptions were tacitly adopted by Plato.

If we take all these into consideration, then it turns out that Plato had a more developed theoretical consciousness than do many present-day sociologists.

Without undertaking here the reconstruction of Plato's sociology, we shall, however, review the issues with which he was concerned when reflecting on the state (society). Even a cursory listing of these issues will show that philosopher's sociological perspicacy. In each case his opinions on what the state should be like are intertwined with diagnoses.

Differentiation of Wealth Within Society. Plato attached great significance to increasing social inequalities and saw in them one of the sources of the decomposition and disease of the state. About existing states, he wrote that

each of them, as the saying runs, is no city, but cities upon cities; two at the least, each other's enemies, the city of the poor and the city of the rich; and in either of these is a vast number of cities which you will be entirely wrong to treat as one.[11]

In the states divided in that manner the interest of parts takes precedence over that of the whole, and the legislator's task is to put an end to such a division. Hence the famous Platonic "communism," which to some extent assumed the abolition of private property and of the family as well, because the latter is another cause of the interests of the community having to yield to the interests of small groups.

Individualization. Plato was alarmed by the fact that increasing individualization threatened the social order, and in his model of the ideal state he
provided for numerous measures that would ensure the citizens' conformity,
both in the sphere of their behavior in public and in that of their thoughts
and feelings. Plato's reflections on this subject are of particular interest
because they prove that his social philosophy included—implicitly, at least
—the belief that every sphere of social life, insignificant as it may seem, is
functional in relation to the entire social system. For this reason he provided
for a detailed supervision of all spheres of individual life in his ideal state,
denying individuals the right to any extravagance, since all extravagances
are a potential danger to the fixed principles of social order.

Division of Labor and Specialization. An important component of
Plato's conception of the state was the belief that all "must be set each to
the task for which nature has fitted him, one man one task, that so each
citizen doing his own particular work may become one man and not many,
and thus the whole city may grow to be not many cities, but one."[12] This
conviction led Plato to singling out, in his ideal state, something like orders
—namely, the sages, the warriors, and the common people (these, however,
were not hereditary). In *Republic* this solution was given extensive justification, using the argument that no human being is self-sufficient and, hence,
the coexistence of human beings must be based on mutual exchanges of
services.

Size of the State. Plato attached much importance to the fact that "the
city be neither small nor of illusory greatness, but of sufficient size and
unity."[13] He even fixed the optimum number of the population at 5,040.
This proves that Plato's sociological imagination was confined to the
Greek *polis*, but, on the other hand, his idea opened the long discussion
of the relationship between the size of a state and its organization. Plato
saw an excessive territorial expansion of the state to pose a particular threat
to its unity.

Location of the State. In *Laws*, Plato took up the problem of the effect
of the geographical location of the state on the condition and morals of
society. "The sea is pleasant enough as a daily companion, but has indeed
also a bitter and brackish quality, filling the streets with merchants and
shopkeepers, and begetting in the souls of men uncertain and unfaithful
ways—making the state unfriendly and unfaithful both to her own citizens,
and also to other nations."[14]

Thus, Plato's views compose, it seems, a coherent whole and confirm
Wolin's opinion that the philosopher treated society as a functioning *system*.
His ideal of the state is that "which most approaches to the condition of the

individual" and, hence, constitutes a kind of organism. In his analysis Plato is also concerned with factors that enhance or impair organic unity. He was most interested in social facts insofar as they had definite consequences for the integration or disintegration of society. And he was concerned above all with discovering conditions that are conducive to social integration and equilibrium.[15]

ARISTOTLE

Aristotle of Stagira (384-322 B.C.) was the other great social theorist in classical Greece. As a philosopher he equaled Plato in influence, and, not without reason, he was believed to have been the most encyclopedic thinker in antiquity. He created a comprehensive system that was to play an important role among philosophers over a dozen centuries after his death. We shall be concerned here, of course, not with Aristotle's philosophy in general (its exposition can be found in every textbook on the history of philosophy), but only with his social philosophy.

Aristotle was a disciple of Plato, and his attitude toward the relationship between the individual and society was anti-individualistic, too. In *Politics* he wrote that "neither must we suppose that any one of the citizens belongs to himself, for they all belong to the state, and are each of them a part of the state, and the care of each part is inseparable from the care of the whole."[16] Like Plato, he strove to ensure equilibrium of the *polis* and saw the processes of social disintegration no less clearly. Yet, the remedies he suggested for the treatment of the diseased city-state differed from the Platonic ones. He also differed from Plato in his research method and his theory of the social whole.

For Aristotle, it was beyond doubt that "the form of government is best in which every man, whoever he is, can act best and live happily."[17] Unlike Plato, he claimed that "the nature of a state is to be a plurality, and in tending to greater unity, from being a state, it becomes a family and from being a family, an individual."[18] In *Politics* we find a fairly detailed criticism of the Platonic Utopia that was made from the position of pluralism.

The difference in method was certainly no less important: Plato was, above all, a visionary; Aristotle, a researcher whose attitude toward social facts resembles his attitude toward natural phenomena, which he also studied with an accuracy unrivaled for centuries. That attitude pervades his immense work on the political systems of the various Greek states, of which only *The Constitution of Athens* has been preserved. There is no doubt that Aristotle, too, looked for a recipe for the perfect system, but he realized that "we should consider not only what form of government is best, but also what is possible and what is easily attainable by all."[19] In *Nicomachean Ethics* we read about sciences that "all of these, though they aim at some good and seek to supply the deficiency of it, leave on one side the knowledge of *the* good."[20] P. Janet wrote in this regard that, as compared to Plato, Aristotle radically changed the relationship between morals and politics and made the latter *la science suprême, la science maîtresse, architectonique.*[21] Thus, even if Plato's social theory was more penetrating and coherent, it yielded precedence to the Aristotelian in the wealth of the data used and in the precision of analysis. Aristotle was a philosopher, but an empirically minded scientist as well. Of course, it is not our intention to show him as a student of society in the present-day sense of the term nor, *a fortiori*, to claim that his social theory was merely a generalization from accumulated data. Such a theory does not happen to exist at all, and Aristotle himself did not treat his "sociological" theory as something independent of his philosophical system and the values that he accepted.

Aristotle's sociological heritage is enormous, so we shall be concerned only with some of the main ideas.

Man as a Social Being. Probably the most famous of all Aristotle's statements appears in Book 1 of *Politics:* "man is by nature a political animal."[22] Similar formulations are to be found in *Nicomachean Ethics:* "Man is a political creature and one whose nature is to live with others" and "man is born for citizenship."[23]

In many translations of Aristotle's works the adjectives *political, social,* and *state* and their equivalents in other languages are used as alternatives. If we are to understand properly both Aristotle and other ancient thinkers, we have to bear in mind that in every case the original employed one and the same Greek word, *politikon,* which probably has no exact equivalent in any modern language. A. F. Łosev, when commenting on the title of Plato's dialogue *Politicus* ("The Statesman"), points to the fact that the meaning of that term is extremely complex, because *polis* is both a city and a state, and also the combination of the two, and above all "the social and socio-political life, organized into a single whole. . . . In other words, the Greek *polis* is to be interpreted as the least *historical unit* that comprehends all that which belongs to social culture in its entirety."[24] Thus, to be "a political animal" means to be a member of a human community of a definite kind, the only one that was known in classical Greece.

When interpreted in this way, the Aristotelian thesis may seem trivial and deserving of attention only as the refutation of the fiction, found in some Sophists' works, of man freed from the "artificial" bonds of social conventions. Furthermore, when isolated, Aristotelian statements that "the state is a creation of nature and prior to the individual" may seem to return to that naive monism which was overcome by Sophistic thought.[25] But to those appearances, Aristotle presents a refined conception that, following a specific interpretation of nature, did not dismiss the problem of

men's creation of the state, which was raised by the Sophists. Aristotle
introduced a teleological interpretation of nature, in accordance with which

the order of actual development and the order of logical existence are always the
inverse of each other. For that which is posterior in the order of development is
antecedent in the order of nature, and that is genetically last which in nature is first.
(That this is so is manifest by induction; for a house does not exist for the sake of
bricks and stones, but these materials for the sake of the house.)[26]

Hence, when he speaks about the state as "a creation of nature," he does
not claim thereby that it has always existed on the same principle as the
sun and the stars, the mountains and the seas, the heat and the cold. Instead, he merely says that man belongs to the state and will inevitably strive
to establish and improve it. This is so because the individual is not self-
sufficient, and to attain his full development he must cooperate with other
men.

There is no man without a woman and no woman without a man; no
person who gives orders without those who obey them; no master without
a slave and no slave without a master—for each of them has his own task
that he can perform only in cooperation with others. This linking together
"of those who cannot exist without each other" gives rise first (it is difficult to say how far Aristotle's exposition of the problem was intended
to be historical) to the family, that is, "the association established by nature
for the supply of men's everyday wants."[27] Then,

when several families are united, and the association aims at something more than
the supply of daily needs, the first society to be formed is the village. And the most
natural form of the village appears to be that of colony from the family. . . . When
several villages are united in a single complete community, large enough to be nearly
or quite self-sufficing, the state comes into existence, originating in the bare needs
of life and continuing in existence for the sake of a good life. And therefore, if the
earlier forms of society are natural, so is the state, for it is the end of them, and the
nature of a thing is its end. For what each thing is when fully developed, we call its
nature.[28]

As can be seen, Aristotle's anthropology had to be the science of the
state, or a *sui generis* sociology, because the social character of man is his
specific feature. This is proved by the fact that man is "the only animal
whom [nature] has endowed with the gift of speech."[29]

The State. According to Aristotle, what is the state? An unambiguous
answer to this question is far from easy. When we look for it, we have to
face the heterogeneity of *Politics*, a text which the experts often refer to as an
unfinished conglomerate of fragments and notes. It is also legitimate to

suppose that Aristotle used different meanings of the term, the *state*, at different times: an organized community of individuals and human groups (including those who have no political rights) who need one another; or merely an essential part of such a state, that is, the community of citizens; or just a political system. On some occasions he spoke about changes in the system of the state, but at other times he claimed that when the system changes, another state comes into being. Problems of interpretation are also due to the vague line between the ideal and the reality and between political principle and political practice.

If we disregard these difficulties (which are, however, worth noting as testimony to the fact that even the key concepts were at that time still in a underdeveloped form), we can say that Aristotle focused his attention on three aspects of the state.

First, self-sufficiency. In Aristotle's opinion, self-sufficiency was the essential attribute of the state: "A city only comes into being when the community is large enough to be self-sufficing."[30] Self-sufficiency is not to be interpreted in the sense of economic autarky, that is, the ability to satisfy the citizens' material needs without outward assistance. Aristotle meant the totality of human needs, whose satisfaction ensures the happiness of individuals and their making full use of their abilities—in other words, existence in accordance with nature, teleologically interpreted. His reflections on the proper "measure of quantity" (he took up Plato's subject—the size of the city-state) show clearly that he meant both moral and economic self-sufficiency.

Second, moral community. Aristotle stated explicitly that "political society exists for the sake of noble actions, and not of mere companionship."[31] His thesis was that a community living on a common territory and linked together by material interests—"exchange, alliance, and the like"—would not form a state if it were not united by a common striving for virtue.

And, finally, variety and complementarity of parts. Aristotle felt it most important that the unity of the state not be pushed too far. He wrote,

the state, as composed of unlikes, may be compared to the living being; as the first elements into which a living being is resolved are soul and body, as soul is made up of rational principle and appetite, the family of husband and wife, property of master and slave, so of all these, as well as other dissimilar elements, the state is composed.[32]

Obviously, Aristotle, like Plato, treated the state as a kind of organism. But while Plato stressed the unity of that organism and the subordination of all its parts to the whole, Aristotle emphasized cooperation of parts. When each part acts in accordance with its nature, the result is a harmonious action of the whole; not only do they retain their relative independence, but they perform their functions properly because of that cooperation.

Social Structure. This anti-Platonic conception of unity in variety is probably the most interesting and the most original part of Aristotle's theory of society. Aristotle has left astonishingly comprehensive comments on social structure.

The Aristotelian picture of social structure is many-dimensional. Viewed from various points, that social structure appears as (1) a conglomerate of families (and, of course, "colonies from the families"); or (2) a system of economic classes (the rich, the poor, and the middle class); or (3) a system of status groups (the common people and the notables); or (4) a set of specific "classes" resembling medieval "estates." Aristotle's *Politics* is a veritable anthology of ideas concerned with the interpretation of social structure. The striking point, however, is that very little notice is made in that work of the division into freemen and slaves, so important from our point of view. This was probably due to the fact that the Stagirite saw the slaves as just "talking tools," who are an essential element of the family, but have no part in the city-state, which was—a fact considered self-evident at that time—a community of freemen.

We shall not discuss again the division of the state into families; however, it is worth noting that Aristotle saw the state as a collection of groups, not of individuals.

The second aspect of social structure, in Aristotle's interpretation, is the division of society according to the functions performed by the various classes of citizens. He says in *Politics*,

States . . . are composed, not of one, but of many elements. One element is the food-producing class, who are called husbandmen; a second, the class of mechanics who practice the arts. . . . the third class is that of traders. . . . A fourth class is that of the serfs or labourers. The warriors make up the fifth class. [The sixth class is that of priests.] There are also the wealthy who minister to the state with their property, these form the seventh class. The eighth class is that of magistrates and of officers. . . . There only remains the class of those who deliberate and who judge between disputants. . . .[33]

Aristotle divided these classes into "the common people" and "the notables."[34]

The third essential aspect of social structure, according to Aristotle, was the division of society into groups that differ by wealth. As mentioned above, in *Politics* he passed from a multiclass structure to a dichotomous division (classes, in the first case, being actually vocational groups). He seems to have attached particular importance to the latter division, for at least two reasons. First, that division is the most clear-cut, for a person cannot be simultaneously rich and poor, whereas he can be simultaneously a husbandman and a warrior, a "mechanic" (craftsman) and a judge. Second, the distribution of power between the rich and the poor has the greatest effect on the stability of the state and its political system. Between these two extremes Aristotle introduced "the middle class," with which he sided, as he saw it to be the bulwark of order and the social foundation of a good system that is capable of avoiding the pitfalls of both oligarchy and democracy.

Classification of Political Systems. Aristotle paid considerable attention to the classification of political systems, which is not surprising if we consider their variety and changeability at that time. The issue had been taken up by Plato, who even tried to discover certain regularities in changes in political systems. Aristotle singled out "three true forms: kingly rule, aristocracy, and constitutional government, and three corresponding perversions—tyranny, oligarchy, and democracy."[35] The issue need not be discussed here, as it has been amply analyzed by historians of political thought. The important point is that Aristotle, when explaining the differences between the various political systems, proves to have been more sociologically minded than any other thinker before Montesquieu. The author of *Politics* wrote that "the reason why there are many forms of government is that every state contains many elements."[36] Those elements may appear in various combinations and proportions, thus making up different political systems. On that occasion he also made an interesting comparison between the component parts of the states and the parts of animals, which confirms our earlier comments on the organicist nature of his social theory.

THE SOCIAL HORIZONS OF THE CITY-STATE

Plato was active at the time when the *polis* was in a state of deep crisis; Aristotle, when it was collapsing. In describing the city-state, they behaved like Minerva's owls, which start flying only at dusk (to use Hegel's metaphor). It is even more striking that neither of them—and no other eminent thinker in classical Greece—could imagine social order as other than the order of the city-state, which was just retreating into the past. Plato failed to do that, even though he pictured his ideal system of government without being excessively concerned with the realities of his times. Aristotle failed as well, even though he had an imposing knowledge not only of the political systems of the Greeks, but also of the modes of life of the barbarians. Thus, it is worthwhile to conclude our comments on classical Greek thought by reflecting on the impassable barriers faced by the "scientific revolution," of which the work of Plato and Aristotle was the culmination.

George H. Sabine is right when he writes that

the Greek city-state was so different from the political communities in which modern men live that it requires no small effort of the imagination to picture its social and political life. The Greek philosophers were thinking of political practices far different from any that have prevailed commonly in the modern world, and the whole climate of opinion in which their work was done was different. Their problems, though not without analogies in the present, were never identical with modern problems.[37]

In looking for the peculiarities of the Greek *polis* and thereby for the answer to the question about the limits of Plato's and Aristotle's sociological imagination, we have to pay special attention to three factors.

First, the *polis* was a society of limited size. For all the differences among the various city-states, the Greeks did not doubt that there was a certain size that should never be exceeded: They imagined the *polis* as a community in which every member of it has all other members within his field of vision and thus has the whole functioning of the state under review. Aristotle wrote that the population of the *polis* should be large enough to ensure it self-sufficiency, but also small enough to "be taken in at a single view."[38] The city-state thus had essential characteristics of a local community.

Second, the social structure of the *polis* was extremely complex, not only because of the numerous stratifications (also known in other types of society) that were discussed at such length by Aristotle. The population of the *polis* included citizens; slaves, treated like things rather than human beings; and *metics*, who were very numerous in some cases. The latter were aliens who played an important role in economic and intellectual life, but had no political rights and did not form "an essential part" of the state. In other words, in the city-states, which emerged from communities based on the family or the gens, the bonds of blood retained their importance. In practice, as Aristotle wrote, only those people who came from families of citizens were citizens.

Third, the *polis* was thus not a community of people who inhabited a definite territory and were subject to the same political authority, but a community of those who enjoyed certain rights by birth, took part in political life, and were capable of discussing the essential problems of the state. This gave rise to the sense of similarity among members of the *polis*, which J. P. Vernant treats as one of the determinants of the "spiritual world of the *polis*."[39] The bonds that linked together the essential parts of the city-state were strong and many. To quote Sabine again,

For the Greeks . . . the city was a life in common; its constitution, as Aristotle said, was a "mode of life" rather than a legal structure; and consequently the fundamental thought in all Greek political theory was the harmony of this common life. Little distinction was made between its various aspects. For the Greeks the theory of the city was at once ethics, sociology and economics, as well as politics in the narrower modern sense.[40]

So, classical Greek thought, especially that of Plato and Aristotle, proved much more sociologically minded than the majority of later conceptions prior to Montesquieu and Hegel. "Sociological" problems had to retreat to the background when the state came to be shaped not as a community of its citizens, but by the authority of the ruler over his subjects. Yet that strength of the Greek thinkers also marked their weakness: It made it impossible for them to distinguish society from the state or to imagine the individual as other than a member of the *polis*.

STOICISM: THE DISCOVERY OF THE SUPRALOCAL COMMUNITY

"In the history of political philosophy," Sabine writes,

the death of Aristotle in 322 marks the close of an era, as the life of his great pupil [Alexander the Great], who died the year before him, marks the beginning of a new era in politics and the history of European civilization. The failure of the city-state is drawn like a sharp line across the history of political thought, whereas from this date forward its continuity is unbroken down to our own day.[41]

That unbroken continuity may be a matter of controversy, but the first part of Sabine's claim can hardly be disputed, because the fall of the classical *polis* marks a radical change in the interests of social thinkers, who adjusted themselves to the situation in which "masses of men, scattered over great distances and differentiated by race and culture, [were] gathered into a single society and governed by a single authority."[42]

Even though Alexander's empire proved to be very short-lived, its very existence changed the ancient world and prefigured the political organization that developed following the expansion of Rome. Not by coincidence, it was Stoicism, born in Hellenistic Greece, that became the most influential philosophy among the Romans. Stoicism was not the only new philosophy in the period that followed the decline of the city-states, but it will be the only one discussed here. It is worth noting, however, that all those trends in philosophy were marked by the tendency to seek a good life rather than a good state—and a good life not so much within the state, as despite the state. Stoics escaped political issues and engaged in ethical issues, as separate from politics.

For that reason, it might seem that Stoicism is irrelevant to the history of social theory. In fact, it did not yield any work that could vie with *Republic* and *Politics*. Nevertheless, we do claim that it affected sociological imagination by contributing to the emergence of concepts without which social thought in later epochs would have been impossible. What, then, was the significance of Stoicism from the point of view of the problems discussed in this book?

Universal Anthropology. Greek thought in its classical period treated man as a being that was predetermined to live in a state. *Man* was synonymous with *citizen*. In Hellenistic thought we notice the concept of man as a member of mankind, a being who, according to the Stoics, is endowed with an innate "social impulse," but is not at all "a political creature" by his very nature. This undermined one of the dogmas of classical thought—namely, the division of human beings into freemen and slaves, citizens and non-citizens. The change in the philosophy of man was followed by the appearance of the concept of universal community, in which all men participate, regardless of their position in the structure of power, privilege, and wealth. In the face of nature there are neither Greeks nor barbarians, neither masters nor slaves; there are only men, equal to one another, though differing in manners and conditions.

Natural Law. That law which is common to all men is not the law of any definite state (although in some Stoics we find the Utopia of the world state governed by the principles of that universal law), nor was it made and written by a definite legislator, nor does it sanction any definite political system. It is the law of eternal reason, which man discovers in himself despite conventions, customs, and legal acts to which he is subjected by his membership in a given political community. The Stoics thus discovered, in opposition to the classical doctrines, the double allegiance of the human individual: On the one hand, he is a member of mankind and, as such, is subject to the standards of the natural law; on the other, he is a member of a state and, as such, is subject to its laws and customs, which infrequently are at variance with the principles of universal reason. In other words, the individual belongs in two different orders: the moral (and reasonable) one, and the political (and not necessarily reasonable) one.

Separation of Ethics and Politics. As has been said, Stoicism turned from political to ethical issues. It did not endeavor to define the new political and social realities in terms of society or the state, but it turned into "a species of moral philosophy, addressing itself not to this or that city, but to all mankind."[43] The Stoics taught virtue, not politics. The underlying cause of that trend was a sense of alienation from existing political structures and of complete helplessness in the face of impersonal fate. The state had ceased to be something one had under control, something known and in a sense one's own:

The former citizen of the Greek *polis* was now left to himself politically and economically, and his fortunes depended on external forces over which he had no control: the whim of the "tyrant," the spontaneous functioning of the market, and politics, which followed its course without his participation and even without his knowledge of what was going on. It is no wonder that under such circumstances the philosopher tended to spin a cocoon about himself, to solve above all his own problems, those of morals, human goals, and the sense of life; he was moving more and more away from general philosophical problems in order to provide for himself and his adherents consolation, moral support, and inner balance that would replace that solid foothold which the *polis* was.[44]

The Social Problems of Stoicism in Roman Thought. These elements of Stoic philosophy found their continuation in the social thought of the Romans, to whom they owe that form in which they were to survive for centuries. The historical transformations of Stoicism are less important here, and so, following Sabine, we shall confine ourselves to indicating the main trends of development. One was the formation of Roman *legal* ideas, and the other trend was the emergence of Roman moral philosophy, which preceded Christian morality. The former was personified by Cicero (and, of course, the codifiers of Roman law); the other, by Seneca. In the case of law, Stoicism included inspirations deriving from classical Greek conceptions, for the point was to renew the theory of the state and to take up once more the problem of the individual's place in the *state*; Stoicism in its pure form, being a philosophy of political indifference and escape from political life, did not serve the purpose. In the case of morality, Stoicism was preserved in its purer form, although it was complemented in a way. At any rate, in both cases an important role was played by the Stoic conceptions of man and natural law.

The social philosophy of Marcus Tullius Cicero (106-43 B.C.) preserved the idea of natural law, "the law of honest reason," which cannot be changed by any other law, nor abrogated in any of its parts, nor abolished completely. We cannot be freed from it by the senate or by the people. It is not one law in Rome and another in Athens, one law now and another later, but it is the law unique of its kind, eternal and changeless, which covers all nations and all epochs alike. Yet the more interesting point seems to be that Cicero, engaged in politics as he was, took up on a large scale the problems of positive law that were dismissed by the Stoics. He was also the first thinker who can unreservedly be termed a *jurist*. As Sabine says, his interests were connected with "the presumption that the state is a creature of law and is to be discussed not in terms of sociological fact or ethical good but in terms of legal competence and rights." Sabine is correct in pointing out that this law-oriented view of the state, so deeply rooted in European thought, did not have any analogue in Greek thought.[45]

Cicero took up the Aristotelian problem of the origin of the state. He ascribed to man the innate impulse to collective life, but thought that laws and authority are necessary prerequisites of the state. He wrote that the state (*res publica*, that is, the public concern) is the concern of the people (*res populi*). The people is not just any collectivity of men brought together, but a large crowd of them that is united by the acceptance of the same law and by the benefits of common existence. The state is a union of citizens based on the provisions of the law. Cicero did not consider the state to be the only form of association (he even extended the Aristotelian triad of the family, the community, and the state by replacing it with a hierarchy of associations from *coniugium* to *societas humana*; in it the *polis* had its analogue in *civitas*, above which there were two other forms of association: *gens* and *societas humana*).[46] But in each case he thought that the law and the authority based on that law were essential and showed little understanding for other aspects of human relations.

Seneca differed from Cicero essentially in one respect: He did not show interest in problems connected with political institutions and saw in natural law a set of moral injunctions rather than a standard that would be useful to makers and reformers of definite legal systems. The human community that Seneca sought was not a political one; it was, as Sabine says, "society rather than a state; its ties [were] moral or religious rather than legal and political."[47] For Seneca the state was at most a necessary evil, not something that could be considered good in itself. In reviving the Utopia of the golden age, he admitted the idea of a human community that would not need any government and laws, as it would be free of the moral decay that marked his contemporaries. It was human cooperation, and not the state as an institution, that was the natural necessity.

It seems, thus, that as compared with the thought of classical Greece, Hellenistic thought and Roman thought (which is usually believed to have lacked originality) considerably extended the limits of sociological imagination by giving the pride of place to the idea of man as the member of communities other than the *polis:* one being mankind and the other being the state, interpreted as the union of citizens based on the provisions of the law. The relationship between these two forms of solidarity became a problem, which was reflected in the separation of ethics and politics as autonomous spheres of thought about man's place among other men. The depth of sociological analyses certainly suffered due to this splitting because none of the concepts of mankind or the state constituted an analogue to the modern concept of society, as the *polis* was.

SOCIETY AS THE COMMUNITY OF VALUES: THE TWO STATES OF SAINT AUGUSTINE

Early Christian ideas represented a distinct stage in the development of social thought. Focused on eschatological issues and seemingly turned away from this world, they included interesting sociological intuitions.

Christian thought certainly referred to Stoicism, but was not simply an extension of this philosophy, as it drew from other (especially Jewish) sources as well. Even more important, it was not an esoteric philosophy, but the ideology of a rapidly growing mass movement. The Christians were acutely conscious of the hostile milieu in which they had to live, but with which they did not want to identify themselves and within which they formed a specific counterculture. That situation gave rise to essentially new problems—namely, problems of a community constituted exclusively by the *values* that it shared. In the eyes of a Christian, the individual's membership in the community that he ranks above all others is no longer determined by circumstances that are independent of him—social status, wealth, power, or ethnic origin—and becomes a matter of his conscious choice of the purpose of life and the way to live it.

The community of faith appeared to early Christian thinkers to be the perfect union; all other bonds lost importance, because they pertained to worldly matters, while unity in Christ opened the path to eternal salvation. The organicist analogy, previously applied to society as a whole, now referred only to the community of values. In some formulations that ideal of perfect unity even assumed that Christians should renounce material goods that differentiated members of their community.

But the most interesting sociological problems in early Christian thought, elaborated most fully in Saint Augustine's *City of God* (*De civitate Dei*), were linked to the endeavors to define the place of that community of men of the same faith in the real social world of late antiquity. Those problems are shown with full clarity in a letter to Diogenetus by Tatianus of Syria (2d century A.D.):

Christians are not distinguished from the rest of mankind by country or language or custom. . . . While they live in cities both Greek and Oriental . . . and follow the customs of the country . . . they display the remarkable and confessedly surprising status of their own citizenship, they live in countries of their own as sojourners, they share all things as citizens; they suffer all things as foreigners. . . . They pass their life on earth; but they are citizens of heaven.[48]

The Christian thus belonged to two orders, the heavenly and the earthly. While he was eager to unite with his brethren in Christ, he did not thereby renounce all connections with the earthly social order. Those problems were becoming more and more topical as the Christians were ceasing to be a small sect that expected the advent of the Kingdom of God any day and was persecuted by fellow subjects who professed another creed. Some Christians would choose monastic life, continuing the evangelic Utopia of perfect unity in Christ, which can make one completely turn away from this world. Others had to find some *modus vivendi* and an ideological formula that would both preserve the ideal of the community in its unimpaired condition and reflect the fact that the members of that community have to live among other people. This formula also had to cover the institutionalization of faith in the form of the church, whose degree of organization was continually increasing.

Such a formula was offered by Saint Augustine (354-430), and in his works we find the most original element of the early Christian social thought. He was also the only one to construct an expanded system of social philosophy that was comparable with the great systems produced by non-Christian antiquity.

His sociology was based on the conviction that every society is in fact a community of values. Such was the starting point of his famous conception of two states, or "cities," which are discussed extensively in *City of God*: "two cities have been formed by two loves: the earthly by the love of self, even to the contempt of God; the heavenly by the love of God, even to the contempt of self."[49] Saint Augustine's mode of thinking was radically theocentric, and this is why he singled out only two cities. Although there may be many different objects of love that can unite human beings and, hence, almost an infinite number of societies (he mentioned robbers' gangs as "small cities"), it is only God that really matters, and it is the attitude toward God that splits mankind into two societies. Seen from that perspective, other divisions are of no importance,

though there are very many and great nations all over the earth, whose rites and customs, speech, arms, and dress, are distinguished by marked differences, yet there are no more than two kinds of human society, which we may justly call two cities. . . . The one consists of those who wish to live after the flesh, the other of those who wish to live after the spirit; and when they severally achieve what they wish, they live in peace, each after their kind.[50]

The separation of these two cities is merely moral, and not physical; their citizens live and would live in mixed groups until the day of the Last Judgment, when they would be separated physically as well. Hence, their description does not correspond to any observable social facts. It serves only to show the two opposing systems of values and the two different kinds of social order. In the description of one city, the point is to give an abstract idea of a society focused on secular values. In the other, we see a community focused on sacred values, which thereby rises above all the particular interests of the individual, the family, the town, and the empire. Accordingly, the inner order of each of these two cities differs completely from that prevailing in the other.

The earthly city is imperfect by its very nature.

The society of mortals spread abroad through the earth everywhere, and in the most diverse places, although bound together by a certain fellowship of one common nature, is yet for the most part divided against itself, and the strongest oppress the others, because all follow after their own interests and lusts, while what is longed for either suffices for none, or not for all, because it is not the very thing. For the vanquished succumb to the victorious, preferring any sort of peace and safety to freedom itself.[51]

Saint Augustine compared that city to the sea, in which fish devours fish; in his opinion, conflict is an inevitable function of organized secular society.

It is otherwise in the city of God:

True peace shall be there, where no one shall suffer opposition either from himself or any other. . . . And in that blessed city there shall be this great blessing, that no inferior shall envy any superior, as now the archangels are not envied by the angels, because no one will wish to be what he has not received, though bound in strictest concord with him who has received it: as in the body the finger does not seek to be the eye, though both members are harmoniously included in the complete structure of the body. And thus, always with this gift, greater or less, each shall receive this further gift of contentment to desire no more than he has.[52]

Saint Augustine thus shows that the two opposing systems of values on which the two antagonistic cities are based have analogues in the two kinds of social order: one based on conflict and the other based on consensus. As W. Stark puts it, "St. Augustine's theory of the *civitas terrena* elaborates a mechanistic and quasi-contractual sociology, as his concept of the *civitas divina* does an organological and quasi-biological one."[53] Of course, analyzing the sociology of Saint Augustine's conception should not be pushed too far, for we have to bear in mind the basically religious nature of his philosophy: Even if the description of the earthly city includes many elements of a realistic description of societies at the time of the fall of the Roman Empire, his reflections on the heavenly city do not refer to this world. But was it otherwise in the case, for instance, of Plato's sociology?

The sharp opposition between the two cities did not mean in the least, in Saint Augustine's formulation, that man has to escape all share in secular life. Man must take care of his material needs; he has his family and his motherland. Even more than that, "the blessings with which the Creator has filled this life, obnoxious though it be to the curse," are beyond doubt.[54] The earthly city is indispensable till the end of our days; hence, it is not participation in it that is evil, but, rather, an attitude toward its values that results in the renunciation of higher values and of the prospect of life in the heavenly city. For, as we have said, man's membership in this or that community was settled by his faith and not by the factors that determined his existence independently of his will.

From the point of view of the historian of sociology, the originality of Saint Augustine's theory consisted not only in the expansion of the conception of society outlined above, but also in his having placed the conflict of the cities in a historiosophical perspective, in the perspective of time, which has its beginning and its end. He vehemently attacked the ancient conceptions of cyclic changes, the eternal wheeling of human affairs. History is governed by providence, and hence history must have its sense and goal, must be an oriented process that follows a straight-line course. There is no doubt that this was a forerunner of the modern ideas of historical development and progress, even though, like all early Christian ideas, it was formulated in a specifically religious language, which accounts for the fact that lay historians of social thought have not paid enough attention to it.

MEDIEVAL ORGANICISM AND SAINT THOMAS AQUINAS

This is not the place to discuss the evolution of Christian thought following the profound socioeconomic and political changes that resulted in the emergence and stabilization of the feudal system. As before, we shall confine ourselves to outlining the final outcome of a long evolution. In this case it was that type of social thought which was represented above all by Saint Thomas Aquinas (1225-1274), author of *De regimine principum* and *Summa theologica*. We assume here that the theory of society formulated by him fully corresponded to the new social order, which had formed in Western Europe after the fall of the western Roman Empire. That social order, and the *Weltanschauung* that accompanied it, are succinctly characterized by Robert A. Nisbet:

The essence of the medieval order was hierarchy, in which each man gave and received what his functional place in the social order demanded. Commonality and membership were central in the medieval scheme of things. The whole order was conceived as a kind of *communitas communitatum*, a community of communities; and whether it happened to be monastery, guild, university, knighthood, manor, fief, or patriarchal family, it was the individual's duty to serve his community. Society was conceived by medieval philosophers as a great chain of being ranging from the simplest organism at the bottom all the way up to God at the top, and each link, however humble, was deemed vital in the divine chain.[55]

This is just the social world depicted by Aquinas's philosophy, which is not to say that his philosophy may be considered typical of the Middle Ages. It cannot be qualified as such primarily because of its formal refinement, which was due to the assimilation of the philosophical system of Aristotle, among other things. Further, Saint Thomas's philosophy developed at a late period, when centrifugal forces were already at work and the Gothic structure of the feudal system had started to crack.

When we compare medieval social thought with that of the early Christian period, we are struck, first of all, by a mitigation of the opposition of heaven and earth, the divine and the earthly orders. Nisbet says that "an ideal—the functionalist-organic ideal of human relationships—which Augustine had located in the hereafter, in the eternal community of the elect, was to become, above all in the writings of Thomas Aquinas . . . the ideal for society in this world."[56] The organicist idea of society, which previously referred to the union of the faithful in Christ, came to be ap-

plied to society as such, to all permanent community. Society did not cease
to be a mystical body, but it proved to be a physical entity, too. Theology
began to mingle with politics, reality with the ideal. The hierarchy of God's
creatures and of the choirs of angels had its analogue in the isomorphic
earthly feudal system; the interdependence of the two systems was to find
reflection in language: While the vocabulary describing relationships between the seignior and the vassal was interspersed with religious terminology, the vocabulary of the theological treatises was often "contaminated"
with terms drawn from documents concerned with the feudal system and
the functioning of the monarchy.[57]

The evolution of the idea of natural law seems characteristic: It was an
idea that in its earlier—and, *a fortiori*, its later—versions assumed a more
or less fundamental opposition between the ideal and reality, the law of
perfect reason and positive law. In medieval social thought that opposition
came to be largely obliterated.

An excellent example of the process by which opposition was removed is
offered by the Thomistic doctrine of three kinds of law. First, it says that
all laws are manifestations of the one divine law and are necessarily in conformity with it, because if they were not, they just would not be laws.
Aquinas introduced into his philosophy the idea of the uniform system of
the laws that govern the world. At the top of that hierarchical system there
is the eternal law, which exists per se; at a lower level there is the natural
law, which reflects the eternal law in the world and in human reason; at
the bottom there is human—positive—law, which merely states the principles of the natural law under given circumstances and is binding only insofar as it agrees with the natural law. The entire order of the world is deduced
here from a single cause and directed toward one goal, which is God. The
law is the incessant order of the Supreme Ruler, to whom everything that
exists is subordinated—from the thrones of the angels to the world of
inanimate nature. "Now the Constitutive Principle of the Universe,"
O. Gierke wrote, "is in the first place Unity. God, the absolutely One, is
before and above all the World's Plurality, and is the one source and one
goal of every being."[58] Since the various kinds of creatures are more or less
remote from God, the structure of the world must be hierarchical.

What applies to the universe applies in the same degree to the human
world, which, being part of the former, reflects the order of the whole (as
do all the other parts, too). Every community has its superior, as the universe
has one, and in every community there is a certain hierarchy. For Aquinas,
hierarchy was synonymous with order. Having taken from the church
fathers and from Aristotle the idea of society as an organism (*corpus natur-
ale et organicum*), he accordingly endowed society with specific features.
He made use of the organicist analogy not only to point to the interdependence of the various parts of society and to the unity that results from the

connections among them, but also, and primarily, to bring out their differentiation and the necessary dependence of the "lower" parts on the
"higher" ones. The head is the source of "feeling and movement" for the
whole body; hence, society without authority would be a dead body. Moreover, the various members of the social body are of unequal importance
for the life of the whole, and this is why the various groups of members of
society are placed at higher or lower levels of the hierarchy. Each of them
has a definite task to perform under the plan provided for the whole, but
can perform it properly only if it obeys its superiors. While society is still
conceived of as a mystical body, individuals participate in it not only as
confessors of one and the same faith (the interpretation of early Christian
authors), but also as human beings who are assigned to the various social
groups that have definite earthly tasks to perform.

The early Christian idea was that men enter the religious community
regardless of their respective places in existing social structures, and even
by abandoning them for the salvation of their souls. According to the
medieval Christian thought, man has to deserve salvation by being active
in that place in society in which he finds himself: service to God does not
mean abandoning the world, but accepting it. To put it briefly, medieval
authors, and especially Saint Thomas Aquinas, adapted the traditional
idea of society as an organism to the requirements of the state organized
into *estates*, in which every individual has his fixed place and his rights and
duties defined once and for all. According to the most popular schema,
which used to be interpreted in detail in various ways, society consists of
those who pray, those who fight, and those who work.

The statement that man is a social being (*animal sociale*) meant in medieval thought something more than it did to Aristotle, even though Aquinas
followed rather closely the Stagirite's argument on the issue. The individual,
who is not self-sufficient by nature, was placed not only within the family,
the local community, and the state, but also within the corporation. Without recognizing this fact, we could not understand medieval society, which
was *pluralistic* regardless of the degree of its political centralization. One
can correctly understand the social system of medieval Europe only by
taking into consideration both the vertical relationships of rule and dependence and the horizontal bonds of corporate bodies. The vassal is personally
subject to his seignior, but he receives his status from his group, from a
sociolegal category, from a corporate body, with which his lord must
reckon, too.

We have stressed very much the religious nature of medieval social
thought. This is substantiated not only by the type of argument used by
official ideologists of the church, because the arguments used by the ideologists of the opposition were religious, too. Thus, for instance, the ideologists of popular heresies, when turning against the very foundations of

the feudal order, did not as a rule go beyond the limits of religious consciousness. This is not to say, however, that all medieval social thought was a kind of applied theology, with no room left for secular arguments. Even in Aquinas himself we often find reflections that refer to utilitarian arguments, to the needs of individuals that cannot be satisfied without social organization, division of labor, and the like. For instance, such was his justification of the institution of private property. The point is, however, that these reflections are always embedded in a context that was basically theocentric and intended to legitimate the existing social order. That context also accounts for the fact that the Thomistic interpretation of Aristotle only in part resembles the authentic Aristotle, the penetrating student of social facts.

NEW HORIZONS OF SOCIAL THOUGHT
DURING THE RENAISSANCE

The concept of *renaissance*, which was fully shaped only in the nineteenth century, was strongly value-oriented and was originally associated with the radically critical assessment of the medieval period. The achievements of Renaissance art, science, and philosophy were supposed to glow against the background of the Dark Ages. Many authors associated the term *renaissance* with return to life, with awakening, with an essential change in the attitude toward the world. Other authors, especially those who in the twentieth century undertook to rehabilitate the medieval period, questioned the idea of the Renaissance as a turning point and claimed, not without reason, that certain ideas considered typical of the Renaissance had been presented in late medieval culture. On the other hand, the Renaissance had its dark aspects, too: After all, it yielded the notorious *Malleus maleficarum* (1486). It seems that the two great camps of the participants in the controversy over the Renaissance were both right to some extent: The Renaissance did mark a turning point, but certainly not so such an important one as its enthusiasts of the last century tended to think.

The overlapping of periods should not, however, veil the fact that the fifteenth and sixteenth centuries saw a sudden acceleration of centrifugal processes in Italy and in other Western European countries (including Poland), processes that were to bring about a total collapse of medieval culture and social structure. The framework of the new culture was being shaped at the same time, accompanied by the transition from a civilization that was predominantly feudal and ecclesiastic in its social, political, and cultural features and agrarian in its economic foundations to one that was predominantly national, urban, and secular, with the economic center of gravity shifting from agriculture to commerce and industry and the primitive money economy developing into capitalism.

But the main point was that no new civilization emerges in a day; it is preceded by a long series of minor changes, often hidden under the surface of official culture and relating to the various social groups, spheres of life, and countries or provinces in varying degrees. Even when it seems to have triumphed fully, such a triumph is usually confined to those centers which we are inclined to treat as the leading ones. This is why our opinion on the depth of the revolution that the Renaissance marked depends largely on the focus of our attention: that which cuts itself most clearly from the medieval background or that which still remains in the fetters of the age-old tradition. Of course, we have to consider both, because otherwise we may take the peak achievements of a given epoch for its average and overlook all that which represented routine and stagnation. It seems to the point to recall those truths here, because the Renaissance was an elitist movement. The Reformation was to play an incomparably greater role on a mass scale: Although it remained within the sphere of religious thinking and did not make any intellectual discoveries, it sanctioned new kinds of activity and new principles of the organization of collective life.

It seems that we cannot treat the Renaissance as a fully shaped cultural formation that suddenly replaced the medieval by producing contrapositions in all fields of life. When we speak about medieval society, we mean a closed and relatively harmonious whole. When we speak about Renaissance society, we refer largely to the same social system—but in a state of increasing crisis. We call it Renaissance society not to reflect its qualitative difference, but to draw attention to the presence of certain new trends, which, however, were far from being dominant everywhere. More profound social changes at first took place in a small section of Europe—namely, Italian commercial cities—or covered small groups. The social ideas of the Renaissance, then, announced changes in social reality rather than summing them up. This accounts for the major role of the heritage of antiquity, which provided patterns that helped in the sorting out of new experience.

The Social Framework of Renaissance Social Thought. When we look for the social conditions of Renaissance thought, our attention is attracted first by symptoms of the collapse of the medieval order, not by any new and already well-shaped structures. The psychological counterpart of the crisis of the traditional social system was the spreading feeling of instability, weakness of human bonds, and changeability of everything except human passions.

Taking its most acute form in Italy—which was favored by the country's location at the crossroads of the principal routes of the world, the growth of cities and commerce, and a lack of strong central authority—that crisis had several dimensions.

In economics, it meant the shrinking of natural economy in favor of marketable production and the intensifying of trade; the world at that time was expanding rapidly, following the great geographical discoveries, with a resulting increase in the scale of navigation. These changes brought about the strong impulse to amass wealth and to put an end, whenever possible, to the medieval regulatory measures applied to economic activity, measures that covered both production (the guild system) and the market (the doctrine of the just price). Even the late Middle Ages in Italy were a period of emergence of vast fortunes, whose owners had a growing influence on social life regardless of the position they had in the traditional hierarchy.

In social organization, the crisis consisted of the undermining of the rigid social order, within which everyone had his place fixed from the moment of birth and a status ascribed to him regardless of his individual achievements and/or talents. The social hierarchy did not, of course, cease to exist, and social contrasts in all probability became even sharper, but this was accompanied by an increasingly quick march up and down the social ladder. Those who were the most talented, the most vigorous, and the least scrupulous were moving up. Society became a playground for competition, with the rivals resorting to all kinds of measures and being guided by the effectiveness of actions rather than by constant moral principles.

In politics, the authority was becoming more and more independent of its religious tasks and was becoming predominantly an instrument for the defense of secular group, dynastic, and—more and more often—national interests (it was then that the concept of the *raison d'état* was born). The result was growing resistance to the church, which was itself undergoing a kind of secularization. F. Tönnies wrote that there was an analogy between societal life and politics; in both the leading roles were grasped by individuals free from prejudice and even from scruples, who, to achieve their ends, availed themselves of all the means they had at their disposal.[59]

In psychological attitudes, we see increased individualism, which resulted from making the individual's position depend more and more on himself and not on his ascribed group membership. That liberation was, however, accompanied by the feeling of a lack of security, security that was provided by the medieval social structure at the cost of restrictions on individual freedom. It might also be said that people in that period were, on the one hand, ready to accept without reservation the thesis of the absolute independence of the individual. On the other, they seemed to have believed in the power of fate, in the face of which the individual is totally powerless.

As has been said, these processes did not embrace all of Europe equally. It is also to be supposed that the comparatively few darlings of fortune availed themselves of the benefits of the changes. Most people had lost the former guarantees to obtain instead only the right to engage in unequal rivalry. Those people who were unsaddled from the medieval system but partaking of no spoils of the Renaissance adventure would later provide numerous supporters of religious reformers. In Western Europe the latter were to bring about an upheaval incomparably deeper and followed by more durable consequences than the Renaissance, even though those reformers on the whole represented grim religious fanaticism accompanied by a low intellectual level.

But for all their limited scope, these trends in economic and social life, in politics, and in psychological attitudes were strong enough to give rise to systems of social thought reaching far beyond the theocentric *Weltanschauung* of the Middle Ages. In those systems, as O. Gierke says, "the State was no longer derived from the divinely ordained harmony of the universal whole; it was no longer explained as a partial whole which was derived from, and preserved by, the existence of the greater: it was simply explained by itself."[60] There is no divine secret behind the social order, which does not need any supernatural sanction. It is simply a work of human art. From the point of view of Renaissance statesmen, politics was not any valuation of moral goals for which politicians strive; rather, it was merely a technical knowledge used to register and to codify those means which are most effective in grasping, consolidating, and expanding power under various circumstances.

Machiavelli. Niccolò Machiavelli (1469-1527), author of *The Prince* (1513), *Discourses about the First Ten Books of Titus Livius* (1513-20), and *History of Florence* (1520-26), personifies probably most fully the aforementioned features of Renaissance culture. He is also one of those thinkers of the past who are known to more than a small group of specialists. The term *Machiavellianism* entered everyday language, denoting attitudes of ruthless and perverse people who are guided by the amoral principle that the end justifies the means. That stereotype of Machiavelli seems justified insofar as his works disavowed the medieval (and ancient) tradition of linking together politics and morality. In many contexts Machiavelli did not ask what was good and confined his inquiry to the most effective means to a given end. This is not to say that Machiavelli did not moralize at all. His work analyzed as a whole, is marked by a striking duality: On one hand, it consists of "amoral," almost natural-science analysis of types of human behavior that result from changeless human nature, which led him to formulate definite recommendations in social engineering (to use a recent term). On the other, he presents very sharp criticism of his own times, carried out in the name of ancient patterns of virtue.

There is no doubt that Machiavelli had a moral ideal, but, when diagnosing his own times, he felt obliged to state that "how one lives is so far distant from how one ought to live, that he who neglects what is done for what ought to be done, sooner effects his ruin than his preservation; for a man who wishes to act entirely up to his professions of virtue soon meets which what destroys him among so much that is evil." Machiavelli was not a philosopher who would rest satisfied with stating what is and then abandon all interference with the course of events. His belief was that "fortune is the arbiter of one-half of our actions, but that she still leaves us to direct the other half, or perhaps a little less."[61] If human actions are to bring desired results, they must be adapted to the circumstances in which they take place and to the characteristics of those people toward whom they are directed. It is possible to discover the rules of effective action because circumstances recur and human characteristics are permanent: Human behavior can be predicted if we have adequate knowledge at our disposal. That knowledge is provided above all by history, which Machiavelli treated as an immense laboratory that allows us to watch human actions and to discover the regularities that govern them. This is why Machiavelli was often called an inductionist. Yet the fact that he was greatly dependent on ancient patterns and often approached history merely to seek confirmation is an argument against labeling him so. But his research procedure was novel in many respects and paved the way for a real observation of social facts.

Machiavelli's discoveries were very rarely sociological in nature, for they referred either to political issues—for example, conditions of action determined by the type of political system: monarchy versus republic, hereditary principality versus new principality, and so on— or to issues that we would now term psychological—various peculiarities of human nature. It may be said that society did not exist for Machiavelli even in that sociologically limited sense in which it existed for Plato, Aristotle, and Aquinas. As Wolin notes, "Machiavelli's political actors take decisions, conflict rages between group and group, there is thrust and riposte between princes, but no reflection of an ordered set of relationships among men of the same social grouping, no sense of shared loyalties, no feel for the continuity of a collectivity extending over time."[62] In Machiavelli we find a vision of a society so individualized that subordination to one and the same political authority proves to be the only bond between men. Moreover, the activities of that political authority are analyzed by him only from the point of view of immediate effects, and not in relation to their lasting consequences— the establishment of a definite social order, which would be of such interest to Hobbes, for one. In Machiavelli's field of vision we find only the ruler and his individual subjects. It is also easy to note that, unlike most earlier thinkers, he did not consider the state to be a natural community; it was for him a work of the ruler who proves strong and wise enough to impose his will upon others.

Bodin. The social theory of Jean Bodin (1530-1596), author of *Methodus ad facilem historiarum cognitionem* (1566) and *La République* (1575), was

different in many respects. The explanation was not only a difference between generations, but also the great variation in the historical conditions
under which the authors lived. Bodin's France was not in state of social
disorganization like that which marked Machiavelli's Italy. In spite of
religious wars, France was a centralized country with a strong royal authority and, moreover, was changing from a medieval monarchy into a
modern national monarchy based on fairly stabilized social structures.
Bodin's work was thus an endeavor to consolidate and legitimize definite
political institutions, and he was very definite in cutting himself off from
all those who wanted to make fine expositions of ideas without any real
foundations.

Like Machiavelli, Bodin referred to history. He drew on a comprehensive
repertory of data (which, by the way, he interpreted rather uncritically)
and considered history not only as a collection of cases from which we can
draw conclusions about human nature, but also as a process that deserves
in itself to be studied and explained in a scholarly manner. His own explanations may seem simplistic (he believed in astrology and was an almost radical
adherent of geographical determinism), but his very formulation of the
problem was far from naive.

Bodin is known primarily as that theorist who introduced into political
thought the concept of sovereignty, which he defined clearly and included
in the definition of the state. In his opinion, one can speak about the state
only when there is an absolute and permanent supreme authority, endowed
with the prerogatives of making laws and punishing anyone who breaks
them. While this idea of Bodin's came to play an enormous role in the history of modern Europe, it is of interet here only to a limited extent, namely
as one of the best examples of absolutist conception, which treated the
state as a work of human art and reduced the basic problems of the state to
those of authority and law.

The sociologist is much more interested in that which resulted from
Bodin's inconsistencies or, in other words, the medieval heritage in his
political doctrine. Unlike Machiavelli, Bodin used a pluralistic conception
of society, and the problems of social relations were for him incomparably
more comprehensive than the relations between the ruler and his subjects.
First of all, he paid much attention to the family as the natural community
that is the foundation of the state and of all other associations as well,
namely, "corporations and colleges," in the sense of various collective
bodies. Society, while subject to an absolute authority, has an intricate
inner structure that in some sense (which was not formulated precisely by
Bodin) makes the foundation of the state. It is with the family that the
institution of private property is connected, which seems to indicate that
the sovereign authority is, contrary to its definition, limited to some extent.
It is also to be noted that Bodin took as his starting point the Aristotelian
schema: the family, the colony of families, and the state. But he thought it

necessary to modify considerably the last link in that chain. The state was not for him just a simple extension of the family, and defining the relation between these two kinds of community posed insurmountable difficulties for Bodin.

Like Machiavelli, Bodin tried to lay scientific foundations for politics. But while the former sought them in the knowledge of changeless human nature, the latter focused his attention primarily on geographical determinants of human character, believing that the knowledge of "anthropogeography" is a necessary condition of reasonable policies and effective government. His use of the concept of the *national* state was a novelty, too.

Renaissance Utopias. At the pole opposite to Machiavelli and Bodin, we can place Renaissance Utopias, the best known of which and the one that gave the genre its name was *Utopia* (1516) by Thomas More (1478-1535). Other works of that kind were *Civitas solis* (*City of the Sun*) (1602) by Thomas Campanella and *New Atlantis* (1626) by Francis Bacon. At first glance they do not have anything in common with the realistic analyses made by politicians of that time. They describe islands of felicity, lost in remote oceans, and offer no direct practical recommendations to their contemporaries. They appear to be products of intellectual play, dissociated from real life. Even more, to the idea of an open and mobile world in which everything is possible they oppose a picture of a closed and stable society, so that some commentators see in them products of a longing for the past and even an idealization of medieval monastic life.

It seems, however, that Utopias were closely linked to the main trend of social thought under the Renaissance. More's *Utopia* shows clearly to what extent they provided answers to questions posed by the epoch. The first part of the work is a realistic analysis of the social conditions prevailing in Renaissance Britain and concludes that political measures cannot solve the basic problems. It is a treatise intended to substantiate the claim that law and its rigorous observance cannot remove existing evil if the conditions that breed that evil remain unchanged. Like nineteenth-century Utopians, More shifted the center of gravity of social thought from politics and law to the socioeconomic organization. While Machiavelli and Bodin sought a remedy in the reconstruction of the state's authority, More sought it in a thorough transformation of the socioeconomic system, particularly in the abolition of private property, the expansion of which resulted in a polarization of society and in poverty that bred crime. In More's opinion, the problem of social order was not one of politics and law. The inhabitants of his Utopian island had very few laws, which, however, proved sufficient, and the islanders blamed other peoples that in spite of their great number of laws, their countries could not be kept in order.

The object, accordingly, was to devise a harmonious and self-regulating social system, and this is the subject matter of Part 2 of the work, which contains a detailed description of the ideal society, in which there is no private property, idleness, conflicts, infringement of the law, and so on and in which all live as it were one great family. Harmony is based primarily on the consensus about the supreme values in human life and the best institutional solutions. Social supervision is almost exclusively self-control. The social order in Utopia is assumed to be stable to the point of perfection, and so its inhabitants keep themselves in isolation from the external world in order to avoid the destructive influence of the latter.

Like other Renaissance thinkers, More was guided in his social ideas by a definite set of assumptions concerning human nature. But he refused to base his idea of human nature on observation of human behavior under conditions which, he thought, had to deform man:

More thought that an empirical analysis of human beings, intended to yield a picture of real man, resulted in falsehoods if one did not take into account all that which in human behaviour and conduct was imposed by social conditions. The real social man under existing condition was not the true man; the true man and the social man can become one and the same only under the system which prevails in Utopia.[63]

According to Machiavelli, we acquire the knowledge of human nature by watching man in the course of history; according to More, we acquire it by discovering what is its permanent substance and what is the product of the social system. It seems that the latter viewpoint was to prevail in modern social thought, which, however, is not to be ascribed to any direct influence by the author of *Utopia*.

Regardless of the ways in which More (and other Utopians) differed from Machiavelli and Bodin, we may speak about some affinity between the two small groups. In particular, all the Renaissance authors whom we have mentioned believed firmly that social order is a work of human art and, as such, can rationally be modified according to the requirements of circumstances and permanent features of human nature, however these be understood. Also typical of the period was the belief that the order received from the past was not the only possible one; to those thinkers, the received order had been sanctified neither by the lapse of time nor by the church, and the problem of how to organize social life remained open.

Digression on the Reformation. The epoch of the Renaissance was also that of the Reformation, which, as we said earlier, changed the manner of thinking of ordinary people much more deeply than did the Renaissance doctrines, in most cases esoteric in nature. We are concerned here with types of theoretical thinking and not with changes in the consciousness of ordinary people (which, by the way, became the passion of many sociologists, beginning with Max Weber). So the Reformation—originated by Martin Luther (1483-1546), John Calvin (1509-1564), and other religious thinkers and theologians—is of interest for us only because the new religious consciousness implicitly included definite patterns of interpretation of social facts. There is no doubt that the Reformation, being a profoundly religious movement, also influenced the way of approaching secular issues, both by criticizing the medieval principle of hierarchy and by preaching the ideal of the church as the community of the faithful. The impact of the Reformation on social thought was, in one respect, strikingly similar to that of the Renaissance: While the latter freed politics from theology, the former —especially in Luther's version—emancipated theology from politics.[64]

Luther, in opposing *Romana tyrannis*, freed the faith from the institutional framework in which it had been enclosed in the Middle Ages and made it the issue of the conscience of the individual, who before God is equal to all other believers. In his contacts with God the individual does not need the intermediary of the office. The church is the community of the faithful, not a hierarchy of prerogatives and offices.

That egalitarian vision of society (like early Christian thought) covered only the sphere of faith: Luther was not a radical in the political or social sense of the term and openly opposed the application of the principle of equality in secular life (glaringly manifested in his hostile attitude toward the popular reformation of Thomas Müntzer). It may even be said that in this case religious egalitarianism favored the acceptance of the need of a strong authority and inequality in earthly matters, because religion showed the individual the path to salvation, but—unlike its role in the Middle Ages— did not provide any pattern for the political organization of secular society. In Luther's opinion, the latter needed an absolute authority, a strong head, if it was not to sink into chaos. Yet those authors, like Hegel, who saw connections between the religious principles of the Reformation and the political ones of the French Revolution were certainly right. The new idea of the religious community was a prefiguration of the idea of society as the community of free and equal individuals, who in their conduct are guided by their own conscience and not by any authorities. In other words, the Reformation provided an important chapter in the history of European individualism.

More intricate problems certainly emerge in connection with Calvin's doctrine, since he was concerned with the institutionalization of faith, the role of authority, and the participation of the church in political life. Great as the role of that doctrine was, we shall not be concerned with it here since Calvinism did not produce any essentially new sociological approach.

SOCIAL THOUGHT IN THE SEVENTEENTH CENTURY: NATURAL LAW AND MANKIND

However far-reaching was the effect of Renaissance and Reformation ideas on the shifts in European social thought, the most important modern theory of society came to take full shape only in the seventeenth century. That theory was the doctrine of natural law, developed in the writings of Johannes Althusius (1557-1638), Thomas Hobbes (1588-1679), Hugo de Groot (1583-1645), Samuel Pufendorf (1632-1694), Benedict Spinoza (1632-1677), John Locke (1632-1704), and many other authors, whose influence ceased only when the nineteenth century witnessed the triumph of historicism and positivism. As Schumpeter says, these authors formulated "a comprehensive theory of society on all its aspects and activities" and gave it the form of a theory of law.[65] Further, it was supposed to answer the question of "how, given definite permanent features of human nature, public life can be organized so that those features be taken into consideration while individuals are guaranteed maximum security and freedom."[66]

That theory (or, rather, those theories) largely retained the secular orientation of the social thought of the Renaissance period, with its individualism and fascination with the problem of sovereignty. At the same time it opposed that heritage by deducing social order not so much from force as from the principles of natural law, which is prior to any authority and anyone's will. According to Machiavelli, law is created only by the authority, and so only positive law exists. But according to the theorists of natural law, a certain kind of law precedes the emergence of all authority and is binding—at least *in foro interno*—regardless of any such authority. The idea itself was, of course, not new and could be found in Renaissance theories, too. For instance, Jean Bodin wrote about the divine law in conformity with which the "law of government" depends, although he thought that the states had had their source and origin in force and coercion. Seventeenth-century theorists expanded that idea extensively and drew all the possible consequences from it. As Schumpeter put it tersely in present-day language, "the ideal of natural law embodies the discovery that the data of a social situation determine—in the most favorable case uniquely—a certain sequence of events, a logically coherent process or state, or would do so if they were allowed to work themselves out without further disturbance."[67] In other words, the theorists of natural law discovered a certain sphere of human relations that is constituted independently of political institutions and positive law and provides, as it were, their foundation. This discovery substantiates the opinion that "social science discovered itself in the concept of natural law."[68]

The Modern Doctrine of Natural Law versus Tradition. A concise exposition of the doctrine of natural law is difficult to make, first, because that doctrine showed much differentiation internally, and, second, because it bore a very complicated relation to the earlier idea of natural law, being both its continuation and its denial.

The inner differentiation of the doctrine manifested itself in the content of its ideas, in the interpretation of the basic concepts (including that of natural law), in the expression of the principal problems of the period, and in the types of practical recommendations deduced from the theory. The last-named ones appeared to be diametrically contradictory, for in some cases they recommended absolute obedience to the authority, while in others they justify resistance to the authority if the latter acted at variance with the absolutely binding natural laws.

Without belittling such differences, we must realize that underneath them lay a common way of thinking, which consisted in the more or less radical refusal to be guided in politics by anything other than rationally established *principles*. Whatever those principles were and whatever conclusions were drawn from them, they were incompatible with the acceptance of sociopolitical order just because it was supported by the authority of tradition. In this sense, all modern varieties of the doctrine of natural law were marked by a kind of radicalism.[69] It was an inevitable result of the distinction between that which should be—natural law—and that which is —positive law. As Gierke put it:

in opposition to positive jurisprudence, which still continued to show a Conservative trend, the natural-law theory of the State was Radical to the very core of its being. Unhistorical in the foundations on which it was built, it was also directed, in its efforts and its results, not to the purpose of scientific explanation of the past, but to that of the exposition and justification of a new future which was to be called into existence.[70]

For all its radicalism (or, at least, its potential for radicalism), the modern doctrine of natural law was a continuation of the medieval theories of natural law, from which seventeenth-century thinkers took both the essential problems and concepts, going back to antiquity, and a large part of techniques of demonstration.[71] In that respect their work was a step backward, as compared with Machiavelli. Of medieval origin was, above all, the assumption that human beings, both individuals and communities, are bound by certain rules of conduct that had not been established by them, but had been given to them together with their human nature.

Comprehension of modern social thought requires noticing, however, not only that continuity, but also the changes that occurred in the doctrine of natural law and resulted in its deep crisis in the late eighteenth century. From a modern perspective those changes seem to have been inevitable, since they were a consequence of the fundamental changes in sociopolitical life and in the general climate of modern thinking. When it comes to the history of the idea of natural law, the turning point was in the seventeenth century. In what did it consist?

First, the concept of natural law became secularized and separated from divine law, from which it had been deduced by medieval thinkers. The substance of natural law was made independent of divine will; for example, de Groot maintained that God cannot change natural law, just as He cannot change the laws of mathematics. Thus, its knowledge ceased to require revelation and became the sphere of philosophy, freed from links with theology. It meant "a transfer of the idea of deism to the reflection on state law. If human nature is a work of God, then that fact is irrelevant for the analysis of its properties; natural law can be deduced from the properties of human nature and *from these only*, and not from divine law."[72] Natural law was assigned the same status as that enjoyed by the laws of mathematics and physics: Even if it was still taught in a scholastic form, its substance was becoming more and more secular.

Second, unlike its medieval antecedent, the modern doctrine of natural law was *nominalistic*. Regardless of whether human individuals were ascribed an innate *appetitus societatis* or, on the contrary, were considered as being naturally asocial, natural law was interpreted as a set of principles applicable to individuals and not to society as a whole. Those principles were supposed to regulate relationships among members of society and only indirectly the functioning of the social organism.[73] Since natural law applies to human individuals as such (and if it does to communities as well, then only to communities that are treated and treat others as individuals in their relationships), its principles can best be analyzed when one mentally suspends the existence of all human bonds that do not result from the properties of human nature, which are equally an attribute of every individual. Hence the growing popularity of the idea of the natural state, expected to help in revealing these properties, which could have been veiled or suppressed by advanced forms of societal life. Theorists of natural law as a rule referred to the very clear distinction between *status naturalis*, on the one hand, and *status socialis*, *status civilis*, and *status culturae*, on the other (the last term being used quite sporadically, for example, by Pufendorf). The nominalism of the modern doctrine of natural law also found manifestation in the conceptions of social contract, intended to explain (1) how individuals, who are independent by nature (even though they have an innate social impulse, according to many authors), come to form a single social body, *persona moralis composita* and (2) how it happens that those who govern and those who are governed emerge from individuals, who are equal by nature because their nature is the same. Civil society can be more or less in harmony with the principles of natural law, but it is not in itself a product of nature.[74]

Third, the conception of man or, in Schumpeter's terms, "metasociology," assumed by modern theorists of natural law, was novel, too. Not only did the concepts of original sin and of the supernatural destiny of man disappear from anthropological considerations, but also that the use of methods typical of natural sciences was believed possible in the study of human nature. It is not by coincidence that Hobbes and Locke are treated as forerunners of scientific psychology. In some cases (especially in Hobbes), that new viewpoint revolutionized the interpretation of the principles of natural law, which came less and less to resemble a moral code and to become "merely a fancied description of the physical order of nature, or a hedonistic and utilitarian precept for the survival of man as a biological creature in the jungle of nature."[75] This was connected with the shift, typical of the modern conceptions as compared with the medieval ones, in interests from duties to rights, from that which man owes to God to that which he needs himself.

Fourth, the modern doctrine of natural law tended to assimilate the patterns of contemporaneous sciences, particularly those of mathematics and physics. This tendency was revealed both in the method of exposition of the subject matter, which often imitated mathematical treatises, and in the assignment of a privileged place to deduction and to the belief that the important point is not so much to accumulate descriptions of facts as to search for general laws that would make it possible to explain those facts. De Groot admitted to have turned his mind away from singular facts when considering problems of law, in analogy of mathematicians who analyze geometrical figures in abstraction from all bodies. Thus, the comprehensive descriptive data to be found in the works of theorists of that epoch were not historical data (in the sense that the word *historical* acquired in jurisprudence at the times of Montesquieu), but served merely as illustrations. It is another issue that the same period witnessed an accelerated development of statistics, indispensable for the modernization of the state.[76]

Finally, it is worth noting that the modern doctrine of natural law was class-oriented, as it offered a theoretical justification of the aspirations of the middle class, which was then developing at a rapid pace. Injunctions and prohibitions of the natural law turned out to be, above all, guarantees of property, freedom of trade, and honesty in adhering to contracts. This can best be seen in the approach to property: For medieval thinkers (Saint Thomas Aquinas, for example) its existence was compatible with, but certainly not imposed by, the natural law. But for modern theorists it became one of the foundations of society, and possession turned out to be one of the principal rights of man, which must be guaranteed to him by society.

Differentiation of Doctrines of Natural Law. The peculiarities of the modern doctrine of natural law, as listed above, did not manifest themselves clearly in all of its versions. The medieval doctrine was most thoroughly destroyed by Hobbes, who in fact transformed the principles of natural law into a set of reasoned conditions for the survival of human beings, conditions that they realize and observe insofar as they fear the consequences of their own "natural" activity. In other authors, especially Althusius and de Groot, but also the otherwise very modern-minded Locke, the relicts of traditional views were much stronger: Natural law was not so openly independent of divine law, and its principles did not result so immediately from a naturalistic analysis of human instincts. On that issue, those authors more often referred to the common consensus, starting from the assumption that whatever is considered indisputable by many people in various times and places must be attributed to a general cause. But for the whole of their social theory it was significant that most modern theorists of natural law stuck to the opinion, deeply rooted in the tradition, that social impulse (*appetitus societatis*) is one of man's attributes. This is an impulse to live together with others, in peace and in an organized manner that corresponds to the properties of the human mind.

Hence they believed, as did Aristotle and Aquinas, that at least some relationships among human beings are natural in character, so that they exist regardless of the advantages those human beings could expect of them. It may be said that two different "sociologies" coexisted within the modern doctrine of natural law. One of them followed Machiavelli and Bodin in assuming coercion to be an indispensable condition of social life, which develops only insofar as egoistic human interests are bridled; the other assumed cooperation to be a natural result of the social impulse, cooperation that is protected and consolidated rather than made possible by the political authority. In the former case the birth of the state was in fact identical with the birth of society, since, as Hobbes claimed, social relations without an authority are inconceivable. In the latter it was believed that the state was formed on the basis of existing social groups of various kinds. One of such groups was, primarily, the *family* (*societas private* or *domestica*), whose existence and development seemed to be totally independent of the state and sometimes was even treated as the nucleus of the latter. Problems of social groups were most extensively discussed by Althusius, who singled out such levels of "symbiosis" as the family, the brotherhood (*Genossenschaft*), the local community (*Gemeinde*), the province, and the state.

Despite all these profound differences both "sociologies" attached immense significance to political authority and were unanimous in the opinion that full-fledged societal life exists only where political authority functions. In the seventeenth century we do not find any thinker who in his social theory would do without the concept of political authority or would treat it just as an appendage to an already shaped society (as was sometimes the case in the eighteenth century). Moreover, it does not seem in the least that the theorists of an innate social impulse represented more advanced sociological consciousness than did the adherents of the other concept. It was rather Hobbes who, by denaturalizing all human relations except for rivalry and strife, paved the way for reflection on them.

Conceptions of the State of Nature: Hobbes versus Locke. This difference of opinions on human nature and on the original conditions of social life manifested itself most clearly in the conceptions of the state of nature, which formed an integral part of the doctrine of natural law at that time.

When concerning ourselves with that important concept, we have to realize first that it was not historical in character. Reflections on the state of nature were not intended to answer the question about the *earliest* state of mankind. As has been noted by E. Barker, "The natural-law thinkers were not really dealing with the historical antecedents of the state; they were concerned with its logical presuppositions."[77] If the factual existence of a state of nature was taken into consideration at all, then that state was treated as something which could have happened in any period in the past or present, under conditions in which human beings have nothing in common with one another except membership in the species. As Wolin says of Hobbes's idea, the concept of the state of nature had the status of "an ever-present possibility."[78] In Hobbes's interpretation every restriction of the sovereignty of the state marked a step toward the state of nature. That concept had a similar status in Locke's system, even though he gave it a quite different interpretation: He was ready to apply it not only to the situation that preceded the emergence of the state (civil society), but also to all situations of crisis and, more interesting still, to the state under an absolutist rule (as the absolute ruler makes himself his own judge, reproducing thereby the state of nature, when every individual administered his own justice).

Obviously, reflections on the state of nature were above all mental experiments intended to reveal what—in a given author's opinion—the state is; this was done through the description of the situation that was supposed to occur if the state did not exist. Those reflections were meant to show the operation of the forces of nature under the experimental conditions of a political (and possibly also social) vacuum—that is, when that which was considered specially significant for the political and social order did not exist. The empirical data used in those reflections served mainly as illustrations and were drawn from diverse sources: basic knowledge of primitive peoples (America in Hobbes and Locke), observation of international relations and relations among citizens of different states, analysis of contemporaneous political crises, and the like. The discussion of the state of nature also had a clearly didactic sense: The point was not only to explain what the state is, but also to demonstrate what it should be to guarantee natural rights.

Very roughly, we can single out two basic concepts of the state of nature, which corresponded rather closely to the two rival concepts of human nature. One of them, represented in the seventeenth century by Hobbes, interpreted the state of nature as one without any bonds between individuals. The other, represented by Locke, for instance, did not exclude from the state of nature the existence of even fairly developed social relations. Further, it shifted the boundary between that state and the social state (in the sense of "civil society" and not of just any association of people) to the time when political guarantees developed to cover relations that emerged spontaneously under the principles of natural law, principles that had been binding earlier *in foro externo* and not only *in foro interno*, as in Hobbes's interpretation.

As one can easily see, the first interpretation of the state of nature was associated with the view of man as a being that is naturally asocial and the view of the interests of the individuals as absolutely incompatible with one another. Since the individuals are equal—that is, they have the same natural rights—rivalry and strife develop, and the participants are at most restrained by the fear of being killed by a stronger rival. Struggle for survival always means here a struggle with another individual. The state of nature is thus inevitably a state of war of all against all, a battle that can be terminated only by a sovereign authority that would be obeyed by all because it ensured life and property in exchange for absolute obedience. Only such an authority guarantees the observance of the orders and prohibitions of natural law, which are discovered by human reason, but deprived of all binding force as long as there is no authority behind them. Only such an authority makes it possible for social relations and society as a *sui generis* collective person to exist.

The other interpretation of the state of nature also had nominalistic anthropology as its underlying idea, but it was the anthropology that assumed that man is a social being and that individual interests are convergent. In the state of nature man is interested in another man not so much as a potential aggressor or an object of aggression, but as a similar being with whom he can establish cooperation that would be to the advantage of both. Man struggles for survival not with other men, but with nature, which he succeeds in mastering by his work. Hence, the state of nature need not be a state of war, but can be "a state of peace, good will, mutual assistance, and preservation. . . . Men living together according to reason . . . is properly the state of Nature."[79]

Thus, the state of nature is here a *social* state (although different from that of "civil society"), marked by observance of the principles of natural law that regulate relationships among individuals and ensure protection of property both in the broad sense of "lives, liberties, and estates" and in the narrow sense that covers only the material goods acquired through work.

We have here, in fact, an idealization of a society of petty owners, each of whom tills his own plot and neither wishes nor needs to appropriate anything that belongs to his neighbor. In Locke's opinion, the state of nature interpreted in this way was markedly better than the conditions prevailing under the absolute rule. Matters came to be more complicated with the invention of money, which made it possible to accumulate more wealth than any person would need to satisfy his needs. But even that did not, in Locke's eyes, put an end to the state of nature as a state of equality in which all authority and jurisdiction are based on reciprocity and no one has more of them than others do. It does turn out, however, that at a certain point in the development of private property, man is always subjected to intrusion by others.

The dangers described by Hobbes were, in Locke's opinion, quite real. They resulted, however, not from human nature as such, but from the level of economic conditions attained by mankind. This led to the necessity of society's transforming itself into a civil society, that is, one in which a single individual does not himself stand guard over his natural rights, but transmits that function to specialized agencies that act on the strength of positive law. "Men give up all their natural power to the society which they enter into, and the community put the legislative power into such hands as they think fit with that trust."[80] Note, however, that establishing civil society is not the first act of aggregation by human beings; it merely secures those guarantees which the existing community began to require in view of the opposing tendencies within it. In Hobbes, the state is needed to put the natural law into effect; in Locke, to prolong the functioning of that law.

The differences described above resulted in differences of another kind. In Hobbes's doctrine, the establishment of political authority was irreversible, because any rebellion against it would mean dissolution of society and a return to the state of anarchy. Hobbes assumed that individuals had to agree to appoint a sovereign, but he meant a single case of consent, which does not ever have to be renewed, regardless of what that sovereign does. His authority is unlimited, and it is that characteristic of it which makes the very existence of society possible. According to Locke, the authority was established by the existing community to carry out specified tasks with which that community was unable to cope. Hence, if the authority fails to carry out those tasks or takes prerogatives that are incompatible with those tasks (for example, acts that threaten the lives and the property of the citizens), then it becomes not only superfluous, but detrimental to society. In such a case the people have the right to revolt and to reorganize their civil society.

The Idea of Social Contract. The concept of social contract, an act that makes it possible to pass from the state of nature either to a social state or to a civil society, was of fundamental importance for all theorists of natural law, especially the modern ones. Regardless of the level at which the origin of human bonds was placed, no one imagined that it would be possible to explain the existence of civil society without assuming a contract between the members of that society. For if those individuals are free and equal by nature, only some kind of agreement among them can explain the limitations and forms of dependence that are typical of societal life.

The concept of social contract has had a long history, requiring a distinction between the idea of the contract of government and that of the social contract proper. Both had been known since antiquity, but in the Middle Ages it was the former that was dominant. In the modern doctrine of natural law the problem of the social contract came to the fore again, linked to growing individualism; it was a contract among the future members of society concerning the principle of the organization of that society and not a contract between the ruler and the ruled concerning the form of that rule.[81] In Hobbes's case the issue does not require any further explanation, because he considered the establishment of society to have been the subject matter of the contract: The individuals merely renounced the rights they had had in the state of nature on behalf of the ruler. When it comes to Locke, the matter is less obvious, because a kind of an agreement between the totality of citizens and the government was involved. The main point, however, was that for Locke the contract was concerned primarily with the principles of the self-organization of society and not with the mutual obligations of that society and the ruler who headed it.

Inconsistencies in Thinking about Natural Law: Locke. The modern doctrine of natural law bridged ancient and medieval thought with ideas and trends typical of modern times and modern society. So it is not surprising that the opinions of many representatives of that doctrine were marked by inconsistencies and, in some cases, even included evident contradictions, which resulted from the desire to bring different world views into agreement. Such contradictions were particularly manifest in the writings of John Locke; one explanation is that as a philosopher he formulated a theory of cognition that was fatal for the assumptions that he was bound to adopt as a theorist of natural law. Thus he came to face an unsolvable problem: There is a natural law, binding on all men, but man, who draws all his knowledge from experience, does not have any source of information about the principles of that law, because that law is by definition different both from the law imposed by the state and from customary law, by which men guide their conduct.

The problem did not exist for the earlier theorists of natural law, for they believed either in the participation of human reason in the divine *lex aeterna*, or in innate ideas, or in the self-evidence of the principles of natural law. The empiricist standpoint made the adoption of any of these three solutions impossible, and hence natural law had to be considered either an arbitrary product of man or a result of some revelation, for which there was no place in Locke's epistemological system. Locke proved unable to cope with that.[82] The first solution meant abandoning an objective substantiation of morality and politics (Hobbes came closest to that position), and the second meant entangling oneself in unsolvable philosophical problems or even returning to the traditional religious *Weltanschauung* (which in the seventeenth century was done by Bossuet). Another difficulty with the modern doctrine of natural law was that the principles of natural law were assumed to be accessible to all normal human beings, whereas in fact one could see a basic disparity between those principles and actual human conduct, which made one question whether one could speak about the universal nature of those principles.

As a result, Locke's writings are exceptionally hard to comment on; they include, in fact, several different conceptions of societal life. Attention should be paid in particular to *An Essay Concerning Human Understanding*, in which human actions are interpreted mainly in terms of customary law, by which most people are guided in practice. Locke says there that

several actions come to find credit or disgrace amongst them [societies, tribes, and clubs of men] according to the judgment, maxims, or fashion of that place. For through men uniting into politics societies have resigned up to the public the disposing of all their force, so that they cannot employ it against any fellow-citizen any farther than the law of the country directs; yet they retain still the power of thinking well or ill, approving or disapproving of the actions of those whom they live amongst, and converse with.[83]

It thus turns out (and Locke confirms it explicitly) that when we study actual human behavior we have to focus attention not so much on natural law as on "the law of opinion or reputation," which is a denial of all universalism, being different in every place, in every time, and in every social group. Locke comments "there is scarce that principle of morality to be named, or rule of virtue to be thought on . . . which is not, somewhere or other, slighted and condemned by the general fashion of whole societies of men, governed by practical opinions and rules of living quite opposite to others."[84]

Thus the belief in the existence of natural law does not yield any feeling of the harmony of societal life, as was the case in medieval thought. On the contrary, it is an arena of conflict between reason and prejudice, between the principles on which civil society is based and those by which its members are guided in everyday life, between universalism and particular interests, between man and the citizen. In Locke's social thought those contradictions remained unresolved and probably not fully realized by him. Locke as a theorist of natural law and Locke as a student of man and human nature looks as if he were two different authors, each of whom wrote on a different topic.

It seems that those contradictions make Locke so very interesting for the student of modern social thought: In the work of this author we can see the beginning of the disintegration of the doctrine of natural law. That disintegration, which was completed in the eighteenth century, resulted in two trends: first, the emergence of the revolutionary idea of natural rights, opposed to existing social institutions, an idea that served as the foundation of far-reaching reformatory measures (the natural law as the norm), and, second, the emergence of the idea of human nature which is given empirically and the knowledge of which can help in practical activity, but provides no clear and universally valid recommendations about what society should be like. In other words, the path from Locke leads both to Rousseau and to Hume [see Chapter 3].

THE SOCIAL PHILOSOPHY OF G. VICO: THE BIRTH OF THE HISTORY OF CULTURE

This cursory review of conceptions and ideas that preceded the budding of the science of society in the Age of Reason can suitably be concluded by reference to Giambattista Vico (1668-1744), author of *Principles of a New Science* (1725). Professor of rhetoric at Naples, he wrote during a period that nearly coincided with the Enlightenment in France—the first works by Voltaire appeared during his lifetime, and the revised third edition of his *New Science* preceded Montesquieu's *Spirit of Laws* by only four years. Because Vico was active at the periphery of the intellectual life of his times, he was not fully aware of contemporaneous discussions on philosophical and social issues. Superstitious and devoutly Catholic, he devised a system of his own that never came to play any major role and found approval only in the romantic period, but included a wealth of ideas that were strikingly ahead of his times. His system appears remarkable when one realizes that no social thinker before Montesquieu, and perhaps even before Herder and Hegel, showed comparable understanding of specifically social problems, different from those discussed in both natural and political sciences.

At the first glance, Vico's work may seem a product of Roman Catholic apologetics; and Vico himself considered his primary task to be refuting the principles of secular social philosophy which had been taking shape since the Renaissance, and reminding his contemporaries that their reason had its limitations and that the world was governed by divine providence. His numerous comments on the social nature of man can also be treated as a simple affirmation of the orthodox Christian views, consolidated one generation earlier by Bossuet (1627-1704), who adapted the traditional argumentation to a new political situation (the absolute system of government) and also revived Christian historiosophy, neglected since Saint Augustine. Such an interpretation of Vico's work would be not completely mistaken, but one-sided. That author is interesting both because of his Roman Catholic orthodoxy (which can, however, give rise to certain doubts) and because of his success in including in his system most striking ideas. These made later commentators see him as the founder of the modern philosophy of history, historicism, "the historical theory of cognition," the philosophy of language and culture, and even the conception of a qualitative difference between *Naturwissenschaft* and *Geisteswissenschaft*.[85] This thinker's work announced many ideas that were to be typical of the late eighteenth and early nineteenth centuries.

Comprehension of Vico's social philosophy requires, first of all, realizing that he was extremely critical of thinking in terms of natural law, which was dominant in his epoch. He blamed his contemporaries for having confused the natural law of nations, which develops together with national customs, with the natural law of philosophers, devised by them through a process of reasoning.

Where the natural law theorists are abstract, Vico is concrete; where they invented fictions, the natural man or the state of nature, he remainded uncompromisingly committed to what he called history, a history which may not have been accurate, but which was time-bound through and through. Where they distinguished morals from politics, he regarded these as one organic evolutionary process, connected with every other self-expression of human beings in society. Where the natural lawyers were individualists, he grasped the social nature of man. . . . For Vico, men acted as they did because their membership in social groups and their sense of this relationship were as basic and as decisive as their desire for food or shelter, or procreation, as their lusts and sense of shame, their search for authority and truth, and everything else that makes men what they are. Where the lawyers were exact, clear, formal, rationalistic, utilitarian, he remained religious, vague, intuitive, disordered, and painfully obscure.[86]

The key issue seems to have been Vico's antirationalism, combined with his criticism of applying methods developed in the analysis of abstract geometrical questions to the study of human problems. He wrote that the regularities that govern human problems are more real than points, lines, planes, and solids. When considering human problems, we are concerned not with a reasoned world, but with one which really exists and in which we participate directly. At that time of growing fascination with mathematics and natural sciences, Vico seemed to rank humanistic knowledge above them, since the latter gives man *self-knowledge* and not only a knowledge of mechanisms of the external world, mechanisms that cannot, in any case, be fully known by man. Vico found it astonishing that philosophers paid so much attention to studying the world of nature, which only God, its creator, can know, and neglected the study of the world of nations, created by man and hence accessible to human knowledge. The author of *New Science* was interested not in that which makes the course of human affairs resemble the natural chain of causes and effects, but in that which makes it differ from it. Vico thought that man's participation in the process of history gives him a special cognitive chance because he takes part in its creation. Humanistic knowledge proves here to be the knowledge acquired by man who creates himself and at the same time is aware of that fact of creation.

Vico assumed that man is naturally a social and—more important still—a historical being. There is no human nature, if that is a substance which is given once and for all. I. Berlin wrote, "In Vico's conception man is not distinguishable from the actual process of his development—at once physical, moral, intellectual, spiritual and equally social, political, artistic. For him the nature of men is intelligible solely in terms of men's relations with the external world and with other men."[87] Conceived in this way, human nature is in a process of incessant growth that proceeds, on a path determined by providence, from a semianimal to a fully human condition. Human nature is accordingly discovered in history and not through abstraction from history, as the theorists of natural law used to think.

That process of the shaping of human nature passed through definite stages, each of which was conditioned by the preceding one and prepared for the one that was to follow. They were governed by specific rules, which Vico imagined as movement along a spiral; hence he cannot be considered as just an early advocate of the idea of progress. There are also other differences between his ideas and the rationalistic historiosophical conceptions: Vico focused his attention not on the development of human cognition, but on the development of man as a whole in his relations with other men. He was interested in the evolution of cognition, language, religion, manners, art, law, political institutions, and so on into a single organic process that has a certain general pattern. In that sense he may be treated as a theorist of the development of culture *avant la lettre*. An important element of his conception was the combination of the universalistic vision of the history of mankind, guided by providence, with the belief that the history of every nation has its own particular features and that the various nations move in the same direction at different paces and along different paths. In that respect he resembles Herder and historiosophers of the Romantic period.

CONCLUSION: HISTORICAL CONDITIONS OF THE SCIENCE OF SOCIETY

This chapter is not, and could not be, a history of social thought from antiquity to the early eighteenth century. Many important ideas have been disregarded, and those which have been not have been discussed briefly and, in many cases, only one-sidedly. The period that it covers is not in itself the subject of our interest, and so this chapter has been conceived as a kind of historical introduction. The choice and the hierarchy of problems have been determined by the principal subject matter of this book, which is a history of sociology and not a history of social thought or of the social sciences in general.

This is why it seemed pertinent to accomplish in this chapter these four tasks:

1. To provide concise information about the views of those thinkers (like Plato, Aristotle, Hobbes, and Vico) who used to attract the attention of sociologists as their predecessors;
2. To disclose certain patterns of thinking that in some form have remained topical in sociology;
3. To show the plurality of the sources of "sociological" reflection and also the circumstances that favored its pursuit;
4. To show certain necessary conditions that had to be met for the postulation of a specialized science of society and its realization.

The last point seems the most important of all: If the old thinkers contributed to the subsequent emergence of sociology, they did so not by formulating conceptions that sociologists could take up and work out, but rather by discovering problems that made such a new discipline necessary. Similarities between concepts used to be realized *ex post facto*, but the problems were being gradually included in the general considerations of the watchers of the human world; this is why we have tried to point to such problems, even if we could not do so explicitly in every case. We have started from the assumption that three kinds of questions were indispensable for the emergence of sociology. First, it was necessary to pose the question, resulting from the dismissal of naive monism, about the order of the human world, which—contrary to what was believed for centuries—is not just part of the general order of the universe. Second, it was necessary to realize the plurality of the orders occurring in the human world and to pose the question about that which is common to them and that which distinguishes each of them. Third, it was necessary to ask what is that order of the human world and how is it preserved. This question was linked to the discovery of the social order as something different than the politico-legal order. In no case is it possible to establish with precision when a given question was first posed. Even if one was formulated with reasonable clarity, it often became obsolete to some philosophers, though remaining viable in the work of others, who adopted another world view and were active under different historical conditions. Even in the eighteenth century not all these questions would be clear to everyone. However, we tried to show in this chapter, it does seem that they had been taking shape in European thought since antiquity.

NOTES

1. See Paweł Rybicki, *Arystoteles: Początki i podstawy nauki o społeczeństwie* (Wrocław: Ossolineum, 1963); Alvin W. Gouldner, *Enter Plato: Classical Greece and the Origins of Social Theory* (New York: Basic Books, 1966).
2. Karl R. Popper, *The Open Society and Its Enemies* (Princeton: Princeton University Press, 1971), 1:57, 60; See Henri Frankfort, Mrs. H. A. Frankfort, John A. Wilson, and

Thorkild Jacobsen, *Before Philosophy: The Intellectual Adventure of Ancient Man* (Harmondsworth: Penguin Books 1961), p. 12.

3. Z. Barbu, *Problems of Historical Psychology* (London: RKP, 1960), p. 72.

4. Ernest Barker, *Greek Political Theory: Plato and His Predecessors* (London: Methuen, 1957), p. 2.

5. See Sheldon S. Wolin, *Politics and Vision: Continuity and Innovation in Western Political Thought* (London: Allen and Unwin, 1961), p. 31.

6. K. Marx, *Das Kapital* (Moscow: Foreign Languages Publishing House, 1954), vol. 1, chap. 12, par. 5.

7. Popper, *Open Society*, 1:55.

8. Wolin, *Politics and Vision*, p. 33.

9. *The Republic of Plato*, trans. A. D. Lindsay (London: J. M. Dent; New York: E. P. Dutton & Co., 1937), p. 213.

10. Ibid., p. 152.

11. Ibid., p. 107.

12. Ibid., p. 108.

13. Ibid.

14. Plato, *Laws*, trans. B. Jowett, in *Great Books of the Western World* (Chicago: Encyclopaedia Britannica, 1952), vol. 7, 705 B.

15. See Alvin W. Gouldner, *The Coming Crisis of Western Sociology* (New York: Equinox Books, 1971), p. 412.

16. Aristotle, *Politica*, trans. B. Jowett in *The Works of Aristotle,* translated into English under the editorship of W. D. Ross (Oxford: Clarendon Press, 1921), vol. 10, 1337a.

17. Ibid., 1264b.

18. Ibid., 1261a.

19. Ibid., 1288b.

20. Aristotle, *Ethica Nicomachea*, trans. W. D. Ross, in *The Works of Aristotle*, 9, 1097a.

21. Paul Janet, *Histoire de la science politique dans ses rapports avec la morale* (Paris: Librarie philosophique de Ladrange, 1872), 1:177.

22. Aristotle, *Politica*, 1253a.

23. Aristotle, *Ethica Nicomachea*, 1169b, 1097b.

24. A. F. Losev, *"Istoricheskie vremja v kulture klassicheskoj Grecji,"* in M. A. Lifsic, ed., *Istoria filosofii i voprosy kultury* (Moscow: Izd. "Nauka," 1975) p. 16.

25. Aristotle, *Politica*, 1253a.

26. Aristotle, *De partibus animalium*, trans. W. Ogle, in *The Works of Aristotle* vol. 5, 642a.

27. Aristotle, *Politica*, 1252b.

28. Ibid.

29. Ibid., 1253a.

30. Ibid., 1261b.

31. Ibid., 1281a.

32. Ibid., 1277a.

33. Ibid., 1290b-1291a.

34. Ibid., 1289b, 1291b.

35. Ibid., 1289a.

36. Ibid., 1289b.

37. George H. Sabine, *A History of Political Theory*, 3d ed. (London: George G. Harrap, 1951), p. 17.

38. Aristotle, *Politica*, 1326b.

39. Jean Pierre Vernant, *Les Origines de la pensée grecque* (Paris: P.U.F., 1962), p. 52.

40. Sabine, *History of Political Theory*, p. 25.

41. Ibid., p. 129.

42. Wolin, *Politics and Vision*, p. 71.

43. Ibid., p. 94.

44. A. B. Ranovic, *Ellinizm i evo istoriceskaja rol* (Moscow-Leningrad: Izdatelstvo Inostrannoj Literatury, 1950), p. 392.

45. Sabine, *History of Political Theory*, p. 145.

46. W. Kornatowski, *Zarys dziejów myśli politycznej starozytności* (Warsaw: PAX, 1968), p. 225.

47. Sabine, *History of Political Theory*, p. 158.

48. See Wolin, *Politics and Vision*, p. 100.

49. Saint Augustine, *The City of God*, trans. M. Dods (Edinburgh: T. & T. Clark, 1872), book 14, chap. 28.

50. Ibid., chap. 1.

51. Ibid., book 18, chap. 2.

52. Ibid., book 22, chap. 30.

53. Werner Stark, *Social Theory and Christian Thought* (London: RKP, 1959), p. 22.

54. Saint Augustine, *City of God*, book 22, chap. 24.

55. Robert A. Nisbet, *The Social Philosophers: Community and Conflict in Western Thought* (New York: Crowell, 1973), p. 192.

56. Ibid.

57. Aron Guriewicz, *Kategorie kultury średniowiecznej* (Warsaw: PIW, 1976), p. 72. See Wolin, *Politics and Vision*, p. 135.

58. Otto Gierke, *Political Theories of the Middle Ages* (Boston: Beacon Press, 1958), p. 9.

59. Ferdinand Tönnies, *On Social Ideas and Ideologies* (New York: Harper and Row, 1974), p. 14.

60. Otto Gierke, *Natural Law and the Theory of Society, 1500 to 1800* (Boston: Beacon Press, 1957), p. 40.

61. N. Machiavelli, *The Prince*, trans. W. K. Marriott, (London: J. M. Dent & Sons Ltd.; New York: E. P. Dutton & Co.), chap. 25.

62. Wolin, *Politics and Vision*, p. 240.

63. Bogdan Suchodolski, *Narodziny nowozytnej filozofii czlowieka* (Warsaw: PWN, 1963), p. 321.

64. See Wolin, *Politics and Vision*, pp. 142-43.

65. Joseph A. Schumpeter, *History of Economic Analysis* (London: Allen and Unwin, 1954), pp. 117-18.

66. Leszek Kolakowski, *Jednostka i nieskończoność: Wolność i antynomie wolności w filozofii Spinozy* (Warsaw: PWN, 1958), p. 515.

67. Schumpeter, *History of Economic Analysis*, p. 112.

68. Ibid.; cf. Gierke, *Natural Law*, pp. 35-36.

69. Hobbes wrote that "an argument from the practice of men, that have not sifted to the bottom, and with exact reason weighed the causes and nature of Commonwealths, and suffer daily those miseries, that proceed from the ignorance thereof, is invalid. For though in all places of the world, men should lay the foundation of their houses on the sand, it could not thence be inferred, that so it ought to be." *Leviathan*, in *Great Books*, vol. 23, pt. 2, chap. 20, p. 112.

70. Gierke, *Natural Law*, pp. 35-36.

71. Cf. Carl Becker, *The Heavenly City of the 18th Century Philosophers* (New Haven: Yale University Press, 1932).

72. See Kolakowski, *Jednostka*, p. 520.

73. Cf. A. Salomon, *In Praise of Enlightenment* (New York: Meridian Books, 1963), pp. 51-53.

74. Gierke, *Natural Law*, p. 40.

75. Peter J. Stanlis, *Edmund Burke and the Natural Law* (Ann Arbor: University of Michigan Press, 1958), p. 23.

76. Cf. Waldemar Voisé, *La réflexion présociologique d'Erasme à Montesquieu* (Wroclaw: Ossolineum, 1977), pp. 135-45.

77. E. Barker, Introduction to Gierke, *Natural Law*, p. xlix.

78. Wolin, *Politics and Vision*, p. 264.

79. See Howard Becker and H. E. Barnes, *Social Thought from Love to Science* (New York: Dover, 1961), 2:444.

80. Wolin, *Politics and Vision*, p. 308.

81. E. Barker, *Essays on Government* (London: Oxford University Press, 1951), pp. 89-90.

82. See Zbigniew Ogonowski, *Locke* (Warsaw: *Ksiazka i Wiedza,* 1972), p. 180.

83. John Locke, *An Essay Concerning Human Understanding* (Oxford: Clarendon Press, 1894), vol. 1, bk. 2, chap. 28, par. 10 (p. 477).

84. Ibid., vol. 1, bk. 1, chap. 2, par. 10 (p. 74).

85. See Isaiah Berlin, *Vico and Herder: Two Studies in the History of Ideas* (London: The Hogarth Press, 1976), p. 88.

86. Ibid., p. 87.

87. Ibid., p. 65.

2

THE ADVENT OF MODERN SOCIETY: SOCIAL PHILOSOPHY IN THE ENLIGHTENMENT

The Enlightenment, also called the Age of Reason, is of particular significance in the history of social thought both because it concludes the process
of secularization of reflection on society and because it opens new prospects,
which in many respects were the starting point of the interests and conceptions that were to become sociology. In the opinion of Irving M. Zeitlin,
"the Enlightenment appears as the least arbitrary and most appropriate
point of departure in the study of the origins of sociological theory. The
eighteenth-century thinkers began more consistently than any of their
predecessors the study of human condition in a methodic way, consciously
applying what they considered to be scientific principles of analysis to
man, his nature, and society."[1] If we also recognize that they postulated a
specialized science of society more clearly than it had ever been done, it is
not surprising that many researchers have seen them as the direct forerunners
of sociology or even its founders.

THE ENLIGHTENMENT DEFINED

The tendency of rationalistic thought to establish a science of society did
not, however, result in anything that we could call a rationalistic "sociology" (*rationalistic* will often be used, for convenience, as the adjective corresponding to *Enlightenment* and *Age of Reason*). It would not be legitimate
to speak about any such sociology both because reflection on society did
not at that time separate itself from philosophy, historiography, jurisprudence, and political economy and because the fairly common strivings to
make social thought scientific yielded results that were not homogeneous
and were sometimes even contradictory.

This is not to say that the Enlightenment was simply eclectic or that it formed an apparent whole, called into existence by historians of ideas who wanted to make their job easier by replacing a description of many different individuals by a description of an allegedly single species, in which all those individuals would be conveniently included. It is a fact that those eighteenth-century philosophers, each so different from the next, generally thought of themselves as members of one group and were seen as such by their contemporaries.

We cannot go here into the intricate problems of the formation of such general concepts, problems that the historian finds both indispensable and embarrassing. But we must realize that, when tracing the evolution of social thought, we too often succumb to the temptation of analyzing it as though the only possible connections among opinions consisted in the agreement of *statements*. In fact, similarities and differences between ideas can, and should be, analyzed not only at the level of the answers given by the various thinkers, but also at the level of the questions they asked themselves.[2] In many cases the fact that various authors made statements evidently incompatible with one another turns out to be less important than the fact that they had a certain common platform of discussion, which might be totally inacceptable to other authors even if the latter could agree with some points in such a discussion.

To comprehend Enlightenment thinking, one must first realize the peculiarities of a way of thinking that differs from that of the founders of philosophical systems in the seventeenth century and even more from that prevailing in the nineteenth century. The description of this way of thinking can probably best be opened with the well-known quotation from Kant's *Was ist Aufklärung?*:

Enlightenment is man's emergence from his self-incurred immaturity. Immaturity is the inability to use one's own understanding without the guidance of another. This immaturity is *self-incurred* if its cause is not lack of understanding, but lack of resolution and courage to use it without the guidance of another. The motto of Enlightenment is therefore: *Sapere aude!* Have courage to use your own understanding.[3]

Kant's formula makes us immediately recognize the feeling of the breakthrough that the epoch marked and that was so typical of rationalistic thought. And it shows the sense of the importance of the mission that the Enlightenment thinkers believed to have been theirs: bringing about an essentially new attitude toward the world.

When looking for what was common to Enlightenment thinking, we find it easiest to identify the targets at which the philosophers aimed their criticism. The claims that the Enlightenment was basically *critical* in nature, if not downright destructive, are certainly exaggerated, but not unsubstantiated.

Rationalistic criticism was aimed against:

1. Traditional religious systems, because it questioned the cognitive value of the Holy Scriptures, revealed the adverse social effects of faith not accompanied by reflection, pointed to the harm caused by institutions created by the various religions, and so on;
2. All those authorities that deprive man of the right to verify for himself the truth of his opinions whenever he thinks such verification to be necessary (in social life this meant the questioning of the authority of tradition);
3. Speculative thinking, metaphysics, "the philosophy of systems"—all those philosophical conceptions which, unlike Newtonian physics, cannot refer to facts;
4. Contemporaneous political and social institutions, particularly "despotism" and tyranny and sometimes even the very principle of social hierarchy and private property.

The total desacralization of society was probably the most essential point: Even if the existing political system was defended, it was done for its supposedly rational character, rather than because the political system should be respected as such. This was why Enlightenment philosophers were often charged with responsibility for the Revolution of 1789.

In fact, no sphere of contemporaneous life and no aspect of the traditional *Weltanschauung* was immune to philosophical criticism. But the positive program of the philosophers was far from uniform, and its description concentrated, as has been said, on problems rather than on solutions or resulting practical recommendations. What were the problems?

First, the crisis of the traditional religious view of the world and its philosophical criticism required taking up anew the problem of *order*, which ceased to be resolvable in terms of Christian theodicy and the metaphysical systems founded in the seventeenth century. They sought an idea of order that would allow explanation of the regularities in observable phenomena and processes without reference to anything that evades reason and the data provided by observation. The new idea of order was to apply not only to the properties of matter, but also to intellectual, moral, and social facts. Order was imagined as a uniform physicomoral order from which nothing that exists can be excluded.

Second, the concept of *nature,* with all its numerous derivatives (natural order, laws of nature, state of nature, human nature, natural laws, and the like), was certainly the key concept in rationalistic thought. The term *nature* always was one of the most ambiguous ones, and hence all efforts to find how it was understood in each case would be in vain. Yet it was a common tendency to pose the question of what, among the facts observed, can be considered primary, necessary, constant, or natural and what is to be taken as secondary, contingent, variable, or artificial. Answers to that question happened to differ diametrically; the best illustration was the mutually incompatible opinions of what are the "natural" social conditions. Nevertheless, rationalistic thought incessantly moved around that pivotal question.

Third, rationalistic anthropology seems radically *sensualistic*, because its major problems centered on the relation between living conditions and the types of sensations, on the one hand, and the characteristics of human individuals, on the other. This was closely linked to the belief that there is one changeless human nature, a belief that impelled the thinkers of that time to look outside human beings themselves for the explanation of all differences among them—namely, in external factors that modify or deform the manifestation of the constant substance. The human individual belongs to the order of nature, but by participating in social life (whose "naturalness" is more or less problematic), he acquires characteristics that cannot be deduced from the natural order. Human ability to experience sensations, and thereby to be susceptible to the influence of the *conditions* in which one lives, is natural; certain other properties or inclinations are natural, too, but what a given person is like depends on the conditions in which he lives. As in the discussion of other issues, rationalistic thought was extremely diverse, tending on some occasions to analyze the changeless characteristics of human nature and on other occasions to analyze only external conditions. But it seemed always to move around the same axis: the human being versus his living conditions.

Fourth, rationalistic social thought was *individualistic*, in the sense best described by G. Simmel, who brought out its inherent conviction that "if man is freed from all that he is not purely himself, if man is found himself, there emerges as the proper substance of his being, man-as-such or humanity. This humanity lives in all individuals. It is their constant, fundamental nature which only empirically and historically is disguised, made smaller, distorted."[4]

Fifth, the concept of *progress* seems to have been one of the guiding ideas in rationalistic thought. It was apparently implicit in the very idea of making man "mature" and hence in the belief that man, by making the proper use of his cognitive faculties, can know more and more and can live better and better. That faith in progress did not always result in the construction of expanded philosophical systems, but it did play an important role in spreading opinions on history and in the valuation of contemporaneous events.

Finally, we have to mention the *Utopian* elements in Enlightenment thinking, that is, its inclination to produce visions of a world that would be an alternative to the world known from human experience. The concept of natural order was just a kind of philosophical Utopia. The Utopian element was even more strongly marked in the concept of nature as applied in the analysis of moral and social problems; by revealing the artificiality of human institutions, it answered the question about what those institutions should be. But Utopianism was not only an aspect of the philosophical thought in the Age of Reason: It contributed to the emergence of numerous literary works on Utopia, which—next to traditional descriptions of travels to islands of happiness, drafts of constitutions that would be in agreement with "the code of Nature," and numberless idealizations of the way of life of primitive peoples (the motif of the "good savage")—included the first known future-oriented Utopias that placed a happy society in a more or less remote future. This was certainly remarkable testimony to the degree to which the idea of progress was being accepted.

These six items, of course, were not all the elements of rationalistic thinking when viewed from its positive, and not merely its negative, side. We should probably mention its utilitarianism, which made itself known both in the ethical ideas of the time and in the spreading manner of evaluating social institutions, and also the feature that makes some researchers refer to the Enlightenment period as "the legal *Weltanschauung*," that is, a focus mainly on those social phenomena which are subject to regulation by law. Some peculiarities of Enlightenment thinking will also manifest themselves later in the discussion of rationalistic thought and of its critics' position. At this point it seems necessary to make an additional comment, one on the *social* nature of the Age of Reason.

When we concern ourselves with the social nature of rationalistic thinking, we have to take several dimensions into account: the consciousness of the thinkers and their position in society, the milieu of the recipients of the ideas formulated by the thinkers, the contemporaneous political and social situation, and the use made of philosophical ideas in ideologies and in politics.

The eighteenth-century philosopher, above all, felt himself in solidarity with other philosophers and considered himself a citizen of the *république des lettres*, which transcends social and national divisions and admits all "enlightened" persons, without, however, succumbing to any group prejudices. Such consciousness could, of course, be false consciousness. Nevertheless, its very emergence was a significant social fact, as it testified to the rise of a social *group* that felt itself alien to the traditional social structure and had a sense of its own special mission.

That new group consciousness had its analogue in a new socioeconomic situation. The author addresses all those who want to read him; he works not for definite persons, groups, or institutions, but for the anonymous market in which his works are a commodity available to all. He tries to write in order to reach impersonal public opinion, on which he becomes dependent.

So it can be said that in rationalistic thought there was a gradual articulation of the moods and aspirations of all those who were not satisfied with the traditional model of life and thought: They certainly included many enlightened bourgeois, but not them alone. It is known that large sections of the French bourgeoisie were very well adjusted to the conditions that prevailed before the French Revolution, while the nonconformist ideas had many followers among the nobility and in court and even ecclesiastic circles. This unprecedented expansion of new philosophical consciousness, which penetrated almost all milieus, would have been unthinkable had it not been for the social crisis, which made the traditional order a problematic one and made people feel the need to find the principles of a new order. The social and political realities of that new order remained totally undefined in Enlightenment thinking. It was to be in agreement with reason and nature, to guarantee individual happiness and a harmony of individual and collective interests, to make man free in it, and so forth. There was, however, no consensus of the philosophers about what system would be the best embodiment of such an order and how could it be established. They thought it more important to preserve a common front of criticism and the general philosophical ideal. Philosophers in the Age of Reason were concerned with politics, but they were not politicians. Moreover, the peak period of the Enlightenment, which in France fell in the mid-eighteenth century, was not a period of political strife, in the present-day sense of the word. Even if some philosophical systems suggested direct political conclusions, such conclusions were not drawn at that time.

Those conclusions were drawn only by the next generation, that of revolutions in America, France, and (if *revolution* is the appropriate word here) Poland. Eighteenth-century philosophy prepared those revolutions in the sense of having made the social order problematic and of having made those concerned—namely, those who were to be transformed from subjects into citizens—responsible for its form. It prepared them also in the sense of having drawn up a list of concepts beyond which the revolutionary ideologies in the eighteenth century were never to advance: natural laws, social contract, freedom, equality. The point is, however, that no eighteenth-century philosophical conception became the ideology of a definite revolutionary group or movement. Links of the ideologies of postrevolutionary bourgeois society with the heritage of the Enlightenment were still looser, even though there was, of course, a certain continuity of social ideas and conceptions.

THE ENLIGHTENMENT IN FRANCE

It was not France, but the Netherlands and England, countries in which John Locke was active, that served as the cradle of Enlightenment thinking; it would also be difficult to maintain that this way of thinking reached its peak in France, because eighteenth-century France yielded only two philosophers, Montesquieu and Rousseau, who could be ranked together with Hume, Smith, Kant, and Herder. The strength of the Enlightenment in

France consisted more in the popularity, variety, and boldness of ideas than in their novelty and originality. Yet the political and cultural role of France at that time accounted for the widespread influence of those ideas; occasionally, views and opinions that had developed elsewhere radiated into other countries through the intermediary of France. Further, works by French authors were, on the whole, more accessible intellectually and were addressed to broader circles of the reading public. Hence, the stereotype usually reflects the Enlightenment in France, and even the professional literature on the subject reveals an inclination to treat those thinkers who were active in peripheral countries during the late years of the Enlightenment mainly as replicas of the various French patterns. The word *philosophe*, too, happened to be used in many languages in its original form. Such a focusing of attention on the Enlightenment in France has strong arguments in its favor, for even if it was not the most ingenious there, it was certainly the most consistent as a trend and had the strongest impact on social consciousness. It was, therefore, not by accident that later critics of the rationalistic ideas would launch their attacks first at the French philosophers.

The social thought of the French Enlightenment was in no sense uniform, so we shall be concerned with its main trends, not with any general characteristics.

Voltaire and the Philosophy of History. Next to the *Encyclopedia* edited by Diderot, the writings of François Arouet (1694-1778), known by the pen name of Voltaire, are certainly the best introduction to the intellectual atmosphere of the Enlightenment in France. He was a poet, playwright, philosopher, and historian, but above all—to use the words of G. Lanson— a "brilliant journalist," who did more than anyone else to popularize the new *Weltanschauung* and to discredit its opponents. He was the originator and the forerunner of many ideas without having fully developed them and without making full use of them. He popularized Newton's philosophy in France, but he left to others its application in science. He was a great critic of religion, but he was unable to philosophize without resorting to the concept of God. He preached liberty and equality, but he himself did not cross the horizon of enlightened absolutism. He did not originate any coherent sociology and influenced the ways of handling social issues indirectly, at most. His influence is linked mainly to his activity as a historian and a philosopher of history (it should be noted here that it was Voltaire who invented the concept of *la philosophie de l'histoire*).

Voltaire's historiography was polemic-oriented: He strove to overcome specified philosophical and political attitudes rather than to reconstruct past events. He showed the catastrophic consequences of obscurantism, superstitions, and lack of toleration, "the folly that prevails on our globe." His historiography lacks the modern concept of the process of history:

Events take the form of an interplay of fate and accident, and the most important factor in them is constant and changeless human nature. The remarkable point is that, unlike many contemporaneous theorists of eternal human nature, Voltaire thought that man had always lived in society, and he accordingly ridiculed the then popular conceptions of the state of nature. To that changeless man Voltaire explained what his natural rights and duties were. For the purpose he found it useful to refer to the history that showed the mistakes committed in the past and instructed how to avoid them. Thus it was a typically pragmatic approach to history, known already to the ancients. On the other hand, his historiography did include four novel elements.

First, Voltaire claimed that *il faut savoir douter* (one must know how to doubt) and promoted criticism of sources, which aimed at the authority of the ancients and of the sacred texts. He formulated criteria of reliability of sources, which make it possible to eliminate from historical narratives all that which cannot be explained by science and common sense.

Second, Voltaire shifted attention from acts of great men to "the great epochs" in the development of civilization: He wanted to write a history of customs, sciences, laws, habits, and superstitions; of peoples and not kings.[5]

Third, Voltaire signally extended the geographical horizon of historiography by making it include not only Russia, but non-European countries as well. He thus strove to give rise to a *universal* history in the full sense of the term.

Finally, Voltaire did much to secularize historical explanations. However trivial and incoherent his own explanations of historical processes were, they always referred to relationships between cause and effect that could be established in a scientific manner. Such was the meaning, for instance, of his search for what he called "small causes," which reduce events of great historic importance to accidental physiological facts that lay at their origins. He ascribed the greatest importance in the life of nations to human instincts, the climate, the political system, and the state of public opinion, thus exhausting practically all the possibilities of the social thought of the Enlightenment.

Montesquieu: Beginnings of Historical Sociology. The social theory developed by Charles-Louis de Secondat Baron de la Brède et de Montesquieu (1689-1755), author of *Les lettres persanes* (1721), *Considérations sur les causes de la grandeur des Romains et de leur décadence* (1734), and one of the masterpieces of social thought in the eighteenth century, *L'Esprit des lois* (1748), carried incomparably more weight. He is sometimes believed to have been not only a forerunner of sociology, but a sociologist *avant la lettre*.[6]

Such opinions are supported by many features of Montesquieu's way of thinking and, above all, by his *method*, which consisted in systematic observation and comparison of facts, thus moving furthest away, in the French Enlightenment, from the deduction-oriented doctrine of natural law that prevailed in the seventeenth century.

The significance of that turn can best be seen in the case of Montesquieu's interpretation of the concept of law. True, it was still not quite uniform and consistent. In some contexts we find the concept of the law of nature to be a constant norm that, once discovered, would serve as the constant point of reference in the assessment of human institutions. But such injunctions of nature were not the main subject of Montesquieu's interest. Human customs and man-made laws can be at variance with such injunctions, but that does not mean that there is no order, no inner regularity in them. The student of social life can concern himself not only with the lack of agreement between social institutions and the laws of Nature, but also with the question of whether violations of those injunctions reveal a certain pattern. Said Montesquieu, "I have first of all considered mankind: and the result of my thoughts has been that amidst such an infinite diversity of laws and manners, they were not solely conducted by the caprice of fancy."[7]

No matter how far the social world has moved away from nature, it is not the exclusive domain of randomness and chaos. Montesquieu's interest was not in learning whether or not human institutions agree with the laws of nature. Rather, he sought their inner necessity, determined by definite conditions in which those institutions had emerged. None of them can in advance be considered absurd; none of them is just a product of ignorance and ill will: every one depends on many conditions and is intertwined with others. Among social facts, as among physical facts, we can discover certain constant relationships owing to which those facts are what they are, regardless of our evaluations, ideals, and expectations. Thus, law as a norm is replaced by law as a necessary relationship, and man-made laws come to be examined not so much from the perspective of what should be based on the laws of nature, as from the perspective of what is and can be under the conditions given.

This change in the interpretation of the concept of law had manifold consequences in Montesquieu's thought. On the one hand, it meant a weakening of social radicalism, which at that time usually consisted in confronting society with nature and in showing that its institutions are not justified by nature. By focusing his attention on given conditions, Montesquieu made the ideal of nature a relative one and paved the way for the approval of all that which is adjusted to those conditions. On the other hand, the change made it possible to notice the variety of social facts, because the knowledge of the necessary relationships had to begin with a recognition of their many possible manifestations.

Popular interpretations turn Montesquieu into a representative of geographical determinism, explaining all peculiarities of the societies he studied by the peculiarities of the soil and climate. But Montesquieu's ingenuity consisted not in pointing to any single decisive factor, but in revealing relationships among the various factors, in pointing to the fact that society is a system. If he ascribed the decisive role within such a system to anything, it was to "the general spirit" of a given nation, a spirit that develops historically under the impact of many influences and requires that legislation be adjusted to it.

Adopting these views meant, first, abandoning the search for a social ideal that would be good to all society and, second, accepting the opinion that society as such is not made by man, but can at best be improved, following a meticulous examination of the conditions under which it exists. This meant, in fact, rupture with most dogmas of the social thought of the French Enlightenment, which—as we shall see—was marked by the strong belief that a good law, by definition, has universal validity and that legislation determines the general state of a given society, rather than adjusting itself to it.

The novel elements in Montesquieu's approach to legislation can clearly be seen in his typology of political systems. He offered the first typology of societies to be found in social thought; he did so not by paying attention to who is in power and how that power is exercised (the distinction between monarchy and absolutism), but by investigating under what social conditions the various political systems can function. This has been pointed out by Durkheim, who wrote that Montesquieu had singled out true "social species."

This interpretation of the political system as dependent on the characteristics of existing social substratum did not win Montesquieu any adherents among the radicals active in the late eighteenth century and even made him popular in some conservative circles. He cannot, however, be treated as a conservative, for he sought not arguments against all interference by legislation with social life (the sphere of customs and manners), but the knowledge that would pave the way for prudent and effective interference. In defining the goals of that interference, he did not differ essentially from his more radical contemporaries. He was primarily a liberal who combined the eulogy of freedom with the fear of all arbitrary legislative action. He also came to influence nineteenth-century liberalism. But his principal role was that of theorist, author of *L'Esprit des lois*, about which Schumpeter wrote that it was "a new departure and methodologically spelled a significant break with natural law ideas: it was sociology based upon actual observation of individual temporal and local patterns, not merely of general properties of human nature."[8]

Rousseau: Natural Law versus Society. The French Enlightenment had its second great social thinker in Jean Jacques Rousseau (1712-1778), author of *Discours sur l'origine et les fondements de l'inégalité parmi les hommes* (1775), *Du contrat Social* (1762), and many other writings that had a far-reaching impact on European thought in the eighteenth century and later. The many aspects of his influence, on people of various political and philosophical orientations, were due to the ambiguity and paradoxicalness of his writings. The essential question posed by Rousseau was: How should one live? He was not a scholar engaged in detached observation of facts, but a man who found himself in an alien world, suffered from loneliness, and searched for a community with which he could identify himself.[9] He has probably remained to this day the best example of a thinker who is concerned with social issues as an insider, not as an outsider.

In Rousseau's social thought the key role was played by an opposition: *l'homme de la nature* ("man of Nature") versus *l'homme de l'homme* ("man as a product of society"). The latter is "artificial and fantastic," deformed and depraved; the former is free, good, independent, equal to other men, and happy. The latter has lost all those attributes, gaining mere appearance instead; all that which civilized people are inclined to value most has been reduced to appearances. That opposition was greatly expanded by Rousseau; it involves theoretical concepts, personality patterns, criteria of moral evaluation, and so on.

The dislike of culture, which is imposed upon *l'homme de la nature*, and of society, which restricts his autonomy, is manifested by Rousseau on all occasions; it results in his piercing sense of the reality of "collective existence," that antinatural world in which all human beings have found themselves. "We are all," he wrote, "parts of a whole, but we have no sense of unity with that whole." That sense of collective existence makes Rousseau rebel against it vehemently and protest against its being accepted as human existence *par excellence*. Man does live in society, but cannot be reduced to it.

When analyzing human problems, we have to separate *culture* from *nature*—what man is as a result of his collective existence from that what he is *per se*. To use Rousseau's own expression, we have to study "man" rather than "men." "Let us begin . . . by laying facts aside, as they do not affect the question."[10] This might suggest a purely speculative conception, and yet Rousseau's was not such, or at least it was no more speculative than the other conceptions current in his time. The point is that he looked for facts other than those which were of interest to Montesquieu. The latter was fascinated by the variation of the human world, while Rousseau was interested in the unity of humankind, the knowledge of which cannot be acquired through observation of any single society. This is why C. Lévi-Strauss sees him as "the father of cultural anthropology."[11] To use a quite modern phrase, we could say that Rousseau looked for culture universals, that is, facts common to all human beings qua human beings.

The concept of the state of nature, exceptionally significant in Rousseau's work, was to serve that purpose in the first place. It was a theoretical model, conceived by Rousseau with his full consciousness of its fictional or idealizational character.

The description of the process of *denaturalization*, which forms a large part of his study entitled *On the Origin of Inequality*, was of the same kind. It was not conceived as a description of past events, and Rousseau stated outright that "the events might have happened in various ways." In any case, he was not interested in the reconstruction of that process, and his point was to formulate a number of hypotheses about how society in its present form, so remote from the natural state, could have developed and how it was possible for men to exist in a way that evidently contradicts all that which man is by nature. Note also that the word *origines* did not have in the eighteenth century the unambiguously genetic sense that it acquired in the nineteenth century.

The answer given by Rousseau is very comprehensive and in many respects impossible to compare with the other conceptions of mankind's transition from the natural to social state. First of all, it is much more sociological in character, since it points not to any single act of the formation of society as a partnership or company, but to a complex process of intensifying inter- actions among individuals, formation of social institutions, and—especially significant in this context—transformation of human beings under the influence of those institutions. Although Rousseau looked for the constitu- tive properties of human nature in the natural state of man, he never thought that their discovery would suffice to explain human behavior in the social state, as Hobbes and even Locke seemed to assume. Man acquires in society a number of new properties, and, as we shall see, the problem cannot be reduced to eradicating them and thus bringing man back to the state of natural innocence.

Rousseau's reflections on the denaturalization of mankind cover various problems and include the emergence of language and thinking, family, labor and means of production (he recognized the revolutionary consequences of metallurgy and agriculture), property, coercion, political power, and so on. Yet the most interesting issue seems to be the gradual formation of various *needs*, including the specific need of society, which Rousseau believed not to have existed in the state of nature. In other words, society as seen by Rousseau does not merely satisfy existing needs, but itself gives rise to new needs that can be satisfied only in society. Those needs, which Rousseau called "artificial," are both growing material needs, whose satisfaction makes the individual dependent on the whole world, and new psychological needs, which make him seek support in others. "The savage lives within himself, while social man lives constantly outside himself, and only knows how to live in the opinion of others, so that he seems to receive the consciousness of his own existence merely from the judgment of others concerning him."[12] Those problems played an enormous role in Rousseau's work, and this is why he seems to have been so far ahead of his times. The loss of natural independence, as he sees it, does not consist merely in the physical coercion of some people by others: It means such a metamorphosis of all people that they accept slavery willingly. It may be slavery under a despot, but it is always slavery under other people, even if the latter have no intention whatsoever to treat anyone as a slave. Man ceases to be himself, loses his *I*, and becomes totally dependent on the social routine, on the requirements of his social status.

The acuity of the invectives hurled by Rousseau at society, combined with his unquestionable idealization of nature, made many of his readers (beginning with Voltaire) treat him as an advocate of the escape from civilization to the state of nature. The truth is far from being that simple. First, Rousseau idealized the state of nature to only a limited extent, as he did not consider it to have been a fully human condition: The happiness experienced in the state of nature was purely animal in character; it was a state that was not considered to be good as much as it existed outside good and evil, since there could not be any moral system in it. Second, while he vehemently criticized social organization, he did not think it possible for mankind merely to go back to the presocial state, because the changes it had undergone were irreversible. Rousseau compared them to senility and likened the social institutions to the crutches that old people have to use, but the necessity of adjusting all practical solutions to those changes was a fact. Hence, the description of the state of nature did not suggest any pattern of the way of life that could have practical validity now, but provided only some elementary knowledge of human nature, a knowledge that politicians ought to take into account.

It is to that knowledge that the idea of *social contract* refers. To the society that he has criticized he opposed not nature as such, but a good society. The good society would restore at least one condition prevailing in the state of nature: The members of society would not be subject to one another. All of them would be subject to law, which is a product of their own and not a product of nature.

Thus, to the opposition of nature and culture Rousseau added the second fundamental opposition—society based on law versus society based on arbitrary will.

Hence, the point is not to bring about the dissolution of society, but to restore the natural equality and independence of individuals. This would become possible through law, to which all members of society would be subjected without, however, being subjected to one another. Such law cannot derive from the will of individuals, the will of the majority, or even the will of all: It must be a product of *general will*, which is not the sum of the will of individuals, but the perfect reflection of those needs of the members of society that are indistinguishable from the needs of the society as a whole. That law, which would replace natural instincts, would emerge as a result of a social contract, but the social ideal associated with it is not in the least individualistic. As a result of the social contract, a democratic Leviathan comes into existence, a society-organism whose parts are inseparable from the whole and in which the will of the individual is dissolved in the general will.

It may be said that Rousseau's works have to do with two separate conceptions of society: the critical one, in which the pride of place goes to revealing the various restrictions that result from the individual's life in an ill-organized community, and the apologetic one, which brings out above all the pleasures of participating in the community. The former refers to the past and the present; the latter, to the future and to those rather isolated cases in the past (such as Rome under the Republic) in which that ideal seemed to Rousseau to have materialized. Liberals who struggled against the tyranny of the majority could make use of the former; revolutionary ideologists who preached the sovereignty of the people, of both. Despite all the differences, these two conceptions had one thing in common: Society was treated as a supraindividual fact. This was one of the reasons that Durkheim saw in Rousseau a "forerunner of sociology."

The Materialists and Social Theory. The production of the French materialists active in the eighteenth century had the fewest "sociological" elements. This claim applies to Claude-Adrien Helvétius (1715-1771) and Paul-Henri Dietrich d'Holbach (1723-1789); Denis Diderot (1713-1784), the renowned editor of the *Encyclopedia*, can be included in that group with some reservations. The poverty of sociological ideas was due primarily to the fact that they studied man as part of nature, treating him as a biological organism endowed with definite permanent needs, relative to which society was merely instrumental. From that point of view the only subject matter of interest was to what extent existing society really facilitated satisfaction of those needs and what conditions it should meet to be able to perform that function. Since human needs are universal by definition, there is no reason that social institutions should be examined from any other point of view. As Diderot wrote about manners, they are neither African, nor Asiatic, nor European; they are good or bad. This is why the materialistically minded philosophers of nature had left exceptionally little sociology.

We could disregard them completely had it not been for the fact that they preached certain ideas that were extremely popular and influential; moreover their works showed a standard application of the idea of natural order in the analysis of social issues. Like all other organisms, man is a mechanism with principles of functioning that are fully knowable; if we know what they are, we are not in a position to predict and control events, but we can explain them scientifically by pointing to their causes and effects. The system of nature, which embraces man, is a system of universal necessity. They saw social problems almost exclusively as problems of tools to fulfill the tasks that result from the order of nature. If those tools are chosen well, then man lives happily in harmony with that order; if they are chosen badly, the harmony is disturbed, but efforts of reason can restore it.

Materialistic sociology, then, was a peculiar combination of determinism and indeterminism: Man is a will-less cog in the mechanism of nature and a product of social conditions shaped contrary to nature, but, on the other hand, whether he acquiesces in his condition depends solely on his reason and experience. Here theoretical fatalism goes hand in hand with practical voluntarism.

When it came to practical solutions, the materialists represented a naive faith in the boundless power of legislation or legislation combined with education. That faith was based on the conviction that man is a *tabula rasa* on which his living conditions can write anything.

Passions or interests are the only motives of human actions. This results in the emergence of society as a gathering of beings who are susceptible and endowed with reason, who desire happiness, and who fear unhappiness. Like most of their contemporaries, Diderot, Holbach, and Helvétius were interested more in the principle of social life than in the origin of society, even though they seem to paint a vast picture of its origin, covering the development of social bonds, economy, law, social stratification, science, art, and the like. In their interpretation, the emergence of society did not change man in any essential way. It changed the means that he had at his disposal when struggling with nature, but his motives of action remained the same: He continued to be, above all, a biological organism that strives for pleasure and tries to avoid pain.

Yet the emergence of society gives rise to new problems: Insufficient consciousness makes society repudiate its mission so that instead of satisfying the natural needs of all men, it serves as a means whereby some people oppress others. The blame for that is laid on a wrong interpretation of one's interests and on nonobservance of the laws of nature. The blame is laid on society, not on nature—on living conditions, not on individuals. Hence, the individuals are not to be punished for the inclinations developed in them by society itself, and the task is to recognize society in order to enable all people to make full use of their natural rights. The materialists referred to those assumptions to criticize social institutions extensively; their criticism was continued by the early socialists and communists in the nineteenth century, who also stressed the effect of social conditions on the characteristics of individuals. The social thought of eighteenth-century materialists at the same time prefigured those numerous sociological conceptions that assumed that the basic motives of action of members of society originate outside society. This is why they appear to have been much less "sociological" than Montesquieu and Rousseau.

Turgot and Condorcet: A Theory of Progress. It is sometimes claimed that the rationalistic *Weltanschauung* found its fullest expression in the theory of progress, expounded by Jean Antoine de Condorcet (1743-1794) in his *Esquisse d'un tableau historique des progrès de l'esprit humain* (1794) and, nearly half a century earlier, by Anne Robert Jacques Turgot (1727-1781) in his *Discours sur l'histoire universalle* (1750). In fact, theories of progress were the best manifestation of rationalistic optimism, unshakable faith in the future of human knowledge and its beneficient consequences, the belief that mankind can soon find a way of life that would be in harmony with its nature, and so on.

This is not to say that theories of progress were widespread in the eighteenth century. Enjoying real popularity was only a general *idea* of progress, in no case to be confused with a *theory*, since the latter included a number of elements that at that time still had not penetrated general consciousness. Those elements were, above all, the belief in the regular nature of social development, the regular succession of its specified stages, the cumulative development of all spheres of life, and the possibility of forecasting further development. Many authors, who were otherwise deeply convinced that everything was going for the better (for example, Voltaire), did not take the trouble to construct a theory that would explain the trend, regularities, and mechanisms of social development. The novel element in the work of Turgot and Condorcet consisted of taking that trouble.

The very idea of progress was still rather new in the eighteenth century, and its acceptance encountered resistance due both to the tradition of religious thinking (the Christian myth of the Fall and of Paradise Lost) and to certain elements of the new lay *Weltanschauung* (idealization of the state of nature and of "the good savage," fascination with patterns drawn from antiquity, and so on). Conditions for the acceptance of the idea of progress were being shaped gradually, and the idea itself came first to be applied to a limited range of facts—namely, the development of human cognition. That idea, developed in the seventeenth century in the controversy between the "ancients" and the "moderns," came to cover the sphere of morals, social life, and politics about one century later.

Progress (the French authors often used the plural: *les progrès)* came to be treated more and more often as characteristic of all spheres of life, which influence one another in that process. Turgot was, however, clearly aware of its being spread unevenly. He singled out four basic fields—technology, science, morals, and art—and stated that progress in the first of them was marked by the greatest degree of continuity (it had not stopped even in the Dark Ages). Furthermore, progress in the first three fields seemed boundless, while progress in poetry, painting, and art encountered limits that cannot be crossed. Nevertheless, neither for Turgot nor even for Condorcet was there a sphere of human life that in the long run could remain unchanged or move backward.

Theories of progress reflected new attitudes toward changes in social life. For a long time, changes were considered undesirable or desirable only insofar as they would result in a perfect state, which by definition would be a stable one. In the eighteenth century such an attitude toward changes was still not rare, even among the advocates of rationalistic ideas. In the theories of progress that attitude changed basically, a shift that can best be seen in Turgot's work. He was not only inclined to consider the degree of mobility of society as one of its principal characteristics (more important than the political system), but even to claim that mobility is always desirable as it brings new experience and thereby an opportunity for amplification of knowledge. An error committed in the search for new solutions is a lesser danger than the imitation of a truth discovered in the past. Human history proves largely to be a conflict between the novel and routine, and a *sui generis* urge to innovate which never lets man rest satisfied with what has already been achieved, is an element of human nature.

In Turgot's opinion, man's ability to bring about progress results in the fact that human history differs essentially from "revolutions" in nature; the latter are subject to certain constant laws and tend to recur, whereas the former "presents a changing spectacle from century to century. Reason, the passions, liberty, produce new events without end."[13] This endless occurrence of new events does not, however, mean that history is not governed by any law whatsoever. It is governed precisely by the law of progress, which determines the trend of the changes and a given succession of stages and epochs. Yet progress turns out to have its origin in nothing other than constant human nature: It is, in fact, the actualization of the possibilities inherent in that nature. Man has the faculty of sensing impressions and associating them with one another, of cumulating acquired knowledge and transmitting it to others, so that the cumulation of knowledge takes place not only in the minds of individuals, but also in the human species. Endowed by nature in this way, man is simply unable not to improve himself, and societies are unable not to progress. Thus, progress is guaranteed by constant human nature. As a matter of fact, the theory of progress made it possible to save the faith in uniform human nature at just the time when more and more facts proving that mankind was greatly differentiated were being discovered (note the rapidly growing preanthropological literature of that period). In the light of the theory of progress, differences among the various peoples proved to be merely differences in stages of progress and, hence, something equally "unnatural" as differences within one's own society.

The theory of progress was thus, in a sense, profoundly antihistorical. While it certainly broadened the sphere of historical interests, stimulated accumulation and comparison of data, and suggested questions about the interpretation of history as a uniform process, it focused attention on the changeless.

The belief that human nature is constant and uniform was the core of the theory of progress. Coming ahead of nineteenth-century evolutionism, that belief made possible the uniform interpretations of diverse anthropological data without abandoning the basic assumptions of the underlying philosophy, which in itself did not require any support by historical research.

Condorcet's *Esquisse* did most to popularize the theory of progress. While he agreed with Turgot on the primary idea of the theory, they differed in many other respects. First of all, Condorcet did not accept the demarcation line drawn by Turgot between the recurrent natural processes and historical processes. On the contrary, he seems to have striven to demonstrate that the latter have the same degree of regularity and necessity. Starting from these assumptions, Condorcet developed his idea of the possibility of founding social mathematics, which would consist of applying the theory of probability to the analysis of social processes and would make it possible to predict such processes with precision. That social mathematics was made possible by the adoption of a radically nominalistic view of society and the assumption that the general progress of mankind is nothing other than a result of individual progress examined simultaneously in the many individuals who combine to form society. Since he viewed individual development mainly as development of cognition, he interpreted development of the human species mainly as development of knowledge and education. In the first parts of *Esquisse* an important place is given to the description of changes in securing livelihood, which resembles Smith's four-stage schema (hunting, pasturage, farming, industry) and is used also by other authors. But later in the text, social changes are analyzed increasingly as changes in consciousness. The conclusion is that at the root of all errors in politics and morals there are philosophical errors, which in turn are related to errors in sciences.

Condorcet's theory of progress had the relatively greatest impact on the sociological conception of Comte, who referred to it directly when formulating his idea of social dynamics.

THE ENLIGHTENMENT IN BRITAIN

Another strong center of Enlightenment thinking developed in Scotland within a large group of representatives of what was called *moral philosophy*: Connected mainly with the Universities of Glasgow and Edinburgh, they contributed much to the formulation and consideration of problems of social theory.[14] Studies in Scottish social thought were somewhat neglected, but the belief in its having been ahead of its time is far from new; it was expressed by many sociologists (for example, L. Gumplowicz, W. Sombart, and A. Small), who drew attention to the fact that members of the Scottish group were forerunners of such widely different trends in nineteenth- and twentieth-century sociology as Marxism, evolutionism, functionalism, and symbolic interactionism.

All statements about the harbingers of ideas are difficult to substantiate, but in this case it seems justifiable to point to elements of permanent value in the views of the Scottish group that certainly were not the common property of eighteenth-century thinkers. Those elements were, first, the formulation, with extraordinary clarity, of the idea of a social science based on experience and observation and being not essentially different from natural science; second, the development of the concept of man as a participant in social life whose actions are never "entirely complete in [themselves] without some reference to the actions of others";[15] the discovery of the "law of unintended consequences"—that is, the statement that whatever occurs in social life is "the result of human action, but not the execution of any human design";[16] finally, the formulation of a theory of social development that differs widely from the French rationalistic patterns, as it does not see the main driving force of historical processes in the progress of education. All these achievements were certainly connected with the reorientation of moral philosophy "from reflection on moral goods to analysis of moral acts."[17]

The distinctive nature of the Enlightenment in Scotland (and in Britain in general, though it did not yield many remarkable works outside Scotland), as compared with the Enlightenment in France, was largely determined by the peculiarities of the social situation of the country, which had already had its own "glorious revolution." It faced not the problem of defining fundamental human rights and finding effective guarantees of them in the political system, but the task of comprehending and improving the already existing "civil society," which seemed to be something quite natural and at the same time to represent the highest stage of social progress. An important role was also played by the strong tradition of British empiricism, from which British thinkers drew their research method and the French only some ideas, which they later adjusted to their rationalistic *Weltanschauung* as a whole.

When describing the galaxy of the Scottish moral philosophers, we have to begin with Francis Hutcheson (1694-1746), whose treatise *De naturali hominum socialitate* (1730) started almost all anthropology and sociology of the Scottish group. Next come the famous philosopher and historian David Hume (1711-1776), the economist and moral and legal philosopher Adam Smith (1723-1790), and the philosophers Thomas Reid (1710-1796) and Dugald Stewart (1753-1828). Finally there are four authors who were concerned mainly with theory of society and social development: Adam Ferguson (1723-1816), John Millar (1735-1801), Henry Home, Lord Kames (1696-1782), and James Burnett, Lord Mondboddo (1714-1799). Many related ideas are also to be found in the historian William Robertson (1721-1793).

They certainly did not form any uniform school; nevertheless, intellectual bonds among them were very strong, and some of them were linked by personal friendship and direct cooperation (for example, Hume with Smith, Smith with Ferguson). We shall later point to differences between some opinions, but we shall be primarily concerned with grasping those common interests and trends that were decisive for the originality of the social thought of the Enlightenment in Scotland.

"Experimental" Science of Human Nature. From at least Hutcheson on, we can watch the fascination of Scottish moral philosophers with the Newtonian model of science as a universal one; in the science of man he is the moral being, different from the rest of the universe, but forming a link in one and the same "vast chain of being."[18] *A Treatise of Human Nature* by Hume (1739), the most eminent philosophical work of the British Enlightenment, bore a characteristic subtitle: *Being an Attempt to Introduce the Experimental Method of Reasoning into Moral Subjects.* We find there the formulation that "there is a general course of nature in human actions, as well as in the operations of the sun and the climate. There are also characters peculiar to different nations and particular persons, as well as common to mankind. The knowledge of these characters is founded on the observation of an uniformity in the actions that flow from them."[19] For all the enormous differentiation of human actions, institutions, and manners, which testifies to the strong influences of education and of the form of government, we can always detect "a uniformity in human motives and actions as well as in the organization of body."[20] That uniformity is based on the stability and sameness of human nature. In *An Inquiry Concerning Human Understanding* (1748) Hume expounded that viewpoint in a radical way. The knowledge of human nature was for him the source of all knowledge, because we come to know not things themselves, but the ideas that people have about them.

The repertory of the concepts used by Hume was typical of the Enlightenment; the same applies to his focusing attention on the issue of human nature. But his conclusions undermined important elements of the rationalistic *Weltanschauung.* Nature, as seen by Hume, was the plurality of phenomena and process that become known through observation and experience, but it ceased to be *the* standard whose discovery endows human reason with the criteria of moral good and evil. Science tells us what we are and in what world we act, but it says nothing about how we ought to act and what we ought to be. On this point, as on many others, Hume proves to have been a predecessor of positivism.

The science of human nature, as formulated by Hume, was psychology above all. His psychologism was not universally accepted by that age's Scottish philosophers, who to a greater or lesser extent were taking the sociological determinants of human actions into consideration. But there was full agreement that the science of human actions can—and must—be a science that enjoys the same status as the natural sciences, which had taken shape earlier. The common tendency was likewise to deprive the concept of nature all normative connotations and to treat everything universal, regular, and constant as "natural."

Reason versus Emotion: The Origin of Society as Seen by Hume. The shift of attention from the rational to the emotional aspects of human nature, characteristic of the Enlightenment in Scotland, was as important as the demand that anthropology be made scientific. It had particularly grave consequences for the understanding of the origin of society. The conception of man used by Hume and other Scottish authors assumed the absolute primacy of emotions over reasoning and instincts over reflection. (This is why the Scottish moral philosophers are sometimes called "sentimentalists," a misleading term in view of the fact that, unlike sentimentalists proper, they did not recommend that people be guided by emotions, but merely claimed that people are in fact guided by them.)

Ferguson questioned the grounds for opposing human societies to animal ones and claimed that "the establishments of men, like those of every animal, are suggested by nature, and are the result of instinct, directed by the variety of situations in which mankind are placed."[21] Similarly, Hume wrote, "It appears evident that the ultimate ends of human actions can never, in any case, be accounted for by *reason*, but recommend themselves entirely to the sentiments and affections of mankind without any dependence on the intellectual faculties."[22]

The role of reason consists in supporting the decisions made, not in making them. Reason is inactive by its very nature. It analyzes what has occurred, but does not create anything by itself. Nor is it reason that sets the standards of moral good and evil: "Reason is, and ought only to be, the slave of the passions, and can never pretend to any other office than to serve and obey them."[23]

This idea, originally applied by Hume in moral theory, acquired a clearly sociological sense in Hume, Smith, Ferguson, and others. They undertook to prove that the fact of association cannot be deduced from the human faculty of reasoning, but must be based on more elementary properties of human nature, to which the consciousness of the advantages of community life is joined only at a later time. This meant putting to question the theory of social contract, which in all its versions was basically rationalistic; it assumed that the individuals who were parties to that contract had a more or less clear consciousness of the goal that was to be attained by the contract and at the cost of the natural inclinations of those individuals. In the opinion of the Scottish moral philosophers there was an essential error in that reasoning; society is possible only if man is pushed toward it by his natural inclinations, regardless of any calculations whatever.

The most comprehensive criticism of the theory of social contract and of governmental contract as well was given by Hume (who, in doing so, pertinently pointed to its political functions) in his *Treatise* and in an essay,

On the Original Contract (1748). He did not, unlike Ferguson, dismiss the problem of the origin of society; nor did he question the belief, typical of the theorists of social contract, that social institutions are "artificial" in character; nor did he cease to consider those institutions as instruments that help satisfy definite human needs; nor did he, unlike the latter conservative critics, try to dismiss the democratic implications of the theory of social contract for politics. His criticism was purely theoretical, based on the antirationalistic anthropology discussed above, which makes us conclude that man "is compelled to maintain society from necessity, from natural inclination, and from habit."[24] Society could not have come into being as a result of a contract, for in such a case the realization of the advantages of collective life would have to precede actual participation in it. Knowledge would then be earlier than experience; reason, earlier than emotions and will.

Hume's philosophy, taken as a whole, requires that the explanation of social life begin with those properties of man which are earlier than all reflection. The sexual impulse—because of which individuals of both sexes desire intercourse, thus creating links between two generations, parents and children—turns out to be the "first and original principle of human society." It shapes the first habits of collective life and gives rise to reflection that enables one to comprehend its advantages. First of all, men acquire the experience showing that the gravest disturbances in their interrelationships are linked to the existence of those goods which can serve everyone, but are too scarce to be equally accessible to all. The result is the establishment of property, which occurs, however, not as a single act, but as a long process analogous to the formation of languages. Safeguarding property was for Hume (as it was, earlier, for Locke) the main condition of the existence of society, and attacks on property were the greatest threat to society. The concepts of justice and injustice come later than property and, hence, cannot serve as its safeguards. They become necessary only when goods that are limited have been distributed, but continue to be desired by all. Thus definite emotions and conditions come into existence first, and the principles used to regulate them develop later.

A question arises: Why do people abide by those principles even though every application of them does not yield direct advantage to everyone? To answer it, Hume did not endow man with a clear comprehension of long-term interests, but ascribed to him the peculiar faculty (also shared by animals) that he called *sympathy*. It consists in the "communication of passions"—man's being guided in his actions not only by that which is of immediate advantage to him, but also by the consideration of other people's response to his actions. What is involved is not the fear of others, but the inclination, inherent in human nature, to place oneself in the position of another; this ability prevents one man from harming another without experiencing himself an intense discomfort.

An important role was also assigned by Hume to custom and habit, owing to which men value things that are known to them more highly than something else.

Different arguments for the governmental contract were adduced by Hume. He claimed that the decisive role had been played by necessity and custom, while the range of the options that average people had was always extremely limited. Obedience to the government, then, resulted not from decisions made deliberately, but from circumstances under which the subjects, for all practical purposes, could not do anything else.

Searching in the sphere of emotions for the basis of men's union in society or under the rule of a given government—and not in the sphere of reason —meant breaking away from the social philosophy dominant in the French Enlightenment. However great was the role ascribed by the French thinkers (as did the materialists) to emotions as the driving force of human actions, emotions were considered (except by Montesquieu) merely to be the "anti-social factor" insofar as they were not subject to the rule of reason. It was quite otherwise in the case of Hume and Smith: Human passions remained the factors of universality, union, and truth and were not those disquieting forces that the rationalists feared.[25] As a matter of fact, in the Scottish philosophers of that period we find the view, later popularized by conservatives, that social life is based on *prejudice*—that is, whatever judgment existed before reflection.

Foundations of Social Life According to Smith. Hume's analysis of human nature had notable sociological implications, yet Hume's sociology was limited in scope. He did state that "we can form no wish, which has not a reference to society," but he did little to analyze that reference.[26] This task was taken up by a friend of his, namely Adam Smith. Known today mainly as a classic of political economy and the author of *Inquiry into the Nature and Causes of the Wealth of Nations* (1776), in the eyes of his contemporaries Smith was, above all, a teacher of the philosophy of morals and law and the author of *The Theory of Moral Sentiments* (1759).

The links between Smith-qua-economist and Smith-qua-philosopher are very close, and his sociology is found in both fields of his scholarly activity. The analyses of the division of labor, carried out by the economist, and the analyses of sympathy, carried out by the philosopher, were concerned with two aspects, economic and moral, of the same fact of association that takes place below the level of reflection, calculation, and planning. These two kinds of analyses are often examined separately, to the detriment of the comprehension of Smith's work as a whole, because in both cases he investigates one and the same elementary relation of mutuality and exchange. In both cases his point is to demonstrate, as summed up by A. Salomon, that "by nature, we all live as potent and productive and also as needy and incomplete beings. By establishing mutuality we create a whole. But we do not create this unity by reasoning.''[27]

Smith's theory of sympathy corresponds, in its essentials, to Hume's theory of sympathy. The development of morals is possible primarily because human beings are "mirrors" for one another, whereby nonegoistic behavior is reinforced. But while Hume did not proceed beyond ascribing to the human individual an innate faculty of recognizing in others emotional states similar to those which he can experience himself, Smith made a detailed analysis of the role of sympathy in the formation of moral reflection. Hume was interested most in the origin of morals; Smith, in their functioning. The former posed the question of how society can come into existence; the latter, how it functions as the mirror by which individuals control their conduct. Those problems were expanded in Smith's concept of "Impartial Spectator," which has much in common with the later concept of the "looking-glass self," formulated by Cooley, and "the generalized other," formulated by G. H. Mead.

The concept described the intricate emotional and intellectual process whereby society influences the individual.

Were it possible [Smith wrote] that a human creature could grow up to manhood in some solitary place, without any communication with his own species, he could no more think of his own character, of the propriety or demerit of his own sentiments and conduct, of the beauty or deformity of his own mind, than of the beauty or deformity of his own face. All these are objects which he cannot see, which naturally he does not look at and with regard to which he is provided with no mirror which can present them to his view. Bring him into society, and he is immediately provided with the mirror which he wanted before.[28]

The individual who lives in society imagines a spectator who watches that individual's conduct from the outside and approves of it or condemns it.

Further, Smith's conception of sympathy was more profound than Hume's, because Smith singled out its various types—original, habitual, and conventional—which correspond to the various types of social groups: the family, the clan or the neighborhood, and the vocational group.

The motif of others as a mirror was conspicuous in the works of J. J. Rousseau, who, however, saw it mainly as a threat to the individual's sovereign status. According to Smith and Hume, the individual is constituted by that mirror alone: There is no human self outside society. In Smith's opinion, even the realization of one's own interest requires living within society. It is, therefore, groundless to attribute to Smith the opinion that at the beginning of society there are ready-made "natural" individuals. In his conception, as in those of other Scottish theorists, the individual is given by nature merely certain potentials whose expansion is possible only within society.

In Smith's *Inquiry* the moral principle of mutuality takes on the form of the economic principle of exchange: The individual needs others not only to win approval for his conduct, but also to meet his material needs. The market is an impartial spectator through which the individual verifies the quality of his work and finds out whether he himself is really needed by society. The market is the mirror by which he views and controls his economic actions in the same way as he controls his moral actions in the eyes of the supposed spectator. Like other human institutions, the division of labor "is not originally the effect of any human wisdom, which foresees and intends that general opulence to which it gives occasion. It is the necessary, though very slow and gradual, consequence of a certain propensity in human nature which has in view no such extensive utility; the propensity to truck, barter, and exchange one thing for another."[29] The division of labor is not based on transactions made by individuals conscious of their respective goals, but develops spontaneously owing to certain inclinations of human nature that take full shape only within society.

This sociological approach to man, characteristic of Scottish moral philosophy, was probably most advanced in the works of Adam Ferguson, author of *Institutes of Moral Philosophy* (1769), *Principles of Moral and Political Science* (1792), and, especially, *An Essay on the History of Civil Society* (1767), the work that L. Gumplowicz called "the first natural history of society." One of the peculiarities of that book (which will be discussed later) was its dismissal of the problem of the origin of society and the naturalness or nonnaturalness of its institutions, which was still of topical interest for both Hume and Smith: ". . . all the actions of men are equally the result of their nature."[30] For Ferguson, whatever exists is part of nature: Human inclinations are natural, as are societies in which men live. He accordingly shifts his attention to society. If Hume represented psychologism, Ferguson was a representative of sociologism, probably the first in history. He wrote: "Mankind are to be taken in groups, as they have always subsisted. The history of the individual is but a detail of the sentiments and thoughts he has entertained in the view of his species: and every experiment relative to this subject should be made with entire societies, not with single men."[31] Although Ferguson, too, started from the theory of moral actions of the individual, he ultimately focused his interests in the *Essay* on a comparative study of the various types of society. He no longer posed the question of how society was possible, but tried to demonstrate how it changes.

Human Actions and Social Order. The emotionalistic conception of society made its advocates face an extremely difficult problem: If the members of society are guided by instincts, passions, sentiments, and ultimately egoistic interests (for even sympathy works on the principle of the individual's trying to avoid discomfort, which is in this case the knowledge of another individual's discomfort), how are social order and the safeguarding of common interests possible? Note that the solution suggested by the doctrine of the law of nature (men discover permanent and rational principles to which they adjust their conduct and their institutions by restraining their natural impulses) was excluded. In the latter interpretation, social order amounted more or less to political order, because only the existence of a government fully guaranteed the protection of common interests. In any case, social order required an act of cognitive illumination, because it had to comply with a more or less deliberately outlined plan: Its spontaneous emergence was excluded. It was shaped as a result of a conscious concern with the whole, and without such a concern it could only be embryonic or defective in form. The Scottish philosophers, in contrast, adopted the assumption that social order emerges spontaneously as a result of individual actions that have individual interests in view and whether or not the individuals are conscious of that fact.

The basic pattern of reasoning appropriate to this issue was to be found in *The Fable of the Bees, or Private Vices, Public Benefits* (1714) by Bernard de Mandeville (1670-1733), who formulated the paradoxical thesis that private vices can turn into public benefits, and vice versa. Blameworthy motives do not deprive human actions of their beneficial social functions, and morally blameworthy actions can contribute to public well-being. Mandeville's work, which in eighteenth-century Europe had a rather scandalous reputation, did not find approval by the philosophers now under consideration, but they, in fact, reasoned in a very similar way. Since they excluded the emergence of social order as resulting from a plan that was accepted or imposed on the members of the community by a despotic government, the only solution left was to assume that such an order emerged spontaneously as the result of individual actions, which were taken without the intention of bringing about such an order. Social order thus emerges as a result of human actions, but not of human intentions.

This manner of reasoning resembles in many respects the later views of Hegel and Marx; it differs from them not only by the acceptance of the spontaneity of social development as inseparable from human nature, but also by clear traces of deism. In the Scottish philosophers we often find such concepts as "the Great Geometer" (Reid), "the great Director of Nature" (Smith), "the invisible hand" (Smith), or the concept of the goals of nature, which materialize because of the action of blind human passions. They also made use of the Aristotelian distinction between the final cause (in this case "the invisible hand" of nature) and the efficient cause (human actions). They thus certainly took up the problem—of key importance for later sociology—of unanticipated consequences of purposive social action and also come close to the distinction, first made by Durkheim, between cause and function. This is why they are sometimes considered to have been the forerunners of functionalism.[32]

It seems beyond a doubt that for the Scottish group it was the capitalist economy that served as the model of society. This can clearly be seen in the *Inquiry*, in which Smith writes of the entrepreneur that he "intends only his own gain, and he is in this, as in many other cases, led by an invisible hand to promote an end which was no part of his intentions."[33] Ferguson is even more explicit when he says that "nations of tradesmen come to consist of members who, beyond their own particular trade, are ignorant of all human affairs, and who may contribute to the preservation and enlargement of their commonwealth, without making its interest an object of their regard or attention."[34] As we shall see later, this model of social order came to be considered by Spencer as typical of industrial societies.

In its practical applications the idea of the invisible hand meant classical liberalism, which is not to say that all Scottish moral philosophers can unreservedly be treated as its representatives, although Smith certainly was.

Theory of Social Development. Hume wrote, "I believe this to be the historical age and this the historical nation."[35] The interest in history, shown by the Enlightenment in Scotland, was certainly very lively. Hume himself was a renowned historian, and his four-volume *History of Great Britain* (1754-1761) was often compared to Voltaire's historical works. Other prominent historians of the period were Edward Gibbon (1737-1794), author of *The Decline and Fall of the Roman Empire* (1776-1788), and William Robertson (1721-1793), author of *The History of the Emperor Charles V* (1769) and *History of America* (1777). Other authors also occasionally engaged in historiography; this applies, for example, to Ferguson, who wrote *History of the Progress and Termination of the Roman Republic* (1783).

Highly creditable as they were, historical studies produced by the Scottish Enlightenment were not its most original and influential contribution to the theory of social development. The major contribution is rather to be seen in what was called conjectural history, pursued sometimes on the periphery of historiography (as was the case of Robertson), but much more frequently in philosophical works or in special texts, the best example of which is Ferguson's *Essay*. Conjectural history was a kind of philosophy of history, concerned less with reconstructing past events than with grasping general trends and regularities. It was linked to historiography only insofar as the latter showed interest in the development of social institutions, and not only in single events and actions of individuals, and provided data necessary for comparative studies. Those engaged in conjectural history were fully aware that the data provided by historical works were absolutely insufficient to enable one to attain new cognitive goals. Hence there was a search for other data, analogous to that undertaken by Enlightenment thinkers in France.

First of all, there was much more interest (though still not widespread) in the social life of animals, discussed for its similarities to the social life of human beings rather than its differences. Second, there was an explosion of interest in primitive societies, and budding ethnological data came to be treated on equal footing with the traditional historical sources. Characteristically enough, the savage appears in the social thought of the Scottish Enlightenment not so much as *le bon sauvage*, whose very existence discloses the artificiality of contemporaneous civilization, as "the ignoble savage," not more natural than the civilized world and not happier than his contemporaries. The French *bon sauvage* was an instrument of social criticism, whereas the ignoble savage of the Scottish philosophers helped promote a theory of social development from savagery to civilization. This theory of progress in many respects resembled the French theories, but it differed from the latter by not taking the progress of science and education as the pivot of social development.

Probably the most popular theory of social development, a product of the Scottish Enlightenment, was that which assigned the key role to changes in the ways of securing livelihood. Hence, "in every inquiry concerning the operations of men when united together in society, the first object of attention should be their mode of subsistence. According as that varies, their laws and policy must be different."[36] Beginning with the 1750s, that theory became almost the standard one. It was Adam Smith, in all probability, who was its proper author; in his lectures he left the most complete schema of social development that singles out the four stages: hunting, pasturage, farming, and commerce. An extremely interesting aspect of that theory is its correlating changes in the mode of subsistence with changes in social relations, property, political organization, and consciousness. Thus, for instance, the emergence of property was associated with the rise of pasturage and farming, and the rise of government with the emergence of property, because, as Smith wrote in his *Lectures on Jurisprudence* (1766), the task of government "is to secure wealth, and to defend the rich from the poor."[37]

The three-stage schema—most fully developed by Ferguson, whose work preceded Morgan's theory—was somewhat different in character. Ferguson singled out the periods of savagery, barbarism, and civilization and discussed them comparatively in his *Essay*. His analysis covered problems of production, but was focused mainly on social and political structure, as much more importance was attached to the distribution of property and, on that basis, the formation of classes with opposing interests.

Ferguson claimed that "in every society there is a casual subordination, independent of its formal establishment, and frequently adverse to its

constitution. . . . this casual subordination, possibly arising from the distribution of property, or from some other circumstance that bestows unequal
degrees of influence, gives the state its tone, and fixes its character."[38]
Ferguson's attention was concentrated not so much on the differences
between societies in their respective modes of subsistence as on the conditions that determine a given form of government (which shows his intellectual
affinity with Montesquieu) and on a given degree of social unity and a
given kind of social bond. Characteristically, he associated the concept of
civilization with a definite type of sociopolitical organization rather than
with a definite level of material standards of living. He also ascribed an important role in the formation of that organization to external conflicts,
which he considered a powerful factor of social integration.

His analysis of the social consequences of the division of labor is probably
the most interesting element of his inquiries, as it fully reveals his sociological insight. Like Smith, he saw in the division of labor the fundamental
mechanism that shapes modern society, but he also noticed aspects of this
division that came to be seen clearly only in the nineteenth century. The
division of labor was for him a factor of far-reaching social differentiation:
"in every commercial state, notwithstanding any pretention to equal rights,
the exaltation of a few must depress the many." In a modern society, "the
members of a community may . . . be made to lose the sense of every connection, but that of kindred or neighbourhood; and have no common
affairs to transact, but those of trade."[39]

In brief, the division of labor was for Ferguson a factor of both social
integration and disintegration that was unknown to primitive societies,
and it formed the basis—the most important one after the innate inequalities
of talent and private property—of the division of society into classes (unlike
Smith, Ferguson did use the term *class*). Probably this explains why we do
not find in his works the liberal faith in the possibility of a spontaneous
emergence of social order; on the contrary, we find doubts whether progress
is really necessary by nature. In any case, the concept of progress used by
Ferguson was much more complex than the ideas of his contemporaries.
Progress attained by society in some field did not have to mean progress
in other fields.

Finally, it is worth noting that of all eighteenth-century thinkers Ferguson
was the most conscious in his use of the pre-evolutionist comparative
method: He put forth quite clearly the major assumptions of that method,
substantiated the use of certain data (the savage as a contemporaneous
image of our remote ancestors and a representative of the universal social
type), and criticized the idea, current in rationalistic thought, that the
"primitive state" was the simple opposite of the contemporaneous conditions. Understandably, his ethnological techniques left much to be desired,
and hence his practical applications of those novel principles can give rise
to many doubts.

Next to Ferguson's *Essay*, historians of social thought often mention *Observations Concerning the Distinction of Ranks in Society* (1771) by J. Millar, and some value it even higher. Millar's work is very interesting in two respects. First, in addition to the subject specified in its title (and discussed in relation to the evolution of political systems), it carries the most comprehensive analysis of the development of forms of family and marriage to be found in rationalistic thought. Second, even more clearly than Ferguson, Millar singled out classes with opposing interests in society and analyzed relations among them as relations of power and dependence. He saw social development largely as the process of institutionalization of social inequalities, a process that takes place in the spheres of both politics and manners. He dedicated particular attention to slavery, whose existence in the eighteenth century seemed to him a testimony of "how little the conduct of men is at bottom directed by any philosophical principles."[40]

Bentham's Utilitarianism. Jeremy Bentham (1748-1832), author of *Introduction to Principles of Morals and Legislation* (1789), at one time enjoyed great publicity. His work was outside the main trend of the social thought of the Enlightenment in Britain, yet it must be considered here both because of its vast influence and because of its affinities with moral philosophy. Bentham's utilitarianism was the link between his ideas and those of Hume, Smith, and Ferguson. This view associated problems of moral assessment not so much with the intentions of the individuals (which were believed to be inevitably egoistic) as with the actual consequences of their actions. Regardless of their underlying intentions, these consequences promote or oppose the general well-being or "the greatest happiness of the greatest number."

Unlike the other philosophers, Bentham was more interested in normative ethics and believed that advances in education would bring about a *sui generis* revolution in morals. He was more concerned with guiding human conduct than with scientific explanations of the moral consequences of human actions. Further, he did not share their opinion on the social nature of man, and followed in that respect the French materialists (he considered himself a disciple of Helvétius), to whom society was purely instrumental from the point of view of individual needs. If utilitarianism is to be treated as a combination of a philosophy of life, a normative ethical system, and a theory of human behavior, then Bentham stressed the first two aspects, while Hume and Smith emphasized the third.[41]

Bentham's system was markedly nonsociological. He was practically not interested in strictly social issues, such as customs. He focused both on ethical problems and on problems of the legislation that would ensure maximum adjustment of the state to essential needs of the individuals and would enable them to live a truly moral life from the utilitarian point of view.

Nevertheless, Bentham's role in the history of social thought was not a small one. It consisted in the destruction of most concepts current in rationalistic thought, such as nature, law of nature, natural rights, social contract, reason, and moral sense. As we have seen, Scottish moral philosophers, and especially Hume, moved in the same direction, but Bentham went much further and constructed a vast program of fighting "fictions." Moreover, he was inclined to treat even society as a fiction, whereas other philosophers were busy working on that concept. Bentham's radicalism in criticizing fictions was closely linked to his assumption of a very much simplified psychology, according to which human beings are in fact guided by two motives only—the striving for pleasure and the avoiding of pain—and all other motives are reducible to these two. The significance of laws and social institutions boils down to their contribution to a greater happiness of a large number of human individuals; hence, it does not make sense to discuss the problems of such laws and institutions being, or not being, natural and rational if we are unable to state how far they serve this purpose. It is worth emphasizing, however, that Bentham's criticism of rationalistic ideas (including *The Declaration of the Rights of Man and of the Citizen*) did not in the least mean a lack of approval of the libertarian ideals of his age. Bentham thought, instead, that he was giving them stronger theoretical foundations. He did much for the formation of liberal ideology, although, unlike Smith, he attached much hope to an active government; diverging from his utilitarian philosophy, he believed, that the government may include people capable of disinterested service on behalf of society.

THE ENLIGHTENMENT IN GERMANY

If the social thought of the German Enlightenment differed considerably from that in France and in Britain, the reasons are to be seen in the situation prevailing in Germany, which in the eighteenth century was incomparably more backward in socioeconomic development and, more over, did not form a single political entity. German thinkers had not, and could not have, experienced themselves living in a "civil society" in the sense of, say, Ferguson's *Essay*. It was for them an abstract requirement projected into an indefinite future, rather than any given or nascent reality.

That backwardness of Germany, however, did not mean intellectual stagnation. Even in the eighteenth century it would be legitimate to say about Germany what Marx said later; namely, the Germans were *philosophically* contemporaneous with the present epoch without being *historically* contemporaneous. Perhaps the position of outsiders to European modernity gave the Germans a specific cognitive opportunity, as it allowed them to reflect philosophically on problems that were lost in discussions of current issues in other countries. Without belittling in any way the contribution of the French rationalists, we may say for them the essential task of the theory was to provide arguments for the advocates of progress, however the latter happened to be understood. But the Germans participated in their contemporaries' dialogue on the future of society with maximum political disinterestedness.

While the social thought of the German Enlightenment approached the realities of that country, it also proved astonishingly restrained on issues that were touchy politically and socially. Culture was the main subject of interest. (Consider Herder, for example.) There was nothing strange in that if we consider that at that time the real bonds uniting German society were language, tradition, and literature, not a common organization or political idea.

Thus in Germany the Enlightenment was the Golden Age of philosophy and literature—and not of politics.

Kant: Philosophical Anthropology and Historiosophy. When writing a history of sociological thought one should not disregard (although this is often done[42]) the renowned German philosopher Immanuel Kant (1724-1804). He was an important source of inspiration for many theoretically oriented sociologists. The Kantian way of thinking affected European thought so much that it penetrated even those spheres in which no direct references to him were made and those in which his views were rejected. Moreover, the image of the Enlightenment would be incomplete without Kant, for it was he who introduced the term *Aufklärung* and contributed signally to its definition. It seems beyond doubt that Kant started from typically rationalistic theoretical dilemmas, although the solutions that he suggested were the origin of quite different ways of thinking.

Kant can be taken into consideration in various ways: as an author who directly touched on sociological issues when writing on historiosophy, ethics, law, and politics, or as an author whose strictly philosophical works revolutionized all spheres of thought. Moreover, one can read his works (as many commentators have done since the time of Heine) from the point of view of the answers, included in his philosophy, to questions that are essentially political and social. His philosophy was said to have been a highly abstract "analogon" of Jacobinism (Marx) or of liberalism (Simmel) or a condensed manifestation of bourgeois individualism (L. Goldmann). Whichever is true, the problem of Kant as a social thinker (like that of Hegel) does not reduce to the reading of his not very numerous statements directly concerned with sociology. These, if taken in isolation, are not particularly interesting and include many current ideas. It may be said that Kant deserves his special place in the history of rationalistic thought to the ability to go beyond its philosophical horizons. By making a revolution in philosophy, he started to carry weight in all those fields which are linked to philosophy.

We shall not discuss the intricate system formulated by the author of

Critique of Pure Reason (1781), *Critique of Practical Reason* (1788), and
Critique of Judgment (1790), but shall point to its two important consequences. Following Popper, we will call them the humanization of science
and the humanization of ethics.[43]

The first of these is connected with Kant's assumption, made in the
Critique of Pure Reason, that in the process of cognition the subject plays
an active role, without which that process would not be possible at all. Kant
eliminated from the theory of cognition the idea of the subject as the passive
experiencer of sensations. Only reason, owing to its categories that exist
a priori, orders the chaos of sensory data and constitutes thereby the object
of cognition. This is not to say that Kant belittled the role of experience;
rather, he disclosed the limited nature of all empiricism, thus crossing the
boundaries of traditional rationalism. In this way he destroyed the faith in
world order that would be independent of man. Kant did retain the idea
of order, but he shifted it into the human mind: He looked for the law that
governs nature not in the world around man, but in man himself, for it is
man, depending on the *a priori* faculties of his reason, who changes the
chaos of sensory data into an intelligible order of nature.

The critique of cognition was inevitably a critique of social cognition.
It is true that it was only Simmel who transferred the totality of Kantian
gnosiological problems to the sphere of reflections on sociological cognition.[44] Nevertheless, the change in the status of the cognizing subject, brought
about by Kant, had been noticed in the social sciences at a much earlier
date and by Hegel and Marx (who made an essential correction in the
Kantian approach by treating that active cognizing subject as a product of
history). Next, Durkheim and his followers took up systematic research on
the social origin of the categories of cognition, whereas present-day struc-
turalists have returned to Kant's point of departure. In any case, Kant
raised problems that no one else did in the eighteenth century and that later,
too, would be ignored by many representatives of the social sciences, who
were inclined to believe that they had to do with ready-made facts that are
simply mirrored by science.

Kant's humanization of ethics, carried out in the *Critique of Practical
Reason*, was no less important. Man is not determined by the external world
either in his cognition or in his actions. All cognition proceeds from theory
to empirical data, not from empirical data to theory. This holds for natural
science and for ethics as well.

Kant was directly inspired by Rousseau, who claimed that the individuals
whom we see in our daily experience reveal their masks, and not their faces;
therefore, true humanity is to be sought somewhere behind the veil of
appearances. Kant adopted that attitude, but he modified it essentially.
In his opinion, the essence of humanity is not contained in human nature
as revealed by an analysis of the hypothetical presocial state (even though

Kant did use the concept of the state of nature), but in nature as interpreted as the moral mission of *Homo sapiens*, which raises him above nature and even opposes him to nature. When seen as part of nature, man is an object; and it is only when he is opposed to nature that he becomes a subject. To individuals described by other theorists, Kant opposed not a man of nature, but a man of reason and morals, and he shifted the emphasis to the *goals* that this man is to attain. In Rousseau, man as a moral being remains part of the natural order, whereas in Kant he transforms himself into a sovereign moral subject who, in fact, has no connection with man as part of nature and as an object of sensory experience. Man as subject lives in the kingdom of freedom; man as object, in the kingdom of causality.

Kant's anthropology was radically dualistic and individualistic. Its dualism consisted in splitting man into *homo phaenomenon* and *homo noumenon*; its individualism, in the claim that for his moral activity man does not need any other men. Every human individual is endowed with reason as the faculty for finding the path of the proper conduct, which consists in obedience to the injunctions of the categorical imperative—that is, conduct that could be made a universal norm. In Kant, man is thus torn between the duties defined by reason and the pressure of the external world in which he lives and which puts a premium on conduct that is incompatible with moral duty. The ethics associated with anthropology was directed, on the one hand, against utilitarian ethics that strove to deduce the principles of morality from experience and, on the other, against those absolutist doctrines which brought into ethics any moral authorities that are external to the individual and thus destroy his autonomy as a being endowed with reason. Kant thus opposed both utilitarianism, so powerful in the rationalistic thought, and the traditional ethics based on religion.

Kant's ethics seemingly did not include any sociological elements. It did not cover any injunctions intended to regulate social relations (except, of course, the principle that every individual is to be respected as an autonomous subject); it was concerned with a most abstract duty and excluded the assessment of human actions relative to their social (and all other) consequences.

There is, however, no doubt that Kant's ethics was closely related to his politics, for it defined the ideal that the latter was supposed to bring into effect. Furthermore, in human history that ideal materializes through culture, which bridles the power of the senses over human conduct and is conducive to the emergence of conditions (civil society) under which the freedom of any individual would not be a threat to the freedom of any other individual. This makes Kant face the problem once faced by Rousseau: How is it possible to make a system of law that would not violate individual freedom without simultaneously paving the way for individual arbitrary will. Rather unexpectedly, Kant assigned the task of bringing about that ideal to nature, whose problem is "that of attaining a civil society which can administer justice universally."[45]

Kant's historiosophy seems to come closest to the views typical of the rationalistic philosophy of progress both because it includes the idea of a natural order *sui generis* and because its system of values does not differ essentially from systems of values underlying other historiosophies of his times. That historiosophy, expounded most distinctly in his *Idea for a Universal History with a Cosmopolitan Purpose* (1784), is based on the conviction that the course of events, which seems to be an aggregate of accidental occurrences, proves to be a process governed by regularities if it is seen from the point of view of mankind taken as a whole. We find in Kant the motif, already known in the Scottish Enlightenment, that announces Hegel: "Individual men and even entire nations little imagine that, while they are pursuing their own ends, each in his own way and often in opposition to others, they are unwittingly guided in their advance along a course intended by nature, they are unconsciously promoting an end which, even if they knew what it was, would scarcely arouse their interest."[46]

The concept of "unsocial sociability of men" *(die ungesellige Geselligkeit der Menschen)*, linked to the dualistic conception of man and intended to explain the mechanism of progress, is probably the most original element of Kant's historiosophy. Every man "seeks . . . a status among his fellows, whom he cannot *bear* yet cannot *bear to leave*."[47] That status seeking means the essential step from barbarity to civilization, the latter being based on socialization. The next step is the transition from society based on coercion to society as a union based on morality. Without that "unsociability," progress would have been impossible and men would have remained at the animal level. It is only conflict that snatches them away from a state of stupor and brings them ultimately to civilization and to society as an union based on morality. Kant thus dismissed the age-old dilemma of whether man's nature is social or antisocial. Society and its progress are possible only because both inclinations are inherent in man.

The problems raised in Kantian anthropology and ethics, like those raised in his epistemology, had numerous offshoots in European social thought. First, its characteristic dualism in interpreting man seems to have become the nucleus of the distinction between *Geisteswissenschaften* and *Naturwissenschaften*, popular not only in Germany.[48] Second, the Kantian problem of bringing into harmony the order of nature and the order of morals inherent in man remained topical. It was with that problem in fact, that Durkheim's sociology originated. Third, Kant's ethical formalism prefigured the later formal sociology, because it gave rise to reflection on human actions as separate from both their psychological motivations and their historical context. Thus, it may turn out that Kant's impact on sociological thought was greater than that of any other thinker in the Age of Reason.

Herder: Cultural Pluralism. The Enlightenment in Germany had its other prominent representative in Johann Gottfried Herder (1744-1803), author of *Ideen zur Philosophie der Geschichten der Menschheit* (1784-1791) and a theorist whose work influenced the later development of social thought.

While Kant represented the most advanced philosophical consciousness within rationalistic thinking and thus started the triumphant pageant of German idealism, Herder's work meant, above all, the expansion of the ideas that we usually call pre-Romantic: the ideas of cultural differentiation of mankind, the spirit of the nation, the role of nations in history, and so on. While Herder was a thinker of much smaller stature than Kant, his role in the history of social thought was important, as it gave rise to modern historicism.

Herder's originality, against the background of the eighteenth-century way of thinking, was so striking that some historians saw him as a critic of the Enlightenment and disregarded all his connections with the thought of his epoch except for those with Montesquieu and other theorists of "the spirit of the nation."

The controversy between Herder and the French *philosophes* focused, it seems, on four fundamental issues. (1) While declaring himself generally in favor of the pattern of science created by Newton, Herder rejected the mechanistic vision of the world and replaced it by a vitalistic or organicist vision, which, of course, led to an essentially different interpretation of nature, symbolized for him by the variety of life and not by the uniformity of the laws that govern it. (2) While retaining the ideas of progress and mankind, Herder revised their most popular versions, declaring himself against men who treat lightly the wisdom of other epochs and against those thinkers who treated mankind as a homogeneous whole or believed its gradual homogenization to be desirable. (3) Without belittling the very idea of reason (as was to be done later by the romanticists), Herder brought out its connections with the other faculties of man, whom he treated as the subject who acts, experiences, and expresses his personality and does not merely receive sensations and think. His anthropology assumed an organic connection between the individual and others, since men need one another simply because they differ from one another. (4) Note also that the distinctive feature of Herder's works was largely determined by his way of writing, marked by an element of poetry, which scandalized Kant.

Herder's social theory can hardly be separated from the whole of his philosophy. Its comprehension requires consideration of some of his ontological and epistemological assumptions. According to the former, the universe is a great organism in which everything is interconnected, following the working of an irrational vital force that penetrates every particle of nature. According to the latter, the process of cognition does not consist in observing the world, which is external to the cognizing subject, but in actively participating in it and in experiencing it in an almost religious manner. Man is capable of knowing the macrocosm because he himself is a microcosm.[49] Thus, Herder's "natural history of human forces, actions, and impulses" differed rather essentially from the other natural histories worked out in the eighteenth century.

Society is not qualitatively different from the rest of the universe, and it is subject to the same laws. It was not constructed like a machine, but is an incessantly growing organism. It is a whole that consists of parts which are different from one another, endowed with unique individual features, but indispensable for one another and dependent on one another. Society consists of individuals, but cannot be reduced to them. An individual cannot be considered solely a participant in society, for he has his own autonomous value and, as such, cannot be replaced. Herder's organicism differed thus, from that of the conservatists, who opposed the very principle of individuality and reduced the variety of the parts of the social organism to the variety of the functions assigned to the various social groups. Society is, however, the natural state of the individual: From the very moment of his birth he is immersed in a community—family, tribe, nation, and the like.

According to Herder, the nation (*Volk*) is the most important human community. He was ahead of his time on this point, because the word meant for him (unlike the overwhelming majority of rationalistic thinkers) not so much an aggregate of people who live on a common territory and are subject to the same laws as a culture community, shaped in the course of history and finding expression in its language.

The problem of language had a special significance in Herder's social philosophy. He often repeated that language is not, and cannot be, the exclusive hunting ground of the grammarians and that "each nation speaks in the manner it thinks and thinks in the manner it speaks."[50] Language is the basic factor of the identity of a given nation: It expresses the character of the nation that survives as long as it can foster the traditions crystallized in language.

This is not to say that Herder did not attach importance to political organization, which so strongly attracted the attention of other rationalistic thinkers. On the contrary, he believed it to be something "natural."[51] However, he treated political organization as secondary and as determined by cultural factors. The essence of the state is not the existence of a sovereign power, but a human community that develops the political organization that it needs. The strength of the state is based on the strength of that community, and hence when the latter weakens, the most powerful government proves helpless. Good laws are not those behind which there is the strength of the state, but those which are based on ancient national customs. This conception has much in common with Montesquieu's, but seems much more consistent: It leaves much less room for a wise legislator, of whom the author of *The Spirit of Laws* thought incessantly. Herder, nevertheless, was not an apologist of existing political conditions. The idea of a national state-organism was Utopia that he opposed to the existing order of things.

The peculiarity of Herder's idea, as compared with the later conservative conceptions, was that the nations remained integral parts of mankind, which was to him a real entity.[52] But the history of mankind is the history of the nations and is contained in the latter. This belief had significant methodological consequences: The task was not to show a single model line of development, but to grasp the whole variety of historical events, the wealth of which determines the wealth of mankind. It also implied considerable caution in classing the various forms of social life as higher and lower, because every nation has its own measures of perfection, which must not be confused with measures developed by other nations. Thus, Herder's *Reflections of the Philosophy of History* are concerned more with the plurality of facts in which the intentions of providence (a fairly important concept in Herder's historiosophy) materialize than with the uniformity of the laws of history. It is only the general objectives of nature that are uniform.

Herder comes closest to other ideas of his time when he analyzes the causes of historical processes. His starting point was the doctrine of geographical determinism. He developed his own "climatology," but he used the concept of climate in such a broad sense that it is legitimate to assume that he had in mind all forms of the environment's influence on individuals.[53]

But in the history of social thought Herder appears above all as the great forerunner of the science of *culture*. Reflection on culture had, as it seems, two principal sources: (1) distinction between nature and all that which in man's environment is the product of his own actions; and (2) recognition of the historical and spatial differentiation of that artificial environment. It it legitimate to suppose that Herder realized problems of both kinds more fully than any of his contemporaries; at the same time, acting counter to the main trend of his age, he in a sense consecrated cultural pluralism.

CONCLUDING REMARKS

By calling this chapter "The Advent of Modern Society," we meant to indicate, first, that the social thought of the Enlightenment had developed before that society took shape and, second, that it had anticipated many of society's problems and dilemmas. Social philosophy under the Enlightenment was in some respect, it seems, superior to nineteenth-century sociological systems, and its heritage has affected all subsequent thinking. However, it could not have been fully assimilated by sociology, because the latter emerged in different historical conditions and strove to solve the problems of the new society that came to be fully formed only after the industrial revolution and the political revolution of the bourgeoisie.

Those who lived in the nineteenth century, however much they owed to their predecessors, had a firm sense of belonging in another epoch, which, by the way, had little in a common with the kingdom of reason envisaged by philosophers. As we shall see later, they carried on an incessant dialogue with those philosophers and adopted many of their ideas, but they could not consider themselves their disciples for several reasons:

1. They attached much more weight to historical variability of human beings and societies.
2. They were fascinated much less by striving for an ideal than by explaining the differences between the old feudal society based on estates and the equally real, new capitalist society based on classes.
3. Issues of social (and national) bonds that evade social control were for them much more important than issues of legal and political systems.
4. New advances in natural sciences made the possibility, and the necessity, of founding social science even more evident to them than it had been to people who had lived in the Age of Reason.

NOTES

1. Irving M. Zeitlin, *Ideology and the Development of Sociological Theory* (Englewood Cliffs, N.J.: Prentice-Hall, 1968), p. vii.
2. Cf. Bronislaw Baczko, Introduction to Dom Léger-Marie Deschamps, *Prawdziwy system czyli rozwiazanie zagadki metafizyki i moralności* (Warsaw: KiW, 1967), pp. 98-99.
3. Hans Reiss, ed., *Kant's Political Writings* (Cambridge: Cambridge University Press, 1970), p. 54.
4. Kurt H. Wolff, ed., *Sociology of Georg Simmel* (New York: Free Press, 1964), p. 68.
5. Voltaire, *Essai sur les moeurs et l'esprit des nations* (Paris: Editions Sociales, 1962), p. 22.
6. Cf. R. Aron, *Les étapes de la pensée sociologique* (Paris: Gallimard, 1967), p. 27.
7. Montesquieu, *The Spirit of Laws*, in *Great Books of the Western World*, vol. 38 (Chicago: Encyclopaedia Britannica, 1952), p. xxi.
8. Joseph A. Schumpeter, *History of Economic Analysis* (London: Allen and Unwin, 1972), p. 136.
9. Cf. Bronislaw Baczko, *Rousseau: Samotność i wspólnota* (Warsaw: PWN, 1964), pp. 11-90.
10. J. J. Rousseau, *On the Origins of Inequality*, in *Great Books*, vol. 38, p. 333.
11. C. Lévi-Strauss, "J. J. Rousseau, *fondateur des sciences de l'homme*," in Lévi-Strauss, *Anthropologie structurale deux* (Paris: Plon, 1973).
12. Rousseau, *Origins of Inequality*, p. 362.
13. Frank E. Manuel, *The Prophets of Paris* (Cambridge, Mass.: Harvard University Press, 1962), pp. 21-23.
14. Gladys Bryson, *Man and Society: The Scottish Inquiry of the Eighteenth Century* (New York: Kelley, 1968), p. 4.
15. D. Hume, *An Enquiry Concerning Human Understanding* (Leipzig: F. Meiner, 1913), chapter 8, sec. 141.

16. Adam Ferguson, *An Essay on the History of Civil Society* (Edinburgh: Edinburgh University Press, 1966), p. 122.

17. Cf. A. Salomon, *In Praise of Enlightenment* (New York: Meridian Books, 1963), p. 203.

18. Cf. Bryson, *Man and Society*, p. 60.

19. Hume, *A Treatise of Human Nature* (London: Longmans, Green, 1898), vol. 2, part 3, chap. 1.

20. Hume, *An Enquiry*, chap. 8, sec. 132.

21. Ferguson, *An Essay*, p. 182.

22. David Hume, *An Enquiry Concerning the Principles of Morals* (LaSalle, Ill.: Open Court Publishing, 1946), p. 143.

23. Hume, *A Treatise*, vol. 2, pt. 3, chap. 3.

24. David Hume, "Of the Origin of Government," in Hume, *Essays Moral, Political and Literary* (London: Oxford University Press, 1963), p. 35.

25. E. Bréhier, *Histoire de la philosophie* (Paris: P.U.F., 1962), vol. 2, pt. 2, p. 433.

26. Hume, *A Treatise*, vol. 2, pt. 2, chap. 5.

27. Salomon, *In Praise of Enlightenment*, pp. 202-18.

28. Louis Schneider, ed., *The Scottish Moralists on Human Nature and Society* (Chicago: University of Chicago Press, 1967), p. 70.

29. Adam Smith, *Inquiry into the Nature and Causes of the Wealth of Nations* (London: Methuen, 1950), book 1, chap. 2.

30. Ferguson, *An Essay*, p. 4.

31. Schneider, *Scottish Moralists*, p. 81.

32. Ibid., pp. xxix-xlvii (Introduction).

33. Ibid., pp. 106-7.

34. Ferguson, *An Essay*, p. 181.

35. See Bryson, *Man and Society*, p. 78.

36. W. Robertson, *History of America*, quoted in Ronald L. Meek, *Social Science and the Ignoble Savage* (Cambridge: Cambridge University Press, 1976), p. 2.

37. See Andrew S. Skinner and Thomas Wilson, eds., *Essays on Adam Smith* (London: Oxford University Press, 1976), p. 158.

38. Ferguson, *An Essay*, p. 133.

39. Ibid., pp. 186, 219-20.

40. See Marvin Harris, *The Rise of Anthropological Theory* (New York: Crowell, 1968), p. 52.

41. Cf. Schumpeter, *History of Economic Analysis*, pp. 132-33.

42. One of the exceptions is Don Martindale, *The Nature and Types of Sociological Theory* (Boston: Houghton Mifflin, 1960), pp. 216-20.

43. Karl R. Popper, *Conjectures and Refutations: The Growth of Scientific Knowledge*, 3d ed. (London: RKP, 1969), p. 181.

44. Cf. Kurt H. Wolff, ed., *Georg Simmel, 1858-1918: A Collection of Essays with Translations and a Bibliography* (Columbus, Ohio: Ohio State University Press, 1959), pp. 337-56.

45. See Reiss, *Kant's Political Writings*, p. 45.

46. Ibid., p. 41.

47. Ibid., p. 44.

48. Cf. Talcott Parsons, *The Structure of Social Action* (New York: Free Press, 1968), pp. 473-87.

49. Cf. F. M. Barnard, *Herder's Social and Political Thought from Enlightenment to Nationalism* (Oxford: Clarendon Press, 1965), pp. 31-42.

50. Ibid., p. 56.

51. Ibid., p. 55.

52. Ibid., p. 88.

53. Ibid., p. 122.

3

POSTREVOLUTIONARY SOCIO-POLITICAL THOUGHT AS A SOURCE OF SOCIAL THEORY

"The fundamental ideas of European sociology," Robert A. Nisbet wrote, "are best understood as responses to the problem of order created at the beginning of the nineteenth century by the collapse of the old regime under the blows of industrialism and revolutionary democracy."[1] It is worthwhile to realize that that problem had become a subject of public debates even before the first sociological systems emerged. The practical importance of this problem accounted for its being taken up in all spheres of reflection on society. One such sphere encompassed the sociopolitical ideologies of the period: conservatism, liberalism, and socialism.

CONSERVATISM

The Concept of Conservatism. When discussing conservatism in this context, we mean only one of the possible meanings of the term *conservatism.*[2] We are not in the least concerned with conservatism as a fairly constant mental disposition to oppose all change, nor with conservatism as that type of ideology which emerges whenever the status quo is threatened in its entirety. We treat conservatism here as an ideology specific to a certain epoch—namely, the epoch of transition from feudalism to capitalism, the epoch of bourgeois revolutions, when certain social groups strove to stop the changes that were taking place or at least to comprehend what at first seemed to be a "dissolution of society" and an almost cosmic catastrophe. It was with such "aristocratic" conservatism, determined by historical conditions, that Karl Mannheim was concerned in *Conservative Thought*, in which he claimed that this conservatism was the first case of an integrated *Weltanschauung*. In fact, the conservatives in the late eighteenth and early nineteenth centuries proved to be the first of those inclined to praise the past who were in a position to develop a specific social philosophy that could vie with other philosophies (especially those of the Age of Reason) and was attractive intellectually.[3]

Obviously, even this brand of conservatism never was, nor could be, fully homogeneous, for its supreme calling was to defend specific, differentiated societies against the inroads of universalistic patterns of political rationalism and revolution.

Further, the campaign against the Revolution of 1789 was led by various social groups and by ideologists of various orientations, who differed in the intensity of their inclinations to reject the very idea of change and to eulogize the prerevolutionary system. From the point of view of social theory, certainly the most interesting among them were those who sought the ways of securing *continuity* in an inevitably changing society, rather than defending specified institutions characteristic of that system. Those thinkers had to consider, to some extent, the realities of the revolutionary period and also to reconcile themselves to the fact that social stability is relative, at best. They also had to recognize that restoration of old institutions was not possible and that they had only to look for certain general *principles* that would make it possible to secure social order under the new conditions. This reorientation, which was not easy to achieve, gave rise to the conservative social philosophy, which was qualitatively different from the half-instinctive resistance to all change.

It is Edmund Burke (1729-1797), an English writer and statesman, who is universally held to be the founder of modern conservatism; he won renown with his book *Reflections on the Revolution in France* (1790). Karl Ludwig von Haller (1768-1854) was active in Switzerland and in Germany. In France, the task of overcoming revolutionary consciousness was taken up by émigré writers such as Rivarol (1753-1801) and Mallet du Pan (1749-1801) and, above all, by Louis de Bonald (1754-1840) and Joseph de Maistre (1754-1821). Among the Germans, among whom conservative thought seems to have been most popular, the pride of place goes to Adam Müller (1779-1829), a representative of so-called political romanticism, and also to the historical school of law, which was initiated by Friedrich Carl von Savigny (1779-1861) and grew from the same stem. Conservatism had numerous less-known advocates in all European countries. The original Russian variation of conservative thought developed rather late, in the second quarter of the nineteenth century, in the form of Slavophilism of Ivan Kireyevsky (1806-1856), Alexei Khomiakov (1804-1860), and others.

We shall now discuss the elements of conservative thought that seem to have spread most widely.

The Anti-Utopian Nature of Conservative Thought. The conservatives saw the revolution, which they opposed, to be a result of the spiritual changes that had been taking place in Western Europe since the Reformation; in their opinion, it consisted especially of unrestrained wisecracking and criticizing, which gradually resulted in the destruction of all authority and tradition, and in questioning everything in the name of principles of abstract reason. That was why they often blamed the revolution on eighteenth-century philosophy, which declared war on "prejudice" and spread the belief in the possibility of a rationalistic policy. They considered the striving for a fundamental restructuring of society on the basis of such universal principles as the natural laws of man and the social contract to have been the basic feature of both the Age of Reason and the Revolution of 1789. They claimed that people who have been educated in the spirit of the Age of Reason were incorrigible Utopians who were busy devising plans for what should be, while neglecting recognition of what is.

In political practice, conservatives opposed the treatment of the French ideas (from *The Declaration of the Rights of Man and of the Citizen* to Napoleon's code) as the universal pattern and questioned the usefulness of such abstractions even for the country in which they developed. In the sphere of theory, they doubted the value of any general social knowledge. "Nothing universal can be rationally affirmed," Burke claimed, "on any moral or any political subject. Pure metaphysical abstraction does not belong to these matters. The lines of morality are not like the ideal lines of mathematics. . . . they admit of exceptions; they demand modifications. These exceptions and modifications are not made by the process of logic, but by the rules of prudence."[4]

The Critique of the Age of Reason's Ideas of Human Nature. That idea of social knowledge was combined, in conservative thinking, with two important assumptions. First, its advocates claimed that human nature includes both rational and—above all—irrational factors, which cannot be in any way predicted, controlled, or even described with precision. Human conduct is governed not only by reflection, but also by sentiment, habit, custom, example, and the like—in a word, by "prejudice," which is earlier than reflection. Writers in the Age of Reason paid much attention to the problems of prejudice, the elimination of which they believed to be their task. Even Montesquieu, who had so much understanding for the problems of prejudice and customs, was primarily interested in ensuring good legislation. According to conservatives, it is neither possible not advisable to put an end to prejudice, because it is on prejudice that all social life and morality are based, and because without it society would become a conglomerate of atomic individuals incapable of any permanent cooperation (see next section). The conception (and the ideal) of man as a thinking being they thus replaced by the conception (and the ideal) of man as a predominantly feeling being.

Second, they interpreted such irrational human nature as dependent on place and time, varying from country to country and from period to period. Some of them even doubted the usefulness of the very concept of nature and used that term only metaphorically to denote empirically given human features which, unlike rationalistic nature, need not be, and in most cases are not, common to all men. Joseph de Maistre wrote, "There are no men in the world. I have seen Frenchmen, Italians, Russians in my life. . . . I even know, owing to Montesquieu, that one can be a Persian. But when it comes to man, I state I have never met him; even if he exists, I know nothing about him."[5] Those concrete features of human beings who are members of particular societies or nations depend on a great many circumstances, above all the specific history of each community. Revolutionary Utopianism consisted simply of disregarding those circumstances, of treating society as a virgin land.

To bring out the specific and unique character of every nation, conservatives—especially the Germans—willingly availed themselves of the concept of "the spirit of the nation" *(Volksgeist)*, by which they referred, to some extent, to Montesquieu and Herder. But the conservative conceptions of the spirit of the nation stressed its irrational character with much greater force: It could be grasped by intuition only, and one had to humble oneself unreservedly before it. Favorite slogans of the conservatives included reference to man's helplessness and to his organic inability to transform or to make social realities, which develop spontaneously like plants or are guided directly by God.

The assumptions adopted by the conservatives, thus, came to determine their sociological interests, which focused on phenomena that are products of a spontaneous growth of the social organism below the level of reflection: language, folklore, customs, customary law, nondogmatic religion, and so on. They also meant those phenomena which are observable in all societies, but take on a specific form in each of them.

Antiatomism of Conservative Social Philosophy. While they demanded that society be treated as a *sui generis* whole, the conservatives also wished to overcome the individualism and nominalism (or "atomism," as they usually called it at that time) of many rationalistic conceptions in use. They claimed that interpreting society as a conglomerate of naturally independent individuals favored the belief, which they considered detrimental, that such individuals can agree time and again on the principles of social organization according to their own will and interests. The conservatives opposed all conceptions of society by which it has merely an instrumental value with reference to human needs. De Bonald's formula—"The schools of modern philosophy . . . have produced the philosophy of individual man, the philosophy of *I.* . . .I want to produce the philosophy of social man, the philosophy of *we*"[6]—can be taken as the declaration of faith of conservative thinkers in general.

The isolated man was believed by conservatives to be a pure fiction. They asserted that man always exists in society, owing to society, and for society and that he would not be what he is, had it not been for the social influence to which he is subject from childhood on. They opposed the Age of Reason's idea of a state of nature and natural man. In Burke's opinion, ". . . art is man's nature,"[7] and Joseph de Maistre claimed that so-called savages were not in the least closer to nature than their contemporary Europeans were. Further, he viewed savagery as a result of decline and degeneration. Men could not have made society, because it was owing to its existence that they became men. This eliminated the problem of the origin of society in the form that it had in seventeenth- and eighteenth-century philosophy. In conservative thought, society was either a divine creation or a result of historical growth whose beginning cannot be established. Men, therefore, have no right to impose their will on a social organism: The beliefs, customs, and institutions that they have received are the embodiment of corporate (or divine) reason relative to which the reason of an individual, and even the reason of all the individuals who are alive at a given moment, has a zero value. Society is an entity that is primary and superordinate with respect to the individual.

This opposition to atomism often took the form of an opposition between *organism* and *mechanism.* A mechanism, the conservatives claimed, is a whole that can be disassembled into its component parts, driven, wound, or stopped. This is how, in their opinion, the revolutionaries imagined society. For themselves, however, society was a susceptible organism—that is, a whole no part of which can be removed or exchanged. A mechanism has no history: It is good or bad, in order or out of order. An organism develops; it can be healthy or ill; it can die; but it cannot be repaired. It has its inner life and its soul, which animates it.

The Pluralistic Concept of Society. Conservative social philosophy was not, however, simply the reverse of the sociological nominalism popular in the eighteenth century. Conservatives were concerned not only with defending the priority of the community (in relation to the individual), but also with incorporating the individual into the system of relationships that covers all spheres of life. Thus, a strong state is not good per se: It is good only if it has a suitable base at the various levels of societal life. Men do not live in a state (society) as such, but in families, communes, parishes, corporations, estates, and the like, through which they participate in a more comprehensive societal whole. The danger of a revolution consists in the fact that both the individual and the state become independent, while the latter abolishes the "intermediate bodies" between itself and the individuals, thus establishing a tyranny. So conservatives were pluralists. They did not deny having been inspired by the medieval society based on estates, even though only some of them dreamed about restoring the basic institutions of that society; others looked, instead, for alternate solutions that would make it possible to put similar principles into effect under new conditions. The latter group made particularly great efforts to defend the thesis that the family is of fundamental importance in society. The groups into which society is divided should be ordered hierarchically, according to the importance of the services that they render to society. Individuals also are not "atoms" because they differ in their rights and duties according to their positions in the whole, conditioned by their membership in a given group.

The Problem of Social Bonds. The fall of the old system was seen by the conservatives as a *sui generis* dissolution of society and the cause of its deep crisis, which was, above all, the crisis of the traditional forms of social bonds. They saw postrevolutionary society as a disorderly conglomerate of egoistically minded individuals, each of whom was in pursuit of profit, regardless of others. Conservatives could be very eloquent critics of capitalism. Their attacks on the bourgeoisie, industrialism, pauperism, and so on were combined, as a rule, with idealizations of feudal society, extolled not only for its agreement with the general principles or order, but also for its human relations. The relation between the lord and his serfs, like that between the king and his subjects, was paternal and familylike. The relation between the capitalist and the workers is one between atoms that are alien to one another. It is a relation based exclusively on interests, on the contract of sale; to such coolly calculated dealings are all relations in bourgeois society reduced. In many conservatives we clearly observe opposition (which anticipates the typology later introduced by Tönnies[8]) between two types of communities: one based on direct bonds between people, on customs, tradition, and religion, and the other based on current interests of individuals, on contracts, on formalized rules, and sometimes just on physical coercion like that manifested in revolutionary terror. According to context and circumstances, bourgeois society as opposed to feudal society, France as opposed to England, town as opposed to country, Western Europe as opposed to Russia, and so forth were considered embodiments of the latter type of society.

Conservatives particularly stressed the criticism of any relations formalized and planned with a specified aim. Society cannot be defined by its goals because—unlike a company, a factory, or an office—it has not been set up to attain a single goal. According to Burke, whose formulation came to be repeated by dozens of later authors, society is "a partnership in all science, a partnership in all art, a partnership in every virtue and in all perfection."[9] Social relations are durable only if men do not realize their nature and live in community on the same principle on which they breathe. This is why written law is evil; it is always based on some rational calculation that refers to varying opinions and interests of individuals. Such law is necessarily superficial, since it can regulate only certain selected spheres of societal life. Society should be governed by historically shaped customs, for they express the true spirit of the nation. If written laws prove indispensable, then the legislator should be a kind of master of records, who merely takes down "the natural constitution" of a given society. Hence we find frequent eulogies of the English legal system, in which precedents are more important than written provisions of law.

In the sphere of social integration, conservatives assigned a major role to religion; they did not confine themselves to repeating the former conceptions of religion as that which sanctifies the authority and ensures obedience by the subjects. It was also considered a foundation of social bonds. Religion was valued for the fact that it penetrated all fields of societal life, from the family to the state, and at the same time came close to irrational "prejudice." The motif of the societal role of religion was particularly marked in French conservatism, whence it found its way to the sociological systems of Saint-Simon, Comte, and Durkheim.

Conservatism versus Social Theory. Conservative thought was above all an endeavor to find practical measures of preventing revolutions and of restoring the old system or reinstating its principles in the new society in those cases in which a revolution already had taken place. Yet in the period now under consideration, conservatism was something more than a political program, and its later effects, too, were at least twofold. On the one hand, it served as a point of reference to politicians and ideologists who sought arguments for an antirevolutinary policy. On the other, various conservative opinions inspired theoretical studies that were much more loosely connected with such policies. Not infrequently various elements of conservative thought were taken over by thinkers whose systems of values were openly opposed to the conservative ideology. In particular, the emergence of inner conflicts within a new society accounted for the fact that conservative ideas could be used in analyzing social problems other than those discussed originally. In this way conservative ideas were being assimilated also by defenders of the bourgeois social order. Still more important, the conservative thought was concerned with important sociological *problems*, which could not be just dismissed. As a result, nineteenth-century sociology—from Saint-Simon, Comte, Tocqueville, and Le Play to Taine, Durkheim, and Tönnies—many a time referred to conservatism, whether directly or indirectly.[10] The most vital conservative ideas were those connected with critiquing Utopianism and abstractionism in social philosophy, with the defending the historical viewpoint, with emphasizing the role of irrational factors in societal life, with treating society as an organism, with interpreting social bonds, with bringing out the importance of small groups, with analyzing religion from the point of view of its effect on social integration, and so on. The assumption that societal life is essentially spontaneous and uncontrollable was also to prove extremely fertile.

LIBERALISM

The Concept of Liberalism. In the case of liberalism, too, we shall be concerned with only one of the many possible interpretations of the term, which in everyday language and in the language of politics and certain social sciences has many different meanings. When speaking about liberalism, we shall mean a sociopolitical trend in the epoch of free-competition capitalism and the still undisturbed belief, shared by advocates of that socioeconomic system, in its unfailing self-regulatory ability. Whatever the opinion of economic historians, from the point of view of the historian of social ideas that epoch ends in the mid-nineteenth century. Of course, systems of liberal ideas would develop in later times, too (in sociology it would be primarily the system formulated by H. Spencer), and many liberal ideas would survive till our times. Nevertheless, that which we could term liberal social philosophy had its purest form in the late eighteenth century and in the first half of the nineteenth century. Even the ideas of John Stuart Mill (1806-1873), author of the classical essay *On Liberty*, are quite often called "modernized liberalism" because of the marked difference between his views and those of early liberalism.

It was Britain that was the motherland of liberalism and the arena of its greatest triumphs. Britain was then the most advanced on the path of capitalist development, which favored political initiatives by the ever more powerful bourgeoisie (or the middle class). The latter, however, was interested not so much in fomenting a political revolution, as was the case of France, as in winning maximum economic freedom through gradual reforms. Liberalism found advocates in many other European countries, but there, as a rule, it differed from the British pattern. Hence, when writing about liberal thought in general, we indulge in considerable simplification. It is even greater when we combine such widely different manifestations as the theory of law and morals of Jeremy Bentham (1747-1832), the political economy of Adam Smith (1723-1790), the moral ideas and social philosophy of James Mill (1773-1836) and John Stuart Mill (1806-1873), and the political ideas and philosophy of Benjamin Constant (1767-1830). In other words, we discuss here the common assumptions underlying the various forms of intellectual activity, each of which could be the subject matter of a separate study. As the most important assumptions we have to take individualism, utilitarianism, a clear-cut demarcation line between the socioeconomic and the political system, and the conviction that the former has an almost unlimited self-regulatory ability. It is these assumptions formulated by liberal thinkers that make their philosophical product most interesting to a historian of sociology.

Liberalism versus Rationalistic Thought. Liberalism may in many respects be treated as a direct continuation, or even a variation, of rationalistic philosophy. The founders of British liberalism (Bentham and Smith) were prominent representatives of the Age of Reason in their country. French liberalism can be traced back to the doctrines of the physiocrats and Montesquieu. In many countries liberals defended the rationalistic heritage against conservative attacks.

While bearing in mind these numerous links between liberalism and the heritage of the Age of Reason (which were particularly strong in Britain), we must not disregard the fact that liberalism was a postrevolutionary philosophy and that it opposed eighteenth-century trends in social philosophy insofar as they suggested a radical transformation of the political system. Hence, liberal critique was aimed at the idea both of man's natural rights (and, generally, of nature interpreted as a norm) and of social contract. Liberals also proved opponents of the 1789 revolution and, in particular, its Jacobinic phase, in which they saw the birth of a new despotism. Liberty, as B. Constant wrote, is a triumph of individuality over both the authority, which would like to govern despotically, and the masses, which demand subjugation of the minority by the majority.[11] The motif was extensively treated in Mill's essay *On Liberty*, in which he argued that "the people . . . *may* desire to oppress a part of their number; and precautions are as much needed against this as against any other abuse of power."[12] Of course, such apprehensions could arise only after 1789, but liberalism from its very inception programmatically favored a middle-of-the-road course in politics: While opposed to feudal reaction, it was also against revolutionary democracy whenever the latter threatened the bourgeois order. That antirevolutionary character of liberalism accounts for the fact that it is sometimes treated as an orientation similar to conservatism. Although such an opinion may seem an exaggeration, the nineteenth century did produce conceptions (see Tocqueville) in which it would be difficult to separate liberal elements from conservative ones.

Individualism and Utilitarianism. As mentioned earlier, the critique of a number of rationalistic ideas, considered fictions that had no analogues in the real world, was an important aspect of liberal thought. What was declared fiction included the natural law and the natural rights of individuals, as listed in *The Declaration of the Rights of Man and of the Citizen*, the social contract and the general will in Rousseau's philosophy, the laws of reason, and so forth. Bentham argued that in all such cases we are faced with meaningless generalities, a confusion of demands and descriptive statements, and a dangerous playing with words that may have disastrous social consequences.[13] Such consequences consisted of imposing solutions invented by abstract reasoning without regard to the empirically given characteristics of human individuals. And the problem is not to invent an ideal that would be maximally attractive, but to ensure maximum happiness to real human beings, who above all strive to satisfy their needs and to protect their own interests. The constant mental properties of human beings are the fundamental fact that a politician must take into consideration. All actions and all institutions should be assessed only on the extent to which they help individuals to minimize suffering and maximize pleasure. All the rest is—according to the principle of utility—a harmful fiction.

This standpoint varied in details and led to various practical conclusions. But the common belief was that discovering the innate dispositions and needs of human beings, who are the only real entities, must be the point of departure in all social knowledge. This was in absolute opposition to all those ideas which treated society as an organism.

Spontaneous Social Order. The adoption of this individualistic standpoint required a conception of social order that would not refer to anything other than actions of individuals who strive to attain their individual goals. Since individuals are egoistic, how is it possible to ensure order and to avoid a war of all against all (about which Hobbes wrote, as he did not see any preventive measures other than the establishment of a strong government)? The liberals were basically opposed to the idea that underlies *Leviathan*, because they assumed that social order can emerge spontaneously from conflicting and divergent human strivings. They assumed that human interests are in mutual agreement and that if they clash, this is due less to the nature of things than to defects of sociopolitical organization. Hence if we let things take their own course, we can expect that harmony will emerge by itself. This assumption can be seen most clearly in Smith's economic ideas: He pointed out that selfish interests induce men to cooperate and to exchange commodities—activities that provide the foundation of socioeconomic organization. Division of labor, which is the most important aspect of that organization, is not introduced deliberately with the intention of ensuring general welfare, but emerges spontaneously as a result of innate inclinations of individuals. Heeding one's own interests thus contributes to the establishment of social bonds.

Not all liberals would go to such lengths as did Smith, the theorist and eulogist of free competition, in suggesting elimination of all governmental interference from societal life. But in all cases the political system was treated as something external to the socioeconomic system, whose emergence does not require any efficient cause, in the form of authority.

In *The Theory of Moral Sentiments* Smith characterized "the man of system" in a way that may be considered as a good summary of the liberal conception of society, as opposed to those conceptions which focus all attention on politics and the state:

He [the man of system] seems to imagine that he can arrange the different members of a great society with as much ease as the hand arranges the different pieces upon a chess board; he does not consider that the pieces upon the chess board have no other principle of motion besides that which the hand impresses upon them; but that, in the great chess board of human society, every single piece had a principle of motion of its own altogether different from that which the legislature might choose to impress upon it.[14]

That social order which results from spontaneous movements of individuals was occasionally termed "natural order" by liberal thinkers. It is worth emphasizing that, unlike many rationalistic conceptions, that concept lost its normative nuance and came to be applied to the sphere of facts alone.

Universalism. In its conception of society, liberalism referred to changeless human nature. The highest authority was seen in psychology and not in history, as the conservatives believed. If history was viewed by liberals with approval, then it was only as a source of additional information about the permanent characteristics of human nature or as an illustration of mankind's progress toward the comprehension of natural order. In that respect, liberalism was deeply rooted in the ideas that prevailed in the eighteenth century and differed essentially from the trends that came to be dominant in the historically minded nineteenth century. This applies, of course, to liberalism as a *sui generis* sociopolitical philosophy; liberalism as a practical program occasionally had adherents whose philosophical opinions differed from the pattern described above.

Liberal Thought versus Social Theory: Liberal sociology was apparently much poorer than its conservative counterpart, and its ingenuity can easily be doubted, especially if compared with the Age of Reason in England. Yet it seems that a historian of sociology cannot disregard liberalism for at least two reasons. First, by consolidating the belief in a spontaneous social order that in its origin and function is independent of acts of political authority, liberalism paved the way for sociologists, even if they did not share the opinions of early liberalism. Liberalism also gave birth to its own sociological systems, of which Herbert Spencer's came to be best known. Second, liberalism left two paradigms that proved exceptionally viable in social thought. One was pointed out by Talcott Parsons, who wrote about the utilitarian conception of man, of which Western sociology began to rid itself only at the turn of the nineteenth century.[15] The other was recently analyzed by J. Bernard, who called it "the paradigm of capitalism": It compared human community to the market, on which individuals make decisions intended to maximize their profits and to minimize their losses, at the same time, however, these decisions ensure a rise in general welfare.[16] That paradigm, too, proved more viable than classical liberalism and came to be consciously or unconsciously adopted by many sociologists. We shall find it, for instance, in the Chicago school's conception of community.

UTOPIAN SOCIALISM AND UTOPIAN COMMUNISM

The Concepts of Socialism and Communism. A general characterization of socialism and communism in the early nineteenth century is very difficult to make because a homogeneous social philosophy cannot be ascribed to those doctrines. It is true that they represent an equally intensive search for a new vision of society, but the results do not form any single pattern. Stress must be laid on common interests and problems rather than on agreement of assumptions and statements.

This feature of socialist and communist thought becomes quite clear when we study their attitude toward the heritage of the Age of Reason. On the one hand, we find endeavors that provide a direct continuation of the social philosophy characteristic of the eighteenth century; on the other, we see endeavors to construct a philosophical system that would be essentially new. There is no doubt that Utopian socialism and Utopian communism in the first half of the nineteenth century were extensions of the age-old tradition, but at the same time they were tentative solutions to problems that marked the new epoch. Socialist and communist ideas finally ceased to be a conglomerate of isolated episodes on the periphery of the main trends in social thought and became a phenomenon of primary social and intellectual importance.

The main reason for this change was that at the turn of the eighteenth century the consequences of two important social phenomena, the bourgeois political revolution and the industrial revolution, came to manifest themselves in a glaring manner. The political victory of "the third estate" inevitably brought about its inner stratification and the appearance of class antagonism between the bourgeoise and the nonpropertied "fourth estate," for which the abolition of feudal privileges was not accompanied by any radical improvement in living conditions. The triumph of the political revolution made clear the fact that the social revolution stopped halfway and also aroused the hopes to bring that revolution to a conclusion. Those hopes then came to underlie innumerable conceptions of an equality that would be not merely formal, but real as well.

The political changes brought about by the French Revolution coincided with the first social consequences of the industrial revolution, which at that time was making most rapid progress in England, but was also intensifying its impact on continental Europe. That revolution meant a quick growth of the proletariat, the class whose underprivileged status did not result from any surviving traces of feudalism, but was due mainly to the new economic conditions in which the bourgeoisie was growing rich. Further, the emergence of large cities resulted in a concentration of poverty and its coming to the public view. Beginning with the second decade of the nineteenth century (in the Luddite movement in Britain), independent actions by workers were becoming more and more frequent and, over the course of time, more and more organized and political in nature. Worker problems and pauperism became topical issues even for those who were not at all inclined to criticize capitalism or were doing so only from the position of the former feudal system. Yet when we speak about socialism and communism, we usually have in mind only those conceptions in which the new social issues were included in the search for a new social order that would come *after* capitalism.

The word *socialism*, which came to be more currently used in the 1820s, was intended to denote a trend opposed to liberalism: It focused its interests not on the individual, not on liberty as such, not on political reforms, but on the organization of society as a whole and, in particular, socioeconomic conditions. In Cole's opinion, it was typical of socialism (or rather, socialisms) (1) to assign the decisive role to the social issue; (2) to assume that solving social problems requires setting up a new social order, one based on association and not on competition and conflict; and (3) to reject or to push into the background purely political measures and to concentrate on production and distribution of goods and also on education.[17] Communism, mentioned somewhat later, was usually ascribed the same characteristics, but the term had other connotations as well. It was sometimes associated with the word *commune*, which denoted a kind of self-governed community (such as French urban communes), and sometimes with the word *communauté*, that is, community, interpreted as a community of possession, an ideal of society without private property. Communism usually had a more radical tinge than socialism had. The majority of the socialists and communists in the period now under consideration favored a program of a peaceful reorganization of society. Note also that here we are disregarding problems of practical activity of socialists and communists and are mainly interested with the social theory associated with practical activity.

The best-known representatives were Robert Owen (1771-1859), Claude Henri de Saint-Simon (1760-1825), and Charles Fourier (1772-1837). But socialist thought in the first half of the nineteenth century included contributions by English Ricardian socialists, disciples of Saint-Simon: Armand

Bazard (1791-1832) and Barthélemy Prosper Enfantin (1796-1864); the re-
belled Saint-Simonists Pierre Leroux (1797-1871) and Philippe Buchez
(1796-1865); the Fourierist Victor Prosper Considérant (1808-1893); the
communists Etienne Cabet (1788-1856), Louis Auguste Blanqui (1805-1881),
and Théodore Dézamy (1808-1850); Pierre Joseph Proudhon, the forerunner of anarchism (1809-1865); the German philosopher Moses Hess
(1812-1875); Wilhelm Weitling (1808-1871). Socialist and communist ideas
also found, in the 1830s and 1840s, adherents among Eastern European
thinkers.

*Utopian Socialism and Its Attitude toward Revolution and the Age of
Reason.* Of the three trends here under consideration, socialism and communism were least critical toward the Revolution of 1789. If the socialists
and the communists questioned its achievements, that was mainly because
that revolution seemed to them neither social nor constructive enough. It
was not social enough because it did not sufficiently improve the position
of the people and did not put into effect its own slogans of liberty, equality,
and fraternity. It was not constructive enough because while destroying
the old system, it did not bring about the establishment of a new one; at
most, it prepared some of its elements. They saw in the postrevolutionary
period merely an extension of a social crisis of long duration and treated
that period as a transition stage that preceded the proper reconstruction
of society on the principles of reason.

To use Engels's formulation, one could say that the Utopian socialists
and the Utopian communists saw that "this kingdom of reason was nothing
more than the idealized kingdom of the bourgeoisie . . . and that government of reason, the Contract Social of Rousseau, came into being, and only
could come into being, as a democratic bourgeois republic."[18] Unlike most
critics of the Great Revolution, the socialists and the communists did not
question its values, but raised doubts about the agreement of facts with the
ideal. The revolution had not solved the problem that it should have solved.

That point of view was not conducive to a revaluation of the social
thought of the Age of Reason: The principles were good, but people failed
to apply them properly. Hence, it was necessary to come back to the principles.

Owen, when formulating *A New View of Society* (1813-1814), directly
referred to rationalistic sensualism and argued that man was shaped by the
conditions he lived in. Further, those conditions had to be changed if human
beings were to be free from the faults that they had. Fourier rejected Owen's
belief in the almost limitless flexibility of human nature, but he, too, made
human nature the foundation of his system by assuming that it is changeless
and that social organization must be adjusted to its permanent requirements;
That is, natural human passions and the laws of the mutual attraction of

human beings must be taken into consideration. Saint-Simon abandoned the concept of human nature, but referred to the rationalistic idea of progress and postulated the compiling of a new encyclopedia. Communist thinkers referred to the rationalistic concept of the code of nature with which a well-organized society ought to comply. Dézamy referred to "the science of human organism, that is, the knowledge of human needs, abilities, and passions," founded by French eighteenth-century materialists, and his principal work, *Code de la Communauté* (1842), by its very title alluded to Morelly's *Code de la Nature* (1755).[19] Similar examples could easily be mentioned, demonstrating the exceptional vitality of rationalistic ideas in socialist thought and in all radical thought in general. Those links with the heritage of the Age of Reason were strengthened by the fact that early socialists and communists usually acted as advocates of abstract humaneness and justice, not as defenders of any specific classes in the new society.

It could be noted, however, that socialist thought tended to go beyond the horizon of the Age of Reason. That trend was, to some extent, evident even in Saint-Simon. Later on, the search for a really new vision of society was to intensify. Exceptionally interesting in this respect is the production of Proudhon, who strove to formulate an original social philosophy, based on an entirely new diadic dialectic (as distinct from Hegel's triadic dialectic) and political economy. Another example of a search for a new social philosophy of communism can be seen in the works of Hess, who availed himself of certain categories of classical German philosophy, such as the category of alienation, in the analysis of the capitalist system. Utopian socialism and Utopian communism did not confine themselves to replicating the well-known schemata of rationalistic thought, but tried to go beyond them, seeking inspiration in new trends in philosophy. This applies in particular to opposing the idea of history to the idea of changeless human nature.

Critique of Bourgeois Society. Socialist thought had its greatest merit in submitting bourgeois society to strict and many-sided criticism, which focused first on the fact that man's natural needs were not respected. It also turned against specific elements of early capitalism by revealing (in Owen's case, for example) poverty and exploitation. Utopian socialists accumulated comprehensive documentation on the position of the working class and also suggested a number of solutions that would radically improve the existing situation. Owen followed the path of social experiments expected to overcome the evil. Bourgeois society seemed to socialists to be a pyramid of all kinds of absurdity.

Existing evil consisted, on the one hand, in oppression by some of the others—oppression by those who govern and are propertied of those who are governed and nonpropertied—and, on the other, in a state of war of all against all, competition instead of cooperation. Bourgeois society is corroded by egoism, anarchy, and demoralization, is split into classes hostile to one another, and dooms the majority to humiliation and poverty. Some authors even claimed that it is not a society at all, because there is no real unity in it as a whole; unity develops only within the various classes. Society is in a state of grave illness that can successfully be treated only by a radical socioeconomic reform, combined with reeducation of all citizens. It is not the case of political reforms alone, since those are of necessity superficial and ineffective.

The Social Ideal. When describing and criticizing the actual state of things, socialists and communists incessantly compared it with their Utopia, an image of the world arranged in agreement with human needs. That social ideal was in no sense homogeneous, and the proposals concerning the ways of putting it into effect were not homogeneous, either. But it seems that there was a common element in them—namely, the concept of association as the social organization that would completely eliminate coercion and competition and replace them by cooperation of free and equal individuals, cooperation based on the principle of voluntary participation. In communist thought, the idea of association has its counterpart in the idea of community.

The ways recommended for the attainment of those goals varied greatly. Some tried to set up model associations and communes on the periphery of public life, while others believed it possible to transform society as a whole gradually. Some disregarded the existing political system, while others counted on its gradual democratization or revolutionary abolition. Some desired the establishment of a new, socialist state, while others, like Proudhon, imagined socialist society as one without state authority, based on cooperation of small associations that were guided in their mutual relations by the principle of reciprocity. Some thought that the new social order would be possible because of the technological achievements of industrial civilization, while others cherished the past-oriented Utopia of small bucolic communities that could do without industry and great urban agglomerations. Yet, in all cases the social ideal was more or less the same: a reorganization of society that would eliminate, on the one hand, all hierarchical dependence or social superiority based on anything other than merit and, on the other, all competition that pits people against one another and makes some succeed at the cost of others, instead of rewarding that which is beneficial to all. Socialists, as a rule, did not believe in any spontaneous social order; rather, they thought that well-planned organizing work of long duration would be necessary to provide conditions in which social cooperation would be possible. In some authors this concept even took the form of detailed supervision intended to oppose possible centrifugal tendencies.

Utopian Socialism versus Social Science. The contribution made by pre-Marxian socialism and communism to social science seems to have been twofold. First, by their very existence those trends suggested new problems to thinkers and set sociological imagination free. Such a role was noticed, for instance, by Durkheim, who wrote that socialism had rendered science greater services than it had received from it.[20] Second, socialists and communists included original thinkers who made an essential contribution to social knowledge in their times. Saint-Simon certainly was one, as were Proudhon, who formulated on interesting program of "positive" social science, and Buchez, who made a promising endeavor to continue Saint-Simon's "science of man" in a way different from Comte's attempt. Analysis of socialist thought could reveal in it many novel ideas that were ahead of their time.

Whatever their weaknesses, socialists and communists of the first half of the nineteenth century contributed to social knowledge by

1. having accumulated ample documentation on early capitalist society, especially on the position of the working class under the industrial revolution;
2. being the first to systematize social problems by bringing out the differentiation and conflicts within society;
3. having made a far-reaching analysis of such concepts as association and community, which were to become the leading ideas in social thought in the nineteenth century;[21]
4. having contributed to a shift of interests from political and legal issues to socioeconomic ones;
5. having offered a vision of a classless socialist and communist society.

By the last point we mean not so much the social ideal, even though it has remained viable, as the strictly cognitive value of that discovery. As Lucien Sebag wrote,

socialism is, perhaps, not a practicable proposition, but the history of our societies would become incomprehensible if such a concept were not introduced. Likewise, it cannot be denied that the model of society in which all forms of alienation and exploitation of labor have vanished has a merely extrahistorical significance, but, nevertheless, the history of industrial societies can be shown in the proper light only through a confrontation with that model.[22]

The point was that formulation of a theory of capitalist society required comprehension of its specific nature; and for that an ideal concept of socialism was no less helpful than the historical concept of feudalism. Conservatives contrasted capitalism with an idealized system based on estates, while socialists contrasted it with a classless society. Of course, conceiving such a society required some knowledge of the mechanisms of social life and also the ability to pose questions that were unthinkable to those who believed capitalism to be the natural system.

We may conclude that the requirement of scientific approach, advanced by many Utopian authors in the nineteenth century, was not merely a purely verbal claim. This is also confirmed by the effect that they had, on the one hand, on Marx and, on the other, on Comte, Durkheim, Tönnies, and many other sociologists who were far from being socialistically oriented. The issue can be shown more clearly when we become acquainted in detail with the views of Saint-Simon.

THE SOCIAL THEORY OF SAINT-SIMON

The works of Claude Henri de Saint-Simon (1760-1825) provide the best example of a transformation of social problems into problems of a new social theory. He was the author of *Lettres d'un habitant de Genève à ses contemporains* (1802), *Introduction aux travaux scientifiques du XIXe siècle* (1807-1808), *Catéchisme des industriels* (1823-1824), *Nouveau Christianisme* (1825), and a great many other writings that can be said, without too much exaggeration, to contain in an embryonic form nearly all that which was novel in social thought in the nineteenth century. His writings, often marked by dilettantism and pure madness, are full of penetrating observations and original proposals concerning the interpretation of facts related to the new industrial society. The very term *industrial society* was introduced by Saint-Simon.

The Epoch of Crisis and the Methods of Its Resolution. Saint-Simon (an army man, speculator, and would-be builder of the Panama Canal before he became a thinker) was convinced, like most his contemporaries, that Europe was in a state of a profound crisis, which, he wrote, was essentially the transition from the feudal and theological system to the industrial and scientific one. Saint-Simon thought that overcoming that crisis required application of measures quite different from those advocated and used by existing political doctrines and parties. He claimed that such a critical state always follows an earlier organic one and precedes a later organic one. A critical state is marked by the fact that all community of thought, all collective action, all coordination vanish and society becomes merely an agglomerate of isolated individuals fighting one another. The crisis had not been solved by the French Revolution, which did play an important role in history but was, unfortunately, mainly destructive in nature. This was why a fundamental reorganization of society was necessary and would be achieved, in particular, by a transformation of consciousness.

Saint-Simon attached the highest importance to the idea of a new encyclopedia, which would integrate all contemporary knowledge and formulate it in a manner that would make it usable for the benefit of mankind. He referred directly to d'Alembert and other eighteenth-century thinkers, but he believed that they had not left a complete work that would fully satisfy contemporary needs. To this end he started working on the construction of a scientific system that would be fully homogeneous and coherent and, thus, useful as the basis for the renovation of society.

Saint-Simon thought that the state of society depended on what ideas are the dominant ones: In the past, different types of thinking had had their analogues in different social systems. The theological and the metaphysical epochs were followed by the positive one, in which scientific ideas would become the dominant ones and social organization would be based on them. Science can play that role only on the condition that it becomes systematic. Saint-Simon's systematization of science was to consist of adopting a single principle that would explain all facts and, hence, refer them to a single fundamental law. He assumed Newton's law of gravity to be such and wrote that the only way of reorganizing the system of our knowledge is to base it on the idea of gravity. That basically scientific orientation did not prevent him, toward the close of his life, from preaching a new religion; however, this did not mean his abandoning the primary idea of finding a philosophy capable of integrating people into an "organic" society. In *Nouveau Christianisme* his intent was to devise a system of beliefs that would perform the role of former religions rather than to restore any specifically Christian ideas, as postulated later by some socialists.

The Idea of Social Science. This is not the place for a detailed discussion of Saint-Simon's philosophy of science or his opinions on physical or biological problems. Being a product of utter dilettantism, they were merely a curiosity in the history of science and, at best, testified to the intellectual atmosphere of the period, resulting from rapid advances in natural science. What deserves attention is the fact that Saint-Simon saw the founding of social science—social physiology or "social physics"—as an indispensable element in a reform of science. This is why Gurvitch calls Saint-Simon, who authored *La Physiologie Sociale* in 1813, John the Baptist of sociology. Other authors share this opinion and bring up the fact that he was a forerunner of that discipline in the version given by Comte, who was Saint-Simon's secretary from 1818 to 1822.[23] In Saint-Simon's opinion, the social problems of his times could not properly be solved and, hence, the system of sciences could not be complete without application of "positive" scientific methods to the study of social issues.

As the very name of this postulated science of society indicates, it was to be modeled largely on natural science, on physics and on "the physics of organic bodies," that is, physiology. Saint-Simon treated society as an organism, whose structure and development are subject to constant regularities that can be discovered and used in practice for predicting social phenomena and for consciously guiding their course.

Having drawn the concept of law from physics and the conceptions of organic whole and development from biology, he did not abuse analogies and did not try to reduce social facts to biological and/or physical ones. His treatment of society as an organism merely meant adopting the view that society is a whole whose parts bear specified relations to one another as long as that social organism is healthy.

His idea of development was even more loosely connected with biology, for he was concerned with only a general analogy to stages of organic development. As a matter of fact, Saint-Simon referred to Condorcet's idea of progress, even though he modified it essentially by emphasizing the variability of human nature. The science of society was for him primarily historical in nature, and when pursuing historical research, he did not have to refer to physics or physiology.

Industrial Society. While the idea of a special social science contributed significantly to strengthening Saint-Simon's position in the history of ideas, and also in the history of sociology, the most interesting part of his work seems to have been the conception of industrial society and his resulting views of the past, the present, and the future of European societies, particularly those of France. It is with that conception, too, that Saint-Simon's fame as a social reformer and socialist has been mainly associated.

Let us note at the outset that his socialism was of a rather peculiar nature. Unlike Owen, who was active in Britain and, therefore, at another stage of industrial revolution, Saint-Simon took up the working-class issue to only a limited extent, and he even failed to notice it at all during a long period of his life. He used to ask "Messieurs les ouvriers" for their support of his actions; he noticed the increasing numbers and importance of that "most numerous and poorest class"; he saw some of the needs of that "still benighted class." But he located the basic social problems in another sphere.

Saint-Simon's main concern was to pave the way for the development of industry—that is, production, on which, as he claimed, all society is based. Industry, in his terminology, covered all that which serves collective needs and, thus, not only the production of material goods, but also science and art insofar as they have the public good in view. The fundamental importance of production in societal life accounts for the fact that the class of industrialists is the most important of all; it can do without all other classes, whereas no other class can do without it. The imperfection of society in his time consisted particularly in the fact that industry was not developing fully and the industrialists continued to be subordinated to nonproductive classes.

The terminology used by Saint-Simon requires a fairly comprehensive commentary, for otherwise his specific conception of social classes and class structure can easily be misunderstood. His conception stands midway between that of Sieyès, who opposed the undifferentiated third estate to the privileged estates in prerevolutionary society, and the proper socialist conceptions, in which society was divided into the nonpropertied and working proletariat (often called "the people") and the propertied and nonworking bourgeoisie ("the rich"). Saint-Simon opposed the working class to the nonworking class and demanded that inequalities be abolished only if social superiority could be substantiated by usefulness to society as a whole.

For Saint-Simon the basic social antagonism was that between "the bees" and "the drones," that is, between producers and consumers who live parasitically on other people's work. He placed at one extreme, as working organizers of production, the proletarian, the scientist, and the artist and also the big industrial entrepreneur and the banker; at the other, he put the aristocrat, the bishop, the courtier, and the "bourgeoisie," in which he included nonworking owners of capital and legists, whom he detested. That schema of class structure underwent certain modifications in details, but its general principles remained the same. Hence, property as such was not interpreted by Saint-Simon as a determinant of class status; the way in which property is used, special emphasis being placed on the amount of services rendered to society, was so considered.

Industrialism versus Militarism. Saint-Simon saw the conflict between producers and nonproductive classes not only in his contemporary France and other modern European societies; he made it the pivot of the whole process of history from the fall of the Roman Empire on. Plekhanov wrote about this that "Saint-Simon was able to trace the mainsprings of the internal development of European societies further than his contemporary specialist *historians*."[24] His treatment of that development was marked, above all, by a very strong stress on class struggle and on the gradual increase in the social importance of the industrialists. To explain the origin of that struggle, he resorted to the hypothesis of the conquest by the Franks of the country of the Gauls, a hypothesis very popular in his times. Further, the final victory of the industrial system, falling into the nineteenth century, marked the principal caesura in history. Saint-Simon claimed that only two systems of social organization that are really distinct from one another do in fact, and can, exist: the feudal, or military, system and the industrial one; in the spiritual sphere, the system of beliefs and that of scientific proofs. The whole time of the existence of civilized mankind must be split into those two basic social systems. The final shaping of the industrial system is a historical necessity that a historian discovers simply by a detailed analysis of facts.

For a sociologist the opposition between the industrial and the military system, which later won publicity through Spencer's efforts, is of particular interest because of the social bonds in those two types of social organization. The most profound difference between the two was the fact that one of them is based on coercion and the other on contract and voluntary cooperation.

In the old system the people were *subject* to their rulers; now they are combined with them. Military commanders were in *command* of them, whereas industrial chiefs only exert *guidance*. In the former case, the people were *subjects*; in the latter, they are *partners*. For the nature of industrial activity is such that all those who contribute to it are real cooperators; all are partners—from the simplest laborer to the richest factory owner and the most educated engineers.[25]

Industrial society as a whole, like its component parts, seemed to Saint-Simon to be an entirely new kind of organization of human relations, one that he usually called *association* and opposed to feudal corporation. As N. Assorodobraj wrote, the term *association*

is a label for the industrial system, as corporation was for the feudal system. It was used to denote a new combination of the various societal elements on the basis of freedom of cooperation mainly for productive purposes, as contrasted with corporation, which symbolized relations based on coercion and holding between socially homogeneous elements on the basis of the automatic operation of the law based on the estate system.[26]

Originality of Saint-Simon's Ideas. In a discussion of Saint-Simon's view, it is worthwhile to point to some of their additional peculiarities, which make the author of *Nouveau Christianisme* a thoroughly original thinker. First, the ideal of industrial society was dynamic in nature; unlike earlier Utopian thinkers, Saint-Simon imagined it not as a perfect situation attained once and for all, but as a point of departure for further development that would infinitely increase men's command of nature. He differed from most Utopian socialists by being interested not so much in a just distribution of the goods already available as in the production of ever increasing quantities of new goods.

Second, Saint-Simon's idea of association was conceived on a national scale, whereas many reformers of his times focused only on organizing small communities within the existing state. In the opinion of Saint-Simon, the whole state should be transformed into a single big workshop for the production of goods, and the authority should be changed from authority over human beings into authority over things. Accordingly, the administration of the state should pass into the hands of scientists and organizers of production—as we would say today, technocrats.

Third, Saint-Simon used to stress emphatically that in the new society the authority should be centralized, should control all production processes, and should ensure unanimity. This is why many researchers call him *authoritarian* (when it comes to his idea of industrial society, although at an earlier stage Saint-Simon sided with the liberals), and Durkheim, for whom Saint-Simon's conception was almost the model of socialism, concluded that the tendency to organize is the determinant of all socialism.[27]

Saint-Simon's Impact on Others. The impact of Saint-Simon's ideas was varied and durable, but it followed two entirely different paths. On the one hand, his ideas (such as the idea of "positive" social science) were taken up by representatives of various trends in both socialist and nonsocialist thought, as will be shown in later chapters of this book. In the nineteenth century, many of them became current concepts, often adopted without knowledge of their origin. Some of them (for example, the so-called law of three stages) were later ascribed to Comte. On the other hand, a certain role was played by Saint-Simonism proper, the set of doctrines developed by people who referred to the whole of the teachings of their master—or, rather, prophet, for his teachings were often treated as a new religion and the school had many features of a religious sect.

Since it is not possible to describe the fortunes of Saint-Simon's school, we shall confine ourselves to mentioning the most serious intellectual undertaking, namely, the lectures given in Paris in 1829 by Armand Bazard and Berthélemy Prosper Enfantin. Their lectures were a successful systematization of Saint-Simon's teachings in the last period of his life, but they also contained numerous additions to and expansions of his views.

After 1830, the Saint-Simonists started referring to the opposition between the bourgeois and the proletarian, a concept that did not play any role in the doctrine formulated by the patron of the school. To put it briefly, they came to be interested in the specific problems of the new society rather than an attempt to overcome the remnants of feudalism. The majority, however, tended toward modernized capitalism rather than toward socialism. And it seems that within the orthodox ideas of Saint-Simon the concept of working-class socialism was unthinkable, which is best proved by the intellectual development of such authors as Pierre Leroux (1797-1871) and Philippe Buchez, whose commitment to the proletarian cause resulted in breaking off with the Saint-Simonists.

It was, in particular, Leroux who demonstrated clearly why he had ceased to be satisfied with the doctrine of Saint-Simon. "The new epoch," he wrote, "will come, but at the present it has come for capitalists only. Saint-Simon's mistake consisted in calling those capitalists industrialists and calling capital industry."[28] Leroux spoke about "a new feudalism" and a profound crisis developing in society already transformed by industrialization. In his *De la plutocratie* (1848) he described the differentiation of French society by singling out seven principal classes, based on income brackets. That picture of class structure was to a large extent a picture of the inequalities within Saint-Simon's "class of producers."

CONCLUDING REMARKS

We have seen in this chapter the three great trends that marked social thought in the early nineteenth century and constituted three different replies to the challenge that the emergence of new society was for politicians and social philosophers. The first reply was marked by hostility to the new society and by a longing for the prerevolutionary order; the second was largely its apology; and the third was a critical response that referred to an ideal projected into the future. It seems to be of particular interest that in all these cases attention was focused on problems of social, and not political, order. Representatives of these three trends believed that taking up theoretical problems in the sphere that later came to be considered the field of sociology was a condition of solving practical problems. It will also turn out that many issues discussed in this chapter will be continued in sociological research and not merely in those social ideologies which were initiated by the concepts considered here.

NOTES

1. Robert A. Nisbet, *The Sociological Tradition* (London: Heinemann, 1967), p. 21.

2. Samuel P. Huntington, "Conservatism as an Ideology," *American Political Science Review* 51 (1957):454-73.

3. Cf. Karl Mannheim, *Essays on Sociology and Social Psychology* (London: RKP, 1953), pp. 74-164.

4. Louis I. Bredvold and Ralph G. Ross, eds., *The Philosophy of Edmund Burke* (Ann Arbor: University of Michigan Press, 1960), p. 41.

5. Cf. Francis Bayle, *Les Idées politiques de Joseph de Maistre* (Paris: Donat-Montchrétien, 1945), pp. 62-63.

6. Cf. Léon Brunschvicg, *Le Progrès de la conscience dans la philosophie occidentale* (Paris: P.U.F., 1953), 2:549.

7. Bredvold and Ross, *Edmund Burke*, p. 61.

8. Andrzej Walicki, *W kregu konserwatywnej utopii* (Warsaw: PWN, 1964), pp. 134-42.

9. Bredvold and Ross, *Edmund Burke*, p. 43.

10. Robert A. Nisbet, "Conservatism and Sociology," *American Journal of Sociology* 58 (September 1952):167-75.

11. See Maxime Leroy, *Histoire des idées sociales en France*, vol. 2, *De Babeuf à Proudhon* (Paris: Gallimard, 1950), p. 175.

12. J. S. Mill, *On Liberty*, in *On Liberty; Representative Government; The Subjection of Women* (London: Oxford University Press, 1954), p. 8.

13. Cf. Maria Ossowska, *Myśl moralna Oświecenia angielskiego* (Warsaw: PWN, 1966), pp. 338-39.

14. Cf. Sheldon S. Wolin, *Politics and Vision*, (London: Allen and Unwin, 1961), p. 299.

15. Talcott Parsons, *The Structure of Social Action* (New York, Free Press, 1968).

16. Jessie Bernard, *The Sociology of Community* (Glenview, Ill.: Scott, Foresman, 1973), pp. 16-21.

17. Cf. G. D. H. Cole, *A History of Socialist Thought*, vol. 1, *The Forerunners, 1789-1850* (London: Macmillan, 1955), pp. 1-3.

18. Frederick Engels, *Socialism Utopian and Scientific* (New York: International Publishers, 1945), p. 6.

19. See Gian Mario Bravo, ed., *Les Socialistes avant Marx* (Paris: Maspero, 1970), 3:155.

20. Emile Durkheim, *Le Socialisme* (Paris: F. Alcan, 1928).

21. Cf. Nisbet, *Sociological Tradition*, pp. 47-106.

22. Lucien Sebag, *Marxisme et structuralisme* (Paris: Payot, 1964), pp. 68-69.

23. Georges Gurvitch, Introduction to Saint-Simon, *La Physiologie sociale: Oeuvres choisies* (Paris: P.U.F., 1965), p. 7.

24. G. V. Plekhanov, *The Development of the Monist View of History* (Moscow: Foreign Languages Publishing House, 1956), p. 49.

25. Saint-Simon, *La physiologie sociale*, p. 112.

26. Nina Assorodobraj, "Elementy świadomości klasowej mieszczaństwa," *Przeglad Socjologiczny* 10 (1949):189.

27. Durkheim, *Le Socialisme*, pp. 26-30.

28. Cf. Henri Mougin, *Pierre Leroux* (Paris: Editions Sociales Internationales, 1938), pp. 183-84.

4

HISTORIOGRAPHY AS THE STUDY OF THE "SOCIAL CONDITION"

When watching the formation of sociological problems in human consciousness in the early nineteenth century, one benefits from reflection on the work of at least some of the historians who concerned themselves with the study of the "social condition" and "civilization." Such sociologically conceptualized historiography had many different variations, some of which have aroused the interest of historians of the social sciences and not merely that of historians of historiography.[1] Much still remains to be done in that field, as there is no doubt that it contains a wealth of sociological ideas. It would be difficult, by the way, to say whether historians had any immediate influence on the authors of sociological syntheses in the nineteenth century. In any case, the work of many historians testifies to the vitality of those problems on which sociology was to focus its attention. But the relationships between these two disciplines are still far from being worked out satisfactorily.

The nineteenth century was a period of impressive advances in the science of history and also one in which history was assigned an exceptionally high rank, for historical knowledge and the ability to use the historical method were considered indispensable to both scholars and people engaged in practical activity. Thinkers in that period often called it the age of history, while the eighteenth century was that of philosophy. This opinion was certainly very simplified, and it helped spread the erroneous belief that the Enlightenment lacked any major interest in history, even though it was eighteenth-century authors—Montesquieu, Voltaire, Hume, Gibbon, Herder, and others—who in many respects had paved the way for the future flourishing of historiography. Nevertheless, there was a grain of truth in it: The Enlightenment was not an age without history, but in its attitude toward history it differed essentially from the nineteenth century and especially from the romantic period.

First, we see a striking difference in the scope of historical interests: In the nineteenth century they were incomparably more diverse, finding reflection in philosophy, political journalism, belles lettres, and so on. Second, we note a decline of so-called pragmatic history,[2] which was replaced by either historiography or historiosophy oriented toward explanation of mechanisms of the process of history, discovery of the laws of that process, and indication of the principal trends in the evolution of society. Third, the place of history in the totality of opinions on the social world of man was changed. In the eighteenth century historical reflection was mainly ancillary to philosophy, as it was intended to advance the knowledge of changeless human nature; for nineteenth-century thinkers history became a matter of interest in itself, as it was expected to reveal and to explain the *changeability* of human beings and societies.

That turn toward history was undoubtedly due to the fact that the first thinkers of the age of history were themselves witnesses of, and participants in, historical events of great import, which they tried to understand. The most important of those events was the French Revolution, which was to become one of the main topics of historical studies and historical journalism for a long time. The feeling of connections between a person's biography and history was extremely strong at that time. As A. Thierry wrote, "There is no one among us who would not know more about uprising and conquests, collapses of empires, falls and restorations of dynasties, democratic revolutions and subsequent reactionary governments than Velly and Mably, and even Voltaire himself did."[3]

Responses to those experiences were taking many forms in European historical thinking. The turn toward history was in many cases dictated by the desire to find in the past something that could be opposed to contemporaneity, assessed as a period of decadence and crisis. It could be an escape into a beautiful dream, in which society was still not yet torn by conflicts and shaken by revolutions. In other cases (on which Small focused his attention), fascination with history was linked to the intention of protecting the principle of continuity and a model of social change that would preclude cataclysms resembling the Revolution of 1789. In still other cases, people resorted to history in order to comprehend such cataclysms by showing how they resulted from the causes that had been accumulating for centuries and to demonstrate thereby that they had been inevitable. Oriented in this way, historiography can be considered a continuation of the rationalistic idea of progress, even though it differed from the latter in many important respects.

We shall confine ourselves to selected aspects of this expansion of history in social thought in the nineteenth century and shall be interested in those authors who were most sociologically minded.

CIVILIZATION AND CLASS STRUGGLE:
FRENCH HISTORIANS UNDER THE RESTORATION

This category usually includes such authors as François Guizot (1787-1874), Augustin Thierry (1795-1856), François Auguste Marie Mignet (1796-1884), and Adolphe Thiers (1797-1877). They are sometimes absorbed into the broader class of French romantic historians together with Léonard Simonde de Sismondi (1773-1842), Jules Michelet (1798-1874), Edgar Quinet (1803-1875), and the like, with whom they had much in common, especially their interest in processes that take place on a mass scale. (However, we shall not discuss here the problem of romanticism in historiography.) The term *historians under the Restoration* is used because the mentality of the members of that group was shaped between 1815 and 1830, under the impact of the specific experiences during that period. Even though those historians remained active for decades after the ultimate fall of the Bourbon monarchy, they later revealed little ability to modify their way of thinking about society; that is, their way of thinking was determined by the dilemmas peculiar to the Restoration period, particularly the dilemma of the old and the new order, which was revived by the fall of the First Empire. Those historians showed strikingly little understanding of the inner dilemmas of the new order, to which socialist thought was pointing more and more explicitly. Like Saint-Simon, the historians of the Restoration period noticed mainly the conflict between the relics of feudalism and the new institutions that had emerged following the revolution. The Restoration seemed to menace the new institutions with which they sided as advocates of the third estate and as liberals, although they could hardly be treated as advocates of the revolution as such. When it came to a confrontation between conservatism and liberalism, they firmly declared themselves in favor of the latter.

Historiography was an important arena for that confrontation. As S. Mellon writes, "The Liberals must find a way to defend the Revolution, while freeing themselves from the charge of *being* revolutionary. . . . They discover a method, and that method is history. History would provide an arena in which the liberals could restage and relive the battles of the revolution, stating their case while remaining invulnerable under the cloak of an impersonal muse."[4] But historiography was not only an instrument of political struggle. There is no doubt that historiography served definite political tasks, at that time more than ever, particularly, resistance to the pressure exerted by the advocates of the Restoration and a *sui generis* validation of the recent revolution by showing it as an inevitable stage in the process of history and not just an episode whose consequences can easily be erased. This validation of the revolution resorted to the claim that it had been a significant *social* fact and not just a *political* act, which can simply be revoked by other political acts. Politics in general seemed to those liberal historians to form a kind of superstructure over social relations.

Thus, for instance, Guizot wrote:

The majority of writers, scholars, historians, or publicists, have attempted to explain the condition of society, the degree or the nature of its civilization, by the study of its political institutions. It would be wiser to begin with the study of society itself, in order to learn and understand its political institutions. Before becoming a cause, institutions are a consequence; society creates them before it begins to change under their influence; and instead of judging the condition of a people from the system or the forms of its government, we must first of all investigate the condition of the people, in order to judge what should be and what could be its government. . . . Society, its composition, the mode of life of individual persons in keeping with their social position, the relations of various classes of persons, in a word, the civil condition of men [*l'état des personnes*]—such, without doubt, is the first question which attracts the attention of the historian who desires to know how peoples lived, and of the publicist who desires to know how they were governed.[5]

This new, sociological trend in historical interests took fullest shape in Guizot's and other authors' interpretations of the process of history in terms of civilization and class struggle.

The Idea of Civilization. In Guizot and others, we note the unwillingness, typical of the majority of prominent historians of that period, to describe events simply in the chronicler's style. Guizot suggested that "historical anatomy," concerned with description and classification, be complemented by "historical physiology" and "historical physiognomy." He wrote, for instance, that "facts do not merely subsist, they support one another; they succeed and generate one another through forces governed by laws. There exists, in other words, an organization and a life of societies as of individuals. That organization has also its science, the science of hidden laws presiding over the course of events. It is the physiology of history."[6]

Without ceasing to be a science of actions of human individuals, historiography should be above all the science of the development of civilization; when accumulating and classifying data, it ought to integrate them and thus to construct a great synthesis. "Human history," Guizot wrote in one of his earlier works, "should not be treated as other than a collection of data accumulated for a great history of human civilization."[7] This idea gave rise to two works by Guizot, probably his most important ones; *Histoire générale de la civilisation en Europe depuis la chûte de l'empire romain jusqu'à la Révolution française* (1828) and *Histoire de la civilisation en France depuis la chûte de l'empire romain* (1829).

Guizot did not define the term *civilization*: He probably relied on the intuition of his contemporaries for whom that term, which had then been in circulation for some fifty years, sounded familiar and evoked an emotional response as the antonym of *barbarism*. The idea of civilization was also strongly associated with that of progress, emphasized by Guizot himself, who in many other respects remained dependent on rationalistic inspirations and counted Montesquieu, Herder, Robertson, and Gibbon among his predecessors.[8]

But the requirement that the history of civilization be the subject of study was given a much clearer methodological sense by Guizot; he formulated with precision the tasks whose implementation that concept was to facilitate. First, when we are concerned with civilization, we mean "a general fact, the hidden one under all the other facts which envelop it."[9] A historian of civilization thus strives to reach something that is not given by direct observation of facts. Second, civilization is a general fact that combines in it all other fact "all the elements of the life of the people, all the forces of its existence."[10] To write a history of civilization is to refer all singular facts to one context, one whole, and one process. Even those facts which seem purely individual and connected with individual experiences can and should be analyzed from the point of view of civilization. The idea of civilization thus provides the principle that integrates the process of history and enables us to turn a disorderly aggregate of events into a coherent whole. Third, within that whole, Guizot assigned a merely relative significance to "moral factors" or to the intellectual improvement of individuals. He claimed that too little attention had been paid to the study of the material conditions of social existence, conditions that have, as they change, a strong impact on the development of civilization. It seems that it was Guizot whom Marx had in mind when he wrote in *German Ideology* about French and English authors who had made first endeavors to base historiography on a materialistic foundation because they wrote the first history of civil society, commerce, and industry.[11] Civilization meant for Guizot both "the internal facts," associated with man's improvement as an individual, and "the external facts," made up of material conditions, social relations, and social institutions. Of course, facts of both kinds should be harmonized, and so the idea of civilization seems to assume a gradual elimination of the uneven development of internal and external facts.

Without going into details, we may say that the idea of civilization made it possible to go far beyond the limits of the traditional historiography as a description of events. It was also to play an important role in the later development of the social sciences, which, however, drew their principal inspiration elsewhere (even so, the significance of Guizot's works was noticed by as influential a thinker as John Stuart Mill). It seems, by the way, that the connections between Guizot's idea of civilization and the theories of representatives of the Scottish Enlightenment or the views of the evolutionists have not been explored systematically.

Class Struggle. The other important aspect of the French historians' turn toward the study of *l'état social* was their striving to describe the fortunes of nations—not of a few eminent personalities—and to tell about events in societal life—not those in individual biographies. So far, history had been a history of the privileged classes, and there had been no true history of the people: "In those vague and pompous narratives, in which a few privileged personages monopolize the historic stage while the mass of the whole nation is hidden behind the mantles of the courtiers, we find neither serious instruction, nor any lessons applicable to ourselves, nor that sympathy which in general interests men in the fate of those who resemble them."[12] The new historiography ought to show the history of that anonymous mass which by its work created civilization and struggled to pave the road to freedom. The new historiography suggested a look at the history of France that would give the pride of place to mass processes, in particular the struggle of the third estate against the nobility, which culminated in the Revolution of 1789. It is said correctly that this conception originated with A Thierry, but in the circles under discussion it was almost a universal idea, even though the various authors differed both in the radicalism of general formulations and in the practical conclusions drawn from them in their works. Guizot managed to offer a sweeping generalization: "New Europe was born of the struggle of social classes."[13]

It was those historians whom Marx had in mind when he wrote to J. Weydemeyer in a letter of March 5, 1852, that the credit for discovering classes in modern society and the struggle of those classes with one another did not go to him. Yet the concept of class used by the French historians differed widely from the Marxian, as it was formed by criteria typical of prerevolutionary society, in which the principal conflict was between the nobility and the third estate, that is, between feudal estates. The Restoration did revive that division, but in the nineteenth century it was becoming more and more anachronistic; thus, Guizot and others knew only to draw the conclusion that society after the bourgeois revolution was essentially a *classless* one. Thierry, whom Marx correctly labeled the father of the theory of class struggle, wrote outright that after 1789 there was in France only one class of citizens, living under the rule of one law, being subject to uniform regulations, and comprised by one order.[14] To the bourgeois ideologists, which includes the French historians under the Restoration, the abolition of feudal privileges seemed identical with the elimination of all social classes. There was a striking disproportion in the acuity with which they saw the class conflicts in the past and the way in which they blurred class conflicts in their own times or treated them merely as relics of the past. When confronted with socialism and its visions of class structure, the bourgeois historians acted (especially after 1848) as ardent advocates of social peace.

While they noticed the class struggle and conflicts of incompatible class interests in the past, they explained their origin by the conquest hypothesis: The conquerors were supposed to have become the privileged class and the conquered population became the oppressed class, the people who had to struggle against their oppressors. That conception, elaborated in detail in many works, resembled strongly the vision of the history of France as outlined in the writings of Saint-Simon. It was also one of the pivotal issues in the controversy between Marxism and the earlier theories.

Regularities in the Process of History. The historiographic production of the group now under consideration was marked by the belief in a kind of historical necessity. Every epoch was thought to be an indispensable link in the chain of events, a link conditioned by all the earlier ones. That linking of facts was supposed to make it possible to understand and to predict them. In this spirit, Guizot wrote that in the history of mankind there were for him immense gaps, but no secrets; that he did not know many things, but understood everything; and that he did not know millions of events, but would not be surprised by any of them.[15]

J. LELEWEL'S "HISTORY OF CULTURE"

A similar trend was represented by Joachim Lelewel (1786-1861), the greatest Polish historian in the romantic period, who claimed that a historian should "penetrate the nature of societies, their political condition, their economy, abilities, and activity, in order to be able, on the basis of statistics and politics, to outline at all times the condition of things human with clarity and, in any case, to prepare himself for penetrating the peculiarities of place and time."[16] Critical of the traditional political historiography, he maintained that the proper subject matter of historical research is to be seen in "human actions in all their variety, that is, human culture in all its details."[17] He wrote that it is impossible to understand political history without insight into the development of culture in its entirety, and by culture he meant all the aspects of national life in their mutual relationships. "The history of culture describes the progress and the varieties of mankind in its religious, moral, and customary formation, in its social system, and in its activity and abilities, as manifested in its manual and mental work."[18] We see here an undertaking quite analogous to Guizot's history of civilization, but taken up independently of the French historian.

From the point of view of the history of sociology, Lelewel's theory and practice of historiography seem extremely interesting for at least three reasons. First, by postulating the study of "the social arrangement of mankind," he took up on a large scale an analysis of the nature of "social bonds" and paid particular attention to "national social bonds," that is, problems to which nineteenth-century sociology was to assign a rather limited place. If we were to trace the emergence and development of the sociology of the nation, we would have to concentrate on the work of historians rather than sociologists. Second, Lelewel's recommendation of *comparative* studies would make it possible to preserve the perspective of universal history, which originated in the Age of Reason, and at the same time to avoid the pitfalls of a speculative philosophy of history. Third, his research program was consciously formulated to encompass studies of contemporaneous Polish society, for he believed that a description of the current condition of societies crowns a historian's work in a natural manner.[19]

A. DE TOCQUEVILLE'S HISTORICAL SOCIOLOGY

Among sociologically minded historians the special place must be assigned to Alexis de Tocqueville (1805-1859), author of *La Démocratie en Amérique* (*Democracy in America*, 1835-1840) and *L'Ancien Régime et la Révolution* (*The Ancien Régime and the Revolution*, 1856). In fact, it seems doubtful that he ought to be called a historian and not a representative of an interdisciplinary *science qui traite de la conduite de sociétés*, created by him but left without a name or any clearly defined program. Today, Tocqueville apparently enjoys more esteem among sociologists and representatives of political science than among professional historians. True, he did not affect nineteenth-century sociology in any notable way, but after his rediscovery in the mid-twentieth century he is more and more often considered a classic of sociology.[20] There is no doubt that in many respects he is superior to Comte and Spencer, and many of his ideas have retained a vitality that can be compared only to that of Marx's ideas. Without engaging in a discussion of the causes of Tocqueville's revival, we shall analyze his ways of investigating social facts. Like other thinkers of his times, his point was above all to comprehend that great upheaval in human history to which he was a witness. "Although the revolution which is taking place in the social condition, the laws, the opinions and the feelings of men, is still very far from being terminated, yet its results already admit of no comparison with anything that the world has ever before witnessed."[21] Both of his principal works were intended to explain the essence, the origin, and the prospects of the new society, which he called *democratic* in opposition to the ancient *aristocratic* one. As we shall see, he imparted to these well-known concepts an original content and at the same time suggested a novel conception of revolution, bringing out the historical continuity between the old and the new regime. His own political standpoint, which combined liberal and conservative elements, was original, too.

Tocqueville's Method. The author of *Democracy in America* has not left any comprehensive texts concerned with philosophical reflection. He rarely made any statements on what society in general is and how societies are to be studied. His views on those matters are mainly implied by his analyses of given societies and social processes. His attitude most resembles that of Montesquieu, to whom he consciously referred, as he shared both the political ideal of the author of *The Spirit of Laws* and his opinions on societal life. It is especially his determinism that he seems to have drawn from Montesquieu. That determinism was interpreted as fatalism by many of his contemporaries, because he often wrote about the inevitability of the processes taking place, about providence that guides them, and so forth. While he pointed to the futility of human efforts undertaken without considering existing conditions, he did not in the least preclude the possibility of success of actions based on a thorough knowledge of those conditions. He could, accordingly, think that it was always possible to preserve freedom from all the threats to it that resulted from the development of democracy. In his *Memoirs* he stated plainly that institutions that are considered necessary are often merely those to which we are accustomed. For him, as for Montesquieu, the problem was that the success of human actions depends on thousands of conditions on which man has no influence whatever.

When a legislator succeeds . . . in exercising an indirect influence upon the destiny of nations, his genius is lauded by mankind, whilst, in point of fact the geographical position of the country which he is unable to change, a social condition which arose without his cooperation, manners and opinions which he cannot trace to their source, and an origin with which he is unacquainted, exercise so irresistible an influence over the courses of society, that he is himself borne away by the current, after an ineffectual resistance.[22]

No reference is made here to any metaphysical necessity: This is simply sociological determinism.

Among the received conditions of human actions, Tocqueville assigned special importance to the social conditions, which he clearly distinguished from the political conditions; he wrote, for instance,

I will never admit that men constitute a social body, simply because they obey the same head and the same laws. Society can only exist when a great number of men consider a great number of things in the same point of view; when they hold the same opinions upon many subjects, and when the same occurrences suggest the same thoughts and impressions to their minds.[23]

Society forms an internally integrated whole (sometimes compared to an organism) and must be investigated as such. The novel element in *Democracy of America* was an analysis of North American society from the point of view of the mutual relationships of laws and manners, thoughts and feelings, politics and economy, family life and the theater, literature and power, the way of conducting research and the disribution of wealth, and so forth.

While stressing the need of studying definitive societies, Tocqueville did not confine himself to describing how they functioned. *Democracy in America* was not merely a monograph of American society, but also represented a study of certain type of society. "I confess that in America I saw more than America: I sought the image of democracy itself, with its inclinations, its character, its prejudices, and its passions, in order to learn what we have to fear or to hope from its progress."[24] Likewise, his book on the *ancien régime* and the revolution cannot be treated simply as a historical monograph concerned with eighteenth-century France, for it is also a sociological case study of the process of centralization. Tocqueville himself used to compare his procedure to Cuvier's reconstruction of long-extinct animals on the basis of their extant fragments. Application of this procedure was possible owing to his acceptance of these deterministic and holistic assumptions.

Democracy and Aristocracy as Types of Society. Tocqueville's generalizations pertained primarily to processes connected with the transformation of an aristocratic society into a democratic one. The terms *democracy* and *aristocracy,* denoting concepts pivotal in his social thought, were very rarely used by him in a purely political sense. In that respect he followed Montesquieu, who transformed the classifications of political systems, known since antiquity, into a typology of societies. As noted by J. Lively, Tocqueville used the term *democracy* "in a social context to describe either the theoretic model of society in which equality of conditions was perfectly realised, or the actual societies in which this model was most nearly approached, or those aspects of existing societies which conformed to aspects of the model."[25] To put it briefly, democracy meant for him an egalitarian society.

Tocqueville did not believe in the possibility of absolute equality. People would always differ from one another by their respective abilities, wealth, or education, but democracy is that social system in which such individual differences are the only essential ones. People do not inherit their social status; they are not born as members of definite higher or lower classes. All posts are open to them, and whether or not they hold them depends solely on their ingenuity and diligence. Nor are there occupations that are better or worse by nature: All are good if they lead to success. There are no privileges; some live better than others, but only because they are this or that as individuals, and society does not raise any impassable barriers.

But he paid most attention to the characteristics of the democratic *ethos.*

The principal role was played in it by the concept of individualism (the term itself was at that time only beginning to enter into circulation). In democratic societies, obedience to and trust in authorities begin to vanish, and individuals are inclined to refer solely to their own reason. There are no authorities sanctified by tradition or a privileged position in society; everyone is the supreme authority for himself. The groups to which an individual belongs are too unstable to appear as treasure houses of wisdom. At the same time, a lack of sharply marked boundaries between groups accounts for the fact that thinking turns toward general concepts and becomes abstract, whereas in ancient society it turned toward the concrete, which differed from class to class. It is now mankind, and not class, which becomes the system of reference for the individual. Since the paths of social promotion are open to all, the belief that an individual can improve and that mankind can make progress is being spread. Feelings in democratic societies are undergoing similar changes. Mutual dislikes among classes give way to universal humanitarianism. Bonds between individuals are weaker than they were under the aristocratic system, but good feelings among them, mutual respect for other people's rights, and appraisal of mutual assistance are possible.

Individualism thus means that people come closer to one another, but at the same time causes their tendency to live in isolation from one another. Both trends are inseparable from democracy. Human beings are equal, but everyone cares above all about his own prosperity; everyone tends to close himself up within his family and shows little interest in public matters. The sense of obligation toward society is weak; what is strong is individual ambition combined with envy of those who have fared better.

His perspicacity can also be seen in his noticing a number of facts that did not fit well the picture that he had painted: the adverse effects of industrialism, which, he deemed, was favored by democracy. Industrialism gives rise to new inequalities. He wrote: "Thus, in proportion as the mass of the nation turns to democracy, that particular class which is engaged in manufactures becomes more aristocratic. Men grow more alike in one—more different in the other; and inequality increases in the less numerous class, in the same ratio in which it decreases in the community."[26] In Tocqueville's opinion, the new aristocracy was only a margin of the new society, and this was why he squeezed those problems, of pivotal significance for socialist critics, into the framework of his dichotomy—democracy versus aristocracy. The new society was for him by its very nature a classless one, for he tended to identify class differences with those which were dominant in feudal society. His sociological imagination did not reach beyond that dichotomy.

Democratic Society and Centralization. This characteristic of democratic society, brilliant as it was in its details and novel in its methodology, is not Tocqueville's only claim to sociological glory. Even more inspiring, perhaps, was his discovery of centralizing tendencies in that new society which used to alarm the majority of contemporaneous thinkers by its "atomization." Tocqueville termed centralization "the democratic instinct," thereby bringing out the inner contradiction contained in the 1789 slogan, "liberty, equality, fraternity." Equality is no guarantee of liberty, but, on the contrary, carries the dangers of new despotism. "It would seem as if every step [the democratic nations] make towards equality brings them nearer to despotism. . . . Thus, two contrary revolutions appear, in our day, to be going on: the one continually weakening the supreme power, the other as continually strengthening it; at no other period in our history has it appeared so weak or so strong." Moreover, it turns out that "these two revolutions are intimately connected together, that they originate in the same source, and that after having followed a separate course, they lead men at last to the same result."[27]

Tocqueville supports that position by referring not only to the case of France, where a democratic revolution twice gave rise to Bonapartism, but also to certain properties of democracy. The individualism that is characteristic of that social system has, he claims, consequences of two kinds. On the one hand, it means liberation for the individual from those group authorities and dependencies that used to play such an enormous role in aristocratic society. On the other, it leaves the individual alone to face the state, which becomes his mainstay whenever he cannot rely on himself only. Isolated, "atomized" individuals easily succumb to the central authority. In its striving for equality, democracy eliminates the old hierarchical organization, which restricted individuals' freedom of action in many ways, but at the same time gave them support and protection against the tyranny of the central authority. Absolutism and revolution, by destroying that organization, paved the way for a new despotism. Members of a democratic society do not rebel against it, for it does not infringe on their beloved equality: All are equally subject to the pressure of the state. An individual can more easily acquiesce to dictatorship than to his neighbor's growing richer. Any endeavors to make a counterbalance of the state seem suspect as attempts at equality—hence the common dislike of corporations (in the sense of vocational organizations), unions, parties, and other collective bodies; hence also the strict control to which they are subject in many democratic countries.

Tocqueville did not confine himself to a diagnosis. He was not a disinterested observer in the controversy over the development trends of the new society. While pointing to dangers, he also looked for the means of averting them, for he was far from being a fatalist. While he considered democratization of societies an irreversible process, he thought that centralization could be prevented by organizing, under the new conditions, analogues of the former "intermediary bodies" destroyed under absolutism. In this way he also contributed to a revival of liberal thought.

Significance of Tocqueville's Work. The greatest significance of Tocqueville's work consisted of his introducing into the analysis of political processes and institutions many concepts and methods that we may call sociological (while admitting a certain anachronism) and also of his closely linking recent political history with the study of the social condition. That undertaking, fully appreciated by present-day sociologists, did not find any direct followers among nineteenth-century sociologists, for the latter, fascinated by the idea of constructing a great system of social knowledge, did not pay practically any attention to the much more circumscribed ideas of the author of *Democracy in America.* Yet, it still remains to be seen how his way of investigating societal facts was analogous to and anticipated the tendencies that marked the first sociologists. More interesting still would be a study of the reasons for Tocqueville's popularity in Western sociology today.

SOCIOLOGICAL INTERESTS OF CONSERVATIVE HISTORIANS

The above examples of historiography's becoming sociological were in the domain of historians who favored the new society or, at least, like Tocqueville, considered its emergence to be a manifestation of historical necessity and an effect of long-accumulating social causes. Historiographers who were conservatively minded in their political ideas and totally critical of the new society were undergoing changes that in some respects were analogous to those described above. What has already been said about conservatism shows that it tended to promote sociological interests perhaps even more than other political trends did. The best example can be seen, of course, in German historiography (and in social sciences in that country in general), which even under the Enlightenment showed much understanding for the issues of the social condition and culture and not only for those of politics and law. Conservative historians started from other assumptions than those made by liberal historiographers, but they arrived at basically the same question about the relation between the political system and the social condition as a whole. But the answer that they gave was outside the conception of historical progress, and when comparing the present to the past, they stressed their similarity and continuity.

It appears that the highest level of sociological self-knowledge was reached in conservative historiography by what is called the historical school of law, represented among others by Friedrich Carl von Savigny (1779-1861), Karl Friedrich Einhorn (1781-1854), and Georg Friedrich Puchta (1798-1846). That school emerged as a protest against the opinion that all law has its source in the legislative activity of the lawmaker. The programmatic work by the first of these authors, *Vom Beruf unserer Zeir für Gesetzgebung und Rechtswissenschaft* (1815), gives the expanded version of the view characteristic of the whole school. It is said that in the earliest written history we find civil law to be distinct in its national character, like language, manners, or political systems. These phenomena do not even have any separate existence of their own, but constitute single functions of the same nation, are closely interconnected with one another, and can be seen as distinct characteristics only when we subject them to analysis. They are combined into a single whole by a nationwide belief, by the same feeling of inner necessity that bars any idea of accidental and free emergence of those phenomena. That organic connection between the law and the life and character of the nation is maintained in the later periods. The law, like the language, develops together with the nation; it is improved together with the latter and finally withers when the nation loses its distinctive personality.

As national culture evolves, the various functions specialize and law, too, acquires a kind of autonomy. However, it can never fully dissociate itself from the whole out of which it has grown, for all law develops in the way commonly (but not very precisely) called *customary*. It is first produced by the manners and beliefs current in the nation and only later by jurisprudence —that is, always by inner latent forces and not by any arbitrary actions of the lawmaker. The task of the student of law is, thus, to trace those inner latent forces and to discover the "organic principle" that unites all the functions of the nation; law, accordingly, cannot be investigated in isolation from other fields. As Small writes when summing up Einhorn's views, "Laws do not exist in a vacuum. They are bone of bone and flesh of flesh in the whole life of their time and place."[28] And he says that history written from that viewpoint must report on the plurality of the factors that affect the life of a given community and on their interconnections.

This standpoint resembles the attitude of certain authors discussed earlier in the text: Legislative activity is treated as an aspect of the more comprehensive whole, which in this case is the nation. This explains why this standpoint, being a manifestation of a cognate theoretical tendency, is discussed in this chapter. Yet the conservative standpoint differs from the liberal on at least two issues. First, its idea of a social whole is basically not completely rational, so we are referred to an "organic principle" that can be grasped by intuition only and takes on the form of national character, that is, *Volksgeist.* Second, the conservatives practically eliminate the idea of development from their general conception. They do not, of course, question the fact that society does and must change, but that is not a scientific problem for them. They are interested, above all, in the identity of the social organism. They try to comprehend not so much the development of society, as the basic conditions and causes of its permanence.

NOTES

1. One of the best-known exceptions is Albion W. Small's book, *Origins of Sociology* (Chicago: University of Chicago Press, 1924).

2. According to Kant, "A history is composed pragmatically when it teaches *prudence*; i.e., instructs the world how it can better provide for its interests, or at least as well as did the men of former times," *Metaphysical Foundations of Morals*, in Carl I. Friedrich, ed., *The Philosophy of Kant: Immanuel Kant's Moral and Political Writings* (New York: Random House, 1949), p. 165.

3. A. Thierry, *Lettres sur l'histoire de France* (Paris: 1836), p. v.

4. Stanley Mellon, *The Political Uses of History: A Study of Historians in the French Restoration* (Stanford: Stanford Universtiy Press, 1958), p. 6.

5. G. Plekhanov, *The Development of the Monist View of History* (Moscow: Foreign Languages Publishing House, 1956), pp. 29-30.

6. Karl J. Weintraub, *Visions of Culture* (Chicago: University of Chicago Press, 1966), p. 92.

7. See Lucien Febvre, *Pour une histoire à part entière* (Paris: S.E.V.P.E.N., 1962), p. 517.

8. Cf. Weintraub, *Visions of Culture*, p. 85.

9. Ibid., p. 92.

10. See Febvre, *Pour une histoire*, p. 518. Cf. B. G. Reizov, *Francuzskaja romanticeskaja istoriografia* (Leningrad: Izdatelstvo Leningradskovo Universiteta, 1956), p. 184.

11. Z. A. Jordan, ed., *Karl Marx: Economy, Class and Social Revolution* (London: Michael Joseph, 1971), p. 95.

12. Cf. Fritz Stern, ed., *The Varieties of History from Voltaire to Present* (New York: Meridian Books, 1956), p. 68.

13. See W. M. Dalin, "Francuzskie istoriki epokhi Restavracji," in E. A. Zelubovskaja et al., eds., *Marks-istorik* (Moscow: "Nauka," 1968), p. 20.

14. Cf. Maxime Leroy, *Histoire des idées sociales en France*, vol. 2 (Paris: Gallimard, 1950), p. 190.

15. Cf. Dalin, "Francuzskie istoriki," p. 16.

16. J. Lelewel, "Jakim ma być historyk," in *Dziela*, vol. 2, *Pisma metodologiczne* (Warsaw: PWN, 1964), pt. 2, p. 551.

17. J. Lelewel, "O historii, jej rozgalezieniu i naukach zwiazek z nia majacych," in ibid., pt. 1, p. 445.

18. J. Lelewel, "Historia, Jej rozgalezienie, na czym sie opiera," in ibid., p. 239.

19. Cf. Nina Assorodobraj, "The Origins of the Polish Studies of Current History," *Polish Sociological Bulletin* (1969) No 1/19, pp. 5-21.

20. Cf. Raymond Aron, *Les Etapes de la pensée sociologique* (Paris: Gallimard, 1967).

21. Alexis de Tocqueville, *Democracy in America* (New York: Schocken Books, 1961), 2:396.

22. Ibid., 1:183.

23. Ibid., p. 469.

24. Ibid., p. lxxxii.

25. Jack Lively, *The Social and Political Thought of Alexis de Tocqueville* (Oxford: Clarendon Press, 1962), p. 49.

26. Tocqueville, *Democracy in America*, 2:192.

27. Ibid., pp. 363, 376.

28. Small, *Origins of Sociology*, pp. 76-77.

5

PHILOSOPHY AS A
SOCIAL THEORY: HEGEL

Problems of revolution, of old and new society, and of the future of European countries, which dominated political and social thought in the early nineteenth century, were also the focus of interest of many authors whose immediate political role in shaping that future was much smaller. The most eminent of them was the German philosopher Georg Wilhelm Friedrich Hegel (1770-1830), the founder of a comprehensive philosophical system whose impact on philosophy and social thought was enormous. We are not interested here in that system as such and shall not repeat that which can be found on the subject in handbooks on philosophy and innumerable special studies. Instead, we shall be concerned with Hegel as a social theorist, even though it is a most controversial issue whether that part of the work of the Berlin sage can be singled out from his whole system without causing extreme distortions of his main ideas.

THE SIGNIFICANCE OF HEGEL'S IDEAS

From Plato and Aristotle to Hume and Kant, philosophy always was the field in which reflection on social life developed abundantly, and we have already discussed that aspect of the history of philosophy. There is also no doubt that, on the whole, social opinions of philosophers were closely connected to the sum total of their views of the world. In Hegel's case we find something more: He created a philosophical system which *of necessity* had to be a sociological system as well and not to include a sociology as only one of its many possible ramifications. The Hegelian "spirit" attains its self-knowledge only in human history, and culture is the highest phase of its development ("absolute spirit"). This is why, as Marcuse says, "the transition from philosophy to the domain of state and society has been an intrinsic part of Hegel's system. His basic philosophical ideas had fulfilled themselves in the specific historical form that state and society had assumed and the latter became central to a new theoretical interest. Philosophy had in this way devolved upon social theory."[1] Hegel is, therefore, of particular interest to the historian of social thought. He created a philosophical system that denies the possibility of a philosophy that would not at the same time be a philosophy of social institutions, the state, and history. This meant a shifting of the theoretical horizon of philosophy and also a theoretical ennobling of social science, without which the basic problems of the development of the spirit proved unsolvable. He can, thus, be considered one of the principal forerunners of sociology even though this opinion varies with the common stereotype of nineteenth-century sociology as a product of positivism. Note that Hegel not only formulated the grounds for pursuing all philosophy as social *philosophy*, but also formulated such a philosophical system himself.[2]

His philosophy had a very strong impact on the development of social thought and sociology both in the first half of the nineteenth century and later. First of all, it was very important for the shaping of Marxism, parts of which (and not only the works of the young Marx) would be difficult to understand out of the context of the Hegelian tradition (for example, Lukács). Hegelianism affected the evolution of many fields of the humanities, especially in Germany, and was one of the main sources of the influential methodological trend usually termed *historicism*. According to Lukács, Hegel paraphrased Aristotle's famous statement on man as "a political animal" by claiming that man is "a historical animal" *(ein historisches Tier)* as well.[3] The affinity between Hegel's ideas and the ideas included in the various sociological conceptions in the nineteenth century—for instance, the conceptions advanced by A. Comte—is a separate issue.[4] Although Hegel's role is evaluated in greatly divergent ways, there is no controversy over its having been enormous, and few thinkers can vie with him in that respect. Yet his influence on the development of sociological thought still has to be examined.

Whatever his significance has been and still is, Hegel is repugnant to many authors because of the seemingly purely speculative character of his system and, still more, because of the notorious abstruseness of his style. For a modern positivist Hegel is the personification of all that is the worst in philosophy. Reading his works is in fact extremely toilsome, and their interpretation is difficult; one faces, on the one hand, the danger of being "infected" by his specific terminology, considered inacceptable today, and, on the other, the danger of a simplified "translation." The result of the latter would be that original author's being treated as merely a representative of one or another *ism* of his times. Realizing all these difficulties, we do not pretend to offer here an exhaustive description of Hegel's sociology. We shall try only to show its major topics and—more important—to present it as a tentative answer to the practical problems posed by his times, an answer comparable to those given by his contemporaneous politicians, reformers, lawyers, historians, economists, and the like. Those questions pertained in particular to the problems of revolution, the regularities of historical changes, the old and the new society, and the state. His seemingly fantastic construction, dominated by objective idealism and found in his successive studies and lectures, was in fact an endeavor to discover the sense of those events in which his generation was involved. Careful reading of Hegel's works shows that he had an astonishingly good knowledge of the political, social, and economic realities of his times. He was an assiduous student not only of contemporaneous political events, such as the French Revolution and the Napoleonic Wars, but also of the new social and economic conditions on which Marx was later to focus his attention.

THE PLACE OF HEGELIANISM AMONG THE IDEOLOGICAL TRENDS OF THE PERIOD

On a superficial reading, Hegel's works reveal a striking similarity to many formulations found in conservative thought (Mannheim treated Hegel, qua the author of *The Philosophy of Right* [1821], as one of its main representatives). These similarities apply to his criticism of the Age of Reason and social atomism, the worship of the social whole, the criticism of abstractionism and Utopian ideas, the idea of "the spirit of the nation," the eulogy of the society divided into "estates," and so on. Some of these ideas had become current in German thought and cannot, as such, be considered exponents of a specific political position, but there is no doubt that in Hegel we encounter a comprehensive syndrome of such ideas. On the other hand, his opposition to many conservative conceptions is noticeable, too. And it was not among the conservatives that he found disciples.

To some extent we could even speak about Hegel's anticonservatism. First, he was an absolute rationalist, although his rationalism differs essentially from that characteristic of the Age of Reason. Hegel was firm in rejecting the belief that social life is basically irrational and in criticizing folklore, beloved by the conservatives, as "befogged consciousness." It was rational law, and not prerational custom, that was his ideal. Second, Hegel believed in the idea of progress, although in a form different from that which it had had in the eighteenth century. In any case, he was far from the conservative denial of it: To the deification of the past he opposed his critical attitude toward it and thought that the past could be justified only insofar as it was a stage in the development of the spirit, a stage in the development of freedom. To "the pallid shades of memory" he opposed "the life and freedom of the present" and demonstrated that every epoch is something specific, that all solutions must originate from it, and that one can learn nothing from the past. Third, his interest was focused on universal history, a concept disregarded by the conservatives, who tended to look for the specific features of the history of the various nations. This is why the concept of the spirit of the nation (*Volksgeist*) is in his philosophy incomparably less important, if not of merely secondary significance. Fourth, Hegel did not look for harmony in societal life. His philosophy of history is an apology of contradictions, strife, and conflicts, from which new historical forms emerge. There are no perfect forms, and each form has in itself the germ of its own end. For all the inconsistencies—for example, Hegel's political opinions concerning the Prussian monarchy—such a historiosophy had to be unambiguously anticonservative, so there is nothing paradoxical in his later popularity with radical circles, even though he himself was not a radical. Finally, in Hegel's works certain terms have entirely different meanings than they do among the conservatives: For instance, the term *estate* does not mean for a feudal estate, because he treats it as an open group membership that is not determined by inheritance. As a matter of fact, it corresponds rather to the term *class*, and present-day authors are probably right in translating his term so into other languages (Note, for instance, that Adam Smith also spoke about modern society's being divided into ''orders'' and not into ''classes''). All this indicates that it would be groundless to categorize Hegel among the conservatives and to see his originality merely in his greater philosophical refinement.

Of what, then, did Hegel's opposition to the rationalistic social thought and his contemporaneous liberalism consist? From this point of view the focal issue was the problem of the relation between the individual and society, the problem of what constitutes the social whole. Hegel dismissed all individualistic (atomistic) answers. As a matter of principle, he questioned all variations of the theory of social contract and also the utilitarian conception, on which the liberal doctrine rejecting the idea of contract is based. The Age of Reason erred by trying to rest the social whole on so unsure and unstable foundation as the will and the interests of individuals. We seemingly encounter here well-known conservative ''antiatomism'' or the idea, much more stable than classical conservatism, of the absolute primacy of the whole over its parts, of society and the state over the individual.

Yet matters are not as simple as that. First, Hegel, unlike the conservatives, assumed some autonomy of the individual and did not mean that it was merely absorbed in the social whole. Second, the process of the socialization of individuals had, in Hegel's interpretation, many levels, and the problem was never reduced to deciding which is the more important of the two: the whole or its parts. One of the gravest errors committed by Hegel's interpreters was their reducing the problems to the dichotomy: the individuals versus the supraindividual whole, which is society and the state. What, in fact, is the most interesting issue in Hegel's views is the overcoming of that dichotomy.

In other words, Hegel was neither a conservative nor a liberal. His analyses cover both society, which emerges as a result of the individuals' strivings for the attainment of their own interests, and the state, which is something more than a political and legal form of safeguarding those interests Hegel's sociological analyses take place at two essentially different levels (three, if we take the family into account) that are rarely distinguished from one another in the social thought of his times—namely, the level of socio-economic relations ("civil society") and that of political and moral relations (the state). What usually were two elements of the same political alternative (independent individuals versus the sovereign state) turn out here to be two forms (and stages) of socialization. In the relations that develop from the egoistic interests of individuals, Hegel did not see (as did the conservatives) the lack of any social bonds whatever, but treated these relations as a specific form of social bonds. Nor did he treat them, as the liberals did, as social bonds *par excellence.* Hegel in a sense synthesized the liberal and the conservative theories of society. But the starting point for him was neither liberalism nor conservatism as definite political positions: Rather, synthesized liberal political economy (Adam Smith) and the related concept of civil society with the preconservative ideas of the state and society, represented mainly by Montesquieu.

CIVIL SOCIETY VERSUS THE STATE

Hegel's originality largely lies in the fact that he focused his attention not on an abstract relation between the individual and the society or the state, but on the society and the state as two basic locations in which the individual undergoes socialization. In the former, socialization is based on interests; in the latter, on reason. (In a third location, the family, it is based on sentiments.) Individuals become members of civil society *(bürgerliche Gesellschaft)* by each one's striving only to satisfy his own egoistic interests and needs. This is not to say, however, that their going outside the family, which is based on altruism, necessarily weakens or breaks bonds among human beings. On the contrary, it is an essential feature of civil society that no individual can have his interests satisfied without the interests of some other individuals being satisfied, too. When viewed from his motives for action, the individual is a totally independent "atom"; but when viewed from his actual functioning in society, he proves to be multiply dependent on others. His dependence is, however, neither conscious nor consciously chosen by him. It is an outcome of necessity: Social production is based on the division of labor, and no one is in a position to satisfy his own needs without availing himself of the assistance of others and without assisting others. An individual's existence also depends on whether all other individuals with whom he is in contact respect his rights, within specified limits, in return for having their respective rights observed. This applies in particular to safeguards of property, which is an outward manifestation of individual labor, because human individuals are able, unlike the animals, not only to assimilate specified goods by destroying them, but also to transform and to reproduce them. Hegel's anthropology on this point strongly resembles the Marxian view. Civil society is thus not only a system of interhuman bonds that develop spontaneously in the course of production and exchange; it is also a system of institutional safeguards of individuals' interests, property, security, rights, and contracts concluded by them. In brief, civil society as seen by Hegel can be defined as the totality of the socioeconomic relations together with their institutionalized legal safeguards.

As can easily be noted, there is nothing strikingly new in this characteristic of civil society. Hegel repeats here elements of bourgeois thinking that had been current since Locke. The idea that egoistic strivings of individuals ultimately yield a certain whole seems to replicate Smith's "invisible hand," which puts chaotic economic actions in order. It is known, by the way, how much Hegel availed himself of liberal political economy and his own observations of the bourgeois economy.[5] Links with that tradition make him differ from the conservatives, for whom any society based on such foundations was unimaginable.

But at the same time Hegel was critical of that tradition and any such society. He paid particularly attention to the negative aspects of civil society and demonstrated that it was a product of uncontrolled economic coercion and not of reason and consciousness; that it was governed by necessity and not by freedom; and that it was inevitably undergoing a process of polarization that accumulates immense wealth at one pole and extreme poverty at the other. As S. Avineri writes, Hegel was "one of the earliest radical critics of the modern industrial system."[6] He gave, for instance, a penetrating analysis of the worker's situation when he has to serve a machine, and he also described the alienation of labor, a process that in his opinion was inevitable. It should also be noted that, unlike the representatives of the liberal tradition, Hegel saw in civil society not just society as such, but a peculiar form of society that developed in the modern times following the expansion of industry and trade. In other words, he associated that special form of relations among human beings not with human nature, but with a definite stage of development of mankind. For all his critical attitude toward civil society, Hegel did not make use of any past-oriented Utopia: Even if he eulogized the Greek *polis*, he did not do so in order to recommend its institutions to his contemporary Europe, because he thought that no solution preserves its advantages forever, regardless of the later advances made by reason.

He avoided Utopias as a rule, being interested in what *is* (or becomes) and not in what *should be*. This was one more reason that he criticized the Age of Reason. Yet it would be difficult not to see in his philosophy an endeavor to set up a positive pattern of social life, a pattern owing to which ancient virtues would be reintroduced into the modern, depraved world. Such a pattern is contained in Hegel's conception of the state as that factor which makes it possible to overcome everything in civil society that calls for criticism. He was, of course, convinced that his ideal of the state is not a Utopia imposed upon the process of history, but that it is found there as a reason, which is necessarily becoming a reality.

It is not easy to say what is Hegel's conception of the state. The current idea of the state as the political and legal framework within which the society or the nation lives turns out to be most misleading in his cause. The state in his conception does not reduce to that framework and brings to mind, rather, the idea of Aristotle's *polis* or Montesquieu's state, which can more readily be associated with our idea of society than with our idea of the state as an organization. Hegel referred to Montesquieu directly and wrote that Montesquieu was that thinker who "proclaimed the true historical view, the genuinely philosophical position, namely that legislation both in general and in its particular provisions is to be treated not as something isolated and abstract but rather as a subordinate moment in a whole, interconnected with all the other features which make up the character of a nation and an epoch."[7] The political and legal system is merely "a moment" in a whole to which many other "moments" contribute: religion, art, philosophy, the whole culture of a given nation, its traditions, morals, and so on.

An individual does not participate in the state as he does in the company or the association; instead, he participates in it as he does in the family (although this comparison fails, too, because the family is particular by its very nature and does not require an equally high level of consciousness). When looking for the most suitable term, we should perhaps call the Hegelian state a *community*, but with the proviso that such a community differs from that recommended by the conservatives as it assumes a high level of consciousness (reason instead of prejudice), the autonomy of the individuals as conscious subjects, and the fulfillment of their freedom (insofar as freedom is not "arbitrary will," but the freedom of reason). When understood in this way, the state is, of course, an infinitely finer link between human beings than that which results from the struggle for the satisfaction of material needs—that is, finer than civil society. We should recall, however, that this is not an apology for the state as such: Not all states recorded in the history of mankind were states of that kind or, to use Hegel's terminology, truly "historical" states.

While opposing the state to civil society, Hegel did not postulate that the latter should be eliminated by the former, nor did he claim that the further course of history, marked by simultaneous advances of reason (freedom) and the state, would lead to that. He seems to have assumed a permanent dualism of the human individual, who "takes care of himself and his family, works, signs contracts, etc., and at the same time he also works for the universal and has it as an end. From the first viewpoint he is called *bourgeois*, from the second, *citoyen*."⁸ As we shall see later, when discussing Hegel's philosophy of history, that dualism is extremely characteristic and makes him differ in that respect from Marx, who looked for the ways of terminating it and of establishing a community at the level of work and production —that is, at the level of society.

How is such coexistence of the particular interests that mark civil society and the universalism of the state possible? It seems that the answer is given by Hegel's conception of classes or "estates" *(Stände)*, a conception that mainly accounts for the fact that Hegel's social philosophy used to be associated with conservatism. Like Adam Smith, the author of *The Philosophy of Right* links the emergence and the existence of classes to the division of labor. His singles out three basic classes: the agricultural class, concerned with assimilating natural products for society; the business class, which transforms those products and owes everything to its own productive activity; and "the thinking class," or the class of civil servants, which is concerned with coordinating the whole and taking care of the public interest. In the Hegelian analysis of the classes in civil society there are quite a few inconsistencies, but they do not affect the fundamental issues. Descriptions of the inner structure of the classes vary, but Hegel's principal opinions on the problems of class structure prove stable and consistent.

They can be summed up in three points. First, the division of society into classes *(Stände)* is inevitable, as are conflicts between the classes. Hegel even says that "the history of the inner politics [of a country] reduces to the history of the formation of the classes, the legal conflicts which oppose individuals to those classes, antagonisms between the classes and between them and the central authority."⁹ This fact, thus, is of essential significance for social life. Second, every class develops a specific group consciousness that corresponds to its living conditions and its position within society. The agrarian class is marked by the particularly strong attachment to the status quo, obedience, a lack of individualistic tendencies, and so on. The industrial class is marked, rather, by the spirit of innovation and inventiveness, individualism, and the capability for reflection and abstract thinking. The thinking class (*denkender Stand*) can free itself from the pressure of particular interests and think in terms of public interest, of which the other two classes are not capable. This is why Hegel usually calls it the "universal" class. And third, every individual is and must be a member of a class, but that membership is not determined by inheritance and depends totally on the abilities of the individual himself. In this sense Hegelian classes are not, and are not intended to be, medieval estates.

It may be said, however, that the function of those classes is in some respects analogous to that of the medieval estates: The individual becomes somebody by being a member of a class and thus starts to participate in the social whole; by joining other similar individuals on the strength of similarity of egoistic interests, he at the same time enters into a relationship with the public interest, which can never be reduced to such egoistic interests. In other words, Hegel sees in the classes not so much a factor that divides the whole into mutually opposing parts, but a factor that links parts into the whole. They are the basic element of universalism in civil society, governed by particular interests. The existence of classes makes it possible to bring individual interests into agreement with public interest and civil society into agreement with the state as imagined by Hegel. The special role is assigned to the universal class, that is, to the bureaucracy of the state, whose members, while belonging to civil society, simultaneously personify the state and deny the atomism of civil society. Note, in this regard, that Hegel was probably the first to outline a theory of bureaucrats as a specific social group.

Hegelian sociology, complemented by a comprehensive conception of political and legal institutions, eliminates "the people" as an important concept, current in the social thinking of the period. Hegel believed it to be too abstract and vague and also politically harmful as a possible ground for revolutionary actions directed against the state.

THEORY OF HISTORICAL DEVELOPMENT

When reference is made to Hegel's enormous influence, it is primarily his philosophy of history that one has in mind (*Philosophy of History*, 1837). It seems to have been the main passion of that philosopher and the crowning to his system. The principal ideas of Hegel's philosophy of history are simple: (1) The world is governed by reason; (2) History is the realization of freedom; (3) There is no reason nor freedom outside the state. His primary intention is also clear: He sought the regularities whose discovery would make it possible to give history some sense and to cease seeing it as an absurd sequence of murders, wars, and revolutions. Hegel wrote thus in a private letter about his *Lectures on the Philosophy of History:*

I maintain that the Spirit of the World *(Weltgeist)* gave our times the order: Onward! That order is being carried out. The Spirit of the World marches irresistibly on like an armored phalanx, and it moves on as imperceptibly as the sun in the skies, regardless of all obstacles. At its wings, light troops are engaged in disorderly skirmishes that sometimes slow down and sometimes speed on its march. Most people do not realize at all what it is all about, and they get knocked on the head as if by an invisible hand.[10]

This quotation sums up the main problems studied by Hegel: the individual versus the process of history, "disorderly skirmishes" versus the whole of which they are parts and which has its inner sense and can be explained rationally.

The regularity that the philosopher sought was to be the inner regularity of the process of history. The Christian idea of providence, which guides human history from the outside, was inacceptable to him. The science of history should not simply register facts, yet the regularities that it establishes must result from facts. If we contact infinity through the intermediary of history, then infinity manifests itself only through the activity of human beings. Of course, the Hegelian spirit or reason can be traced back to the Christian God in the same way that all historiosophy can ultimately be traced back to theodicy. But that spirit was thought by Hegel to act in human history and not to exist outside that history.

We can say, like Hegel, that history is "the exhibition of spirit in the process of working out the knowledge of that which it is potentially."[11] But we can also say, in full agreement with his texts, that history is the exhibition of the gradual development of human freedom on the basis of what human beings say and do. For Hegel, these were two formulations of one and the same idea. The East did not know the freedom of man at all, and it was only the ruler who was free. Ancient Greece knew about the freedom of some people, leaving others in the position of slaves. The Germanic peoples acquired in Christianity the consciousness of the fact that man qua man is free; the knowledge of that came slowly to penetrate the sphere of secular life. The further stages of that process were marked by the Reformation and political revolutions in modern times, particularly the French Revolution, which Hegel analyzed with exceptional perspicacy.

It does seem, however, that posing the question about the basic mechanisms of the process of history was much more important than indicating its general trend. Hegel did not want to judge, nor did he intend to moralize. He was inclined to think that human behavior is guided by passions and by egoistic and narrow interests. It does not make sense to deplore that or to expect that one day people can be turned into saints. The real problem is that "in history an additional result is commonly produced by human actions beyond that which they aim at and obtain, that which they immediately recognize and desire. They gratify their own interest; but something further is thereby accomplished, latent in the actions in question, though not present to their consciousness, and not included in their design."[12] As Hegel says, "knowing Reason" stays in the background and lets passion act for itself. The world moves on, the costs being paid by individuals: History is a vast graveyard of their aspirations, hopes, and interests. If some individuals win and become historic personages, this is not because they are of a different kind of clay, but because their particular interest coincides, at a given moment of history, with the trend in which the world is evolving. It was probably in this sense that Hegel, as the story goes, called Napoleon I "Reason on horseback." But even these victories prove to be of a short duration. As Kroński summed up Hegel's ideas, "a given system survives only as long as there is freedom in it; transition of the consciousness of freedom to a higher level again turns the once flourishing and vigorous institutions into ashes that merely slow down the progress of freedom."[13]

CONCLUDING REMARKS

Hegel's ideas have been presented here only in part and greatly simplified at that. Yet even this simple version allows one to realize that he tackled key problems and did so in an original way. We saw him take up a number of key issues of the social thought of his times and to offer, within his philosophical system, the solution that has proved to be one of the most stable paradigms of social philosophy. These problems were, above all, man versus society; man versus history; regularities in the process of history and its driving forces; variability of social institutions; and connections among the various spheres of national life. The solution suggested by Hegel was, it seems, three specific features. First, it tended to reveal processes that take place regardless of the intentions and consciousness of those who participate in them. Second, it was absolutely holistic in nature, as it assumed that comprehending anything in social life requires examining that social life as a whole that, of course, has various aspects and moments, but cannot be broken down into autonomous parts. Third, it was based on historicism, which precluded any possibility of handling human problems outside their historical context. On all these points Hegel proved to have been ahead even of many later authors who subjected his philosophy, as a whole or in part, to fundamental criticism.

NOTES

1. Herbert Marcuse, *Reason and Revolution: Hegel and the Rise of Social Theory*, 2d ed. (New York: Humanities Press, 1954), p. 251.
2. George H. Mead, *Movements of Thought in the Nineteenth Century* (Chicago: University of Chicago Press, 1939), pp. 147-48.
3. Georg Lukács, *Der junge Hegel* (Berlin: Aufbau-Verlag, 1954), p. 536.
4. Cf. Oskar Negt, *Strukturbeziehungen zwischen den Gesellschaftslehren Comtes und Hegels* (Frankfurt: Europäische Verlag, 1964).
5. Cf. Lukács, *Der junge Hegel*, pp. 369-89.
6. Shlomo Avineri, *Hegel's Theory of the Modern State* (Cambridge: Cambridge University Press, 1972), p. 93.

7. Georg Wilhelm Friedrich Hegel, *The Philosophy of Right*, trans. T. M. Knox, in *Great Books of the Western World*, vol. 46 (Chicago: Encyclopaedia Britannica, 1952), p. 10.

8. Avineri, *Hegel's Theory*, p. 104.

9. See Eugène Fleischmann, *La Philosophie politique de Hegel: Sous la forme d'un commentaire des "Fondements de la philosophie du droit"* (Paris: Plon, 1964), p. 222.

10. See Kuno Fischer, *Hegels Leben Werke und Lehre*, pt. 1 (Heidelberg: Winter, 1901), pp. 97-98.

11. Hegel, *The Philosophy of History*, trans. J. Sibree, in *Great Books*, vol. 46, p. 161.

12. Ibid., p. 165.

13. Tadeusz Kroński, *Rozwazania wokól Hegla* (Warsaw: PWN, 1960), p. 127.

6

HISTORICAL MATERIALISM: MARX AND ENGELS

The founders of historical materialism participated in the same great discussion of the crisis and the future of Western European societies that was described in previous chapters, and this is why their conception could not be comprehended without knowledge of its historical context. Yet Marx and Engels differ from their contemporaries by having survived, in present-day social science, not only as eminent thinkers of the past, but also as living authorities. There are no more Comtists and no Spencerians; there are not even Weberians and Durkheimists; but there are Marxists. This fact makes us pay a special attention to Marxism, but at the same time makes the historian's task complicated.

HISTORICAL MARXISM AND PRESENT-DAY MARXISM

A clear distinction must be made between Marxism as a present-day sociological theory and Marxism as a nineteenth-century social conception. Every continuation is inevitably selective, and it is not all the ideas of the initial doctrine that come to be developed, but only those which best comply with the needs of the epoch and the country in which those who continue the doctrine are active. Some ideas are forgotten, while others acquire importance that they did not have originally. Note also that continuation often consists in clarifying those statements whose original formulations were so ambiguous and general that they lent themselves to different interpretations.

The historian's task must be to reconstruct historical Marxism as a conception that lends itself to various interpretations and complementary theories, which sometimes are incompatible with one another. When reading Marx, we should question not so much who came to be the best guardian of his heritage, but rather what are the causes of the fact that both Kautsky and Lenin, both Plekhanov and Lukács, both Bukharin and Gramsci could be Marxists. We should also reflect on how it was possible for Marx to have been interpreted in various ways also outside the trend that he founded. To understand Marx's role in the history of social thought, one has to assume that Marx did not construct a closed system and left many important questions far from being settled unambiguously.

The reconstruction of Marx' conception for the history of sociology faces additional obstacles and in a sense requires abandoning the principle of focusing on historical Marxism. The point is that, contrary to what we find in many handbooks, Marx was *not* a sociologist—not only because he did not use the term *sociology* and his opinion of Comte could hardly have been worse. It seems that Marx could not have been a sociologist for essential reasons and that those Marxists who, on behalf of their master, questioned the sensibility of pursuing sociology as a separate and autonomous field of research were right.

First, historical materialism was to be a science or, rather, *the science of society*, but not sociology as distinct from philosophy, history, or political economy. In their works Marx and Engels took up the majority of those issues with which sociologists were concerned, but they themselves did not want to be sociologists. Note also that the author of *Kapital* did not call himself an economist, either, but referred to himself as a "critic of political economy." Thus, when describing Marx's sociology, we resort to an interpretive operation that consists of projecting into the past the present-day division of intellectual labor into the various disciplines. Thus we should bear in mind, and also pose from time to time, the question of whether we can sensibly continue speaking about Marxism once a certain level of specialization in research has been reached.

Second, Marxism had been conceived not as only a research discipline, and not even as a discipline that, once established, becomes an instrument of practical activity, but instead as a sublimated expression of the needs and aspirations of the proletariat. A thinker was also a leader and an ideologist (in the present-day sense). The shaping of sociology as a separate discipline was also a departure from Marx in the sense that it required a separation of those roles whose unity had been assumed by him in accordance with the historiosophical conceptions of the working class' role that extended also to the sphere of epistemology. As specialization progressed, a Marxist scholar was becoming a person who could draw inspiration from that historiosophy, but would not identify his knowledge with the consciousness of the class that had acquired its specialized spokesmen in the appropriate political parties. Those parties had also become intermediaries between scholars and the social movement, which happened to breed essential difficulties in defining the place of Marxist sociology in relation to other methods of revolutionizing society. However such difficulties may be overcome, the status of the present-day Marxist sociologist must differ quite essentially from the status that Marx had assigned to himself.

While pointing to certain peculiarities of Marx's thought, which make it difficult to show him as just a sociologist, we do not intend to claim that his standpoint was unique. In fact, all nineteenth-century sociology was neither specialized nor academic. Nevertheless, the main, positivistic trend of nineteenth-century sociological thought differed from the Marxian.

But the most profound difference between Marx and the nineteenth-century sociologists was that in a postrevolutionary society they saw a new society (or at least its nuclear form), while he considered it to be the old society doomed to inevitable destruction. Sociology was bourgeois-minded, for it did not reach with imagination beyond bourgeois society, improved as it was; in contrast, for Marx the constant system of reference was the new socialist society. This essential difference gave rise to many others.

TRANSITION FROM ANTHROPOLOGY TO A THEORY OF SOCIETY: STRUGGLE AGAINST "IDEOLOGY"

The beginnings of the intellectual formation of Karl Marx (1818-1883), and also of Friedrich Engels (1820-1895), with whom Marx closely collaborated from 1845 on, were linked to the young Hegelian movement and Hegelian philosophy, transformed by that movement into an instrument of radical social criticism. While retaining the highest esteem for Hegel throughout his life, Marx rather early quarreled with young Hegelians and arrived at formulating his own philosophy. Its first and most complete exposition was *The German Ideology* (1846), written jointly by Marx and Engels. In the evolution of Marx's views an important role had been played by his studies of the 1789 revolution, French socialism and communism, and English political economy.

Marx began his discussion of Hegel and Hegelianism by his *Contribution to the Critique of Hegel's Philosophy of Right* (1843) and articles in which he developed his thesis on the limitations of all political revolution that "dissolves civil society into its elements without revolutionizing these elements themselves or subjecting them to criticism."[1] Political emancipation, thus, can be only partial emancipation, and political changes prove superficial because "civil society," the material base of the state, remains intact. The state must not be analyzed as a factor of its own, independent of its "natural base" in the form of that society. Those opinions meant a declaration in favor of communism, which called for revolutionizing that base. They also meant rejection of all sociological explanations, which assigned to the state a role independent of society and to ideas and political programs a role independent of interests.

The concept of civil society, taken from Hegel (and indirectly from the Scottish philosophers of the Age of Reason), failed to satisfy Marx, who accordingly undertook intensive study of its anatomy, which consisted in political economy, he concluded. The first results of those studies took the form of *Economic and Philosophical Manuscripts of 1844*, concerned mainly with the analysis of alienation under the system of private ownership of means of production. The concept of alienation, formulated by Hegel and Ludwig Feuerbach (1804-1872), was extended by Marx to cover economic phenomena. In God, created by himself, man sees a power independent of him; likewise, under certain conditions, human labor and its products seem to human beings to be something external to them.

In the criticism of capitalism, presented in the *Manuscripts*, a considerable role was played by Feuerbach's concept of the "species-being" of man. Capitalism is unhuman because it deprives man of his "essence," his calling, which consists in conscious and free creative activity, in an all-around development of human physical and spiritual abilities, in a limitless enrichment of the individual within the human community. Marx sometimes even used the concept of human nature, which, however, is misleading here, because it suggests a similarity to those who criticized capitalism from the point of view of "natural" rights and needs. Marx was firm in rejecting such criticism, and his ideal of man was based on the conception of historically expanding needs, which was a novel element in the history of socialism (and, especially, of communism). In bringing out the importance of the individual and in rejecting the opposition between society and the individual, Marx was also opposed to traditional communism.

Clear as they are in their main ideas, the *Manuscripts* as a whole constitute an obscure text liable of widely divergent interpretations. They are more important as a stage in the evolution of Marx's ideas than as a theoretical achievement.

The Holy Family (1844), the first joint work by Marx and Engels, is interesting to sociologists as it contributes to the characteristic of civil society that bears out the problems of social bonds. Counter to the numerous critics of capitalist society who spoke about its "atomization," Marx wrote about the "natural necessity" of social relations, which in capitalist society do not vanish, but, instead, take on the form of reified relationships. Important, too, was the rejection of that idea of history as a "metaphysical object" (as in Hegel), and, hence, as something more than "the activity of man pursuing his aims."[2]

The German Ideology (1846), written jointly with Engels and preceded by the aphoristic *Theses on Feuerbach* (1845), crowned Marx's campaign against philosophical (or "ideological," a term he then started to use) abstract concepts of the state, society, history, and also man. Engels's somewhat earlier study entitled *The Condition of the Working Class in England* (1845) was an important item both in the history of social surveys and in the history of Marxism: It seems to have contributed to overcoming the speculative nature of the philosophical communism of the *Manuscripts* and to bringing it closer to facts. Beginning with that work, the proletariat in Marxist thought ceased to be merely a philosophical concept that brings the solution of "the puzzle of history."

In *The German Ideology* Marx and Engels turned against philosophy as such and suggested that it be replaced "at the most . . . [by] a conspectus of the general results, which are derived from the consideration of the historical development of men."[3] Antiphilosophical criticism was directed against Feuerbach and his "true socialism" based on his humanism and also at Max Stirner (1806-1856), who used to criticize Hegel from the position of radical individualism. All these conceptions and the interpretations of history known to Marx and Engels were covered by them by the common term *ideology*. They used that term without definition, ambiguously, so that it can be said with certainty only that for them the term was strongly derogatory and denoted a deformation of reality in the process of thinking, a deformation that on other occasions was called "false consciousness." According to Marx and Engels, that deformation consisted in particular in (1) believing that thought is independent or other forms of human activity; (2) ascribing to consciousness the role of efficient cause in social life and identifying social change with a change in the way of thinking about it; and (3) ascribing absolute validity to one's own opinions, which in fact are always conditioned by a given epoch and class membership.

For Marx and Engels the fundamental problem was finding those properties of the social world that make ideological alienation (and other forms of alienation as well) both possible and inevitable. Their point was not so much to disclose the prejudices of the various philosophers as to examine the situations in which ideology becomes the dominant form of consciousness.[4]

Philosophical *anthropology* came thus to be replaced by *sociology*. In his polemic with Feuerbach, Marx wrote that "the essence of man is not an abstraction inherent in each particular individual. The real nature of man is the totality of social relations," while the "abstract individual . . . belongs to a particular form of society."[5] Feuerbach, according to Marx, "remains in the realm of theory and conceives men not in their given social connections, not under their existing conditions of life which have made them what they are."[6] The dichotomy of "human" versus "inhuman" was replaced by a historical variability of human relations. Feuerbach's naturalistic materialism was transformed into historical materialism. It is true that man is a product and part of nature, but nature itself is, in Marx's opinion, "the product of industry and of the state of society.''[7] The real knowledge of man must, accordingly, include the relation between men and nature, on the one hand, and that between men and men, on the other. Both relations must be studied, for they have changed over the course of history.

But *The German Ideology* was not confined to polemics. Its first chapter included a fairly expanded exposition of Marx and Engels's conception of society, particularly that part of it which will later be discussed as the theory of socioeconomic formations and the theory of social consciousness. In fact, *The German Ideology* contains all the essential ideas of historical materialism.

When we analyze the destructive part of Marx's early production, we have to mention his polemic with Proudhon in *The Poverty of Philosophy* (1847), which was Marx's first public appearance as a theorist of political economy. That work reveals his criticism of all modes of thinking that make use of ahistorical concepts, in particular, that of the naturalness of social relations.

The works by Marx and Engels discussed so far can be treated primarily as their attempt to settle accounts with the philosophical tradition, intended to prepare for the construction of their own theory of society and history and their own communist policy. Those polemics reveal the problems and inspirations that shaped historical materialism. As often noted, those inspirations included Hegelianism, Utopian socialism and communism, and political economy in the version offered by Adam Smith and David Ricardo. The influence of French historians active under the Restoration is less often taken into account, although studies by Thierry, Guizot, and others had contributed much to the shaping of Marx's views of the process of history and the role of class struggle. Those various influences were transformed by Marx and Engels into an original whole, to be supported later by an imposing amount of empirical data accumulated in *Kapital*.

THE THEORY OF SOCIOECONOMIC FORMATION

The concept of socioeconomic formation seems pivotal in historical materialism, for it constitutes the most general framework of the analysis of both social structure and social development. The concept itself was left undefined by Marx, and its use offers many problems of interpretation. Yet the basic assumptions that supported its introduction into the theory of society seem clear.

First, Marx assumed that society is an internally intertwined *whole*. Its components came in the form of the various kinds of human activity (production, exchange and consumption, social system, politics, social consciousness, science, and the like), which had previously been analyzed independently of one another or considered to be linked to one another by ideas, consciousness, or the spirit that is inaccessible to observation (in Hegel). Marx thus rejected both a pure description of those elements treated in isolation and a speculative reflection on society in general, and he suggested that the relations between the various elements of that social whole be investigated.

Second, Marx assumed that a researcher's concern is not with society in general, but with many different societies that differ from one another in their component elements and in relations between those elements. Such societies make up several basic *types*, which follow one another in a specified order, each being a whole of its own.

And third, Marx assumed that a specified mode of production is the base of every society. This assumption has been placed last in order not to avoid the implication that historical materialism is essentially *economic* materialism—that is, a doctrine claiming that all social phenomena are unilaterally determined by their economic base. It is true that numerous passages in the writings of Marx and Engels favor that latter interpretation, which has also been the most frequent in the history of Marxism, but that interpretation is far from being the only possible one. In the opinion of some authors, historical materialism is essentially a conception that assumes interconnection between the various levels of social life and the various aspects of historical praxis and does not insist on an absolute primacy of any factor.

It seems that the thesis on the decisive importance of the mode of production must be understood mainly as a methodological principle. In his introduction to *A Contribution to the Critique of Political Economy* (1859), the most concise exposition of historical materialism, Marx wrote:

The distinction should always be made between the material transformation of the economic conditions of production which can be determined with the precision of natural science, and the legal, political, religious, aesthetic or philosophical—in short ideological, forms in which men become conscious of this conflict and fight it out. Just as our opinion of an individual is not based on what he thinks of himself, so can we not judge of such a period of transformation by its own consciousness.[8]

This was a summing up of the earlier polemics with ideology that led the founders of historical materialism to the study of the social facts that lend themselves best to rigorous observation. Such facts were adopted by them as the independent variable in the description of the process of history and came to serve them as the basis of the typology of societies (which also was a general division of human history into periods) and as the point of departure for characterizing all social wholes.

Since the conception now under consideration was formulated ambiguously, it led to two essentially different sociological theories: that of a causal conditioning of all social facts by the economic base and a theory of the structural relationship between economic facts and all other social facts.

Marx singled out the Asiatic, the ancient, the feudal, and the modern bourgeois formations and, less distinctly, also the primitive and the communist formations. The last-named one was to take shape after the proletarian revolution. But his systematic studies covered only the capitalistic formation, both its origin and its functioning—not only because it was contemporaneous with him and the explanation of its functioning was practically important, but also because he saw that understanding it was the indispensable point of departure for the explanation of other formations. In that respect Marx differed considerably from the evolutionists, who sought the key to the comprehension of their contemporaneous society in the understanding of earlier and simpler societies. The results of Marx's studies of the capitalistic formation were included in *Kapital* (volume 1, 1867; volumes 2 and 3, published posthumously by Engels in 1885 and 1894). Marx had been preparing gradually for this, his main opus, moving from *The Poverty of Philosophy* (1847) to *Wage Labor and Capital* (1849), to *A Contribution* (1859), mentioned earlier in this chapter, and to the comprehensive *Grundrisse der Kritik der Politischen Oekonomie* (1857-1858), which came to be known only in 1940. *Kapital* gave Marx the renown of an economist, but it is also the fundamental source for his methodology and social theory.[9]

... Marx ... did not confine himself solely to "an economic theory" in the ordinary sense of the term ... while *explaining* the structure and development of a given form of society *exclusively* in terms of relations of production, he nevertheless everywhere and always went on to trace the superstructure that corresponds to these relations of production and clothed the skeleton in flesh and blood.[10]

Other socioeconomic formations were not worked out by Marx so systematically, but his achievements in that field are much more comprehensive than it was believed not very long ago. This is proved by the lively discussion of the so-called Asiatic mode of production and precapitalistic formations in general. The exceptions are the primitive formation, in which Marx became interested rather late and which could not be fully examined for the scarcity of anthropological data,[11] and the communist formation, about which Marx said little because of his unwillingness to engage in Utopian fantasies about the future.

Like other conceptions of this type, constructed in the nineteenth century, the theory of socioeconomic formations as interpreted by Marx had both typological and historiosophical aspects, for Marx often referred to socioeconomic formations as a succession of "epochs." He wrote in the preface to the first German edition of *Kapital* that "the country that is more developed industrially only shows, to the less developed, the image of its own future."[12] He also maintained that no society could skip the natural phases of its own development. The abundance of such statements favored the interpretation of historical materialism after the pattern of historio-sophical schemata, typical of the nineteenth century, which singled out certain phases through which every society must pass.

This interpretation of Marx's conception is far from being indisputable if we recall its main outline was based on facts drawn from the history of Western Europe. Marx realized that when, in his letter to the editor of *Otecestvennye Zapiski*, he engaged in a polemic with Mikhailovsky: "He feels he absolutely must metamorphose my historical sketch of the genesis of capitalism in Western Europe into an historico-philosophic theory of the general path every people is fated to tread, whatever the historical circum-stances in which it finds itself. . . . But I beg his pardon (He is both honour-ing and shaming me too much)."[13]

Marxian theory of formations can in its historiosophical aspect be inter-preted in two ways: as a universal schema of historical development, like the laws of three stages formulated by Saint-Simon and Comte, or as a general hypothesis based on facts drawn from European culture and to be verified by other data. There is no doubt, for instance, that the ancient formation was a peculiarity characteristic of a small part of Europe and that the precapitalistic development of other countries followed an entirely different course. From this point of view, the Marxian interpretation of social development would be, commented A. Jasińska, "not unilinear, but unidirectional in the sense accepted by modern conceptions of eveolution."[14]

SOCIAL CLASSES AND CLASS STRUCTURE

The theory of socioeconomic formations provided only a most general framework of an analysis of society and social development in terms of historical materialism. The relations of production are relations between classes, that is, groups of people some of whom possess means of produc-tion, while the others do not; some of whom have functions of control, while the others are subordinated; some of whom receive great parts of the national product while others receive little. Even in his criticism of the Hegelian philosophy of law, Marx referred to classes as components of the civil society; in his later works that concept continued to gain in importance. *The Communist Manifesto* (1848) opens with the statement that "the his-tory of all hitherto existing society is the history of class struggle."[15] The historical studies by Marx and Engels, mostly concerned with the experience of the revolution of 1848—*The Class Struggle in France* (1850) by Marx,

The Peasant War in Germany (1850) by Engels, *The Eighteenth Brumaire of Louis Bonaparte* (1852) and *Revolution and Counterrevolution in Germany* (1852) by Marx—were above all analyses of historical events in terms of conflicting class interests and class struggle. Marx himself did not overestimate his achievements in that respect, pointing to the fact that bourgeois historians had preceded him in presenting the development of class struggle and bourgeois economists had already examined "the economic anatomy of the classes." He believed that his merit was to have proved that the existence of classes was connected only with specified socioeconomic formations.[16] Nevertheless, Marx's contribution to that field of research has been enormous and his impact continues to this day, even outside Marxist theory. Nor is there any doubt that earlier conceptions have influenced present-day sociology mainly through the intermediary of Marx; this can easily be explained by the fact that it was Marx alone who applied those conceptions to the analysis of bourgeois society, whereas his predecessors confined their interpretation to society based on estates. The modern concept of social classes is connected with a society in which there are no formal inequalities between its members.

Marx and Engels have not left any systematic exposition of their conception of social classes, nor have they even defined them. The reading of their works is particularly difficult, because the term *class* does not have a constant meaning, although it invariably refers to groups of people singled out relative to a distinct economic position and, accordingly, to distinct group interests.

But the problems connected with the Marxian conception of social classes do not reduce simply to the issue of one or another definition. The most important of these problems are discussed below.

Class Consciousness. Some contexts in Marx's writings seem to indicate that in his opinion, as S. Ossowski puts it, "an aggregate of people which satisfies the economic criteria of a social class becomes a class in the full meaning of this term only when its members are linked by the tie of class consciousness, by the consciousness of common interests, and by the psychological bond that arises out of common class antagonisms."[17] Even though such statements are not numerous, they do reveal a very important aspect of Marx's conception. In his opinion, the existence of an aggregate of human beings who satisfy certain economic criteria suffices for their being called a class, but in general a class is something more, and the role played by social classes in social life depends on whether a common economic position gives rise to corresponding common attitudes. This idea is best expressed by the distinction between a class *in itself* and a class *for itself*, made in *The Poverty of Philosophy*. In other words, Marx's con-

ception differs basically from those numerous conceptions that single out
classes by subjective criteria (the sense of class membership), but it is in no
way confined to objective (economic) criteria. In particular, when Marx
was concerned with classes of specified societies he was most interested in
attitudes and behavior of members of those classes. But even when he was
engaged in a model analysis (as was the case of *Kapital*), he seemed to
assume that (class) consciousness is at least a potential attribute of social
classes.

Class Structure. A theory of social classes as a rule includes a specified
conception of class structure. Social classes cannot be described in isolation,
especially if the very concept of social class assumes, as in the case of the
Marxian interpretation, interdependence of classes within the framework
of a given mode of production or, at another level of analysis, interdependence within the framework of a given political community (state). Schemata
of interpretation of class structure vary greatly, and it is important to
establish which schema Marx was inclined to adopt. Many authors thought
that he had given preference to the dichotomous schema, which treats class
structure in terms of the opposition of two classes: the propertied and the
nonpropertied. In the opinion of those authors Marx was only minimally
interested in the issue of "the middle class," and in social stratification
based on criteria other than the economic one.

These opinions are justified to some extent, because Marx, in fact, was
engaged in the sociology of social *antagonism*, not in the sociology of
social *stratification*. In his case that interest was substantiated in many
ways. First, the Marxian theory of socioeconomic formations was a study
of models, and hence the simplification, in certain stages of analysis, of the
schema of class structure did not have to be identical with the actual class
structure of any given society. In their works concerned with the analysis of
specific events, Marx and Engels used a different, and extremely complex,
schema of class structure. Second, the Marxian conception of capitalism
included a forecast of an increasing simplification of class oppositions as a
result of the process of annihilation. In that respect Marx was the antithesis
of Tocqueville, who thought that the middle class would be the only class to
remain. Third, Marx believed that in every society, whatever the degree of
complexity of its class structure, there are two basic antagonistic classes.
The relationship between them was decisive—especially in periods of
revolutions—for the behavior of members of the other classes (for instance,
the attitude of the petite bourgeoisie during an intensifying conflict between
the proletariat and the bourgeoisie) and also for the intensification of conflicts within each of the basic classes (for instance, the unification of the
various propertied classes and their otherwise quarreling sections in the
face of a threat by the nonpropertied majority).

This "polar" model of class structure, wrote J. Hochfeld, "did not by itself sufficiently map all social divisions. It merely singled out 'the ideal type' of a certain specific social relation which is of fundamental importance." A concrete description of any society and also a historical description of the course of class struggle absolutely require the use of "schemata of expanded class structure."[18] One must take into account the inner stratification of each class that is "basic" for a given formation, the existence of those classes which are survivals of earlier formations or the nucleus of the new formation, the existence of the class of small producers in its "interformation" status, and also the existence of such specific social groups as the lumpenproletariat, the bureaucracy, and the intelligentsia. Note also that his analysis of model situations, given in *Kapital*, need not be confined to the two basic classes and offers opportunities for making further distinctions.

The General and the Particular Concepts of Social Class. Marx's conception of social classes referred above all to capitalism; Marx even happened to claim that classes had been formed only under capitalism. However, the concept of class was much more general and was intended to apply to all societies in which there was private ownership of means of production. As S. Ossowski puts it, "changes in social reality may . . . involve changes in the conceptual apparatus, not only to enable one to describe the new phenomena but also to formulate general hypotheses which will take the old and the new experiences into account."[19] The general hypothesis was in this case concerned with the economic substratum of all significant social divisions and, hence, also divisions into estates and castes, whose basis had often been sought only in the political superstructure. This had important consequence for socioeconomic history, although Marx himself engaged mainly in the study of capitalism and did not investigate issues of the class structure of precapitalistic societies on any broader scale. In any case, Marxian ideas included two concepts of class: the general one, which pertains to all societies in which there has been private property, and the particular one, applicable to capitalist society, in which the division of society on the economic basis can be seen in its purest form. In the case of bourgeois society, the term *class* is used directly in the description of facts; in the other cases, it is an analytic concept that makes it possible to reveal the economic substratum of social divisions.

The Origin of Social Classes. As compared with many other contemporaneous thinkers, Marx was less interested in the problem of the origin of the division of society into classes; yet it seems that his opinions on the issue were quite clear-cut. First, he linked division into classes to the division of labor, thus remaining faithful to the traditions of English political economy. Second, he was firm in rejecting the explanation of class division by references to conquests, an explanation that was quite popular in his times. In his opinion, the differentiation into those who govern and those who are governed was derivative of the differentiation into those who are propertied and those who are not, and not vice versa. On this point Marx broke with the traditions of French bourgeois historiography, from which he drew the idea of class struggle. This also makes him differ from the other representatives of the so-called conflict theory, who were active in the nineteenth century.[20]

THE STATE

The problems of the state were among the key issues in Marxian sociology. This was due to both practical and theoretical reasons: On the one hand, Marx's communism, unlike many earlier communist doctrines, was markedly political in nature; on the other, historical materialism was a theory of the social *whole*. Full-fledged class struggle was for him a political conflict. Marx's sociology was outstandingly political in character, but his theory of politics was markedly sociological in nature, as it gave the pride of place to the social origin and the social function of the political institutions, especially the state, and not to the formal issues of the legal system.

Marx and Engels's theoretical reflections on the state followed two paths, which were to some extent separated from one another. We can find comments on the state as both "a special organism separated from society through division of labour"[21] and as "the organized power of one class for oppressing another."[22] In some cases Marx was interested in the state from the viewpoint of the relation that it bears to society as a whole; on other occasions he examined it from the viewpoint of the relation of one part of society to its other parts. In other words, Marx's political theory covers both the theory of bureaucracy and the theory of class domination. Both theories were interconnected in many ways, but they may be separated from one another for analytical purposes.

Beginning with his earliest works, Marx pointed to the fact that in modern states the political system of the state has developed into a peculiar reality that exists next to the real life of the nation, and he analyzed the process whereby the state became "independent" of society. Those problems were most comprehensively discussed in his studies of French politics in 1848-1851 and 1870-1871, and in many respects their interpretation resembles Tocqueville's reflections on the centralization proper to modern societies. Marx wrote, for instance, that in France "the executive power . . . constantly maintains an immense mass of interests and livelihoods in the most absolute dependence. . . . through the most extraordinary centralization this parasitic body acquires a ubiquity, an omniscience, a capacity for accelerated mobility and an elasticity which finds a counterpart only in the helpless dependence, in the loose shapelessness of the actual body politic.''[23] The Paris Commune was greeted by Marx as ''the re-absorption of the power of the state by society.''

Marx did not think, however, that the alienation of the state can be explained by itself, regardless of economic and social conditions. Both he and Engels emphasized that the independence of state power was relative or even illusory. It seems that the originality of the Marxian conception of bureaucracy (unlike those of Hegel and many later authors) resulted from its having been formulated in a close connection with the theory of class struggle and class domination.

The idea of the class-conditioned nature of state power can be seen very clearly in Marx's works; it was used by him to substantiate the thesis that it was necessary for the proletarian revolution to destroy the bourgeois state. It was developed most comprehensively by Engels in his *Origin of the Family, Private Property and the State* (1884). While Marx was mainly concerned with the nature, functioning, and transformations of the bourgeois state, Engels took up the problem of the state in general and tried to demonstrate a relationship between its existence and the class division of society. Anthropological and historical reflections led him to the same conclusions as observations of current political life.

This thesis, so important for historical materialism, must not be oversimplified and misinterpreted to mean that every class-based society is *governed* directly by the economically dominant class. Such an interpretation is refuted by almost everything that Marx and Engels did in their research work: Many a time they described the struggle for power among the various sections of the economically strongest class, and they even pointed to a relative independence of the machinery of the state from the claims of the various classes at any given time.

In most general terms, within historical materialism the state can be presented as an instrument of class domination, which under certain historical circumstances becomes relatively independent of the various sections of the dominant class and reveals a tendency to grow at the cost of society as a whole. Marx and Engels visualized the proletarian revolution as an act of abolishing the class domination of the bourgeoisie and the bureaucracy alike. The result would be a dictatorship of the proletariat (at that time *dictatorship* referred to the content, and not to the form, of government), intended to create a classless society and thereby to prepare conditions for the withering away of the state.

From the point of view of the founders of historical materialism, the state was a historical phenomenon in a twofold sense. First, it was supposed to exist only in those socioeconomic formations in which society is divided into classes. Second, as it occurs in the various countries and in the various epochs, it must have different forms.[24]

SOCIAL CONSCIOUSNESS

The most important conclusion that Marx and Engels reached when criticizing ideology was this:

Morality, religion, metaphysics, and other ideologies, and their corresponding forms of consciousness, no longer retain therefore their appearance of autonomous existence. They have no history, no development: it is men, who in developing their material production and their material intercourse, change, along with their real existence, their thinking and the products of their thinking. Life is not determined by consciousness, but consciousness by life."[25]

Such statements, understandable in the course of the polemics in which Marx and Engels were engaged when the foundations of historical materialism were being shaped, could lead to the conclusion (at which Marx's successors often arrived) that those authors claimed consciousness to be merely an epiphenomenon of social life. There is no doubt that in their research they did their best to demonstrate that consciousness depends on its material substratum ("social life"); this viewpoint also found reflection in their specific terminology: *base* and *superstructure*. Only toward the close of his life did Engels, having realized that Marxism had been distorted into absurdity by some of its overzealous adherents, try—unfortunately, not too successfully—to make corrections in the current interpretation of his own and Marx's views by emphasizing the fact that social consciousness is marked by a certain amount of independence and that it is determined by material conditions "in the last analysis" only. For all his efforts, continued by many Marxists in the twentieth century, the problems connected with Marx's opinions on social consciousness (and the role of ideologies) have remained to this day some of the most controversial issues in historical materialism. This is why, in the history of the Marxist theory, we can single out at least two rival trends: One consists of interpreting social consciousness merely as a reflection of social life; the other, of ascribing social consciousness an important role in human history.

Social Life and Social Consciousness. Marx and Engels have not left any complete and orderly theory of social consciousness. What we have at our disposal is confined to a number of suggestions, in most cases formulated either during discussions with ideologists or in connection with analyses of specific manifestations of social consciousness: political, religious, philosophical, literary, and legal ideas.

There is no doubt that the opinions on social consciousness that marked historical materialism were attractive largely due to their one-sidedness. Treating consciousness as a dependent variable was a novelty in social science, especially when seen against the background of the philosophy of those times, dominated by the tradition of the Age of Reason and, in contrast, by Hegelian philosophy. In some cases, it has remained such a novelty till the present day. In fact, those Marxian one-sided views gave rise to sociological studies of consciousness, which are today termed sociology of knowledge, sociology of religion, sociology of morals, sociology of art, or sociology of culture and which sometimes form an integral part of studies in general history, in the history of literature, and so on. This was so because such studies required the assumption, which in Marx's times was far from self-evident, that "consciousness is . . . from the very beginning a social product, and remains so as long as men exist at all."[26]

The novel element in Marx's position was that he did not confine himself to decreeing the truth or the falsehood of ideas, to rationalistically separating truth from prejudice, but treated all human ideas as the *expression* of specified historical situations in which human beings enter into relations with one another. The statement that an idea is false does not settle the question, because next to the epistemological problem there is always a sociological problem: Why do people under various conditions produce various ideas and why are they inclined to adopt them? The question was important for the future of the social science, but the danger of vulgarization was immediately lurking behind it: It was the danger that all problems of the study of consciousness might be reduced to the search for the social conditionings of consciousness and to the assumption that similar social conditions necessarily produce similar forms of consciousness. This was the course followed by many who continued Marx's thought, while others opposed that vulgarization only by repeating that consciousness, after all, enjoys some independence and plays an active role.

It seems that many comments on Marxian statements about social consciousness are burdened by the alleged alternative disjunction: Consciousness is either a simple reflection of social life or an active factor in the process of history. But, for Marx these two fields were merely two aspects of one and the same human praxis.[27] In history, we never are concerned either with pure consciousness or with pure existence. As Engels wrote, "in the history of society . . . the actors are endowed with consciousness, are men acting with deliberation or passion working toward definite goals; Nothing happens without a conscious purpose, without an intended aim.

Those actors are always determined societally and the problem consists in finding out in what social conditions they think in this way or other."[28] But this problem is in no way identical with the question about the relation between abstract "existence" and abstract "consciousness."

False Consciousness. Marx's attention was largely focused on the analysis of the phenomenon that he had termed *false consciousness*, by which he did not mean falsehood in the gnosiological sense, but the notorious inability, on the part of human beings, to identify their places in the process of history. Historical analysis reveals numerous illusions that accompany the mental grasping of social reality by people who belong to the various epochs, classes, and groups.

Marx and Engels describe facts that could be defined as the false consciousness of the epoch. They refer, for instance, to the modes of thinking characteristic of those societies which are governed by mechanisms of the market economy, to the peculiarities of the periods of "immature class relationships" and revolutionary breakthroughs, to the consciousness typical of societies under the slave and the feudal systems. Every epoch that follows unmasks the false consciousness of the preceding one by revealing the real consequences of human actions in that preceding epoch and by demonstrating, by its own existence, that everything believed to be natural and eternal not long ago is just transitory.

Marx and Engels were concerned with the false consciousness of social classes. Thus, for instance, a petit bourgeois is supposedly prone to placing himself above class antagonisms; a bourgeois would believe the capitalist conditions to be the only possible ones; and so forth. This kind of false consciousness reveals its illusory nature when confronted with the consciousness of members of other classes. Although the latter, too, is probably illusory, it usually forms a sufficient system of reference for recognizing the "conscious existence" of a specified social class. An example is provided by the conservative criticism of the revolutionary bourgeoisie. Marx and Engels assigned the privileged status to proletarian class consciousness, which, being the consciousness of the class that has nothing to lose, is free from the limitations typical of the consciousness of all propertied classes.

Marx and Engels also analyzed the false consciousness of the ideologists, which is a special case of group consciousness that develops with the progressive division of labor (another case being the specific bureaucratic consciousness of members of the administrative machinery). As has been mentioned, they paid very much attention to the criticism of ideologies. The very fact that there had emerged, within society, specialized groups of thinkers, separation of mental work from manual work, and finally separation of theory from practice marked the beginning of the domination of false consciousness: "From this moment onwards consciousness *can* really flatter itself that it is something other than consciousness of existing practice. . . . From now on consciousness is in a position to emancipate itself from the world and to proceed to the formation of 'pure' theory, theology, philosophy, ethics, etc."[29] The longer the tradition of any such sphere of activity, the stronger the feeling of autonomy. An ideologist is primarily concerned with his attitude toward the ideas of his predecessors, reflecting neither on whose "conscious existence" they are, nor on relation of his own field of activity to social practice. The history of thought becomes separated from the history of human beings and also splits into spheres that are independent of one another and determined by the actual division of intellectual labor. This gives rise to two problems: the relation between ideologists and social classes (What does it mean, for instance, to be an ideologist of a class?) and the relationships between the various spheres of ideology, which, by the way, are linked with social practice in different ways (religion and philosophy are linked with it less directly than are law and political theory, for instance).

Marx and Engels assumed that—regardless of how remote human ideas appear to be from social practice—appropriate analyses can reveal their social origin and function and thus can comply with the requirement that social processes be described with the precision of natural science. They attached particular significance to the establishing of relationships between those ideas, on the one hand, and the interests of the various classes and the very fact of the existence of classes and class conflicts, on the other. This is why the concept of class consciousness was certainly the pivotal concept in the Marxian theory of social consciousness.

Class Consciousness. This concept is not quite clear; in present-day sociology it is often used in a sense remote from the Marxian— namely, to denote the empirical consciousness of the members of a class that is singled out in a certain way. In the Marxist theory itself the meaning of the term is rather vague. In some cases, it is used to refer to the social class with which a given thinker consciously identified himself; sometimes, to the class in which a given idea had most adherents; sometimes, to the class to which it could be the most advantageous. It seems that for Marx the concept of class consciousness was in the category of ideal types.

For him, class consciousness was not, and could not be, identical with the empirical consciousness of members of a given social class. Such identity is a purely theoretical possibility, because the transformation of a class in itself into a class for itself is never, in fact, complete. When reference is made to the class consciousness of the proletariat, "it is not a question of what this or that proletarian, or even the whole proletariat, at the moment considers as its aim. It is a question of what the proletariat is, and what, in accordance with this being, it will historically be compelled to do.''[30]

Some authors here introduce the concept of potential consciousness, which is distinguished from real consciousness and is empirically given as the views of the individuals who are members of a given class. In historical materialism this distinction seems to be of fundamental importance. All analyses of concrete manifestations of social consciousness carried out by Marx and Engels assume a specified model of potential consciousness. If they speak about false consciousness, they do so because such and such views are not an adequate interpretation of the situation of those who formulate those views. False consciousness is born, above all, from the hiatus between what people think of themselves and what really is in social life. The procedure regularly used by Marx in his study of social consciousness was to pose questions as to what that consciousness would be if—for reasons that can be explained historically—it adequately diagnosed the social situation in which the thinking subjects lived. In fact, we see here the same procedure of idealization that Marx used when investigating class structure and the state as the instrument of class domination. Historical facts are not, and cannot be, in agreement with the ideal type that serves as an instrument of analysis.

Of course, the use of that instrument involved certain dangers, which, by the way, let themselves be felt in the history of Marxism. The theoretical danger results from a naive confusion of instruments of analysis with the results—that is, in the case under consideration, the confusion of potential consciousness with empirical consciousness, caused by disregarding what the latter is. Especially when one makes use of the idea of historical necessity, one can easily be trapped by a *sui generis* Platonism, which takes into account only the idea of class and not the people of whom that class consists. The practical danger is that there may appear individuals or groups who usurp the sole right to decide what is class consciousness and what is not.

SOCIAL DEVELOPMENT

Like the overwhelming majority of social ideas in the nineteenth century, historical materialism tended to explain the development of society. While the various parts of the doctrine—such as the theory of social classes and the theory of social consciousness—could and can function by themselves, they were originally just aspects of a homogeneous whole that had been clearly conceived as a historiosophical construction.

It is, therefore, necessary to examine Marxism from that point of view, especially because that aspect of the theory has given rise to quite a number of misunderstandings. It has been mentioned previously that socioeconomic formations were interpreted by Marx and Engels not only as types of societies, but also as "particular stages of development in the history of mankind."[31] The direction of that development was outlined by them very clearly, although they omitted details on those points for which empirical data were unavailable (the future communist society). There are major doubts about how far Marx and Engels were inclined to adopt the conception of unilinear development, notoriously ascribed to them by popularizers of Marxism. Yet the most essential controversy has been over the mechanisms of social development.

Historical Necessity. Clearly, this concept played an enormous role in historical materialism, as it did in other conceptions of that time. Owing to Marx it was introduced into socialist thought, which, as we have seen, had long remained under the influence of the ahistorical schemata current in the Age of Reason and had resisted the spreading of historicism (except for Saint-Simon and some minor writers). For Marx, socialism ceased to be a requirement of eternal reason or changeless human nature and became a "necessary" result of the process of history. That way of thinking originated, of course, with Hegel, but current observations concerning the discrepancy between human intentions and actual effects of human actions signally contributed to the final shape of the idea. Marx was one of those numerous nineteenth-century authors who took up the problem of objective conditioning of human actions and their consequences. In his case it was also the problem of the conditions for a success of the communist revolution: Promoters of such a revolution before Marx usually represented the voluntaristic approach. It seems that the problem of conditions of actions was the focus of Marx's reflections on historical necessity.

He was not a fatalist who believed that all historical events are inevitable and must occur in a certain way only. He also protested against hypostasizing history and treating it as a force external to human beings. Nor did he think that history unfailingly guaranteed the victory of the cause with which he was linked. Since he thought that society forms an internally intertwined whole, he concluded that a change in some of its parts must result in a change in the others. For the same reasons, human actions are confined within certain limits: Political institutions that would be desirable from a certain point of view cannot be made to work if they are not compatible with the existing configuration of social forces and economic system; opinions that are otherwise justified cannot be expected to spread if they are at variance with dominant interests; and so on. Historical data, generalized as the theory of socioeconomic formations, seemed to indicate that such dependences are exceptionally strong; this referred in particular to dependence on the system of production. The thesis on historical necessity,

though often formulated in a language close to Hegel's, thus seems trans-
latable into a number of particular statements about structural and causal
relationships between facts which are liable to scientific investigation. The
problem of the truth of such statements is essentially different from belief
or disbelief in the fate of history. Later propaganda needs and numerous
unfortunate formulations caused Marx often to be imagined as a prophet
who predicted the advent of communist society in the same way that ancient
prophets predicted the advent of the kingdom of God.

The proper understanding of the Marxian interpretation of historical
necessity requires other limitations, which have not always been taken into
account. First, it does not seem that Marx's position authorizes us to make
any forecasts on particular issues. His theses on the necessity of the process
of history referred to the most general trends and not to the course that the
process should take in a given country or a given period. Marx realized
that a great number of factors were involved and was, accordingly, rather
cautious and flexible in his opinions. Second, the belief in the necessity
of the process of history does not necessarily lead to the conviction that in
given situations individuals or even social classes would behave in a specified
manner. One can, of course, expect with some probability what the members of certain classes would not do and what limits they would not cross,
but one must not claim that they would act in precisely one way or another.
In particular, historical materialism does not claim to say anything conclu-
sive about motivations underlying actions by individuals, and it confines
itself to forecasts about the most likely results of collective actions on the
historical scale.

History as a "Natural Process" Engels's formulation that the process of
history resembles phenomena described in natural science is certainly one
of the most controversial statements in the theory of historical materialism.
Engels's statement used to be interpreted in two ways. According to some
authors, it is purely metaphorical and means only that the process of history
is not an arbitrary product of those who participate in it. Instead, like
natural processes, it has its own objective laws that can be known, but
cannot be abolished. According to others, his statement says that society
is to be treated as part of nature and that the explanation of at least some
social processes must be sought in the laws of natural science. It was especially toward the close of the nineteenth century, as Darwinism was becoming popular, that the latter interpretation won many advocates among
Marxists, some of whom were inclined to associate Marx with Darwin and
Spencer rather than with Hegel. Engels's views probably evolved in that
direction, too. Of course, this self-adjustment of Marxism to the dominant
climate of opinion was quite natural; we shall watch a similar trend at the

time of the antipositivistic reaction. The point, however, is not to find whether Marxism was subject to the influence of evolutionistic naturalism, but to establish to what extent that process could result from the inner logic of Marx's doctrine.

Naturalistic motifs can certainly be found in it, first in Feuerbach's and later in Darwin's version. In the *Manuscripts* we can read that Marx was interested in "corporeal man with his feet firmly planted on the ground, inhaling and exhaling all the powers of Nature,"[32] and in *The German Ideology* "living individuals" with a specified physical constitution are the point of departure for the formulation of the theory of society. These statements, however, do not go beyond generalities and, moreover, they are weakened by the emphasis Marx laid on the interpretation of nature as a product of human activity. This was modified somewhat by the impact of Darwinism, greeted by Marx as a great scientific discovery and the formulation of a scientific view of nature. But on other occasions, Marx protested against an excessive generalization of Darwinism, since he saw it primarily as a doctrine that, when applied to society, was an image of free-competition capitalist society, that is, a transitory socioeconomic formation.[33] Further, both for Marx and for Engels, history remained, in accordance with the Hegelian tradition, the development of self-knowledge; they were greatly interested in human actions as conscious activity, for which little room was left in a Darwinian conception of society.

All this induces us to be rather cautious in interpreting the thesis on historical development as analogous to processes investigated in natural science, although it would, of course, be anachronistic to see in Marx's works manifestations of antinaturalism in the present-day sense of the term.

Driving Forces of the Process of History. Historical materialism emerged as a result of discussions with the idealistic conceptions of history, and its founders used to stress with exaggeration (as Engels concluded many years later) their first principle: It states that social life is primary with respect to social consciousness; social life is the base of social consciousness which is only its superstructure. In their striving to explain social changes and revolutions, both contemporaneous examples and those known from history, the founders of the Marxist theory consistently avoided reference to the intentions and aspirations of the participants in those changes and revolutions. Human actions were for them the main factor of social development; those actions, however, do not correspond (or at least do not correspond exactly) in their course and results to what was conceived and planned by the human agents concerned.

It may be said that they analyzed those actions at several levels without, however, paying the same attention to every such level. This made it possible for their later readers to interpret Marx's and Engels's views of the driving forces of social development in different way.

The first of those levels was the role of technological progress, that is, the impact of changes in forces of production on the whole of social life. Agreeing with many other thinkers from the period of the industrial revolution, Marx and Engels always thought that mutual relations among human beings depend to a great extent on their mastering the forces of nature, which is synthetically manifested in the level of technology in a given period. Marx wrote in *The Poverty of Philosophy* that "social relations are closely bound up with productive forces. In acquiring new productive forces men change their mode of production, and in changing their mode of production, in changing their way of earning their living, they change all their social relations. The handmill gives you society with the feudal lord; the steam-mill, society with the industrial capitalist."[34] Many such statements can be found in the works by Marx and by Engels, yet it does not seem justified to interpret historical materialism as a variety of technological determinism.

When discussing the issue of the driving forces of social development, Marx and Engels most often focused their attention on the mode of production—a complex concept that covers both a specified level of productive forces and those social relations (relations of production) into which men enter when engaging in the production of material goods. They also assumed a correspondence of the level of productive forces and the system of social relations; if that correspondence is disturbed—and the dynamic character of production, especially under capitalism, makes such disturbances both inevitable and permanent—then the result is a revolution, reflected in all spheres of social life. For Marx and Engels this was certainly the focal problem; nevertheless it does not seem justified, as it was often done at the turn of the nineteenth century, to interpret historical materialism as economic determinism and to assume a strict and undirectional dependence of changes in society as a whole on changes in the economic system.

Marx's stress on economics seems doubtful largely because of the role that he ascribed to class struggle. It is true that the foundation of class struggle is purely economic in nature and that the relations among the classes are, in the last analysis, relations of production. No class struggle brings about a change in the social system if the economic conditions are "immature." The "maturity" of those conditions was in itself a necessary, but not a sufficient, condition of a social revolution. Conditions of other kinds had to be satisfied if such a revolution was to take place: namely, an appropriate configuration of political forces and an appropriate state of social consciousness, which do not emerge spontaneously as the economy develops.

One must remember that, according to Marx, the durability of a given mode of production is guaranteed not merely by its economic effectiveness, but also by the ability of the class that is dominant economically to dominate politically and ideologically as well. A revolution means an upheaval in all these spheres and depends in each of them on a number of extraeconomic factors. Marx was far from assuming that a society economically "mature" for a revolution must necessarily enter a higher stage of development: Inner contradictions may result equally well in its regression or a catastrophe. In the case of any particular society, progress is a chance, but not a necessity. In this sense, neither productive forces nor economic changes in general, but revolutions are "the locomotives of history."

In the above comments we have tried to give the Marxian idea of social development a relatively unambiguous interpretation, yet it is very easy to notice in Marx's conception certain inner dilemma that could later result in the emergence of various orientations within Marxism. The major dilemmas were fatalism versus voluntarism; explanation of the totality of social changes by one factor only or by a plurality of factors; and the scope of possible forecasts. As we will see later, in most cases those dilemmas were not specific to Marxian thought, although they came to be particularly important in the controversies over the interpretation of Marx's ideas.

THE MARXIAN METHOD

The modernity of Marx's ideas, seen against the background of nineteenth-century thought, is attributable in part to the fact that he not only studied society, but also reflected on the best *method* of studying it. Except for him, only Comte and John Stuart Mill were at that time fully conscious founders of a methodology of social sciences.

This is not to say that Marx wrote comprehensive treatises on methodology, comparable with Mill's *System of Logic.* His statements on methodological issues are in most cases scattered,[35] and only when combined with an analysis of his own research practice (especially as reflected in *Kapital*) do they form a sufficient basis for the reconstruction of Marx's methodology with its all originality.

Without going into details, we have to discuss it briefly, as it in a sense opposed the trends dominant in nineteenth-century methodology. This was certainly due to the fact that Marx shaped his social thinking in the sphere of Hegelian inspiration, whereas most sociological doctrines of the period were based on positivism.

One peculiarity of Marx's research method consisted in its historicism. The concept is not very clear in itself, and this is why Marx's historicism requires a fairly comprehensive comment.[36]

First, Marx revealed historicism in assuming a *sui generis* anthropology that, being a refutation of rationalistic atomism, treated man as "a totality of social relations" and rejected the possibility of explaining anything in social life by reference to human nature, that is, those properties which are attributes of human individuals qua human individuals, regardless of the conditions determined by time and place. It was in terms of just that anthropology that Marx and Engels criticized both the earlier socialist and communist conceptions and the social philosophy that supported the classical political economy and treated the human individual not as a product of history, but as the point of departure of history.

Second, Marx's historicism manifested itself in analyzing all social facts as parts of more comprehensive wholes, on the assumption that no fact can be explained as long as it is treated in isolation from the other social phenomena occurring at the same time and interacting with it.

Marx observed the principle of the integrated examination of the facts that he studied both in detailed economic analyses and in formulations of general theorems of historical materialism and of the theory of socioeconomic formations. Observance of this principle made Marx resist, for instance, the extension of the concept of capitalism beyond specified historical limits, even if he noted elements of the capitalistic economic in earlier socioeconomic formations.

And third, Marxian historicism was also connected with an assumption about the status of the cognizing subject. He understood cognitive activity to be historically conditioned and the cognizing subject to be inevitably rooted in the same social facts as the study with which he is concerned.

This kind of historicism was fairly common, or perhaps even dominant, in Marx's times. It can be found in various formulations in conservative social philosophy, in Hegelianism, in the doctrines of historians and philosophers of history, and so on.

The essential originality of Marx and Engels's approach consisted not in going in that direction, but in combining these assumptions with a number of methodological rules that are not found in the other doctrines based on historicism. It seems particularly characteristic of Marx to have broken away from the tendency, very strong in these doctrines, to treat the process of comprehending an isolated historical whole as an essentially intuitive grasping of the mass of facts that spontaneously impose themselves on the researcher's perception. In this field Marx undoubtedly had a predecessor —Hegel—as a critic of romantic social philosophy.

One of the fundamental principles both in Hegelianism and in Marxism was the distinction between the historical and the logical methods. The point is not, and cannot be, that of a simple reconstruction of the real course of events, since that leads neither to the understanding of their essence nor to the separation of that which is important and consequential from that which is accidental and devoid of lasting significance.

For that reason, when concerning himself with the state of political economy, Marx explicitly opposed to one another the two modes of study, one of which reaches the inner meaning, while the other merely describes, registers, discusses, and places among the schematic definitions that which appears on the surface of the process of life.

Accordingly, it may be said that Marx's historicism was rationalistic and antiphenomenalistic; simultaneously, it turned against treating social cognition as an intuitive process of penetrating the essence of the historical whole and against reducing cognition to the ordering of immediate empirical data, which was characteristic of the positivistic, or, in Marx's terminology, "vulgar" social science.

Marx was a determined adherent of antiphenomenalism—that is, the view that the true object of science is not that which is immediately given in experience. In this regard, Marx's method has been correctly compared with that of Galileo who was probably the first to realize that a scientist does not describe specific states of affairs as much as he tries to find out what the processes would be like if they were free from any disturbances whatever.

In natural sciences, maximum approximation to the essence of things can be achieved under experimental conditions. Marx realized that a student of social life has very limited possibilities in that respect: "in the analysis of economic forms . . . neither microscopes nor chemical reagents are of use. The force of abstraction must replace both."[37] Discovery of laws thus requires application of other procedures, which, resembling those used in natural science by their precision, take into account the peculiarities of that specific subject matter of cognition which is social life.

Marx thought that that goal could be reached in two principal ways. The first was investigation primarily of those stages in the development of society and those societies in which the processes can be seen in a relatively pure form. "The physicist," he says in the preface to *Kapital*,

either observes physical phenomena where they occur in their most typical form and most free from disturbing influence, or, wherever possible, he makes experiments under conditions that assure the occurrence of the phenomenon in its normality. In this work I have to examine the capitalist mode of production, and the conditions of production and exchange corresponding to that mode. Up to the present time, their classic ground is England. That is the reason why England is used as the chief illustration in the development of my theoretical ideas.[38]

Of course, the use of such a procedure required the assumption, which Marx and the majority of his contemporaries almost unquestionably adopted, that the social sciences are *nomothetic* in nature; that is, they discover laws.

The essence of the social process that is being sought is not the essence of a historical individual entity such as a nation or an epoch, but the essence of the whole class of such individual entities.

Second, Marx systematically resorted to the procedure that he himself termed *abstraction* and that is nowadays usually called *idealization* and *concretization*.[39] That method can be defined as based on a *sui generis* mental experiment, since it consists in producing, by means of abstraction, certain ideal conditions that will never be encountered in fact, and it allows us to see what an undisturbed process looks like.

Thus, for instance, in *Kapital* Marx deliberately adopted a number of idealizational assumptions and investigated the capitalist economy as if the prices of the commodities corresponded to their respective values, the supply equaled the demand, foreign trade did not exist, society consisted of capitalists and proletarians only, and so on. In later parts of his opus those assumptions are removed, one by one, and the abstract model comes closer and closer to the empirical data, although in no phase of the analysis does it cease to be a model that intentionally simplifies facts to make them easier to understand.

Scientific thinking differs from everyday thinking, among other reasons, because social facts as given in everyday, accidental, and reflection-free experience are not, and cannot be, its point of departure. Marx wrote,

The correct procedure seems to involve commencing with the real and concrete, with the objectively valid assumptions of any problem. For instance, in the case of political economy, one would begin with population which is the basis and the agent responsible for the entire process of social production. However, on closer examination this proves to be wrong. Population is an abstraction if we ignore, e.g., the classes of which it consists. . . . If we start out, therefore, with population, we have only a chaotic conception of the whole, but by dividing it into less comprehensive attributes we will analytically arrive at progressively simpler concepts; thus we shall be proceeding from what was perceived as concrete to finer and finer abstractions until we get at the simplest attributes. . . . For instance, the economists of the seventeenth century always started out with the living whole, with population, nation, state, several states, and so forth, but in the end they invariably discovered, by means of analysis, certain determining, abstract and general relations, such as division of labour, money, value, etc. As soon as these separate aspects had been or less established by abstraction, there arose the system of political economy which started from simple conceptions, such as labour, division of labour, demand, exchange, value, and concluded with state, international exchange and world market. Clearly the latter method is scientifically correct. The concrete is concrete, because it is composed of many attributes, i.e., it is a unity of manifold elements. In our thought it therefore appears as a process of synthesis, as a result, and not as a starting point, although it is the actual starting point and, therefore, also the origin of perception and general ideas. In the former method the complete conception passes into an abstract attribute; in the latter, the abstract attributes lead to the reconstruction of the concrete subject in the course of reasoning.[40]

In the discussions concerned with historical materialism many misunderstandings have been, and still are, due to a lack of comprehension of the specific method used by Marx and Engels. Those misunderstandings are of two kinds: They consist either in making the Marxian method resemble positivistic phenomenalism or in interpreting it in terms of Max Weber's method of ideal types, although it differs from the latter (among other reasons) by the fact that abstractions are intended to reproduce phenomenal reality, not only to serve as instruments for understanding that reality. In his polemic with Hegel, Marx emphasized that a concept, or category, "can have no other existence except as an abstract partial relation *[einseitige Beziehung]* within an already given concrete and living whole."[41]

Comparisons of the proper method of social science to the methods used in natural science, which are frequent in Marx's writings, are not to be taken literally. Marx assumed that, as Kolakowski interprets it, "social life produces new values which are irreducible to natural ones and are not accessible to immediate perception, but are nevertheless real and serve to define the processes of history."[42] Thus, for instance, the fact an object is a commodity is determined not by its physical properties, but its having been produced for the market.

Likewise, the attributes of human beings qua members of society remains imperceptible as long as we analyze them outside a given system of relations. On the other hand, the cognizing subject is rooted in society, too, and hence his attitude toward the subject matter of his study is not as direct as that of a natural scientist toward the object he observes. Understanding social life takes place under the domination of false consciousness, so cognitive success does not depend alone on whether the scholar has the appropriate method at his disposal.

In Marx's opinion, it is equally necessary for the social scholar to hold a position in society that enables him to free himself from the world of appearances and to arrive at the essence of things. This is why the Marxian criticism of, say, classical political economy aimed not only at its errors, but also at the class-based limitations of its viewpoint. That is also why Marx treated his own access to the working-class movement as a way of acquiring a clearer vision of bourgeois society. Marx believed, too, that the abolition of the capitalist system would make social relations more "transparent."

In brief, whatever description of Marx's scientific method we use, we have to take into account the fact that for him the theory of social cognition was invariably the sociology of knowledge.

NOTES

1. Karl Marx, *Selected Writings in Sociology and Social Philosophy*, ed. T. B. Bottomore and M. Rubel (London: Watts, 1961), p. 235.

2. Ibid., pp. 219-20; Z. A. Jordan, ed., *Karl Marx: Economy, Class and Social Revolution* (London: Michael Joseph, 1971), p. 192.

3. Marx, *Selected Writings in Sociology*, p. 76.

4. Louis Althusser, *Pour Marx* (Paris: Maspero, 1967), pp. 233-34.

5. Marx, *Selected Writings in Sociology*, pp. 68-69.

6. Jordan, *Karl Marx*, p. 85.

7. Ibid., p. 83.

8. Marx, *Selected Writings in Sociology*, p. 52.

9. Cf. Louis Althusser et al., *Lire le Capital*, 2 vols. (Paris: Maspero, 1967).

10. V. I. Lenin, *What the "Friends of the People" Are and How They Fight the Social-Democrats: Selected Works in Two Volumes* (Moscow: Foreign Languages Publishing House, 1952), vol. 1, pt. 1, p. 109.

11. Cf. L. Krader, ed., *The Ethnological Notebooks of Karl Marx* (Assen: Van Gorcum, 1975).

12. K. Marx, *Capital* (Moscow: Foreign Languages Publishing House, 1954), pp. 8-9.

13. Jordan, *Karl Marx*, p. 206.

14. A. Jasińska, "Mikro- i makro-spoleczne determinanty myśli Karola Marksa," in *Studia Socjologiczne* 20 (1966):35.

15. Marx, *Selected Writings in Sociology*, p. 200.

16. Cf. Jordan, *Karl Marx*, p. 148.

17. Stanislaw Ossowski, *Class Structure in the Social Consciousness* (London: RKP, 1963), pp. 72-73.

18. Julian Hochfeld, *Studia o marksowskiej teorii spoleczeństwa* (Warsaw: PWN, 1963), pp. 166, 178.

19. Ossowski, *Class Structure*, p. 10.

20. Cf. Don Martindale, *The Nature and Types of Sociological Theory* (Boston: Houghton Mifflin, 1960), pt. 3.

21. K. Marx and F. Engels, *Basic Writings on Politics and Philosophy*, ed. Lewis S. Feuer (Garden City, N.Y.: Doubleday, 1959), pp. 129, 402.

22. Ibid., p. 29.

23. K. Marx, *The Eighteenth Brumaire of Louis Bonaparte* (Moscow: Progress, 1967), pp. 50-51.

24. Cf. Jordan, *Karl Marx*, p. 272.

25. Marx, *Selected Writings in Sociology*, p. 75.

26. Ibid., p. 71.

27. Lucien Goldmann, "La Réification," in Goldmann, *Recherches dialectiques* (Paris: Gallimard, 1959), p. 66.

28. Marx and Engels, *Basic Writings*, p. 230.

29. See Jordan, *Karl Marx*, p. 98.

30. Ibid., p. 144.

31. Marx, *Selected Writings in Sociology*, p. 147.

32. Karl Marx, *Early Writings*, ed. T. B. Bottomore (London: Watts, 1963), p. 206.

33. K. Marx to F. Engels, 18 June 1862, K. Marx and F. Engels, *Briefwechsel* (Berlin: Dietz-Verlag, 1949-1950), vol. 3, pp. 94-95.

34. Jordan, *Karl Marx*, p. 186.

35. Cf. *Karl Marx: Texts on Method*, ed. and tr. T. Carver (New York: Barnes and Noble, 1975).

36. J. Szacki, "On the So-Called Historicism in the Social Sciences," *Quality and Quantity* 5 (December 1971): 281-96.

37. Jordan, *Karl Marx*, p. 107.

38. Ibid., p. 108.

39. Cf. Leszek Nowak, *U podstaw marksowskiej metodologii nauk* (Warsaw: PWN, 1971).

40. Jordan, *Karl Marx*, pp. 105-6.

41. Ibid., p. 107.

42. Leszek Kolakowski, *Główne nurty marksizmu* (Paris: Instytut Literacki, 1976), p. 323.

7

EARLY POSITIVISM AND THE BEGINNINGS OF SOCIOLOGY: COMTE, MILL, AND QUÉTELET

In the genealogy of sociology, a special place is held by the positivistic thought of the first half of the nineteenth century, both because Auguste Comte, the principal theorist of that trend, coined the name of the new discipline and outlined the fairly vast program of its pursuit and because it was positivism (though not necessarily Comte's version) that had a very strong impact on sociology. Herbert Marcuse is right in stating that "sociology originated in . . . positivism and through its influence developed into an independent empirical science."[1]

Those links between early sociology and positivism can be explained by at least three factors:

1. The vast sphere of positivistic influence in nineteenth-century thought in general and, in any case, in French and English thought;
2. The unofficial, nonacademic, and reform-oriented nature of both positivism and early sociology, which, accordingly, was eager to accept it as *the* philosophy of the future;
3. The scientism of the positivists, who, by extending the standards of science over all spheres of thought, were more explicit than anyone else in defending the belief that human actions can, and should, be made a subject matter of scientific study.

Since science is the only authority that can be relied on in all times and all places, establishment of a science of social life, opposed to common-sense reflection and traditional social philosophy alike, seemed indispensable from both theoretical and practical points of view. It is not surprising, therefore, that the first sociologists took positivism (termed and understood in various ways it is true) as a theoretical revelation and that the main founders of positivism—Comte, Mill, and others—became cofounders of sociology. That was why the later critics of positivistic sociology, beginning with W. Dilthey, often acted as antisociologists and not only as antipositivists.

THE CONCEPT OF POSITIVISM

When making such statements about positivism, we inevitably appeal to the reader's intuitions, because the term *positivism* is believed to be less unambiguous than it really is. In summing up the practice in recent years, a contemporary author wrote that "the word 'positivist' . . . has become more of a derogatory epithet than a useful descriptive concept, and consequently has been largely stripped of whatever agreed meaning it may once have had."[2] This situation does not in the least seem to be new, nor does a peculiar paradox: Antipositivists believe positivism to be a very influential trend, while the authors considered by them to be positivists rarely define themselves so. Neither J. S. Mill, nor H. Spencer, nor A. Quételet, nor W. Wundt, nor G. Tarde, nor E. Durkheim, nor G. Lundberg —to mention only those whose positivism has probably never been questioned—has called himself a positivist. Some of them even explicitly disclaimed that in order to mark their independence from Comte and to indicate that they represented simply science and not any school. This is why we can today describe all positivists by the statement once made by John Stuart Mill about the positivists of Comte's school: "It is not very widely known what they represent but it is understood that they represent something."[3]

When reference is made to the nineteenth century, many misunderstandings over positivism are usually due to the insufficiently clear distinction between the two extensions of the term *positivism:* the positivism of Comte and his more or less faithful adherents and successors versus positivism as a philosophical orientation.

In the former case, positivism is a scientific (and not only scientific) school that called itself so; in the latter it is a type of thinking that we construct ourselves and call positivism because opinions of the authors whom we take into consideration in many important respects resemble those of the authors of the positivistic school. The thinkers thus included in a single general group did not have to avow solidarity with, or even experience any direct influence of, the author of *Cours de philosophie positive.*

Of course, the boundaries of that group happen to be marked in different ways. Yet there is a stable tendency to treat positivism as a phenomenon that is incomparably broader than the Comte school.

In this book positivism is interpreted in that extended sense, although we shall be careful to avoid exaggeration, which usually takes on the form of identifying positivism with the tendency to question the value of any knowledge that is not scientific (in the sense specific to modern natural science). Luckily, there is the broader concept of scientism, which often proves quite sufficient.⁴ When discussing the Comte school, we shall refer to Comte's positivism or just to Comtism.

What, then, are the peculiarities of positivism as a *type of thinking*, so popular in nineteenth-century sociology and—as some of its critics claim—in twentieth-century sociology as well?

Anticriticism. In its original use by Comte, who had in this a predecessor in Saint-Simon (whom some believe to have been the real founder of the trend), the word *positive (positif)* had many meanings combined into a single syndrome opposed to the syndrome of those properties which they thought undesirable. Opposed to what is negative, fictitious, insipid, unsound, vague, and destructive was what is positive—that which is real, useful, certain, precise, and constructive.⁵

Positivism was opposed not only to religion or bad philosophy, but to philosophy that could result in stagnation and petrification or in social disorganization and anarchy. In other words, nineteenth-century sociological positivism took up directly the topical problems of the social crisis of its time and looked for knowledge that would be useful in organizing the new society that had emerged from revolution and still could not find its balance, knowledge that would be as useful as religion had been in consolidating feudal society. Early sociological positivism turned against all varieties of critical philosophy that led to a confrontation of what *is* with what, according to philosophical principles, *should* or *could be*.

Criticism of "Metaphysics" and Phenomenalism. Positivism criticized traditional philosophy for its having abandoned certainty of cognition for the illusory ideal of finding answers to so-called fundamental questions to which science cannot provide answers. Positivists assumed, as L. Kolakowski described it, that "we are entitled to register that which is in fact revealed in experience; all opinions about hidden entities whose existence would supposedly be experienced through their manifestations do not deserve credit, and controversies between standpoints over issues that go beyond the sphere of experience are purely verbal in nature."⁶ Metaphysics consists simply in looking for such entities hidden beneath the surface of phenomena, for some supposed essence of things. Science is concerned with phenomena alone.

This principle of phenomenalism, as interpreted by Comte, turned against the principle of causality, to which he opposed the requirement of discovering laws as constant relationships—co-occurrence or sequence—between phenomena observed. That principle was directed against studying the problem of "first causes" or goals of the processes taking place and also against establishing absolute principles, like the rationalistic laws of nature, independently of observation of facts.

Natural Science as the Model Discipline. Positivism meant naturalism, in both the normative and the descriptive senses. It assumed that the methods used in social science do not, and should not, differ essentially from those used in natural science. Positivists were convinced that human knowledge is one and the methods of its acquisition are uniform, even though in the early stage they were not as inflexible in that respect as later positivists and logical positivists were. Both Comte and Mill paid much attention to the problem of differences between social and natural science without, however, opposing one to the other.

Positivistic naturalism was supported by (1) the intention of applying in social science those methods which had already proved to be effective and were believed to be the only scientific ones; (2) the belief that only that science which complies with the standards used in natural science—that is, science *tout court*—can serve as the foundation of effective social engineering; and (3) the conviction that only science plays an educational role that deserves support, as it develops attitudes that are the most desirable in modern society: the matter-of-fact approach, openness to rational argumentation, resistance to the temptations of methaphysics, unwillingness to engage in unresolvable controversies, and so forth. For Comte the community of men of science was the prefiguration of the general societal unity that would emerge if people abandoned the nonsensical controversies in which they engaged.

Social Facts as Things. First-generation positivists assumed (unlike those of the second generation) a sharp demarcation line between the cognizing subject and the object of cognition. They considered the sphere of social facts to be a set of phenomena that is totally independent of the observer and seen by him from the outside. In that sense even early positivism complied with Durkheim's requirement that social facts should be considered as things. A student of social life acts as an observer, not as a participant. This was combined with the conviction that he can free himself from—to use Bacon's terminology—the idols of the markets by acting as a researcher and nobody else. Advances in social knowledge are the work of man reduced to his cognitive functions and free from the passions that move men of action. On that point, positivists differed both from Marxists and from pragmatists and other thinkers who came to voice their opinions in the period of modernism.

Antinormativism. Positivists presumed, even though they did not necessarily observe that in practice, that evaluation of the phenomena studied is not a task of the scientist and that finding what is does not lead to any recommendations as to what should be. Cognitive activity is neutral relative to controversies over values and does not provide the parties to such controversies with any arguments whatever.

First-generation positivists (and probably all positivists in general) were inconsistent in having introduced latent evaluations into their social conceptions. Such latent evaluations usually took the form of statements about human needs, or about trends in historical development, or, finally, about such and such "normal" relations. When they formulated their social prognoses, they in fact often voiced their opinions about what was most desirable. All nineteenth-century positivists resorted to some kind of social Utopia. They differed from the earlier Utopians not so much by not propagating any ideal (*qua* scientists), as by doing so shamefacedly, pretending that their ideal was becoming a fact, which allegedly could be seen through nonprejudiced observation.

Early positivists were marked by an inner tension between their good scientistic intentions and their practice, which was largely conditioned by tradition and the climate of nineteenth-century public opinion, so affected by controversies over the values of new society. J. Habermas is right in writing that "the knowledge that Comte invokes in order to interpret the meaning of positive knowledge does not itself meet the standards of the positive spirit. This paradox disappears as soon as we discern the intention of early positivism: the pseudo-scientific propagation of the cognitive monopoly of science."[7] That which is often called the inconsistency of early positivism was actually one of its constitutive elements.

Science as the Foundation of Social Engineering. Practical orientation was an important feature of positivistic thought: Science was to make prediction possible, and prediction, in turn, was expected to help control societal processes and to put an end to their spontaneity and destructiveness. Francis Bacon's dreams that the knowledge of laws of nature should give man power over nature took, for the positivists, the form of a dream of the same power over society. This led them to various practical conclusions: Comte was an advocate of strictly controlled society, whereas Mill and Spencer represented the trend that is typical of liberalism and strove to restrict such control maximally. But in all cases we are concerned with one and the same conception, namely, practical applications of the science of society. This was a conception later to be termed *piecemeal engineering* by Popper; he opposed it to the conception of *Utopian engineering*, which is oriented toward attaining, in societal practice, the highest imaginable good. An advocate of piecemeal engineering does not pose any questions about the ultimate goal of his efforts to improve society, but merely tries to solve the most urgent problems by those means which are available to him at the moment. That strategy is certainly in fullest agreement with the general positivistic tendency of avoiding metaphysical problems and concentrating on improving the existing or the spontaneously emerging social order. In positivistic social engineering there are no questions about what should be done in general; the only question is how and by what means the existing problems should be solved.[8]

Of course, in the early stage of positivism that feature was not yet clearly marked, because at that time no centers of power showed any willingness to follow the suggestions made by positivists to make them experts in social engineering. Thus, the positivists were forced, contrary to the inner logic of their doctrine and contrary to their own recommendations, to plan a society in which the role of sociologists as experts would be both possible and indispensable. In other words, positivists had to form a Utopia of society without Utopia. In this endeavor they were helped by their historio-sophy, which enabled them to present that Utopia not as an arbitrarily formulated ideal, but as a result of objective processes of development, processes that are independent of human will. This also enabled them to present themselves as the discoverers of the laws that govern those processes, and not as planners of the best possible world. They did not identify them-selves with any of the two principal blocs in postrevolutionary Europe: They were both against revolution and against reaction. They presented their escape from specified ideologies as an escape from ideology in general; this does not mean, however, that they did not themselves form an ideology.

THE SOCIOLOGY OF AUGUSTE COMTE

Auguste Comte (1798-1857), author of *Cours de philosophie positive* (six volumes, 1830-1842), *Discours sur l'esprit positif* (1844), *Discours sur l'ensemble du positivisme* (1848), *Système de politique positive* (four volumes, 1851-1854), and *Catéchisme positiviste* (1852), certainly was the most important representative of early positivism. A mathematician by training—he studied in the renowned Ecole Polytechnique in Paris, but never finished—he went in for somewhat dilettantish philosophizing. The result was a comprehensive system conceived as the synthesis of all available knowledge, its necessary complement in the form of the foundation of sociology, and an exposition of the reliable method of acquiring knowledge. The system was conceived also as the program for the improvement of society, which, unlike the rival ideologies, would be *ni anarchique ni rétro-grade*, owing to its basis in a set of scientific dogmas.

Comte's system was a genuine system of systems, which covered practic-ally everything that might interest the educated man of that epoch and was constructed with a pedantic concern for having each detail properly elabo-rated and linked with others. That makes the reading of Comte's works a laborious task, but also accounts for the fact that they are among the best documents of the period. In intellectual history, Comte holds the ambiguous position of a classic who is not being read: Almost everyone has heard about him, but only specialists know his works. Comte's system is an astonishing combination of philosophical minimalism with philosophical maximalism. While it advocated studying facts at the roots and strove to replace "Heaven by Earth, the vague by the positive, and poetry by reality,"[9] it was at the same time an endeavor, on a Hegelian scale, to bring into a single system everything that makes up the subject of reflection. That duality of Comte's idea was due to the fact that, on the one hand, he tried to establish an ideal of verifiable and reliable knowledge and, on the other, strove to save the unity of knowledge at the time of the growing specialization of science. While remaining in agreement with the result of "the positive sciences," he wanted to bring those results into a single whole and to make them the basis of the *Weltanschauung* of the new society's members.

Social Crisis and Philosophy. Although Comte's philosophy was largely a philosophy of science, its point of departure was not reflection on the difficulties that science in his times had to face. Like almost all positivists, he was very optimistic about the state and the prospects of scientific knowledge. His anxiety had its source elsewhere: He thought that society was in a state of a profound crisis, and he expected science to put an end to it. His reflections on the shortcomings of science were then derived from making it face important practical tasks. The scope of those tasks, which went far beyond what is expected today of science by its most ardent admirers, was in Comte's case determined by the basically rationalistic faith (taken over directly from Condorcet) that the consciousness of individuals is the fundamental factor of social change.

The diagnosis of the great crisis given by Comte, beginning with his youthful *Opuscules de philosophie sociale* (1820), was primarily a diagnosis of the state of consciousness. In his opinion, following the five centuries of critical activity by the various "metaphysicians" (and as a result of advances in positive knowledge), both the old system of beliefs—namely, medieval Catholicism (and theology in general)—and the political analogue that it had in the feudal (or, more generally, the military) system had decomposed. Comte claimed that "the collapse of theological philosophy and its counterpart in the form of the spiritual power has left society without any moral discipline whatever."[10] The author of *Considerations sur le pouvoir spirituel* maintained, as conservatives did, that society had disintegrated. The new institutions, emerging in large numbers, were provisional by their very nature and did not produce any durable bonds between human beings. Matters were made still worse by the protracted conflict between the two parties into which postrevolutionary society was split: the defenders of the old regime and its opponents, who tried to make revolution continue indefinitely. The former made the crisis deeper by trying to reverse the course of history and by denying society the right to progress; the latter did the same by their efforts to destroy all bulwarks of social order. That deep schism of modern society paralyzed it completely and threatened it with destruction, for there can be no society without some common values. As can be seen, Comte was one of those thinkers who considered society to be, above all, the focus of moral life. That was why postrevolutionary society seemed to them to be in danger, although it had its unquestionable successes in the economic sphere and managed to provide for the material needs of individuals better than any other society.

According to Comte, the only way out of crisis and the only basis of a social construction would be the introduction of a system of beliefs that would put an end to the controversies that were ruining society, but would not be just a replica of the anachronistic theological system. The founder of positivism thought that science promised such a system. If science was to play its role as a factor in social reconstruction, it must be transformed to that end in the spirit of the positive method, and in particular it must apply this method to social, political, and moral problems; that is, it must establish sociology as a scientific discipline.

It could seem that Comte merely suggested to his contemporaries one more rival ideology, positivistic or scientific instead of theological and metaphysical. But Comte assigned to his opinions a status quite different from that of the views he criticized.

First, he considered his own opinions to be scientific *par excellence* and, hence, to be intersubjectively verifiable and determined by the very nature of those facts to which they refer. Simultaneously, he claimed the opinions of his opponents to be quite arbitrary in nature.

Second, Comte gave his opinions the sanction of historiosophy. He maintained that the process of cognition inevitably had, on both the individual and the societal scales, three main stages (the famous law of three stages, which he took over from Saint-Simon): theological, metaphysical, and scientific, that is, positive. Comte thought that his times were the epoch of the great crisis that separated the initial or preparatory phase of social order from the final or definitive one—the phase of unanimity based on religion from that based on science. After the age-long expansion of the areas of social consciousness governed by science, the time comes when science can, and must, make its kingdom cover the totality of human problems so that mankind enters, once and for all, the new epoch of order. In that sense, Comte believed himself to be the executor of the will of history and not just the inventor of one of the many possible conceptions of the world and one of the many possible ideologies. In that respect Comte resembles Marx and, especially, some of the Marxists.

The necessary evolution of human spirit thus led to the point at which a scientific system must, in fact, emerge. Hence, the emergence of sociology, which would complete and crown the system, is necessary, too. According to Comte, sociology is an independent discipline intended to provide knowl-

edge of the laws governing that sphere of facts which had been the least
known of all fields. Still more important, it is also part of the system that—
owing to that part alone—becomes a system and starts influencing society,
not only communities of scholars. The significance of the new science is
thus twofold: It provides knowledge of a specified segment of the world and
also qualitatively modifies the totality of our knowledge by finally turning
it into a system. And in Comte's opinion, it is only within a system that our
abstract concepts acquire certainty and constancy.

Over time, Comte gave to his system of science the features of a religious
system, a new religion of mankind based on the dogmas of science. In this
tendency, some of his disciples, and also some historians of positivism, saw
Comte's abandoning the scientific ideals that he had cherished in his youth.
While we should not disregard the turning point in Comte's opinions, we
have to say that it consisted in making his opinions subjective and sentimental
rather than religious. The turn toward a lay religion was nothing essentially
new for him: Since his youth, he repeated obsessively that society, in order
to shake off the chaos of the transition period, needs a uniform system of
beliefs very badly. What many of his readers found repulsive in a social
system based on a positivistic religion was not so much the fact that philosophy was transformed into religion, but the fact that—according to that
philosophy—science was to assume the social functions of religion.

Sociology in Comte's System of Philosophy. Comte's positive method
will not be discussed here in any greater detail. But it is proper to realize the
inner structure of the system of positive philosophy and the place of sociology as the last of the theoretical disciplines in that system. We shall also
have to consider the features of the positive method that Comte believed to
be characteristic of its applications in sociology.

In the opinion of the author of *Cours de philosophie positive*, the place
of each science in his system is determined historically and logically. The
sciences form a hierarchy that depends, on the one hand, on the order in
which they emerged (since each science paves the way for the next and is a
sine qua non of the latter's emergence) and, on the other, on the way in
which we can order them most logically, according to the degree of their
generality and interdependence. These two orders, the historical and logical,
correspond to one another most closely. The sciences form the following
hierarchy: mathematics, astronomy, physics, chemistry, biology, sociology.
Such is also the correct order of the development of the disciplines, which
Comte himself observed.

The sciences listed above were ordered by him by the following logical
criteria: (1) the degree of decreasing generality and abstractness; (2) the
degree of increasing complexity; (3) the degree of practical importance.
Thus, mathematics is that science which is the most abstract of all, the

simplest, and the most remote from direct practical applications, whereas sociology is the most concrete of all, the most complex, and the most directly related to practice. A mathematician does not have to avail himself of results obtained in any other science (and this is why mathematics emerges first as a positive science), whereas a sociologist has to make use of results obtained in all other science (and this is why sociology emerges last).

The above classification of sciences was one of the many that people developed throughout the nineteenth century as they felt, more and more strongly, that the knowledge of the world is so complete that it must be presented as an interrelated whole.

As compared with other classifications, Comte's conception did not have any special features except for its inclusion of sociology. That innovation was, however, full of methodological consequences. The general requirement that the knowledge of society be turned into the science of it did not suffice any longer. The similarities and the differences between that new science and the others had to be analyzed methodically because all points unclear in that respect inevitably reflected on the value of the system as a whole.

The problem of the relation between sociology and the other positive sciences seems to have been one of the main problems faced by Comte and is essential for an understanding of his positivism. Comte seems to have assumed, on the one hand, that sociology is scientifically helpless without sciences that precede it, particularly biology. It could not have emerged before those sciences did, and it takes their theorems as premises that it could not do without. On the other hand, Comte did not doubt that sociology, like all the sciences included in his classification, has *ses faits propres*; its peculiarities account for the fact that research procedures used in sociology are sometimes not only specific, but actually opposed to those used in other sciences (except perhaps in biology, which also has to do with organisms). The point is that in biology and sociology, unlike the sciences concerned with inanimate nature, decomposition of the object of study into its component parts is "profoundly irrational."

Society, like any biological organism, is a complex entity, irreducible to its component parts; this is why the method adopted by the sciences concerned with inorganic bodies fails here and must be replaced by a reverse procedure: not from the knowledge of the parts to the knowledge of the whole, but from the knowledge of the whole to the knowledge of the parts. The concept of system must be the point of departure both in sociology and in biology. In his methodology, Comte generalized the opinions that in social philosophy had been voiced with increasing frequency since Montesquieu and that emphasized the contextual nature of all societal facts. Comte himself went very far in that direction by taking into account as Hegel did, both synchronic and diachronic relationships between those facts.[11]

As a result, Comte's hierarchy of disciplines is cut across by a sharp line, separating the sciences concerned with organic bodies (including the science of society) from those concerned with inorganic bodies. From that point of view sociology turns out to be a close relative of biology. This is not to say that the findings of biology have a direct bearing on the sociologist's work, because Comte assumed a qualitative difference between singular and collective organisms. The latter cannot be said to consist just of individuals, and hence sociological statements are not, and cannot be, conjunctions of statements about the individuals of which society is formed. "Society," Comte wrote, "cannot be decomposed into individuals any more than a geometrical surface can be decomposed into lines, or a line into points."[12] If society can to some extent be analytically decomposed into parts, then the final limit of such a division is found in the family, that is, in the smallest social organism.

Comte's antireductionism also came to determine his firmly negative attitude toward the two disciplines that in his times received enormous publicity—namely, psychology and political economy. Not only did he not find any place for them in his system, but he subjected both of them to fundamental criticism. His unwillingness to incorporate them into his system was partly due to his critical attitude toward introspection, which at that time was the most important (if not the only) method in psychology, and to his lack of understanding of the methods of idealization, which was more or less consciously used in political economy. But even more, it was due to his programmatic anti-individualism and antireductionism. Comte believed that breaking up social entities in order to analyze their components was a relic of metaphysical thinking, the elimination of which was a necessary condition for progress in social science.

As mentioned earlier, the idea of the unity of science was, in Comte's case, in no way identical with the idea of an absolute unity of the methods used in the various disciplines. He pointed out that the methods of social research must differ from the methods used in the other positive sciences because of the specific nature of their subject matter. That distinctive nature of the methods used in sociology was twofold: (1) when using methods known in other sciences (pure observation, experiment, comparative method), the sociologist should always remember that society forms a whole, and that fact restricts or modifies the applicability of such methods (for example, the experiment); (2) when using such methods, the sociologist must add the historic method to them. This method is specific to sociology and the most suitable for it. It consists of comparing "the consecutive states of mankind" and not the states of different societies at the same time (which is the task of the comparative method).

Therefore, sociology is a positive science not because it avails itself of ready methods evolved in disciplines of longer standing, nor because it explains the facts that it studies by laws discovered by other disciplines, but because it overcomes the relics of theological and metaphysical thinking, accumulates knowledge that can be verified empirically, and discovers laws that enable one to predict the further course of the processes and to influence it.

The Subject Matter and the Tasks of Sociology. Sociology thus appeared in Comte's system as a result of reflection on the crisis of society and as the complement of his philosophical system, which, owing to sociology, was supposed to acquire practical social significance. But sociology was also a *sui generis* summing up of investigations made by Comte's predecessors, so the claim that Comte was the founder of that discipline certainly is not beyond dispute. The only unquestionable fact is that he coined the name of the new science, that "barbarous" (as it was called) neologism consisting of the Latin element *socio-* and the Greek element *-logia.* That term was introduced by him in the fourth volume of his *Cours de philosophie positive* (1837), when the term he had been using, *social physics,* which was borrowed from Saint-Simon, turned out to have been adopted by Quételet, with whom Comte did not want to be associated. Note also that he used the term *sociology* alternately with many others, such as *social philosophy* and *political philosophy.*

It seems that Comte, contrary to his deepest conviction, was not one of those thinkers who are inventors and whose role is to suggest new ideas (as was the role of Vico, Kant, and Hegel). Rather, he was one of those whose originality consists in a creative and laborious continuation combined with the ability to link previously known elements into new wholes.

Comte was, above all, a successor to the ideas of Saint-Simon, whose secretary he had been for nearly seven years. As mentioned earlier, Saint-Simon formulated—explicitly, though merely in outline—such important ideas, sometimes believed to have been Comte's inventions, as positiveness, social physics, the three stages of the development of mankind and the ways of overcoming social crisis through the reconstruction of unanimity based on science or on a scientific religion. Many other ideas advanced by Comte were current in his times or had originated in the works of such well-known eighteenth- and nineteenth-century authors as Montesquieu, Rousseau, Condorcet (the idea of progress), de Bonald, and de Maistre (the idea of order). Comte also drew on earlier authorities, of whom he apparently valued Aristotle and Hobbes most. He did not conceal his intellectual indebtedness to others, passing over in silence only his obligations to Saint-Simon.

Comte's work consisted of formulating a synthesis and expanding it into a system intended to include all human knowledge and hence to provide support for a moral, social, and political renewal, which, in his opinion,

French society needed very badly. That practical program also was a synthesis because it referred in many points to conservative and socialist ideologies of the period. Comte's most original contribution was the articulation and systematization of current opinions, which he succeeded in integrating into a single and coherent theory of society and a single and coherent positivistic ideology.

That characteristic of Comte's thought can best be seen in the pivotal element of his doctrine, which certainly was the linking of the concepts of order and progress into an inseparable pair, in contrast with the earlier theories, especially social ideologies, in which those concepts were opposed to one another.

Comte's positivistic ideology was a recipe for concord between the adversaries and the advocates of the bourgeois order: To the former it guaranteed preservation of elementary conditions of societal equilibrium and harmony, and to the latter it offered a guarantee against returning to the feudal system and blocking progress. During the national movements in 1848, Comte even had something to offer the socialists, whom he was inclined to assure that "socialism is spontaneous positivism, and positivism, systematized socialism."[13] He submitted that offer to representatives of well-shaped political blocs, but above all to the sections of new society that had not yet participated in political life (professionals with technological training and workers).

Comte's elimination of the greatest dilemma in post-1789 French social thought had its most important consequences not in politics, but in sociology. His political offer, rejected by all except a handful of his adherents, made it possible to take up the analysis of the concepts of order and progress as two necessary aspects of every conceivable society. And Comte's sociology, with its static and dynamic parts, was exactly nothing other than such an analysis. The basic theoretical issue in Comte's sociology was that of bringing these two perspectives into line—discovering the laws both of a relatively stable structure of social organism and of its incessant growth, the laws both of spontaneous social order and of equally spontaneous social progress.

This approach to that problem of sociology which Comte believed to be the basic one must have determined the many other peculiarities of his sociology. If, for instance, he defined its scope very broadly, he did so mainly because the questions that sociology had to answer pertained to the social organism as a whole, to global society as an emerging system. Sociology was for him the only social discipline not because he did not think of other social sciences, but because he questioned their ability to grasp "the common consensus of the social organism."

This is why "there can be no scientific study of society, either in its conditions or its movements, if it is separated into portions, and its divisions are studied apart." Comte goes on:

I have already remarked upon this, in regard to what is called political economy. Materials may be furnished by the observation of different departments; and such observation may be necessary for that object, but it cannot be called science. The methodological division of studies which takes place in the simple inorganic sciences is thoroughly irrational in the recent and complex science of society, and can produce no results. The day may come when some sort of subdivision may be practicable and desirable; but it is impossible for us now to anticipate what the principle of distribution may be; for the principle itself must arise from the development of the science; and that development can take place no otherwise than by our formation of the science as a whole.[14]

To that holistic principle was linked another peculiarity of Comte's sociology: the belief that every consecutive state of society was inseparably connected with an earlier state and a later one. Today's social order is not a refutation of the bygone order (as conservatives claimed) nor will it be refuted by the future order (as socialists asserted). All along, our concern is one and the same social order undergoing gradual changes. To use the language developed much later, we could say that Comte was interested in changes *within* the system and not in changes *of* the system, because he believed the essential requirements of the social order to be permanent.

The third peculiarity of Comte's sociology was that it did not study any specific society, but considered the social organism as such, that is, mankind. As Harris wrote, Comte "took over Condorcet's fatal invention, 'the device of supposing a single nation to which we may refer all the consecutive social modifications actually witnessed among distinct people.'"[15] In that respect Comte's sociology was a total denial of the various forms of historicism in his times, with which it did, however, share the belief that all spheres of social life are interdependent and that every state of society is conditioned by its past. This is not to say, of course, that the society about which Comte wrote lacked all reality and was transformed into an abstract system. The theorems that he formulated were applicable to all mankind not because the level of their generality excluded the differences between various societies, but because for Comte mankind consisted of very few societies. To put it briefly, he was interested in Western European industrial societies, which were for him identical with mankind.

Social Statics. Social statics is concerned with a methodical study of the social order, that is, of the interrelations between the various parts of the social system and, thereby, the factors that determine formation of social consensus. We could also follow J. Laubier and term it Comte's "theory of institutions," because it covers the same sphere of facts that Spencer will call *institutions* in *Principles of Sociology*. In statics, it is the problems of the family, property, division of labor, the state, and also language and religion that come to the forefront. They are examined by him prefunctionalistically to determine how each of those institutions affects, or contributes to, the maintenance of the system. Comte, Coser wrote, "studies the balance of mutual relations of elements within a social whole. There must always be a "spontaneous harmony between the whole and the parts of the social system." When such harmony is lacking, we are confronted by a pathological case."[16]

Comte's attention was especially focused—as was the case of other defenders of order—on the family, which, in his opinion, was *la moindre société, le véritable élément sociologique*. He wrote about the family that it is "an *association* which is the least extensive and the most spontaneous. Now, decomposition of mankind into individuals in the strict sense of the term is nothing other than an anarchical analysis, as irrational as it is immoral, which tends to dissolve social existence instead of explaining it."[17]

That pushing of the family to the fore was in Comte's system substantiated in many ways. An analysis of a family was to yield an explanation of the origin of the other associations that, according to Comte, emerged on the same basis (the tribe, the nation, and so on). It was expected to result in the refutation of the individualistic, utilitarian, and contractual conceptions of society by pointing to the most primitive form of association, which developed spontaneously, regardless of any rational calculations. It was also expected to call attention to the problem of man's socialization, a problem that in the period of metaphysics had been superseded by the problem of man's supposed independence. The family was for Comte the most permanent element of society and, accordingly, the best instrument of the social reconstruction.

Another factor that makes people associate spontaneously is, as Comte claims while he refers to Aristotle, the division of labor, which results in a growing complexity of the societal system and in its ever increasing inner differentiation into professional groups and classes. Without the division of labor, "even under the condition that settled life prevailed, there would be no veritable association of the various families, but a mere agglomeration. It is the division of labor that makes all the difference between the political order, based on cooperation, and the purely domestic order, based on mutual liking."[18] While he believed the division of labor to be a requirement for the existence of a social system and an important factor in the development of human abilities, moral sentiments, and solidarity, Comte—unlike the liberals—did not think that division of labor would work by itself. He considered a government that would use some coercion in order to guarantee a harmonious cooperation of the various groups of society to be an indispensable institution. In that respect he thought Hobbes to have been right, as he ascribed strong egoistic inclinations to human beings in general.[19] Thus, next to the family, *la cité* turns out to have been the second basic form of association; it was a politically organized community that corresponded roughly to what Hegel, for instance, called civil society.

Yet economic bonds, even if strengthened and consolidated by a political organization, did not seem to Comte to be a sufficient foundation of social coherence and equilibrium. Such a foundation is formed only by the unity of feelings, and that can be provided by religion alone. In fact, that which ensures such unity is treated as religion, whether or not any supernaturalistic beliefs are involved. Without unity of feelings, centrifugal forces would inevitably make themselves felt, and this is why "every government supposes a religion to consecrate and regulate commandment and obedience."[20] Hence the church is the third and final form of association by which society enters the stage of full development. Religion is closely linked with language, the means by which the emergence of a community of emotions becomes possible.

It is proper to pay some attention to the psychological assumptions of social statics. We have mentioned Comte's dislike of psychology. That dislike did not make him abandon all psychological assumptions. On the contrary, both social statics and social dynamics would have been inconceivable without a fairly large number of such assumptions, referring, for instance, to the social nature of man, the domination of emotions over intellect, that of egoistic emotions over altruistic ones, and so on. Comte's sociology adopted *la théorie positive de la nature humaine* as one of its premises.[21] The attitude toward the requirements of that human nature determined whether a given social system was "normal" or "pathological." Both Comte's social statics and his social Utopia rested on the conviction that there are permanent human needs. His antipsychologism accordingly did not take the form of rejecting all psychological assumptions, but assumed, first, that such assumptions do not suffice to explain societal life, and second, that the laws of sociology cannot be deduced from psychological knowledge (classed by him in the sphere of biology).

Social Dynamics. The main assumptions of the second part (or, rather, the second aspect) of Comte's sociology—his theory of progress—have already been mentioned, but they deserve a brief restatement:

1. Social development is based on regularities.
2. Its most important law is that of three stages: the theological, the metaphysical, and the scientific explanations of the world.
3. In accordance with the principle of interdependence of all parts of the social system (consensus), changes in consciousness, to which that law directly refers, are correlated with changes in all fields of societal life: Every state of social consciousness is associated with a specified state of manners, social organization, production of goods, political system, and the like, so that each stage can be described relative to the various aspects of the social system and not only as a specific way of thinking. Nevertheless, Comte, did not have the slightest doubt that it is "ideas which

govern and shake the world, so that, in other words, the whole social mechanism is ultimately based on opinions."²²
4. History means materialization of perfect social order, which will ensure stabilization without stagnation and evolution without revolution.
5. It is mankind as a whole that is the subject of history.

Comte expanded greatly his exposition of social dynamics because he strove to include in his schema the whole of his vast, albeit dilettantish, historical knowledge. He was interested not only in a good description of the trend of the development of mankind, but also in an interpretation of the various historical facts. As a result, he had to introduce additional divisions and distinctions in the description of every stage; this can best be seen when he divides the theological stage into the periods of fetishism, polytheism, and monotheism and when he singles out the various forms of polytheism.

Yet that is not what seems to be the most interesting aspect of Comte's social dynamics. The pride of place goes rather to the set of hypotheses on correlations between changes in consciousness and those in societal organization. Theological consciousness has its counterpart in a rigid organization, set to keeping society within an established framework; methaphysical consciousness means, in fact, social disorganization; and scientific consciousness means its reorganization, ensuring a stable social order without depriving society of its ability to change. The evolution from theology to positive science is simultaneously the evolution from militarism to industrialism. On this point Comte took up the issue raised by Saint-Simon and later most successfully developed by Spencer.

Industrial society, whose emergence was inevitably brought about by history, is a society given to peaceful production; owing to the scientific organization of work, it has at its disposal a wealth of goods, and its basic social classes are those of entrepreneurs and wage earners. Comte believed deeply that such society had unlimited opportunities for progress, which would make it possible to put an end to crises and conflicts still observable in the early period of that stage and resulting from the relics of the past. That was why Comte declared himself firmly against socialist tendencies (in particular against communism, which questioned private property) that were set to continue criticism or revolutionary activity. In his opinion, there arose in Europe sufficient conditions for further progress that would be peaceful and slow.

On the other hand, Comte was not in agreement with the liberally minded glorifiers of the new society, in which he saw much evil and whose bourgeoisie he assessed critically. Nor did he think that the situation could improve without any conscious organizational work. In accordance with his belief in the leading role of ideas, he thought that such work would be effective only if socioeconomic reorganization were preceded by a spiritual reorganization; otherwise, the equilibrium of the system would be disturbed.

Comte found himself in opposition to all trends in the social thought of his times. He was against conservatism, as he declared himself in favor of the new industrial society; he was against liberalism, as he was very critical of the actual state of that society; and he was against socialism, as he refused, in his criticism of the new society, to go beyond capitalism. This resulted in his isolation, which was increased by the fact that even many positivists turned their backs on him because they thought that Comte's competing with the prophets of the ideal society was reneging on the calling of scientist.

JOHN STUART MILL'S LOGIC OF SOCIAL SCIENCE

John Stuart Mill (1806-1873), theorist of liberalism, economist, and logician, was the most eminent representative of positivism in England. He was also one of the foremost initiators of the new social science in the nineteenth century, which he called *social economy, political ethology, sociology, politics, social science,* or *social sciences.* He was very consistent in pursuing that subject, even before the appearance of volume 4 of Comte's *Cours de philosophie positive.* It is true, however, that as early as the 1820s he was becoming familiar with some works by Comte, Saint-Simon, and Saint-Simonists.

Mill's most important "sociological" text is, beyond all doubt, Book 6 of his *System of Logic Ratiocinative and Inductive* (1843), which presents the adaptation of the methods already tested in natural science to the needs of those disciplines which had not yet reached the standard of scientific knowledge. But sociological problems are raised in all of Mill's works, beginning with his earliest essays, and play an important role in them. It seems that the presence of those problems in his works largely accounts for the fact Mill cannot be dismissed as a trivial liberal, a utilitarian, or a representative of vulgar political economy. He rises above the mediocrity through his extremely clear understanding of the fact that *homo oeconomicus* is at best an epistemological fiction that can serve certain purposes, but is not a real fact in any society whatsoever. Insufficient investigation of that aspect of Mill's thought accounts for his being notoriously ignored as one of the founding fathers of sociology.[23]

The Search for a Social Economy. Before we discuss Mill's program of sociology as outlined in his *System of Logic,* we shall consider the sources of his interest in sociology. The most important one was his dislike of utilitarian anthropology in its Benthamite version.

In one of his essays Mill criticized Bentham and claimed that such philosophy of man "can teach the means of organizing and regulating the merely *business* part of social arrangements," while it completely disregards

". . . that which alone causes any material interests to exist, which alone enables any body of human beings to exist as a society"—that is, the national
character.[24] In his essay entitled "Coleridge" (1840), Mill formulated—while
criticizing rationalistic philosophers and glorifying philosophers of the
reactionary school for their contribution to the philosophy of human
culture—the fundamental conditions of a "permanent political society"
and "the elementary principles of the social union": (1) the upbringing
that develops restraining discipline; (2) the existence of something that all
hold to be sacred; and (3) the strength and the active character of the bonds
between the members of a community or a state.[25] It was the reactionary
school that was the first, in Mill's opinion, to reveal those conditions of
social order and to investigate them from a philosophical standpoint and
in the spirit of Baconian thought.[26]

No less interesting is his essay on the subject of political economy (1836),
containing the statement that at the time of his writing that discipline covered
only part of those problems of social economy that it ought to investigate.
Social economy is interested in "every part of man's nature in so far as
influencing the conduct or condition of man in society." Its task is to
discover the social laws, i.e., the "laws of human nature in the societal
state."[27] As we shall see later, Mill, who inclined toward reductionism, did
not think that such laws would be numerous.

Mill listed many problems specific to social economy:

It shows by what principles of his nature man is induced to enter into a state of
society; how this "feature" in his position acts upon his interests and feelings, and
through them upon his conduct; how the association tends progressively to become
closer, and the cooperation extends itself to more and more purposes; what these
purposes are and what are the varieties of means most generally adapted for further-
ing them; what are the various relations which establish themselves among human
beings as the ordinary consequence of the social union; what are those which are
different in different states of society; what historical order those states tend to
succeed one another; and what are the effects of each upon the conduct and character of man.[28]

That discipline, which he also called "speculative politics" and "the natural
history of society," was supposed to fill the gap resulting from the fact that
political economy had concentrated on the abstract concept of the economic
man and hence on "the merely *business* part of social arrangements."

This is not to say that Mill criticized political economy. On the contrary,
in his opinion the representatives of that discipline were the first thinkers to
have come close to a clear idea of social science. In the case of Bentham,
Mill criticized bad philosophy; in the case of political economy, he merely
pointed to the limitations of a *science* that deliberately adopted certain
idealizational assumptions, as a result of which it is concerned with man

"solely as a being who desires to possess wealth, and who is capable of judging of the comparative efficacy of means for obtaining that end. . . . It makes entire abstraction of every other human passion or motive."[29]

But whatever the differences between poor philosophy and good science, their effects were the same: An important sphere of the human world remained outside the reach of scientific investigation, and it was the sphere affecting the business part of social arrangements and the manifestations of the general laws of human nature. Although convinced that such laws are stable and universal, like all liberals were, Mill nevertheless had learned the lesson of historical and cultural relativism. This, it seems, explains in his interest in the reactionary school, in Continental historians from Herder to Michelet, in Saint-Simon's doctrine, and above all in Comte's sociology.

Mill versus Comte. Mill never was a Comtist, even though for some time he considered *Cours de philosophie positive* to be one of the greatest works of the century and corresponded extensively with Comte, occasionally referring in his letters to "our common philosophy." Mill propagated Comte's works in England, and he probably contributed much more than Comte's ardent followers did to the French positivism that was appearing in English intellectual life. Mill was the author of a small book entitled *Auguste Comte and Positivism* (1865), which is still one of the best analyses of Comtism. By the time of its writing, Mill was already very critical of Comte. When discussing the latter's sociology, Mill credited him with historical merits, but claimed that Comte had "done nothing in sociology which does not require to be done over again and better."[30] Mill's intensified criticism was due to Comte's engaging in the founding of positivistic religion and politics, which were quite inacceptable to Mill. But even earlier Mill was not uncritical of Comte's philosophy, praising its *partie critique* rather than its *partie organique.* He declared his respect for the positive method, but questioned many of its applications by Comte.

Mill agreed with Comte on the basic rules of the positive method and on the possibility and necessity of constructing a complete system of scientific knowledge that should form a hierarchically structured body of laws with a varying degree of generality. Like Comte, he claimed that "this blot on the face of science," which was the lack of social knowledge that deserved the name of science, had to be wiped away quickly.[31] Like Comte, he believed that the goal was to be achieved by a reasonable use of the patterns supplied by natural science. He accepted Comte's law of three stages of the development of the human mind, even thought he named them differently. He was equally critical of their contemporaneous state of social philosophy, political practice, and public opinion. Following Comte, he divided sociology into social statics and social dynamics, parallel to the distinction between the laws of co-occurrence and those of sequence. He used the concept of social consensus worked out by Comte and even claimed that that consensus was "so complete (especially in modern history) that in the filiation of one generation and another, it is the whole which produces the whole, rather than any part a part."[32] Mill also agreed with Comte that the development of "the speculative faculties of mankind" is the basic factor of progress. The list could be made longer, but it is comprehensive enough to substantiate the claim that Mill agreed with the author of *Cours de philosophie positive* on as many points as some sociologists who considered themselves to have been Comtists.

But there is at least one essential difference between the two great positivists: Mill was a sociological nominalist, while Comte was a realist. The former seemed to think (although not without some inconsistencies) that so-called social laws can ultimately be reduced to the laws of behavior of human individuals, while the latter believed society to be a *sui generis* reality, an organism that is governed by its own laws, though not by them alone, of course.

Mill maintained firmly that "the laws of the phenomena of society are, and can be, nothing but the laws of the actions and passions of human beings united together in the social state. Men, however, in a state of society, are still men; their actions and passions are still obedient to the laws of individual human nature."[33] To put it briefly, in the case of Mill and Comte was find the first version of the sociological controversy between psychologism and sociologism and between reductionism and holism.

This difference of opinions between two eminent positivists had important consequences. One was that Mill placed the science of individual man —that is, psychology and ethology[34]—before sociology in the system of sciences, as he considered the former to be a more general discipline. Mill also excluded the possibility of explaining any societal facts without referring to laws of psychology. Many passages in his writings seem to indicate that Mill was most interested in social phenomena because they add complexity to the mechanisms of changeless human nature. However universal are the laws of individual psychology, "every individual is surrounded by circumstances different from those of every other individual; every nation or generation of mankind from every other nation or generation; and none of these differences are without their influence in forming a different type of character."[35] The emphasis laid on the varying circumstances in which permanent human nature manifests itself did not in the least undermine Mill's conviction that all phenomena of society are phenomena of human nature. Hence, the laws that he called sociological have a much weaker explanatory force than those of psychology. The former explain not human actions as such, but rather their deviations from the universal standard due to a specific historical or cultural context. Mill did not, however, exclude the possibility of the emergence of other sciences akin to political economy, that would investigate human behavior regardless of that context.

Sociology is needed, accordingly, not because of the existence of a specific category of social facts, but rather because of the fact that man cannot be observed in a pure state. Sociology is, therefore, expected not so much to provide independent knowledge as to protect us against errors having two opposite sources: extrapolation of results of empirical observations onto all possible situations and speculation on human behavior in concrete cases that is based on properties of human nature taken *in abstracto*.[36] This attitude placed Mill inevitably in opposition to Comte who, in spite of the use he made of the concept of human nature, was precisely in search of laws that apply to society in general.

Mill's Program of Sociology. However limited and subordinate was the role assigned by Mill to sociology as compared with psychology, his conception of sociology deserves close examination both because of its originality and because of its being, on many points, ahead of the times.

Its originality consisted of the endeavor to bridge the gap between two kinds of interests that have alwyas been in social thought: first, the interest, dominant in the eighteenth century, in the permanent features of human nature that are characteristic of every individual in the same degree; and, second, the interest, more and more noticeable in the nineteenth century, in the variable features of societies as wholes. Mill's conception preserved the human-nature approach and saw the chance for a scientific explanation of human behavior in the new achievements of psychology. At the same time, he rejected the belief that psychology, even at its best, could provide a satisfactory explanation of all those social phenomena with which politicians and students of social life must deal. This is so because one may know all the motives of human behavior and yet be unable to explain certain behavior in specified circumstances. On the other hand, study of those circumstances alone provides fragmentary knowledge, deprived of the universality that should mark truly scientific knowledge. For Mill, psychology turns out to be an inductive science, while the social sciences become deductive as they try to explain the behavior of particular individuals by reference to general laws.

Unfortunately, Mill's ideas on this topic remained undeveloped and failed to find any broad application. Political economy was the only science that he pursued systematically. It was the discipline that could cause him the least methodological trouble, as it was one of those "hypothetical or abstract" social sciences that assume that human beings are always guided by the same motives regardless of circumstances. Mill believed that it was the only social science at that time about which one could say that "whoever knows the political economy of England, or even of Yorkshire, knows that of all nations, actual or possible.''[37] Thus his experience qua economist and the author of *Principles of Political Economy* (1848) had little bearing on sociology, which he left in the sphere of proposals. The only thing that he did equally with Comte was to pose the problem of the *method* of sociology.

The study of methodological problems was favored by the naturalistic approach of the first sociologists: Since the task was to found a social science similar to natural science, it was necessary to find out *how* the latter manages to succeed and to consider whether the same procedures can be applied in the study of society. That is the essence of both Comte's and Mill's methodology.

Mill's methodology of the science of society seems to be of particular interest in two points.

First, the author of *A System of Logic* took up the problem (later critically discussed by Durkheim in his *Règles de la méthode sociologique* [1894]) of the possible application in sociology of his renowned inductive methods. On having examined, one by one, the methods of difference, agreement, concomitant variations, and residues, Mill came to the conclusion that their application is extremely limited by the fact that the social sciences, unlike the experimental disciplines, are not in a position to isolate the various factors affecting the emergence of a given phenomenon. Mill used to repeat in an almost obsessive manner that social reality is almost infinitely complex, so that

the mode of production of all social phenomena is one great case of Intermixture of Laws. We can never either understand in theory or command in practice the condition of a society in any one respect, without taking into consideration its condition in all other respects. . . . There is, in short, what physiologists term a *consensus*. . . . We can never, therefore, affirm with certainty that a cause which has a particular tendency in one people or in one age will have exactly the same tendency in another.[38]

This reasoning strengthened Mill's conviction that only inductive psychology was possible, while sociology had to be confined to the study of peculiarities in the manifestation of psychological laws in specified historical circumstances. But on the other hand, the discovery of the phenomenon termed *consensus* must have encouraged Mill to search for a "natural correlation" among the various elements of "a state of society." Such a correlation ("natural law") occurs for instance, "between the form of government existing in any society and the contemporaneous state of civilization." Mill also referred to a possibility of "discovering the law of correspondence not only between the simultaneous states, but between the simultaneous changes, of those elements.''[39]

In other words, Mill could not make up his mind whether to assign the status of general laws to the laws of psychology alone or to those of sociology as well. In the last analysis, he tended toward the former solution and thought that sociology could go beyond historical and common-sense empirical laws only if it would resort to deduction. Mill's proverbial clarity is less obvious when he discussed the social sciences.

Second, Mill's most important contribution to sociology (regardless of whether his approach was psychology-oriented or sociology-oriented) was the formulation of some simple truths about the nature of the laws of human behavior as discovered by the social sciences and in particular the statement that those laws are statistical in character. In that respect Mill had forerunners in Condorcet, as the founder of "social mathematics," and in Quételet, his contemporary, who started to use such mathematics, but probably did so unconsciously. Mill's reasoning, repeated by Durkheim many years later, was extremely simple: Since "men's actions are the joint result of the general laws and circumstances of human nature and of their own particular characters,"[40] the explanation of those actions depends above all on whether we succeed in finding a method of separating that which is general from that which is particular or accidental. Statistics provides such a method, because it enables us to assume that when we consider sufficiently great masses, then accidental deviations cancel one another out. Statistical laws do not allow us to forecast the behavior of single individuals in specific circumstances, but they reveal those trends which inevitably manifest themselves on a mass scale: "that which is only probable when asserted of individual human beings indiscriminately selected [is] certain when affirmed of the character and collective conduct of masses."[40] The science of society is thus "principally concerned with the actions not of solitary individuals, but of masses, with the fortunes not of single persons, but of communities."[41]

The almost universal interest in masses assumed a quite different form in Mill's case than that observed in most other authors. Masses here are not collective subjects like mankind, nation, people, or class, but merely large sets of individuals to which the laws of large numbers apply. Instead of popular masses, in Mill's works we have statistical masses; this is totally in harmony with his political opinions as a liberal and a theorist of representative government. Mill was interested not in social movements, but in strictly individual behavior, which falls, however, into a specific and constant distribution, of which a wise politician should be aware. This tendency, still very weakly marked in Mill's case, will find a forceful manifestation in the works of Quételet.

QUÉTELET'S SOCIAL PHYSICS

If sociological positivism is interpreted broadly, we have to conclude that Lambert Adolphe Jacques Quételet (1796-1874), the Belgian mathematician and statistician, also was a representative of that trend, even though he had never called himself a positivist and probably did not even know Comte's works. Despite his Renaissance-like variety of interests—from painting and poetry to mathematics, physics, and astronomy—he was never concerned with philosophy. And for all his profound understanding of social issues, he was not fascinated, as was Comte, by the task of reconstructing society. He would leave that task to governments, reserving for himself the role of expert, who provides data about facts and, more important still, knowledge of the laws of social life. Quételet's position in the history of science is connected mostly with his achievements in statistics.

Quételet's point of departure differed completely from Comte's and even Mill's. He was an academically minded mathematician who from the very beginning of his career enjoyed the highest recognition from his contemporaries. Although he recognized the opportunity to expand the sphere of applications of his knowledge, he aspired neither to saving mankind nor to founding an all-inclusive philosophical system.[43]

Yet, his work in that limited field produced a *sui generis* social positivism that we are tempted to call spontaneous positivism. That philosophy corresponded better to the main requirements of the positive method advocated by Comte than the social philosophy of Comte himself, which was a kind of positivistic metaphysics. Quételet's critique of metaphysics was much more consistent and agreed with his own experience qua theorist. Nevertheless, he produced more than just a number of statistical studies and improvements on statistical methods. He in fact founded, under the label of social physics, a sociology that was much more the forerunner of twentieth-century sociology than Comte's, despite the fact we ascribe the title of the father of sociology almost exclusively to the latter.

Quételet expounded the foundations of his sociology in *Sur l'homme et le développement de ses facultés: Physique sociale* (1835); its ideas were repeated, expanded, and reformulated in *Du système social et des lois qui le régissent* (1848) and in *Physique sociale ou Essai sur le développement des facultés de l'homme*, his best known book (two volumes, 1869). Each of these included a fairly large portion of traditional sociophilosophical issues, such as the problems of progress, revolution, nation, morals, social ideas, and the like; but since Quételet's sociology is under discussion, we have something else in mind. Nor are his reflections on actions and reactions, states of equilibrium and disequilibrium, and gravitation within society—scattered all over his works and concerned with analogies between the *corps social* and bodies of other kinds—of particular importance. They merely prove that Quételet interpreted the term *social physics* rather literally and was inclined to explain the various states of a given social system by direct reference to the laws of physics, which we encounter neither in Comte nor in Mill. In fact, in his numerous texts Quételet appears as the first *physicalist* in sociology.

But the most interesting point in Quételet's sociology is the way in which he arrives at the refutation of current voluntaristic philosophy, which was such a great roadblock on the sociologists' path to the discovery of laws. Since human individuals are endowed with free will, as the voluntarists argued, then looking in their actions for regularities that are typical of natural phenomena cannot succeed, because free will by definition is something whimsical and incalculable. This standpoint was criticized by Comte, Mill, and, most extensively, Spencer, all of whom confined themselves to purely philosophical arguments. Quételet drew on empirical data in his argument: What can be more dependent on free will of human individuals, he wrote, than marriages, crimes, and suicides? And yet statistical data show that all those phenomena are marked by a striking regularity.

Oh, sad condition of mankind. We can say in advance how many individuals will sully their hands with the blood of their neighbors, how many of them will commit forgeries, and how many will turn poisoners with almost the same precision as we can predict the number of births and deaths. Society contains in it the germ of all the crimes that will be committed. In a sense it prepared those crimes itself, and those guilty of them are merely the instruments that commit them. Every social state thus presupposes a certain number and a certain order of crimes that follow as a necessary result of its organization.[44]

The statistical data that Quételet had at his disposal were still comparatively poor (he was the first to initiate statistical studies on the national scale and to organize research institutions for the collection of data). But in his opinion they were promising enough to suggest that in the course of time all human actions would become observable not only from the point of view of the motives and intentions declared by individuals, but also from the point of view of their objective causes and social consequences. This is not to say that Quételet denied the free will of human individuals or questioned the existence of important individual characteristics. But he stated that as scientist he was not interested in such individual variations. "Nature," he wrote, "is here considered from the most general point of view. We analyze here man as shown by philosophy, and not an individual, who belongs in literature and the fine arts."[45]

This formulation recalls Rousseau's idea that we ought to study not men, but man. Quételet, however, attained his goal not by dissociating himself from observable facts, but by choosing a specific method of investigating them. In his opinion, "general facts" are revealed when we begin to handle data about large masses of people, instead of remaining satisfied with fragmentary observation of individuals. He claims that "the greater the number of the individuals we observe, the more [fully] specifically individual features are . . . obliterated and yield place to a series of general facts, owing to which society exists and extends its existence." On another occasion he said: "By depriving [man] of his individuality, we eliminate all that is merely accidental."[46]

The basic difficulty in the science of man, accordingly, does not lie in the distinctiveness of its subject matter; it is, in fact, an essentially technical difficulty of accumulating an adequate amount of data and of applying adequate mathematical methods of handling them (probability theory). That difficulty is surmountable, although Quételet did not belittle it; he realized the disproportions between the actual possibilities of statistics and his own aspirations for an empirical theory of all human actions and all communities, including mankind as such. Whatever the degree of difficulty, the subject matter itself does not differ essentially from physical objects, which, like human individuals, are never identical and yet are subject to laws.

By handling great masses of people, and not individuals, and by thus eliminating from science those individual variations that cancel out one another *en masse*, Quételet formulated the concept of average man (*l'homme moyen*), which was to be an analogue of the physical concept of the center of gravity.[47] In the nominalistic theory of society, that concept has a similar meaning to Comte's conception of society as something other than the sum of individuals and all their peculiarities. The concept was arrived at by abstraction from everything in human behavior that deviates, upward or downward, from the statistical mean. Such an average man can be found for every group, and for every country, and even for mankind as such. It is only when we have such an abstraction available (it is true that Quételet sometimes tended to personify it) that we can sensibly speak about variations and deviations and can explain them properly.

Quételet saw the principal instrument of such explanation in the law of accidental causes *(loi des causes accidentelles)*, which states that all properties are subject to fluctuations around a certain average state, and those changes which are due to accidental causes occur with such accuracy and regularity that they can be numerically distributed in advance. Every social state has its proper *état moyen*, determined by the operation of constant causes (or forces) such as age, sex, occupation, religion, and economic institutions. Those causes operate with unchanging intensity and always in the same direction. Another category of the forces that ultimately contribute to the fixing of a given state is that of variable causes *(variables)*, which operate always in the same direction, but with a varying intensity (for example, the cyclic phenomena such as the succession of the seasons of the year). The constant causes have their opposites in accidental or perturbative causes *(perturbatrices)*, which account for the fact that not everything remains at the average level and that fluctuations continually take place (for instance, some people reveal stronger inclinations to commit crimes than others do). It is the task of "moral statistics" to discover both the limits of such fluctuations and the mechanisms underlying them. It was with that end in view that Quételet set in operation an apparatus of statistical analysis that was quite refined for his times.

We shall not be concerned here with the purely technical aspect of the problem, nor shall we try to assess the relation of Quételet's endeavors to present-day mathematical sociology, which makes use not only of a broader range of techniques, but also of a mathematics that differs significantly from what was available to Quételet.[48] Nor shall we discuss precisely what Quételet had in mind when formulating his laws. It is known that by the term *law* he meant statements of at least three kinds: (1) on trends, (2) on relationships between phenomena, and (3) on distribution of properties. It is worth nothing only that his conception does not include historical laws in Comte's sense, even though his works reveal a certain historiosophy that assumes the progress of mankind from savagery to civilization and ascribes to science the principal role in that progress, since science replaces belief in miracles by the knowledge of laws of nature. This differs from Comte's historiosophy by the specific statements rather than by essentials.

But it is worthwhile to examine Quételet's specific system of values that is latent in the concept of the average man. The concept was far from being neutral in the axiological sense: It applied not only to a statistical average, but to a societal *standard* as well, namely, that standard which under given conditions seemed the most desirable to the statistician. Quételet did not leave any doubt on that point, as he wrote:

I have said earlier that the average man in every epoch represents the type of the development of mankind in that epoch; I have also said that the average man always was whatever it was possible and required for him to be in a given place and in a given time, and his characteristics were developing in perfect equilibrium and in perfect harmony, being equally far from excess and from shortage of any kind, so that under given circumstances he must be treated as the type of all that which is beautiful and good.[49]

The average man thus turns out to be the statistical "natural man," who, however, differs from his rationalistic analogue, first, by changing as mankind progresses; second, by being adjusted to the various societies into which mankind is divided; and third, by not being an Utopian ideal to be striven for, but a fact that can be established by a scientist if the latter can use the proper methods of social research. The appearance of this *type de la vulgarité* in European social thought was, by the way, an interesting testimony of how far Western European societies had evolved, following the decomposition of feudal structures. The vision of society in Quételet's writings is a one of a world which is extremely individualized and in which the supreme virtue is keeping up with the Joneses. It was also a recipe for social integration, but radically different from the recommendations advanced by Comte, who suggested expansion of new social institutions that would take over the functions of the old religions.

POSITIVISM AND THE FURTHER DEVELOPMENT OF SOCIETY

The foregoing review of the sociological conceptions of Comte, Mill, and Quételet makes it possible to see better both the general assumptions of positivism in sociology, and its internal differentiation. It was, in fact, a general (and, often, merely vague) option for a philosophy of the social sciences, made when other such philosophies did not exist. Marxism was still in its formative stage and was, at best, known as a variant of socialism. Humanistic sociology had not yet been conceived, if we disregard its remote prehistory in the form of romantic hermeneutics. When the social sciences, and sociology in particular, were in the embryonic state, the very requirement of founding a positive social science that would be free from metaphysical speculations and would discover laws following a methodical observation of facts was clear, self-evident, and attractive. Early positivism was above all a reflection on the need for a science of society and was not the theoretical and methodological self-knowledge of a mature discipline that must explicitly lay down its assumptions and theorems. The scattering of research also contributed to the fact that the sphere of those opinions common to all (or at least to many) was rather small. Thus, early positivism was a kind of *l'état d'esprit*, a "silent knowledge" of the conditions of success of cognitive activity rather than a set of strictly defined rules of research procedures or a uniform theory of society. Endeavors to change the situation in that respect continued throughout the nineteenth century, evolutionism in sociology and social anthropology being the first of them; it will be discussed in the following chapter. In further chapters it will be shown that there were many such endeavors, but none of them was fully successful. This failure paved the way for the antipositivistic revolution in the social sciences.

The early stage of positivism was marked by those basic dilemmas which later were to make their existence known continuously and to result in a further differentiation of standpoints. The first of them was that of *realism* versus *nominalism* in sociology, closely associated with the problem of the nature of the laws discovered by sociology: Are they laws of the structure and growth of the social organism as a whole, analogous to other living organisms? Or are they laws that refer to the characteristics of human individuals and, hence, psychological laws that enable us to explain individual behavior or statistical laws about the order of occurrence of certain characteristics in specified populations and about the distribution of those characteristiscs? The issues of sociologism versus psychologism and of holism versus reductionism were associated with this first dilemma, although not identical with it. In its early stage, positivism as such did not settle those questions.

The second dilemma was that of the *dynamic* versus the *static* point of view. In early positivism they occurred side by side, as a rule, or even seemed to be inseparable from one another. Yet their unity was guaranteed only by organicism, in which the concept of life of necessity assumed both a specified structure and specified changes in the process of growth. In all those cases in which the organicist analogy did not play any important role (which was quite frequent even in positivistic sociology in the nineteenth century), these two different points of view could be separated from one another. One of them found its fullest manifestation in evolutionism and in the postevolutionist theories of development; the other found expression in the theories of the social system that strove to reveal the changeless conditions of its equilibrium and showed minimal interest in the problems of evolution (classical functionalism being the peak of that trend).

Finally, the third dilemma was related to the social tasks of sociology. Positivism always implied the question that was later to be formulated in the title of Lundberg's book, *Can Science Save Us?* There were two different replies in the affirmative. One of them, formulated most clearly by Comte, linked the saving of society by science with science's transforming social consciousness and taking over from old religions their functions. Apart from its purely technical applications, science in this case was to play an impòrtant role as the educational factor that would change society. The other reply restricted the tasks of science to expertise for those who are in power and actually make the decisions concerning society. It can be said that the former reply was given when the positivists were not yet ashamed of their aspirations to become ideologists and leaders, while the latter was used when they retreated to the position of supposedly neutral scholars. But it is proper to note that sociological positivists were always marked by inner tension between an impatience to have the final say in the controversy over the future of society and the anxiety not to compromise themselves as passionless students of society.

NOTES

1. Herbert Marcuse, *Reason and Revolution: Hegel and The Rise of Social Theory*, 2d ed. (New York: Humanities Press, 1954).

2. Anthony Giddens, ed., *Positivism and Sociology* (London: Heinemann, 1975), p. ix.

3. John Stuart Mill, "Auguste Comte and Positivism," in *Collected Works*, vol. 10, *Essays on Ethics, Religion and Society*, ed. J. M. Robson (Toronto: University of Toronto Press, London: RKP, 1969), p. 263.

4. W. M. Simon, *European Positivism in the Nineteenth Century: An Essay in Intellectual History* (Ithaca, N.Y.: Cornell University Press, 1963), p. 3.

5. A. Comte, *Discours sur l'esprit positif* (Paris: Union Générale d'Editions, 1963), pp. 71-73.

6. Leszek Kolakowski, *Filozofia pozytywistyczna od Hume'a do Kola Wiedeńskiego* (Warsaw: WP, 1966), p. 11.

7. Jürgen Habermas, *Knowledge and Human Interests* (Boston: Beacon Press, 1972), p. 71.

8. Karl R. Popper, *The Open Society and Its Enemies* (Princeton: Princeton University Press, 1971), 1: 157-59.

9. Pierre Arnaud, *La Pensée d' Auguste Comte* (Editions Bordas, 1969), p. 29.

10. Ibid., p. 19.

11. Ibid., p. 141.

12. Auguste Comte, *Sociologie: Textes choisis par J. Laubier* (Paris: P.U.F., 1969), p. 25.

13. See B. Skarga, *Ortodoksja i rewizja w pozytywizmie francuskim* (Warsaw: PWN, 1967), p. 70.

14. See J. H. Abraham, *The Origins and Growth of Sociology* (Harmondsworth: Penguin Books, 1973), p. 109.

15. Marvin Harris, *The Rise of Anthropological Theory* (New York: Crowell, 1968), p. 63.

16. Lewis A. Coser, *Masters of Sociological Thought* (New York: Harcourt Brace Jovanovich, 1971), p. 10.

17. Comte, *Sociologie*, p. 25.

18. Ibid., p. 55.

19. Ibid., p. 56.

20. Quoted in Coser, *Masters*, p. 11.

21. Cf. Arnaud, *La Pensée de Comte*, p. 156.

22. Raymond Aron, *Les Etapes de la pensée sociologique* (Paris: Gallimard, 1967), p. 128.

23. The most important exception is Ronald Fletcher as the editor of *John Stuart Mill: A Logical Critique of Sociology* (London: Nelson, 1971).

24. John Stuart Mill, "Bentham," in *Essays on Ethics, Religion and Society*, p. 99.

25. John Stuart Mill, "Coleridge," in ibid., pp. 134-35.

26. Ibid., p. 139.

27. John Stuart Mill, "On the Definition of Political Economy and on the Method of Investigation Proper to It," in *Collected Works*, vol. 4, *Essays on Economics and Society* (Toronto: University of Toronto Press, London: RKP, 1967), p. 320.

28. Ibid.

29. Ibid., p. 321. Cf. Mill, *A System of Logic, Ratiocinative and Inductive*, 6th ed. (London: Longmans, Green, 1856), pp. 191-92.

30. John Stuart Mill, "Auguste Comte," p. 327.

31. John Stuart Mill, *System of Logic*, vol. 2, book 6, chap. 1, par. 1, pp. 412-13.

32. Ibid., chap. 10, par. 6, p. 519.

33. Ibid., chap. 7, par. 1, p. 464.

34. Ethology was conceived by Mill as "science which determines the kind of character produced, in conformity to these [psychological] general laws, by any set of circumstances, physical and moral." Ibid., chap. 5, par. 4, p. 452.

35. Ibid., chap. 5, par. 2, p. 447.

36. Ibid., chap. 9, par. 2, p. 489.

37. Ibid., chap. 9, pars. 3-4, pp. 495.

38. Ibid., chap. 9, par. 2, pp. 488-89.

39. Ibid., chap. 10, pars. 2, 5, 7, pp. 504-5, 514, 521.

40. Ibid., chap. 9, par. 1, p. 528.

41. Ibid., chap. 3, par. 2, p. 428.

42. Ibid., book 3, chap. 23, par. 7, pp. 136-37.

43. According to Quételet, "The more advanced the sciences have become, the more they have tended to enter the domain of mathematics, which is a sort of center toward which they converge. We can judge of the perfection to which a science has come by the facility, more or

less great, with which it may be approached by calculation." Quoted in D. Landau and Paul L. Lazarsfeld, "Quételet," in *International Encyclopedia of Social Sciences*, 13:250.

44. Adophe Quételet, *Physique sociale, ou Essai sur le développement des facultés de l'homme* (Brussels: J. Issakoff, 1869), 1:97.

45. Ibid., p. 132.

46. Ibid., p. 93.

47. Ibid., 2:369.

48. Cf. Paul F. Lazarsfeld, "Notes on the History of Quantification in Sociology: Trends, Sources and Problems," *Isis* 52 (1961):294-311.

49. Quételet, *Physique sociale*, 2:391.

8

THE EVOLUTIONIST SOCIOLOGY

Evolutionism was one of the most influential doctrines of nineteenth-century social thought, and it prevailed in the general trend of thought of those days. There is no doubt that evolutionism has contributed more than any other concept, earlier or later, to the development of social anthropology and sociology, being —with the exception of sociography—the only realization of the program outlined by the founders of positivism up to the time of Durkheim and Tönnies. Even ideas clearly opposed to evolutionism (for example, psychologism) have essentially grown under its influence. Evolutionism has created a body of notions, hypotheses, and methods that for quite a long time were regarded as a property not of a specific school of social science, but of social anthropology and sociology as such.

THE CONCEPT OF EVOLUTIONISM IN THE SOCIAL SCIENCES

The real meaning of the above statements depends, however, on our understanding of evolutionism. In the social thought of the nineteenth century, expressions such as "evolutionism," "the theory of evolution," and even "the idea of evolution" did not have a clear-cut meaning and were often conceived either too narrowly or too broadly. In the former case, evolutionism in social science was identified with Darwinism, that is, with concepts that, in one way or another, derived from the idea of biological evolution formulated by Charles Darwin (1809-1882). In the latter case, the term *evolutionists* applied to all thinkers who had shown major interest in problems of social development and who claimed that discovering its laws and course was the primary objective of social science. From this point of view, practically all social thought of the nineteenth century was evolutionist. The evolutionists were not only Darwin and Spencer, Tylor and Morgan, Bastian and Frazer, but also Hegel and Marx, Guizot and Tocqueville, Saint-Simon and Comte, Michelet and Newman.[1]

This expanded understanding of evolutionism has been facilitated by the fact that for a long time, the very term *evolution* was not indicative of any specific group of scholars, being used rather freely in place of such terms as *development, growth, change*, and *progress*. Evolutionists, even in a most limited sense, did not compose a school, and thus attempts to include one or another thinker into that group could lead to an unresolved controversy.

There are sound arguments to support both the narrow and the broad views of evolutionism. Darwinism has, in fact, exerted a far-reaching (albeit not necessarily direct) influence on social science, and many ideas of social evolution that had arisen independently from it owed it their final shape; furthermore, in the eyes of the public they were backed by the prestige and authority of the great biologist. There also appeared certain sociological concepts—even though of no real importance—that simply applied some of Darwin's ideas (natural selection, in particular) to interpret social processes. More significantly, a number of theories of social development, especially English, that were not based on Darwinism show a distinct kinship with his conceptions of science and scientific methods. Viewed in this light, the ties linking Spencer with Darwin, for instance, are very close indeed.

Accentuating the ties of evolutionism in social science with Darwinism has, however, its pitfalls, as it tends to ignore some historical facts. First, the most important ideas of its leading representatives are older than Darwinism. Second, these ideas had their origins in the eighteenth and early nineteenth centuries, not only in the ideas of Malthus—which Darwin, too, made use of—but also, if not originally, in the theories of social development expounded by Ferguson and Monboddo as well as Turgot and Condorcet. Essential also were the accumulation of ethnological material and the progress of archaeology, which in the first half of the nineteenth century was able to present a convincing picture of the sequence of the Stone, Bronze and Iron Ages. Third, all the major evolutionistic ideas in the social sciences differed considerably from Darwin's doctrine (Spencer's Lamarckism, for example), both in their propositions and in the focus of interest. Finally, many evolutionistic social theoreticians openly stressed their independence from Darwin. In the light of these facts, even the British evolutionists cannot be unreservedly regarded as Darwinists.

It seems, therefore, necessary to extend the meaning of the term *evolutionism* beyond Darwinism, but not far enough to cover all authors of the schemata of social development. Such an extension of the term's meaning would make it useless for an analysis of the internal dilemmas of the nineteenth century's social thought.

Without going into detail, we shall examine two theses concerning the specific nature of the evolutionistic orientation, as opposed to the other theories of social development, in which the nineteenth century abounded. According to the first, evolutionism was a naturalistic orientation, whereas according to the second, evolutionism meant antihistoricism. The former is merely obvious, but the latter may seem paradoxical, considering that the evolutionists were concerned with history, though conceived in a particular manner. Both theses need some comment.

Classical evolutionism was a naturalistic doctrine in both ontological and methodological meaning. It proclaimed the fundamental unity of the universe and uniformity of the laws that govern the universe, and it insisted that the methods of studying all phenomena could and should be the same as those applied in the natural science. This is not to say, however, that all evolutionists were inclined to identify social phenomena with, say, biological ones. The antihistoricism of the evolutionists consisted of their lack of interest in the actual social processes. Rather, they searched for a single model process, free from any accidental deformations and deviations, and reduced to its "fundamental" features. Thus, they continued the Enlightenment's tradition of philosophical, conjectural, and reasoned history. Evolutionism did have certain common points with nineteenth-century historicism, but only insofar as the latter was concerned with studying the history of societies and, consequently, rejected the idea of history being steered by the hand of God, or by heroes and monarchs. If the historicists sought to discover the laws of the process of history, they did so by studying the history of existing societies. The evolutionists, on the other hand, were not interested in historical processes as such, but saw them only as a raw material for study aimed at discovering general laws. Their primary concern was not so much what had really happened, but what would have happened if the process had gone undisturbed. They did not attempt to explain individual historical facts, nor did they seek to study the peculiarities of individual countries or cultural groups. Consequently, for many of them a nation did not exist (at most they recognized national prejudices), and the basic category was for them—as for the philosophers of the Age of Reason—mankind.

The evolutionists searched for the laws of social evolution, which was conceived as a universal process, and treated the histories of individual countries as raw material for building "a Comparative Sociology, and for the subsequent determination of the ultimate laws to which social phenomena conform."[2] The comparative method—called the historical method by Comte—served to reveal not differences, but basic similarities. In a sense, evolutionism was an attempt to restore the belief in the uniformity of human nature, and history was necessary for the purpose only insofar as it facilitated finding one and the same man in different societies and in different periods. Spencer wrote: "until you have got a true theory of humanity, you cannot interpret history, and when you have got a true theory of humanity you do not want history."[3] This, however, is not to say that evolutionism was completely unattractive and useless for historians. Yet only one outstanding historical work could be mentioned as being fully compatible with evolutionistic assumptions: Henry Thomas Buckle's *History of Civilization in England* (1857). The evolutionists felt best as students of primitive societies, sociologists and philosophers of universal evolution, segregating historical data according to logical criteria provided by some theory of evolution rather than according to historical criteria of time and space. This, however, did not prevent them from regarding themselves as historians, though they were fully aware that they were concerned with a history of different kind.

Obviously, this summary of characteristics of evolutionism is rather insufficient and will have to be complemented with a description of typical assumptions and research procedures. But we are unable to determine any definition so precise that every thinker could be included in evolutionism or excluded from it without any doubts. We shall certainly include Herbert Spencer (1820-1903), Louis Henry Morgan (1818-1881), Edward B. Tylor (1832-1917), John F. McLennan (1827-1881), John Lubbock (1834-1913), Johann J. Bachofen (1815-1887), Adolph Bastian (1826-1905), James Frazer (1854-1941), John Robertson Smith (1846-1894), and Edward Westermarck (1867-1939). No serious objections would arise if we called evolutionists such scholars as Henry Sumner Maine (1822-1888) and Numa Denis Fustel de Coulange (1830-1889), though their views cannot be accepted as typical because they bear elements of historicism. Open to doubt are Comte, whom we include among evolutionists, and Gumplowicz, whom we shall discuss in the chapter devoted to sociologism. Also doubtful is where we should place Engels, as the author of writings based on Morgan's works, and all those Marxists who not only applied procedures similar to the evolutionists' in their research, but even approved one or another theory of evolution.

Our rule seems to be as follows: We use a certain model constructed with ideas developed by the authors listed above. Every one of them could be atypical in some of his opinions. On the other hand, in the works of many authors who followed other theoretical orientations (for example, Marx and Engels) there could have been elements of evolutionism. This was quite natural considering how influential the evolutionistic trend was and how attractive its promise of a social science of the same kind as natural science must have been at that time.

THEORETICAL ASSUMPTIONS OF EVOLUTIONISM

The evolutionists did not form a cohesive group or school, and hence we would search in vain for programmatic statements on which all of them would agree. Undoubtedly the most programmatic were the works by Spencer, but even they could not be accepted as fully representative because other evolutionists voiced reservations about them, and, above all, because the author of *Principles of Sociology* had philosophical aspirations that the others did not share. In fact, he alone was the theoretician of cosmic evolution, whereas all the others studied the evolution of society and—even more frequently—of given social institutions or given aspects of culture (most often family and religion). Consequently, any synthetic exposition of the assumptions of evolutionism must result from a partly arbitrary reconstruction taking into account both programmatic pronouncements and research practice. Classical evolutionism accepted ten assumptions, a discussion of which follows.

Unity of the World. From the philosophical point of view, the evolutionists were positivists and, hence, also naturalists. This is not to imply that they were followers of Comte's philosophical system (rather strongly criticized by Spencer) nor that they identified themselves with any other philosophy. We call them positivists *ex post*, in view of their acceptance of the fundamental rules of the positive method and, more important, of the conviction that they cherished about the unity of the human and natural worlds and of the knowledge of them (hence the criticism of religions, voluntarism, and the like).

Regularity. The incorporation of human reality into the world of nature was linked with the assumption that it is governed by the same laws. "Our thoughts, wills and actions" wrote E. B. Taylor, "accord with laws as definite as those which govern the motion of the waves, the combination of acids and base and the growth of plants and animals."[4] The same idea has been explicitly stated in Spencer's *System of Synthetic Philosophy*, which was a treatise providing a uniform interpretation of all phenomena then known. The first principles, described in a book by that name, were equally applicable to astronomy, physics, chemistry, and biology as to psychology, sociology, and ethics. The laws discovered by science are of two kinds: concurrence and sequence, structure and function. If definite conditions are fulfilled, phenomenon A is invariably accompanied by phenomenon B and is succeeded by phenomenon C. If we fail to notice this, it proves not the absence of regularity, but the imperfection of our methods of observation.

Geneticism. The evolutionists attached particular importance to discovering genetic interdependencies, supposing that explaining a phenomenon means, first of all, finding its genesis. This reminds us both of the Enlightenment's fascination with the problem of origins and of the identification of the origin with the essence of the matter, so common in the Age of Reason. In this respect evolutionism was in opposition to the later functionalism. Evans-Pritchard claimed that the most appropriate name for evolutionist social anthropology would be "genetic anthropology."[5]

Uniformity of Human Nature. The search for the invariable laws governing human realities required the assumption that irrespective of the incessant
changes that this reality is undergoing, it does have some permanent characteristics. The evolutionists accepted the existence, within certain limits, of
an unchangeable human nature. This does not mean to say that they believed,
like Hobbes or Bentham, in the fundamental stability of the human psyche,
if only because this would rule out the conviction about the universal nature
of evolution. They often expressed the opinion that, for example, our
knowledge of contemporary man's psychology is of no use in explaining
primitive man. They assumed, however, that the general principles of the
functioning of the human mind—or, as Bastian said, certain *Elementargedanken*[6]—were constant; otherwise, one could not expect that under definite
conditions the same cause would always bring the same effects. This problem, by the way, has been a source of a permanent nuisance to the evolutionists, because in addition to the common traits of various societies they
also had to explain the differences between them (if only the difference in
the pace of evolution) and their peculiar traits (what Bastian defined as
Völkergedanken). Hence, in view of the dominant tendency towards universalistic explanations, there occasionally appeared among the evolutionists certain racialist ideas, which were evidently opposed to the fundamental premise that held that under the same conditions every man behaves
in the same way.

Changeability. One of the evolutionist dogmas was that everything that
exists is in motion, undergoes changes, and develops. For them evolution
was simply a fact confirmed by all sciences, the all-embracing law of the
universe; and if anything required explanation, it could only be the rare
states of stagnation and immobility. Perhaps only Maine—who lived for
many years in India—considered immobility of societies as a rule and
progress as a fortunate exception. Typical for the evolutionists, instead, was
a conviction about the omnipresence of change. And presumably for this
reason they were concerned with studying the direction and the mechanism
of change rather than with discovering its presumed causes.

Direction of Changes. From the evolutionists' point of view, any change
has a direction. Even though they did not exclude the possibility of regres-
sions and recurrences, in their final accounting change was identical with
progress. Any deviation from the way of progress was seen as a departure
from a normal course of events. It could happen, but only in the case of
individual societies that, as a result of unfavorable circumstances, found
themselves stagnating or even regressing to an earlier phase of development.
Yet, such phenomena in no way altered the conviction that a normal sequence of phases is from a lower to a higher level.

Thus, the evolutionists continued the Enlightenment's idea of progress, though they added new elements to it. Above all, they put an effort into formulating precise and objective criteria of superiority and inferiority, thus considerably weakening the emphasis laid by Comte and Mill on the development of consciousness as the core of all progress. This idea may have been present in their thinking, but much more widespread was the opinion, expounded by Spencer in his polemics with Comte, for instance, that development of consciousness is secondary in relation to changes in other spheres. The criteria of progress adopted by the evolutionists were basically objective and remained the same whether applied in social or in natural sciences. Of such a character was Spencer's concept of evolution: a change "from an indefinite, incoherent homogeneity to a definite coherent heterogeneity."[7] The fundamental difference between superiority and inferiority was thought to be the difference of structure and function. The more complex is the structure of an organism and the more numerous are the separate functions within it, the more advanced is its evolution. The same principle is applicable to the inorganic world and to the superorganic, that is, social world. In the latter, this progress means also the progress of consciousness and knowledge, but that is not the decisive factor. This approach to the question of the direction of evolution resulted in some authors (for example, McLennan) in a peculiar notion of age "in structure,"[8] which has nothing in common with chronology.

In the course of deliberation on the subject of social development, this general—and often ambiguous—criterion of progress has, of course, been considerably particularized. Taken as measures of the maturity of societies and cultures were the development of material culture, the division of labor, the social structure, the political organization, and also the development of consciousness. Just as archaeology has distinguished the Stone, Bronze, and Iron Ages, so the students of social evolution have distinguished the great periods of human history using sociological criteria. In some cases the epochs were distinctly separated; the most popular was the division of human history into savagery, barbarism, and civilization, originated by Ferguson and then elaborated in greater detail by Morgan. In others, scales were made to enable the grouping of societies according to their progressiveness, but without cutting any clear lines across history (Maine's scale from status to contract, Morgan's scale from *societas* to *civitas*, or Spencer's scale from militarism to industrialism). The most typical of the evolutionist ideas concerning the direction of the societal evolution were those of the development of the family, from primitive promiscuity to the present monogamy; of the economic system, from primitive communism to the contemporary forms of ownership; of religion, from animism to monotheism; of social bonds, from kinship to territorial community; and of knowledge, from magic to science. These ideas supplemented, rather than excluded, each other.

A common characteristic of evolutionists was the tendency to treat Western European societies (England, in particular) as the most advanced in their evolution and other societies as "retarded," but marching in the same direction. Yet, this opinion did not entail either disrespect or contempt for the lower cultures, because these were regarded as equally natural, though at an earlier stage of evolution. Nevertheless, such division into periods by the evolutionists did have a tinge of evaluation: "Industrialism, democracy, science, and so forth were good in themselves. Consequently the explanations of social institutions they put forward amount, when examined, to little more than hypothetical scales of progress, at one end of which were placed forms of institutions or beliefs as they were in nineteenth-century Europe and America, while at the other end were placed their antitheses."[9]

It is questionable, however, to what extent one should attribute to the classical evolutionists (as it has often been done) the belief that the roads of development of all societies had to be identical in every respect. In other words, it is not at all clear whether the belief that the evolution of all mankind moves in the same direction was identical with the conviction that progress is of a unilinear character. Spencer, for instance, was firmly opposed to such a conception of evolution.

The Global Nature of Change. Since social life is governed not only by the laws of sequence, but also by laws of concurrence, and since society is a certain whole (an "organism"), a change in any sphere is followed by changes in other spheres. The evolutionists often resorted to the following kind of reasoning:

A full explanation of the origin of exogamy [wrote McLennan] requires it to be made out that wherever exogamy prevailed, totemism prevailed; that where totemism prevailed, blood-feuds prevailed; that where blood-feuds prevailed, the religious obligation of vengeance prevailed; that where the religious obligation of vengeance prevailed, female infanticide prevailed; that where female infanticide prevailed, female kinship prevailed. A failure to make good any one of these particulars would be fatal to the entire argument.[10]

Though some evolutionists have not been particularly interested in the development of society or culture as a whole and have studied only its separate fragments, they all were in agreement that coexistence of social institutions or elements of culture belonging to different phases of development was, in the long run, impossible. Thanks to this belief, they could—with bits of archaeological and ethnological data—hypothetically reconstitute the earliest phases of development in a way similar to that in which Cuvier reconstructed the appearance of prehistoric animals on the basis of the preserved fragments of their bones. Thanks to this belief, they could also anticipate the further course of the evolution of society as a whole, even though they knew certain phenomena only in their "embryonic" stage. The belief in the global nature of change has made it possible to use the important notion of "survivals," social and cultural phenomena that were openly incompatible with the prevailing state of society as a whole. The existence of survivals and the uneven development (frequently mentioned by the evolutionist) of both societies and the various spheres of social life could, of course, put into question the infallibility of the laws of concurrence. Nevertheless, such doubts have never violated this fundamental premise, thanks to which early functionalism could refer directly to evolutionism even though it rejected the idea of evolution.

Unevenness of Progress. All human societies are governed by the same laws and are advancing in the same direction. But the pace of evolution varies in a double way. First, the different "sectors of mankind" are advancing at different speeds; second, the pace of the development of a single society is different in the various phases of evolution. The first thesis was of special significance, because on its acceptance depended the possibility of applying the comparative method—that is, in the case of evolutionists, inferring the future of one society from the present of others. As a matter of fact, only the combination of the thesis of universality of evolution with that of the unevenness of its pace has made evolutionism possible.

Continuity and Gradualness of Progress. The evolutionists assumed that social change, just like any other change, is never violent and that the higher stages of evolution are separated from the lower ones by countless intermediate stages. Hence arose the inclination to use scales or—as Morgan did with great partiality—to divide specific periods into subperiods and sub-subperiods. "The conditions of man at the lowest and highest known levels of culture," wrote Taylor, "are separated by a vast interval; but this is so nearly filled by known intermediate stages, that the line of continuity between the lowest savagery and the highest civilization is unbroken at any critical point."[11] In social development, every higher form emerges gradually from the directly preceding form. There is no place for any act of creation.

Immanence of Change. The students of evolutionism in social sciences disagree whether its adherents regarded changeability as an immanent attribute of all societies and any outside element as being a root of evil that complicated the natural and necessary process, or whether they believed that change was a result of mutual interdependence of a society and its environment (and those of other societies). The very essence of the controversy around the immanence of change can be reduced to the question of the role of culture contact and diffusion. Counter to the opinions of their later critics, the evolutionists were fully aware of the important role of diffusion. Moreover, they sometimes even argued that this role is statistically greater than the role of independently made inventions. Tylor, for instance, wrote that civilization is "a plant much oftener propagated than developed."[12] Besides, to argue otherwise would be in glaring contradiction to the facts known by the evolutionists. The point, however, is that their strategy of research has not been orientated toward finding out how a prevailing social need was being satisfied, but had concentrated, instead, on how that particular need has arisen and why it has to be satisfied. Diffusion is a result not of accidental borrowing, but of a given society's reaching the level at which a new element of culture has become indispensable. On this matter the evolutionists accepted Ferguson's opinion that "any singular practice of one country . . . is seldom transferred to another until the way be prepared by the introduction of similar circumstances."[13] If that is so, there always is a great probability that the necessary element would be independently invented, irrespective of culture contacts. The idea of the immanence of change was for the evolutionists a principle of methodology rather than an assertion that every social change has exclusively internal roots and thus, in the final analysis, originates in human nature as a quality vested equally in members of all societies. Evolutionism did not exclude autogenesis in social life, but did not accept it as a universal law of evolution.

THE COMPARATIVE METHOD

The evolutionists called the method that they applied in investigating social phenomena the *comparative method.* They did not, however, deem it necessary to give it any specific characteristics, perhaps assuming that the requirements of that method are evident and need no explanation.

The basic premise of the comparative method was the aforementioned belief that the study of some contemporary phenomena makes it possible to reach conclusions concerning phenomena that took place long ago and thus cannot be observed directly. If all phenomena are governed by invariable laws, then we can infer from the known phenomena about the unknown ones. In his *History of British India,* James Mill wrote that "by conversing with the Hindus of the present day, we, in some measure, converse with the Chaldeans and Babylonians of the time of Cyrus, with the Persians and Egyptians of the time of Alexander."[14]

The thesis that the savages are "our living forefathers" has been repeatedly stated by the evolutionists in a multitude of variants. In this way they have ennobled the studies of primitive societies. These studies proved to be of great significance as a source of knowledge about the past of European societies, the laws of social development, and also human nature, which, being basically homogeneous, could be studied just as well through ethno-

logical data as through any other. The former even have the advantage that
they make it possible to come down to elementary phenomena that could
not be traced otherwise. Evans-Pritchard wrote that for the evolutionists
the interest in primitive societies lay "not so much in themselves as for the
use they could make of them in the hypothetical reconstruction of the
earliest history of mankind."[15]

The evolutionists were, of course, aware of the fact that the primitive
societies accessible to their observations (mostly indirect) were only relatively primitive. Therefore, they sought to form an opinion about the earliest
phases of evolution on the basis of other sources, primarily archaeology,
which in the nineteenth century was passing through its golden age. A
combined analysis of archaeological, ethnological, and historical data was
to have provided the foundation for reconstructing the development of
society and culture from the earliest time to the present and the future, for
if the laws were invariable, there was no reason to stop at the present.

The discovery of societies and cultures at various stages of evolution was
not in itself a proof that they were parts of one and the same sequence. The
transposition of differences in space into differences in time required adequate tools. The general criterion of the complexity of a structure was
inadequate for this purpose, especially because the very thesis about evolution's taking precisely that course had to be empirically proved. The major
difficulty lay not so much in locating given societies in one of the great
stages of evolution, but in establishing the sequence of those numerous
transitional phases. Called to help in overcoming that difficulty was the
so-called theory of survivals, such elements of culture that at present
perform no function (hence the subsequent attacks on the theory by the
functionalists) or else perform a function basically different from that
which they were presumed to perform originally. According to Tylor, these
survivals "are processes, customs, opinions, and so forth which have been
carried out by force of habit into a new state of society different from that
in which they had their original home, and they thus remain as proofs and
examples of an older condition of culture out of which a newer has been
evolved."[16] The evolutionists claimed that these "proofs and examples"
gave the opportunity to draw conclusions about conditions immediately
preceding the existing ones.

This theory was a source of many misapprehensions. However useful it
may have been for carrying out the objectives of investigations, it was
dangerous for the evolutionistic theory, striking at the idea of society as
coherent whole. It was probably not by accident that the theory of survivals
was most fully developed by Tylor, who was the most ardent antiquary of
all evolutionists, and not by Spencer, who was a theoretician of social
systems.

HERBERT SPENCER'S SOCIOLOGY

The most eminent representative of evolutionism was Herbert Spencer (1820-1903), the author of *Social Statics* (1855); *The Study of Sociology* (1873); the monumental *System of Synthetic Philosophy* (ten volumes, 1862-1896), part of which is a three-volume set, *The Principles of Sociology* (1876-1896); and countless other papers that enjoyed tremendous popularity in his time. He was also the initiator of a collective work, *Descriptive Sociology*, whose seventeen volumes appeared between 1873 and 1933. Spencer's role was at least equal to Comte's in the history of sociology.

Nevertheless it would be difficult to insist that Spencer exerted an exceptionally strong influence on the progress of evolutionism in the social sciences. Probably Burrow was right when he wrote that Spencer's works were "the symbol rather than the inspiration of evolutionary social theory."[17] Very strong, however, was Spencer's influence on the intellectual life of the Victorian era. He fascinated his contemporaries by unfolding before them a picture of a world arranged in a perfect order without the assistance of any traditional authorities, a world understood by people who believed only in science. During his lifetime Spencer was an esteemed scholar and, above all, a much-admired teacher of a new generation of intelligentsia, which was shaking off the influence of religion and Toryism.

Vicissitudes of Spencerism. Rarely do we witness such deep contrast between the successes achieved by a thinker during his lifetime and the oblivion, if not infamy, into which he fell after his death. This author, once regarded as one of the greatest thinkers of all times, is today ignored by many historians or, at best, quoted only as a good illustration of some antiquated "isms": individualism, liberalism, organicism. True, the sociologists acknowledge him as one of the founders of their discipline, but all they find in his works (if they ever read them) is a warning about how not to pursue it. But it must be remembered, as Cooley mentioned, that almost everyone who began to study sociology between 1870 and 1890 did so under the influence of Spencer.[18] But later the author of *The Principles of Sociology* was almost entirely forgotten, and only the last decade has witnessed serious attempts at his rehabilitation as a scholar. These resulted partly from the growth of general interest in the classics of sociology and partly from the expansion of neo-evolutionism initiated in social anthropology by L. A. White.

The reasons for Spencer's posthumous defeat were not unlike those of his triumphs. His system was so superbly suited to the needs and the way of thinking of the Victorian era that it just could not outlive it. Its strongest sides soon proved to be its weaknesses, probably the greatest of which was that it sought to provide a uniform explanation of all phenomena, in the belief that science already knows all that can be known (everything else was regarded as a mystery impenetrable by human mind). Another weakness was that on every occasion Spencer called upon detailed data. Spencer's vast erudition eventually turned against him, as his arguments became but museum pieces. His sociological works contained an imposing array of minute information. They were not a product of pure speculation, like the works of many of his predecessors, and thus they were an indubitable step forward. But twenty-five years of systematic ethnological studies were enough to change that collection into useless antiques.

Yet, in spite of all their shortcomings, his sociological works were not without value. They contained many statements that, when first formulated, advanced the development of sociology and referred to social evolution, social institutions and their functions, social structure, and the society as a system. His sociology was not merely a theoretical foundation of the laissez-faire ideology, though their links are, of course, beyond dispute.

Spencer's direct influence on the development of sociology was rather limited, even if it seriously affected Durkheim and early American sociology. Nevertheless, MacRae was right when he wrote that Spencer was an author "whom no one reads, all abuse, and to whom all are indebted."[19] Spencer was the classic of evolutionism and the forerunner of its numerous offshoots and continuations. But he was also the precursor of functionalism, even though only few of its adherents acknowledged that rather inconvenient heritage. It is also beyond doubt that Spencer invented the great part of the sociological vocabulary, introducing or popularizing such terms as *social structure*, *function*, *organization*, and many others that are still used today. All this requires devoting more attention to Spencer than to other evolutionists.

The Idea of Superorganic Evolution. We do not intend to dwell on Spencer's entire philosophical system, which has long been buried, nor are we going to repeat all that has already been said about evolutionism in general. It should be stressed only that Spencer, like all other evolutionists, accepted the basic unity of the world and of the laws that govern it as one of the premises of the theory of social development. Further, he held that the real subject of scientific investigation was not an isolated sphere (even if it were as big as social life), but the world as a developing whole.

Spencer differentiated three phases and three kinds of evolution: inorganic, organic, and superorganic. He did not distinctly separate these phases, claiming that all transitions were effected by imperceptible steps (*Principles of Sociology*, section 1). The laws of the three phases of evolution are identical; this is not to say, however, that phenomena occurring in the higher phase could be reduced to the phenomena of the lower phase. Thus, in analyzing superorganic evolution, we are dealing with a certain category of facts that do not appear in the organic or, even more assuredly, in the inorganic world. Therefore however essential the biological foundation of social processes may be, sociology is concerned with specific facts. This belief was all the stronger since Spencer, unlike other utilitarians, assumed the changeability of human nature—that is, a man as a member of a society is different that a man as a representative of a biological species. Even though some origins of social life appeared in the animal world, Spencer argued that the first human groupings could barely be called societies. Step by step, man became a social animal and thus changed his primary nature. Thus, Spencer raised the question of the origin of society, which to many of his contemporaries already seemed completely anachronistic, and excluded a possibility of any answer that society was consciously made.

How does it come into effect? Spencer found an answer to this question in Malthus: The main factor in the process of the formation of society was the growth of population. Its pressure "compelled the people to enter into the social state, made social organization indispensable and developed social feelings" (*Principles of Sociology*, section 373). It caused man to develop his intelligence, proficiency, and inventiveness, without which he could not adapt himself to new conditions and would perish. The emergence of society is a long, spontaneous process, the most important element of which is the gradual socialization of man.

Social Institutions. From this point of view, the pivotal issue is Spencer's analysis of institutions, which is regarded as an important achievement. Spencer did not define the term *institution*, and he often used it interchangeably with such terms as *relations, organization, government, control, regulation,* and *system of restraints.* Social institutions were for him those factors which stimulated the adaptation of the naturally unsocial man to an equally natural cooperation with other men. This cooperation was becoming a necessity as the earth's population grew. The greater was the number of people, the better organized they had to be, in accordance with the general law that an increase in population invariably causes complication of structure and differentiation of functions.

But Spencer did not confine himself to generalities. He spoke little about socialization and organization in general, but a good deal about various types of institutions that were developing in the course of social evolution. He began his analysis of institutions with the family, that is, with domestic institutions. Subsequently, he proceeded to ceremonial institutions, which he considered to be the most powerful, the earliest, and a constantly regenerating (though waning in modern societies) form of regulation of human relations. Spencer's discussion of ceremonial institutions concerned the category of social facts that in the earlier theories were called "customs." Spencer also paid attention to political institutions, and this was linked with his conviction about the leading role of wars and conflicts in the development of society. The emergence of social organization was, in fact, a transposition of the struggle for survival from the sphere of relations between individuals to that of relations between societies. Spencer even wrote that "social cooperation is initiated by joint defence and offence, and from the cooperation thus initiated, all kinds of cooperation have arisen" (*Principles of Sociology*, section 438). Being a fanatical opponent of wars and strong state organization, Spencer did not extend his feelings of hostility to the past. He believed that only the modern times have created premises for a fundamental change of the organization of society and its function. The emergence of society meant for Spencer the beginnings of the social division of labor and of class structure, resulting from a gradual differentiation of tasks within a society forced into military action. The fourth type of institution discussed by Spencer was the ecclesiastical, considered chiefly as an element preserving collective ideas and feelings and consolidating the society, even though he explained the origin of religion in psychological terms. It seems relevant to note how much attention Spencer devoted to parallelism in the development of political and ecclesiastical institutions and to their mutual ties. The last two types of institutions were professional and industrial. In this case Spencer concentrated on the problem of the development of the division of labor and of corresponding social structures that gradually gain ever greater independence from the political organization and may, in the future, almost completely replace it.

The deliberations on the emergence and development of social institutions were supplemented by the analysis of the simultaneous evolution of language, knowledge, art, ethics, and human intellect. All this served to provide an answer to the question of how the hypothetical primitive man has changed into contemporary man.

Society as an "Organism." Spencer's conception of a social institution is based on four assumptions: (1) No institution has been invented and consciously introduced into being. According to Peel, the essence of Spencer's method was "to explain institutions not in terms of the motives and purposes, either of the actors whose actions compose the institutions, or of the creators of the institutions, but in terms of the functions they fulfill, that is of their effects or consequences for the whole system of which they form a part within the environment to which they are adapted."[20] (2) The understanding and explanation of social institutions and their functioning are impossible without taking into consideration their origin and the transformations that they have undergone—that is, their evolution. (3) All institutions are closely interrelated, making up one social system whose functioning depends on cooperation of its individual parts and subsystems. Between these parts—Spencer repeated Comte—there is a consensus, and the derangement of any one of them may disturb the functioning of the whole. (4) Every social institution performs its definite functions. If it takes upon itself the performance of functions of other institutions, the danger arises of disturbing the balance of the entire system and of its regressing to the state in which these or other functions were not yet separated. Hence is government's interference in economic life, customs, family relations, and religious beliefs and observances so dangerous.

All four assumptions constitute the conception of society as an organism, which is given so much prominence in Spencer's works that some readers have hardly noticed anything beside it. The status of this conception is, however, not very clear. In one context Spencer seems to treat it as an absolutely literal analogy; in another, as a didactically useful trick; and in still another one (as Peel insists[21]), as a formal theory of systems. Doubtless, Spencer was quite aware of the dangers inherent in organismic analogy. In any case, he never claimed—as did certain other organicists—that societies were organisms. But in accordance with his philosophical thesis about the unity of the world, he persistently argued that the "principles of organization" or else the "general law of organization" of biological and social organisms were one and the same. It is also significant (though seldom noticed by sociologists) that he used to compare not only societies to biological organisms, but also biological organisms to societies. His biology contains as many social analogies as there are biological analogies in his sociology.

Spencer's organicist analogy referred to five basic similarities between societies and organisms:

1. Both are characterized by augmentation of mass.
2. Parallel with their growth occur differentiation of parts and complication of the internal structure.
3. In both there occurs differentiation of functions.
4. Their different parts are mutually dependent in both, and the functioning of any of them is impossible without the functioning of the rest.
5. In both, that which is indispensable for life is the performance of definite functions and not the constancy of parts that at the moment are performing these functions; therefore, the whole is more enduring than any one of its components.

After presenting similarities, Spencer proceeded to discuss the differences. This discussion was of considerable importance, because it brought into dispute the whole organist tradition. He tried to accomplish a seemingly impossible task, namely, the combination of organicism—always an extremely anti-individualistic theory—with an extreme individualism that characterized him as a fanatical liberal.

Spencer distinguished four fundamental differences between societies and biological organisms:

1. Society does not have a specific shape or a definite outward form; whatever we could say about its structure would be more or less metaphoric.
2. Society is a discrete whole, dispersed in space; thus cooperation between its parts demands symbolic communication.
3. In a society, differentiation of functions is considerably restricted, because no organ in which feeling and consciousness would concentrate could develop within it. Spencer claimed that every unit of a social organism has an almost equal capacity for happiness and misery and that there could be no social well-being that would not be shared by each member of the society as an individual.
4. The separate parts of the society are not attached to any definite points in space, but have some mobility.

Hence, the most serious limitations of organicist analogy result from the idea that human individuals have autonomy, whereas the component units of any biological organism do not. That idea in particular determined Spencer's originality in the history of organicist thought, in which this autonomy of human individuals has always been questioned in the name of superior reasons of a social whole.

Society and Individuals. Spencer, the organicist, consistently argued that "a society is but a collective name for a number of individuals" (*Principles of Sociology*, section 212). This combination of organicism and nominalism was one of the major theoretical problems of Spencer's sociology. Embodied in sociology was the dilemma that later would lead to the appearance of two opposing orientations—Tarde's and Durkheim's. On the one hand, Spencer advanced the thesis that characteristic features of the whole could be traced to the characteristic traits of its components; but on the other, he stated—and for him this constituted one of the reasons for the very existence of sociology—that "the effects which can be achieved only by the joint actions of many, we may distinguish as social. At first these are obviously due to accumulated individual efforts, but as fast as societies become large and highly organized they acquire such separateness from individual efforts as to give them a character of their own."[22] Spencer persistently tried to resolve this dilemma, though he was probably only partially conscious of it. How, then, did Spencer go about solving this problem?

We must, first of all, notice that his nominalistic theories were far from being theoretically unequivocal. The statement that "the character of the aggregate is determined by character of the units"[23] could mean many different things, as could a statement to the opposite. Sometimes Spencer spoke only of "essential" qualities, but on other occasions he claimed that the characteristics of the units designated only "the limits" within which the characteristics of the whole are contained. There is an evident inconsistency in his sociology: He was tempted by the Bentham-style utilitarian anthropology, which made it possible to explain all social activities by characteristics vested in individuals, and at the same time he refused to accept this anthropology because it simply destroyed his entire theory based on the assumption that human characteristics emerge as a result of the influence of society. In turn, the acceptance of an antinominalist explanation, which was later given by Durkheim, was out of the question in view of both scientific reasons (the concept of a society as a superindividual existence would be tantamount to introducing a metaphysical fiction into philosophy) and ideological reasons (the anti-individualistic consequences of all kinds of sociological realism).

The only solution to the dilemma was to accept the formula of mutual interaction: the characteristics of the whole are derived from those of its units, which, in turn, are molded under the influence of the whole and of the changes that it is undergoing. Spencer wrote:

As soon as a combination of men acquires permanence there begin actions and reactions between the community and each member of it, such that either affects the other in nature. The control exercised by the aggregate over its units tends ever to mould their activities and sentiments and ideas into congruity with social requirements: and these activities, sentiments and ideas, in so far as they are changed by changing circumstances, tend to remould the society into a congruity with themselves. In addition, therefore, to the original nature of the individuals and the original nature of society they form, we have to take into account the induced natures of the two. Eventually, mutual modification becomes a potent cause of the transformation in both (*Principles of Sociology*, section 10).

The Direction of Social Evolution. "Social organisms," Spencer wrote,

like individual organisms, are to be arranged into classes and sub-classes; though not, of course, into classes and sub-classes having anything like the same definiteness or the same constancy. . . . And just as biology discovers certain general traits of development, structure and function, holding throughout all organisms, others holding throughout certain great groups, others throughout certain sub-groups . . . ; so sociology has to recognize truths of social development, structure, and function that are some of them universal, some of them general, some of them special.[24]

It goes without saying that these classes and subclasses could be fitted into the general scheme of evolution and that they are differentiated by such criteria as size of the organism, its internal differentiation, complexity of structure, separation of functions, and so forth.

In dealing with the question of the direction of superorganic evolution, Spencer applied two different approaches: classification and typology.

The former represented an exact equivalent of the biological classifications mentioned in the quotation above; the latter appeared to have been something new and peculiar to sociology. The former divided the known societies according to the degree of their complexity into simple, compound, double-compound, and treble-compound, while the latter presented two extreme types of "pure" societies—the military and the industrial—that all known societies only approximate to a greater and lesser degree. The former spoke of a continuum of societies from the simplest to the most compound ones; the latter introduced two extremes. The former provided, above all, the framework for collecting and arranging empirical data for subsequent generalizations and comparisons (compare his *Descriptive Sociology*); the latter was an instrument with which to interpret this data and to explain the fundamental social structures and processes. The former stated merely that within individual societies there existed subsystems; the latter defined relations between these subsystems. The former was ideologically neutral; the latter was an instrument for evaluating social systems and for propagating Spencer's social ideal.

Nevertheless, there are some links between classification and typology. Societies closest to the industrial type are at the same time generally the most complex; this does not mean, however, that all highly complex societies must necessarily be industrial societies. Spencer did, in fact, speak of the inevitable process of demilitarization of societies (that, after all, is the meaning of social progress). Nevertheless, he also mentioned highly advanced militant societies (Russia and Germany) and observed militarization of England (calling it "rebarbarization") in connection with its imperial expansion. He also admitted the possibility of the emergence of a military society in countries committed to peaceful production (he argued that such would be the effect of carrying socialist Utopia into practice). But, in general, we can assume that Spencer regarded the transformation from militarism to industrialism to represent the same iron law of social evolution as the growing complexity of the structures and functions of social organisms and that he found any deviations from it to be transient and—in a historical perspective—to have minor significance.

Classification of Societies. We shall not pay much attention to Spencer's classification, because it is much less important than typology. Let us, therefore, restrict ourselves to essentials. The point of departure for Spencer —just as it was later for Durkheim—was the concept of a "small and incoherent social aggregate," all units of which directly cooperate with each other, either without any controlling center or with only a nucleus of such a center. In other words, it is a group that is not divided into any subgroups. The larger aggregates differ from the simple societies primarily because its members are parts of simple aggregates that make up a larger aggregate, though preserving their distinctive structure. Each one, therefore, has its own controlling center, which, in turn, is subordinated to a single center controlling the whole society. The double- and treble-compound societies have a correspondingly more complicated structure. Within this fundamental framework, the author of *The Principles of Sociology* considered a number of other variables. The most important was the development of political organization, sedentary life, and division of labor.

Typology of Societies: Militant and Industrial Societies. The main premise of Spencer's typology was the juxtaposition of two kinds of social organization, of which "one arising directly from the pursuit of individual ends, and indirectly conducing to social welfare, develops unconsciously and is non-coercive; the other, arising directly from the pursuit of social ends, and indirectly conducing to individual welfare, develops consciously and is coercive" (*Principles of Sociology*, section 447). We could also speak of the contradictory nature of two kinds of actions that they pursue: the first embraces "growth actions" and the other includes "manufacture actions."

The question to which Spencer's typology provides an answer could be formulated thus: What would a society that was fully engaged in a struggle against other societies look like, in contrast to a society fully committed to ensuring the highest possible level of well-being for its members?

This mental experiment is feasible, because Spencer ascribed to societies consensus, using Comte's meaning of the term; that is, he argued that there was a close homology between the various spheres of social life, in particular between the predominant kind of activity pursued by the members of the society, its organization, the prevailing system of values, and the psychic features. Spencer believed also that one could define the conditions under which the different types of societies are molded.

These conditions—if we ignore the less essential ones (for example, tradition, ethnic composition, culture, and the like)—are, above all, the existence or nonexistence of external conflict. As we have said, such conflict had played a major role in the process of primitive socialization. The accompanying circumstances were isolation, lack of trade exchanges, and so on. On the other hand, a feeling of security and the cessation of conflicts with other societies constituted the principal premise for the development of an industrial society.[25]

An external threat causes all activities to be subordinated to one goal. Every man able to carry arms fights; all others toil to sustain the fighting. The result is the division of society into warrior-masters and worker-slaves, or people dependent on the warriors. The economic foundation of that dependence was landed property—so abhorred by Spencer. It also means— and to this point Spencer devoted the greatest attention—the creation of such an organization of collective life in which the main principle is regimentation, that is, the extension of military organization to the society at large.

Consequently, the military society has only one center, which exercises control over all its members and over all spheres of their activity, not only prohibiting certain actions, but also deciding what should be done. Such a center wields power over religious and lay people, military and civic, political and economic. Each member of the society is assigned a position "in rank, in occupation and in locality"; he remains in a permanent hierarchical relationship of submission to those above him and of superiority to those below him. In other words, everyone has a definite status, which is mostly inherited, but certainly bears no relation to whatever an individual does. Nobody is rewarded for his work, and each person is allocated only the means of subsistence that are indispensable for the proper execution of his tasks and that accord with his status. Social structure is rigid and provides proof against change. The government's control over the individual members of the society, extending also to their thoughts and beliefs, causes a complete uniformity. The development of any voluntary organizations is out of question; if any organizations do exist, they can be only an integral part of the unified social organization and remain under the strict surveillance of the controlling center. The law does not serve to safeguard the interests of individuals, but is concerned primarily "in regulating status, maintaining inequality, enforcing authority" (*Principles of Sociology*, section 535). The source of the law is not the members of the society (contract), but the power and the will of the rulers, presented usually as having a supernatural sanction.

Members of a military society have specific mental features. This element has been rather strongly emphasized by Spencer because he excluded the possibility of a society's existing without an appropriate basis in the thoughts and feelings of individuals. The mental features peculiar to the members of a military society are conformism, obedience, loyalty, acceptance of routine, lack of initiative, dependency on authority, and also belief that actual conditions both are natural and are the only possible conditions.

A society composed of such people is inevitably conservative and hostile to innovations, inflexible and difficult to reorganize, characteristics that to Spencer constituted a most serious deficiency, because he assumed the necessity of constant adaptation to the changing conditions. The societies approximating the military type were ancient Egypt, Sparta, Peru, Russia, and many others, because—in Spencer's opinion—this type has always been prevalent.

The industrial society is basically an exact opposite of the military society. Only for this reason, by the way, is it possible to say anything at all about it, because there have been only few historic examples of it, and even these could be mentioned only with reservations (Athens, the Hanseatic towns, the Netherlands, North America, and England). An industrial society was, above all else, an ideal presented as the ultimate result of evolution.

The main elements of this ideal were as follows: in place of centralized control, decentralization conducive to self-regulation of social processes; in place of positive regulation, only negative regulation; instead of subordination of individuals to the state, the defense of their interest as the supreme duty of the state; in place of uniform beliefs, a heterogeneity of beliefs and opinions; instead of regimentation, a multitude of voluntary associations; in place of status, the rewarding of real merits; instead of isolation, international cooperation; in place of a law sustaining status, a law protecting contracts between individuals; instead of a uniform authority extending over all spheres of life, a variety of controlling centers and the exclusion of the greatest possible number of individual actions from social control; instead of conformism, a feeling of independence and the striving for change; in place of the cult of authority, the respect for the rights of other people; instead of attachment to status and place, mobility; in place of conservatism, a spirit of innovation; instead of external coercion, force of personal convictions; in place of subservience, partnership.

Spencer's typology, like other typologies of that kind, can be analyzed in two different ways (leaving aside its ideological aspect). On the one hand, it is a conception of transition from the old to the new society—transition that from the beginning of the century fascinated many thinkers and focused the interest of Hegel, Saint-Simon, Comte, Guizot, Tocqueville, and a number of other authors. Many elements of that theory were very popular: for instance, the idea of a new industrial civilization coming in place of the old civilization of war and conquest, or that of a new social organization eliminating the old subordinations and restrictions of individuals. Spencer's theory as a conception of a historical process was only one of many. It looks, however, much more interesting if seen as a theory, the essence of which is the isolation of certain models of social order. When viewed in this way, it was surpassed only by Tocqueville's concepts of the aristocratic and democratic order.

It is somewhat paradoxical that those elements of Spencerism which were most loosely linked with his evolutionism proved to be most enduring. What was fruitful in this case was not the evolutionist system as such, but only those of its many aspects that facilitated the analysis of social phenomena at a more general level. It was precisely this kind of analysis—and not the all-embracing vision of evolution or the descriptive sociology, overloaded with facts—that represented the strongest side of Spencer's thought.

Determinants of Social Evolution. The last problem that we intend to raise in examining Spencer's sociology is that of the main determinants of social evolution, especially those which he conceived as specific to the super-organic world. As mentioned earlier, this world was for Spencer a specific reality to which the general laws of evolution were, of course, fully applicable, but which they did not fully explain. The problem that he met first was that of culture (even though he used the term only a few times), as something which is created exclusively by men, but which "philosophically speaking is no less natural than all other products of evolution" (*Principles of Sociology*, section 12).

Seeking to explain the mechanisms of social evolution, Spencer faced two dilemmas that proved unsolvable within the framework of his system. First, there was the dilemma of natural and sociological interpretations; and second, the already mentioned dilemma of nominalistic and realistic interpretations. On the one hand, he tried to explain everything in society by biological and mental characteristics of human individuals who, after all, make up every social aggregate; on the other hand, however, he had to consider phenomena that have emerged only at the superorganic level. On the one hand, he wanted to see society determined in every respect by natural conditions; yet on the other, he observed that society was modifying these conditions by creating on "artificial" environment whose importance increased parallel with evolution. In effect, he argued that whatever was going on within society, its origins were either in nature or in nature modified by human beings or eventually in the human beings themselves. This is a very extensive formula, indeed, one which—just like the formula of interaction of individual and society—contains practically everything. Spencer's theory of determinants of social evolution is, in fact, highly eclectic, even though at first sight it looks like one-sided biologic determinism. In this respect, eclecticism is characteristic for evolutionism in general, and this is why evolutionism became the starting point for the various schools of sociology.

Spencer divided determinants of social evolution into two basic categories: primary and secondary. The former included both "outer" determinants, such as climate, soil, flora, and fauna, and "inner" determinants, such as physical traits of individuals, their level of intellect, character, and the like. These primary determinants do not explain everything; with the progress of civilization an ever greater role is played by secondary determinants, which limit the influence of both the natural environment and all that is typical of the human species. The environment is modified by human activities, and as a result there occurs "accumulation of super-organic products," or that which Tylor will make the object of his "science of culture." This additional environment eventually becomes more important than the primary and consequently the society advances onto a "higher stage" (*Principles of Sociology*, section 12).

The modified environment is the habitat of the changing man. Though the primitive traits of individuals are not completely obliterated, new ones are emerging that are linked with the participation in social life, which, in turn, makes it possible to overcome the egoistic instincts of the presocial man.

True, Spencer did not expound this concept in any greater detail and used it rather sparingly. Fascinated as he was with the problems of primitive (but at the same time elementary and universal) human traits and of the unity of nature and culture, he attached relatively little importance to the study of secondary phenomena, which were peculiar to individual societies. But what seems essential is that he was by no means as one-sided as is generally assumed. His sociology did not become only a blind alley of contemporary naturalism, which was the fact that befell many attempts at more precisely defining the main determinants of social evolution or even at indicating a single decisive determinant.

THE EVOLUTIONIST SOCIAL ANTHROPOLOGY

However numerous were the theses accepted by all evolutionists in social science, they did not represent a uniform school. They differed from each other in many respects, and they were fully aware of the differences. Undoubtedly, the major difference was that between Spencer's philosophical system and the efforts of those scholars who at that time laid the foundations of the science of culture, which grew, thanks to their endeavors, "from nothing to perfection."[26]

Spencer's sociology was also (and it had to be) social anthropology, for it used the same kind of data and embraced all matters with which the anthropologists were concerned. It appears also that the author of *Principles of Sociology* was by no means a second-rate anthropologist, compared to his more specialized contemporaries, and that the historians of this discipline have devoted less attention to him for purely formal reasons rather than on the grounds of merit. It should be remembered, nevertheless, that the just emerging science of culture (a term adopted by Tylor) had no specifically marked limits and that most of its cocreators did not refer to themselves under any common name. None of them (except Morgan, to some degree) pursued field research on the primitive societies, which, by the time of Boas, became a mark of distinction for a social anthropologist. Even if Spencer showed himself to be a dilettante in his statements about culture (though he did not actually use the term), he was certainly no more a dilettante than some of the "social anthropologists." Thus, going from sociology to anthropology, we are not crossing any wall separating the two disciplines: Both were then only at the stage of formation and came largely from the same substance. Evolutionism promoted this lack of separation, as it required compliance with certain general principles and acceptance of certain philosophical assumptions. Besides, in England (of which we are speaking primarily) the borderline between social anthropology and sociology has never been very strongly marked, because the former was, to a large measure, a science of social institutions.

Nevertheless, already during the period of classical evolutionism there appeared a noteworthy divergence of interests, which was to have serious consequence for both the later division of labor in the social sciences and the idea of superorganic evolution. Side by side with Spencer's tendency to pursue an all-embracing philosophy there appeared a distinct trend toward specialization, represented above all by the students of culture. Specialization was the inescapable result of the aspiration to consider more and more facts. This attitude was popular among evolutionists who investigated not social evolution in general, but the evolution of the family, religion, moral ideas, and so on. Such specialization could be avoided, without abandoning the ideal of inductive science, only at the price of limiting investigation to separate societies and cultures in a given place and at a given moment—that is, at the price of renouncing the fundamental assumptions of evolutionism.

Tylor's "Science of Culture." The man who probably exerted the greatest influence on the progress of specialization was Edward B. Tylor, author of *Primitive Culture: Researches into the Development of Mythology, Philosophy, Religion, Art and Custom* (1871). His role stemmed, on the one hand, from his formulation of the program of the science of culture and, on the other, from his detailed studies, in which he proved himself to be the most cautious and critical of all his contemporaries in utilizing the still dubious and incomplete data that were then available to anthropologists. Tylor's program and his research practice were in opposition to Spencer's method of pursuing social science. Whereas the latter studied the development and the functioning of societies as wholes, Tylor broke up this whole into component parts and analyzed only some of them in detail, using the comparative method. Carneiro argued, stretching the point a bit too far, "throughout much of his published work . . . Tylor showed himself to be a good deal more of a cultural historian than an evolutionist."[27]

Tylor claimed that any student of culture should begin with division of culture into elements and classification of these elements. In stipulating such classification, Tylor, like Spencer, referred to the example of biological classifications; his postulate applied, however, not to society, but to the elements of culture. He did not claim that society was an organism, and though he called culture "a complex whole," he defined it in such a way that it was above all a collection of elements.[28] His comparative method served to study the evolution of these elements and not the evolution of culture as a whole.

Tylor's strategy had its strong and its weak sides. Its strength was that it enabled later writers and thinkers to avoid some of the pitfalls of the speculative philosophy of history. Wrote Tylor,

The philosophy of history at large is in fact a subject with which, in the present state of knowledge, even genius aided by wide research seems but hardly able to cope. Yet there are departments of it which, though difficult enough, seem comparatively accessible. If the field of enquiry be narrowed from History as a whole to that branch of it which is here called Culture, the history not of tribes or nations but of the conditions of knowledge, religion, art, custom and the like among them, the task of investigation proves to lie within far more moderate compass. We suffer still from the same kind of difficulties which beset the wider arrangement, but they are much diminished. The evidence is no longer so widely heterogeneous, but may be more simply classified and compared, while the power of getting rid of extraneous matter and treating each issue on its proper set of facts makes close reasoning on the whole more available than in general history.[29]

By concentrating on more particular problems, Tylor was able to reduce the risk of dilettantism; and by separating culture as a whole into homogeneous and comparable elements, he enabled the application of new techniques of investigation—for example, statistics—propagated by Quételet.[30]

Yet, while avoiding some of the pitfalls of evolutionism, Tylor fell into others. The study of the evolution of separate elements of culture led to his manipulating them at will without due consideration "for date in history or for place on the map."[31] If the functionalists later criticized evolutionism for pulling facts out of their context, the criticism was leveled first against Tylor, who built his evolutionary sequences while paying no attention to where the separate fragments came from. As a matter of fact, that was a sin of all evolutionists (it was the original sin of the comparative method), but Spencer (and, even more so, Robertson W. Smith) at least partly compensated for it with his analyses of the internal links of the social system. Tylor, as Harris remarked, "failed to achieve an understanding of socio-cultural phenomena as a functional-causal system."[32]

That is the main reason that in the history of sociology Tylor—irrespective of his attainments as the initiator of the science of culture—is but a figure of minor importance. But the road that Tylor took was not the only road of evolutionist anthropology, as was proved chiefly by the work of Morgan, among the first generation of evolutionists.

Morgan's Sociological Anthropology. Lewis Henry Morgan (1818-1881), the American scholar-amateur whose *Ancient Society* (1877) quickly won worldwide fame, was one of the most interesting representatives of evolutionism. He has never been completely forgotten, largely because his principal ideas were popularized by Friedrich Engels, who also incorporated some of them into historical materialism. Since then the work of Morgan has benefited from the enduring liveliness of Marxism, in which, with the passage of time, it has gained the status of an almost canonical anthropological text. Much has been done for his rehabilitation as a scholar by the neo-evolutionists, especially by Leslie A. White, who even claimed that social science owes as much to Morgan as biology owes to Darwin.[33] But Morgan really was a great scholar even though the subsequent development of social anthropology revealed some glaring faults in his works and his conception of social evolution is full of contradictions and inconsistencies.

Undoubtedly, the major fault was his theory of the development of the family, from the primitive group marriage to the present monogamous family, which was elaborated in excessive detail on the basis of only fragmentary and erroneously interpreted data.

Yet, when we speak of Morgan as an original and outstanding scholar, we have in mind something other than his speculations about the development of the family. Morgan's importance stems, above all, from (1) his recognition of technological and economic development as one of the basic variables in societal evolution; (2) his stress on the relation between political organization and the development of private property and on the evolution of property and its social consequences; and (3) his attempts to determine the correlations between the transformations of different social institutions. Morgan's theoretical efforts were not crowned with complete success, though his attitude seems to have been more fruitful than that represented by Tylor.

Many statements in the first part of *Ancient Society* indicate that the primary aspect of social evolution, according to Morgan, was the changing ways in which people procured their means of subsistence. He wrote: "the great epochs in human progress have been identified, more or less directly, with the enlargement of the sources of subsistence." In his elaborate and detailed division of history into periods of savagery, barbarism, and civilization, Morgan assumed that "the successive arts of subsistence which arose at long intervals will ultimately, from the great influence they must have exercised upon the condition of mankind, afford the most satisfactory bases for these divisions."[34] This discovery of "historical materialism" was in fact the cornerstone of both Morgan's general division of history into periods and the division of the first two "ethnical periods" into subperiods.

Of course, the originality of Morgan's scheme was limited, but it certainly was the most comprehensive attempt, outside of Marxism, to discard the prevailing conception of social evolution (the development of consciousness) from a position other than the biologistic. Morgan's inconsistency—which was at the root of the rather absurd controversy over whether he was a materialist or an idealist—lay in his changing his philosophy of history, and when passing from the development of technology to the development of social institutions, he returned to the idea of "mental principle" as a determinant of social progress. He wrote that "out of a few germs of thought, conceived in the early ages, have been evolved all the principal institutions of mankind. . . . The evolution of these germs of thought has been guided by a natural logic which formed an essential attribute of the brain itself."[35] Consequently, we observe in Morgan's works two independent evolutionary paths running, as White remarked, along two parallel but different lines: One was a series of technical inventions made under the pressure of material needs, while the other was the growth of social institutions emerging gradually from ideas conceived in mankind's earliest history.[36]

Nonetheless, this idealistic side of Morgan's evolutionist doctrine contains interesting ideas. In the first place, these are ideas concerning the development of property and the subsequent development of social stratification and political organization. Part of the same syndrome was, for Morgan, the transformations of the family that were mentioned earlier.

Because of these ideas, the scheme of the evolution of social institutions presented in Morgan's works—especially of the family, private property, and the state—bears only partial resemblance to other such schemata. Morgan laid particular stress on the importance of the transformations of the forms of property in this process. He held, for example, that social evolution is a process of transition from common property (so-called primitive communism) to private property, from equality and brotherhood of the former gens to the division into classes and to competition born of the greed for possession common to members of modern societies. Transformations of the system of property were exerting a far-reaching influence on all aspects of social life and, in particular, on the political organization. Morgan wrote that "government, institutions and laws are simply contrivances for the creation and protection of property."[37] He defined the whole process as the transition from *societas* to *civitas*. Commentators are puzzled by his almost complete omission of ideological problems and especially of religion, which attracted attention of many other evolutionists.

Morgan's vision of social evolution had yet another original attribute. He was probably the only one of the great evolutionists whose works show a nostalgic apologia of the primitive society and of the presumed equality and brotherhood of its members. Morgan believed that the inevitable, though on the whole beneficent, process of evolution has nevertheless destroyed something valuable, and he hoped that the future would bring a rebirth of the values shared by our distant ancestors who knew no private property nor quest for profit. In this respect, his vision of the very origins of human society differed considerably from Spencer's; the latter, we recall, was inclined to accept the struggle of all against all as the starting point of social evolution. But Morgan's romantic nostalgia brought him closer to the socialist thought in general, insofar as it was motivated by a retrospective Utopia. It should be noted, however, that Morgan himself had nothing in common with socialist or communist ideology.

The last question that we should consider when discussing Morgan's ideas is his aspiration to reveal the correlation between the changes that take place in different spheres of social life. Although he actually gave up on linking the growth of social institutions with the progress of technology, he regarded society as an internally related whole and sought to present evolution as "the overall movement from systems based on sex and kinship to those based on territoriality and property."[38] But Morgan's holism was essentially different from Spencer's. Like Tylor, Morgan also represented a strong tendency toward specialization and, counter to appearances, did not study social evolution as such. Morgan's specialization lay in his subject's always being a given society (Iroquois, Aztec, Greek, Roman) and not societies in general. True, he always regarded them as *pars pro toto*. But he was primarily a student of given societies, and, as such, exceeded both Spencer and Taylor.

In this light, it seems accurate to say that just like Tylor initiated American cultural anthropology, so Morgan initiated English social anthropology. In fact, however, we are dealing with two distinct styles of pursuing evolutionistic anthropology (or anthropology in general), which competed with each other in different countries. Thus, they contributed—each in its own way—to specifying the subject and the method of this new discipline, which, under different names, has greatly extended the traditional interest of anthropology.

DETERMINANTS OF SOCIAL EVOLUTION: THE SOURCES
OF THE DISINTEGRATION OF EVOLUTIONISM

As we have already said, the evolutionists were much more concerned with the direction of evolution that with the question of what is it that sets the societies in motion and determines the changes of their culture. If changeability was seen as an attribute of everything that existed, then the question should be how and why everything changes. Nevertheless, the problem of the causes of evolution, its "determinants," must have been present in the evolutionist thoughts in connection with two important questions: (1) how to interpret the great similarities between societies and cultures whose influence on each other is either totally impossible or not very likely; and (2) how to explain the differences in the pace of evolution of different societies and cultures, as well as their deviations from the general pattern. The evolutionists found it particularly difficult to explain why some societies advanced to the stage of civilization while others remained even to that day at the stage of savagery.

They had no doubts that they must exclude all theological and voluntarist interpretations, with which they argued frequently and not ineffectually for the further development of social sciences. But they were not agreed on what kind of interpretation would most comprehensively meet the postulates of science. As a rule they emphasized, either explicitly or implicitly, the multitude of causes influencing social life. On that score they were in accord with John Stuart Mill, who wrote in his *System of Logic* that "the circumstances . . . which influence the condition and progress of society are innumerable, and perpetually changing; and though they all change in obedience to causes and therefore to laws, the multitude of the causes is so great as to defy our limited powers of calculation."[39] One effect of this approach was overt eclecticism, occasionally leading to the exposition on two successive pages of diametrically opposed theses.

The matter would not in itself be worthy of greater attention if it were not for the fact that these difficulties in determining the causes of evolution were largely responsible for the disintegration of classical evolutionism in the social sciences and for the emergence of a number of sociological schools, each of which concentrated on a different aspect of social evolution.

As a matter of fact, there is no sphere of social life that some evolutionist would not, in some context, single out as the basis of the changes in all other spheres. Many referred also to various extrasocial determinants of social processes. The most we can say about individual authors is that they gave preference to one or another interpretation. Such interpretations could be divided into four main groups.

Determinants of Evolution: Man. In the efforts to interpret social evolution, its determinants were often frequently sought in specific qualities of human individuals—what Spencer called "inner" and "primitive" determinants of social evolution. Favoring this line of research was undoubtedly the essentially nominalistic orientation of evolutionism as well as the often manifested tendency to eliminate anything metaphysical from science. Consequently, social evolution was attributed to the existence in man of some "inherent tendency" (Taylor), "instinct of progress" (Comte), or "germs of thought" (Morgan). And though such hypotheses were opposed by Darwin and Spencer, they were never totally abandoned. Even if they did not provide the answer to the question about the "ultimate" cause of evolution, they were extensively used with the view to interpreting the universality of the evolutionary process. It should be accepted that there is, among men, a basic psychical similarity or—as Brinton wrote—"the one and unvarying psychical nature of man."[40]

Acknowledging human nature as the primary determinant of social evolution and did not contribute to solving the problem of differences between societies that develop at an uneven pace, though subjected to the of solutions: intellectualist and instinctivist. The former concentrated on the similarity of ideas formed by men; the latter, on the similarity of passions that guided them. The two diametrically opposed views on the matter were represented by Comte and Spencer. But is seems that the theory that attributed particular importance to ideas and the man's ability to accumulate knowledge predominated. That latter element played a special role, and some even professed what could be called sociological Lamarckism, which held that the abilities developed by men were hereditary.

All these views and opinions served first to explain the unity of social evolution and did not contribute to solving the problem of differences between societies that develop at an uneven pace, though subjected to the same general laws. The only explanation for these differences, outside of "external" and "secondary" factors of social evolution, could have been the hypothesis of inequality of human races, which was most extensively expounded by Arthur Comte Gobineau (1816-1882) in his *Essai sur l'inégalité des races humaines* (1853-1855). It seems that to include Gobineau among evolutionists would not be quite correct, even though in some respects the basic questions of his social philosophy considerably resembled the evolutionist approach. He differed from the evolutionists in his conviction that humanity was falling into decadence and also in his one-sided emphasis on the differences between societies and cultures. At the same time, however, we find strikingly similar arguments also among the evolutionists.

Thus, for example, Morgan spoke about "inferior mental capabilities" of North American Indians as compared with Aryans, thus reiterating Gobineau's thesis. (It is hard to say whether he did so consciously.) Spencer differentiated "superior" and "inferior" races, while Frazer maintained that "different races [are] differently endowed in respect of intelligence, courage, industry and so forth."[41] The evolutionists had little use for racist ideas and had many reservations about them, yet this inclination should not be ignored. The term *race* was then itself ambiguous and could mean both anthropological as well as ethnic race (Gobineau himself was not very explicit on that score). In the first case we are dealing with a false interpretation of cultural differences, fraught with dangerous social implications; in the second, with a purely tautological interpretation. One way or another, tracing a distinct borderline between some ideas of the evolutionists and the ideas of the so-called racial-anthropological trend in sociology may prove difficult.

Determinants of Evolution: Nature. Although the evolutionists attached great importance to the qualities of individuals as determinants of evolution, they by no means assumed that actualization of the potentialities of human nature could take place irrespective of circumstances or, as Spencer called them, "external" determinants. People have always lived in a given environment, and its influence on the social organism—as well as on individual organisms—is one of the basic premises of the theory of evolution. The writers whom we are discussing were most often concerned with relationships of mutual interdependence of men and circumstances, though occasionally, especially in reference to the earlier phases of evolution, they were inclined toward one-sided environmental determinism; social life was thus determined by natural conditions in which people have found themselves. In effect, a whole new sociological discipline emerged, making its primary objective the discovery of the most important natural determinant of social evolution. It was but another blind alley into which the evolutionists ventured in the quest to determine the laws of social life.

Determinants of Evolution: Society and Culture. In general, the evolutionists were aware of the inherent vulnerability of the two interpretations. They spuriously started from the assumption that the characteristic traits of individuals and of the environment were permanent, while ignoring the fact that both were undergoing profound changes in the course of their evolution and also that a new, artificial environment was being created, which Tylor named culture. Counter to widespread opinions, the evolutionists were genuinely concerned with this problem, which can be found in Spencer's notion of superorganic evolution and in Morgan's detailed dissertations. Of course, we are not dealing with any coherent doctrine, but the fact is that an intensive search was made with a view to discovering the determinants of social development that that development itself creates. Mentioned first should be the hypothesis of the demographic determinant, that is, the influence of the number and density of population on the forms of social life. According to Spencer, this determinant provides the prime force that starts the process of social evolution. But the demographic determinant was also used in order to give the causal explanation of its subsequent stages, and the French theoretician Adolphe Coste (1842-1901) presented a comprehensive theory interpreting the whole social evolution in categories of demographic determinism as a sequence of settlement, town, metropolis, state capital, and the capital city of a federation.

Another hypothesis concerned the specific role that the methods of procuring means of subsistence have played in social evolution. Morgan was certainly not the only advocate of this theory, which was extensively expounded in numerous deliberations on, for instance, the influence of agriculture on the organization of social life and the importance of new inventions for social evolution. Such ideas are usually described as technological determinism. In postevolutionist sociology it had such outstanding exponents as Thorstein Veblen (1857-1929) and William F. Ogburn (1886-1959), author of the concept—so popular in the United States—of "cultural lag," which assumed absolute primacy of technological development, to which all other spheres subsequently adapted themselves.

Still another hypothesis—though somewhat akin to technological determinism—spoke of the overwhelming influence exerted on social life by economic relationships. Some elements of such economic determinism appeared in Morgan's deliberations on the institution of property. Many similar elements can be found in Spencer's conceptions, particularly in the parts pertaining to the growth of the industrial society. Therein lies the way to confront evolutionists with Marxists, at least if historical materialism is given the economic interpretation popular at the turn of the century. Very characteristic from this point of view are the writings of the Italian economist Achilles Loria (1857-1943), who tried to explain the evolution not only of laws, but also of morality and poetry, by economic transformations. Similar attempts to cross the border between the evolutionist economic determinism and historical materialism can also be observed in the works of some Marxists, especially those of Karl Kautsky.

Yet another hypothesis suggested by the evolutionists (mainly Spencer and W. G. Sumner) brought some of their pronouncements closer to sociology, which sought to find an explanation of social transformations in the arrangement of social relations. Evolutionists reflected on the subject of social institutions, folkways, and customs, which determine human behavior and the further course of a given society's evolution.

Determinants of Evolution: Conflict and Struggle. We distinguish the fourth group of evolutionist interpretations of social growth according to somewhat different principles than the former three, because it could coexist (at least theoretically) with practically any one of the competing determinants. It is distinguished not so much by its preference for one or another of them, as by the conviction that in every case the driving force of social evolution is conflict and struggle. From such a theoretical perspective, the origin of conflict (though a subject of considerable interest) seemed much less relevant than the conflict itself. The course of social evolution, it was claimed, is such and no other because it constitutes a precise balance of opposing forces. Why these forces are in opposition to each other is a related, but different, problem, and an answer to the question concerning the causes of evolution did not have to provide a solution for it.

The most appropriate term for this group of interpretations of social evolution is social Darwinism, a name that we preferred to avoid so far. This does not imply, however, that these interpretations necessarily conformed with the Darwinian theory. It means only that the basic tenets of this theory (the struggle for survival, natural selection, and so forth) were extensively applied in them.

In classical evolutionism this kind of interpretation of social growth was not of primary importance, but it can be found in Spencer, who wrote about the role of conflict in the process of the emergence of societies and pointed to war and conquest as a source of domination of the militant social type in the hitherto history. The advancement of such interpretations to a position of prominence resulted in the emergence of the original theory of conflict which was, to some extent, opposed to classical evolutionism and of which Ludwig Gumplowicz (1838-1909) was the most outstanding advocate.

SUMMARY OF EVOLUTIONIST SOCIOLOGY

Evolutionism was a crossroads at which the social thought of the latter half of the nineteenth century arrived. Its founders formulated a comprehensive program of a social science, but its implementation led inevitably to the disintegration of evolutionism. Classical evolutionism contained so many threads that its disentanglement into many separate trends was unavoidable. These numerous ramifications of evolutionist sociology, of which we mentioned only some, did not have the same importance or the same cognitive value.

In the social sciences, evolutionism was—and still is—a subject that evokes a great variety of opinions, ranging from outright enthusiasm to absolute negation. The latter prevailed especially during the interwar period and the immediate postwar years, when the orientation initiated by Franz Boas dominated American anthropology and Malinowski's and Radcliffe-Brown's functionalism was gaining predominance in Europe, though their opposition to evolutionism was not quite so total. But even earlier, the scientific reputation of the evolutionists was impaired by the diffusionists—chiefly German—who, like Boas, focused their attention on investigating ethnological details, abandoning the ambition to arrive at any synthesis. Evolutionism was criticized still more profoundly in sociology, not only because a different research strategy was set in opposition to it (by Durkheim, for one), but also because the entire scientific concept that lay at its foundation was put under question by the criticism of naturalism in social science. From the point of view of humanistic sociology, evolutionism not only gave false answers, but also posed wrong questions. At the same time, the scope of interests and the investigation techniques used in most sociological studies (so-called empirical sociology) were undergoing such far-reaching changes that many opinions held by the evolutionists proved simply to be unrelated to the subject. An average sociologist did not even denounce the basic premises of evolutionism; he just dismissed them altogether, viewing them as relics of outdated social philosophy. A rather paradoxical situation arose in the Marxist thought: Although carefully preserving part of the evolutionist heritage, it quite often dissociated itself from evolutionism because of its antisocialist political options and its concept of social progress without revolution.

As we have already mentioned, the last few decades have witnessed a basic change of attitudes toward evolutionism among both sociologists and social anthropologists. More and more frequently there prevails the opinion that the main mistake of the evolutionists was not so much their selection of questions and the direction in which they sought the answers, but their use of unreliable material and speculations about the inevitability of one or another course of evolution. Even if the range of evolutionism is still very limited, especially in sociology, at least the climate has become propitious for a more balanced and just evaluation of classical evolutionism.

While making such an assessment, however, one should realize how vast was the influence of evolutionism on the mode of thinking about social processes, even at the time when it was most criticized or rejected. Some elements of the evolutionist comparative method were invariably present in everyday thinking, as well as in the social sciences, in the form of such notions as a more or a less developed or advanced country or a more or less modern society. In the final analysis, all attempts to escape from this pattern of reasoning (for example, by otherwise correctly avoiding the term *primitive society*) proved unsuccessful, unless a sociologist locked himself in a laboratory, a small group, or his study, where he could peacefully meditate on some abstract models of a social system. Donald G. MacRae wrote that "so long as the problem of social change remains—and must remain—central to the understanding of social life, so long will the question whether certain kinds of change can be called evolution or explained by evolutionary concepts remain."[42]

Quite extensively accepted were certain categories introduced by the evolutionists, not only the notions of structure and function, but also the concept of social system, which in Radcliffe-Brown's works preserved visible links to the concept of organism. The theory of needs elaborated by Malinowski, who turned to social anthropology under the influence of the evolutionist Frazer, seems to have been taken in its entirety from evolutionism. Paradoxical as it may sound, one could say that the whole early functionalism was but evolutionism without the idea of evolution—that is, it preserved evolutionist sociology while repudiating the philosophy of history and the related methods of research.

Considering the detailed studies of evolutionists (and these occupied a very important place in classical evolutionism), we must reach the inevitable conclusion about the enduring nature of the evolutionistic heritage. Relevant is the following passage from Evans-Pritchard:

Thus to Morgan we owe the inception of the comparative study of kinship systems which has since become so important a part of anthropological research. McLennan not only brought together a great mass of evidence to show how common is the rite of marriage by capture in the wedding ceremonies of the simpler societies, but he was also the first to show that exogamy (he invented the word) and totemism are widespread features of primitive societies and thereby to give us two of our most important concepts; and to him and to Bachofen is due the credit of being the first to draw attention, against the overwhelming bias in favour of patriarchal origins of the family at that time, to the existence of matrilineal societies in all parts of the world, and of recognizing their great sociological importance. Tylor, among many other achievements, showed the universality of animistic beliefs and established the term animism in our vocabulary. Frazer likewise showed the universality of magical beliefs and that their logical structure can be reduced by analysis to two elementary types, homeopathic magic and contagious magic; and he brought together a great number of examples of divine kingship and other institutions and customs, and by so doing brought them into relief as widespread social and cultural patterns. Moreover, their research was much more critical than that of their predecessors.[43]

Finally, it should be noted that under the banner of evolutionism both sociology and social anthropology began to acquire the status of sciences like all others. This status may later have been frequently questioned, and even today, with regard to sociology, it gives rise to serious doubts; nevertheless, the evolutionists were the first to popularize—though not to invent —the ideal of social sciences as those which discover objective regularities.

We can thus state that this opinion has outlived sociological naturalism. Once demarcated, the line between science and art has never been obliterated, even thought the views on this science and on the possibilities of its practical application have changed with time. Initiated also during the evolutionist period was the institutionalization of sociology and social anthropology.

NOTES

1. Cf. Robert A. Nisbet, *Social Change and History: Aspects of the Western Theory of Development* (New York: Oxford University Press, 1969), chaps. 4-6.

2. See Ronald Fletcher, *The Making of Sociology: Beginnings and Foundations* (London: Nelson, 1972), 1:251-52.

3. See J. D. Y. Peel, *Herbert Spencer: The Evolution of a Sociologist* (London: Heinemann, 1971), p. 158-59. Cf. Kenneth E. Bock, *The Acceptance of Histories: Toward a Perspective for Social Sciences*, University of California Publications in Sociology and Social Institutions, vol. 3, no. 1 (Berkeley: University of California, 1956).

4. E. B. Tylor, *Primitive Culture* (London: J. Murray, 1871), 1:2.

5. E. E. Evans-Pritchard, *Social Anthropology* (London: RKP, 1951), p. 43.

6. Cf. Robert L. Carneiro, "Classical Evolution," in Raoul Naroll and Frada Naroll, eds., *Main Currents in Cultural Anthropology* (Englewood Cliffs, N.J.: Prentice-Hall, 1973), pp. 70-71, 88-90.

7. H. Spencer, *First Principles* (London: Williams and Norgate, 1863), p. 216.

8. Cf. I. W. Burrow, *Evolution and Society* (Cambridge: Cambridge University Press, 1970), pp. 12-13.

9. Evans-Pritchard, *Social Anthropology*, p. 41.

10. J. F. McLennan, *Studies in Ancient History*, second series (London: Macmillan, 1896), p. 28.

11. Carneiro, "Classical Evolution," p. 73.

12. See Marvin Harris, *The Rise of Anthropological Theory* (New York: Crowell, 1968), pp. 173-79.

13. Adam Ferguson, *An Essay on the History of Civil Society* (Edinburgh: Edinburgh University Press, 1956), p. 169.

14. See Burrow, *Evolution and Society*, p. 47.

15. Evans-Pritchard, *Social Anthropology*, p. 37.

16. Tylor, *Primitive Culture*, 1:14-15.

17. Burrow, *Evolution and Society*, p. 182.

18. C. H. Cooley, "Reflections upon the Sociology of Herbert Spencer," in *Sociological Theory and Social Research* (New York: Holt, 1930).

19. Donald G. MacRae, *Ideology and Society: Papers in Sociology and Politics* (London: Heinemann, 1961), p. 33.

20. Peel, *Herbert Spencer*, p. 183.

21. Ibid., pp. 179-80.

22. Quoted in Fletcher, *Making of Sociology*, 1:291.

23. Herbert Spencer, *The Study of Sociology* (London: C. Kegan Paul, 1880), p. 48.

24. Ibid., pp. 58-59.

25. Our discussion of military and industrial societies is based mostly on Spencer's *Principles of Sociology*, especially pt. 2, pars. 257-66; pt. 5, pars. 434-577; and pt. 8.

26. S. Tax, "From Lafiteau to Radcliffe-Brown: A Short History of the Study of Social Organization," in Fred Eggan, ed., *Social Anthropology of North American Tribes* (Chicago: University of Chicago Press, 1955), p. 466.

27. Carneiro, "Classical Evolution," p. 61.

28. "Culture or civilisation is that complex whole which includes knowledge, belief, art, morals, law, custom, and any other capabilities and habits acquired by man as a member of society." Tylor, *Primitive Culture*, 1:1.

29. Ibid., pp. 5-6.

30. Ibid., p. 10.

31. Ibid., p. 6.

32. Harris, *Rise of Anthropological Theory*, p. 204.

33. Leslie A. White, "L. H. Morgan: Pioneer in the History of Social Evolution," in Harry Elmer Barnes, ed., *An Introduction to the History of Sociology* (Chicago: University of Chicago Press, 1948), p. 138.

34. L. H. Morgan, *Ancient Society* (New York: Holt, 1877), pp. 19, 9.

35. Ibid., pp. 59-60.

36. White, "L. H. Morgan," p. 141.

37. See ibid., p. 153.

38. Harris, *Rise of Anthropological Theory*, p. 182.

39. John Stuart Mill, *A System of Logic, Ratiocinative and Inductive*, 6th ed. (London: Longmans, Green, 1856), book 6, chap. 6, par. 2.

40. Carneiro, "Classical Evolution," p. 89.

41. See Harris, *Rise of Anthropological Theory*, chap. 4.

42. MacRae, *Ideology and Society*, p. 137.

43. Evans-Pritchard, *Social Anthropology*, pp. 32-33.

9

PSYCHOLOGISM: PSYCHOSOCIOLOGY AND THE RISE OF SOCIAL PSYCHOLOGY

Among the still positivist trends that emerged from evolutionism as its partial or total denial, psychologism and sociologism deserve special attention. Both had had a long prehistory, their nuclei being noticeable in evolutionist sociology and in still earlier social thought. However, the opposition between the two was fully evident as long as attention was focused on regularities in social evolution.

THE CONCEPT OF PSYCHOLOGISM

By singling out psychologism among the various sociological trends and dedicating a separate chapter to it, we do not in the least intend to suggest that any uniformity of views prevailed. The term *psychologism*, in fact, includes a great variety of views, many of which were formulated independently of one another and based on the theoretical conceptions in which psychology abounded at the time of its own scientific revolution; in some cases, too, such views were formulated *ad hoc* to explain certain facts in human behavior. The term itself was coined *ex post facto* as the epithet denoting fascination with psychology as the fundamental science of man, a fascination felt not only in sociology, but also in philosophy, historiography, literary theory, linguistics, and the like. The term *psychologism* is used in this book to denote that mode of thinking which "starts with the psychical characteristics of an individual, takes them as variables, and tries to interpret social phenomena as their derivative or manifestation."[1]

Understood in this way, psychologism has a long prehistory. It originates with a common-sense belief: Since it is human individuals who participate in social processes, the explanation of those processes is possible only if and when we come to know the permanent nature of those individuals. However, psychology was not in a position to give social thinkers any significant assistance, so they were forced to avail themselves of current psychological experience or to invent substitutes for scientific psychology (as was done by Spencer on a scale that was typical of him). Quite understandably, this trend must have intensified with advances in scientific psychology.

It is, however, worthwhile to record the interesting phenomenon of *psychological evolutionism*, represented by Benjamin Kidd (1858-1919), Lester F. Ward (1841-1915), nicknamed the American Aristotle, and others. Without essentially modifying the evolutionist paradigm, they moved the focus of their interest from the evolution of the social organism as such to the evolution of its spiritual aspects, which, it was believed, make it differ from animal organisms. A similar trend can be found in the work of the Russian advocates of the subjective method in sociology, namely N. M. Mikhailovsky (1843-1904) and Pyotr L. Lavrov-Mirtov (1823-1900). F. N. House may be right in claiming that there is a *general* tendency to replace physical and biological explanations by psychological ones.[2] That tendency was seen in all its clarity in the 1890s, when a group of authors claimed, as Small did, that "nothing is social which is not psychical."[3] Those authors suggested not psychological corrections to evolutionistic sociology, but a rival theory in form of psychosociology.

That tendency was supported by the scientific evolution in psychology, which consisted of (1) the rise, owing to Wilhelm Wundt (1832-1920) and other scholars, of experimental psychology, which promised to end "metaphysical" speculations on the human soul and/or human nature as a result of methodical observation of real psychical processes and which was expected to acquire the rigor of observations carried out in natural science; (2) the treatment of psychical facts as the only reality that is immediately given to the researcher and the establishment of the experiment as a basic concept in psychology, which was expected to make that science the way of acquiring knowledge of all humanistic facts; (3) the approach to man as "a subject endowed with will and thought"[4] and not only with the ability to perceive and to associate impressions—an approach that opposed the deeply rooted tradition of English empiricism; and (4) the replacement of the psychology of the conscious by the psychology of the unconscious. These changes in approach were not equally marked in all founders of the new psychology, but they were visible enough to make that discipline an object of increased interest. Psychologism in the social sciences would have been unthinkable without that peculiar atmosphere.

Yet, it does not seem proper to class all those theorists who reacted strongly to the possibilities revealed by the advances in psychology as psychologists in sociology or as psychosociologists. It is necessary to restrict the meaning of the term *psychologism* so that it denotes a clearly defined type of sociological theory. We want to make a distinction between, on the one hand, psychologism as an endeavor to explain all social problems by reference to psychological variables and, on the other, all those standpoints according to which sociology must avail itself of some kind of psychology, but cannot rest satisfied with psychological explanation. Thus, for instance, Max Weber's interest in the problems of motivation does not make him a representative of psychologism. Further, psychologism as we understand it has had five other peculiarities.

Positivism. The psychological trends remained within the positivistic philosophy of science. Reducing humanistic facts to psychological ones did not by itself mean that they are qualitatively different from the facts investigated by the natural sciences. Only a few authors (Wundt) would take up the general issue of the distinctive nature of the "logic of the humanities" (*Logik der Geisteswissenschaften*) and try to draw methodological conclusions from the statement that man, as a subject endowed with will and the ability to think, is an important factor to be considered.

Retreat from Evolutionism. It could not be said that all psychologists were antievolutionists, for at least some of them continued the study of traditional evolutionistic problems. In most cases we find a different emphasis rather than a radical change of interests. Nevertheless, it was psychologism that started to destroy evolutionism as a way of thinking within sociology, and it did that by assuming that society, as an aggregate of psychical individuals, does not undergo any unidirectional changes and should be investigated primarily from the point of view of what is recurrent and permanent in it. The laws discovered by the psychologists pertained to the behavior of human individuals, and it was only in a secondary manner that they could serve to explain evolutionary processes.

Sociological Nominalism. Psychologism was an individualistic and nominalistic trend. Hence, the term is not used here to cover all forms of interest in the psyche in all the senses of that word (such as collective psyche, "social soul," *Volksgeist*, and so on); instead, it means only interest in the psychical characteristics of individuals that had to be understood if the study of society was to be undertaken. The conceptions that referred to a collective psyche as an irreducible whole (traditionally connected with the various forms of organicism) are interpreted here as *sociologistic*.

Noninteractionism. Only those conceptions in sociology that explain social facts by reference to psychical characteristics of human individuals without, however, taking up the issue of their interaction—that is, the impact of social relations on the emergence and modification of such characteristics—are considered here as psychologistic. According to representatives of psychologism, social relations merely determine the way in which psychical processes manifest themselves; they can also suppress the natural dispositions of individuals, but they are in no case to be seen as their origin. In other words, in the interpretation adopted here, psychologism is not only antisociologism, but noninteractionism as well. This is why we do not class Cooley, Thomas, and Mead as representatives of psychologism; according to those scholars, essential psychical characteristics of individuals develop in social life.

Anti-intellectualism. The tendency to concentrate attention on unconscious psychical processes also seems characteristic of psychologism in sociology. It was only Wundt who continued to treat psychology as the science of the conscious. For the others, it was emotions, instincts, the unconscious, suggestion, hypnosis, libido, psychical residues *(residua)*, and the like that became the basic psychological concepts. This was due both to changes within psychology itself and to the change in the intellectual atmosphere in Europe at the end of the nineteenth century. It was marked by the breakdown of the faith in a relatively harmonious social progress that is controlled by human reason, which comes to comprehend the direction of that progress and the laws governing it.

FOLK PSYCHOLOGY

Next to psychological evolutionism, the first symptom of growing interest in psychosociological problems was the emergence in Germany of so-called folk psychology *(Völkerpsychologie)*, first represented by Moritz Lazarus (1824-1903) and Heymann Steinthal (1823-1899), founders of the renowned *Zeitschrift für Völkerpsychologie und Sprachwissenschaft* (1860-1890), "Their aim," Tönnies wrote, "was to establish, besides individual psychology, a psychology of socialized man or of human society."[5] The idea itself was certainly not new. On the one hand, it referred to the tradition of Herder and romanticism, still vivid in Germany at that time, and, on the other, it took up the problem of *Elementargedanken* and *Völkergedanken*, that is, those features of human mentality which are species-conditioned and culture-conditioned, respectively, a problem of concern to many evolutionists. The individual is a member of the human species and, as such, has features that are common to all other human beings. But he is also a member of a certain people *(Volk)* and, as such, has features specific to only one group within the species. Thus, a distinction between psychic characteristics of organic origin and those which are the product of a given culture was assumed. This accordingly meant the assumption that acquiring the knowledge of man requires cooperation of two different disciplines: psychology as the science of the individual man, and the psychology of peoples, which avails itself of ethnological data. But *Völkerpsychologie* was not just a study of cultures: The knowledge of a given culture was, rather, a path to acquiring the knowledge of the human psyche, which was in turn to help grasp the "spirit of the whole" *(Allgeist)*, specific to every culture. Note, however, that *Allgeist* was interpreted by the advocates of *Völkerpsychologie* nominalistically, as the name of the psychical characteristics specific to the members of a culture group.

The ideas of the folk psychology was systematized and developed by Wilhelm Wundt in his monumental *Völkerpsychologie* (1900-1909); "Its problem," he wrote, "relates to those mental products which are created by a community of human life and are, therefore, inexplicable in terms merely of individual consciousness, since they presuppose the reciprocal action of many. This will be for us the criterion of that which belongs to the consideration of folk psychology."[6]

In practice, folk psychology (which was the earliest manifestation of social psychology, the science that investigates those features of human individuals which they develop under the influence of group life) failed to keep its promise; it was mainly concerned with accumulating descriptive data or using them, as did Wundt himself, to construct one more hypothetical history of mankind in the manner of psychological evolutionism. *Völkerpsychologie* did help to popularize psychology in the social sciences, but it was not the trend that gave rise to psychologism as a theoretical approach in sociology.

CROWD PSYCHOLOGY AND THE PSYCHOLOGY OF THE PUBLIC

The second endeavor to focus sociological research on psychological issues was crowd psychology, exceptionally fashionable at one time. Apparently invented by the Italian criminologist Scipio Sighele (1868-1913), it was popularized by Gustave Le Bon (1841-1931), the French archaeologist, anthropologist, physician, traveler, and inventor, whose book *Psychologie des foules* (1895) was one of the greatest sociological best-sellers. At the turn of the nineteenth century, many authors were concerned with the problems of crowds, but a distinction must be made between the study of those problems within a more comprehensive sociological theory (Tarde, Durkheim, and Park) and the specific psychosociological theory according to which observation of crowds' behavior can explain all social facts. Le Bon was a representative of just such a theory.

Crowd psychology started from common-sense observations of differences between the ordinary behavior of an individual and his behavior when he is among other individuals and, as it were, succumbs to their hypnotic influence and becomes able to commit acts that he would never commit individually. Crowd psychologists thus took up, at a new level, the age-old problem of the origin of society and formulated it as the problem of the observable transformation of the individual under the impact of his contact with other individuals. The very manner of formulation was affected by a specific political viewpoint, antiliberal and antidemocratic, which can best be seen in the writings of Le Bon himself.

He claimed that "the era of crowds" was approaching, and that "the philosophy of number seems the only philosophy of history."[7] Behind him was the experience of the French Revolution, which he described in *La Révolution française et la psychologie des révolutions* (1912); ahead of him was the horrors of a new revolution, which Le Bon depicted in *Psychologie du socialisme* (1898). There was no room left for illusions: In the light of crowd psychology, "it can be seen how slight is the action upon [crowds] of laws and institutions, how powerless they are to hold any opinions other than those which are imposed upon them, and that it is not with rules based on theories of pure equity that they are to be led, but by seeking what produces an impression on them, and what seduces them."[8]

This diagnosis of contemporaneous society, opposing the optimistic forecasts by Comte, Mill, and Spencer, lay at the foundation of crowd psychology and largely determined it. Crowd psychology was a sociology of conservatives who had already lost all hope.

Le Bon was not concerned with crowds in the ordinary sense of the word, but with what he called psychological crowds; for example, gatherings of people who, subject to collective suggestion, develop a "soul" *sui generis*. The term *crowd* applies to any collectivity whose unity consists of an irrational readiness to act that is due to the individuals' being lost in the mass of others and having abandoned all self-control. The emergence of such a unity is thus identical with the suppression of individual consciousness. As Freud pertinently presented Le Bon's ideas, "the mental superstructure, the development of which in individuals shows such dissimilarities, is removed, and . . . the unconscious foundations, which are similar in everyone, stand exposed to view."[9] For Le Bon, a psychological crowd is both an accidental assemblage of people in the street and the staff of a factory, a class, a nation, a political party, or a parliamentary club.

Crowd psychology thus becomes the all-embracing theory of social life, politics, power, social change, and revolution. According to Le Bon, really important historical events took place in an atmosphere of uncontrolled human emotions, and it is *le fond héréditaire des sentiments d'une race* that is the most durable determinant in social life.

Le Bon realized that his concept of the crowd was extremely broad and was often criticized on that account; therefore, he introduced a fairly detailed classification of crowds. This, however, did not eliminate the basic obscurities connected with the concept of *crowd* (or *mass*), and hence later authors would use that term with caution and in a much narrower sense.

The first step in that direction was made by Gabriel Tarde (1843-1904), who in his book *L' Opinion et la foule* (1901) suggested that the term *crowd* be used only in the case of physical proximity of a number of human individuals. More important still, he postulated a psychology *of the public*, which he believed to be a kind of community much more characteristic of recent times than a crowd is. In his opinion, the public is marked by spatial dispersion combined with spiritual proximity, which develops as the means of exchange of opinions improve. When writing about "suggestion at a distance," Tarde formulated many opinions that bring him close to the American social pragmatists who laid special emphasis on problems of communication. In his interpretation of the problem of the public, Tarde was in fact an interactionist, which helped his ideas to be received favorably by the Chicago school of sociology.

TARDE'S THEORY OF IMITATION

Labeling Tarde's views as psychologism and reducing them to that would be unjust. Apart from his dubious psychologistic doctrine, Tarde's work comprises a number of ideas that count among permanent achievements of sociology.[10] Those ideas include certain recommendations concerning comparative studies and application of statistical methods in sociology (which he successfully did in his studies of criminality) and also brilliant criticism of evolutionism and organicism.

The core of his sociological theory, which was an aspect of his general philosophy, consisted of the conception of imitation, in which he saw a manifestation of the more common phenomenon of repetition.

Physics [he wrote] studies facts reproduced by periodic movements, undulations, and gravitations; biology studies physico-chemical events reproduced by internal or external generation; sociology must study psychological events reproduced by imitation, and as soon as it has thus found its own area of repetition, numeration, and measurement, its autonomy is assured without the necessity to think up tyrannical and fantastic formulas of evolution.[11]

Let it be added at once that, for all the naturalism of those formulas, Tarde stressed that imitation differs from repetition in nature. He thought that the underlying factors of the former are beliefs and desires, which, though measurable like physical forces, are different in nature from them. On the nature of beliefs and desires, however, he did not have much to say.

The basic elements of individual mentality were to Tarde the only conceivable foundation of all social facts. Tarde excluded from his sociological conception all that which cannot be reduced to basic psychical phenomena, Power, moral norms, law, labor and its division, Durkheim's collective ideas—all these were for him abstractions that are meaningful only insofar as it can be shown how they originate from individual psychical experience. "Collective psychology," he wrote, "*inter-mental* psychology, that is, sociology, is thus possible only because individual psychology, *intra-mental* psychology, includes elements which can be transmitted and communicated from one consciousness to others, elements which, despite the irreducible hiatus between individuals, are capable of uniting and joining together in order to form true social forces and quantities, currents of opinion or popular impulses, traditions or national customs."[12]

The main problem of Tarde's sociology thus seems to be this: What is given is, on the one hand, certain states of individual consciousness and unconsciousness and, on the other, facts that are called social and that have so far been presented by the social sciences in their reified form of supra-individual entities. Tarde's sociology was an endeavor to resolve that dilemma. The solution took on the form of the concept of imitation: Society exists owing to the repetition of individual acts, each of which retains its sovereign nature, but at the same time imparts uniformity and regularity to the various instances of human behavior. Every human action in fact replicates something and is a kind of "interpsychical photography." Imitation is the basic and—in the last analysis—the only social relation; this is why the knowledge of so-called social laws reduces to that of the laws governing imitation.

Tarde did not rest satisfied with the general formula on the significance of imitation. He investigated the logical and extralogical laws of imitation and formulated such theorems as the imitation of ideas precedes that of the ways of expressing them; the imitation of ends precedes that of means; and those individuals whose position in the social hierarchy is low imitate those whose position is high. He also made a distinction between the two basic types of imitation: custom and fashion. This makes it possible to describe, in the language of his interpsychological conception, the difference between a traditional and an innovative society, a difference that used to fascinate all sociologists.

But taking imitation to be the fundamental social fact resulted in an essential difficulty: In its extreme version this conception would yield a vision of society in which nothing new occurs and everything moves within the sphere of routine. Tarde rejected this (as a philosopher he was a supporter of individuality) by introducing the concept of invention, owing to which all social modifications take place. (In his system the term *modification* replaced the term *evolution*.) Forward movement takes place not because there are hard and fast laws of development, but because individuals come to face ever new alternatives that reveal various new possibilities. In fact, every individual is *une humanité nouvelle en projet*.[13] An invention is always made by an individual and not by the masses; an innovator is a leader of the crowd that imitates him and not an agent acting on behalf of a community. Tarde's comments on the issue are interesting as an endeavor to overcome the doctrine of historical necessity, the evolutionistic vision of history without alternatives.

When it comes to alternatives, we have to mention the second general law formulated by Tarde (next to the law of imitation): the law of general opposition. Since there are always many patterns to be imitated, this inevitably brings about conflicts between individuals who differ in their options. The waves of imitation that follow opposing courses clash in conflicts, rivalry, or discussion. This ultimately brings about mutual adaptations so that social equilibrium is achieved (the law of adaptation). It may also be said that conflicts favor inventions, which in turn make adaptation possible.

Tarde's schema was worked out in great detail and with great consistency. He did not for a moment leave the ground of interpsychology: Social processes are, in the last analysis, interactions among individuals. While many of Tarde's ideas have remained his exclusive property, his path proved attractive to early social psychology and interactionistic sociology. Psychologism did not prevent him from investigating processes of interaction, for it was not as dogmatic as the psychologism of Le Bon or other authors, who were mainly interested in the psychical driving forces of human activity and not in the mechanisms of their actions.

MCDOUGALL'S INSTINCTIVISM

Interest in the psychological aspects of social life took on different forms in the United States, where it resulted—due to Dewey, Cooley, Thomas, and Mead—in the rise of interactionistic social psychology, which in many respects opposed European psychologism. But before that, psychologism had enjoyed some popularity in the United States. Thomas as a young man was an advocate of *Völkerpsychologie*, and Tarde was one of the greatest authorities in the eyes of Edward Alsworth Ross (1866-1951), an influential American sociologist at the turn of the nineteenth century, whose book *Social Psychology* (1908) contributed signally to the rise of social psychology as a special discipline dealing with the psychic interplay between man and his surrounding society.[14] In the propagation of social psychology, an important role was also played by Charles A. Ellwood (1873-1946), who popularized the opinion that "the social" is no distinct realm in itself, but is evidently a certain combination of biological and psychological factors."[15]

But in the English-speaking world, psychologism had its fullest expression in the renowned works by William McDougall (1871-1938), an Oxford-trained psychologist who started work at Harvard University in 1920 and was the author of *An Introduction to Social Psychology* (1908), *The Group Mind* (1920), and other books. The first of these happened to be one of the greatest best-sellers in the history of the social sciences (sixteen printings in ten years) and was sometimes thought to have opened a new epoch.[16] It has also been a target of endless criticism as the supposedly model example of how human behavior is explained by reference to a limited number of innate instincts with a total disregard of social interaction and social structure. Such criticism can hardly be considered well deserved if one takes account of McDougall's other works and his reservations concerning the preliminary and hypothetical nature of the main theses formulated in *An Introduction.* Nevertheless, he certainly tried to produce a theory of human social behavior based on the assumption that "the human mind has certain innate or inherited tendencies which are the essential springs or motive powers of all thought and action, whether individual or collective, and are the bases from which the character and will of individuals and nations are gradually developed under the guidance of the intellectual faculties."[17]

The adoption of this assumption enabled McDougall to construct what Jesse R. Pitts has described as "a sort of molecular theory of behavior,"[18] instincts being treated as such molecules. According to McDougall, an instinct is "an inherited or innate psycho-physical disposition which determines its possessor to perceive, and to pay attention to, objects of a certain class, to experience an emotional excitement of a particular quality upon perceiving such an object, and to act in regard to it in a particular manner, or, at least, to experience an impulse to such action."[19] This concept was to be the basis of a uniform theory of behavior, a theory whose character was programmatically naturalistic and which bore out connections between human and animal psychology. It was only that theory which was expected to allow a scientific explanation of complex psychological and social facts.

There would be no point in a detailed discussion of that theory, now completely obsolete. If it deserves mention, that is only because it is one of the purest specimens of psychologism as a theory of human social behavior.

McDougall's instinctivism ("hormic psychology," as it has been called by some authors) assumed the possibility of reducing social facts to the psychical molecules of instincts. Thus religion would be explained by assigning to human beings the instincts of flight, curiosity, and self-abasement; capitalism, by the instinct of acquisition; urbanization, by the instinct of gregariousness; and so on. It was not particularly difficult to criticize such a theory. It sufficed to demonstrate that the instincts described by McDougall were not empirically confirmed facts, but, at best, hypotheses that do not explain much since they merely provide terms with which to label a number of unconfirmed facts. Further, even if human nature were such as McDougall and other instinctivists thought, Znaniecki's reservation, that the main error of the instinctivists consisted in replacing a real human being who participates in social processes by a human being who represents a biological species, would remain valid.[20]

Note, however, that the schema of explaining social facts, as suggested by McDougall, was far from being so simple that it could be inferred from *An Introduction to Social Psychology* alone. In the light of his second book, *The Group Mind*, McDougall's conception proves much more complex, for at least two essential reasons.

First, for McDougall, the task of social psychology is not only to discover those components or elements of human nature that have the decisive effect on social life, but also to study the impact of the group on the individual. What is more, only the knowledge of the psychical life of social groups can be the point of departure for the explanation of individual life in all its concrete forms. Even in *An Introduction* we can find statements proving that his social psychology was not as totally opposed to the social psychology of the interactionists as one might infer from the theory of instincts taken in isolation.

And second, *The Group Mind* abounds in antireductionist formulations, including a polemic with Spencer. McDougall criticized traditional psychology for having focused its attention on individual man, without regard to social relations. There are statements that a group's collective psychical life is to be interpreted nominalistically, but a large part of the book is concerned with national character, which usually is not discussed in individual psychology.

The point is not to blame McDougall for inconsistencies. It seems that his conception deserves attention as providing an example of radical instinctivism and also of showing the difficulties that social psychology had to face at the time when its advocates had at their disposal only a certain doctrine of individual psychology and a certain sociological doctrine, but not any theory of the formation of social personality. This was why McDougall's conception, like many other theories within psychologism, "tended to oscillate between the limits of individual psychology on the one hand and of systematic sociology on the other."[21]

FREUD'S PSYCHOANALYSIS VERSUS SOCIOLOGY

The conception of the Viennese psychiatrist Sigmund Freud (1856-1939), most often referred to as *psychoanalysis*, was undoubtedly the most influential of those psychologistic theories that emerged at the turn of the nineteenth century. Its influence was not confined to any single sphere of intellectual life. Apart from psychiatry, which was the main field of Freud's theoretical and therapeutic activity, his theory had a strong impact on psychology, social and cultural anthropology, history, sociology, art theory,

literary theory, and belles lettres. In some countries, Freudianism contributed to the emergence of a climate of opinion that distinguished the
twentieth century from the nineteenth. Note, however, that in many cases
the influence was extremely superficial, so that the popularity of some of
Freud's ideas was not necessarily accompanied by any thorough knowledge
of them. Both the enthusiasts and the opponents of psychoanalysis have
tended to interpret in a very simplified manner. This can be explained partly
by the fact that many assumptions of psychoanalysis are obscure, that
Freud modified his views many times, and that he had many disciples, each
of whom claimed to be the only correct interpreter of the master's doctrine.
Hence, describing the whole of the Freudian theory with all its ramifications
and inner contradictions would be an extremely difficult task, which we do
not intend to undertake here.

Sociological Implications of Freudianism. Psychoanalysis as such is,
obviously, not our subject matter. It is of interest here only because it has
sociological implications and possibly also because Freud has left a *sui
generis* theory of society and culture. It is not claimed in the least that psychoanalysis has been and must necessarily be any definite kind of psychosociology. On the contrary, it developed as an endeavor to dissolve problems of individual psychology. As has been written by contemporary advocates of "psychoanalytic sociology," Freud

did not see the necessity for systematically investigating the problem of social
structure. This traditional psychoanalytic position paid hardly any attention at all to
those economic and political structures that historians and sociologists typically
regard as significantly determinative of man's life in society. Freud stressed the
essentially unchanging content of human wishes rather than the "apparently"
changing form of institutions and practices.[22]

The rise and autonomy of Freud's sociological interests were hindered by
the fact that he was above all a clinician, and it was only later that the
adoption as an axiom of a questionable analogy between the development
of the individual and that of the masses made it possible to bridge the gap
between individual psychology and psychosociology and/or social psychology. Yet the writings of the founder of psychoanalysis contain many elements that are clearly *sociological* in nature and later came to be extracted
meticulously and discussed in detail by his followers.

Those elements were of two kinds. First, over the course of time Freud
developed an interest in the role played by external factors, such as the
individual's social milieu, in shaping the human psyche. This is why some
commentators claim that "his psychology involves culture in its very essence."[23] Freud himself wrote on this issue,

It is true that individual psychology is concerned with the individual man and explores the paths by which he seeks to find satisfaction for his instincts, but only rarely and under certain exceptional conditions is individual psychology in a position to disregard the relations of this individual to others. In the individual's mental life someone else is invariably involved, as a model, as an object, as a helper, as an opponent, and so from the very first individual psychology is at the same time social psychology as well.[24]

Second, by making use of this method of analogy, Freud tried to explain collective behavior by reference to certain traits of individual mentality. In his works on the origin and evolution of society he spoke directly on matters of interest to the social sciences (social evolution, crowd psychology, the origin and essence of culture, and so on). Next to social psychology he thus formulated a kind of psychosociology.

In many of his psychological studies we find statements with sociological implications, which Freud himself, perhaps, did not fully realize. Apart from that, he left such sociological studies as *Totem and Taboo* (1913), *Group Psychology and the Analysis of the Ego* (1920), *The Future of an Illusion* (1927), *Civilization and Its Discontents* (1930), and *Moses and Monotheism* (1939), which were on the periphery of his principal interests, but prove his fairly good knowledge of sociological and anthropological literature, though limited to the works of evolutionists and early representatives of psychologism.

However interesting these works may be, to a sociologist, Freud's importance in the history of sociology seems to be largely independent of what he wrote in them. Probably none of them (except for *Civilization and Its Discontents*, with its truly novel ideas) would attract the attention of sociologists so much had they not been written by the great founder of psychoanalysis, who was already well known for his achievements in individual psychology. It is his psychology, and not his sociology, that includes truly novel ideas that in one form or another were to become permanent additions to the social sciences. As Kardiner and Preble wrote, "paradoxically, it is Freud's early work in the field of individual psychology, and not his later sociological studies, that contains something of value for the social scientist."[25]

Freud's Theory of Personality. The foundation of Freud's theory is the discovery that "mental processes are essentially unconscious, and that those which are conscious are merely isolated acts and parts of the whole psychic entity."[26] By continuing the work of Schopenhauer, Nietzsche, and other authors, Freud finally destroyed the rationalistic vision of man as a predominantly thinking being, and he denied consciousness the status of the real motive force in human behavior, which is—according to him—driven by irrational elements embodied in the nature of man as a species. The applications of psychoanalysis to sociology and the turn toward the unconscious marked a *sui generis* revolution in sociology, and its effects can be seen to this day.

Freud's description of those irrational elements underwent many changes. Thus, the concept of *libido*, introduced in Freud's earliest works, first referred to the sexual impulse, later covered the whole of vital energy (whose sexual nature was much less evident), and finally became—under the label of *id*—merely one of the factors that shape human psychical life. While these and similar changes probably did not affect Freud's therapeutic practice, they meant a remarkable metamorphosis of his theory. Freud at first used the idea of a man-machine, activated from the inside by the energy of instincts that are trying to find an outlet (characteristically, Freud availed himself of terminology of hydrodynamics and electrodynamics). The human individual is guided exclusively by the pleasure principle; that is, he incessantly strives to satisfy his impulses and to avoid whatever would prevent him from doing so. This extremely simple (not to say simplified) conception of man as an animal guided by instincts was never totally abandoned by Freud, although the body of concepts and explanations used by him was being expanded all the time, so that his theory is far from being just one of the many instinctivist theories.

Those changes are of interest here insofar as they made Freud increase his attention to those social factors which affect the formation of the character and behavior of the human individual. Not all his interpreters agree about whether in his evolved theory he actually succeeded in taking into account the significance of the social situation. In any case, the sociological content of Freud's psychoanalysis was gradually amplified, particularly when Freud started intensively studying the principle of reality, the *ego*, and the structure of character.

In his early works Freud was interested in the individual's external world, represented by the set of objects around him, some of which come to be desired by him, and the set of obstacles that the individual encounters when trying to satisfy his desires. But Freud did not consider in any greater detail the psychological consequences of the individual's relations with the external world and, *a fortiori*, the ways in which he copes with the problems that result from those relations. In other words, until the 1920s he did not have any theory of the formation of personality. Formulating such a theory required singling out, in human psychical life, elements other than omnipotent instincts (the totality of which now came to be termed *id [das Es]*): namely, *ego* as a *sui generis* mediator between id and the reality, and *superego*, which is that part of ego that consists of the internalized requirements of the social milieu, in particular the family.

Ego functions to ensure equilibrium between id and superego. That equilibrium is, of course, unstable, because the three elements of personality that Freud singled out are in a constant conflict with one another. There is an incessant struggle between id and superego, which can always bring about the destruction of culture by instincts, or the destruction of the individual by the milieu. The antagonism between the individual and society is transferred here into the human psychical life and declared essentially unsurmountable.

Freud's theory of personality, like his other conceptions, is open to many different interpretations, with which we cannot concern ourselves here. Note, however, that some of them (for instance, those by Marxists and Marxist-influenced neo-Freudians) bear out the instinctivist elements of that theory, while others tend to point out that "internalization of the sociocultural environment provides the basis, not merely of one specialized component of the human personality, but of what, in the human sense, is its central core."[27] It seems that this divergence of interpretations reflects the inner tension in the theory itself.

Freud's Theory of Culture. The theory of culture (civilization) formulated by the founder of psychoanalysis poses exactly the same problems. That theory transfers, by analogy, the conclusions pertaining to the microcosm (the individual) to the macrocosm (the society). Freud wrote outright about "the similarity between the process of civilization and the libidinal development of the individual" and claimed that "the community, too, evolves a super-ego, under whose influence cultural development proceeds."[28] But Freud was induced to concern himself with problems of culture not only by that highly questionable analogy, but also by his desire to explain the mechanisms of the formation of human psychic life, in which biological and social influences clash.

It seems that Freud's theory of culture has two important features that result from his conception of man. First, human nature is marked by aggressive cruelty, and "in circumstances that are favourable to it, when the mental counterforces which ordinarily inhibit it are out of action, it also manifests itself spontaneously and reveals man as a savage beast to whom consideration towards his own kind is something alien."[29] Second, human instincts are irremovable and unchanging and the energy inherent in them is a constant quantity, so all that is possible is a change of the forms in which unchanging nature manifests itself.

In accordance with these assumptions, Freud noticed two basic aspects of culture: repression and sublimation. On the one hand, "the whole course of the history of civilization is no more than an account of the various methods adopted by mankind for "binding" their [human] unsatisfied wishes."[30] On the other, the history of civilization is the story of impulses manifesting themselves in sublimated forms. In the former case, culture reveals itself as the denial of nature; in the latter, as its continuation and transformation. This duality in approach to culture seems very characteristic of Freud: It testifies to his links with the still surviving philosophy of progress, but simultaneously discloses his grave doubts.

Freud's reflections on culture originated from works by evolutionists such as Bastian, Tylor, Frazer, and Darwin. He was entirely within the sphere of that heritage when he wrote that "the word 'civilization' describes the whole sum of the achievements and the regulations which distinguish our lives from those of our animal ancestors and which serve two purposes —namely to protect men against nature and to adjust their mutual relations."[31] Similarities between minor points of Freud's reflections and those of the evolutionists are numerous, too. Yet his conception as a whole seems to be thoroughly original, resulting not from the psychologism that pervades Freud's explanations, but from an essential change in the assessment of the consequences of the development of culture.

Even if Freud did not totally abandon the idea of progress (some of its elements can clearly be noticed in *The Future of an Illusion*), he did not think that mankind's achievements in mastering the forces of nature and in organizing social life are permanent or irreversible in any way. Culture is an edifice erected on a building plot with mines buried underground: "The primitive, savage, and evil impulses of mankind have not vanished in any individual, but continue their existence, although in a repressed state . . . and they wait for opportunities to display their activity."[32]

Even if Freud accorded mankind certain durable achievements in the field of technology, he refused to recognize any in the field of social organization or the ability of mankind to ensure happiness for itself. Culture, indispensable as it is to mankind, proves to be a source of suffering: "In fact, primitive man was better off in knowing restrictions of instinct. To counterbalance this, his prospects of enjoying this happiness for any length of time were very slender. Civilized man has exchanged a portion of his possibilities of happiness for a portion of security."[33]

As we have said, Freud assigned to culture mainly repressive functions; superego, which comes into being owing to culture, watches the individual's instincts "like a garrison in a conquered city."[34] No harmonious progress is possible. Freud has, therefore, sometimes been compared to Rousseau, who in a similar way dispersed the rationalists' illusions about progress. The essential difference between the two thinkers is that Freud's pessimism comprehended both culture and human nature. In fact, if mankind still has some hopes, this is due to culture alone, which, by repressing impulses, provides opportunities for their sublimation. Freud's philosophy of culture is thus an unlikely combination of unquestionable radicalism, seen in the assessment of the state of society, with a *sui generis* conservatism, which denied the possibility of any essential improvement and did so by referring to axioms on invariable human nature. Culture is a source of suffering, but that is not an exorbitant price to be paid by mankind for its escape from self-destruction.

This ambivalence of the Freudian philosophy of culture, which was one of the most eloquent manifestations of the exhaustion of bourgeois optimism, seems to have been decisive in determining its originality and attractiveness. It appealed to many European intellectuals, although students of culture (including Malinowski) often pointed to its original sin—taking that which was the result of definite historical conditions to be the destiny of man and humbling oneself in the face of the dark forces of biology, although very many human characteristics are in fact products of culture.

But while the basic—essentially philosophical—issues raised in *Civilization and Its Discontents* cannot be dismissed easily (especially after the experience of two world wars and the technological progress of the twentieth century, forced by state economies regardless of the dimensions of human suffering), particular problems of culture are discussed by Freud in an anachronistic manner, varying with virtually all that can sensibly be said about the mechanisms of the development of culture. This applies in particular to Freud's speculations about the origin of culture, which even his adherents mention only with embarrassment.

Significance of Freudian Theory. More or less the same can be said about the majority of sociological speculations in which Freud indulged. Looking for the essence of all masses (including highly organized communities, such as the church and the army) in the original libidinal ties, explaining a group's dislike of aliens by narcissism, explaining the status of the leader by transference of the attitudes developed within the family—all these are examples of arbitrary interpretations and dogmatism that marked Freud's sociological thinking, which became increasingly arbitrary as he moved further away from the proper field of his studies, individual psychopathology. Freud's impact on the social sciences was the strongest where his instinctivism was the least intrusive and his theory the least speculative.

Freud's heritage is a still active source of inspiration. Without him, our contemporary social sciences would not be what they are. It is true that he probably did not formulate any theorems or theories that could today be accepted unreservedly, but he contributed significantly to the formation of two views whose importance reaches far beyond psychoanalysis, even in the broadest possible sense of the term. These views have become so commonly accepted that they may now seem trivial.

The first view, closely connected with the new interpretation of psychical life as something broader than consciousness, tells us not to attach too much importance in our studies of man to what people say, because they may tell deliberate lies. The individual turns out to be incomparably more complicated than it was assumed in the nineteenth century. Freud was one of those who encouraged the social sciences in the twentieth century to go beyond the surface description of what has been observed and who thus helped to destroy the positivist ideal of science in which he himself believed.

According to the second view, human personality has its own social history. Thus, to understand an individual's behavior, we must consider not only his position in the social structure and his innate characteristics, but also his individual biography, which is governed by intricate mechanisms that require a separate study. We owe to Freud the discovery of a new dimension that is inevitably linked to major social processes, but cannot be reduced to them. Freud made the discovery during his studies of the development of personality, one which ran counter to the instinctivistic assumptions of his doctrine.

THE PSYCHOLOGISTIC SOCIOLOGY OF VILFREDO PARETO

Psychologism in sociology has probably its most outstanding representative in Vilfredo Frederico Damaso Pareto (1848-1923), an Italian economist and social thinker. Trained as a technologist, he was for many years active in business, as a railway manager, and in politics, and from 1893 to 1907 he was professor of political economy at the University of Lausanne, Switzerland. He wrote much (the thirty volumes of his *Oeuvres complètes*, edited by G. Busino, began to appear in 1964), including four works of fundamental importance for sociology: *Cours d'économie politique* (1896-1897), *Les systèmes socialistes* (1902-1903), *Manuale di economia politica* (1906), and *Trattato di sociologia generale* (1915-1916).

Written rather late as a result of many years of experience and reflections, which led him to abandon the progressive views that he had held in his youth, these works are among the most ambitious intellectual undertakings of the early twentieth century. On the one hand, they gave him the ambiguous reputation of the Karl Marx of fascism; and on the other, they made him one of the most influential thinkers in circles that had nothing in common with fascism. Both aspects of his popularity were probably due to the fact that his works (fairly abstract in the majority of formulations) were a total criticism of the ideas underlying bourgeois democracy. Pareto refuted—in a firm and apparently scientific manner—the conception of rational man and of the society that follows the path of uninterrupted progress. He succeeded in imparting to his own doubts, caused by his failure in activities conducted under the banner of classical liberalism, the dimension of a theoretical system, attractive to all those who eventually decided (as did L. J. Henderson's Boston group in the 1930s) that "few of the important phenomena of recent history can be seen as the result of logical actions."[35]

Pareto's importance in sociology is also due to his introduction of a number of theoretical concepts that were to play a considerable role. We mean here above all his concepts of system and social equilibrium, so important in sociological functionalism, and that of elite, which was not his exclusive invention, but owed to him the form in which it came to be adopted in sociology and political science. Yet the pride of place goes to his theory of nonlogical actions, which is a kind of a clasp that holds his intricate sociological system together.

Treating Pareto as a representative of psychologism is a simplification, for he did not think it possible to explain societal life by indicating a single decisive factor. He much more willingly referred to the formula of interaction, which he believed to be cognitively more fertile than the concept of causal nexus. Yet we associate Pareto with psychologism, first, because he focused his attention on psychological elements of social life (his *Trattato* is not so much a system of sociology as a monograph of nonlogical actions) and, second, because his most original and influential opinions pertain to psychological aspects of social life, particularly to the significant role of irrational factors that have their source in changeless human nature. This is not to imply that he had much to say on psychology. Like other sociologists of his times, he was a dilettante in that field.

The Ideal of Science versus Social Facts. Pareto's way of thinking was formed by the sciences, in which he had begun his studies at the School of Technology in Turin, and by patterns provided by positivist naturalism, which in his youth exerted an overwhelming influence. The author of *The Mind and Society* (the title of the English translation of his *Trattato*) never ceased to be a positivist. If he criticized, say, Comte or Spencer, he did so not for having been positivists, but for having been imperfect positivists, contaminated by "metaphysics."

Pareto tried to rid himself of all the inconsistencies of early positivism: He endeavored to eliminate from his language all vague and ambiguous expressions and also those which do not lend themselves to operationalization, and he even postulated that certain expressions be replaced by neutral symbols so that we can free ourselves from the "illusions of language." He strove to save the idea of pure science, which studies society, but does not strive to change it. As a positivist he had a sense of solidarity not with the seekers of secular salvation, which the first positivists were, but with such scientists as H. Poincaré, E. Mach, K. Pearson, and C. Bernard, who are usually reckoned as representatives of so-called second positivism. He retained unshaken faith in the progress of science, but no longer believed in the progress of society. In this way he turned not only against the founders of positivist sociology, but also against Marxism, which was a much more influential opponent around 1900. Note in this regard that Pareto, next to Durkheim and Max Weber, was one of the first sociologists for whom an attitude toward Marx and his followers was a major theoretical problem.

Pareto's methodological program was radically naturalistic, which can best be seen from a commentary that he made on *The Mind and Society* in one of his lectures:

It was driven by the desire to bring an indispensable complement to the studies of political economy and inspired by the example of the natural sciences that I determined to begin my *Traité de Sociologie*, the sole purpose of which—I say sole and I insist upon the point—is to seek experimental reality, by the application to the social sciences of the methods which have proved themselves in physics, in chemistry, in astronomy, in biology, and in other such sciences.[36]

This is why Karl Mannheim calls Pareto's sociology "formal social mechanics" and P. Sorokin classes it—though not without reservations—in the "mechanistic" school.[37] Interestingly enough, Pareto's mechanism co-occurred with a *sui generis* organicism, but the latter did not play any major role in his system because the mechanistic model of society was more in line with the ideal of mathematics, which Pareto placed before all mature sciences.

But in his case mechanics, serving as a model for a science of society, was not allowed to resort to a number of spectacular analogies, with which the majority of now forgotten representatives of the mechanistic trend in sociology—such as H. C. Carey (1793-1879) and L. Winiarski (1865-1915) —remained satisfied. Pareto did not strive to explain social processes by reference to the laws of mechanics, but saw in mechanics an example of a universal scientific method, which he termed *logico-empirical.* That method consisted of two principal procedures: (1) methodical observation of facts and discovery of regularities (laws) and (2) deduction, based on logical operations, which makes it possible to extend the knowledge thus acquired over fields that were not subject to direct observation.

The logico-empirical method opposed the extremes of the two methods most common in the social sciences: the purely deductive method of political economy and the historical method, which was in fact nonscientific, as it confined itself to description and did not discover laws. Like mechanics, the social sciences investigate two kinds of motions: real motions, immediately shown to us through observation, and virtual motions, which take place only under certain special conditions that as a rule never occur in practice.

The second kind of motions (that is, acts of behavior of human "molecules") had for a long time been studied by pure political economy, which uses the simplified model of *homo oeconomicus*. However legitimate and indispensable are the deductive reasonings of this discipline for the explanation of human behavior, that behavior remains incomprehensible as long as we abstain from studying the behavior of real human beings, whose motivations are more complex than assumed in the idealizational concept of *homo oeconomicus*.

It is the task of sociology, as the most "synthetic" discipline, to acquire the knowledge of that real behavior. Sociology should be open

to all facts, whatever their character, provided that directly or indirectly they point the way to discovering a uniformity. Even an absurd, an idiotic argument is a fact, and if accepted by any large number of people, a fact of great importance to sociology. Beliefs, whatever their character, are also facts, and their importance depends not on their intrinsic merits, but on the greater or fewer numbers of individuals who profess them. They serve furthermore to reveal the sentiments of such individuals, and sentiments are among the most important elements with which sociology is called upon to deal.[38]

Assigning sociology such tasks accounts for the fact that in Pareto's interpretation it is primarily a science of nonlogical actions. He ascribed great significance to such actions and excluded the possibility that people would ever be able to guide themselves in their life by anything other than "religions." In Pareto's social philosophy, which was elitist by assumption, vanish the last traces of the faith that it is the calling of the rationalists to turn all people into rationalists. No other thinker has probably ever drawn such a sharp demarcation line between science and life, between theory and practice. He demanded of the scientist that he rid himself qua scientist of all passions that are inevitably his share qua human being. It seems that Pareto was an incomparably more determined advocate of value-free sociology than Max Weber was. Science and practical activity were for him two separate spheres of human actions. In Pareto's opinion, the higher were the requirements that a theory should meet, the more hopelessly irrational practical activity seemed to be. Science does not aspire to show society the path that it should follow; it merely retains for itself the privilege of understanding what happens and possibly of commenting—to those in power—on how to attain goals defined by instincts, sentiments, and interests. This is why the label *Machiavellian*, applied to him by J. Burnham, seems very much to the point.

Social Life as the Domain of Nonlogical Actions. The opposition between science and life, between logico-experimental and everyday thinking, in his sociology takes the form of a dichotomy of human actions into logical and nonlogical. The former comply with the patterns of scientific activity, while the latter form the enormous rest—human actions governed by a faith that derives from sentiments and instincts. This latter kind of actions is the main sphere of Pareto's interest, and the endeavor to construct a comprehensive theory of such actions seems to be the greatest asset of his sociology.

Pareto took sentiments and instincts as a given, something about which not much can be said. He was interested in them not so much for themselves as for their "manifestations," which ultimately restructure and disturb logical thinking or even eliminate it from practical life. He was, above all, fascinated by the problem of why the human being's hunger for thinking is usually allayed in a way so remote from the pattern of logico-experimental thinking.

This in many respects recalls Marx's conception of false consciousness: He also shifted the focus of his interest from the logical value of the opinions commonly accepted under given historical conditions to the determinants of the popularity of such opinions, independent of their logical value. Pareto's conception, however, was in opposition to Marx's, as it precluded any possibility of a change in that state of things.

This is so because the dominance of nonlogical motivations of human actions is a characteristic of the human species and cannot be, in Pareto's opinion, explained by the peculiarities of historical conditions. The latter merely determine the self-deception to which people resort to impart the appearance of logic to actions dictated by impulses. The "hunger for thinking" mentioned above is in fact hunger for substantiations, for "rationalizations" in the Freudian sense of the term. When seen from this vantage point, man does not undergo any essential changes: Only his ideological masks are historically variable. As Pareto put it, "Derivations change, residues endure."[39] He accordingly tried to disclose and to systematize those enduring residues and also to reveal the mechanisms of formation of changeable derivations and to reduce their large number, observable in human history, to several basic types. This was supposed to give rise to a science of nonlogical actions that would equal in precision the science of logical actions.

Pareto characterized nonlogical actions as those which "originate chiefly in definite psychic states, sentiments, subconscious feelings, and the like."[40] He stressed that nonlogical actions are not to be confused with illogical ones; that is, they are not to be identified with actions that are at variance with logic. Logical actions are marked (as in Max Weber's conception) by an adequacy of the means to the ends, such adequacy being considered not only from the point of view of the agent, but also from the point of view of competent observers. The basic difference in the case of nonlogical actions lies either in the fact that the relation between means and ends does not hold at all (a purely theoretical possibility to Pareto) or in the fact that the agent is not aware of it, or imagines it in a wrong manner, or does not take it into account when he begins to act. However it may be, nonlogical action originates from a specified psychic state and not from logico-experimental thinking.

Comprehension of those psychic states would seem to be the key issue, yet Pareto confined himself to stating that it is a task of psychology to study them. The conception of nonlogical actions was intended to explain the theory of residues and derivations, which is the most important part of Pareto's sociology and which we want to discuss briefly.

First, let us consider residues. The concept of residues is not quite clear, and its interpretation has worried historians of sociology. The term itself may have been coined to point to the existence of an irrational remainder that resist the requirements of logico-experimental thinking. Pareto commented on the relative importance of that remainder in human life, but did not characterize it in any comprehensive manner. To make matters worse, we find in *The Mind and Society* statements that it would be difficult, if not impossible, to bring into agreement with one another.

It would certainly be tempting to assume that the residues are nothing other than, in Sidney Hook's words, "a fancy synonym for instincts."[41] But the matter does not look that simple, because in many contexts Pareto makes a clear distinction between residues and instincts. Moreover, nothing indicates that the knowledge of residues could be acquired by psychological research like that undertaken by McDougall; that knowledge can be obtained, rather, through studying facts of culture and discovering their most durable elements. Don Martindale refers to residues as "the recurrent features of action," as distinct from its "variable elements."[42] And H. Stuart Hughes is right in saying that Pareto interprets residues sometimes just as biological instincts and sometimes as a kind of ideal types of human value-orientations.[43]

All these interpretations seem tenable, but it is imperative to realize that Pareto's definitions of the residues are operational only. Pareto was interested not so much in *what* the residues are as in *how* they manifest themselves in observable human behavior. The basic theoretical schema remains the same whether we call the residues instincts or make a clear distinction between the two categories. Pareto's psychologism consists merely of assuming some relationship between the constant features of human actions and human psychic states. It does not, however, cover any specified conception of those states and, hence, does not assume any comprehensive psychological doctrine. This results in an essential weakness of Pareto's sociological theory: While availing himself of a schema of explanations that is typical of psychologism, he abandons all precise definitions of phenomena that are essential from that point of view. He merely offers a fairly detailed classification of the residues.

Their classes are: (1) residues of combination; (2) residues of group persistence; (3) residues of expressing sentiments by external acts; (4) residues connected with sociality; (5) residues of integrity of the individual; (6) residues of sex. Their detailed analysis is supposed to reveal what is "virtually constant in social phenomena,"[44] regardless of all fluctuations to which human actions and their ideological substantiations (derivations) happen to be subjected. For all the endless variety of the substance of history in all possible situations, we find that human beings are marked by the same inclinations and aspirations—the only difference being that they combine in various ways and in varying proportions. They are the substratum on which ideologies develop.

And there were derivations. As the very word indicates, he considered them to derive from more fundamental facts, and that was why he criticized those authors (whom Marx called "ideologues") who confined their study of social life to the sphere of derivations, without posing themselves the question about what underlies them. This is not to say that Pareto belittled the role of derivations. He thought that definite derivations are part of all specifically human actions (with which he was solely concerned, for he disregarded purely instinctive actions common to human beings and animals alike) except for the logical actions, whose sphere is rather limited:

The animal does not reason, it acts exclusively by instinct. It uses no derivations therefore. The human being, however, wants to think, and he also feels impelled to keep his instincts and sentiments hidden from view. Rarely, in consequence, is at least a germ of derivation missing in human thinking. . . . Residues and derivations can be detected every time we look at a theory or argument that is not strictly logico-experimental.[45]

The inclination to mystify is, in Pareto's opinion, part of human nature. Human society can be represented neither as a herd of animals, in which only instincts matter, nor as a learned society, in which everything depends on the logical value of argumentation.

What are derivations as understood by Pareto? One of the few direct answers given by him is this: "The derivations comprise logical reasonings, unsound reasonings, and manifestations of sentiments used for purposes of derivations. They are manifestations of the human being's hunger for thinking."[46] In his interpretation of derivations one point seems to be of special importance: He usually distinguishes derivations from logico-experimental thinking not because of their formal properties (it being possible, though infrequent, that a derivation as a "theory" meets the requirements of scientific thinking), but because of their goals and the func-

tions that they have in social life. Contrary to some statements made by
Pareto himself, it is legitimate to suppose that the derivational status of a
given theory is determined not by its unscientific or pseudoscientific nature,
but by its being accepted or rejected regardless of its logical value, merely
on the strength of its agreement or disagreement with the residues that are
dominant in a given community at a given moment of history. Obviously,
such a derivation always veils the real motives of human beings and, hence,
is resistant to all scientific criticism and argumentation. Quite understandably, from that point of view the social role of ideas has nothing to do with
their logical value; or the utility of theories, with their truth. One may say
that Pareto, when discussing the social role of ideas, abrogates the rules of
logic, which hold when the cognitive values of ideas are analyzed, and seeks
other regularities in association and acceptance of given opinions.

To do so, he bases his classification of derivations on the criterion of the
nonlogical principle on which they are accepted. He singles out four classes
of derivations: (1) those which refer to simple assertion of facts and/or
duties ("It is so and that is that" or "It must be so"); (2) those which refer
to an authority (personal or group authority, tradition, custom, deity, and
so on); (3) those which refer to accords with sentiments or principles (interests, law, metaphysical concepts, and the like); and (4) those which make
use of unclear language, vagueness of terms, persuasive force of language,
metaphors, allegories, or analogies.[47] In all four cases it seems that the main
point is why certain statements or injunctions—despite their evident variance
with facts and logic—are unreservedly accepted by those persons and/or
groups to whom they are addressed. Pareto, however, was interested not
so much in the skill of ideologues, as in the correspondence between derivations and the soil in which the seed is sown by ideologues. Differences
between the classes of derivations have their analogues in different historical
conditions and, to some extent, in different classes of residues. This is why
the rulers and the ideologues have a very limited room for maneuvering.
As Pareto says, "the art of governing lies in manipulating residues, not in
trying to change them. . . . the art of governing lies in finding ways to take
advantage of such sentiments, not in wasting one's energies in futile efforts
to destroy them, the sole effect of the latter course very frequently being
only to strengthen them."[48]

Finally, we should consider interaction between residues and derivations.
It might seem, in the light of what has been said, that Pareto demonstrated
a one-sided dependence of derivations on residues, of the ideological superstructure on the psychological base. He did, in fact, put the main stress on
that, which can easily be explained by his belief that both the social sciences
and politics are burdened by the dangerous faith in the omnipotence of
ideologies. Yet any monocausalism would contradict Pareto's basic meth-

odological assumptions. He never ceased to argue that there are no reasons for a sociological theory to assign a privileged position to any single factor.

In *The Mind and Society* we find statements proving that he was far from belittling the effect that derivations have on residues. When writing that residues are causes of derivations, he put the word *causes* within single quotation marks and added that derivations, too, can be causes of residues. He thought on the whole that residues can have social causes, and in any case he considered unsettled the issue "whether it is living in a certain class that produces certain residues in individuals, or whether it is the presence of those residues in those individuals that derives them into that class, or, better yet, whether the two effects may not be there simultaneously."[49] Such statements must make us cautious in labeling Pareto as a representative of psychologism. In fact, his psychologism was as limited and ambiguous as Marx's economism was.

Social System and History. In the opinion of some commentators, Pareto's reflections on the general form of society and the social equilibrium in history form the main part of his sociological work. They are to be found in the last volume of *The Mind and Society*, so the preceding volumes—concerned with nonlogical actions, residues, and derivations—must be treated as a gigantic introduction to those issues. From this point of view, the concept of social system is of focal importance; as L. J. Henderson wrote, it is "the central feature of Pareto's sociology."[50] Such an interpretation of *The Mind and Society*, though one-sidedly functionalistic, seems to help us to comprehend properly the integrated theory of society that it contains.

It is legitimate to say that *The Mind and Society* is based on the following schema: It begins with an analysis of nonlogical actions that is intended to reveal the potent impact of instincts and sentiments on social life; the next stage is a study of residues and derivations, based on the assumption that those instincts and sentiments can be investigated only through the intermediary of their manifestations, which, however, sometimes require at least a taxonomical ordering; the whole is crowned by a model of social system that would be useful in the study of societies as wholes. In other words, Pareto's theory of human actions turns out to be the foundation of his theory of a social system.

It does not suffice to consider human molecules alone. While society has no existence other than that as the vast aggregate of molecules of which it consists, its functioning cannot be explained until we take into account the interactions of those component elements. This holds for both the social molecules—that is, human individuals with their instincts, sentiments, interests, and so forth—and all other elements that determine the form of society, even though for the sake of simplicity we can disregard them, as they always act through the intermediary of psychic states of individuals. Whichever elements we consider, we have to assume that "they constitute a system, which we may call the 'social system' " and that we have to investigate "the nature and properties" of that system.[51] In other words, the task is not only to assign specified properties to social molecules as such, but also to demonstrate how those molecules function within a more comprehensive whole.

Of course, the very concept of a system (and even the term *social system*) was not novel in sociology, and we have encountered it previously in connection with those thinkers who used a model of social organism. But in historicism and evolutionism the concept of social system was marked by two characteristics. First, there was a relatively low level of abstraction; a system just meant society as such (the Marxist theory of socioeconomic formations being one of the few exceptions), and the ontological, not the methodological, interpretation of social system marked even the functionalism of Malinowski and Radcliffe-Brown. Second, there was a lack of a theoretical framework (the Marxist theory being again the notable exception) that could accommodate the inner contradictions of a system and the conflicts among its component elements: By definition, a social system was, in most cases, dominated by concord, cooperation, and solidarity. Pareto revolutionized the theoretical approach in both respects; his revolution was analogous to the Marxian, although his conclusions were antipodally different.

Pareto's concept of social system—probably influenced by his preference for mechanics as a model—is maximally abstract as a result, first, of a deliberate limitation of the number of elements subject to analysis and, second, of a programmatic disregard of the issues of evolution. He was, of course, aware of both the endless variety of social life and its incessant changes, but he was interested solely in the interactions of specified elements at a given moment. This is why he has been accused by some authors of ahistoricism; they claimed that Pareto's method was "to deny historical change and cultural differences."[52] Pareto's imposing historical erudition meant, in fact, merely the knowledge of known cases of the functioning of certain mechanisms. He was not interested in history as a process or as a context. Historiography was for him what a description of experiments is for a natural scientist. What is involved here is not a research procedure chosen with a strictly defined goal in view; instead, it is a deeply rooted philosophy that made him prefer the knowledge of the permanent substance of social life to the knowledge of its changing forms.

In the social sphere, as seen by Pareto, there is neither progress nor development, except within a narrow domain of logical actions—science, technology, and so on. Changes are undulatory in nature, and hence the issue is to find, as precisely as possible, the point from which the consecutive changes ("oscillations") are deviations. The more we focus attention on the most persistent and the deepest content of social phenomena, the more we can abstract from their variability. The state of a social system at a given moment is, accordingly, the state of equilibrium, to which the system incessantly returns. In the last analysis, it is human instincts, sentiments, and interests that maintain that equilibrium.

Further, in Pareto's approach, an essential aspect of every social system is its being a unity of opposites—to use the formulation due to Hegel and Marx. A system's equilibrium does not, in any case, lie in its being marked by an inner perfect harmony of opinions, interests, and aspirations. To Pareto such a condition was simply inconceivable, and this was why he criticized those thinkers who assumed that it would be possible to eliminate conflicts and strife from social life. He states plainly that that conflicting interests contribute to the emergence of a state of social equilibrium, which can result from incessant action and reaction. Every society, he wrote, is inevitably heterogeneous.

The term *social heterogeneity*, as it occurs in *The Mind and Society*, has numerous meanings and is applied to various facts in individual psychology, social psychology, sociology, and politics. Even a single human individual is not a homogeneous and conflict-free whole, being influenced by impulses incompatible with one another: Some of them favor cooperation, while others favor rivalry; some of them favor strengthening the existing social conditions, while others favor changing them. At the level of society, homogeneity is unattainable *a fortiori*. First, human beings are unequal by nature; second, there are always conflicts of interests among them, because the goods that are equally desired by all cannot be distributed equally among all; third, every society is divided into those who govern and those who are governed. Further, even the classes into which societies are split are not, and cannot be, homogeneous, and so the governing class also has a government of its own. Pareto claims that every difference means a potential conflict, and struggle is the universal law of life. As he wrote in *Les Systèmes socialistes*,

The struggle of life or well-being is a general phenomenon for living things, and everything we know about this leads us to recognize it as one of the most powerful forces for the conservation and amelioration of the race. It is therefore extremely improbable that men will be able to transcend this condition. . . . All our efforts can never result in a fundamental change of this condition, only in slight modifications of its forms.[53]

It is thus correct to say that Pareto's ideas include elements of what has been termed social Darwinism.

In his study of class struggle, Pareto focused his attention not on the classes in the Marxian sense of the term, but on the elites and the masses, that is, on such classes which exist in all societies regardless of the mode of production. In his polemic with the Marxist theory he wrote:

Suppose collectivism to be established and that "capital" no longer exists; then only a particular form of class struggle will have disappeared and new ones will emerge to replace it. New conflicts will appear between the different kinds of workers and the socialist state, between the intellectuals and the non-intellectuals, between the various politicians, between the politicians and those they administer, between innovators and conservatives, etc.[54]

Pareto assumed that the eternal division of every society into elites and masses is based on the natural inequality of human beings and the essential changelessness of their psychical characteristics. While he thus referred to the age-old conservative thought, he did not confine himself to reaffirming existing formulations on that issue, but added at least two essential corrections, which give a certain originality to his ideas. The first correction consists in the neutralization of the concept of elite, which he treated simply as "a class of the people who have the highest indices on their branch activity."[55] The governing elite, in which Pareto was interested most, is part of the class that by violence or persuasion (Pareto refers here to Machiavelli's distinction of "lions" and "foxes") succeeds in ensuring for itself an effective control of the behavior of the masses. An elite means people who are superior to others in their technical efficiency in competing with others and not those who are the best in any absolute sense of the word. His second correction consists of the adoption of the concept of circulation of elites—a sui generis historiosophy stating that every elite is replaced by another one when the energy that enabled it to occupy a privileged position is exhausted. The state of equilibrium is disturbed following "the accumulation of superior elements in the lower classes and, conversely, of inferior elements in the higher classes." "Aristocracies do not last. Whatever the causes, it is an incontestable fact that after a certain length of time they pass away. History is a graveyard of aristocracies."[56] The social structure, while always based on inequality, is thus subject to the universal law of oscillations. The equilibrium of a social system is always more or less in danger, but its restoration in a new form, resulting from given conditions, is assured. No social group is predestined once and for all to be an elite or a mass, but there are specific psychic predispositions to win or to lose in the struggle for existence, owing to which individuals come to occupy high or low positions in the social hierarchy and thus to form, respectively, successive elites and masses.

While Pareto's conception of the circulation of elites is often claimed to have been his principal contribution to sociological theory, it certainly does not form the core of his system of sociology, for his primary intention was to explain the permanence of social systems, not their changes. His conception of the circulation of elites seems to have been a limited concession to historical facts that testify to social change and to theories that explain those facts, a concession made by a theorist who owes his place in the history of sociology mainly to the study of the changeless.

PSYCHOLOGISM IN SOCIOLOGY: A BALANCE SHEET

It is difficult to draw a balance sheet of psychologism in sociology, because psychologism was an intermediate and somewhat eclectic trend. It was a product of the increasing erosion of organicism and evolutionism, but also to some extent at least, a manifestation of new interests and an announcement of new viewpoints. This is why there are items on the debit side of its theory that per se did not have to be listed there. This applies, for instance, to Freud's evolutionist speculations and to Pareto's mechanism, on the one hand, and to Pareto's prefunctionalism, on the other. Some elements of the doctrines subsumed under psychologism were relics of earlier trends, while others were harbingers of new orientations. Further, even psychologism proper was extremely heterogeneous.

Its heterogeneity consists both in the fact that one term covers a number of different theories and in the fact that the various theories represent different trends. One such trend was to seek new explanations of sociological problems by using real or supposed advances in new psychological theories. The other was to formulate new problems when the influence of society on the psychic life of the individual came to be noticed. In the former case, we are talking about *psychosociology*, which in the last analysis means a continuation of thinking about society in terms of human nature as something given once and for all. In the latter, the subject is *social psychology*, a new discipline that takes up those aspects of individual behavior that prove inexplicable as long as they are analyzed apart from the individual's life in society. Psychosociology was an endeavor to solve sociological problems by resorting to individual psychology, and social psychology was an endeavor to demarcate a new field of research situated between individual psychology and sociology. At the turn of the nineteenth century these two spheres of interests were rarely distinguished. Scholars were prone to see primarily that which was common to both: namely, the conviction that sociology cannot do without psychology, because social phenomena are psychic in nature. They are intersubjective, but not objective. Psychosociology proved to be one of the blind alleys of monocausalism, while social psychology was to branch off into a separate discipline, of whose achievements sociology has been availing itself for a long time.

Sociological psychologism, with which we have been concerned here, unfortunately did not go far beyond psychosociology, even though it gave social psychology its name and helped that new discipline to acquire much popularity. Freud was the only scholar to have left an intellectual heritage that really counts in social psychology. The other thinkers discussed in this chapter are valued as sociologists and not at all for that which they themselves valued most in their achievements. Pareto is the best example: He is commonly considered a classic within sociology, but his claims to glory include nearly everything except that which made him a representative of psychologism. And there is nothing extraordinary in this, for psychologism as a theoretical trend in sociology proved quite insipid. If we discuss it here at great length, this is not because of its contributions to sociology, which were almost nil. Rather, it was an important link between evolutionistic sociology in the nineteenth century and the trends that came to be characteristic of twentieth-century sociology, and some of its representatives had something important to say, regardless of their basic theoretical assumptions.

Psychologism encountered strong criticism not only from authors who were inclined to belittle the psychic aspects of social life. For instance, the famous Polish sociologist L. Petrazycki (1867-1931) criticized that doctrine because he firmly believed that a "psychological approach" was necessary; he blamed representatives of psychologism for accepting at face value the offer of psychology as a universal discipline, whereas in fact

psychology as it is now proves completely uninspiring and . . . cannot serve as a foundation on which we could construct such theoretical and practical disciplines concerned with man's spiritual life as the theory of law and morals, aesthetics, pedagogy, and so on. If we want properly to construct those and other humanistic and spiritual disciplines *(Geisteswissenschaften)* that require a psychological foundation, we must first of all reconstruct contemporary psychology.[57]

In a word, the very foundation on which representatives of psychologism tried to reconstruct the social sciences came to be questioned. Characteristically enough, representatives of psychologism themselves often referred not to the generally accepted achievements of psychology, but to a psychology of their own making. The existence of scientific psychology still remained a matter of faith.

Other critics attached less importance to the state of psychology, for they thought that even a scientifically blameless knowledge of the psychic life of the individual would be of little use to the student of social facts. This applies, above all, to Durkheim. He maintained that society is an entity *sui generis*. Accordingly, all knowledge of society must be derived from the study of society itself, as it is not deducible from the knowledge of individual facts, whether biological or psychological in nature. The criticism launched by Rickert and other adherents of historicism came from other quarters. He claimed that the conclusions provided by psychology as a generalizing science are of no use for a student of a definite society, who needs "historical psychology," that is, knowledge of individual men or definite masses of men at definite times."[58] In this case, the refutation of psychologism comes from the position of antinaturalism, diffident of all statements that claim the universal validity of laws of nature. Still another type of criticism was represented by Znaniecki, who maintained, first, that culture has its own inner order and hence cannot be reduced to a simple accumulation of "facts of consciousness" and, second, that the sociologist should start with observation of social actions and not with deduction that takes psychological features of the individual as the point of departure.

But psychologism was dealt the decisive blow by psychology itself, in which behaviorism, represented by John B. Watson (1878-1958) and other scholars, started gaining in popularity soon after 1910. That trend moved the focus of interest from inquiry into the constant characteristics of human psychic life to the observation of what man really *does*.[59] Moreover, behaviorism put an end to speculations on the innate features of human psychic life by stating that they are quite insignificant as compared with what man learns. This opened quite new prospects for advances in social psychology, even though behaviorists often confined themselves to studies in animal psychology or studies of simple responses by human individuals to environmental stimuli. Since the rise of behaviorism (if we disregard the still vigorous Freudian theory), the problem of the usefulness of psychology for explaining social facts has been more and more closely linked to the controversy over the attitude toward behaviorism, and the present-day psychological theories in sociology are behavioristic *par excellence*.

NOTES

1. See Pitirim A. Sorokin, *Contemporary Sociological Theories* (New York: Harper and Row, 1928), p. 600; Joseph A. Schumpeter, *History of Economic Analysis* (London: Allen and Unwin, 1972), p. 27.

2. See Floyd Nelson House, *The Development of Sociology* (Westport, Conn.: Greenwood Press, 1970), p. 179.

3. See Roscoe C. Hinkle, Jr., and Gisela J. Hinkle, *The Development of Modern Sociology: Its Nature and Growth in the United States* (New York: Doubleday, 1954), p. 57.

4. Wilhelm Wundt, *Logik: Eine Untersuchung des Prinzipien der Erkenntnis und der Methoden wissenschaftlicher Forschung*, vol. 3, *Logik der Geisteswissenschaften*, 3d ed. (Stuttgart: F. Enke, 1908), p. 17.

5. Ferdinand Tönnies, *On Social Ideas and Ideologies* (New York: Harper and Row, 1974), pp. 154-55.

6. Wilhelm Wundt, *Elements of Folk Psychology. Outlines of a Psychological History of the Development of Mankind* (London: Macmillan, 1916), p. 3.

7. Gustave Le Bon, *The Crowd: A Study of the Popular Mind* (London: T. Fischer Unwin, 1909), pp. 15, 19.

8. Ibid., p. 31.

9. Sigmund Freud, *The Group Psychology and the Analysis of the Ego, The Major Works*

of Sigmund Freud, in *Great Books of the Western World*, vol. 54 (Chicago: Encyclopaedia Britannica, 1952), p. 666.

10. Terry N. Clark, ed., *Gabriel Tarde on Communication and Social Influence* (Chicago: University of Chicago Press, 1969), pp. 12-15 (Introduction).

11. Ibid., p. 103.

12. Ibid., p. 95.

13. Cf. J. Milet, *Gabriel Tarde et la philosophie de l'histoire* (Paris: J. Vrin, 1970), p. 342.

14. Ibid., pp. 339-40.

15. Charles A. Ellwood, *An Introduction to Social Psychology* (New York: Appleton, 1921), p. 12.

16. Cf. Gardner Murphy, *An Historical Introduction to Modern Psychology* (London: Kegan Paul, Trench, Trubner, 1930), p. 293.

17. William McDougall, *Introduction to Social Psychology*, 26th ed. (London: Methuen, 1945), p. 17.

18. Cf. T. Parsons et al., eds., *Theories of Society: Foundations of Modern Sociological Theory* (New York: Free Press, 1961), p. 747.

19. McDougall, *Introduction*, p. 25.

20. Florian Znaniecki, *Wstep do sociologü* (Poznan: Gobethner i Wolff, 1922), p. 81.

21. Kimball Young and Douglas W. Oberdorfer, "Psychological Studies of Social Processes," in H. E. Barnes, Howard Becker, and Frances Bennett Becker, eds., *Contemporary Social Theory* (New York: Russel and Russel, 1971), p. 329.

22. Fred Weinstein and Gerald Platt, *Psychoanalytical Sociology* (Baltimore: Johns Hopkins University Press, 1973), p. 3.

23. Cf. Hans Meyerhoff, "Freud and the Ambiguity of Culture," in Bruce Mazlish, ed., *Psychoanalysis and History* (New York: Grosset and Dunlap, 1971), p. 56.

24. Freud, "The Group Psychology," p. 664.

25. Abram Kardiner and Edward Preble, *They Studied Man* (Cleveland and New York: World Publishing, 1961), p. 240.

26. Sigmund Freud, *Introductory Lectures on Psychoanalysis, The Major Works*, in *Great Books*, vol. 54, p. 452.

27. Talcott Parsons, *Social Structure and Personality* (New York: Free Press, 1965), p. 113.

28. Sigmund Freud, *Civilization and Its Discontents* (New York: W. W. Norton & Co., 1962), pp. 44, 88.

29. Ibid., pp. 58-59.

30. Cf. Paul Roazen, *Freud: Political and Social Thought* (New York: Vintage Books, 1970), p. 255.

31. Freud, *Civilization*, p. 36.

32. Cf. H. Stuart Hughes, *Consciousness and Society: The Reorientation of European Social Thought, 1890-1930* (New York: Vintage Books, 1958), p. 143.

33. Freud, *Civilization*, p. 62.

34. Ibid., p. 71.

35. George C. Homans and Charles P. Curtis, Jr., *An Introduction to Pareto: His Sociology* (New York: Knopf, 1934), p. 51.

36. See ibid., p. 291.

37. Karl Mannheim, *Ideology and Utopia: An Introduction to the Sociology of Knowledge* (London: RKP, 1954), p. 123. Werner Stark, *The Fundamental Forms of Social Thought* (London: RKP, 1954), p. 124.

38. Vilfredo Pareto, *The Mind and Society: A Treatise on General Sociology* (New York: Dover, 1963), par. 81.

39. Ibid., par. 1454.

40. Ibid., par. 161.

41. S. Hook, "Pareto's Sociological System," in James H. Meisel, ed., *Pareto and Mosca* (Englewood Cliffs, N.J.: Prentice-Hall, 1965), p. 59.

42. Don Martindale, *The Nature and Types of Sociological Theory* (Boston: Houghton Mifflin, 1960), p. 103.

43. Hughes, *Consciousness and Society*, pp. 263-64.

44. Pareto, *Mind and Society*, par. 850.

45. Ibid., par. 1400.

46. Ibid., par. 1401.

47. Ibid., par. 1419.

48. Ibid., pars. 1748, 1843.

49. Ibid., par. 1732.

50. Bernard Barber, ed., *L. J. Henderson on the Social System* (Chicago: University of Chicago Press, 1970), p. 181.

51. Pareto, *Mind and Society*, par. 2066.

52. Cf. Irving M. Zeitlin, *Ideology and the Development of Sociological Thought* (Englewood Cliffs, N.J.: Prentice-Hall, 1968), pp. 183-84.

53. Ibid., p. 165.

54. Ibid.

55. Pareto, *Mind and Society*, par. 2031.

56. Ibid., pars. 2055, 2053.

57. L. Petrazycki, *Wstep do zagadnien prawa i moralnosci* (Warsaw: PWN, 1959), p. 21.

58. Heinrich Rickert, *Science and History: A Critique of Positivist Epistemology* (Princeton: Van Nostrand, 1962), p. 65.

59. John B. Watson, *The Ways of Behaviorism* (New York: Harper and Brothers, 1928), pp. 1, 8.

10

SOCIOLOGISM: SOCIOLOGY AS THE FUNDAMENTAL SOCIAL SCIENCE

The conceptions discussed so far usually emphasized the need to establish sociology as a separate discipline, but were largely intended to seek solutions of the principal sociological problems outside such a discipline. True, they cut themselves off from philosophy, especially in its speculative version, but not from natural science—in particular, neither from biology nor from psychology. The emerging opinion, however, was that sociology must explain social facts as consequences of predominantly social factors and that it not only can do so without assistance by other disciplines, but in some cases (those of philosophy and psychology) is actually in a position to help them. The advocates of the view here termed *sociologism* believed that sociology should become the new queen of the sciences of man, the *magistra* of philosophy, ethics, historiography, jurisprudence, political science, art theory, and the like. That was directed against psychologism in the first place.

THE CONCEPT OF SOCIOLOGISM

Sociologism had two meanings. First, it was a sociological theory connected with a set of rules of the sociological method, which instructed how social facts are to be investigated and explained. Second, it was (especially in Durkheim's case) a philosophical doctrine that claimed the right to make statements on issues that could not be classed as sociological. In the latter sense, C. Bouglé wrote about sociologism as "a philosophical attempt, that is to crown the objective, comparative and specialized studies of sociologists with a theory of the human spirit."[1]

The term *sociologism* in both senses is generally applied to Durkheim and his school, although Sorokin includes Cooley, Gumplowicz, Marx, and even the German formalists in that school. He starts from the assumption that all those authors, so different from one another, were linked together by the acceptance of social facts as a reality *sui generis* and by their reluctance to accept the reductionism that marked psychologism.[2]

The prehistory of sociologism obviously includes all of those antiatomistic conceptions according to which society is not reducible to its component parts and is "primary" or "superior" in relation to them; this applies, for instance, to social philosophy of the conservatives at the turn of the eighteenth century. Sociologism, however, is something more than just antiatomism or anti-individualism, also known as sociological realism in social philosophy. Sociologism means a complex of theorems and assumptions that either did not appear at all in the earlier realistic conceptions or were merely implied by them. It is to be noted first that sociologism developed in the sphere of positivistic naturalism and also took for granted the existence of sociology as a separate discipline covering the study of all social problems. The following is an endeavor to list and to explain the major features of sociologism.

Sociologistic Naturalism. Like psychologism, sociologism was one of the numerous ramifications of positivistic sociology. While its representatives often strove to free themselves from the "positivistic metaphysic" of their predecessors and to renounce their dogmatism, it was for them beyond a doubt that the first step toward a scientific sociology had to be the acceptance of the essential resemblance of social facts and natural phenomena: Social facts, too, are subject to constant laws. The representatives of sociologism considered the main assumptions of positivism to be well founded in practical cognitive activity. The controversy between them and naturalistic dogmatists was thus a family quarrel. The issue was to eliminate from the social sciences the practice of explaining social facts by *a priori* subsuming them under other categories of facts. Social facts are subject to general laws, but they also have their specific characteristics, which only a methodical study can reveal.

The Specific Nature of Social Reality. Sociologism assumed that social facts form a distinct class of natural phenomena. They can, however, be explained on a limited scale if we confine ourselves to referring to other classes of phenomena. Representatives of sociologism strove to draw a demarcation line between facts of individual life and those of collective life and to demonstrate that no reliable knowledge of the latter can be deduced from the knowledge of the former. Sociologism is thus a radically antireductionist approach.

The Autonomy and Self-Sufficiency of Sociology. The opinion that sociology is, and ought to be, a separate and independent discipline was a natural consequence of the conviction about the specific nature of social facts. Since social reality is something specific and qualitatively different from individual reality, sociology has its own subject matter of research. Its success largely depends on whether it can assert its independence from other disciplines and can handle that subject matter without succumbing to dogmas taken from other sciences.

Sociology as the Fundamental Social Science. Sociologism was also marked by the tendency to subordinate to sociology all those disciplines that are concerned with the various spheres of social reality, the tendency often called "sociological imperialism." One of the virtues of sociology was seen in its popularizing the idea that social facts studied by the various disciplines are closely intertwined with one another. Sociology was thus supposed to provide the key to the comprehension of all social facts from both the theoretical and the practical points of view. In the extreme, it was even expected to solve traditionally philosophical problems.

The Overcoming of Evolutionism. Like psychologism, sociologism marked a departure from evolutionism. Problems of social development ceased to be the focus of interest of sociology, which came then to concentrate on permanent and recurrent relationships among social facts, on social types, and on the like. The place of evolutionist schemata was taken by comparative studies. The antievolutionist attitude characteristic of sociologism had many sources, and the principal ones certainly included the rejection of the assumption that human nature is one and the same.

THE SOCIOLOGY OF GUMPLOWICZ

Ludwig Gumplowicz (1838-1909), "the most reasonable and the least extreme" of social Darwinists,[3] was the first sociologist to apply sociologism as the viewpoint. A Polish-born scholar of Jewish origin, he lectured at Graz University from 1875 on, after failing to obtain a chair at the Jagellonian University in Cracow. His main works—*Der Rassenkampf* (1883), *Grundriss der Soziologie* (1885), *Die Soziologische Staatsidee* (1892), *Soziologie und Politik* (1892), and *Sozialphilosophie im Umriss* (1910)— were published in German and, as F. Tönnies noted, were among the first books in German to have in their titles the term *sociology.* As a theorist, Gumplowicz has been underestimated and very often misinterpreted. He is considered at best to be one of the classics of the theory of conflict; much less often is he cited as an author who "proclaimed the autonomy of the social no less trenchantly than Durkheim"[4] and "was one of the first to achieve full emancipation of sociology from the nonsocial sciences by insisting that social phenomena are distinctive and can be understood only by reference to social causes."⁵ His sociological system is rarely viewed as an original one and not as just a standard application of the principles of social Darwinism.

Note that he was one of the last founders of such a system. Like his predecessors, among whom he valued Spencer most, he sought in sociology a theoretical formula that would be applicable to all facts known from human history, would agree with the scientific standards set up by modern natural science, and would be recognized as universal by the positivist philosophy of science.

Monism and the Specificity of Social Facts. Gumplowicz termed his standpoint *monistic* (which corresponds fairly well to the term *naturalistic* used in the present book) and maintained that the task of sociology is to discover the laws that govern social facts. In that respect he was faithful to the positivist tradition, but he saw the fundamental issue in the distinctive nature of social facts as compared with other categories of natural phenomena. He held that "these universal laws govern phenomena of all kinds . . . but for each particular kind they are manifested in a particular way." Hence, "the function of sociology consists in showing that universal laws apply to social phenomena in pointing out the peculiar effects produced by them in the social domain, and finally, in formulating the special social laws."⁶

The social process was for him a natural process *sui generis.* This led to the recommendation to avoid all reductionist explanations and to seek purely social laws, which are not deductible from general laws, but must be discovered by the study of facts. For instance, the general law of causation means merely that every social fact must have a cause of its own. But sociology itself must discover that cause, while the sociologist must bear in mind that "every social phenomenon, whether political, juridical, or economic, must have a sufficient cause in one or more social agencies."⁷

It is from these positions that Gumplowicz criticized his predecessors (Comte, Quételet, Spencer, and others) and blamed them for the inclination to deduce social laws from general ones or from laws discovered by observation of nonsocial facts. That criticism, however, was leveled first against the individualistic conceptions of human nature: Gumplowicz thought that no knowledge of human individuals would bring us closer to the knowledge of social facts, which have their specific features. Note also that he was critical of statisticians, who, in his opinion, failed to notice the essential difference between *individual* facts, which are counted, compared, and grouped together by statisticians, and *social* facts—such as the subjugation of one nation by another, the rise and fall of the various states, emancipation of estates, the decline of the supremacy of the nobility or the gentry, and so forth—which are the subject matter of sociology.[8]

On the other hand, Gumplowicz was also extremely critical of organicism and praised Spencer for not having taken his own analogies too literally. In both cases he was disgusted by the practice of squeezing social facts into a framework conceived outside sociology and intended to explain facts other than social. While standing for monism, he defended the principle of the plurality of "worlds of phenomena" and maintained that "sociology has discovered a new world of phenomena. In that social world we have to investigate natural phenomena and movements and establish the existence of valid laws. Should it later turn out that the framework within which the modern philosophy of nature has locked its image of the world is too tight, let it burst."[9]

In Gumplowicz's system it had to burst in order to make possible the establishment of a specific subject of sociology, for that discipline was qualitatively different from the sciences concerned with human individuals. Sociology is not interested in the individual. The individual is a product of a social group, and hence we have to study concrete groups and not abstract individuals, who are simply nonexistent in social life.

But it was not only rejecting the abstract concept of the individual as existing outside society that was characteristic of Gumplowicz. He was equally vigorous in opposing the abstract idea of mankind and society, which was so important, for instance, in Comte's sociology. It is a group that is the proper subject of sociological research: Sociology is concerned only with those facts which result from the division of mankind into heterogeneous groups. In that respect, Gumplowicz's viewpoint was in exact opposition to evolutionism.

Sociology as the Science of Social Groups. Gumplowicz attached particular importance to his hypothesis of *polygenism*, according to which mankind must be considered to be not a single whole, but a conglomerate of heterogenous groups, each of which has its own origin and nature. That hypothesis, to which he stuck almost until the end of his life (he abandoned it only under the influence of his American friend Lester F. Ward), was not so important by itself, but it constituted the shortest way to making the group the basic datum in sociology.

Gumplowicz thus opposed both individualism and collectivism. Man is a gregarious animal, but his social instinct has definite limits that are identical with the limits of the groups of which he is a member.

Smithian economics and materialistic philosophy considered egoism and self-interest the source of social development and the motive of human behavior. Others pointed to the self-sacrifice of the individual. . . . The real truth was overlooked. Neither one alone and neither to the degree supposed is the cause and motive of social development. If we preface each with the adjective "social" giving it the meaning not of the abstract whole but of the limited social circle . . . we shall have found the middle way which social philosophy has hitherto missed.[10]

The polygenism hypothesis was useful in maintaining that standpoint, for it introduced groups as "natural social elements," but the standpoint itself is logically independent of that hypothesis.

Gumplowicz rejected the idea of independence of the individual as a fiction, but he also rejected the vision of society as a homogeneous organism. In his opinion, at most the primitive tribes that had emerged in the remote past, independently of one another, could comply with that vision. All those societies which are known in human history are inevitably hetero-geneous because they emerged, and continue to emerge, through the amal-gamation of different groups, each of which strives to subordinate the remaining ones. This is why sociology can be neither the science of human individuals nor the science of human society as such: Its subject matter is social *groups* in the process of their mutual interaction. It is only in that process that the individual is shaped and comes to be determined by it.

Gumplowicz's Concept of "Race." Since interaction between social groups was, to Gumplowicz, the principal subject matter of sociology, a more precise definition of those groups and relationships among them acquired essential significance. The issue has led to many misunderstand-ings, because the author of *Der Rassenkampf* introduced into his system the unfortunate term *race*, as a result of which he was blamed for support-ing vulgar racialism and even for paving the way for fascist ideology.[11] Such interpretations are completely groundless, for if there was any connection between Gumplowicz's ideas and racialism (which he criticized as a fantasy devoid of any scientific foundations), it was only the acceptance of inter-group antagonisms as a natural, and not merely a historical, fact that thus—counter to the expectations of Marx and other socialists—essentially cannot be eliminated from human life. Characteristic of Gumplowicz's approach to the problem of race were his firm rejection of any division of human races into better and worse ones, so typical of racialism, and his interpretation of race as a fact of culture, rather than biology. In his peculiar racialism the unity of blood was secondary to the unity of culture. Any other approach would also be in glaring contradiction with Gum-plowicz's antireductionism. He himself did not leave any doubt about it when he wrote, "I have given up the strictly anthropological concept of race and use the term . . . more for social groups which form, not an anthro-pological, but a social unity."[12]

The cultural interpretation of the concept of race resulted in Gumplowicz's opinion that what is permanent is mankind's division into races, but not the existence of any single race. *Amalgamation*—that is, combination of races that yields "historical bonds" that in the course of time result in a "common circulation of blood"—is one of the fundamental social processes. That common circulation of blood, however, is derivative from the emergence of a new group solidarity (*syngenism* in Gumplowicz's terminology).

When we draw attention to the peculiarities of Gumplowicz's interpretation of race, we should not overlook the significance of that term's occurrence in his system of sociology. It is certainly an interesting testimony to the difficulties faced by those who strove to make sociology independent of natural science, but did so on the basis of the naturalistic philosophy of science. The fortunes of the concept of race in Gumplowicz's sociological system are a good illustration of the striving, typical of sociologism, to preserve the status of sociology as a natural discipline and simultaneously to guarantee its autonomy in accordance with the nature of its subject matter.

The Sociology of Conflicts and "The Struggle of Races." Gumplowicz assumed not only a permanent division of mankind into races, but also a permanent antagonism among them. Solidarity within each group has its analogue in the hostility shown by every group to the remaining ones; the altruism of individuals within their own group is paralleled by their absolute egoism when confronted by members of other groups. Gumplowicz's image of the social world makes us think of the Hobbesian vision of the war of all against all, the parties in this case being groups and not individuals. The interests of the various groups are incompatible with one another, and hence "it is not a bucolic state of peace . . . but one of incessant war, which has always been the standard condition of mankind. Both the past and the present of mankind show a picture of unending conflicts among tribes, peoples, nations, and states."[13] That incessant war is a "law of nature," so only its forms change. At all times and in all places, one social group is striving if not to exterminate, then to subjugate, enslave, and exploit another group. Unlike Comte, Spencer, and Marx, Gumplowicz excluded any possibility of a change in that state of things, thus questioning an essential part of that era's idea of progress. At most, he considered it possible that after amalgamation, antagonisms within the various states might become less acute, but that issue did not really attract his attention. He was a theorist of eternal conflict.

Gumplowicz deduced that all major social institutions, the state in particular, had arisen from strife among groups (races). He discussed the problem of the state at much greater length than Comte or Spencer did and held the science of the state to be a component part of sociology. The emergence of the state was a turning point in human history, for it occurred when extermination of enemies came to be replaced by their exploitation: The captives, instead of being killed, were turned into slaves or serfs. The state and the law did not emerge from ideas about common welfare or justice; they are instruments of the rule of the stronger over the weaker. But violence yields not only the enforced obedience of the vanquished; it also yields culture, which "contributes to the uniformity of the varied social elements within the state and in the course of time transforms the various component parts of a people into a uniform nation."[14] Despite the progress in amalgamation, the population of the state does not become fully homogeneous and its original racial differentiation survives as differences of estates, castes, and classes. The dichotomous division of the population into the upper and the lower classes largely corresponds to the former differentiation into the conquerors and the conquered; the "buffer" middle class, too, has its origin in its different ethnicity.

Gumplowicz's sociology can certainly be explained by a very long tradition that goes back at least to Ibn Khaldun. Nevertheless, it seems that the direct observation of the conditions prevailing in the Austro-Hungarian monarchy, which Gumplowicz experienced throughout his life, was no less important. He lived in society which was differentiated ethnically and in which ethnic divisions often coincided with class divisions; the state was felt by many national groups to be an instrument of domination of an alien minority over the native majority. It may thus be said that Gumplowicz's contribution to sociology was the specific experience of a multinational state, unknown to French, British, and even German sociologists.

The Significance of Gumplowicz's Ideas. Gumplowicz's originality lay, above all, in his sociologistic conception of sociology as the science of the specific group reality, a science that must become independent of all other disciplines concerned with other categories of facts and must also become the foundation and the binding element of all disciplines dealing with social facts: anthropology, political science, law, history, political economy, and linguistics. Gumplowicz was an advocate of sociologism before Durkheim.

His influence, however, proved to be limited. He was fairly well known outside Poland and the German-language area (his works were translated into Russian, French, and English), and he was valued by certain contemporaries whose opinion carried weight (Ratzenhofer and Ward). But he had a noticeable influence on only Franz Oppenheimer (1863-1943), whose works have been of marginal significance. This has been due to (1) the inconsistencies and weaknesses inherent in Gumplowicz's system; (2) the fact that the area in which he was active was peripheral to the intellectual centers in Europe at that time; and (3) the ideological ambiugity of his views. Gumplowicz was too radical for the conservatives and too conservative for the radicals. Moreover, his most interesting ideas were much better expounded by others, independently of his influence; this applied to sociologism as developed by Durkheim and to the theory of conflict as handled by Marx and his followers.

THE SOCIOLOGY OF DURKHEIM

Sociologism had its most eminent representative in Emile Durkheim (1858-1917), professor of sociology in Bordeaux and later in Paris and author of such classic works as *De la division du travail social* (1893), *Règles de la méthode sociologique* (1895), *Le Suicide* (1897), and *Les Formes élémentaires de la vie religieuse* (1912). Durkheim is one of those unquestioned classics of sociology whose impact has proved to be multidirectional and durable. Not only did he create an original sociological conception, but he also knew how to apply it in empirical research (the study of suicide), to expound it in an exceptionally coherent manner, to group around him and his ideas a team of talented coworkers, to provide them with an appropriate institutional framework of activity (the periodical *L'Année sociologique*, which was first published in 1898), and to pave the way for sociology in French universities and even in schools of a lower rank.[15]

It seems that he has done more than anyone else to establish the status of sociology and to secure it a permanent position among the other social sciences. He also enabled the country of Comte to become, for several decades, a sociological center of primary importance. Even though there are no Durkheimists today, interest in his work has not abated and has actually increased in English-speaking countries.

Durkheim and the Heritage of the Nineteenth Century. Durkheim's sociology, novel as it was, was strongly linked to the heritage of nineteenth-century social thought and sociology. The problems discussed by Durkheim, both theoretical and ideological, cannot be understood if they are viewed without the proper consideration of their historical background, formed both by the discussions concerning the crisis of society that had been going on since 1789 and by the recurrent endeavors to lay scientific foundations for the overcoming of that crisis. Durkheim's works were an unending dialogue with conservatism, liberalism, and socialism, accompanied by intense work on constructing the foundations of "scientific rationalism," which would make it possible to solve practical problems more effectively than had the doctrines of Comte and Spencer.

Durkheim's principal issue was to define, in theory and in practice, the relation between the individual and society. He strove for a balance between the aspirations of the individuals freed from the bonds of tradition and the needs of society as a whole. He believed that emancipation was both desirable and irreversible, but at the same time he was alarmed by the fact that society had not produced anything that could control the forces of anarchy set free by that process.

Durkheim had not accepted any great ideology of his times. He could not acquiesce in liberalism, according to which society is merely, as Bentham put it, an alleged body consisting of individual persons. He blamed the liberals for having wrongly reduced man to *homo oeconomicus* and reduced the tasks of society to ensuring maximum independence and material well-being to individuals. To Durkheim, man must be educated and society organized: Neither task can be left to the operation of the forces of nature. Hence, he saw liberalism as a doctrine that was both wrong and dangerous.

Durkheim opposed socialism, too, although he showed much interest in it and realized the social significance of that trend better than most of his contemporaries did. From Durkheim's point of view, socialism as a doctrine had some affinity with liberalism, which aimed to turn the state into an instrument of economic life. Yet the main cause of Durkheim's dislike of socialism came from his shifting those social facts out of the analysis from which modern socialism grew to the margin of social pathology and from his believing that the possibilities of a further development of capitalism had been far from exhausted.

Is Durkheim, then, to be considered a conservative? However much he drew from conservative tradition (not only in the sphere of the diagnosis of the social and moral crisis), he represented a trend that was basically opposed to the conservatism of his times. He was a programmatically lay thinker (and took an active part in the drive to laicize French schools), a defender of Dreyfus, and an ardent propounder of the principles of *The Declaration of the Rights of Man and the Citizen.* Together with the conservatives he opposed an individualism that reduces society to a mechanism of production and trade, but he stood for the traditions of Kant, Rousseau, and the French Revolution.

Durkheim thought that in modern society the ways of solving social problems should be indicated by science. He thus referred to positivism, but he was not in full agreement with any of the positivists, who had earlier advanced scientific programs of social reconstruction. He blamed scientific ideologies and sociopolitical ones alike for being satisfied with ready-made doctrines, without entering the path of a "direct contact with things."[16] His sociology was to be the first social discipline that would start from things and not from ideas. Comte and Spencer, as Durkheim saw them, had still been satisfied with an "ideological analysis."

Social Facts as "Things." Durkheim's much publicized demand that social facts be treated as things was thus a cornerstone of his sociology, which he considered to be identical with the social sciences in general. It was a methodological requirement. Durkheim often formulated the reservation (not always properly understood) that he did not want to decide in advance what is the essence of social facts, but merely intended "to assume a certain mental attitude toward them."[17] His point was to make the sociologist approach the subject of his study without any emotions and *praeonotiones* (preconceptions) whatever and to renounce all ideas that he had uncritically brought along from everyday thinking, dominant ideologies, and dogmatic philosophical systems: "When he penetrates the social world, he must be aware that he is penetrating the unknown; he must feel himself in the presence of facts whose laws are as unexpected as were those of life before the era of biology; he must be prepared for discoveries which will surprise and disturb him."[18] Durkheim's fundamental requirement was thus one of methodological ignorance. He himself willingly compared this procedure to Bacon's criticism of the idols and to Descartes's methodological principle of doubting. It was an endeavor to find a sociological *cogito*—the point at which the construction of the edifice of truly reliable knowledge could begin.

Durkheim's epistemological Utopia makes us assume that we face facts about which we know nothing. We have rid ourselves of all preconceptions, and only phenomenal reality is given to us. We do not, and cannot, know morals, but merely the moral standards observable in the various collectivities. We know nothing about crime as such, but we can state that in every collectivity there are acts that are condemned and punished. We have no *a priori* knowledge of religion, but we can study religious beliefs and practices. In each case, the point is not to restrict such studies in advance by our apparent knowledge of their subject matter. Hence, it was typical of Durkheim to formulate definitions and to single out the subject of research by referring to outermost characteristics of the facts that are observable and verifiable at the intersubjective level. As a result, Durkheim's definitions usually differ strikingly from current ones. Further, their task is not to reveal any supposed essence of things, but to pave the way for an objective study of things. Durkheim thus drew the farthest-reaching conlusions from the assumptions of positivist phenomenalism.

But the requirement that social facts be treated as things has another aspect. Since a thing is external to the cognizing subject, it cannot be known by him through introspection. The issue here is the criticism of psychologism in sociology, which admitted the possibility of explaining social facts by introspective knowledge of individual mental life. Durkheim excluded such a possibility and saw the only scientific method in external observation, as used by natural scientists.

Durkheim considered his requirement to be philosophically neutral and free from connections with any social ontology. This belief, however, gives rise to profound doubts. He himself was fairly positive about what social facts are and did not confine himself to explaining how they are to be studied. The first chapter of *The Rules of Sociological Method* is concerned with the answer to the question, "What is a social fact?" His famous definition this: "A social fact is every way of acting, fixed or not, capable of exercising on the individual an external constraint; or again, every way of acting which is general throughout a given society, while at the same time existing in its own right independent of its individual manifestations."[19]

Thus, methodological recommendations were complemented by a definite philosophy of society. That option for sociological realism had two justifications in Durkheim's thought, a philosophical one and a quasi-scientific one. He stuck to it all his life, despite all the changes that his interpretation of the subject of sociology underwent.

The Philosophy of Dual Man. Durkheim's philosophical anthropology, most explicitly formulated in his paper "The Dualism of Human Nature and Its Social Conditions" (1914),[20] was an important element in his sociology and in his ethical and educational ideas as well. Man, he claimed, is marked by a striking duality *(homo duplex)*, which has always been reflected in religious, philosophical, and moral systems that show man as a being split into soul and body, senses and reason, instinct and consciousness. Current experience shows us "two aspects of our psychic life": At one pole there are sensory data, instincts, and dispositions connected with purely physical needs of the human organism; at the other are conceptual thinking, morality, religion, and the like—in a word, all that which is common, which is shared with other men. We may call these two aspects "personal" and "impersonal," "egoistic" and "altruistic," "individual" and "universal," or "singular" and "social."

Durkheim thought that there is a permanent antagonism between the two. When he wants to act morally, man must violate his animal nature, for animals have no sense of self-denial and sacrifice, without which there is no moral act. When grasping the world in terms of general concepts, man must to some extent dismiss the testimony of his own senses, which show him merely single phenomena and things. Durkheim rejected all monistic solutions, which evade the problem instead of solving it: Moral and reason cannot be deduced from any properties characteristic of man as a biological organism; nor can man be treated as a purely spiritual being and his links to the animal world be totally disregarded. Durkheim accordingly poses the question: How is it that abilities and dispositions so widely different as reason and morality, on the one hand, and animal desires and instincts, on the other, can coexist in man?

Perhaps it was just this problem that gave rise to Durkheim's interest in religion. He assigned a particularly important role to it in social life, since he thought that man, when he engages in religious life, takes on a different nature and becomes a different person. Owing to religion, something that goes beyond the limits of sensory experience enters into human life: Above the sphere of *profanum* is formed that of *sacrum*, in the face of which the individual experiences respect and fear that make him restrain his natural responses and renounce satisfaction of the needs of his organism.

It is society that, by influencing the individual from the outside, turns him into a being endowed with reason and a sense of morality. Thus, the dichotomy of sense and reason, instincts and morality, egoism and altruism, *profanum* and *sacrum*, is finally the dichotomy of the *individual* and the *social*.

Thus sociology [Durkheim wrote] appears destined to open a new way to the science of man. Up to the present, thinkers were placed before this double alternative: either explain the superior and specific faculties of man by connecting him to the inferior forms of his being, the reason to the senses, or the mind to matter, which is equivalent to denying their uniqueness; or else attach them to some superexperimental reality which was postulated, but whose existence could be established by no observation. What put them in this difficulty was the fact that the individual passed as being the *finis naturae*—the ultimate creation of nature; it seemed that there was nothing beyond him, or at least nothing that science could touch. But from the moment when it is recognised that above the individual there is society, and that it is not a nominal being created by reason, but a system of active forces, a new manner of explaining man becomes possible.[21]

This is why Durkheim saw in sociological realism a hypothesis necessary for the solution of traditional philosophical problems.

Society as a Reality Sui Generis. Durkheim was convinced that the thesis on sociological realism can, and ought to, be substantiated empirically. He believed that the very existence of sociology depended on such a substantiation, since sociology has its *raison d'être* only insofar as there are "phenomena of which this society is the specific cause, phenomena which would not exist if this society did not exist and which are what they are only because this society is constituted the way it is."[22]

Durkheim used four types of arguments to support his interpretation of society.

First, he employed analogies drawn from natural science. If two chemical elements, when combined, form a compound whose properties differ from the properties of both its components, and if biological processes cannot be explained by the properties of the cells of which a given organism consists, then there is no reason to suppose that society has only those properties which are attributes of the individuals of whom it consists. Even though such reasoning is found quite often in his works, there is no reason to believe that he attached to them any major importance in the sense of proof value.

It was rather a *façon de parler*. The statement that society is a reality *sui generis* was a working hypothesis, which offered better opportunities for explaining facts, but need not be preserved in the future.

Second, Durkheim availed himself of the discoveries of crowd psychology to point to the fact that individuals gathered in a place behave differently than they do in isolation. People never live in complete isolation, and this is why such "psychic epidemics" of varying scope and intensity develop continuously and, more important still, tend to be fixed in the form of social ideals and collective ideas. Of course, there were significant differences between Durkheim's sociology and crowd psychology, for Durkheim did not share the opinion that the fact of gathering triggers whatever was potentially inherent in the individuals. Besides, he was mainly interested in the fixed results of social influence.

Third, Durkheim maintained that social reality for the individual is the reality *received* by him. Man does not create the language he speaks, but learns it from his group; he does not invent the methods of work he applies, but takes them over from his milieu; he does not invent his own religion, but professes one of those which already exists. In a word, he must adjust his ways of thinking, feeling, and acting to the ways accepted by society. If he does not do so, he encounters from society a response that varies in form: from legal sanction to public disapproval. It is by this external and coercive nature that social facts differ from individual ones.

And fourth, Durkheim emphasized that individual consciousness always is false consciousness. Human activity is conscious, but the consciousness involved is not adequate to reality. We do not realize even fairly simple motives for our actions. *A fortiori*, there must be a discrepancy between intentions of individuals and effects of their actions.

The Meaning of the Principle of Sociological Realism. Durkheim's principle of sociological realism aroused many doubts on the part of social scientists, and it is in fact far from clear. The critics of that principle usually strove to demonstrate that Durkheim's concept of society (and that of collective consciousness as well) was a hypostasis and was nothing better than Comte's concept of mankind and that of *Völksgeist*, formulated by the German romanticists.[23] Such criticism usually called for elimination of unfortunate metaphors, in which Durkheim's works abound, and dismissal of certain problems. Criticism of collective consciousness often indicated abandoning the classical problems connected with the study of social systems and social structures in favor of studying only individual human behavior. Durkheim's works ought to be read in the belief that his theory of society was concerned with real problems, even though formulated in an unfortunate manner.

Durkheim frequently protested against ascribing to him the intention to make collective consciousness substantial or ontological. He wrote that "one cannot, following idealistic and theological metaphysics, derive the part from the whole, since the whole is nothing without the parts which form it." Society, "while it surpasses us . . . is within us, since it can only exist by and through us."[24] And in *The Elementary Forms of the Religious Life* we read:

Social life . . . moves in a circle. On the one hand, the individual gets from society the best part of himself, all that gives him a distinct character and a special place among other beings, his intellectual and moral culture. If we should withdraw from men their language, sciences, arts and moral beliefs, they would drop to the rank of animals. So the characteristic attributes of human nature come from society. But, on the other hand, society exists and lives only in and through individuals. If the idea of society were extinguished in individual minds and the beliefs, traditions and aspirations of the group were no longer felt and shared by the individuals, society would die.[25]

To avail ourselves of H. Alpert's formulation, we could say that Durkheim's sociological realism was *relationistic*; that is, it assumed the real existence of durable relations among human beings, of institutions, to be interpreted as all those modes of thinking, feeling, and acting that the individual receives ready-made and gradually takes over in the process of his socialization. To use more recent terminology, fully developed only by British and American cultural anthropology, we could say that Durkheim tried to use his specific terminology to bring out the problems of culture,[26] the latter being interpreted not as the material attainment of the community, but as its regulatory function applied to individual behavior. This does not mean, of course, that all statements ever made by Durkheim on collective ideas may unreservedly be translated into statements on culture, but there is no doubt that the basic problems raised by that sociologist can be presented, as done by Parsons, as problems of "*interpenetration* of social system, personality, and culture."[27]

In order to understand properly the meaning of Durkheim's sociological realism, we have to realize what the word *individual* really means in his texts.[28] When Durkheim said that society is "external" to the individual and when he proved that society cannot be explained in terms of concepts applicable to individuals only, he meant the individual as an abstract biological individual taken completely in isolation. From that point of view, the proper meaning of opposing the society to the individual is making a distinction between "natural dispositions" and "social system," between nature and culture. On other occasions Durkheim referred to a given social individual, with respect to whom the thesis that society is external to the individual can have a limited application only. The more he is socialized— the more he has internalized the modes of thinking, feeling, and acting that are accepted in a given society—the less that society is external to him. One of the aspects of the development of social consciousness, as described by Durkheim, is the gradual disappearance of collective consciousness as a force external to individuals. Of course, man can never rid himself completely of his animal nature (he always remains *homo duplex*), so full internalization of collective consciousness remains a purely theoretical possibility.

His conception was certainly not very fortunate. Parsons is right in stating that "the analytical distinction between "individual" and "social" cannot run parallel with that between the concrete entities "individual" and "society.""[29] When modifying the traditional platform of the controversy over the relationship between society and the individual, Durkheim did not fully succeed in freeing himself from the old terminology and from the pressure of false alternatives. Nevertheless, his theory paved the way for the study of important problems.

Social Solidarity and Its Transformations. Those problems can best be seen in Durkheim's studies in changes in social solidarity. Being a scholar of vast historical knowledge and interests, he noticed the extreme differentiation and variability of social bonds and, accordingly, shifted the discussion of the relationships between the individual and society from the level of philosophical generalities to that of sociological facts. He was one of the first sociologists to speak less about society in general and to pay more attention to an analysis of specified societies and groups. Even the very concept of society seemed too broad to him: "What exists and really lives are the particular forms of solidarity, domestic solidarity, occupational solidarity, national solidarity, yesterday's, today's, etc. Each has its proper nature. . . . general remarks in every case give only a very incomplete explanation of a phenomenon, since they necessarily omit the concrete and the vital."[30]

But Durkheim did not go to the other extreme: While he opposed the all-embracing constructions advanced by philosophers, he also rejected the tendency, typical of historians, to consider societies to be "many heterogeneous individualities, not comparable among themselves." In *The Roles of Sociological Method*, he claimed:

It seems . . . that social reality must be merely subject matter of an abstract and vague philosophy or for purely descriptive monographs. But one escapes from this alternative once one has recognized that, between the confused multitude of historic societies and the single, but ideal, concept of humanity, there are intermediaries, namely social species. In the latter are united both the unity that all truly scientific research demands and the diversity that is given in the facts, since the species is the same for all the individual units that make it up, and since, on the other hand, the species differ among themselves. It remains true that moral, legal and economic institutions, etc., are infinitely variable; but these variations are not of such a nature that they deny all scientific treatment.[31]

In his book entitled *The Division of Labor in Society*, Durkheim tried to be neither a philosopher nor a historian. He was not interested in the problem of social solidarity as such, because some kind of solidarity is given to man together with his specifically human existence; nor was he attracted by the description of definite societies as a goal in itself. His intention was to study social species.

How are we to study social solidarity? How can we subject it to close scrutiny as a fact in the sphere of morals, but a social, and not a psychological, one? In accordance with those principles of the sociological method discussed earlier, it is necessary to find an objective (observable from the outside) indicator that would make it possible to study and to measure solidarity. Durkheim took law to be such an indicator.[32]

In his reflection on law, Durkheim came to the conclusion that there are two essentially different kinds of legal provisions, whose weight is not the same in the various societies. One is penal law, whose provisions involve repressive sanctions. The other is cooperative law, in which there are only restitutive sanctions, intended not so much to punish the guilty person as to restore the state of things before the infringement of the law. This applies to civil, commercial, and administrative law. The difference between these two kinds of provisions is due to the fact that the former applies to actions that violate the modes of thinking, feeling, and acting common in a given society, whereas the latter applies only to those which affect individuals or certain sections of society. This difference, in Durkheim's opinion, reflects the difference between two types of social organization and two types of social solidarity. The importance of penal law diminished over the course of human history.

We can single out societies in which penal law dominates; nearly all life of the individual is subject to social supervision. There is in such societies a fairly uniform set of beliefs and feelings that are mandatory for all members of the society, and all individual deviations from the accepted standards are punished severely. Such deviations, by the way, cannot be frequent, because the individual there is "a simple reflection of collective life" and does not yet have his own personality. The scope of individual consciousness is in principle identical with that of collective consciousness. Society is not differentiated internally and thereby, as Durkheim put it, its relationship with the individual is direct. Solidarity in such societies may be termed *mechanical*. It is in inverse ratio to the degree of the differentiation and individualization of society. Such solidarity, based on the similarity of individuals, has its analogue in the social structure that is a "system of segments that are homogeneous and similar to one another."[33] By analogy to arthropods, Durkheim termed such societies segmentary; they are marked by communism in the sphere of goods, domination of religion, traditionalism, and so forth. But from the point of view of Durkheim's typology, the basic fact is that they lack division of labor.

Societies in which cooperative law prevails are marked by the fact that solidarity is based on division of labor. While in societies based on mechanical solidarity the categorical imperative is "Do what others do," here the principle is "Be able to perform usefully a given functin!" Divided labor evades supervision by collective consciousness, which coincides less and less with the consciousness of the various individuals. Specialization contributes to the emergence of personality. Individuals have the sense of solidarity because they differ from one another and need one another. Such solidarity has been termed *organic* by Durkheim; it is in direct ratio to the degree of differentiation and individualization of society. It has its analogue in society (modern industrial society, at least) as "a system of different organs each of which has a special role and which are themselves formed of differentiated parts."[34] The community no longer supervises all spheres of the individual's life; this is reflected, for instance, in the fact that penal law is almost exclusively concerned with the protection of persons and their property. Beliefs and practices more and more lose their religious nature; the importance of rational thinking increases; the system of morals, which formerly was uniform, gives place to differentiated systems of morals characteristic of the various groups, and so on. Individualism becomes more and more common and wins social approval as an attitude.

Durkheim sometimes formulated his distinction between the two kinds of solidarity as a "historical law" that reflects the general trend in the evolution of human societies. He spoke about "higher" and "lower" societies, about transition from "simple" to "complex" forms, thus paying homage to evolutionism, which was so popular in his times. For this reason it must strongly be emphasized that his was not a schema of the development of mankind, but a typology constructed with a view of comparative studies. In all existing societies, except for the simplest ones, both kinds of solidarity co-occur, and hence this typology can be applied not only in the analysis considering primitive and modern societies to be the opposing wholes, but also in the analysis of the various aspects of life of single societies, where it serves to disclose the double source of social solidarity.

Durkheim's typology in many respects resembles that advanced by Spencer, to which the former referred explicitly. In Spencer, the difference between military and industrial societies also was that between uniformity and differentiation, between collectivism and individualism. Yet, the two conceptions differed from one another considerably. Durkheim questioned Spencer's thesis that the homogeneity of military societies was due to the restriction of individuality through coercion: Human beings (in Durkheim's opinion) resembled one another not because they were forbidden to think, to feel, and to act as each of them would like, but just because they were still unable to be independent. Individualism was not a result of the weakening of the community's pressure on the individual who is born a modern liberal, but rather a product of the evolution of society.

Nor did he agree with the Spencerian description of industrial societies, which stated that individuals enjoy complete freedom in them and that the free play of their interests spontaneously yields social harmony. He did share Spencer's and other liberals' admiration of the spontaneity of social development; but following the conservatives, he was inclined to interpret it as the spontaneity of the development of the social whole, which always restricts the freedom of the individuals to some extent. In his opinion, nothing seemed to indicate that the emergence of organic solidarity would make the regulatory functions of the community vanish: "If society no longer imposes upon everybody certain uniform practices, it takes greater care to define and regulate the special relations between different social functions, and this activity is not smaller because it is different."[35] Durkheim pointed to the prolific growth of restitutive law, to the expanding scope of the activity of the state, to the development in the new society of specific moral codes, and so on. Moreover, not only did he notice the growth of regulatory functions, but he postulated their expansion (for example, in the form of founding vocational organizations) in order to counteract the adverse effects of individualization. The social crisis was a result of an excessive loosening of social supervision of the individuals, especially of their economic activity.

The Problem of the Substratum of Social Facts: Social Morphology and Physiology. We have so far pointed to Durkheim's conviction about the interdependence of all spheres of social life (*consensus* in Comte's terminology) without posing the question whether—following his contemporaries —he singled out any fundamental sphere. Durkheim neither dismissed the question nor gave an unambiguous answer to it. As compared with other conceptions popular in the nineteenth century, Durkheim's procedure was first to reduce causes that are essential from the sociological point of view to *social* causes. The important principle of the sociological method was that causes of social facts are to be sought exclusively in other social facts. This meant the rejection of all biological or psychological explanations, but did not decide in the least which social facts would be considered general enough to be used for explanation of other social facts.

Durkheim agreed with Marx that

social life must be explained, not by the conception of it held by those who participate in it, but by profound causes which escape consciousness; and we also think that these causes must be sought chiefly in the way in which the associated individuals are grouped. We even think that it is on this condition, and on this condition alone, that history can become a science and sociology in consequence exist. For, in order that collective *representations* should be intellegible, they must come from something and, since they cannot form a circle closed upon itself, the source whence they derive must be found outside them. Either the *conscience collective* floats in the void, like a sort of inconceivable absolute, or it is connected with the rest of the world through the intermediary of a substratum on which, in consequence, it depends.[36]

Thus, one of Durkheim's tasks was to find the substratum of collective consciousness. The study of that substratum, its connections with collective ideas, and its forms of collective behavior was to be the subject of a special branch of Durkheim's sociology, termed *social morphology*.

Durkheim defined its scope as "the study of the material forms of society" and listed such issues as the size of the territory; the location of a given society, that is, "its peripheral or central position in regard to 'continents' and the way it is enclosed by other societies, and so on"; the form of its frontiers; and "the total mass of the population in its numerical size and density." He also pointed to the necessity of studying "secondary groupings which have a material basis," such as villages, cities, districts, and provinces, which should be studied from the point of view of their size, population, transport facilities, and the like. Problems of migrations would fall under the same branch of sociology.[37] Social morphology thus covered vast problems of demography, ecology, and anthropogeography. Including in it problems of social structure as well, he termed social morphology "the part of sociology which has for its task the constitution and classification of social types."[38]

It would, however, be erroneous to seek in Durkheim's works the assumption that the whole of social life, or even the totality of social institutions, is determined by morphological facts that constitute its substratum. First of all, in his later works his interest in social morphology abated markedly and yielded place to his almost exclusive interest in the problems of collective consciousness. Second, even in his earlier works we find statements limiting the role of morphological variables.

It may be said that Durkheim was more interested in discovering the interconnections among the various elements of the social system than in finding the one whose change determines a change in all the rest. And most of all, he was interested in the collective consciousness in its working on individual consciousness: in society as, primarily, a body of ideas and "the center of moral life."[39] The naturalist Durkheim did not hesitate to declare that he was in fact concerned with a category of spiritual phenomena.[40]

This aspect of Durkheim's sociology, which fully agrees with his philosophical anthropology discussed earlier, was brought out in full relief in *Le Suicide*, *Les Formes élémentaires de la vie religieuse*, and *L'Education morale* (lectures delivered in the academic year 1902-1903 and published posthumously in 1925). But elements of it can be found in almost all his works. He stated that morphological changes, which—according to the analysis he had carried out—should have brought about the emergence of organic solidarity, had until his times resulted merely in a state of disorder and crisis. "Indeed," he wrote, "history records no crisis so serious as that in which European societies have been involved for more than a century. Collective discipline in its traditional form has lost its authority, as the divergent tendencies troubling the public conscience and the resulting general anxiety demonstrate."[41]

This situation, which he depicted most vividly in his study of suicide, made Durkheim think that ultimately everything is decided in the sphere of consciousness and that "collective psychology is the whole sociology."[42] Changes in social structure, and *a fortiori* in economic life, do not themselves determine anything. Even the division of labor is conditioned by "a community of beliefs and emotions." Durkheim did not abandon problems of morphology, but he assigned them a less and less important role. He became interested above all in the formation of social norms and/or institutions and in their effect on individuals and also their function, which is to consolidate the group by ensuring the supremacy of centripetal forces over the centrifugal ones.

Institutionalization of Human Behavior and the Dangers of Its Absence. According to the definition formulated by P. Fauconnet and M. Mauss and approved by Durkheim, "an institution is a set of fixed actions and ideas, which individuals receive as something ready-made and imposed upon them more or less irresistibly."[43] In Durkheim's system, defining sociology as "the science of institutions"[44] also meant focusing that discipline on problems of collective consciousness, studying the process of crystallization of that consciousness and its effect on the individual. Disturbances of such processes were, of course, a matter that equally deserved investigation and attracted Durkheim's attention.

From Durkheim's point of view, *religion* was the institution that, as Poggi puts it, was treated as "paradigmatic."[45] This accounts for his special interest in religious phenomena, dating from about 1895. Hence, the study of totemism in Australia was not an ethnological periphery of Durkheim's sociological system, but, on the contrary, a foundation for the essential parts of that system. By studying totemism, he wanted to comprehend religion as such; and by comprehending "the elementary forms of the religious life," he wanted to find the point of departure for explaining social life in general. When studying religion in its simplest forms, we come to know social institutions in their pure form. It must, of course, be recalled that religion as understood by Durkheim had little in common with the current interpretation of that concept, which associates all religion with belief in supernatural phenomena. Durkheim defined religion not by reference to the content of beliefs, which varies in the course of history and is far from always being theological in nature, but by its function, which consists of integrating society and regulating individual behavior. In this sense, Durkheim's often repeated statement that social facts always are more or less religious in nature seems evidently pleonastic.

A good example of Durkheim's interpretation of the functions of religion is his analysis of the religious cult found in *Les Formes élémentaires de la vie religieuse*.[46]

First, according to Durkheim, the individual's initiation into collective life takes place through religious rites. A system of prohibitions ("negative cult") trains the individual in restraint and self-denial, thus preparing him for the "positive cult," in which the individual starts to participate after attaining a certain age. Religious cult is thus the elementary form of discipline.

Second, religious rites also contribute to integrating the community and are the means whereby the social group reaffirms itself periodically. Everyday life makes the individuals more distant from one another, resulting in the shrinking of group ideals; periodical rites and ceremonies are needed to make the individuals feel their moral unity again and to solidify their links within the group by experiencing that moral unity intensely. In modern life, a similar role is played by national days, congresses, and meetings.

Third, the function of rites also lies in perpetuating traditions of the group, which to some extent are decisive for its distinct "moral physiognomy as a community." Wrote Durkheim,

The mythology of a group is the system of beliefs common to this group. The traditions whose memory it perpetuates express the way in which society represents man and the world; it is a moral system and a cosmology as well as a history. So the rite serves and can serve only to sustain the vitality of these beliefs, to keep them from being effaced from memory and, in sum, to revivify the most essential elements of the collective consciousness.[47]

The linking of the present to the past is concurrently the linking of the individual to the group.

Finally, religious rites also perform the "euphoric" function—supporting the individual at the times of breakdowns and crises, which may be exemplified by funeral and mourning rites.

These were Durkheim's real contributions to the knowledge of religions, being the final victory over the rationalistic attitude to religion as superstition and humbug. His analyses revealed certain durable social and—for all his reservations—psychological needs that must be satisfied under all conditions, although not always in the same manner. The eternal presence of religion in one form or another is due to the fact that the individual, when deprived of the moral support of the group, ceases to be capable of normal life; and societies that are incapable of extending moral protection to and supervision over individuals face decomposition, a condition that Durkheim termed *anomie*.

There is a very close link between *Les Formes élémentaires de la vie religieuse* and Durkheim's works concerned with his contemporaneous industrial society. Already in his work on the division of labor in society he wrote about the social consequences of the lack of all regulation of economic activity and of the opinion that regulation is the private business of the individuals involved. He claimed that "this lack of regulation does not permit a regular harmony of functions,"[48] and in the preface to the second edition of that work there is a nostalgic reference to vocational corporations as regulatory devices in economic life. In the same work we can read about big industry, which severs the worker from his family and also opposes him to his employer, thus breaking existing ties and disturbing social balance. We are also told there that the class division of society renders the emergence of the sense of solidarity difficult; when society is so divided, the division of labor is forced and does not correspond to the natural distribution of abilities.

Durkheim's book on suicide can be interpreted as an answer to the question, What happens to those societies in which social control has weakened considerably, societies that have freed themselves from strict regulation of all spheres of life, but have failed to develop new institutions that would perform the functions of former religions and political organization? Durkheim was interested in suicide as a symptom of disturbed relationships between the individual and the group in modern society. In his opinion, suicides cannot be explained in psychological terms: "When society is strongly integrated it holds individuals under its control, considers them at its service and thus forbids them to dispose wilfully of themselves. Accordingly it opposes their evading their duties to it through death."[49] In modern society, that condition of social integration is no longer satisfied, and hence the suicide rate rises steeply.

We shall not discuss here Durkheim's analysis of suicides (which was novel in the application of statistical methods to verify theoretical hypotheses and in the considerable refinement of those methods). But we shall reflect on one of the types of suicide that he distinguished (he spoke about altruistic, egoistic, and anomic suicides)—that which occurs under social anomie. It is the kind of suicide that "results from man's activity lacking regulation and his consequent sufferings." This takes place at the time of rapid economic changes, as the transformation of the social organization and moral consciousness lags behind: "appetites, not being controlled by a public opinion become disoriented, no longer recognize the limits proper to them." "From the bottom of the ladder, greed is aroused without knowing where to find an ultimate foothold. Nothing can calm it, since its goal is far beyond all it can attain. . . . A thirst arises for novelties, unfamiliar pleasures, nameless sensations, all of which lose their savor once known. Henceforth one has no strength to endure the least reverse."[50]

Durkheim's analyses of anomic suicide show the consequences of a lack of social regulation of individual behavior. From the theoretical point of view, they are an interesting contribution to his conceptions of institutions and of the development of organic solidarity, formulated in *The Division of Labor in Society*. We can see in this connection the great significance that Durkheim attached to the state of social consciousness; he was disinclined to reduce it to an epiphenomenon of changes in social morphology. From the practical point of view, his analyses best illustrate his view of capitalism, in which he saw a precursor of the best organization of human relations (organic solidarity), which, however, in his times was not yet developed enough to meet essential social needs. In is opinion, the problem was in the moral lag of society, in which the "normal" development of the division of labor should have produced by itself a state of general harmony. He thus saw the best countermeasures in moral education, which under new economic conditions would yield social discipline as effective as that in traditional societies.

Organicism and "Functionalism" in Durkheim's Sociology. Durkheim adopted without reservation the recommendation of naturalism: He associated the ideal of the study of society as a reality *sui generis* with the conviction that the method of that study must comply with the standards typical of the natural sciences, which were for him *the* sciences. The spiritualization of society, which increased in his works with the lapse of time, did not weaken his conviction that these spiritual facts can successfully be investigated only be methods used in the natural sciences. Such a belief was typical of all adherents of sociologism, who in a way used to reify society. It is even legitimate to claim that Durkheim also retained the organicist approach of his predecessors. That mode of thinking was favored by his radical anti-individualism and antireductionism, combined with the notorious slovenliness and methaphoric nature of his language. His terminology was often unreservedly organicist: He used to speak about "social organism," "morphology," and "physiology," "anatomy," "soul," "body," "nervous system," and so on. It would probably be possible to demonstrate that the idea of society found in Durkheim's works (and especially in *The Division of Labor in Society*) is totally compatible with Spencer's organicist analogy.

Durkheim's organicism can best be seen in two assumptions within his sociology. One of them referred to the strict interconnection between all parts of the social organism, provided that the latter is in its normal state; the other, to the existence of specific needs of that organism, which must necessarily be satisfied and which are something other than the needs of its parts.

On the former issue Durkheim did not go far beyond Comte's ideas. But on the latter he proved more original, which makes him a forerunner of functionalism, even if he was not a functionalist *avant la lettre*. He was the first sociologist to formulate explicitly the requirements of functional analysis. He wrote in his *Règles de la méthode sociologiquue* that *"when . . . the explanation of a social phenomenon is undertaken, we must seek separately the efficient cause which produces it and the function it fulfills.* We use the word 'function,' in preference to 'end' or 'purpose,' precisely because social phenomena do not generally exist for the useful results they produce." And further, he continues that defining the function of a social phenomenon is "necessary for the complete explanation of the phenomena. Indeed, if the usefulness of a fact is not the cause of its existence, it is generally necessary that it be useful in order that it may maintain itself."[51]

Sociology as the All-Embracing Social Science. Durkheim made a great effort to formulate precisely the subject matter of sociology. As compared to Comte, he did significantly restrict its scope, in order to make it only one of the social sciences, in which there is also room for political economy, jurisprudence, history, and other disciplines. Nevertheless, the subject matter of sociology was still strikingly extensible, which seems to have been due not to defective definitions, but to a deliberately adopted program of research. If we recall Durkheim's definition of a social fact, we must immediately realize that his program could not have been otherwise.

Sociology has at its disposal the most comprehensive knowledge of social facts, and hence it cannot remain neutral to any of those disciplines which also are concerned with social facts. It should bridge the gaps between them, inform them about the sociological method, disclose relationships disregarded so far between the various facts, and so forth. However much sociology can contribute to historiography, jurisprudence, ethnography, linguistics, and political economy, it would not in any case undertake a "disinterested" reform of those disciplines. Cooperation must be based on reciprocity. The social sciences as a whole need new ideas; sociology needs facts.

The remarks above reflect Durkheim's dislike, manifested on various occasions, of sociology interpreted as speculative social philosophy concerned with society as such. He claimed that it was time to specialize and to concern oneself with definite social facts in the sphere of law, morals, economics, and history. This standpoint gave rise to *L'Année sociologique*, a periodical that was simultaneously the organ of a definite sociological school, a collection of data that school required, and the training ground for methodological experiments intended to reconstruct the totality of the sciences of man in accordance with the principles of the sociological method.

For Durkheim it was not essential that a sociologist be concerned with something other than a historian, or an economist, or an ethnographer, or a linguist is. His point, rather, was that the sociologist should handle the same facts in a different manner, applying the sociological *method*. While defending the autonomy of sociology, Durkheim did not strive to set it apart from the other social sciences, but he opposed the way of thinking typical of all social sciences to that typical of psychology, philosophy, theology, and the like. He wanted not only to reconstruct the methods used in them, but also to found a new philosophy that, by availing itself of sociological knowledge, would free itself from false alternatives and apparent problems. If man learns how to think from society, then sociology is in a position to make statements about the laws governing human thinking. Another prospect that the renewed sociology was supposed to open was that of a science-based moral system and science-based politics.

The greatest danger of that ambitious program was that all those facts in which sociology was interested were treated as social facts only, which meant replacing psychological reductionism by sociological reductionism. Nevertheless, it is to the one-sidedness of that program that we owe the emergence of one of the few genuine schools in sociology, a school dedicated to a methodical continuation and development of the ideas of its founder and to verification of his hypotheses. The role of that school in the humanities, especially in France, was considerable enough to be discussed separately.

THE DURKHEIM SCHOOL

Schools in sociology are extremely rare, if we mean not a loose, sometimes quite accidental similarity of views, but a group of scientists who deliberately carry out a specified research program, agree on basic issues, and have some kind of institutional support. As a matter of fact, the history of sociology knows only two such schools, both of them extremely influential—the Durkheim school and the Park school (also called the Chicago school). The former, also called the French school of sociology or the clan of *L'Année sociologique* (see G. Davy), gathered a group of researchers who proved capable of applying the general principles of sociologism to the various social disciplines, developing the ideas of their master, and also systematically consolidating the institutional foundations of their activity. While it did not represent the totality of French sociologist (not only Tarde, Durkheim's main opponent, but also René Worms [1867-1926], the vigorous founder of the International Institute of Sociology, remained outside that school), the Durkheim school came to be dominant in France over a fairly long period.[52]

The emergence of the school was possible owing to a number of circumstances. First, Durkheim's sociology did not form a closed system, but was —despite the dogmatism of certain views—a set of questions, problems, and methodological suggestions applicable even in fields that were fairly remote from Durkheim's direct interests. Second, the rise of the school was favored by the sociopolitical situation in France at that time: Durkheim's research program proved extremely attractive to a group of young men, some of whom favored socialism, who were deeply interested in social reforms and could not find any place in existing political and governmental structures. And third, the important factor was that Durkheim, as Coser remarked, "tried to make sociology legitimate not only through intellectual argument but through the tactic of organization."[53] Thus, his disciples gained an opportunity (quite exceptional at that stage of the development of sociology) for careers in university schools and, perhaps even more important still, an excellent center of information, cooperation, and mutual examination of the results obtained—namely, L'Année sociologique (1898-1913 and 1923-1924).

L'Année sociologique. The role of that periodical was highly significant and almost unrivaled in the history of the social sciences. Clark is not wrong when he compares it to a research institute.[54] M. Mauss recalled that "the Année was not only a publication. . . . Around it was formed . . . a "group" in the full sense of the word. Under the authority of Durkheim . . . it was a sort of society fully developed both on the intellectual and on the spiritual side. A great number of investigations and ideas were being elaborated. . . . We practised a true division of labor."[55]

Durkheim's authority within the group around L'Année was unquestionable, and the exchange of ideas among the coworkers was so lively that it is extremely difficult to establish what was the contribution of each of them. No monograph of the Durkheim school has been written so far, nor are there even any monographs of its various members, which would enable us to find out whether, or how far, they differed among themselves on theoretical grounds. Moreover, L'Année used to carry papers by joint authors, some of them being as important for the development of the school as the study by Durkheim and Mauss on primitive forms of classification (1901-1902) and by Hubert and Mauss on the general theory of magic (1902-1903). It seems safest to assume that the members of the school were united by a fairly strong uniformity of theoretical and methodological opinions.

Differences among the Durkheimists were not about viewpoints on fundamental issues, but about special interests and competences that would make it possible to verify the general hypotheses in the light of data drawn either from various fields of social life (religion, law, economics, morals, demography, and so on) or from various cultures (in this regard, compare M. Granet's works on Chinese thought and civilization). Contributors to *L'Année* included not only professional sociologists, but also representatives of the various specialized disciplines who—as far as we can judge today—were less interested in the theoretical possibilities of Durkheim's sociology as a whole than in the applicability of its statements to the solution of definite problems. The main divisions within the *L'Année* school were those of specialization.

The striking fact, however, is that specialized studies were not for the Durkheimists a goal in itself; in fact, they criticized that approach in traditional historiography and other humanities. While founding for the first time distinct sociological subdisciplines and assigning them special columns in *L'Année*, they stood for the unity of sociology as a whole. The binding principle, concisely formulated by Mauss, was that "there are no social sciences, but *one* science of societies."[56] The point was to preserve the ideal of sociology as the theoretical science that explains the functioning of society as a whole and to combine that ideal with the conviction that no social fact can be understood in isolation from others.

Thus, the strategy of *L'Année sociologique* was to establish a solid general sociology based on the results of specialized research conducted according to a uniform plan by both professional sociologists and representatives of other social sciences who have mastered the sociological method and ceased to see facts in isolation from one another. The intention was to ensure conditions conducive to the accumulation of results, which in earlier (and often also in later) sociological research took place on a very small scale.

An additional testimony to that striving for research based on a given theory was the scrupulousness with which world literature on the subject was reviewed in *L'Année*. The distinctive character of the school was not based on the ignorance of what was being done by others; on the contrary, it assumed the duty of a matter-of-fact appraisal of all achievements in the contemporaneous social sciences. The works of the Durkheimists prove that they did know how to use those achievements. For instance, they made ample use of the findings by contemporaneous anthropologists, so that their opinions of preliterate societies were far from dilettantish, despite the fact that they did not do their own field work. For example, Mauss was able to assimilate critically the work of Boas. On the other hand, the Durkheimists had much less understanding for "alien" theoretical conceptions; they not only had a rather superficial knowledge of such theories, but were also incapable of thorough discussions.

L'Année had several dozen fairly regular contributors, but when we speak about the school, we usually have in mind these scholars: Antoine Meillet (1866-1936), Marcel Mauss (1872-1950), François Simiand (1873-1935), Paul Fauconnet (1874-1938), Maurice Halbwachs (1877-1945), Robert Hertz (1882-1915), Georges Davy (1883-19?). Marcel Granet (1884-1940), and Henri Hubert (1885-1954).[57] Out of Polish sociologists, it was Stefan Czarnowski (1879-1937) who was closely connected with that group; his book *Le Culte des héros et ses conditions sociales* (1919) may be considered a classical application of the Durkheim theory.

We shall be concerned here only with Halbwachs and Mauss. Both were ardent followers of Durkheim, but the works of each of them reveals a somewhat different possibility for developing his ideas.

Halbwachs as a Disciple. As compared with Durkheim, Halbwachs strikes us as a *sui generis* philosophical ascetic. Trained as a philosopher, like many other members of the school, he availed himself on some issues of inspiration by philosophers (Bergson, for example), but we would look in vain in his major works for anything that would be an analogue of *Règles de la méthode sociologique* or *Sociologie et philosophie*. To use the terminology that was introduced later, Halbwachs represented "the middle range" of the Durkheim theory. He was marked by a strong empirical orientation, manifested in the study of family budgets, in his approach to problems of social morphology (study in urban sociology), in his ample use of statistical data and techniques, and in *Les Causes du suicide* (1930), which was a direct continuation, but also a revision, of Durkheim's renowned study. Like other members of the school, Halbwachs willingly made use of historical data; on the other hand, he did not reveal any marked interest in anthropological issues, on which Mauss's work was focused.

The two principal spheres of Halbwachs's interest were collective memory and social classes. In both cases, he referred directly to Durkheim's idea of collective consciousness, but he went far beyond the problems considered by his master. On the first issue we notice a change in the attitude toward individual psychology: The belief that it is completely useless for the sociologist gives way to an attempt to reconstruct it thoroughly in the spirit of sociologism. His approach to the second issue is an interesting endeavor to take into account, within Durkheim's sociological theory, those facts about capitalist society to which Durkheim glaringly failed to give proper consideration.

Halbwachs discussed collective memory in *Les Cadres sociaux de la mémoire* (1925), *Mémoire et société* (1949), and *La Mémoire collective* (1950). They were intended as contributions to the psychological study of memory (even though Halbwachs was a dilettante as a psychologist), and they marked a step forward in the sociological study of tradition. Halbwachs's theory of collective memory demonstrated that memory is not a mechanical ability to register facts and to preserve impressions and observations, but consists in the incessant reconstruction of the past by the recollecting subject. Halbwachs strove to prove that a human being is capable of such a reconstruction only as a member of a definite social group, which provides the "framework" for every process of recollecting past events. The individual remembers facts owing to his being a member of his family, his church, his class, his nation, or any other groups with which he identifies himself. A change in the individual's group membership results in a "reconstruction" of his recollections. The peculiarities marking the various social groups in the various epochs of history affected such or another scope and nature of collective memory. This idea also led Halbwachs to take up problems of so-called social time and the like.

Halbwachs's studies of social classes yielded such works as *La Classe ouvrière et les niveaux de vie: Recherches sur la hiérarchie des besoins dans les sociétés industrielles contemporaines* (1913), *L'Evolution des besoins dans les classes ouvrières* (1933), and *Esquisse d'une psychologie des classes sociales* (1955). They contain one of the most original theories of social classes, though it is little known in present-day sociology.

Durkheim's sociology left little room for a theory of social classes: It was a sociology of solidarity, not one of social conflict, and was naturally focused on the factors that unite society, not on those that divide it. Unlike Marx, Durkheim failed to notice the disintegrating consequences of the division of labor. For Durkheim, there was no problem of social classes in the Marxian sense, and so Halbwachs revolutionized Durkheim's theory by taking up that problem. He demonstrated that the social crisis consisted not only of an excessive individualization of society, but also of the alienation from society of large groups of people—namely, the handicapped classes. The differences between Halbwachs and Durkheim were, however, not as great as it might seem, because in the last analysis Halbwachs's theory of social classes remains within the framework of Durkheimism, even though it is an important complement to the latter. The idea of society as "the focus of moral life" remains the starting point of that theory, even though it tries to explain those differences in participation in moral life that are independent of the innate characteristics of individuals.

As interpreted by Halbwachs, social classes—which by definition form a hierarchical order—are facts in the sphere of social consciousness. He wrote that it would be self-contradictory to assume the existence of a class that does not realize its own existence. Even more characteristic was his interpretation of class consciousness or, more precisely, of collective ideas, which may be termed the consciousness of classes. In Halbwachs's opinion, in every society there is a set of generally accepted values, but access to those values is not equally open to all; and there are large groups that are forced periodically to leave society and, being deprived of the possibility of implementing the general social ideal, cease to accept it. In contemporaneous industrial society the working class, above all, was in such a state of temporary alienation. In Halbwachs's conception of classes the focal place is held by the concept of need, a clear distinction existing between material and social needs. Studying the class hierarchy in a given society means studying the kinds of needs and the degree of their satisfaction. Thus the problems of class differentiation are shifted from the sphere of production, where it was located by Marx, to that of consumption.[58]

The strong point of Halbwachs's studies of the problem of social classes lies certainly in his ideas concerning the social origin and conditioning of human needs and also in his endeavors to measure those needs by investigating family budgets. His "sociological theory of needs," while obscure on many points, seems to be of some topical interest even now, although it may prove interesting less for the students of class structure as for those of life styles. Remarkable, too, are Halbwachs's ideas concerning the collective memory of the various social classes and the role of tradition in the formation of class consciousness. Yet from the point of view of the historian of sociology, the most interesting point in his work is that it clearly shows the limits of Durkheimism as a theory.

Marcel Mauss: Durkheimism Modified. Mauss certainly was Durkheim's closest coworker and, after his death, the accepted leader of the school. He was the first president of the French Institute of Sociology, founded in 1925. It was Mauss, too, who strove to renew the publication of *L'Année sociologique* after World War I. Though his production was not very imposing in size (during his lifetime he did not publish a single book of which he was the sole author), it was of great significance. His erudition was enormous, and he lacked not ideas, but patience to work on them, so that many of his texts resemble prospectuses rather than finished papers. They are open to divergent interpretations and reveal nuclei of various sociological orientations. Mauss exerted a very strong influence as a teacher. His interests covered primarily anthropological problems, but in the Durkheim school those problems were considered to be sociological *par excellence.*

We shall disregard here Mauss's cooperation with Durkheim, when Mauss was mainly concerned with social morphology, religions, and the sociology of knowledge, and shall refer mainly to the later period of his activity, when he paid much attention to methodology and general sociology. In those works he formulated the requirement of studying "total" social phenomena *(les faits sociaux totaux),* a requirement that is rather obscure, but has key importance for understanding Mauss's work, his place in the Durkheim school, and his later influence on the social sciences and the humanities in France. This requirement was Mauss's response to the growing specialization and disintegration of the social sciences and, as such, can be seen as the defense of Durkheim's ideal of integrated sociology. On the other hand, some of his views make it legitimate to consider Mauss a reformer, rather than one who continued Durkheim's ideas.[59]

In his essay on the gift, *Essai sur le don, forme archaïque de l'échange* (1924), certainly his best work, Mauss wrote that historians were right in blaming sociologists for resorting to farfetched abstractions and for separating one component of society from another. Sociologists should proceed like historians do, observing that which is given. That which is given is Rome, Athens, an average Frenchman, a Melanesian from a specified island—and not prayer and law in itself. After the time of separating and abstracting, now is the time for reconstructing the social whole in motion, in the transient moment when society and individuals acquire the emotional consciousness of themselves and of their situation relative to others.

This striving for the concrete in social life is manifested in Mauss's works in two ways. First, the sociologist should concern himself not with single cases of human behavior, not with events, not even with institutions, but with their definite "systems."[60] And second, the participant in social life should be analyzed as the total man *(l'homme total)*, as the being who is simultaneously social, psychical, and biological. The sociologist who really wants to comprehend man cannot confine himself to an interest in the social aspect of human behavior and must also investigate his physiological and emotional aspects. Hence, Mauss's turn toward biology and psychology and his tacit rejection of the Durkheimist dualism in philosophical anthropology. Hence, too, the important program of investigating the ways that people use their bodies *(les techniques du corps)* and the culture-based differentiation of physiological reactions. It is on that point—bringing the individual and his material and physiological characteristics into the orbit of interests of sociologists—that we notice Mauss's disloyalty to Durkheim. However, this was not a rebelling against sociologism, but, on the contrary, a bringing it to the extreme. The anti-Durkheimist element lay, rather, in abolishing the primacy of collective ideas and including in sociology the vast sphere of problems connected with individual actions and experiences as integral parts of total social facts. Thus, when reference is made to total social facts, what is meant is both a systemic approach to social facts and the despiritualization and internalization of those facts.

These ideas, which reappear in many of Mauss's works, but are found in their most developed form in his essay on the gift, are, unfortunately, at the level of intuition rather than that of a methodological program. Mauss says, for instance, that the individual is the source of every action and experience, but he leaves unanswered the question about the meaning of that statement in research practice, nor does he draw any conclusion from it. Mauss postulated investigating the whole, but he failed to explain what that whole was, since, unlike the English-speaking anthropologists, he did not engage in monographic studies of definite societies. We do not know whether this was so because he did not overcome the abstractionism that he questioned or because he used a different, and otherwise more modern, concept of the whole. Nor is it certain whether the concrete that he wanted to reconstruct was interpreted by him to be a result of a gradual process of cognition, or something given in direct observation.[61]

But the most obscure point is Mauss's recommendation to investigate social facts as whole: Sometimes the recommendation concerns the manner of investigating all social facts, but at other times it concerns the manner of selecting the facts subjected to investigation. In the former case, we would deal with one of the numerous versions of sociological holism, with the "heuristic element" that makes it imperative to refer every fact under investigation to the system of which it is a part; in the latter, the point would be to discover within a given system its essential, constitutive facts, which in some cases "concern the whole of society and its institutions."[62] Mauss's approach to exchange as a total social fact, which is found in his essay on the gift, supports the latter interpretation; however, this is undermined by other, fairly numerous statements scattered through his other writings.

It seems that in his recommendation to study total social facts Mauss combined many different issues, thus outlining Utopian sociology that would be in a position, like historiography, to show concrete individuals and communities in their actions; like psychology, to make use of the concept of the total human being; like linguistics, to be both descriptive and generalizing. As far as we can judge, Mauss strove to find the most general theoretical formula that would make it possible to define the place and tasks of sociology in view of the accelerated advances in and specialization of the social sciences. He could no longer afford Durkheim's arrogance toward nonsociological social sciences, but was also unwilling to abandon the exorbitant ambitions of sociologism. As a result, he left a collection of comments and ideas that could work as inspirations, but could in no way form a theoretical system.

The Impact of Durkheimism. The impact of Durkheimism was certainly very uneven: Enormous in France, it was rather limited outside that country, even though ignorance of it was not always as complete as Max Weber's. It is also remarkable that *L'Année* had few foreign contributors and that international cooperation focused rather around the International Institute of Sociology, founded by R. Worms, from which Durkheim kept aloof.

The fact that the influence of Durkheimism on world sociology remained limited was certainly due to several causes. First, Durkheimism was deeply rooted in the French intellectual tradition, which went back to Saint-Simon and Comte and which, for various reasons (anti-individualism, positivism, and so on), failed to be accepted everywhere. Second, it was an answer to questions posed by practical social problems in France, which differed essentially from those in America, Britain, and Germany. And third, it was a doctrine of an independent and institutionalized sociology that was able to play the leading part within a broad intellectual movement. At that time such sociology was not to be found anywhere outside France.

Durkheimism was accordingly seen mainly as the French school of sociology. In France, however, its impact was enormous and covered not only sociologists, but linguists, historians, educators, and economists as well, and even spread to nonacademic milieus (which was facilitated by sociology's coming to be taught even in secondary schools). Yet as a distinct theory, Durkheimism withered in France in the late 1930s, even though references to it were made later, too—for example, by Georges Gurvitch (1894-1965), a prominent French sociologist active after World War II.

Durkheimism (in this case the doctrine of Durkheim himself, rather than the theoretical achievements of the school) owes its worldwide renown mainly to functionalism. Radcliffe-Brown, the British social anthropologist, was the first to refer to him, and next Parsons raised him to the status of a classic of contemporary sociological theory, ranking him with Pareto and Max Weber. It is self-evident that Durkheim qua functionalist was no longer the old Durkheim, but the important point was that he again became an object of interest to sociologists. He came to be seen as the founder of modern empirical sociology, the forerunner of modern theories of culture (collective consciousness as culture, in the sense used by recent cultural anthropologists), and the thinker who came close to symbolic interactionism.[63] He also anticipated comparative studies, which have become increasingly popular in sociology. In a word, he has become a classic in the full sense of the term: an author in whom one can find nearly all possible inspirations without, however, having to accept his work as a whole.

SOCIOLOGISM: THE BALANCE SHEET

As E. Benoit-Smullyan writes, sociologism developed as a specific synthesis of positivistic methodology and the view that he terms *agelecism* (from Greek *agele*, "a group," "a crowd")[64] and that we have termed *sociological realism*. It can easily be noticed how much sociologism was a continuation of earlier ideas, particularly the sociological theory formulated by Comte. There is also no doubt that to it apply the objections raised against Comte, who was blamed for hypostasizing the concept of society and for usurping for sociology the right to speak on all human issues.

Representatives of sociologism not only supported Comte's attitude, but even strengthened it in some cases. This was so because sociologism, especially in its French version, also was the professional ideology of sociologists; in their striving to legitimize the new academic discipline, they emphasized excessively the importance and the qualitative distinctiveness of the subject matter with which that discipline was to concern itself. Also at stake were more general political and moral considerations, which made socially active sociologists, even those who did not disapprove of the principles of the French Revolution, stress the importance of social norms and authorities; breaking with classical individualistic liberalism and adopting the idea of guided democracy had an additional justification in the claim that society is something more than the sum of individuals. Sociologism, like the individualistic trends, was still burdened by the "dualistic" fallacy, typical of nineteenth-century thinkers (except for Marx). About this fallacy Ruth Benedict wrote that it gave rise to the erroneous idea "that what was subtracted from society was added to the individual and what was subtracted from the individual was added to society."[65]

The radicalism of most programmatic statements on the relationship between the individual and society made by representatives of sociologism makes it the purest case of what D. Wrong defined as "the oversocialized conception of man."[66] This standpoint consists of making the individual primarily the result of societal factors and of disregarding or belittling the extrasocietal determinants (on which an excessive stress was laid by psychologism) and also the autonomy and creativity of individuals (emphasized by representatives of what is called humanistic sociology). For this reason some systematizations of sociological theories see in sociologism, and especially in Durkheim's doctrine, one of the fundamental paradigms of sociology, of which functionalism is the modern version.[67]

But the role of sociologism was not to reaffirm the thesis of sociological realism, but to reformulate it and make it concrete in at least two respects. First, the abstract (mankind, society in general, and the like) or essentially unknowable (the romantic *Geist*) whole was replaced by definite societies and groups, each of which required separate studies, and the validity of generalizations was made dependent on comparison of the data collected during such studies. This had to result in a rejection of evolutionism as the theory for which mankind was a uniform object of study and which extrapolated the results obtained in the study of one society to all other societies. This also dismissed the organicist analogies, which could still be tempting as a source of ready-made models of all live wholes (as was true for Durkheim, though Mauss would look for the model of social system in linguistics), but did not entitle one to state *a priori* how society functions. Second, representatives of sociologism did not in the least block the study of interactions and even demanded concrete studies of the relations between the individual and the group. The conception of institution, which referred back to Spencer, was especially helpful for such studies.

Sociologism was, indeed, set to investigate facts. Some of its representatives also linked their definite philosophical hopes to it, and all of them availed themselves of existing ethnological, historical, and statistical data without undertaking empirical research, in the modern sense of the word. But sociologism produced the first theoretically minded sociologists who had at their disposal reliable scientific methods and not just a collection of random data and common-sense observations. This was the argument that claimed sociology to be both needed and possible as a separate discipline and that made the term *sociology* no longer associated, in some countries at least, with a blend of second-rate philosophy, historiosophy, and social prophecy.

Sociologism was not a fully homogeneous trend. There were two basic possibilities inherent in it, which we tried to point out by presenting first the views of Gumplowicz and then those of Durkheim and his school. When working on the assumption that groups and institutions are the principal variables explaining social facts, one can consider society (the group) either as an isolated system or as a system that interacts with other societies (groups). One can, concentate on intergroup conflicts, as was done by Gumplowicz, or on problems of intragroup solidarity, as was done by Durkheim. These options have remained of topical interest in sociology.

NOTES

1. Celestin Bouglé, Introduction to E. Durkheim, *Sociology and Philosophy* (New York: Free Press, 1974), p. xxxvii.

2. Cf. S. N. Eisenstadt with M. Curelaru, *The Form of Sociology: Paradigms and Crises* (New York: Wiley, 1976), pp. 86-87.

3. G. Duncan Mitchell, *A Hundred Years of Sociology* (Chicago: Aldine, 1968), p. 36.

4. John Torrance, "The Emergence of Sociology in Austria, 1885-1935," in *Archives européennes de sociologie* 17 (1976): 187.

5. Alvin Boskoff, "From Social Thought to Sociological Theory," in H. Becker and A. Boskoff, eds., *Modern Sociological Theory in Continuity and Change* (New York: Dryden Press, 1957), p. 12.

6. Ludwig Gumplowicz, *Outlines of Sociology* (New York: Paine-Whitman Publishers, 1963), p. 158.

7. Ibid., p. 151.

8. Ludwig Gumplowicz, *System socjologii* (Warsaw: Spólka Nakladowa, 1887), p. 50.

9. See F. Mirek, *System socjologiczny Ludwika Gumplowicza: Studium krytyczne* (Poznan: I. Zamecznik, 1930), p. 22.

10. Gumplowicz, *Outlines*, p. 238.

11. G. Lukács, *Die Zerstörung der Vernunft: Der Weg des Irrationalismus von Schelling zu Hitler* (Berlin: Aufbau-Verlag, 1955), p. 542.

12. See Werner Stark, *The Fundamental Forms of Social Thought* (London: RKP, 1962), p. 56.

13. Gumplowicz, *System socjologii*, p. 229.

14. Gumplowicz, *Outlines*, p. 236.

15. Terry Nichols Clark, *Prophets and Patrons: The French University and the Emergence of the Social Sciences* (Cambridge, Mass.: Harvard University Press, 1973).

16. Emile Durkheim, *The Rules of Sociological Method* (New York: Free Press, 1962), p. 143.

17. Ibid., p. xliii.

18. Ibid., p. xlv.

19. Ibid., p. 13.

20. E. Durkheim, "The Dualism of Human Nature and Its Social Conditions," in Kurt H. Wolff, ed., *Emile Durkheim, 1858-1917: A Collection of Essays with Translations and a Bibliography* (Columbus, Ohio: Ohio State University Press, 1960), pp. 325-40.

21. Emile Durkheim, *The Elementary Forms of the Religious Life* (London: Allen and Unwin, 1976), p. 447.

22. E. Durkheim, "Sociology and Its Scientific Field," in Wolff, *Emile Durkheim*, p. 363.

23. Cf., for example, Georges Gurvitch, *Traité de sociologie* (Paris: P.U.F., 1958), 1:49.

24. Durkheim, *Sociology and Philosophy*, pp. 29, 55.

25. Durkheim, *Elementary Forms*, p. 347.

26. Cf. Paul Bohannan, "Conscience Collective and Culture," in Wolff, *Emile Durkheim*, pp. 77-97.

27. T. Parsons, "Cooley and the Problem of Internalization," in Albert J. Reiss, Jr., ed., *Cooley and Social Analysis* (Ann Arbor: University of Michigan Press, 1968), p. 58.

28. Harry Alpert, *Emile Durkheim and His Sociology* (New York: Columbia University Press, 1939), pp. 135 ff.

29. T. Parsons, *The Structure of Social Action* (New York: Free Press, 1968), p. 337.

30. Emile Durkheim, *The Division of Labor in Society* (New York: Free Press, 1969), pp. 66-67.

31. Durkheim, *Rules*, pp. 76-77.

32. Durkheim, *Division of Labor*, p. 65.

33. Ibid., p. 181.

34. Ibid.

35. Ibid., p. 205.

36. Quoted in Steven Lukes, *Emile Durkheim: His Life and Work: A Historical and Critical Study* (Harmondsworth: Penguin Books, 1975), p. 231.

37. Durkheim, "Sociology and Its Scientific Field," pp. 360-62.

38. Durkheim, *Rules*, p. 81.

39. Cf. Bouglé, Introduction to *Sociology and Philosophy*, p. xl.

40. Durkheim, *Sociology and Philosophy*, p. 34.

41. See Robert A. Nisbet, *The Sociological Tradition* (London: Heinemann, 1967), p. 303.

42. See Lukes, *Emile Durkheim*, p. 234.

43. See Gurvitch, *Traité de sociologie*, 1:10; Marcel Mauss, *Essais de sociologie* (Paris: Editions de Minuit, 1969), p. 16.

44. Durkheim, *Rules*, p. lvi.

45. Gianfranco Poggi, *Images of Society: The Sociological Theories of Tocqueville, Marx and Durkheim* (Stanford: Stanford University Press, 1972), p. 237.

46. Alpert, *Emile Durkheim*, p. 181.

47. Durkheim, *Elementary Forms*, p. 375.

48. Joachim Israel, *Alienation from Marx to Modern Sociology: A Macrosociological Analysis* (Boston: Allyn and Bacon, 1971), p. 136.

49. E. Durkheim, *Suicide: A Study in Sociology*, in T. Parsons et al., eds., *Theories of Society* (New York: Free Press, 1961), p. 214.

50. Ibid., pp. 920-21. Lewis A. Coser and Bernard Rosenberg, *Sociological Theory: A Book of Readings* (New York: Macmillan, 1964), p. 547.

51. Durkheim, *Rules*, pp. 95-97.

52. Cf. Claude Lévi-Strauss, "La Sociologie française," in Georges Gurvitch and Wilbert E. Moore, eds., *La Sociologie au XXe siècle* (Paris: P.U.F., 1947), p. 513.

53. Lewis A. Coser, *Masters of Sociological Thought: Ideas in Historical and Social Context* (New York: Harcourt Brace Jovanovich, 1971), p. 164.

54. Clark, *Prophets and Patrons*, pp. 181-95.

55. Cf. Emile Benoit-Smullyan, "The Sociologism of Emile Durkheim and His School," in Harry Elmer Barnes, ed., *An Introduction to the History of Sociology* (Chicago: University of Chicago Press, 1948), p. 521.

56. Marcel Mauss, "Division concrète de la sociologie," in Mauss, *Essais*, p. 51.

57. The renowned student of primitive mentality, Lucien Lévy-Bruhl (1853-1939)—author of *La Morale et la science des moeurs* (1903), *Les Fonctions mentales dans les sociétés inférieures* (1910), and *La Mentalité primitive* (1922)—is also included by some historians in the French school of sociology. However, in spite of essential similarities between Lévy-Bruhl's ideas and Durkheim's, this problem necessitates a separate discussion. A concise presentation of Lévy-Bruhl's point of view is found in Gurvitch, *Traité de sociologie*, 1:52-54.

58. Cf. G. Gurvitch, *Etudes sur les classes sociales: L'Idée de classe sociale de Marx á nos jours* (Paris: Gonthier, 1971), pp. 166, 168, 170.

59. Elzbieta Tarkowska, *Ciaglosc i zmiana socjologii francuskiej: Durkheim, Mauss, Levi-Strauss* (Warsaw: PWN, 1974), p. 148.

60. M. Mauss, "Essai sur le don," in Mauss, *Sociologie et anthropologie* (Paris: P.U.F., 1960), p. 147.

61. Cf. C. Dubar, "La Méthode de Marcel Mauss," in *Revue française de sociologie* 10 (1969).

62. Mauss, "Essai sur le don," p. 274. Cf. Roscoe C. Hinkle, Jr., "Durkheim in American Sociology," in Wolff, *Emile Durkheim*, pp. 267-95.

63. Cf. Gregory P. Stone and H. A. Faberman, "On the Edge of Rapprochement: Was Durkheim Moving toward the Perspective of Social Interaction?" in *Sociological Quarterly*, 8 (1967): 149-64.

64. Benoit-Smullyan, "The Sociologism of Durkheim," p. 499.

65. Ruth Benedict, *Patterns of Culture* (New York: Mentor Books, 1959), p. 218.

66. Dennis H. Wrong, "The Oversocialized Conception of Man in Modern Sociology," in Coser and Rosenberg, *Sociological Theory*, pp. 112-22.

67. Eisenstadt with Curelaru, *Form of Sociology*, pp. 82-110; George Ritzer, *Sociology: A Multiple Paradigm Science* (Boston: Allyn and Bacon, 1975), pp. 35-82.

ABSOLUTE HISTORICISM: THE ANTIPOSITIVISM TURN IN SOCIOLOGY

The four preceding chapters have been concerned with different variations of sociological positivism in a broad sense of the term, as the trend that dominated the first stage in the development of sociology. We indicated also the first symptoms of a disintegration of positivism.

In sociology there has never been any definitive overcoming or collapse of positivism, which has changed its form many a time, but has survived to this day as an exceptionally influential trend. It is to be noted that sociology is not a discipline in which any really popular way of thinking has ever vanished completely. This is why it is sometimes labeled "a multiple paradigm science."[1] Nor is it a discipline whose evolution can be explained by its inner dynamics alone. Essential innovations in sociological thinking usually had their sources not in a discovery of new facts that could not be explained within the adopted paradigm, but in interference by external factors: other ideologies, new patterns of scientific thinking, new philosophies, or other intellectual traditions.

This can best be illustrated by the so-called antipositivist breakthrough in sociology that took place in Germany, a country that remained at the periphery of the main trends in sociology until the late nineteenth century. That antipositivist turn had its origin outside sociology itself and was often directed against that discipline as such. While it had analogues in some other countries, it was basically a German invention and remains incomprehensible if analyzed apart from German intellectual history, which reveals many unique features at least from romanticism on, since the impact of romanticism on German thought was exceptionally strong. We interpret romanticism in Cahnman's words:

the revulsion against uniformity, generality, calculated simplicity, and the reduction of living phenomena to common denominators; the aesthetic antipathy to standardization; the abhorrence of platitudinous mediocrity. More positively: the attentiveness to the detailed, the concrete, the factual; the quest for local color, the endeavor to reconstruct in imagination the distinctive lives of peoples remote in space, time, or cultural condition; the cult of individuality, personality, and nationality, indulgence in the occult, the emotional, the original, the extraordinary.[2]

Regardless of the influence exerted on German thinkers by French and British positivist doctrines (the Germans themselves had an eminent positivist thinker in W. Wundt), romanticism interpreted as above did not vanish from the German humanities during the nineteenth century and saw its revival after 1875 owing to the so-called philosophy of life, which was programmatically opposed to all schematism, and owing to the various "historical schools." The attention of a historian of sociology is drawn in particular by the historical schools in political economy, represented by Wilhelm Roscher (1817-1894), Karl Knies (1821-1898), and Gustav Schmoller (1838-1917). In historiography the pride of place must be given to Johann Gustav Droysen (1808-1884), who was probably the first to formulate the basic issues in the discussion on the peculiarities of historical cognition. This discussion broke out in Germany at the close of the nineteenth century.

This specific approach of the German humanities, which rejected the vision of the ordered world of positive disciplines, is often termed *historicism*. It is said that "almost all social and humanistic studies in Germany were placed on historical foundations. Historical study replaced systematic analysis."[3] "The historicist principle," Karl Mannheim wrote in 1924, "not only organizes, like an invisible hand, the work of the cultural sciences *(Geisteswissenschaften)*, but also permeates everyday thinking. . . . It is just historicism, and historicism alone, which today provides us with a world view of the same universality as that of the religious world view of the past."[4]

THE CONCEPT OF HISTORICISM

Making use here of the term *historicism* is somewhat risky because of its ambiguity. Arthur C. Danto notes correctly that it is used nowadays either very vaguely or arbitrarily, in the sense assigned to it by Popper in *The Poverty of Historicism* (1944-1945).[5] Popper thought historicism to be represented by thinkers as different as Marx, Spencer, Mill, Toynbee, and Mannheim, because he mainly considered their belief in the existence of so-called historical laws and in the predictability of historical processes.

The ambiguity of the term *historicism* is due to several reasons. First, the term has often been used to denote not definite theory or doctrine, but a fairly general option in favor of taking the historical context into consideration when man and social life are discussed. In this sense, reference is made to historicism whenever we consider a protest against thinking in terms of

natural law or an analysis of social problems apart from their spatiotemporal context.

Second, the term *historicism* happens to be used both as a name of a
Weltanschauung and as a name of a postulated method of studying social
facts. This is why a distinction is sometimes made between philosophical
and methodological historicism.

Third, both philosophical and methodological historicism appeared in
historiography in many different forms. In some cases it was oriented
toward grasping general regularities of the process of history; in others,
toward grasping characteristics of the various stages of that process. This
was noted by Popper, who made a distinction between *historicism* and
historism.[6] Hence, what to some scholars is historicism pure and simple
seems to others to be "pseudo-historicism" or "vulgar historicism" or
"a crisis of historicism." It would probably be more reasonable to speak
about *historicisms*, rather than historicism, and to make distinctions between its various types. Thus, for instance, Jerzy Topolski lists "general
historicism," "absolute historicism" (also termed "relativism"), "Popper's
historicism," "historicism as synonymous with 'the philosophy of history,'"
"existential historicism," and "dialectical historicism."[7]

Our task, however, is not to follow the vicissitudes of the term itself.
We are interested solely in that variety of historicism which was particularly
popular in the German humanities and which Topolski calls *absolute
historicism*. In the English-language literature of the subject it is increasingly being called *historism*, to distinguish it from historicism.[8] One could also
speak about an individualizing historicism as distinct from a generalizing
one. Note, however, that some authors were inclined to attach the greatest
importance to that variety of historicism as they saw in it "the greatest
spiritual revolution which occidental thought has undergone" (Meinecke)[9]
or reckoned it to be one of "the two great scientific creations of the modern
world,"[10] naturalism being the other. In fact, no other variety of historicism
had such far-reaching aspirations, and in no other was the reference to
history so abundant in philosophical consequences.

The following ideas may be considered constitutive of German historicism.

Historicization of Life. Probably the most important feature of absolute
historicism, shared by it with other varieties, was the belief that no fact can
be explained as long as it is treated as something changeless and given once
and for all. As Ernst Troeltsch (1865-1923), a German historian, theologian,
and philosopher, wrote in *Der Historismus und seine Probleme* (1922),
"Here everything is seen as existing in the river of becoming, as unconfined
and continual individualization, determined by the past and directed towards
an unknown future. State, law, morality, religion, art, are all dissolved in
the stream of history's becoming and are intelligible to us only as constituent
parts of historical developments."[11]

Historical Life as a Totality. Karl Mannheim (1893-1947), one of the late representatives of historicism and its most prominent advocate among professional sociologists, noted that historicism is not only the consciousness of the incessant flow of events, but also the ability "to penetrate the *innermost structure* of this all-pervading change."[12] Proper research work begins only when we pose ourselves the question of what is the place of the fact we are studying within a given *totality*.

The Individualizing Approach. Representatives of absolute historicism were, in opposition to naturalists, advocates of an individualizing approach to all social facts *(eine individualisierende Betrachtung)*. According to Friedrich Meinecke (1862-1954), a *sui generis* codifier of this variety of historicism, its essence

is the substitution of a process of *individualising* observation for a *generalising* view of human forces in history. This does not mean that the historical method excludes altogether any attempt to find general laws and types in human life. It has to make use of this approach and blend it with a feeling for the individual; and this sense of individuality was something new that it created.[13]

In spite of the reservation made by Meinecke, absolute historicism was one-sidedly oriented toward the study of historical individuals, both persons and such individuals as the state, nation, epoch, and so forth. Historical facts deserve attention as such, not merely as elements of species and sequences of causes and effects. This approach was decisive for the generally critical attitude toward sociology, to which historicism opposed historiography as a discipline endowed with "a sense of individuality."

Blurred Demarcation Line between Scientific and Everyday Consciousness. By treating all social facts as parts of concrete historical totalities and man as *animal historicum* (a historical animal), absolute historicism blurred the demarcation line, drawn by the positivists, between the subject and the object of social cognition, between scientific and everyday consciousness. Social knowledge is considered to be inevitably the historical self-knowledge of a man who belongs to a given epoch, culture, nation, social group, and so on. It is understood as the expression of life and not as the reflection of a reality independent of the observer. Hence the concept, characteristic of that mental stance, of *Weltanschauung*, analyzed in terms of historical adequacy and not in terms of truth and falsehood, in the classical sense of these concepts. To the idea of pure reason is opposed the idea of historical reason, according to which "all historical knowledge is value-charged,"[14] because man comes to know the world in his capacity of an "integrated spiritual entity," a personality rooted in a given culture. From this point of view, there is no qualitative difference between the cognitive activity of a scholar and that of the members of the communities that he studies.

Specific Features of Historical Cognition. All this led to the conviction
that the naturalistic philosophy of science was quite useless for the humanities. As Dilthey put it, in the world of nature man creates a world of history
as *imperium in imperio*,[15] governed by values rather than causes, by will
rather than necessity. The knowledge of that world requires specific procedures whose essence lies in establishing a special spiritual bond between
the cognizing subject and the object of cognition, a bond that was usually
interpreted as *understanding (Verstehen)*. Understanding must not be
reduced—which is sometimes done—to the psychological process of acquiring the knowledge of other persons' mental states. As noted by W. McDougall,
in *geisteswissenschaftliche Psychologie*, as interpreted by representatives
of German historicism, the true psychological cognition was secondary
relative to the historical cognition of products of culture.[16] Historicism was
not, and was not intended to be, psychologism, even though its representatives were quite concerned with psychology. When studying "the expressions of life," they placed the objectified world of culture at the forefront
and tried to comprehend its inner structure, since, claimed Dilthey, "there
exists here . . . a relationship between the parts and the whole in which
the parts acquire significance *[Bedeutung]* from the whole and the whole is
given its meaning *[Sinn]* by the parts."[17] The operation of understanding,
however it was defined by representatives of absolute historicism, was
intuitive by assumption and resembled an act of producing poetry rather
than the procedures used by natural scientists. The point was to grasp, as
fully as possible, the unrepeatable historical individuality.

Relativism. Advocates of absolute historicism were, on the whole, consistent relativists (or relationists, as some of them preferred to style themselves). They thought that in order to make meaningful statements about
something one has to consider the appropriate historical context. Ideas and
actions cannot be assessed from the point of view of any absolute criteria
or subjected to any ever valid rules. Max Horkheimer wrote that Dilthey's
conception testified to the abandonment by bourgeois liberalism of the
aspiration to discover the absolute: A critical appraisal of earlier doctrines
is replaced in it by their being considered merely as different "expressions
of life," and different world views, which are just different, none of them
being better or worse than any other.[18] There is no doubt that absolute
historicism was very closely linked to the crisis of the belief in social progress, the collapse of confidence in existing institutions and ideals, the
waning of the attitude that had been termed "historical optimism." Absolute historicism taught people to understand the world of history, while
dismissing the questions about the direction and the possibilities of changes.
German absolute historicism, which grew from an irrationalistic philosophy of life, differed markedly from other forms of historicism, with which

it shared the opposition to thinking in terms of natural law. It was a firm rejection of all those conceptions that introduced into history the concept of law (in the sense of regularity) and explained historical processes in the way in which it is done in natural science. That rejection of laws ensured it a place in the history of the social sciences, for it gave rise to one of the most important discussions concerning the foundations and tasks of those sciences, a discussion that has not yet ended.

Absolute historicism did not produce any sociological conception (except for that formulated by Mannheim, who cannot be treated unreservedly as one who continued Dilthey's ideas). This was not a coincidence. The individualizing approach to social facts made the representatives of that trend engage in historiography rather than in sociology, because the latter had looked for theoretical generalizations since its very inception. One could ask outright whether a sociology based on the principles of absolute historicism would even be possible. The example of the historical school in political economy suggests a negative answer. Historical political economy, in fact, was transformed into economic history, and historical sociology would have to become identical with history—and thus superfluous. It is also significant that even those sociologists who in a sense referred to absolute historicism (Simmel, Max Weber, and Znaniecki) refuted it at the same time.

Nevertheless, reflection on absolute historicism seems to the point in a handbook of the history of sociology. First, in historicism we find a continuation and/or analogue of the criticism of the rationalistic and utilitarian model of man, criticism so often encountered in sociology. Second, absolute historicism became the frame of reference, even if often a negative one, for important theoretical undertakings in sociology. Third, it contained a number of ideas that become topical whenever suprahistorically oriented trends—which abstract from spatiotemporal conditions, the context of human actions, and so on—gain the upper hand in sociology. The importance of those ideas was pointed to, for instance, by C. Wright Mills in *The Sociological Imagination.*

DILTHEY'S PHILOSOPHY OF THE SOCIAL SCIENCES

Wilhelm Dilthey (1833-1911) was certainly the most eminent representative of absolute historicism, even though we do not find the term *historicism* in his works. Professor at the universities in Basel, Kiel, and Wroclaw, he became professor at Berlin University in 1882; his works include the fundamental *Einleitung in die Geisteswissenschaften* (1883), many philosophical writings of a programmatic nature, and studies in the history of philosophy and of literature (for example, *Leben Schleiermachers* [1870]). He is not an easy author to read. Problems in the interpretation of his writings are connected with the peculiarities of his style, which continued the worst traditions of German idealism; his changing opinions, although he himself considered his work to be a consistent implementation of the task that he had set himself in his youth; the various influences reflected by his works (Kant, the romantic authors, Hegel, Ranke, the positivists, and, in later years, even Husserl); programmatic lack of orderliness; and, finally, the fact that he often failed to finish what he had begun, leaving the most important conclusions to be guessed at by the reader (for this reason he was called *Mann der ersten Bände*). The paths along which he influenced others proved as tortuous as his ways of thinking. Having become popular only toward the close of his life and after his death, he did not found any major school, although reference is sometimes made to the post-Diltheyan humanities and although there is no doubt that some of his ideas (understanding, *Weltanschauung*, connections between personality and culture, cognitive role of biographies, and so forth) have come to play an important role even in sociology, which he himself disliked heartily. True, in antipositivist thought some of his ideas have been adopted anonymously or have been linked to him without any endeavor to locate them in the broader context of his philosophy. To make matters worse, prevalent ideas about his philosophy do not go beyond stereotypes.

Dilthey's "Positivism" and Antipositivism. These stereotypes can be seen especially in the view that Dilthey's philosophy was a total denial of positivism and a reversal of all its basic principles. There is nothing more erroneous than that. Dilthey's point of departure was a specific "positivism," which found expression in his slogan of *unbefangene Empirie*—that is, approaching facts without any metaphysical assumptions made in advance, which could deform the researcher's picture of reality (an idea extremely popular in the whole "philosophy of life"). As C. Antoni wrote, "Dilthey's originality lay in the fact that he turned the criteria of the positivists against themselves and thus undermined their intrusion into the historical sciences. More positivistic than the positivists, he refused to subordinate empirical facts to laws and methods not growing out of the facts themselves."[19] In Dilthey's opinion, the principal sin of the positivist humanities was having *a priori* conceptions and approaching the facts to be examined with a ready-made standard of science, a standard whose usefulness had never been even tentatively verified. Such a procedure is at variance with the conclusions that can be drawn from advances in modern natural science. Dilthey summed up these conclusions thus: The humanities must start from the most general concepts of general methodology and work up to the elaboration of specified methods well adapted to the subject matter under investigation, proceeding in that respect in the same way as the natural sciences do. We let ourselves be known as true disciples of eminent natural scientists and thinkers not by transfering the methods that they have invented to our fields of study, but by making our cognition comply with the nature of our research and by adopting the same attitude toward it as they adopt toward theirs.

Dilthey dismissed the question about the principles of the scientific method as such. Methodological problems can meaningfully be studied only in close connection with reflection on the nature of the facts under consideration. Further, he denied methodology its traditionally normative character. For him, the methodologist acts as a historian rather than as an instructor. Dilthey does not say how the humanities *should* be pursued and prefers to ask about how they *are* pursued. He wants to provide the humanists with methodological self-knowledge and not to teach them what they should do in order to comply with the abstract standards of a science. Reflection on the research procedures used in the humanities reveals both the specific nature of the world studied by those disciplines and the epistemological status of that world, which differs from that of the world of nature. We come to realize that nature is alien to us; it is a mere exterior, lacking any inner life for us. Society is our world. Dilthey strove above all to disclose the many consequences of that simple discovery, which canceled one of the major dogmas of positivist thought.

The Geisteswissenschaften *and the Issue of Sociology.* Dilthey took the difference in the relationship between the cognizing subject and the object of cognition as the criterion for distinguishing two groups of disciplines—the natural sciences and the humanities *(Geisteswissenschaften)*[20]—and focused his attention on the latter group. That group includes "history, economics, law, politics and psychology and the study of religion, literature, poetry, architecture, music and philosophic world views and systems. All these studies refer to the same great fact: mankind, which they describe, recount and judge and about which they form concepts and theories. . . ." Dilthey also described the subject matter of those disciplines and claimed that it ranges "from individuals, families, composite associations, nations, ages, historical movements or evolutionary series, social organizations, systems of culture and other sections of the whole humanity, to humanity itself."

It is striking that sociology is missing from that list; "the description of the contemporary state of society" is included in historiography.[21] This omission was not due to his ignorance of that discipline, but was caused by his aversion to it, expressed in his numerous comments on Comte's views. Dilthey saw in sociology an extreme case of naturalistic metaphysics. Yet his antisociologism should not be identified with a lack of interest in sociological issues.[22] Dilthey just believed that the study of the problems of the "social system" in which he was interested did not require a separate discipline. The perspective that he suggested might be called *historical psychol-*

ogy or, to use his own term, *descriptive psychology*, the word *descriptive* denoting here the striving for maximum respect for the integrality of facts to be studied.

The Perspective of Historical Psychology. That *unbefenagene Empirie*, toward which the humanistic disciplines aware of their mission were to turn, amounted in Dilthey's interpretation to human life itself, which inevitably evades all definitions and schematizations. "Life," he wrote, is the fundamental fact which must form the starting point for philosophy. It is that which is known from within, that behind which we cannot go. Life cannot be brought before the judgment seat of reason. . . . It is only possible to grasp it through the reconstruction of the course of events in a memory which reproduces not the particular event but the system of connections and the stages of its development." The concept of life *[leben]* was for him closely connected with that of experience *[erleben]* and, hence, with the inner world of human individuals conceived as "psychological wholes," not as systems of separate mental faculties: "We must start from the reality of life; in life all the aspects of the mind are involved."[23]

Dilthey claimed that it had been an unpardonable error of the sociologists to have lost sight of the experiencing human individual and to have reduced the cognizing subject to discursive reason and the object of cognition to something external to that cognizing subject. Life and human mentality are inseparable from one another, and this is why the path leading to the knowledge of life must go via *psychology*. In this sense, Dilthey stands for psychologism and says that psychology is "the first and the most elementary humanistic discipline, and the truths it provides make the foundation of the whole edifice."[24] It would, however, be erroneous to think that Dilthey acceded to psychologism in the form that we discussed previously. What he had in common with such psychologism was merely the belief in the key significance of psychology, which he conceived in a totally different manner, however. He sought a psychology that would, first, be concerned with mental life as a whole that could not be decomposed to any components and, second, would grasp human personality in its unity with the social world defined in historical terms.

Writes Makkreel,

According to Dilthey, psychology should describe the psychophysical complex in such a way as to preserve it as the basic unit of, while showing it to be inseparable from, social and historical life; the individual is not the hypothetical aggregate of some elementary givens, like his sense impressions. Nor is society the mere aggregate of the individuals that can be located in it. Instead, the individual is the ultimate element of a historical society, and in being conscious he is already an embodiment of that society. He is a self-subsistent whole who in turn points to a larger whole as a microcosm reflects a macrocosm.[25]

The idea of the historicity of mental life, essentially alien to all psychologism, was of great significance to Dilthey. In his opinion, the human psyche has certain universal traits that make it possible to understand people from other epochs and other cultures, but the knowledge of man as such is quite insufficient in the humanities. "The course of a historical personality's life is a system of interactions in which the individual receives stimuli from the historical world, is moulded by them and, then, in his turn, affects the historical world."[26] On another occasion Dilthey referred to the individual as the *Kreuzungspunkt* ("meeting point") of the various systems of social interaction.

Thus, for all his stress on psychology as the fundamental humanistic discipline, the focus of his interests was situated far from that of the psychologists. He was fascinated not so much by man endowed with permanent mental features, but by man in history, shaped by changing social influences. His point was "to understand the whole life of an individual as it expresses itself at a certain time and place."[27] This was probably why Dilthey, like later students of interconnections between personality and culture, assigned so much cognitive value to autobiographical data.

Objectifications of Life. According to Dilthey, psychology is as necessary for acquiring the knowledge of the human world as it is insufficient. This is so because life becomes objectified (here he refers to Hegel's conception of the objective mind) in the process of producing relatively permanent structures of interactions among human beings in the form both of cultural systems (religion, art, philosophy, science, law, economy, language, and education) and of external organizations of society (the family, the state, the church, and corporate bodies of various kinds).

Dilthey made it a point not to assign to those structures an autonomous existence, relative to human individuals. They were for him, as Makkreel put it, "functional structures activated by individuals rather than autonomous superpersonal entities."[28] All cultural systems and external organizations of society emerge from a living composition *(Zusammenhang)* of human mentality and, hence, can be comprehended on that basis only. Nevertheless, psychology does not fully explain such phenomena: They are more durable than an individual, each having an inner order of its own, and they make the researcher face problems other than those raised by the experiences of the individuals. Moreover, experiences of individuals are not comprehensible to us, either, if taken in isolation from the systems of culture and the external organizations of society. The individual exists for the humanistic disciplines only in unity with culture.

Every single human expression represents something which is common to many and therefore part of the realm of objective mind. Every word or sentence, every gesture

or form of politeness, every work of art and every historical deed are only understandable because the person expressing himself and the person who understands
him are connected by something they have in common: the individual always experiences, thinks, acts, and also understands in this common sphere.[29]

Man thus acquires the understanding of himself through acquiring the
knowledge of culture—that is, "fixed expressions of life." Hence, even
though the ultimate humanistic reality is that of the mental experiences of
individuals, and though culture is genetically linked to them, the world of
the objective mind is far from being the fiction that Dilthey would like to
eliminate from the humanities.

On the contrary, it seems that as his views evolved, Dilthey was moved
farther and farther away from the psychologistic reductionism in the interpretation of culture. Outhwaite says that "the emphasis shifts from the
empathetic penetration or reconstruction of other people's mental processes
to the hermeneutic interpretation of cultural products and conceptual
structures."[30]

Dilthey's views, however, were inconsistent. His works reveal a constant
tension between psychologism and culturalism, between subjective and
objective idealism in the interpretation of culture. Without the conception
of culture as the objectification of life, he could not have fully overcome
naturalistic psychologism, but the total abandonment of psychology would
mean the denial of the main assumptions of "the philosophy of life," including the belief that the specific feature of culture, as compared with
nature, is the fact that culture is *experienced* by individuals. "Interpretation
would be impossible," Dilthey wrote, "if the life-expressions were totally
alien. It would be unnecessary if there were nothing strange about them.
It therefore lies between these two extremes."[31] It is on this paradox that
Dilthey's entire system was based, and this accounts for both the originality
and the ambiguity of that system.

In Dilthey's system two kinds of interest coexist all the time. On the one
hand, there is a profusion of ideas concerning the "projection" of individual mentality, the common content of individual experiences and analogies between the individual and his system of culture. On the other, we find
statements about the inner order of the products of culture, an order that
combines them into coherent supraindividual wholes that are capable of
attaining their own goals and creating new values. Every system of culture,
he says, has "a focal point within itself,"[32] and this explains why its understanding does not consist in reproducing the mental experiences of those
individuals who participate in that system.

The Idea of Understanding. The inner tension of Dilthey's conception
visibly affects his interpretation of understanding, which he considered to
be the instrument of cognition that is specific to the humanistic disciplines.

That those disciplines can, and have to, make use of such an instrument is due to the fact that culture, being—unlike nature—a product of man, is not totally alien to him. The subject and the object of cognition are in this case in one and the same world and make a community *sui generis* even if they are remote from one another in time and space. "Certainly the humanities have an advantage over all knowledge of nature in that their subject matter is not a phenomenon given in the senses, a mere reflex of a real thing in a consciousness, but is itself immediate inner reality."[33] For this reason, we need not confine ourselves to observing facts—as the positivists recommended—but have an opportunity to reach that which is concealed behind them, that is, *ein Inneres*. The facts studied by the humanities are signs of a deeper reality, whose knowledge is the proper task of those disciplines. In a most general formulation, understanding is the procedure of revealing that which is hidden under the surface of the human world, the surface itself being observable in the way that one uses in the natural sciences. "Understanding and interpretation is the method used throughout the human studies and all functions unite in it. It contains all the truths of the human studies."[34]

Explaining the principles of that method, which later became the foundation of so-called humanistic sociology, is one of the most difficult tasks faced by the historian of the social sciences. He finds in the literature of the subject many divergent interpretations, each of which is to some extent supported by Dilthey's writings, which abound in obscure passages and, moreover, reflect the evolution of Dilthey's views. It would be useful to follow Outhwaite in making a distinction between two methods of understanding—namely, psychological understanding and hermeneutical understanding. Such a distinction was never made by Dilthey himself, nor was one made between his descriptive psychology and his science of culture.

There is no doubt that psychological understanding is most clearly outlined in Dilthey's works. It is based on what R. Aron calls the trivial theory of analogy.[35] Dilthey assumed a correspondence between the researcher's own mental life and that of all other cognizing subjects—hence, also those who are the subject matter of his investigations.

Individual differences are not in the last analysis determined by qualitative differences between people, but rather through a difference in the degree of development of their psychic processes. Now inasmuch as the exegete tentatively transports his own sense of life into another historical milieu, he is able, within that perspective, to strengthen and emphasize certain psychic processes in himself and to minimize others, thus making possible within himself a reconstruction of an alien form of life.[36]

In this case, to understand is to place oneself in another person's position and to experience, in one's imagination, that which the other person experiences and in this way to guess what the other person's observable behavior

means. Since human nature is uniform, we may assume that the ratio between expression and that which is expressed is a constant, and thus, by
observing expression, we can draw some conclusions about the mental
states of other people, even though those states are not subject to our direct
observation.

However important was the role played in Dilthey's work by that simplest
idea of understanding, he did not consider it sufficient, and he made the
distinction between understanding *(Verstehen)* and empathetic reconstruction *(Erlebnis)* and tried to remove the limitations of the latter—its subjective
character and unverifiability. He also noticed that the "expressions of life"
that are subject to understanding are of two kinds: Some of them can be
comprehended by a simple analogy, while others require intricate intellectual
operations and vast extrapsychological knowledge. We come to understand what a person's tears mean in a different way from that in which we
come to understand the meaning of a phrase in a given language, a literary
work written in a certain convention, or the actions undertaken by a historical personality. In such cases insight into our own mental life, while it may
help, proves to be insufficient. We must then refer to our knowledge of
the historical context and also to the possibly vast general knowledge accumulated by the various humanistic disciplines. To understand is not to
experience in one's own mind that which was earlier experienced by others,
but to locate the fact under investigation within a definite whole—a language, a culture, a social system—such a location being achieved by a
number of mental operations. In the latter case we speak about hermeneutic
understanding or simply about hermeneutics, which Dilthey thought to be
a kind of knowledge, while psychological understanding was considered by
him to be an art.

That distinction was not always clear in Dilthey's writings. When he was
concerned with life as such, he stopped at the level of psychological understanding, but when he passed to the objectifications of life, he shifted the
focus of his interests to hermeneutical understanding. In the former case
he tried to discover the relationship between an individual's expression
and his mental state; and in the latter, the relationship between a fixed form
of an expression and the whole of "objectified life." As Outhwaite notes,
"In the case of complex 'spiritual' phenomena what is involved, according
to Dilthey, is not psychological understanding but 'recourse to a conceptual
construction with its own structural regularity.'"[37]

Note, however, that understanding, as interpreted by Dilthey, was in
both senses largely *irrational*. The relevant point is that in one case we enter
into the spirit of people's experience; in the other, into the spirit of a given
whole (an epoch, a work of art, and so on).

Dilthey's Significance in the Social Sciences. Dilthey's activity is believed
by many authors to have marked a kind of revolution in the humanities.

In fact, his philosophy, even though it still contained some traces of positivism, was the first declaration of independence made on behalf of the humanities and the social sciences. That independence had its source, according to Dilthey's claims, in the essentially different nature of the subject matter of the humanities. In those disciplines the object of cognition is not a *thing* opposed to the cognizing subject. For this reason, it requires a different method of research, namely, that of understanding, which assumes a kind of community between the student and that which he studies. Dilthey's ideas gave rise to a new trend in the methodology of the humanities, a trend that is vital to this day and has influenced European sociology whenever the universal validity and direct usefulness of the pattern of natural science were questioned. But to be able to play that role, Dilthey's ideas required far-reaching modifications; in their original form they had included too many obscurities and inconsistencies and had also been too contaminated by the irrationalism of "the philosophy of life," from which they had originated. Those modifications had their principal source in neo-Kantianism, which in its Baden-school variety focused on the methodology of the humanities and the social sciences and did not continue Dilthey's philosophy (which is claimed too often), but managed to overcome it. Dilthey's role was essentially destructive: He questioned the basic assumptions of the positivist humanities, but failed to advance in his own program beyond certain intuitions. Nor did he formulate any coherent theory of humanistic cognition, particularly one offering a foundation on which sociology could be constructed.

HISTORY AS A CULTURAL SCIENCE

The task of formulating such a conception was undertaken by such neo-Kantians as Georg Simmel (1858-1918) and Heinrich Rickert (1863-1936), author of *Die Grenzen der Naturwissenschaftlichen Begriffsbildung* (1902, revised in 1931) and *Kulturwissenschaft und Naturwissenschaft* (1899), which was translated into English as *Science and History*. The work that they started came to be crowned by Max Weber's "interpretative sociology." While they retained the essential elements of absolute historicism, they strove to free that orientation from irrationalism and extreme relativism and, above all, to put an end to the illusion, cherished by "the philosophy of life," that cognition can grasp life as such.

Rickert's Individualizing Method. Both the neo-Kantians and Dilthey rejected the belief that historical facts can be ordered or classified like specimens of biological species and explained by reference to general laws. Rickert wrote: "Whoever speaks of 'history' pure and simple always means the nonrepeatable, individual course of an event."[38] Later, he claimed that "there are sciences that do *not* aim at the discovery of natural laws or even at the formation of *general* concepts. These are the *historical* sciences in the broadest sense of the term. They do *not want* to produce merely 'ready-made' clothes that fit Paul as well as they do Peter; they purpose to represent reality, which is never general, but always individual, in its individuality.''[39]

In these statements, Rickert followed his master, Wilhelm Windelband (1848-1915), who in a famous lecture, "Geschichte und Naturwissenschaft" (1894), made a distinction between the nomothetic and the idiographic sciences. The former are concerned with the general and, thus, strive to discover laws, whereas the latter are concerned with single events. Yet it does not seem that Rickert saw any theoretical problem in that distinction, since he considered it to be self-evident. He was, however, alarmed by the imprecision of the concept of individuality and, perhaps even more, by the formlessness of the subject matter with which the historical sciences would have to deal if that concept remained imprecise. At the time when he engaged in polemics with Dilthey and Windelband, he was aware of the defects of both naturalism and absolute historicism.

Rickert made the difference between history and natural science a relative one, stating that opposing one to the other because of the alleged difference between their subject matters was wrong: "I myself speak rather of a *generalizing* and of an *individualizing* method, and I have always emphasized that what is involved here is not a question of an absolute antithesis but of a relative difference.''[40] The opposition is a methodological, and not an ontological, one. What we are concerned with is "not two different *domains* or reality, but the same *reality* seen from two *different points of view . . . Empirical reality becomes nature when we view it with respect to its universal characteristics: it becomes history when we view it as particular and individual.''[41] It can be said only that reality is many-faceted; this justifies the plurality of methods used in science, which complement one another. Natural science and history are two polar extremes between which there is room for research procedures that are more or less remote from either. It is to be supposed that while Dilthey completely denied the existence of sociology, Rickert would place it somewhere between these extremes.

Rickert was primarily interested in the various ways, actually encountered in research practice, of articulating or conceptualizing the empirical reality that in itself seemed to him to be a formless and undifferentiated whole. In that sense he did not question the validity of the naturalist approach, but merely proved its one-sidedness.

The historical sciences were the focus of Rickert's work, and he claimed that they had been most neglected methodologically among all disciplines. He was interested in concept formation in historiography, which, even though it concentrates on individuality, does not grasp the historical reality as such, but must separate its subject matter from it. In every science—and history is no worse than natural science—the key issue is to select facts and to find the criterion for sifting out that which is important from that which is not. The scholar must know "first, which *objects* it has to represent among the enormously heterogeneous multitude constituting the real world, and, secondly, which of the vast multiplicity of parts constituent of every single object are *essential* for it."[42] The historian, deprived of the concept of law, must thus carry out operations analogous to those performed by the natural scientist. In the historian's case, the purpose of those operations is to make a distinction between "two kinds of individuality," "historically *significant individualities*" and "mere heterogeneity" or "unessential differences."[43]

When seeking the appropriate criterion, Rickert made his most important discovery from the sociological point of view: He introduced the concept of value-relevance *(Wertbeziehung)*, which simultaneously was to serve as an additional criterion for making a distinction between history and natural science and for defining historical individuality "as something unique, *sui generis*, and irreplaceable by *any* other segment of reality."[44] In other words, he defined the historical sciences as the sciences of culture, because culture for him—unlike the evolutionists—was just the sphere of values: "Culture comprises . . . whatever is either produced directly, by man acting according to valued ends or, if its is already in existence, is at least fostered intentionally for the sake of the *values* attaching to it."[45]

Culture and Values. The concept of culture, like that of value, is not very clear in Rickert's writings, but the course that it is to point out to the humanities can be seen distinctly. To put it in general terms, culture is a fairly accurate counterpart of Dilthey's objective spirit, except that Rickert separated it from mental life, however the latter be interpreted. He stated explicitly that "cultural sciences are not to be restricted to the investigation of psychical events and that, consequently, it is not very appropriate to describe these disciplines as sciences dealing with manifestations of the human 'spirit' if the latter term is understood to refer exclusively to inner, psychical life."[46] The cultural sciences are concerned not with what is experienced by individuals (that is the subject matter of psychology, which can be pursued as a natural science), but with what is meaningful for them or bears a tangible relationship to values. The latter do not exist in any physical or mental sense of the verb *to exist*, but are binding in the way that moral norms are. "A cultural value is either actually accepted as valid by all men, or its validity . . . is at least postulated by some civilized human being."[47] These sciences are not interested in the mental phenomena that accompany valuation, and their sole concern is that valuation owing to which historical reality acquires a definite structure, loses its formlessness and anonymity, and becomes ordered.

The order in the human world, discovered in this way, is in no sense an absolute one. While Rickert sometimes mentions suprahistorical values, he is interested primarily in "actually *accepted* values, which are as changeful as the waves of the ocean."[48] Every society and every epoch are marked by their specific configurations, which the historian strives to reconstruct. Further, according to the sphere that he studies, these or other values come to the fore, and the picture is different each time. The world appears in one way to a historian of economics, in another to a historian of law, and in still another to a historian of art. No one picture is truer than any other; nor is there any possibility of integrating them. Rickert, nevertheless, insisted on the ideal of the historian's objectivity. The values involved are those discovered in the process of history and not contributed to it from the outside following an arbitrary decision on the part of the scholar. Rickert made a distinction between value-relevance and valuation (*Wertbeziehung* versus *Wertung*). Historical individuality is constituted by a relationship between a given object and given values, not by the historian's own assessment. He is supposed to abstain from valuation, and his task is to find out how other people valuate things.

While he removed the concept of law (regularity) from the humanities, Rickert retained the concept of causality. As he put it, "history too, with its individualizing method and its orientation to values, has to investigate the causal relations subsisting among the unique and individual events with which it is concerned."[49]

Culture and Forms. Equally remarkable as an attempt to go beyond the horizon of absolute historicism was the philosophical production of Georg Simmel. (Simmel's sociological views will be discussed later.) His limited popularity qua philosopher among sociologists—despite the fact that philosophy was the main field of his scholarly activity—can partly be explained by the heterogeneity of his writings and the ambiguity of his principal conclusions. Simmel is usually seen either as a trivial representative of "the philosophy of life" or merely as the founder of so-called formal sociology, commonly believed to be on the margin of the main trend of humanistic sociology, which followed the course marked by Dilthey, Rickert, and Max Weber. Weber himself, although a close friend of Simmel, clearly underestimated his work.

Simmel deserves the credit for an interesting endeavor to overcome absolute historicism by imposing on the flow of historical experience a definite structure, owing to which its rational cognition would be possible. That endeavor essentially converged with the one undertaken by Rickert. It differed from the latter by the fact that Simmel made statements not only on the methods of acquiring the knowledge of reality, but also on that reality itself. He did not exclude the possibility of answering the question about the structure of that reality which the historian studies.

Rickert's assumption was that the object of historical cognition is constituted by the researcher, who conceptually orders the empirical reality, which is formless by definition. Simmel assumed that social reality—unlike nature—has an order of its own, because it is composed of actions undertaken by conscious agents who inevitably produce order.

Society is an objective unity which does not require [for the establishment of its unitary character] an observer uncontained in it. . . . the things of nature . . . are further from each other than [human] souls; the union of one man with another which lies in understanding, in love, in common effort—there is no analogue to it in the spatial world, in which every entity occupies its own place which cannot be shared with any other.[50]

Thus Simmel assumed, reverting in that respect back to Dilthey, that the difference between the humanities and the natural sciences is both in the method and in the subject matter.

In Simmel's philosophy the concept of form is pivotal:

We speak of culture whenever life produces certain forms in which it expresses and realizes itself; works of art, religions, sciences, technologies, laws and unnumerable others. These forms encompass the flow of life and provide it with content and form, freedom and order. But although these forms arise out of the life process, because of their unique constellation they do not share the restless rhythm of life, its ascent and descent, its constant renewal, its incessant divisions and reunifications. . . . They acquire fixed identities, a logic and lawfulness of their own; this new rigidity inevitably places them at a distance from the spiritual dynamic which created them and which makes them independent.[51]

Culture has a history; it is also marked by an unceasing tension between the eternal flow of life and the fixed forms. Convinced that culture was threatened by the boundless striving for change, Simmel attached both theoretical and practical importance to the relative stability of forms.

Simmel's concept of form was not free from ambiguities, nor did he make use of it in all his works. Yet, it was worked out sufficiently to justify a reference to an original philosophy of culture, the more so as Simmel took up extensively the problems of the origin of forms, their various "levels," the relationships between culture and personality, and the like.

PREREQUISITES OF HUMANISTIC SOCIOLOGY

The thinkers discussed in this chapter were, except for Simmel, concerned with sociology only as its critics, even though they did not lack interest in sociological issues. Problems of society, society's impact on the individual, culture, social development, and so on were the focus of their scholarly interests. Likewise, the dilemmas of sociological thinking, to which we pointed in previous chapters, were not alien to them. (This applies, for instance, to a modified version of the controversy between psychologism and sociologism.) The point was, however, that those sociological problems were so regrouped in the idealistic German humanities that in many cases it would be difficult to speak about their having been solved anew; it would perhaps be more appropriate to speak about their having been rediscovered in the light of a different intellectual tradition, a different hierarchy of scholarly values, and different aspirations in research and academic teaching.

Here we came across a different kind of social knowledge, one whose assimilation by sociology faced serious obstacles not only because its theorems were different from those which sociology was accustomed to accepting, but also because it demanded an essential difference in the ways of thinking. To use Dilthey's terminology, we could say that we are concerned with two opposing *Weltanschauungen*, not with two comparable systems of theorems. Even today one can see how difficult it is for the heirs of the positivist tradition and the heirs of German idealism to find a common language. It has turned out that the latter can more easily engage in a meaningful dialogue with the Marxists, because Marxism also does not accept the positivist conception of science, which the German humanities tried to overcome.

Those humanities have as their foundation the rejection of positivist naturalism, which meant the acceptance of the equal status of all kinds of cognition, the declaration of a search by the humanities for their own standards of what is scientific, the refusal to consider those disciplines' objects of cognition as things, and so forth. The *pars destruens* of the new philosophy of the humanities can be noticed quite clearly. It also accounts for philosophy's attractiveness to some sociologists, namely, those who noticed the disproportion between the promises and the achievements of positivist sociology.

The affirmative program may prove much more intricate. It can be summed up in two words: understanding, the procedure that is more useful for the humanists than the explanation used in natural science; and culture, conceived, first, as a property of historically given communities and, second, as a configuration of nonmaterial forms or values, constituted and preserved by purposive human actions. But the implementation of that program encountered obstacles connected with the imprecision of the basic concepts and the insufficient consistency of the systems based on them. The first difficulty, illustrated by Dilthey's case, lay in bringing into agreement certain statements about culture as the sphere of the objective spirit that is relatively autonomous with respect to individuals and other statements about human experiences as the ultimate empirical reality. In other words, the advances of the new theory of culture (and, hence, of a new sociology as well) required the resolution of the problem of psychologism, which only Rickert tried to do consistently.

The second difficulty resulted from the conflict between the endeavor to comprehend the world of history in its totality and its full changeability and the awareness that this object cannot be comprehended. As a result, a student of history had inevitably to solve the problem of selecting data, although the instruments of selection that natural science provides were dismissed. This was why absolute historicism assumed the shape of formalism, which promised something stable in the flow of historical experience.

In other words, faced with the dilemmas of psychologism versus culturalism and absolute historicism versus formalism, the idealistic philosophy of the humanities had to solve the problem of the objective nature of culture and that of its relatively stable order, which could be studied in a scientific manner, different from that in which the order of nature is investigated, but equally precise. The future of humanistic sociology depended on the same issue.

NOTES

1. George Ritzer, *Sociology: A Multiple Paradigm Science* (Boston: Allyn and Bacon, 1975), chap. 1.

2. Werner J. Cahnman, "Max Weber and the Methodological Controversy in the Social Sciences," in Werner J. Cahnman and Alvin Boskoff, eds., *Sociology and History: Theory and Research* (New York: Free Press, 1964), p. 104.

3. Georg C. Iggers, "Historicism," in Philip P. Wiener, ed., *Dictionary of the History of Ideas: Studies of Selected Pivotal Ideas* (New York: Scribner's, 1973), 2:459.

4. Karl Mannheim, "Historicism," in Mannheim, *Essays on the Sociology of Knowledge* (London: RKP, 1952), pp. 84-85.

5. Arthur C. Danto, *Analytical Philosophy of History* (Cambridge: Cambridge University Press, 1968), p. 308.

6. K. R. Popper, *The Poverty of Historicism* (London: RKP, 1961), p. 7.

7. Jerzy Topolski, *Methodology of History* (Dortrecht/Boston: Reidel, 1976), pp. 158-59.

8. Thus, the 1972 translation of the fundamental work by F. Meinecke, *Die Entstehung des Historismus*, is entitled *Historism: The Rise of a New Historical Outlook* (London: RKP).

9. Dwight E. Lee and Robert N. Beck, "The Meaning of Historicism," *American Historical Review* 59 (April 1954): 569.

10. See Carlo Antoni, *From History to Sociology: The Transition in German Historical Thinking* (London: Merlin Press, 1962), p. 75.

11. See ibid., p. 75.

12. Mannheim, "Historicism," p. 86.

13. Meinecke, *Historism*, p. lv.

14. Maurice Mandelbaum, *The Problem of Historical Knowledge: An Answer to Relativism* (New York: Liveright, 1938), p. 31.

15. Cf. Carl Heinrichs's introduction to F. Meinecke's *Historism*, p. xxvii.

16. William McDougall, *The Group Mind* (Cambridge: Cambridge University Press, 1927), pp. xv-xvi.

17. See William Outhwaite, *Understanding Social Life: The Method Called Verstehen* (London: Allen and Unwin, 1975), p. 33.

18. Max Horkheimer, *Critical Theory: Selected Essays* (New York: Herder and Herder, 1972), pp. 11-12.

19. Antoni, *From History to Sociology*, p. 18.

20. This term is different than that of Rickert [see note 38], who uses the term *Kulturwissenschaften* ("cultural sciences"). It seems that the term *Geisteswissenschaften* first appeared in the German translation of *A System of Logic* by J. S. Mill for "moral sciences."

21. Cf. H. P. Rickman, ed., *Wilhelm Dilthey: Pattern and Meaning in History: Thoughts on History and Society* (New York: Harper and Row, 1961), p. 68.

22. Ibid., pp. 17-18.

23. Ibid., pp. 73, 125.

24. Wilhelm Dilthey, *Gesammelte Schriften*, vol. 1, *Einleitung in die Geisteswissenschaften* (Stuttgart: B. G. Teubner, 1922), p. 33.

25. Rudolf A. Makkreel, *Dilthey: Philosopher of the Human Studies* (Princeton: Princeton University Press, 1975), p. 56.

26. Rickman, *Wilhelm Dilthey*, p. 90.

27. Ibid., p. 79.

28. Makkreel, *Dilthey*, p. 67.

29. Outhwaite, *Understanding Social Life*, pp. 26-27.

30. Ibid., p. 26.

31. Ibid., p. 34.

32. Rickman, *Wilhelm Dilthey*, pp. 129-30.

33. W. Dilthey, "The Rise of Hermeneutics," in Paul Connerton, ed., *Critical Sociology* (Harmondsworth: Penguin Books, 1976), pp. 104-5.

34. Rickman, *Wilhelm Dilthey*, p. 110.

35. Raymond Aron, *La Philosophie critique de l'histoire* (Paris: J. Vrin, 1969), p. 79.

36. Makkreel, *Dilthey*, p. 250.

37. Outhwaite, *Understanding Social Life*, p. 41.

38. Heinrich Rickert, *Science and History: A Critique of Positivist Epistemology* (Princeton: Van Nostrand, 1962), p. 60.

39. Ibid., p. 55.

40. Ibid., p. xii.

41. Ibid., pp. 56-57.

42. Ibid., p. 79.

43. Ibid., pp. 83, 85.

44. Ibid., p. 83.

45. Ibid., pp. 18-19.

46. Ibid., p. 25.

47. Ibid., p. 22.

48. Ibid., p. 137.

49. Ibid., p. 94.

50. Cf. Werner Stark, *The Fundamental Forms of Social Thought* (London: RKP, 1962), p. 215.

51. Donald N. Levine, ed., *Georg Simmel on Individuality and Social Forms* (Chicago: University of Chicago Press, 1971), p. 375.

12

THE FIRST SYSTEMS OF HUMANISTIC SOCIOLOGY: TÖNNIES, SIMMEL, AND WEBER

The tendency to question the need for sociology as such, characteristic of the new humanities in Germany, and the disillusionment with the results of positivist sociology, which was observable in many countries, strengthened the resistance in traditional academic circles to officially accepting the new discipline, but did not stop its further expansion. There were not only continuations of earlier enquiries and initiations of new ones in various countries, but also, much more important, endeavors to reconstruct sociology on the basis of accepted achievements of the idealistic criticism of positivist social sciences. The same period that saw the birth of psychologism and sociologism witnessed the rise in Germany of the first systems of humanistic sociology, which were both a denial of the positivist tradition and a critique of absolute historicism. They were, above all, the systems founded by Ferdinand Tönnies (1855-1936), Georg Simmel (1858-1918), and Max Weber (1864-1920). These sociologists, for all the differences between them, share a similar point of view regarding both the subject matter of sociology and the research methods considered most suitable for that discipline.

The trend represented by those systems, especially by Max Weber's system, is here called *humanistic sociology*, the term being chosen arbitrarily from among several possibilities—*interpretative sociology*, *social actionism*, *social definition paradigm*, and so on.[1]

We do not claim that the trend discussed here was in every respect opposed to the positivist one. Some conceptions advanced by its representatives had certain points in common with psychologism and sociologism. This has been shown, for example, by Talcott Parsons, who in *The Structure of Social Actions* analyzed similarities between Weber's ideas and those of Pareto and Durkheim. Tönnies also was deeply involved in the heritage of positivist thinking. Nevertheless, there does seem to have been a specific trend, which has to some extent remained popular to this day.

THE CONCEPT OF HUMANISTIC SOCIOLOGY

Humanistic sociology is more difficult to define than many other trends. This is so because it is largely a set of metasociological views, which can be given concrete forms in many different ways, and also because attention was focused much more on its criticism of other trends in sociology than on its positive program and its research practice. The following assumptions have been most commonly accepted.

Antinaturalism. One of constitutive features of humanistic sociology was the opinion that social facts are not things that can, or should, be investigated by methods developed in natural science. It was a continuation of Dilthey's criticism of naturalism, but was free from the latter's theoretical radicalism, obscurities, and irrationalism.

Interactionism. Unlike the earlier conceptions, humanistic sociology has been, and still is, the science of social interaction. To quote the Polish representative of this trend, F. Znaniecki (1882-1958),

Instead of beginning with the assumption that the total life of the people who compose a territorially circumscribed, politically organized society is integrated, or with the assumption that every human collectivity is merely a combination of individual human beings of an essentially similar nature, [humanistic] sociologists limit their task to comparative studies of certain specific phenomena which are observable in many diverse collectivities and yet are not reducible to human biology or psychology.[2]

In its definition of the subject matter of sociology (human interactions), humanistic sociology opposes both sociologism and psychologism, both organicism and individualism.

The Subjective Nature of Social Interactions. Humanistic sociology has been concerned with only those human interactions in which individuals participate as conscious subjects. We can speak about social interaction only if, in their own actions, the interacting individuals take into account the actions of others and try to influence them. Interaction is not a simple sequence of stimuli and responses; it takes place in the sphere of meanings and not in that of instincts and/or reflexes.

The Requirement of Understanding. Since the attention of humanistic sociology is focused on social interactions interpreted as above, acquiring the knowledge of social facts only from the outside is excluded. Representatives of that trend are interested not only in the behavior of the individuals, but also in the goals that those individuals set themselves; not only in the situations in which such behavior takes place, but also in the way in which the acting individuals visualize those situations. It is thus necessary to resort to the operation called *Verstehen*. However obscure that requirement happened to be, it meant the definitive rejection of the procedure of explanation that is characteristic of natural science and was recommended by positivists.

Social Knowledge as the Source of Self-Knowledge. Sociology pursued in this way could not yield results that could in turn become the basis of social engineering of any kind—that dream of every variety of positivists. Sociological knowledge could only provide self-knowledge to those who take part in social processes; it could increase their wisdom, but not their technical effectiveness.

FERDINAND TÖNNIES'S "ECLECTIC SYNTHESIS"

The first great system in German sociology was attributable to Ferdinand Tönnies (1855-1936), author of *Gemeinschaft und Gesellschaft* (1887), one of the epoch-making books in the history of sociology. His work is a very intricate matter for a historian to handle. On the one hand, it was—to use Durkheim's formulation—an "eclectic synthesis" of many ideas of modern social thought; on the other, it included many ideas that were ahead of the later sociological systems. Tönnies's production is, as it were, the ark of the covenant between the all-embracing sociological doctrines of the nineteenth century and the analytic sociology of the twentieth century; between the speculative social philosophy that developed in Germany and positivist sociology in France and Britain; between theoretical sociology and sociography. This was so because Tönnies, a programmatically philosophically oriented thinker, claimed (and confirmed by his work) that "empirical sociology is just as important as theoretical sociology."[3] Note also that Tönnies was one of those authors who (second only to representatives of what was called *Kathedersozialismus*) ennobled Marx in German academic circles and even considered himself to have been a Marxist to some extent.

Tönnies cannot be treated as a representative of any definite theoretical orientation. He embodied a rather amorphous formation typical of a transition period, a formation in which elements of positivist and evolutionist sociology coexisted with those of humanistic sociology, in which psychologism lived next door to sociologism and historicism next door to formalism. This was due both to his intellectual inclinations—he was an encyclopedist and a synthesist by temper—and to the fact that he was active for fifty years during an epoch that abounded in new ideas and books, which he studied with unrelenting enthusiasm.

But Tönnies was not just an eclectic. There are reasons to think that his innumerable reference to other authors (whom most other sociologists simply did not read) were subordinated to the primary task of expanding and improving the conception that he had formulated at the very beginning of his activity; and this conception cannot be denied originality, even though it was certainly an elaboration—from a new theoretical and ideological viewpoint—of the earlier issue of a *community* that decomposes under the impact of capitalism.

Tönnies was, in a sense, the author of just one book. True, he has many other books to his credit, including *Thomas Hobbes: Leben und Lehre* (1896), *Die Sitte* (1909), *Marx, Leben und Lehre* (1921), *Kritik der Oeffentlichen Meinung* (1922), and *Einführung in die Soziologie* (1931), and numerous articles collected in the three volumes of his *Soziologische Studien und Kritiken* (1929). But, in fact, he spent all his life elaborating the ideas formulated in *Gemeinschaft und Gesellschaft.* And it was these ideas that proved decisive for Tönnies's place in world sociology, which assimilated the typology included in that book, while disregarding his other conceptions and the connections between that typology and his system as a whole.

It seems that Tönnies's role qua sociologist was to be the first to make a specific synthesis of the attainments of British and French positivist sociology and the heritage of presociological German thought and also to have partially overcome the positivism in which he had been brought up. Thus, he paved the way for Simmel and Weber, a less tortuous path than the one indicated by Dilthey, who criticized all contemporaneous sociology from the outside.

Tönnies's Inspirations. Tönnies drew from many sources, the most important ones being:
1. Seventeenth-century ideas of natural law (predominantly Hobbes);
2. The positivist sociology of Comte and Spencer;
3. The philosophy of Schopenhauer (1788-1860), in particular the conception of will;
4. Socialist ideas, from Rodbertus to the *Kathedersozialisten* and especially Marx, whom he considered to be "the most remarkable and profound of the social philosophers";[4]
5. The works of such evolutionists as Morgan and Bachofen, who were of interest for him not as theorists of universal evolution, but as students of the earliest (and hence community-based) forms of relations among human beings. For the same reason his attention was attracted by Georg Ludwig von Maurer (1790-1872), the student of the old German *Mark* ("community") who was active in the 1850s and later, and Otto von Gierke (1841-1921), the renowned student of medieval law.

The variety of those sources of inspiration was due partly to his intention to bring different theoretical traditions into agreement and partly to the fact that the task that he had set for himself was extremely vast. This task focused on the two key issues in nineteenth-century sociology: the nature of the bonds between the individual and society and the development that had brought European societies to their condition at that time. On both issues Tönnies went far beyond the solutions advocated by his forerunners.

Conception of Sociology. Tönnies thought that there are three basic approaches to man's social life—the biological, the psychological, and the sociological—that have their counterparts in three separate disciplines: social biology, that is, anthropology; social psychology; and sociology. Although he did not erect walls between these disciplines, he made it a point to draw clear demarcation lines.

The psychological view of human social life regards attraction and repulsion, aid and combat, peaceful association and warlike conflict by themselves as equally important and relevant. The biological view is concerned with all such differences only because of the effect they have on increasing or reducing, stimulating or preserving life. The sociological view, as distinct from both, is essentially and in the first instance concerned with those facts that I call facts of reciprocal affirmation. Sociology investigates these specific and restricted social facts, analyzes their motives, and, in doing so, I maintain, must give particular attention to the difference whether reciprocal affirmation is based more on motives in feeling, or more on motives in reasoning.[5]

Sociology is interested in that aspect of social relation which is not only experienced, but also approved, by the individuals.

It belongs to the essence of every social relation as a mutual relationship approved by both parts that each of the persons involved makes and asserts a claim to a certain —regular or occasional, more or less permanent—conduct of the other person or persons; in other words, that conduct is expected as originating from their free will and conforming to the wish and will (the self-interest) of those who expect it.[6]

This is why Tönnies considered it meaningless to reflect on societies of animals or states of insects; he held that the subject matter of sociology is determined by reason and thought.

On another occasion Tönnies introduced the concept of exchange *(Tausch)* as the simplest case of social bonds and defined all coexistence as an exchange of services and gratifications *(Leistungen und Förderungen).*[7] For the same reason he criticized Durkheim's conception of social coercion as a factor that is external to both parties of any social relation. Tönnies's ideas, which ultimately reduce to the belief that social facts must be explained by reference to the attitudes of individuals, were often expressed in the language of psychologism.

Tönnies's ''Psychologism'' and ''Sociologism.''

I attempted [he wrote] to understand *[verstehen]* psychologically all non-rational and somewhat less than rational modes of thought and I concluded that they could never be absolutely unreasonable [unvernunftig], that they must carry their own meaning and that this meaning ultimately was reducible to human volition. I arrived at the generalization that what is social emanates from human willing, from the intention to relate to each other, a together-willing [Zusammenwollen], as it were; and I set myself the task of penetrating to the essence of this willing.[8]

Tönnies believed volition to be the most primitive phenomenon, in which he followed Schopenhauer. However, he differed from the latter by taking volition to be something specifically human and not necessarily irrational. All social relations can be deduced from the will of those individuals who enter into such relations. This is why he sided with the seventeenth-century theorists of natural law, although he blamed them for identifying will with rational will, which clearly distinguishes the ends from the means of action. We can speak about society only if there are individuals who want society to exist.

Social reality does not exist in the same way as natural reality does:

Relations and associations must be understood as existing in the will of those that are related and connected by it. They are immediately present only in consciousness (Bewusstsein) of the participants. . . . They are a product of thought in the sense that the very fact of their being entities entirely depends upon the minds of their members, of whom one can rightly state what Bishop Berkeley applied to the whole of the external world: esse = percipi (to be is to be perceived).

Social reality exists only inasmuch as it is "perceived, felt, imagined, thought, known and willed, primarily by individuals."[9]

This viewpoint did have consequences for the theory of cognition of social facts. As Tönnies wrote, "we can of course observe the life of human beings, and consequently their social life, from the "outside," but it is only from the "inside" that we can understand it."[10]

Tönnies's psychologism made him oppose all varieties of positivist organicism, which assumes that the social body exists regardless of human will. Tönnies was particularly critical of superficial analogies, as he saw in them "a matter of rhetoric and poetry but not of science."[11] This is not to say that he completely dismissed the issue of organicism together with its rational elements. In his opinion, the issue remains real insofar as society is seen by its members as a "psychical or moral body, capable of willing and of acting like a single human being."[12] The problem is of special importance when sociology focuses its attention on corporate bodies as such products of will, in which that will is fixed and, in effect, reified. Such products, treated by individuals as sources of their obligations, thus acquire a kind of independent existence. A corporate body is, of course, a fictitious one, but its existence is not merely nominal. It has a life of its own, ascribed to it by its members, who have not been aware that all social relations are products of their own will. This view, which he himself defined as "conceptualistic realism," was Tönnies's contribution to the sociological controversy over the universals.[13]

Regardless of his statements about deducing social facts from mental ones, he could not be called a representative of psychologism. His concept of will turns out to be a philosophical construction that has little in common with any psychological conception and, moreover, proves of little importance when he proceeds to analyze social processes, which he considers to be essentially irreducible to mental processes of individuals. Characteristically enough, Tönnies sought a compromise between Tarde and Durkheim. The basic question in Tönnies's sociology was about the essential mechanisms of social relations (exchange of services and gratifications) and not about their prime cause, which the representatives of psychologism used to seek.

Two Types of Social Bonds. Tönnies's sociology was focused on social bonds. He tried to synthesize the two traditionally opposed viewpoints: atomism and organicism. Society is neither a company founded by rationally acting individuals who want to attain specified goals nor an irrational collective entity that comes into being regardless of human aspirations. "Tönnies resolves the conflict between the two philosophical schools of thought by showing that each of them saw only *one* of the two spheres of social reality, taking it for the essence of the whole."[14] From Tönnies's point of view, the resolution of this conflict is possible if we assume that human nature has two aspects; thus, man is neither exclusively rational nor exclusively irrational.

There are, he says, two kinds of human will: one that comes from the depth of human self and is not accessible to reflection and one that results from reflection and calculation. We may term them organic or natural will *(Wesenwille)* and arbitrary will *(Kürwille)*. The latter is sometimes termed rational will (see Loomis's English translation of Tönnies's work), but this seems misleading, because organic will, too, according to Tönnies, contains an element of rationality and is not to be interpreted as a blind instinct. The point is, rather, that in the former case thinking is inseparably linked to life, emotions, and the totality of human experience; in the latter it is independent. Either kind of will is associated with a different type of human action: Organic will means action due to an inner drive; arbitrary will means action relative to some external goals to be attained thereby.

Social relations are shaped by both kinds of will, but in each case we come across relations of a different kind: Organic will gives rise to a community *(Gemeinschaft)*, while arbitrary will gives birth to a society *(Gesellschaft)*. These two concepts are pivotal in Tönnies's sociological system, where they play a role at least as important as that of the military and industrial societies in Spencer's sociology or the mechanical and organic solidarity in Durkheim's sociology. Tönnies gave a detailed list of the characteristics that are decisive in distinguishing community from society. Thus, the dominant bonds are kinship, fraternity, and neighborhood in the case of community; contract, exchange of material goods, and calculation, in the case of society. The former brings people together as individuals; the latter, as roles relative to a single function. In the former, social control is based on custom and tradition; in the latter, on formalized law. In their conduct, the members of a community are guided by faith; those of a society, by consideration of public opinion. Community has land and collective property as its economic foundation; in society that function is performed by money and private property.[15]

The Status of the Concepts of Gemeinschaft *and* Gesellschaft. While clear in its outline, the conception just described gave rise to considerable problems of interpretation, especially as it underwent various modifications and reformulations. In particular, it is not quite clear whether we are dealing with an evolutionistic approach, according to which *Gemeinschaft* would in the course of history yield its place to *Gesellschaft*, or with a typological approach, which merely reveals the permanent forms of socialization that coexist throughout human history. Further, in some cases it is difficult to decide whether it is a typology of whole societies or a typology of relations among individuals.

Without entering into the details of these debates, we may say that Tönnies's conception takes on three different meanings.

First, it was certainly historiosophical in nature, especially in his earlier writings: It tended to demonstrate the changes in European societies under the impact of capitalism. On that point Tönnies largely followed Marx, who pointed to the decomposition of the old community bonds and to the emergence of social relations under which people see one another as means to their respective private ends. But unlike Marx, he considered trade to have been the mainspring of economic change and was inclined to see in the development of capitalism the effect rather than the cause of the decomposition of traditional communities.[16] His conception also converged with the opinions of some evolutionists (for instance, his views on the evolution of law).

Second, it was markedly ideological, as it pointed to the collapse, in the capitalist world, of certain social values and demonstrated that no social relation can be really durable without the spirit of community. It was on this conviction that Tönnies's socialist faith was based.

And, finally, it was theoretical in nature, since it was intended to provide universal concepts that would be useful in the analysis of all manifestations of social life. When emphasizing the allegedly valuation-free nature of his dichotomy, Tönnies wrote that he did "not know of any condition of culture or society in which elements of *Gemeinschaft* and elements of *Gesellschaft* are not simultaneously present," that "both kinds of unions are universal," and that a pure *Gesellschaft* is something imagined rather than real.[17] All real societies have features of *Gemeinschaft* and *Gesellschaft* as well. It would, accordingly, be erroneous to use these two concepts as instruments of classification.

Tönnies's Method. To comprehend Tönnies's sociology, one has to realize that for him the most important part of this discipline—namely, so-called pure sociology—was not intended to describe facts.[18] In his opinion, the principal task of theoretical sociology was to conceptualize social relations, which as such are not subject to immediate observation: "only thought is capable of discerning them. They are a product of thought because they are abstracted from real life situations, that is, from the facts of social interaction."[19] In *Gemeinschaft und Gesellschaft* reference is made to *forms* that elude the senses; at a later stage Tönnies will speak, following Max Weber, about ideal types. As long we are concerned with pure sociology, we remain at the level of abstraction; it is only at the levels of applied and empirical sociology, listed by Tönnies as two other branches of this discipline, that we come closer to the reality. In doing so, we make use of the concepts that are available to order the mass of empirical data. In this respect Tönnies's conception seems related to his contemporaneous neo-Kantian ideas.

Tönnies's Significance in Sociology. *Gemeinschaft und Gesellschaft* has been one of the most influential books in the history of sociology, even though its author has now been eclipsed by Simmel and Max Weber and is not a classic whose work could directly be continued. But the impact of his work is hardly to be exaggerated. Hans Freyer claimed outright that all history of German sociology could be reduced to the history of the two concepts introduced by Tönnies.[20] His original ideas were subjected to numerous modifications and were given ever new interpretations and uses. His popularity came to extend far beyond the frontiers of Germany, the United States being a notable case. Yet, his popularity was somewhat one-sided, as it was confined to the typology offered by him in *Gemeinschaft und Gesellschaft*. He was much less often noticed as a thinker who had suggested a new viewpoint concerning the pursuit of sociological theory and the subject matter of sociology.

SIMMEL'S FORMAL SOCIOLOGY

Philosopher Georg Friedrich Simmel (1858-1918) went in the same direction as Tönnies. He even proved to be much more consistent and ingenious in founding a new sociology, although he, too, failed to produce a complete system. Simmel confined himself to outlining his basic theoretical ideas and writing brilliant essays that were merely more or less adequate illustrations of his proposals.

Simmel's Lack of Methodicalness. Simmel was one of the least methodical authors who ever wrote on sociology. This can be explained to some extent by his program, which dismissed the possibility of doing anything more than "to begin and to point out the direction of an infinitely long path."[21] But there were at least four other reasons:

1. His unstable philosophical standpoint, which evolved from positivism through neo-Kantianism to "the philosophy of life," which reminds one of Bergson;
2. The unbelievable scattering of his interests, which covered philosophy, historiosophy, visual arts, music, ethics, religion, literature, and theory of culture, in addition to sociology;
3. A lack, noted by Tenbruck, of "the proper tools for an adequate conceptualization of a new perspective that [Simmel] has discovered";[22]
4. His addressing simultaneously the academic circles (Simmel started lecturing at Berlin University as a *Privatdozent* in 1885; he became a professor in just fifteen years and in 1917 became a full professor at Strasbourg University) and the nonacademic public for which he founded, to use L. von Wiese's phrase, "a sociology for the literary salon."[23]

But the principal reason for Simmel's lack of methodicalness was his fascination with the multifaceted nature of reality, not the possibility of ordering it—illusory, in his opinion. Social reality seemed to him to be multifaceted, too; this was why his sociology was intended not to exhaust it, but merely to look at it from one of the many possible viewpoints.

Simmel was a prolific writer: He left several hundred articles and nearly thirty books, some of which concerned the work of thinkers and artists. Important books were *Ueber soziale Differenzierung: Soziologische und psychologische Untersuchungen* (1890), *Die Problem der Geschichtsphilosophie* (1892), *Einleitung in die Moralwissenschaft: Eine Kritik der ethischen Grundbegriffe* (two volumes, 1892-1893), *Die Philosophie des Geldes* (1900), *Die Religion* (1906), *Soziologie: Untersuchungen über die Formen der Vergesellschaftung* (1908), *Hauptprobleme der Philosophie* (1910), *Philosophische Kultur: Gesammelte Essais* (1911), *Grundfragen der Soziologie* (1917), *Der Konflikt der modernen Kultur: Ein Vortrag*

(1918), *Lebensanschauung* (1918), and *Vom Wesen des historischen Verste-hens* (1918).

Some of these are entirely concerned with sociology, and it is on them that the exposition of Simmel's sociology is commonly based. While not abandoning this tradition, we want to point to the fact that Simmel, in advocating a definite interpretation of sociology, did not reduce the number of those social problems that he considered to be worth studying. Narrowing down of the subject matter of sociology, so typical of Simmel, did not mean dismissing the social issues that he would leave outside the sphere of sociology. When writing about sociology, Simmel would make statements not about what is to be studied in general, but about what is to be studied by sociology as a distinct humanistic discipline.

The Subject Matter of Sociology. Sociology need not aspire to grasp everything that is "social" in the current sense of the word and that has long been of interest to such social sciences as history, political economy, and the like. Sociology resorts to abstraction, which consists of singling out from "the whole of historical life as it is formed societally" the special dimension that is not studied systematically by any other discipline—namely, "the purely social aspects of man."

Simmel questioned the principle that sociology is the science of society, or he gave the term *society* a meaning other than that traditionally assigned to it. He wrote that

the concept "society" has two denotations which scientific treatment must keep strictly distinct. The first designates society as a complex of societalized individuals, the societally formed human material as it has been shaped by the totality of historical reality. The second denotes society as the sum of those forms of relationship by virtue of which individuals are transformed into "society" in the first sense of the term. . . . When using "society" in the first sense, the social sciences indicate that their subject matter includes everything that occurs in and with society. But when using the term in the second sense, social science indicates that its subject matter is the forces, relations, and forms through which human beings become sociated.[24]

Sociology is, thus, not the science of society in the broad sense of the term, which it was for Comte, Spencer, and Durkheim. The very concept of society seemed so doubtful to Simmel that instead of speaking about society *(Gesellschaft)* in the narrower sense of the word, he preferred to use the term *sociation (Vergesellschaftung)*. This was linked not only to his intention to restrict the subject matter of sociological research, but also to his tendency to study processes rather than their fixed results, that is, "the large systems and the super-individual organizations."[25] We may say that Simmel both narrowed down and extended the subject matter of sociology.

He wrote, for instance, that

sociation continuously emerges and ceases and emerges again. Even where its eternal flux and pulsation are not sufficiently strong to form organization proper, they link individuals together. That people look at one another and are jealous of one another; that they exchange letters and dine together; that irrespective of all tangible interests they strike one another as pleasant or unpleasant; that gratitude for altruistic acts makes for inseparable union; that one asks another man after a certain street, and that people dress and adorn themselves for one another—the whole gamut of relations that play from one person to another and that may be momentary or permanent, conscious or unconscious, ephemeral or of grave consequence (and from which these illustrations are quite casually chosen), all these incessantly tie men together. Here are the interactions among the atoms of society.[26]

That sociology which in *Grundfragen* is called "pure" or "formal" sociology is distinct from "general sociology" (interpreted as the sociological study of historical life) and from "philosophical sociology" (interpreted as the epistemological and metaphysical aspects of society). It becomes the study of societal forms, thus turning, first, from the study of social life as a whole and, next, from macrosociological issues.

The Concept of Form. The operation of abstraction that we perform when engaging in pure or formal sociological research consists of distinguishing form and content in social phenomena.

Social groups which are the most diverse imaginable in purpose and general significance, may nevertheless show identical forms of behavior toward one another on the part of their individual members. We find superiority and subordination, competition, division of labor, formation of parties, representation, inner solidarity coupled with exclusiveness toward the outside, and innumerable similar features in the state, in a religious community, in a band of conspirators, in an economic association, in an art school, in the family. However diverse the interests are that give rise to these sociations, the *forms* in which the interests are realized may yet be identical.[27]

Counter to the prevailing opinion, Simmel did not claim that all sociology was to study the forms of sociation in abstraction from local and historical conditions, but there is no doubt that he considered that task to be the most important of all. The nature of sociology lay in its being the "geometry" or "grammar" of social life. The concept of form was of basic significance, but unfortunately, was not very clear. Simmel handled it too casually and, to make matters worse, added that "what is form in one respect is content in another; and upon closer scrutiny, the conceptual antithesis between the two dissolves into a merely gradual opposition."[28]

As mentioned previously, the concept of form was introduced by Simmel as a *philosophical* notion to be used to refute absolute historicism by pointing to the emergence, in the flow of history, of permanent elements that lend themselves to control by reason. But form was not something that the human mind discovers in reality: Instead, in agreement with the Kantian tradition, it was something imposed by the mind on reality. Reality as such is not split into form and content: "In every given social situation, content and societal form constitute a unified reality."[29]

A pertinent description of the procedure used by Simmel has been given by F. R. Tenbruck:

Abstraction for Simmel is not—it could not be—abstraction from content-*phenomena*, in which the forms inhere and through which alone they *can* be set forth, but abstraction from a content-*perspective*. . . . The forms are by no means generalizations which retain only the most common characteristics of all contents. . . . Forms are not general concepts arrived at by generalization and abstraction, and formal sociology is not the analysis of such general concepts. "Abstracting" must be understood in the radical sense of extracting or extricating from reality something which is not a directly observable and common element in it. In abstracting the forms of sociation, the wealth of phenomena is no more disregarded or repressed than in any other science.[30]

It may be said that the procedure used in this case is one based on the concept of ideal types.

When we speak about the pure forms of sociation, we are treating social facts as if they existed irrespective of their historical context and/or the motivations of those individuals through whom they take place, but this does not mean that we assume the existence of a specific social reality that has a distinct ontological status. This is why the Durkheim's criticism of formalism seems totally misdirected.

The task of Simmel's formalism was to introduce into the social sciences a new approach to social reality as a totality, an approach different from both that advanced by historicism and that advocated by psychologism.

Formalism versus Psychologism: Sociology and Psychology. Since sociology is, ultimately, concerned with interactions among individuals, it cannot make a declaration of disinterest in the sphere of mental experiences, outside which such interactions would be totally incomprehensible.

In *Die Probleme der Geschichtsphilosophie*, Simmel wrote outright that

all external events, political and social, economic and religious, legal and technical, would be neither interesting nor comprehensible to us if they did not derive from and engender psychological processes *[Seelenbewegungen]*. If history is not to be a puppet-show it must be the history of psychic processes, and all external events which it describes are nothing but the bridges between impulses and acts of will on the one hand, and on the other the emotional reactions *[Gefühlreflexe]* which are released by these external events.[31]

In his *Soziologie*, Simmel called history "an exercise in psychological knowledge";[32] he also wrote that social interaction is . . . "a psychological phenomenon."[33]

There are, however, reasons to think that Simmel considered mental phenomena to be a necessary, but far from sufficient, condition of social facts. Psychology, indispensable as it is for a sociologist, cannot—in Simmel's opinion—serve as a basis of valid sociological inference, because psychology is concerned with individuals and not with interactions among them (social psychology was unimaginable for him). Social facts cannot be described and understood without recourse to psychological concepts. But from the sociological point of view, we are interested not in mental processes as such, but in social interactions that are possible owing to the former. "In this sense . . . the givens of sociology are psychological processes whose immediate reality presents itself first of all under psychological categories. But these psychological categories, although indispensable for the description of the facts, remain outside the purpose of sociological investigation."[34]

Simmel's Interactionism. Simmel was opposed to psychologism from the position of interactionism. He blamed earlier sociology for two fundamental misconceptions: first, linking social facts to the existence of a specific substance called society (sociological realism) and, second, deducing those facts from such properties of individuals qua individuals considered in abstraction from relationships among them (sociological nominalism). Simmel was interested in interactions and processes of sociation, which he thought to be different both from society as such, which is in the sphere of interest of philosophers and historians, and from actions of individuals, which are a subject matter of psychology. Sociologists focus their attention on that which develops *among* individuals when they associate with one another.

Such an association is by definition a mutual relationship.

Most relationships among men can be considered under the category of exchange. Exchange is the purest and most concentrated form of all human interactions in which serious interests are at stake. Many actions which at first glance appear to consist of mere unilateral process in fact involve reciprocal effects. The speaker before an audience, the teacher before a class, the journalist writing to his public— each appears to be the sole source of influence in such situations, whereas each of them is really acting in response to demands and directions that emanate from apparently passive, ineffectual groups. . . . Now every interaction is properly viewed as a kind of exchange.[35]

As long as we are not dealing with exchange, we cannot speak about the form of sociation. From this point of view, the reciprocity of the relationship is more important than its durability. In this respect Simmel's stand-point corresponded fairly well to that of Tönnies and Max Weber.

By being concerned with interactions among individuals, Simmel kept moving away from psychology. The sociologist is not interested in man as seen in the totality of his life experience, but in man as seen only in relation to that aspect of his personality which is manifested in his relationship to another man. At this point Simmel comes close to the discovery of the concept of role, which became pivotal in later interactionistic conceptions.

The Philosophy of Culture: Simmel's "Sociologism." His pure sociology, which focused attention on the interactions among the atoms of society, did not mean that Simmel failed to notice the problems that we might label Durkheimist. When taking up the problems typical of general sociology, he wrote that "in order to understand certain facts one must treat [the group] as if it actually did have its own life, and laws, and other characteristics."[36] He also maintained that "the facts of politics, religion, economics, law, culture styles, language, and innumerable others can be analyzed by asking how they may be understood, not as individual achievements or in their objective significance, but as products and developments of society."[37]

As a student of social life, Simmel did not confine himself to the abstract forms of sociation and did not dismiss the traditional sociological problems of the large systems and the superindividual organizations.

These problems did not follow logically from the assumptions made in Simmel's sociology and discussed above. They were, rather, a result of his reflection on the state and development of Western European societies, which in his opinion were marked by a hypertrophy of objective culture: "The deepest problems of modern life derive from the claim of the individual to preserve the autonomy and individuality of his existence in the face of overwhelming social forces, of historical heritage, of external culture, and of the technique of life."[38] Man becomes enslaved by his own products, which appear to him to be an external power. Freed from the old medieval bonds, he is tied by new ones, which are primarily effects of the division of labor. Marx's theory of alienation proves true when applied to culture as a whole.

Simmel dedicated to these problems many brilliant pages of his texts (in *Die Philosophie des Geldes*, for example). But one cannot consider Simmel—who is alleged to have dismissed the problems of history and reduced cognition of society to an analysis of abstract forms—to be the prisoner of sociological formalism. Like other sociologists, Simmel was also a diagnostician of his contemporaneous society.

Simmel's Influence on Sociology. Simmel's impact on sociology, espe-cially in Germany, was quite strong, even though it has not yet been examined systematically. Some of his contemporaries—for instance, the author of the entry "Society" in the 1909 *Handwörterbuch der Staatswissenschaften*—saw in him "the most important German sociologist"; as far as we can judge, his popularity exceeded that of Max Weber, whom, by the way, he had influenced, too. Simmel's influence has continued to this day, and interest in his work has even witnessed a certain revival, primarily because Simmel has been discovered as a theorist of conflict.[39] Yet there has never been any Simmel school. This has been due both to the properties of his style of writing and to his marginal academic status, but the decisive factor must be the fact that his writings constituted a collection of ideas rather than any uniform system or program.

Simmel's influence on sociology was threefold. First, there was the reception of his philosophical and metasociological views, which helped to destroy the patterns of sociological thinking that had been dominant throughout the nineteenth century and to popularize the new, interactionist and humanistic point of view. Simmel significantly contributed to the overcoming of the relics of organicism and evolutionism by replacing the science of society with the science of social interaction and the natural-science viewpoint with the humanistic one.

Second, some theorists were influenced by the idea of pure sociology. *Soziologie* gave rise to so-called formalism in sociology, which consists of turning sociological theory into a system of terminology and classification that would be universally applicable in descriptions of social facts. Formalism was an extension of the idea of the forms of sociation to a closed and detailed system. That trend was represented in its purest form by Leopold von Wiese (1876-1969), professor at Cologne University, organizer of sociological studies in Germany, and author of *System der allgemeinen Soziologie als Lehre von den Sozialen Prozessen und den sozialen Gebilden der Menschen* (1924). Other representatives of the formalist trend include Célestin Bouglé (1870-1940), Robert E. Park (1864-1944), Alfred Vierkandt (1867-1953), and Georges Gurvitch (1894-1965).[40] They did not represent any school, and notable achievements by some of them were not connected with formalism. Formalism as a doctrine threatened sociology with sterile scholasticism and at best only helped to make its terminology richer and more precise. It was criticized from the position of historicism by Hans Freyer (1886-1969), who wrote that "the fact 'society' with which sociology is concerned is not a multiplicity of relational and structural forms that repeat themselves identically, and that can therefore leave their particular historical situations and be systematized purely as forms. The fact 'society' is much more an *irreversible* succession of total situations, through which the stream of historical life moves."[41] This criticism applies to Simmel himself only to a small extent.

And third, some of Simmel's ideas proved to be interesting taken in isolation from the rest. Thus we can see in him the author who took up microsociological issues from the theoretical point of view by investigating "the quantitative aspects of the group," who penetratingly analyzed certain social relations (for example, conflict) and societal types (for example, deviants), and who suggested ideas, popular in present-day sociology, on the approach to social structure and so forth.

WEBER'S INTERPRETATIVE SOCIOLOGY

It was, however, Max Weber (1864-1920) who formulated the theoretically most comprehensive and most influential system of humanistic sociology. He is, as MacRae puts it, "the paradigmatic and exemplary sociologist,"[42] who is quoted probably most often of all and whose works are known almost without being read because the basic concepts of his theory became standard during the last thirty or forty years. He has also been the subject of many comments that, even if extremely critical, contributed to giving him an exceptionally high rank that has almost never been questioned. Max Weber's unique position in contemporary sociology is justified by the wealth of issues that he raised in his work (which was completed as a system) and by the fact that parts of his work have been continued by sociologists of different, and even opposing, orientations (both Talcott Parsons and C. Wright Mills referred to him). Further, his ideal of objectivity proved useful as a professional ideology for sociologists at the time when they were increasingly finding their place in academic structures and abandoning excessive aspirations for reform.

Max Weber was marked by a phenomenal erudition and range of interests. He was concerned with law, economic history, comparative history of religions, political economy, theory of political activity, methodology of the social sciences, and, of course, sociology, although he became professor of sociology, first in Vienna and later in Munich, only two years before his death. In the first stage of his academic career (interrupted for a long time in 1897), he lectured on law in Berlin and on political economy at Freiburg and at Heidelberg.

While he clearly defined the epistemological tasks of sociology, he always considered it to be an integral part of *Sozialwissenschaft*, of which political economy, for example, was another integral element. This interdisciplinary approach also marked the *Archiv für Sozialwissenschaft und Sozialpolitik*, a periodical founded in 1903, of which he was a coeditor and in which he published his principal papers, including *Die protestantische Ethik und der Geist des Kapitalismus* (1904-1905). His main works are *Wirtschaft und Gesellschaft* (1922) and the papers collected in *Gesammelte Aufsätze zur*

Religionssoziologie (three volumes, 1920-1921), *Gesammelte politische Schriften* (1921), *Gesammelte Aufsätze zur Wissenschaftslehre* (1922), *Wirtschaftsgeschichte* (1924), *Gesammelte Aufsätze zur Soziologie und Sozialpolitik* (1924), and *Gesammelte Aufsätze zur Sozial- und Wirtschaftsgeschichte* (1924). Many selections of his writings and separate publications of parts of his comprehensive works are available, especially in English.

The Source of Weber's Social Science. Max Weber's social science was a successive endeavor to overcome positivist naturalism from the position of historicism. (We shall hereafter speak just about his sociology, but one must always recall that his sociology was set in a broader context.) It was also a successive attempt (after Rickert and Simmel) to overcome the radicalism of historicism by reference to neo-Kantian formalism. Some authors even see in Weber's sociology a return to certain elements of positivism, because his conception of science excluded any absolute opposition of the humanities and natural science. C. Antoni claims outright that Weber's conception of ideal types was linked to the hope of restoring the naturalistic concept of law to the science of economy. Weber's views also involve "positive criticism of historical materialism," which was a very important system of reference for him.

Weber called himself a disciple of the historical school and stressed that his point was to acquire the knowledge of social facts in their specifically historical aspect. He maintained that

laws are important and valuable in the exact natural sciences, in the measure that these sciences are *universally valid.* For the knowledge of historical phenomena in their concreteness, the most general laws, because they are devoid of content, are also the least valuable. The more comprehensive the validity—or scope—of a term, the more it leads us away from the richness of reality since in order to include the common elements of the largest possible number of phenomena, it must necessarily be as abstract as possible and hence *devoid* of content.[43]

The social sciences as seen by Weber were historical *par excellence.* Systematic sociology was for him, in a sense, an auxiliary historical discipline, and methodology—which is sometimes incorrectly considered to be his principal interest—was intended above all to promote the historian's self-knowledge and to improve his instruments for the study of historical facts.

Yet Weber, while he referred to the historical school (mainly in its economics-oriented version), was extremely critical of many assumptions and practices of absolute historicism, which he voiced in his work *Roscher und Knies und die logischen Probleme der historischen Nationaloekonomie* (1903-1906). In his opinion, absolute historicism took a wrong course to acquire the knowledge of that richness of reality, which Weber strove to grasp, too. The mistake consisted, first, of the attempt to grasp the historical whole intuitively by abandoning the precision of instruments of research and, second, of the belief that assumption-free cognition of facts was possible. Turning away from the patterns of natural science does not free the student of social life from the requirements of precision and rational thinking.

In declaring himself against the radical measures of the historical school, Max Weber referred to neo-Kantians, particularly Rickert and Simmel, and took up a problem typical of those two authors: selecting historical data and organizing them into a meaningful whole that would not simply mirror facts, but would be a creation of the cognizing subject, who is endowed with appropriate tools of research and uses precise methods. The difference between the humanistic understanding of historical processes and their explanation in the manner typical of natural science need not, and should not, be a difference in the degree of rationality of cognition.

Marxism was the third source of Weber's ideas. Weber was, in fact, the first eminent sociologist who not only had a thorough knowledge of Marx's works, but also considered them to be a mainstay of social science. Weber's relation to Marx is extremely intricate and cannot be understood if we disregard the evolution of Weber's views and the interpretation of Marx's views; this is why it cannot be discussed here extensively. Note only that Weber, beginning with his early studies in the economic history of the ancient world, both made use of Marx's hypotheses on particular issues and engaged in a discussion with him on the main issues of historical materialism. Further, the key problems with which Weber was concerned—namely, those of the development of capitalism—were Marx's problems *par excellence*, although Weber came to solve them in a different way. That difference lay in their opinions on such issues as property and classes and in their approaches to the strategy of research. Weber rejected Marx's conception of causality and historical laws. Marxism, interpreted as *economic* materialism (which it often really was in the late nineteenth century) was seen by Weber as one of those doctrines that strive to explain everything by reference to one factor only and are, thus, threatened by dogmatism. Weber did think, however, that the hypothesis of the economic conditioning of social processes had considerable heuristic value and, when corrected, could successfully be defended as a justifiable "one-sided analysis of cultural reality from specific 'points of view.'"[44] The most important issue, however, seems to be Weber's general statement that all theory of modern society must take into account the achievements of Marx and his school.

Weber's social science appears, then, to be both continuation and rejection of three influential trends in German thought: absolute historicism, neo-Kantian formalism, and Marxian historical materialism.

The Chaotic World versus Orderly Knowledge. Weber's sociology started from the vision of social reality as chaos and endless fluctuation. This vision varied both with the "will-to-believe of naturalistic monism"[45] and with Marxism and Hegelianism—that is, with all the varieties of "historical optimism" (or historicism, in Popper's terms).

Weber himself wrote pathetically:

The fate of an epoch which has eaten of the tree of knowledge is that it must know that we cannot learn the *meaning* of the world from the results of its analysis, be it ever so perfect; it must rather be in a position to create this meaning itself. It must recognize that general views of life and the universe can never be the products of increasing empirical knowledge, and that the highest ideals, which move us most forcefully, are always formed only in the struggle with other ideals which are just as sacred to others as ours are to us.[46]

History does not have any immanent sense: It is simply the arena of the struggle among human individuals and human groups endowed with the will to overcome all resistance and to achieve their goals. There is no chance of bringing into agreement those antagonistic aspirations which Weber, following Nietzsche, has linked to the permanent characteristics of human nature. Nor is there any hope that any particular ideal could ever become the universal norm (on that point Weber argued against the socialist position on more than one occasion) and the foundation of stable social order. We can merely take cognizance of chaos and struggle.

But Weber did not want the scientist to accept extreme relativism. Weber professed the ideal of knowledge that is objective and the same for everybody: "It has been and remains true that a systematically correct scientific proof in the social sciences, if it is to achieve its purpose, must be acknowledged as correct even by a Chinese—or—more precisely stated—it must constantly *strive* to attain this goal, which perhaps may not be completely attainable due to faulty data."[47]

Because of that ideal cherised by Weber and because of his incessant opposition to "the constant confusion of the scientific discussion of facts and their evaluation," some authors speak about positivist relics in his thinking.[48] That positivism seems dubious however. What was characteristic of Weber was not his requirement of scientific objectivity, but his consciousness of an unsurmountable antinomy between the vision of the social world, split into parts according to conflicting ideals, and the program of the social sciences, which, while being of this world, are to remain free from the valuations that result from these ideals and are to offer equally reliable knowledge to everybody. Max Weber's philosophy of the social sciences is nothing other than a series of endeavors to resolve that antinomy in order to protect the scientist against both indifference and partiality.

Weber thought that he had attained that by making a distinction between evaluation *(Werturteil)* and value-relevance *(Wertbeziehung)*, which are two different ways of articulating empirical reality. The former should be absolutely avoided in the social sciences (and in science in general). But without the latter, science would be impossible, because it is only values that constitute *culture*, which he defined as "a finite segment of the meaningless infinity of the world process, a segment on which *human beings* confer meaning and significance."[49] If we did not profess some values, we would be deaf and blind to historical facts, nor would we be able to select the subject matter of our research. "Empirical reality becomes 'culture' to us because and insofar as we relate it to value ideas. It includes those segments and only those segments of reality which have become significant to us because of this value-relevance."[50]

The requirement of the objectivity and the axiological neutrality of the social sciences does not refer to formulation of the research problem. The question about what is important can be answered only by reference to certain values, which, in the last analysis, we choose quite arbitrarily. No social facts are important by themselves; they become so by being related to *our* values.

But the point is that the social scientist, when making such a choice, does not accede to any of the conflicting groups and does not declare himself in favor of any ideal other than that of scientific truth. After having singled out the subject of his research, he adopts toward it the attitude of a natural scientist. When it comes to the study of historical facts, "an empirical science cannot tell anyone what we *should* do—but rather what he *can* do—and under certain circumstances—what he wishes to do." Science poses the question about the human goals, about the adequate technical means for and the chances of attaining those goals, about the side effects and/or costs of implementing given projects, and so on. Science is also concerned with the inner consistency of the various human ideals and helps

the acting willing person in attaining self-clarification concerning the final axioms from which his desired ends are derived. It can assist him in becoming aware of the ultimate standards of value which he does not make explicit to himself or, which he must presuppose in order to be logical. The elevation of these ultimate standards, which are manifested in concrete value-judgements, to the level of explicitness is the utmost that the scientific treatment of value-judgements can do without entering into the realm of speculation.[51]

The social sciences, as the sciences of culture, are concerned with human value judgments. However, they do not themselves formulate any such judgments and remain, in this sense, free from any partiality, if we disregard the arbitrary choice of the subject matter, a choice based on value-relevance. Once he has passed the gate of science, the scientist is obliged to take only facts into account, which he must investigate with maximum precision, comparable with that of the natural sciences. His precision must be arrived at by other methods, for he pursues a historical science of culture. But this science, as in Rickert's case, can harbor even the concept of causality, which was banned from the humanities by absolute historicism.

Ideal Types. The implementation of the tasks of the exact social sciences, as formulated by Weber, was to be achieved by using ideal types. In Weber's opinion the social sciences always avail themselves of that instrument of research whenever they arrive at valuable results. Weber found examples of the use of ideal types in Marx, for instance. But he claimed that his predecessors had used ideal types without necessary methodological comprehension of their application, which resulted in their confusing ideal types with historical laws and generalizations.

His opinion that ideal types had been used earlier probably accounts for the fact that Weber did not consider it necessary to present his idea in greater detail and primarily confined himself to explaining how ideal types are *not* to be interpreted. Thus he stressed that they should not be tinged by valuation and that they have "nothing to do with any type of perfection other than a purely logical one."[52] He warned against confusing them with generic concepts, that is, against considering them to be systematized sets of properties that are attributes of all the objects in a given class or to be statistical averages. But he probably protested most vigorously against considering an ideal type to be the constant "essence" of a thing, discovered by the investigation of that thing. An ideal type does not indicate what is: It indicates what could be. As R. Keat and J. Urry put it, "no concrete phenomenon precisely corresponds to an ideal-type, for three main reasons. First, any such phenomenon will have many features that are not included in the ideal-type. Second, those features that are included are represented in an ideal-typed or 'purified' form. Third, not all the features of the ideal-type are present in each concrete exemplification of it."[53]

Weber saw an ideal type to be an instrument constructed by the researcher and used by him to structure reality, which is amorphous per se, and thus to comprehend it:

An ideal type is formed by the one-sided *accentuation* of one or more points of view and by the synthesis of a great many diffuse, discrete, more or less present and occasionally absent *concrete individual* phenomena, which are arranged according to those one-sidedly emphasized viewpoints into a unified *analytical* construct *[Gedankenbild].* In its conceptual purity, this mental construct *[Gedankenbild]* cannot be found empirically anywhere in reality. It is a *utopia.* Historical research faces the task of determining, in each individual case, the extent to which this ideal construct approximates to or diverges from reality.[54]

Such Utopias can be constructed without end. Unlike the laws of natural science, no such Utopia is definitive in nature. Weber speaks about "not only the transiency of *all* ideal types *but* also at the same time the inevitability of *new* ones."[55] This is so because "in the cultural sciences concept-construction depends on the setting of the problem, and the latter varies with the content of culture itself." Self-understandably, ideal types are neither true nor false: Whether their construction is, or is not, a mere intellectual game fully depends on whether they prove useful in research, namely, "in revealing concrete cultural phenomena in their interdependence, their causal conditions and their *significance.*"[56]

Understanding of Social Actions. Weber was essentially interested in human actions, that is, individual behavior that is assigned a subjective meaning by the actor. He tried to draw a clear demarcation line between meaningful action and merely reactive behavior. Sociology, as he defined it, is "a science concerning itself with the interpretative understanding of social action and thereby with a causal explanation of its course and consequences."[57]

Only a human individual can be a social actor. While Weber's statements about social wholes refer to the organicist tradition, he was aware, like Tönnies and Simmel, of the metaphorical and merely auxiliary nature of such terms. His comment was that "this functional frame of reference is convenient for purposes of practical illustration and for provisional orientation," but it was accompanied by the warning that its cognitive value had been overestimated and that such a frame of reference could be risky. Furthermore, he saw in it solely the starting point of a genuine sociological analysis. Weber was a nominalist or a methodological individualist in his sociological theory: He considered the individual to be an "atom" of social reality and the only carrier of meaning.

For sociological purposes there is no such thing as a collective personality which "acts." When reference is made in a sociological context to a "state," a "nation," a "corporation," a "family" or an "army corps," what is meant is . . . *only* a certain kind of development of actual or possible social actions of individual persons. . . . In sociological work these collectivities must be treated as *solely* the resultants and modes of organization of the particular acts of individual persons, since these alone can be treated as agents in the course of subjectively understandable action.[58]

Weber's atomism—which was based on his vision of the world, which excluded the existence of any order independent of individuals—differed markedly from the traditional doctrines of individualism. The point was that Weber did not ascribe to human individuals any properties on the basis of which one could state anything *a priori* concerning social reality. Social action is by definition oriented toward other people, so such action always depends on those other people rather than on the immanent characteristics of those who act. Weber showed very little interest in psychology, which can be seen clearly when his theory of social actions is compared with the corresponding conception of Vilfredo Pareto. The individual, as seen by Weber, lacks any sociologically relevant properties as long as he is considered outside the cultural and historical context of interactions. This is why we consider Weber to be a representative of antisociologism and of antipsychologism as well.

After having thus defined the subject matter of sociology, Weber designated *understanding* as its most important procedure. In that respect he referred to Dilthey, whose approach, however, he modified by enumerating the various levels of understanding; by introducing the concept of explanatory understanding *(erklärendes Verstehen)*, connected with the concept of causality; and by formulating the problem of the validity or intersubjective verifiability of the cognitive results obtained by understanding. It seems that his principal intention was to make that somewhat dubious procedure, to which the positivists would at best concede a heuristic value, as rigorous as possible.

The author of *Wirtschaft und Gesellschaft* made a distinction between direct observational understanding *(aktuelles Verstehen)* and explanatory, or motivational, understanding.[59] The former, which comes closest to Dilthey's conception of understanding, covers all those situations in which the meaning of observed human actions can be grasped by the observer through some evidence—logical, psychological, and so on. In such cases it suffices to watch a person's action to know what it means. It is in this way that we understand facial expressions, conventional gestures, and mathematical operations. In Weber's opinion, such understanding corresponds to the most elementary level of the comprehension of human actions, even though it requires some knowledge on the part of the observer and cannot be attained by intuition alone. The latter represents a higher level of cognition of human actions. It is oriented not toward revealing the meaning of the action itself, but toward acquiring the knowledge of the motives by which the agent was guided. In this case, the point is not to know what individuals do, but why they do it.

Weber was convinced that causal hypotheses can be constructed on that matter and subsequently verified like any other hypotheses, although in the case of the sciences of culture only mental experiments are possible: One can only imagine what would have occurred if a given cause had not been at work. The key role was assigned by Weber to historico-comparative studies, whereby one can test the operation of a given cause by comparing a case with similar ones that differ from it, however, by the absence of the hypothetical cause. As R. Keat and J. Urry put it, the necessity of a rigorous verification of all hypotheses about social actions is due, to the fact that first the apparent conscious motives may conceal, from both the agent and the observer, the "real driving force" of the action. Second, the agent may be subject to different, and conflicting, motives, so that it is difficult to ascertain their relative strength or importance. Third, the agent and the observer may perceive the agent's situation differently, so that what seems a plausible motive to the observer may be based on a mistaken identification of how that situation appears to the agent.[60]

In any case, one ought not to suppose that Weber's concept of understanding can be reduced to uncontrolled empathy and an arbitrary imputation to others of one or another motivation.

Yet, the most interesting element of Weber's conception of the ways of acquiring the knowledge of human actions and their meanings consists not of his reflections—both general and far from clear—on understanding and its kinds, but of his introduction of the concept of rationality. From Weber's point of view, the understanding of social actions would be impossible, had it not been for the fact that—owing to the ideal-type method—we are in a position to imagine fully rational actions, to which all observable actions are more or less approximated.

For the purposes of a typological scientific analysis it is convenient to treat all irrational, affectually determined elements of behaviour as factors of deviation from a conceptually pure type of rational action. . . . Only in this way is it possible to assess the causal significance of irrational factors as accounting for the deviations from the type. The construction of a purely rational course of action in such cases serves the sociologist as a type ("ideal type") which has the merit of clear understandability and lack of ambiguity. By comparison with this it is possible to understand the ways in which actual action is influenced by irrational factors of all sorts, such as affects and errors, in that they account for the deviation from the line of conduct which would be expected on the hypothesis that the action were purely rational.[61]

This lengthy quotation (which, by the way, sheds extra light on the conception of ideal types as instrument of cognition in the social sciences) allows us to realize that Weber's interpretation of understanding means an indirect understanding, a procedure that requires—in addition to empathy—intricate intellectual operations. As a result of this, a sociologist can acquire a better comprehension of the meaning of a given human action than the actor himself, since the actor is very rarely capable of behaving consistently and of singling out various factors that affect what he does.

It was the possibility of constructing an ideal type of rational action on which Weber based his hope that causal explanations are applicable in sociology and his very original idea of social determinism. The more rational a given action is, the better it can be predicted, in the sense that a specified cause yields a specified effect. If that sequence of causes and effects is disturbed, we are in a position to formulate the question "Why was it so?" and then to point to the circumstances that would answer the question.

Reflections on determinism of human actions start from the assumption that man is free, that is, endowed with an unlimited ability to choose his ends and the appropriate means, in which rational actions consist. As a matter of fact, only the actions of a free subject can be explained fully in causal terms.[62] Obviously, this meant the rejection of the schema of reasoning that had been absolutely dominant in sociology.

This focusing of attention on rational actions was purely methodological. Weber was far from claiming that rational factors are dominant in human life, and his intention was to find a system of reference for the study of all actions, which become comprehensible only when compared with purely rational ones.

Weber's "Formal" Sociology. The role of rationality in Weber's sociology can be seen equally well in its both main sections, social and historical sociology. When we speak about Weber's "formal" sociology, we mean an intricate system of concepts presented in his *Economy and Society*, in which, as Herbert Marcuse says, "the method of formal definitions, classifications and typologies celebrates true orgies."[63]

Although this system was conceived as a foundation for sociology as a primarily historical discipline, there are no reasons to oppose Weber as a systematist to sociological formalism and to Simmel. We are inclined to agree with T. Abel, for whom, "clearly, Weber and Simmel share a common outlook and a common approach."[64] As said earlier, formalism in sociology developed as an endeavor to solve the problems raised by absolute historicism rather than as the rejection of the historical approach as such. In Weber's case, the formalistic tendency was reinforced by his ideal of scientific rigor, which made him seek liberation from the pressure of everyday language and construct precise concepts that could be used for unambiguous definitions. Weber constructed his own vocabulary and the catalogue of social forms that he termed "pure" types.

The cornerstone of his system is the concept of social action as individual behavior (outward or not, since it also includes abstention from all behavior that would be noticeable to others) that in its origin and progress is oriented toward past, present, or expected future behavior of other individuals. Social actions do not cover all individual behavior and not even all behavior evoked by other individuals (such as behavior described by crowd psychology). Merely reactive behavior was not classed by Weber as social action. Social action occurs only when an individual has a minimum of consciousness (which, by the way, is not easy to define), owing to which his behavior is endowed with meaning.

Weber distinguished four kinds of social actions according to their distance from "the borderline of what can justifiably be called meaningfully oriented action."[65] Closest to that borderline he placed rational actions, which he divided by the same criterion into rational goal-oriented *(zweckra-tional)* and rational value-oriented *(wertrational)* ones; and farthest away were traditional *(traditional)* and affectual *(affektuell)* actions.

Traditional actions are performed in accordance with fixed habits, but with at least minimum consciousness that makes them something intended and desired. Affectual actions result from the urge that makes one behave in a given way regardless of the consequences, but they are not a mere release of tension, lacking any degree of consciousness. Both traditional and affectual actions border, on the one side, on purely reactive behavior, and on the other, on rational actions, the latter insofar as the actor consciously chooses the appropriate means by having their maximum effectiveness in view. Those rational actions which are marked by a conscious choice of the most effective means while the ends themselves are left outside the sphere of the agent's reflection are termed rational value-oriented by Weber. In the case of rational goal-oriented actions, he means those rational actions in which maximum consciousness of both ends and means is involved. The human actions that come closest to the ideal type of rational goal-oriented ones are easiest to understand, and this is why Weber focused his attention on them in accordance with his methodological assumptions. They were for him the frame of reference in the analysis of other types of action.

Social actions are unidirectional by nature. While they are always oriented toward other people, they do not imply any necessity, but merely the probability, of evoking a response. Only when such a response takes place and thus initiates a series of mutually oriented actions by two or more individuals does a social relationship develop. The latter is the second principal concept in Weber's formal sociology. Weber spells out the various types of social relationship, the legitimation of such relationships, the various types of social groups and social orders, authority, and so on. The best-known elements of that system are the concepts of charisma and bureaucracy and also those of class, status (or estate—*Stand*), and party.

Without going into the details of the intricate architectonics of this system (which on many points was inspired by Tönnies and Simmel), we want to stress, first, that all its elements are ultimately reducible to the basic ones, namely, social actions, and, second, that the concept of rationality retains its fundamental importance at all levels of this system. Thus, for instance, the four types of social actions have their exact analogues in the four types of legitimacy of social order. We can also single out three types of authority—rational (legal), traditional, and charismatic—of which the first refers to legal principles; the second, to tradition; and the third, to the emotions associated with the person of the leader.

Historical Sociology. However great was the importance attached by Weber to his formal sociology, its system of concepts was ancillary to the primary task of analyzing real historical processes. This system was never fully exploited by Weber, who constructed it late in life, when he already had had vast historical and philosophical studies behind him. Weber did not start with working out the set of concepts that would later be applied in the discussion of specified subjects; he proceeded in reverse order. Note also that *Economy and Society* can in no way be reduced to a pile of typologies and classifications. Many parts of that work (for example, "The City" and "The Sociology of Religion") are historical *par excellence.* Weber was fascinated by history because, like many other sociologists, he wanted to explain the peculiarities of his contemporaneous capitalist society.

When comparing the present with history, Weber made it a point not to construct any universal schemata of social development, which had been so attractive to the earlier generation of sociologists. Like Durkheim, Tönnies, and Simmel, he sought at most a general trend in social changes and dismissed the question about the firm laws of the process of history. As J. Freund notes: "Nothing was more alien to him . . . than the establishment of general laws of development which professedly teach us how humanity has passed from one stage to the next before arriving, in an unforeseeable future, at some ultimate stage."[66] Such considerations were for him merely veiled valuations, which science can never substantiate. In his opinion, only the concept of probability—and not that of necessity—can be applied to history, which consists of free actions by individuals who strive to implement conflicting ideals. Hence, theoretically, every historical situation has infinitely many outcomes, and it can never be known in advance which one will materialize.

This is why the general schema of social change used by Weber is non-directional. At any moment there may appear a charismatic leader whom his followers believe to be "endowed with supernatural, superhuman, or at least specifically exceptional powers or qualities"[67] and who may thus release latent revolutionary forces and drive society out of its rut. Charisma later will be routinized, and charismatic authority will be transformed into traditional or rational one. None of them, however, has its permanence guaranteed: Even if traditionalism is not abolished by a new charismatic movement, it is always threatened by rationalism, and vice versa. All outcomes remain possible: Creativity is always opposed to routine; ingenuity of outstanding individuals, to fixed institutions; spontaneity, to tradition. But then the creative forces become exhausted. Thus for Weber, as for Pareto, change is undulatory in nature. This is why it is impossible for any philosophy of history to answer the question, Whereto?

Yet many authors point to the fact that Weber's reflection on history does include the idea of unidirectional change. It can be found in his conception of capitalism and in his vision of the all-embracing rationalization and bureaucratization that are typical of Western civilization—that is, in his vision of the process of "the world's disenchantment" *(Entzauberung der Welt)*, which is correctly held to be the pivotal issue in Weber's historical sociology. In fact, his vast studies of other cultures (China, India, the Moslem world, and the like) were intended to help him grasp the specific problems of Western civilization. As Marianne Weber wrote,

this recognition of the particular character of Western rationalism and the role it played in Western culture constituted for Weber one of his most important discoveries. As a result, his original question of the relation of religion to economics became the wider, more general question of the particular character of the entire Western culture. Why does rational science which produces verifiable truths exist only in the West? Why only here rational harmonic music, or architecture and plastic art which employ rational construction? Why only here a rational state, a trained bureaucracy of experts, parliaments, political parties—in a word, the state as a political institution with a rational constitution, and rational law? Why only here the fateful power of modern life—namely, modern capitalism? Why all this only in the West?[68]

The search for answers to these questions gave rise to Weber's conception of the process of history, a conception that, while intentionally confined to one culture area and free from the idea of any necessity whatever, nevertheless seems in many respects comparable to those produced by the evolutionists and especially to that of Marx and Engels. Weber's conception was programmatically in opposition to all of them, as it was intended to overcome monocausalism and philosophical speculation. Further, Weber made it a point to grasp changes in individual motivation, for only individuals were actors in the drama of history. His fundamental questions could be formulated thus: How is it that, in the activities of Western man, rational elements have priority over traditional and affectual ones? Why have all the spheres of human life become disenchanted so that "there are no mysterious incalculable forces that come into play" and that, accordingly, "one can, in principle, master all things by calculation"?[69] In other words, he is concerned with the sociopsychological conditions of the rise of modern capitalism, which, in Weber's opinion, is primarily the socioeconomic system organized on the principle of rationality.

As S. Kozyr-Kowalski writes,

according to Weber, the specifically Western type of capitalist activity is manifested in two principal spheres: in business organization and in labor organization. . . . The specific character of Western capitalism lies not only in the rational organization of the enterprise, which makes profits owing to regular and free exchange of the commodities on the market, but also in production, which is based on a formally free organization of labor. Political coercion has ceased to be a necessary condition of the social process of production.[70]

Weber's conception of capitalism bears much resemblance to Marx's, but it also differs from the latter in many essential respects. First of all, Weber emphasized the role of ideas in the formation of new economic relations, which can easily be understood if one recalls that human actions endowed with meaning were his ultimate point of reference. But it would be a mistake to think that Weber just reversed Marx's historical materialism and made ideas the mainspring of social development (Protestantism as the "cause" of capitalism). The author of *The Protestant Ethic and the Spirit of Capitalism* made it clear that his intention was not "to substitute for a one-sided materialistic [concept] an equally one-sided spiritualistic causal interpretation of culture and of history. Each is equally possible, but each, if it does not serve as the preparation, but as the conclusion of an investigation, accomplishes equally little in the interest of historical truth."[71]

Aron offers a good interpretation when he writes that according to Weber, "Protestantism is not *the* cause, but *one* of the causes of capitalism, or rather, it is *one* of the causes of *certain aspects* of capitalism."[72] Weber did not oppose to historical materialism an essentially different philosophy of history as much as he chose a different strategy of research, one associated with his particularly strong interest in changes in motivations and with his almost obsessive idea of multifaceted social reality, which cannot fully be grasped by any single theory. Seen from this viewpoint, Weber's conception was a denial of historical materialism only insofar as the latter claimed—as Marx's disciples sometimes did—to be a doctrine of a single factor. It was thus a criticism of those Marxists who were his contemporaries rather than of Marx himself.

Unlike Marx, Weber did not try to formulate a theory of social development, nor did he even strive to explain the functioning of capitalism as a whole. Instead, through comparative studies, he sought partial explanations by pointing to the various conditions evoking the phenomena in which he was interested. Such exactly were his studies in the sociology of religion, which emerged from his reflections on the spirit of capitalism. Weber was not interested in religion as such. He simply investigated some of its socio-psychological consequences, its positive or negative effect on economic activity and, particularly on the pace of rationalization of human actions that was typical of modern capitalism.

What also made Weber differ from Marx was his bringing out that organization of society that was characteristic of capitalism: bureaucracy. He attached to it equally great importance as Marx did to the private ownership of the means of production. Bureaucracy (the term was used by Weber without implying any value judgment) means the rationalization of social organization through the replacement of the authority of tradition and of individuals by the authority of formalized rules. Weber described his ideal type of bureaucracy in great detail.[73] He assigned to bureaucracy the following primary characteristics: (1) subordination of behavior of the members of the group to impersonal rules; (2) strict division of duties and prerogatives in accordance with the specialization of functions; (3) hierarchical system of posts within an organization; (4) professionalization; (5) accessibility of all posts to all those who are competent enough; and (6) exchangeability of post holders.

The originality of Weber's idea of bureaucracy depends largely on the fact that he did not confine it to the machinery of the state, but extended it over all organizations in the disenchanted world. Commented A. Z. Kamiński:

Such organization can successfully be used in all spheres of human activity. It is more rational than the other types of organization that we have known in human history, for it ensures the predictability and calculability of effects of actions. The functioning of bureaucracy is subordinated to rationally established impersonal rules. Written documentation makes it possible to accumulate experience concerning past organizational situations and to avail oneself of that experience when a similar situation arises. A bureaucratic organization is thus capable of "learning", that is, of increasing the efficiency of its actions as the experience of its staff increases following the discharge of their duties. The existence of documentation makes it possible to transmit experience to successors.[74]

The development of bureaucracy seemed to Weber to have been the fate of Western civilization. Even though modern man has created science and technology at a level unprecedented in his earlier history and has developed the most effective methods of economic activity, he has become even more helpless and dependent than his ancestors were. As Weber wrote, "The increasing intellectualization and rationalization do *not* . . . indicate an increased and general knowledge of the conditions under which one lives."[75] Weber was critical of the civilization that he described, but he was unable to imagine any alternative to the capitalist system. Fully conscious of his decision, he rejected the prospects of socialism—both as a bourgeois and as a sociologist who studied the mechanisms governing modern society.

As the above outline shows, the range of problems covered by Weber's historical sociology was quite broad despite his dismissal of a number of questions posed by nineteenth-century theorists of social development. Weber proceeded to solve his problems by using the refined apparatus of his methodology and formal sociology, owing to which he constructed something more than just another historiosophical schema, namely a set of hypotheses that could largely be verified in the course of further research. He must also be given additional credit for an idea of comparative studies that was directed against both evolutionism and absolute historicism. Parsons wrote about Weber's comparative method that it was "the direct methodological equivalent of experimentation in the laboratory sciences.

Only by studying cases which are similar in some respects but different in others would it be possible to arrive at a judgment of the causal influence of any factor."[76] Weber's studies in the sociology of religion, authority, organization, and so on seem fully to corroborate that.

Class, Status, and Party. When discussing Weber's work, one cannot disregard his interpretation of social structure, which has left permanent traces in sociology by initiating the practice of distinguishing the various dimensions of social stratification. When analyzing the problem of classes, Weber opposed vulgarized Marxism, which saw the determining factor of all features of any given group and the substratum of all collective action in economic status alone. Weber wrote that "every class may be the carrier of any one of the possibly innumerable forms of 'class action,' but it is not necessarily so."[77] Moreover, he singled out, in addition to classes, two other kinds of groups: status groups *(Stände)* and parties.

Weber's interpretation of class does not differ essentially from Marx's, although after property classes *(Besitzklassen)* he introduces acquisition classes *(Erwerbsklassen)*, which have no analogue in Marx's system, and he stresses the links between "class situation" and "market situation." Yet, despite all these modifications, a class for Weber is an economic class and roughly corresponds to what Marx defined as a "class in itself." The concept of status group, however, is quite novel. As Weber wrote, "we wish to designate as 'status situation' every typical component of the life fate of men that is determined by a specific, positive or negative, social estimation of *honor.* . . . Status honor need not necessarily be linked with a 'class situation.' On the contrary, it normally stands in sharp opposition to the pretensions of sheer property."[78] While class situation is determined economically, status situation is determined culturally: Associated with it is a specified style of life that is expected to mark everyone who wants to be a member of a given status group. "One might thus say that 'classes' are stratified according to their relations to the production and acquisition of goods; whereas 'status groups' are stratified according to the principles of their consumption of goods as represented by special 'styles of life.'" Weber also referred to two kinds of order: the economic order and the social order.

Finally, Weber distinguished *parties,* which are goal-oriented associations set on securing for their members the influence on the political machine: "In any individual case, parties may represent interests determined through 'class situation' or 'status situation,' and they may recruit their following respectively from one or the other. But they need be neither purely 'class' nor purely 'status' parties. In most cases they are partly class parties and partly status parties, but sometimes they are neither."[79]

In Weber's interpretation, social structure has three dimensions—the economic, the cultural, and the political—each relatively independent of the others. The knowledge of one of them, taken in isolation, does not enable us to draw conclusions about the peculiarities of the other two, because there is no strict correspondence among them. In this way, Weber initiated a vigorous trend of studies in social stratification, which differed from the Marxian approach to social structure (and not only the Marxian, because the dominant trend through the nineteenth century was to divide society into a small number of basic groups) in two important respects: Its representatives did not ask which type of social divisions determines all the remaining ones, and they were inclined to consider social structure to be a system of various overlapping hierarchies.

Weber's Impact on Sociology. The rank assigned to Max Weber in present-day sociology is exceptionally high. Coser claims that sociology is divided into pre-Weberian and post-Weberian and that all modern sociology has experienced his influence.[80] Since there has never been any Weber school, his impact has never been all-embracing. Weber has proved a great inspirer, from whom people took the various ideas without much concern about their place in his system or even about their correct interpretation. Everyone availed himself of Weber's work, but in a sense no one did: Everyone would find in his writings something that would suit him, but few were bold enough to face that Minotaurus (Gouldner's term) in his own field. And there is nothing strange in that. During the last sixty years the process of specialization in sociology has become so advanced that today no one is in a position to grasp—without detriment to the quality of his research—all that which was, for Weber, of fundamental significance in sociology.

Hence it is that methodologists discuss his conception of ideal types; advocates of modern humanistic sociology, the idea of interpretative sociology *(verstehende Soziologie)*; theorists of modernization, his analysis of the process of traditionalism being driven out by rationality; theorists of organization, the concept of bureaucracy; sociologists of political relations, his theory of authority and power; and so on. It may be said that the work of that great encyclopedist of sociology was turned into the small change of present-day sociological subdisciplines and was also adjusted to suit fragmentary problems that result from research based on assumptions that have little to do with Weber's ideas.

This is perhaps the best testimony to the permanent greatness of that scholar in Western sociology who has proved to be the only classic who may never be disregarded, even though his work may raise grave doubts and evoke vigorous protests. Adopting some attitude toward Weber has become a kind of professional duty of every sociologist. As R. Aron wrote, "Max Weber is still our contemporary, more than Emile Durkheim and Vilfredo Pareto are."[81] But that popularity came to him rather late: His work was assimilated fully only after World War II.

GERMAN HUMANISTIC SOCIOLOGY: A BALANCE SHEET

The significance of the German humanistic sociology (if we disregard the achievements of individual authors in specialized fields) comes primarily from being the first endeavor to reconstruct sociology on foundations that differed essentially from those established by positivism and evolutionism. Tönnies, Simmel, and especially Weber demonstrated that it was possible to pursue sociology through observing requirements of scientific rigor, but without idolizing the patterns provided by natural science and without reifying social facts. Note that this rigor was quite high and that the criticism of positivism did not result in speculation and arbitrariness, as it not uncommonly does now. In fact, even in the light of the positivist criteria the works of representatives of humanistic sociology not only stand comparison with Comte and Spencer, but are even superior to them in many respects. It is also to be noted that Tönnies, Simmel, and Weber, while criticizing their predecessors, succeeded in preserving many of the problems discussed by the latter: For instance, while they rejected the idea of evolution, they did not dismiss the problems that resulted from reflection on social development.

Their novelty lay mainly in placing the problems of social actions in the center of interest; this meant discovering for sociological research conscious human actors who form society through their interactions. Society ceased to be an object viewed from the outside and turned into an incessant process of sociation that goes on as long as its members remain active. This meant overcoming both sociologism and psychologism.

Bridging the gap between the two opposing schools in the sociology of those times involved problems that have not been fully solved. The first issue, common to German humanistic sociology and to other varieties of sociological interactionism, was due to the insufficiencies of the set of concepts used in describing the processes of institutionalization of human actions. The apparent wealth of concepts used in formal sociology could not replace the expanded conception of social system, a conception destroyed by the critique of organicism. The second problem, probably even more serious, was due to the lack of a firm psychological foundation for the conception of motivation that was assumed in the theory of social actions. By dissociating itself from psychologism and by considering psychology to be a discipline within the sphere of natural science, German humanistic sociology found itself in a paradoxical situation: It directed attention to the experiences of the individual without trying to formulate an adequate psychological conception, as had been done in the case of social pragmatism. These problems have probably contributed to the fact that none of the great doctrines of German humanistic sociology has ever received continuing attention in its entirety.

Yet, the most bothersome of all was the concept of understanding, which has given rise to various doubts to this day. If sociology is to investigate human consciousness, it certainly must accept that procedure. But, unfortunately, the founders of the first systems of humanistic sociology have not left any satisfactory program for its application, even though they formulated a number of basic questions linked to that issue.

NOTES

1. This latter term has been introduced recently by George Ritzer in *Sociology: A Multiple Paradigm Science* (Boston: Allyn and Bacon, 1975), chap. 3.

2. Florian Znaniecki, *Social Relations and Social Roles* (San Francisco: Chandler, 1965), p. 15.

3. Werner J. Cahnman and Rudolf Heberle, eds., *Ferdinand Tönnies on Sociology: Pure, Applied and Empirical* (Chicago: University of Chicago Press, 1971), p. 238.

4. Ibid., p. 22.

5. Ibid., p. 89.

6. Ibid., p. 134.

7. F. Tönnies, "Gemeinschaft und Gesellschaft," in Gottfried Eisermann, ed., *Soziologisches Lesebuch* (Stuttgart: F. Enke, 1969), pp. 51 ff.

8. Cahnman and Heberle, *Ferdinand Tönnies on Sociology*, p. 4.

9. Ibid., pp. 102-3.

10. Ibid., p. 88.

11. Ibid., pp. 123-24.

12. Ibid., p. 113.

13. Ibid., p. 102.

14. Rudolf Heberle, "An Introduction," in Werner J. Cahnman, ed., *Ferdinand Tönnies: A New Evaluation: Essays and Documents* (Leiden: E. J. Brill, 1973), p. 50.

15. Don Martindale, *American Social Structure: Historical Antecedents and Contemporary Analysis* (New York: Appleton, 1960), p. 230.

16. Robert A. Nisbet, *The Sociological Tradition* (London: Heinemann, 1967), p. 78.

17. Cahnman and Heberle, *Ferdinand Tönnies on Sociology*, pp. 10, 77.

18. Ibid., p. 91.

19. Ibid., p. 93.

20. See Armand Cuvillier, *Manuel de sociologie* (Paris: P.U.F., 1954), vol. 1, p. 44.

21. Leopold von Wiese, "Simmel's Formal Method," in Lewis A. Coser, ed., *Georg Simmel* (Englewood Cliffs, N.J.: Prentice-Hall, 1965), p. 53.

22. F. H. Tenbruck, "Formal Sociology," in Kurt H. Wolff, *Georg Simmel, 1858-1918: A Collection of Essays, with Translations and a Bibliography* (Columbus, Ohio: Ohio State University Press, 1959) pp. 64-65.

23. Wiese, "Simmel's Formal Method," p. 56.

24. G. Simmel, "The Problem of Sociology," in Wolff, *Georg Simmel*, pp. 318-20.

25. Kurt H. Wolff, ed., *The Sociology of Georg Simmel* (New York, Free Press, 1950), p. 10.

26. Ibid., pp. 9-10.

27. Ibid., p. 22.

28. See Rudolph H. Weingartner, "Form and Content in Simmel's Philosophy of Life," in Wolff, *Georg Simmel*, p. 34.

29. See Tenbruck, "Formal Sociology," p. 72.

30. Ibid., p. 75.

31. See William Outhwaite, *Understanding Social Life: The Method Called Verstehen* (London: Allen and Unwin, 1975), p. 44n.

32. Simmel, "The Problem of Sociology," p. 329.

33. Theodore Abel, *The Foundation of Sociological Theory* (New York: Random House, 1970), p. 87.

34. Simmel, "The Problem of Sociology," pp. 332-33.

35. Donald N. Levine, ed., *Georg Simmel on Individuality and Social Forms* (Chicago: University of Chicago Press, 1971), p. 43.

36. Wolff, *Sociology of Georg Simmel*, p. 26.

37. Ibid., p. 18.

38. Ibid., p. 409.

39. Cf. Lewis A. Coser, *The Functions of Social Conflict* (New York: Free Press, 1964); Hermann Strasser, *The Normative Structure of Sociology: Conservative and Emancipatory Themes in Social Thought* (London: RKP, 1976), chap. 7.

40. Cf. Don Martindale, *The Nature and Types of Sociological Theory* (Boston: Houghton Mifflin, 1960), pt. 4.

41. Cf. W. E. Mühlmann, "Sociology in Germany: Shift in Alignment," in Howard Becker and Alvin Boskoff, eds., *Modern Sociological Theory in Continuity and Change* (New York: Dryden Press, 1957), p. 664. Cf. Gabor Kiss, *Einführung in die Soziologischen Theorien*, 3d ed., 2 vols. (Opladen: Westdeutscher Verlag, 1975), 1:88-104.

42. Donald G. MacRae, *Weber* (London: Fontana/Collins, 1974), p. 17.

43. Max Weber, *The Methodology of the Social Sciences* (New York: Free Press, 1949), p. 80.

44. Ibid., p. 71.

45. Ibid., p. 86.

46. Ibid., p. 57.

47. Ibid., p. 58.

48. Cf. H. H. Gerth and C. Wright Mills, eds., *From Max Weber: Essays in Sociology* (London: RKP, 1948), p. 59.

49. Weber, *Methodology*, p. 81.

50. Ibid., p. 76.

51. Ibid., p. 54.

52. Ibid., pp. 98-99.

53. Russel Keat and John Urry, *Social Theory as Science* (London: RKP, 1975), p. 198.

54. Weber, *Methodology*, p. 90.

55. Ibid., p. 104.

56. Ibid., pp. 105, 92.

57. Max Weber, *Economy and Society: An Outline of Interpretative Sociology* (New York: Bedminster Press, 1968), 1:4.

58. See Werner Stark, *The Fundamental Forms of Social Thought* (London: RKP, 1962), p. 246.

59. Weber, *Economy and Society*, pp. 8-9.

60. Keat and Urry, *Social Theory*, p. 146.

61. Weber, *Economy and Society*, p. 6.

62. Cf. Karl Löwith, "Weber's Interpretation of the Bourgeois-Capitalistic World in Terms of the Guiding Principle of 'Rationalization,'" in Dennis Wrong, ed., *Max Weber* (Englewood Cliffs, N.J.: Prentice-Hall, 1970), pp. 111-12.

63. Herbert Marcuse, *Negations: Essays in Critical Theory* (Boston: Beacon Press, 1969), p. 203.

64. Abel, *Foundation*, p. 114.

65. Ibid., pp. 24 ff. Weber, *Economy and Society*, pp. 24-26.

66. Julien Freund, *The Sociology of Max Weber* (New York: Vintage Books, 1969), p. 133.

67. Weber, *Economy and Society*, p. 241.

68. Cf. Irving M. Zeitlin, *Ideology and the Development of Sociological Theory* (Englewood Cliffs, N.J.: Prentice-Hall, 1968), p. 155.

69. Gerth and Mills, *From Max Weber*, p. 139.

70. Stanislaw Kozyr-Kowalski, *Max Weber a Karol Marks* (Warsaw: KiW, 1967), pp. 229-30.

71. Max Weber, *The Protestant Ethic and the Spirit of Capitalism* (London: Unwin University Books, 1965), p. 183.

72. See Freund, *Sociology*, pp. 204-5.

73. Weber, *Economy and Society*, pt. 3, chap. 6.

74. Antoni Kamiński, *Wladza a racjonalność: Studium z socjologii współczesnego kapitalizmu* (Warsaw: PWN, 1976), pp. 21-22.

75. Gerth and Mills, *From Max Weber*, p. 139.

76. Talcott Parsons, "Max Weber's Sociological Analysis of Capitalism and Modern Institutions," in Harry Elmer Barnes, ed., *An Introduction to the History of Sociology* (Chicago: University of Chicago Press, 1948), p. 295.

71. Gerth and Mills, *From Max Weber*, p. 184.

78. Ibid., pp. 186-87.

79. Ibid., pp. 193-94.

80. Lewis A. Coser, *Masters of Sociological Thought* (New York: Harcourt Brace Jovanovich, 1971), p. 234.

81. Aron, *Les Etapes*, p. 564.

13

HISTORICAL MATERIALISM
AFTER MARX VERSUS SOCIOLOGY

Marxism developed from reflection on the same social crisis on which nineteenth-century sociology focused its attention, but it took shape and evolved independently of the latter. For a fairly long time, that independence was such that neither party felt the need to engage in a thorough discussion with the other. Even when declaring their attitude toward socialism, nineteenth-century sociologists usually had in mind orientations other than Marxism. Further on the whole they were interested in socialism as an ideology rather than a theory that offered original solutions to sociological problems. It was only the generation of Durkheim, Pareto, and Weber that discovered Marx to be a partner at theoretical discussion and the founder of a system that offered answers to sociological questions. On the other hand, the Marxists, beginning with Marx and Engels, showed minimal interest in the sociological systems of their times and saw in them at most an apology for bourgeois domination. They even avoided the term *sociology*.

*REASONS FOR THE DIVERGENCE BETWEEN MARXISM
AND SOCIOLOGY*

This separation of Marxism from sociology, and vice versa, is difficult to understand if we consider points of contacts, or at least potential points, between these two great trends. Each strove to find a scientific explanation of a similar set of facts and to overcome the same patterns of thinking. Each criticized liberal political economy, metaphysics, ideology, voluntarism, and so forth. Each was intended to be an instrument for the reconstruction of society and was in opposition to contemporaneous academic science, forming a kind of counterculture in science that was barred from universities and from respectable scholarly periodicals. Note also that Marxism and sociology had some common ancestors (for example, Saint-Simon).

All these affinities did not, and could not, suffice as grounds for a rapprochement, for several reasons (we disregard here the otherwise important fact that Marx's popularity outside the socialist movement came rather late).

First, sociology was, as a rule, a bourgeois discipline: All its early representatives had in view an improvement of the capitalist system, while its abolition was demanded by Marx and his disciples, who were united in an antibourgeois party and deliberately isolated from their ideologically hostile environment. Second, sociology strove to construct a "positive" social science that was independent of philosophy and as specialized as possible. Marx, in contrast, considered his task to be the reconstruction of the whole of social knowledge, together with its philosophical foundations, and he remained a philosopher. Third, Marxism was an activist doctrine, whereas sociology, especially in its positivist and evolutionist versions, was oriented toward outside observation of objective processes, observation that can and should yield practical conclusions, but in itself is not part of social praxis. This is not a complete list of all the essential differences between Marxism and nineteenth-century sociology. But the three mentioned above were enough to block any rapprochement between Marxism and sociology without reshaping one or the other.

At first, Marxism and sociology did not have a meeting ground, because they addressed different audiences and gave priority to different problems. Yet a confrontation was inevitable because sociology was gaining in popularity and significance, and Marxism, as a result of the Second International (1889-1914), had changed into the doctrine of a powerful mass movement. On an increasing scale it strove for its own position on all issues that could be a matter of public interest and also accommodated itself gradually to functioning within existing sociopolitical structures. These changes in both bourgeois sociology and Marxism took place in approximately the same period, the twenty-five years that preceded World War I.

It was then that the first confrontation took place. Marxism was noticed by non-Marxist and anti-Marxist social theorists as a sociological conception, and it started to formulate its own attitude toward sociology. It is still to be determined how much this confrontation—in which such prominent thinkers as Pareto, Durkheim, Tönnies, Weber, B. Croce, R. Stammler, and W. Sombart took part—affected the social thought of the period. In any case, it gave rise to references to "Marxist sociology" and to Marx as a sociologist. Marxists themselves started admitting that they were sociologists, and Max Adler even claimed that Marxism and socioogy are one and the same thing.[1]

This terminological novelty should not be overestimated. In some cases it simply amounted to labeling historical materialism "the Marxist sociology." This did not mean a real dialogue with sociologists. It still remains to be shown whether such a dialogue was established and what was its scope.[2] The active role played by Kazimierz Kelles-Krauz (1872-1905), a prominent Polish Marxist, in the work of the International Institute of Sociology and the writings of Ludwik Krzywicki indicate the tendencies to rapprochement, but on the other hand, there are examples of overt attacks on sociology as such. It is tempting to advance the hypothesis that various attitudes toward sociology were derivatives of various interpretations of Marxism. We may say that at the turn of the nineteenth-century Marxism was coming closer to sociology, as it was becoming nonpartisan, nonphilosophical, and nonactivist.

THE "POSITIVIST" AND "EVOLUTIONIST" MARXISM OF THE SECOND INTERNATIONAL

The salient characteristic of Second-International Marxism was the tendency, originated by Engels, to popularize and to systematize the doctrine. The most prominent and best-known representatives of that orientation endeavored to integrate Marxian ideas into a uniform system that would allow interpretation of all sorts of facts and would satisfy the intellectual needs of people who were living at the close of the nineteenth century and had been brought up in the climate of deference to natural science. Although most Second-International theorists represented Marxist orthodoxy and strove to be faithful to the teachings of the founders of historical materialism, they nevertheless adapted them to a new situation, new issues, and a new climate of opinion. A. Gramsci also drew attention to the intellectual consequences of Marxism's becoming a mass movement—namely, its adaptation to the popular ways of thinking, in which *sui generis* fatalism was deeply rooted.[3] Note also that the period under consideration was marked by a peaceful development of the worker's movement in Western Europe, which favored theories of social evolution rather than social revolution. Moreover, the Second International developed within it a revisionist trend, which was initiated by Eduard Bernstein (1850-1932) and whose representatives deliberately rejected or modified some ideas of Marx and Engels. They assumed that capitalist society had undergone such far-reaching changes that the principles formulated fifty years earlier had become anachronistic.

Second-International Marxism was due primarily to such writers and social leaders as Karl Kautsky (1854-1938), author of *Ethik und materialistische Geschichtsauffassung* (1906), *Die materialistische Geschichtsauffasung* (1927), and a great many other political, historical, and economic writings; George V. Plekhanov (1856-1918), author of *The Development of the Monist View of History* (1894), *The Role of the Individual in History* (1898), *Unaddressed Letters* (1899-1900), *The Fundamental Problems of Marxism* (1908), *Art and Social Life* (1912-1913), and other works; Heinrich Cunow (1862-1936), author of *Die Marxistische Geschichts-, Gesellschafts-*

und Staatstheorie (1920-1921); Eduard Bernstein, author of *Evolutionary Socialism* (1899); and the Austrian Marxists: Max Adler (1873-1937), author of *Kausalität and Teleologie im Streite um die Wissenschaft* (1904), *Marxistische Problems* (1913), *Lehrbuch der materialistischen Geschichtsauffassung* (1930), and *Das Rätsel der Gesellschaft* (1936); Otto Bauer (1881-1938), best known as the author of *Die Nazionalitätenfrage und die Sozialdemokratie* (1907); and Rudolf Hilferding (1877-1943), author of *Das Finanzkapital* (1910).

Though the list is far from complete, we have intentionally listed together thinkers who differed markedly among themselves and even quarreled over basic theoretical issues—the orthodox Kautsky and the revisionist Bernstein, the materialist Plekhanov and the neo-Kantian Max Adler—because it seems that for all their differences they fit along a common theoretical horizon. It is outlined by the striving to win for historical materialism the status of *science* in the positivist sense of the word and also to link Marxism to the tradition of Darwin rather than that of Hegel. However, this was not the only theoretical horizon of Marxism at that time. There were also other orientations, represented, for instance, by Antonio Labriola (1843-1904), author of *Essays on the Materialistic Interpretation of History* (1896) and promoter of Marxism in Italy, and by the French thinker Jean Jaurès (1859-1914). The period now under consideration was on the whole marked by liveliness of Marxist thought.

Marxism as "a Kind of Positivism." One important feature of Second-International Marxism was its tendency to bring historical materialism closer to positivist and evolutionist ideas. Not all of the authors went as far as Enrico Ferri (1856-1929), the Italian theorist who in his book *Socialism and Positive Science* (1894) considered Marxian socialism to b a simple application of the principles of positive science to social issues. Popular expositions of historical materialism, increasing in number at the turn of the nineteenth century, not only made use of the data accumulated by evolutionist sociology and social anthropology, but also formulated answers to questions posed by those disciplines. In many cases they even adopted those answers in readymade form. Thus, for instance, Bernstein was inclined to consider Marxian dialectics to be a deplorable "survival" of Hegelianism and saw in evolutionism a much sounder basis for socialist theory. Kautsky stressed his links to Darwinism and strove to extend the materialistic interpretation of history, in order to make it border on biology. He wanted to find out whether the development of human societies was internally connected with the development of animal and vegetable species; if so, the history of mankind would have to be interpreted as a special case in the history of the organic world and as a process governed by its own laws, which are, however, connected with the general laws of that world. On the issue of the origin of social classes, Kautsky adopted Gumplowicz's standpoint and reduced the dialectics of the process of history to interaction between the organism and its environment, between the individual and society. While they verbally opposed the one-factor fallacy, Second-International Marxists exerted themselves to demonstrate which single factor determines the course of social development and coined the term *economic* materialism.

This tendency varied in strength from case to case, but was common enough to substantiate the later doubts that it had resulted in distortion of Marx's original ideas by both the revisionists and the representatives of the orthodox. In Karl Korsch's opinion, "the fluid methodology of Marx's materialist dialectic freezes [in the case of Second-International thinkers] into a number of theoretical formulations about the causal interconnection of historical phenomena in different areas of society—in other words it became something that could best be described as a general systematic sociology."[4] According to Herbert Marcuse, "the critical Marxist theory the revisionists thus tested by the standards of positivistic sociology and transformed into natural science. In line with the inner tendencies of the positivist reaction against 'negative philosophy,' the objective conditions that prevail were hypostatized, and human practice was rendered subordinate to their authority."[5]

The Sphere of Facts and the Sphere of Values. Making Marxism "scientific" raised a barrier, unknown to Marx, between science and ideology, between scholarship and partisanship, between the sphere of *sein* and that of *sollen*, between pure cognition and all kinds of group interest. Science is one and universal by its own nature, and hence, as Bernstein wrote, "no *ism* is a science."[6] Kautsky wrote in his *Ethik* that

even Social Democracy as the organization of the proletariat in its *class struggle* cannot do without the ethical ideal. . . . But this ideal has nothing to do with *scientific* socialism, which is the scientific study of the laws of the evolution and motion of the social organism. . . . It is, of course, true that in socialism the investigator is always also a militant, and man cannot be artificially cut into two parts with nothing to do with each other. Even in a Marx the influence of a moral idea sometimes breaks through in his scientific research. But he rightly sought to avoid this as far as possible. For in science the moral ideal is a source of error. Science is always only concerned with the knowledge of the necessary."[7]

The Discovery of Neo-Kantianism. This way of interpreting Marx paved the way for neo-Kantianism, which gave theoretical substantiation to a moral ideal. As a matter of fact, neo-Kantianism was an inevitable consequence of the scientism that marked Second-International theorists. Once it had been concluded that the moral ideal was not deducible from factual statements, any penetrating theorist had to ask about its validity. The only available answer was to be found in the conceptions of the neo-

Kantians of the Marburg school. These conceptions were most vigorously popularized among the social democrats by Karl Vorländer (1860-1928).

While accepting the separation of facts from values, the neo-Kantians in the Marxist camp pointed to the importance of the latter and protested against placing man in the enclosure of necessity, as understood in the sense of natural science. Socialism can be validated because man is free by his very nature and in full consciousness chooses his goals; in doing so, he is guided by his own conscience and not by the knowledge of any necessity that is external to him. This gave importance to the problem of the relationship between causality and teleology in social life, a problem whose analysis could result in a reformulation of the whole conception of society. That, however, did not occur. Marxism in the period of the Second International tended, rather, to split into naturalistic determinism—which, in fact, dismissed the "active aspect" of Marx's philosophy—and so-called ethical socialism, which was inclined to belittle the role of external determinants of moral decisions. This dilemma was extremely significant from the political point of view, as it was linked to problems of party strategy and tactics. On the other hand, the resulting controversies did not contribute much to purely theoretical discussions on pursuing the science of society. Thus, Second-International Marxism practically did not respond to the problems of the specific nature of humanistic cognition, which were taken up by the neo-Kantians of the Baden school and even earlier by Dilthey, although their writings were not totally unknown to the Marxists.

Max Adler came closest to tackling those issues and was the only thinker in the group under consideration who concerned himself seriously with the methodology of the social sciences. He tried in his theory of the social sciences to make use *a priori* of Kantian transcendentalism in answering Simmel's question, "How is sociology possible?" But he, too, rejected the proposals advanced by Rickert and Windelband, as he did not see any reason for opposing the social sciences to the natural ones. He did not disregard the new problems and proved that he understood Kantianism better than those who specialized in complementing Marxism with Kantian ethics.

Marxism under the Second International: A Balance Sheet. The period now being discussed was marked by strivings to make Marxism more popular, but not more profound theoretically. Incomparably more effort was expended to make it widely known than to work out the details that Marx and Engels had left unfinished. It is also to be recalled that many works by the founders of historical materialism were not yet known. Most important, however, was the general intellectual atmosphere, which made even those who were orthodoxly minded interpret Marxism unorthodoxly. Even without realizing it, they included in their interpretations many elements of positivism and evolutionism and were gradually transforming Marxism into one of the postevolutionist sociological schools. This had two consequences for the further relationships between Marxism and sociology. On the one hand, Marxism was becoming known and comprehensible to people brought up in the spirit of scientism, since they were no longer repelled by the Hegelianism that marked classical Marxism. On the other hand, modernized Marxism appeared at the moment when sociology, and the humanities in general, started retreating from scientism and when the elements just assimilated by Marxism were becoming anachronistic. This fact, together with the political reasons mentioned above, had to contribute to the critical attitude toward Marxism of such men as Max Weber. Marxism under the Second International, though intended to find an understanding with sociology, failed completely in this respect. Moreover, it had no really prominent work to offer that would gain new attention, as Marx's *Kapital* had done in the earlier period. As a result, there were quite a few scholars who were influenced by Marxism, but the impact of orthodox Marxism was slight outside the milieu of social democrats. The situation changed, at least in Austria and Germany, only after World War I.

This is not to say that the achievements of Second-International Marxists may be dismissed completely. However we assess them, there is no doubt that these thinkers, especially members of the orthodox group, had a decisive influence on the still current version of historical materialism, which was codified by Nikolai Bukharin (1888-1938) in *Historical Materialism: A System of Sociology* (1921). Nor is there any doubt that under their impact Marxism came to be considered a genuine sociological conception. Often criticized as it was, it still began to make its presence known in the official social sciences, and it gave rise to the lasting process of discovering Marx.

L. KRZYWICKI: A CASE OF MARXIST SOCIOLOGY

Ludwik Krzywicki (1859-1941), one of the founders of sociology in Poland, was one of the most prominent Marxist theorists of the time. Krzywicki differed from the rest of representatives of positivist Marxism in one essential respect: He was not only a popularizer and systematizer of Marxism, but also—and primarily—a scholar who tried to use that theory in sociological, economic, demographic, anthropological, and historical studies. His attention was focused not on Marxism as such, but on its possible applications. He was a researcher rather than an ideologist; this accounted for his Marxist orthodoxy's being questioned on various occasions. T. Kowalik writes that "Krzywicki had at his disposal an enormous amount of data from the various spheres of social life and from the various periods and he confronted it with Marx's sociological theory in order to formulate the principles of historical materialism in a form that would be liable to verification."[8] Krzywicki's vast knowledge in various fields enabled him to avoid the traps of dilettantism, the misfortune of Kautsky and Plekhanov, who always referred to the achievements of science, but were not well-trained researchers themselves.

In his many works—which included *An Outline of Ethnical Anthropology* (1893), *Physical Races* (1897), *Psychical Races* (1902), *Social Development in Animals and in Man* (1905), *Socioeconomic Systems under Savagery and Barbarism* (1914), *Sociological Studies* (1923), and *Primitive Society and Its Vital Statistics* (1934), all except the last in Polish—he was mainly concerned with the theory of social development. Brought up in the spirit of evolutionism (he valued Morgan's works most), he remained faithful to it to the end of his life, although he did not fail to be critical of many standard evolutionist ideas that he considered at variance with recent data provided by social anthropology. Thus, for instance, when discussing the periods of savagery and barbarism, he claimed that it was a variety of forms and paths of development, and not any uniform pattern, that was the rule. He also vigorously opposed organicism and biologism, in which he saw instruments of an apology for the existing social order. When pointing to similarities between animal and human societies, Krzywicki used to bring out the peculiarities of the latter, and on this point he referred to the ideas of Marx, of which he was a firm, though quite original, advocate. In adopting the Marxian conception of the course of human history, Krzywicki strove to avoid all schemata, as he did in the case of evolutionism; he did so by stressing the spatiotemporal limits of the validity of his statements.

Krzywicki's originality within the Marxist orientation rested in his conception of territorial societies, which he claimed to have followed tribal societies historically. This conception, while not in contradiction with Marx's writings and even largely due to Marx's inspiration, focused on the changes in social bonds; thus, it resembled Tönnies's ideas, formulated roughly at the same time. Tribal societies are seen to be based on direct contacts between men, whereas a territorial society is "a system of objective bonds," an organization of people through the intermediary of things.

The concept of territorial society denotes all class societies and, consequently, those in which private property exists. Marx's idea of the reification of relationships among human beings is thus broadened considerably. The development of territorial societies is spontaneous and uncontrollable. Krzywicki considered historical materialism to be a theory of that development, thus restricting its applicability to other types of societies, that is, to the preterritorial clan society and the postterritorial socialist society. As Krzywicki wrote,

the rules expounded above, which guide social development, are not . . . hard and fast law, valid in every period of history. They mark the territorial system, they were born and came to evolve fully only when that system had emerged and destroyed the clan-based bonds of community life; if and when the territorial system yields its place to a classless one, based on production that is regulated in full consciousness on the national scale, that spontaneity will disappear together with the rules that we have formulated.[9]

Krzywicki's analysis of mechanisms of social change, which went far beyond popular Marxist formulations, is original, too. It covers the role of social ideas, tradition, and mental factors. Krzywicki did not question Marxist formulations concerning base and superstructure (even though he did not use that terminology himself), as he was little concerned with conforming to them. Rather, he studied the variety of factors that make the relation between base and superstructure a complicated one. He labeled production "an eternal revolutionary," but was very far from explaining all social changes by changes in production. He thought that a "wandering of ideas" (exemplified by the spreading of Roman law) can result in an acceleration of social development out of proportion to changes in its material substratum.

But it is his idea of historical substratum that is known best. He stated that

every phase of social development leaves a heritage that merges with that of earlier periods. Amalgamation of those elements, some of which originated in the remote past and some in the recent past—in general, amalgamation of historical survivals with institutions that no longer meet the needs of a given period although they are still extant—yields an influential category of factors of historical development,[10]

as a result of which "the existing order of things only in part corresponds to the existing productive forces (that is, economic relations and material relations in general), because it is shaped to some extent by the past, too."[11]

Summing up, we may say that Krzywicki proved that Marxist sociology was possible.

REVOLUTIONARY MARXISM

The positivist and evolutionist interpretation of historical materialism, typical of Marxism under the Second International, was opposed by the orientation that is called either Leninism or Third-International Marxism. These two terms, however, differ in their extended versions, and each of them is misleading in its own way. The former can be too easily associated with the codified and even petrified form that Lenin's conceptions were given after his death. The latter may suggest that we mean something like an official doctrine of the Third International, whereas, in fact, the works of such important representatives of this trend as Georg Lukács (1885-1971),

Karl Korsch (1886-1961), and Antonio Gramsci (1891-1937) never acquired such a status and came to be criticized quite strongly by leaders of the International. It was Bukharin who enjoyed great popularity among the communists in the 1920s (next to Lenin, of course). As a theorist, however, he was a posthumous representative of the Second International, and for that he was attacked vehemently by Lukács and Gramsci.

If we seek a common label for all those conceptions that intended to supersede Second-International Marxism, the term *revolutionary* Marxism seems to be most suitable of all. By this, we mean both political attitudes, which came to manifest themselves clearly in 1917 and were marked by the faith in the advent of a world revolution, and—the most important point for us— a peculiar manner of organizing the problems covered by historical materialism.

The revolutionary manner of handling the subject is well illustrated by the opening sentences in Lukács's small book on Lenin, published in 1924:

Historical materialism is the theory of the proletarian revolution. It is so because its essence is an intellectual synthesis of the social existence which produces and fundamentally determines the proletariat; and because the proletariat struggling for liberation finds its clear self-consciousness in it. The stature of a proletarian thinker, of a representative of historical materialism, can therefore be measured by the depth and breadth of his grasp of this and the problems arising from it: by the extent to which he is able accurately to detect beneath the appearances of bourgeois society those tendencies towards proletarian revolution which work themselves in and through it to their effective being and distinct consciousness.[12]

This passage seemingly does not contain anything to which the orthodox followers of the Second International could not subscribe, but the language was new, and so was the viewpoint: The stress was shifted from the knowledge of the laws of social development to the organization of the forces that were to speed it up; from the knowledge of the mechanisms of that development to the self-consciousness of participants in historical processes; from sociology to politics.

Certainly, we do not come across a complete break in continuity, both because they were merely two different articulations of one and the same theory, formulated by Marx, and because representatives of revolutionary Marxism (Lenin in particular), brought up on the works of their predecessors from the period of the Second International, did not immediately break off with them definitively. Further, a political break did not have to mean an equally deep schism in the interpretation of historical materialism, especially when theorizing was not a fully autonomous pursuit. Second-International interpretation of Marxism was attacked most vehemently by those authors who had reached revolutionary Marxism via neo-idealistic philosophy (Lukács, Korsch, and Gramsci) and advocated the return to the

dialectical sources of Marxian thought forgotten by the preceding generation. On the other hand, Lenin emphasized the need to revive Marxian
materialism, although he, too, studied Hegel, which is proved by his
Philosophical Notebooks (1914-1916). On the whole, revolutionary
Marxism seems to have been marked by an intensity of interest in philosophy
and by the opinion that sociology was part of a more comprehensive whole.

Lenin and Sociology. Vladimir I. Lenin (whose original family name was
Ulianov; 1870-1924) was the most eminent representative of revolutionary
Marxism, the theorist to whom other thinkers of this orientation referred,
even though they disagreed with him. S. Kozyr-Kowalski wrote about Lenin
that he was "a sociologist who has not yet been fully discovered" and
pointed to the difficulties connected with reconstructing Lenin's sociology,
which was never expounded by him systematically.[13] It is, however, beyond
doubt that Lenin did attach much importance to sociology and was one of
the first authors to whom the existence of a Marxist sociology was evident.
This was probably due to the emphasis that he, following Marx, put on
interpreting economic relations as social relations. The following ideas,
elaborated most fully during Lenin's polemics with the subjective sociology
of the Narodniki, seem to be of special importance in his sociology.

Lenin did not write on historical materialism in general, but concentrated
on using that theory in solving problems of a specific country. This applies
above all to *The Development of Capitalism in Russia* (1899), about which
P. Anderson wrote that it was "the first serious application of the general
theory of the capitalist mode of production set out in *Capital* to a concrete
social formation, combining a number of modes of production in an articulate totality."[14] In general, the salient feature of Lenin's works was the
tendency to emphasize the historicist orientation of historical materialism.
This tendency can be seen in Lenin's criticism of non-Marxist sociology.
In "What the 'Friends of the People' Are and How They Fight against the
Social-Democrats" we read:

to begin by asking what is society and what is progress, is to begin from the end.
Whence are you to get your conception of society and progress in general when you
have not studied a single form of society in particular, when you have been unable
even to establish this conception, when you have been unable even to approach a
serious factual investigation, an objective analysis of social relations of any kind?
. . . The gigantic step forward which Marx took in this respect consisted precisely in
the fact that he discarded all these discussions about society and progress in general
and gave a *scientific* analysis of *one* society and of *one* progress—capitalist society
and capitalist progress.

And also: "Every historical period has its own laws. . . . The old economists
misunderstood the nature of economic laws when they likened them to the
laws of physics and chemistry."[15]

Lenin put particular stress on "the dialectical method which obliges us to regard society as a living organism in its functioning and development," on investigation of social facts as interconnected phenomena, and he thought that Marxists deserved great credit because they "were the first Socialists to insist on the need of analysing all aspects of social life, and not only the economic."[16] It was this that had in mind when he argued in favor of dialectics and against metaphysics. This was also why he paid so much attention to the theory of socioeconomic formations.

While his approach was holistic—he even used the term *organism*—Lenin thought that the primary objective of social analysis was to reveal the class division, the characteristics of a given society, and the balance of power of the classes. He explicitly opposed the concept of class to that of group, which was becoming common in sociology, and he wrote in *The Economic Meaning of the Narodniki Movement* (1894) that the latter concept was too "vague and arbitrary," because "there is no permanent property on the basis of which one could . . . single out such or other 'groups.' On the contrary, the theory of class struggle is an immense achievement of the science of society just because it defines the way of reducing that which is individual to that which is social with utmost accuracy and precision." And he goes on:

Actions by "living individuals" . . . actions which are infinitely varied and, it would seem, evade all systematization have been generalized and reduced to actions by groups of individuals, groups which differ from one another by the role they played in the system of relations of production, by conditions of production, and hence by their living conditions and their interests resulting therefrom—in a word, they have been reduced to actions by *classes*, whose struggle determined the development of society.[17]

The pivotal role assigned by Lenin to class struggle in his conception of society enabled him to cope in a way with the dilemma of what is and what should be (*sein* and *sollen*), which, as we have seen, worried Second-International thinkers.[18] Lenin believed that it was possible to unite a precise scientific description of social processes with the formulation of the slogan: he specified the ideal as "a demand by a certain class, born of certain social relations (which are liable to an objective study)."[19] Wrote Lenin,

An objectivist, when proving that a given series of facts was necessary, always risks straying to a position of an apologist for those facts; a materialist reveals class oppositions and defines his viewpoint thereby. . . . He does not confine himself to pointing to the necessity of the process, but explains which socioeconomic formation accounts for the meaning of that process, namely, *which class* determines that necessity. . . . materialism, I would say, implies partisanship, by imposing on one the obligation of backing openly, in all evolutions of events, the standpoint of a definite social group.[20]

A Marxist, thus, is objective, because he studies facts without any *a priori* valuation whatsoever. But at the same time he is a party man, because while getting to know the facts, he declares himself for a certain class.

The principle of theoretical partisanship was closely linked by Lenin to that of practical membership of a party; in other words, he was in favor of making Marxist social knowledge the ideology of a political organization and of the class that it allegedly represented and, thus, of transforming that knowledge into a social force capable of changing existing conditions. From this point of view his book *What Is to Be Done?* (1902) is of basic importance: It was concerned with the question of how to bridge the gap between theory and practice, between Marxist social knowledge and the spontaneous labor movement. The answer to this question was thought by Lenin to be a *sine qua non* of the success of the revolution. Lenin was the Marxist who emphasized the role of the subjective factor—ideology and politics—in the processes of social change. This was probably the most essential difference between him and Second-International Marxists, who, acting under different conditions, counted more on the effects of spontaneous development and gave preference to education before organization.

Lukács's Criticism of Sociology. The collected studies published by Georg Lukács, the Hungarian philosopher and aesthetician, under the title *History and Class Consciousness: Studies in Marxist Dialectics* (first published in German in 1923) were the extreme manifestation of revolutionary Marxism. The book, which was one of the most ambitious intellectual undertakings in the history of Marxism, enjoys much publicity even now, surpassing in that respect Lukács's earlier writings, although they included such prominent works as *Theory of the Novel* (German edition, 1920) and *The Young Hegel: Studies in the Relation between Dialectics and Economics* (German edition, 1954). The book mentioned first is the most interesting when it comes to the history of sociology, if we disregard the monumental, but practically still unknown, *Zur Ontologie des gesellschaftlichen Seins*, on which Lukács was working toward the close of his life. *History and Class Consciousness* was a brilliant attempt to reconstruct Marxism as a dialectical method and as a philosophy of history, free from the influence of positivism and evolutionism (unlike Lenin in his *Materialism and Empiriocriticism*, Lukács rejected Engels's idea of "the dialectics of nature").

In making that reconstruction, Lukács introduced into Marxist thought the problems, earlier taken up shyly by Max Adler, of the antipositivist turn in the social sciences. This can be explained by the fact that he had studied under Simmel and Max Weber and began his activity in the spirit of neo-Kantianism, from which he turned toward Hegel and Marx. He added to those problems the dimension of the sociology of knowledge: He did so by posing the question, Under what social conditions does scientism inevitably become the dominant way of thinking about social life? Opposition to scientism was identified by him with the striving for a renewal of the revolutionary essence of Marxism, contrary to the theorists influenced by the Second International, whom he considered to be carriers of the same reified consciousness that marks bourgeois philosophers. As L. Goldmann wrote, in his polemic with the Second-International version of Marxism, Lukács was opposed mainly to the belief that there may be an objective Marxist sociology and to the separation of facts from values.[21] By identifying, like Hegel, the subject and the object of social cognition, Lukács reduced all knowledge of society to the self-consciousness of social classes, thus eliminating the conceptions of both the researcher who stands outside the investigated process and the moralist who brings into history a moral ideal from the outside. In a word, Lukács attacked both scientism and the Kantianism of the Second International, both objectivism and subjectivism.

What other ideas are exposed in *History and Class Consciousness?* In Lukács's opinion (here he refers to Marx's commodity fetishism), under the capitalist economy, whose mechanisms are hidden from the acting individuals, there develops a peculiar way of thinking that turns all human products into "things" that are independent of the cognizing subject, isolated from one another, and changeless. Human beings see even their own activity as something subject to an external necessity, which can at most become known to them in the same way as the laws of nature can. Science, he wrote, "uncritically accepts the nature of the object as it is given and the laws of that society as the unalterable foundation of 'science.'"[22] Accordingly, he held that naturalism in the social sciences was a product of reified consciousness and "an ideological weapon of the bourgeoisie. For the latter it is a matter of life and death to understand its own system of production in terms of eternally valid categories."[23] That reified social world with the corresponding forms of consciousness is inevitably ahistorical, atomized, and reduced to quantitative and abstract relations of exchange of commodities. Bourgeois thought is incapable of grasping society as a changing *totality*; this is reflected, for example, in the distintegration of social knowledge, which has split into political economy, history, jurisprudence, sociology, and so forth.

Hence the goal of social knowledge is not, and cannot be, the cognition of changeless laws of social life and causal relationships among facts. The superiority of Marxism over bourgeois science does not, in any case, consist in Marxism's better implementation of the same ideal of science. The essential difference is in the method, in the viewpoint adopted, and not in the various theoretical statements: "It is not the primacy of economic motives in historical explanation that constitutes the decisive difference between Marxism and bourgeois thought, but the point of view of totality."[24]

That "concrete totality," as Lukács usually calls it, is not immediately grasped through observation, but must, as Marx claimed, be reconstructed following a long mental process. The error of "vulgar materialism" (Lukács used the term very broadly, so that it covers all forms of scientism) lies in not going beyond separate observable facts and in believing that in this way it comes to know reality, whereas in fact it remains closed in the sphere of abstraction. The limitation of bourgeois thought is its inability to rise above the apparent concreteness of observable facts and to determine their connections with the concrete historical totality. These comments, although addressed mainly to historians and economists, can well be applied to sociologists. They are certainly the most radical criticism of empirical sociology ever formulated.

The best example of the procedure for studying social reality that Lukács suggested is seen in his approach to class consciousness, to which he gave most attention in *History and Class Consciousness*. He criticized those researchers who had focused all their attention on empirically given, individual or mass psychological consciousness, on what individuals and/or groups of individuals think, feel, or will at a given moment. He did not deny the value of such "naive description," but claimed that "it remains after all merely the *material* of genuine historical analysis." The latter begins only when we make use of the concept of totality, that is, when we are in a position to interpret the observed facts in the context of a socioeconomic formation. Seen in this perspective, empirically given consciousness proves to be false consciousness, as it does not correspond to the objective situation of its carriers, the situation that ultimately will be decisive for "historically significant actions of the class as a whole." Empirically given psychological consciousness of members of a social class is contrasted by Lukács with the concept of possible class consciousness, which is "neither the sum nor the average of what is thought or felt by the single individuals who make up the class." In his opinion the real process of history can be understood only if that "objective possibility" is taken into account.[25]

According to Lukács, grasping the concrete totality does not depend solely on the researcher's individual perspicacity. While traditional social knowledge expresses, in fact, the viewpoint of the bourgeoisie, which is interested in preserving the fiction of the social world as something changeless like the laws of nature, the new social knowledge is the self-knowledge of the proletariat, the other pure class in bourgeois society, which is interested in solving all the puzzles of history. "The self-understanding of the proletariat is therefore simultaneously the objective understanding of the nature of society."[26] The process whereby the proletariat becomes a class in itself means a change of society and advances in social knowledge. The barrier is abolished between the object and the subject, practice and theory, ideology and science.

Gramsci's Criticism of Sociology. Analyses carried out by Antonio Gramsci, a prominent Italian Marxist, followed a very similar path, although his road to historical materialism was different and led through the neo-Hegelianism of Benedetto Croce (1866-1954). Like Lukács, Gramsci represented a vehement antipositivist reaction, reflected in his many-sided criticism of the Second-International interpretation of Marxism and in his criticism of sociology. In most cases the author of *The Modern Prince* identified sociology with its positivist and evolutionist version, to which he opposed not a different kind of sociology, but an essentially different kind of social knowledge. Gramsci's theoretical views were recorded in his *Prison Notebooks* (1926-1937). They contain mostly notes and passages that are far from a final formulation, since Gramsci made them for his own use. Those writings, arranged in order and published only after World War II, present Gramsci as a truly original thinker. His impact on Marxist thought has been growing, especially in Western Europe.

Gramsci's notes cover politics, philosophy, sociology, literary history, history, and the like. His criticism of sociology is to be found primarily in "Critical Notes on 'An Attempt at a Popular Presentation of Marxism' by Bukharin."

Gramsci was opposed to philosophical materialism, as he saw in it a relic of religious thinking, based on the assumption that there is a reality independent of the cognizing subject. He also declared himself against determinism (which he identified with fatalism), because, in his opinion, it eliminates human activity from the vision of the world and tries to cram the wealth of facts into a single schema. The deterministic conception of society must be false "since one cannot leave aside the will and the initiative of men themselves."[27] It can be valid only as long as the masses remain passive or are considered to be such and the dominant system functions without major changes and distrubances. Comprehension of history as a process that cannot be stopped and comprehension of great turning points in human history (and it is in these that Gramsci, as a revolutionary, is interested) require the adoption of a quite different vision of the social world, one in which objectivity does not mean independence of human actions and "foresight reveals itself therefore not as a scientific act of knowledge, but as the abstract expression of the effort one makes, the practical method of creating a collective will."[28] In this sense Gramsci opposes sociology to politics or, more broadly, to Marxism conceived as the philosophy of action, not as the knowledge of objective laws.

Sociology, as seen by Gramsci, is the quintessence of all the defects of the *Weltanschauung* that he criticized.

Sociology has been an attempt to create a method for historico-political science, dependent on an already elaborated philosophical system (evolutionary positivism), on which sociology has reacted, but only partially. Hence it has become a tendency on its own, it has become a philosophy of the non-philosophers, an attempt to describe and classify historical and political facts schematically, according to criteria modelled on the natural sciences. Sociology is therefore an attempt to deduce "experimentally" the laws of evolution of human society in such a way as to be able to "foresee" the future with the same certainty with which one foresees that an oak will develop out of an acorn. At the basis of sociology is vulgar evolutionism and it cannot grasp the transition from quantity to quality, a transition which disturbs every evolution and every law of uniformity in the vulgar evolutionist sense.[29]

On another occasion Gramsci linked the career of sociology to "the decadence of the concept of political science and political art" and said that "what is really important in sociology is nothing but political science."[30] Gramsci deplored the fact that the distinction between society and the state had become too sharp.

Gramsci deliberately defended the opinion, advanced by the antipositivist trends, that the methods used in the natural science are not applicable in the humanities. "The point must be settled that every research has its own determined method and constructs its own determined science, and that the method is developed and has been elaborated together with the development and elaboration of that determined research and science with which it is one."[31] This was not, however, a defense of the academic humanities against the deformations that could result from copying patterns of natural science. It was primarily a program of social knowledge developed through participation in that social movement which—by changing the fixed ways of life—makes the standard research methods fallible. It was characteristic of Gramsci that he considered that new knowledge indispensable at the time of revolutionary turning points, while in periods of stabilization the traditional methods of studying social facts could prove relatively adequate. Unlike Lukács, he felt that the new social knowledge was not a consequence of a methodological turning point alone: It resulted from changes in social reality itself and from changes in the position occupied in it by the researcher himself, who turns from a witness of historical events into their active coauthor.

Gramsci's criticism of determinism is not to be understood as his joining the camp of subjectivism or voluntarism. In his reinterpretation of historical materialism he turned against both "economism," which overestimates "mechanical causes," and "ideologism," which overemphasizes "the voluntarist and individual element."[32] The point is that the relation between human activity and objective conditions is not one between an effect and the cause that necessarily determines that effect. We may speak only about probability, and it becomes known only *ex post facto* whether that activity really was, in Gramsci's terms, "historical" or "organic." The only possible method is that of trial and error, which shows which class becomes dominant in society. The truth or rationality of social ideas ultimately depends on whether they are capable of taking hold of the masses and thus influence the course of history.

Gramsci's approach to the issue of social ideas is probably the most interesting element of his conception. It was a *sui generis* analogue of the views expanded by Lenin in *What Is to Be Done?* The point of departure of Gramsci's sociology of ideas was the distinction between "the philosophy of common sense"—that is, "the world conception absorbed uncritically by various social and cultural circles in which the moral individuality of the average man is developed"—and the critical *Weltanschauung*, "the philosophy of philosophers." The former, the product of an overlapping of diverse influences and traditions, lacks coherence and consistency; the latter is "a homogeneous, that is, a coherent and systematic philosophy."[33] Each corresponds to different historical conditions: The former spreads when society is passive and disintegrated; the latter becomes possible when it is active and integrated. The problems of changes in consciousness— which make the people ready for a revolution and are in turn conditioned by that readiness—seem to have been the focus of Gramsci's interests.

Revolutionary Marxism: A Balance Sheet. Revolutionary Marxism, whose three, somewhat independent varieties have been discussed above, marked a turning away from the thinking characteristic of the theorists of the Second International. From a theoretical point of view, which is what we are interested in, the change consisted above all in making *revolution* the pivotal concept of historical materialism and in subordinating other issues in social theory to the problems of revolution. Of course, none of the Marxists mentioned here dismissed the idea that the process of history is governed by certain regularities, the belief in the dominant role of economy, or the thesis that the superstructure is dependent on the base. Yet, the hierarchy of problems did change: Everything was made subordinate to the problem of what the decisive factor is in the advance of a revolutionary movement and how these advances can be accelerated. Hence the pride of place given to problems of class consciousness and political organization; hence the opposition to objectivity and the eulogy of the spirit of the party; hence the strong antinaturalistic trend (of which only Lenin was free), the activist attitude, and the interpretation of the process of history in terms of practical human activity rather than historical laws; hence also the dislike of sociology identified with a positivist study of facts independent of historical praxis. Revolutionary Marxism, which some of its representatives labeled "the philosophy of practical activity," was a *sui generis* antipositivist revolution within Marxism itself. As such, it contributed to an increased attractiveness of the Marxist theory during the period that witnessed an aggravating crisis of positivism and evolutionism.

Yet the theoretical possibilities of this variety of Marxism were not exploited to the full. Revolutionary Marxism failed to remove from Marxist social thought the relics of the orthodox Marxist theory that marked the Second International, and some of its fertile ideas did not evoke any wide interest—at least until the late 1950s. This was due to a number of historical circumstances, above all the development of a new orientation within the communist movement after the triumph of the revolution in Russia and Lenin's death. Changes in the Marxist theory of society in that period have still to be examined penetratingly, because we often fail to realize how lively the discussions on sociology were and how widely different the opinions being formulated were, especially in the 1920s.[34] From our point of view, we have to note that the dislike of sociology as a distinct discipline became markedly dominant, even though Lenin, whose authority became unquestionable in the communist movement, did not criticize sociology as such, as was done for instance, by Lukács.

However this attitude arose, beginning with the 1930s we can see what J. Hochfeld called

a growing mistrust of sociology and its very name, developing in the Marxist theorists in the communist camp; a resistance to detailed social studies of the contemporaneous world; the considering such studies to be a "subordinate part" of philosophy; a purely ideological approach to all description, all analysis and all interpretation of social facts; the belief in the strong links between theory and political practice, but understood as an essentially pragmatic thesis on the instrumental subordination of the theory to the requirements of politics; the belief that dialectical and historical materialism is "the universal truth", *the* measure of the truth of statements and of the correctness of actions, that measure being brought down from the clouds of "the borders of consciousness" of the revolutionary proletariat to the solid ground of "the *Weltanschauung* of the Marxist-Leninist party."[35]

It would be absurd to blame Lukács or Gramsci for the long degradation of sociology in the Marxist camp, but there is no doubt that their transformation of all social knowledge into the self-knowledge of social classes was, or could be, a prerequisite for the denial of all verifiable knowledge outside the camp of unhesitating believers in that self-knowledge. Such a denial paved the way for dogmatism, which deprived Marxism of its original critical abilities.

ARMCHAIR MARXISM OF THE FRANKFURT SCHOOL

Opinions of representatives of the so-called Frankfurt school, which we call here armchair Marxism, were a *sui generis* continuation of certain ideas characteristic of antipositivist and antievolutionist Marxism. The concept of armchair Marxism, or "Marxism without a proletariat," may seem inconsistent, because the most prominent representatives of Marxism were as a rule both students of social life and party leaders. There have probably never been Marxist scholars of any import who would set themselves purely cognitive tasks. They differed in the way of interpreting the links between theory and practice rather than in opinions on the necessity of such links. It was one of the peculiarities of the Frankfurt school that, while inspired by the Marxist theory, it revealed less and less connection with political practice and never identified itself with any political party, making at most declarations of solidarity with socialism as such or resting satisfied with the rhetorics of a socially nondescript emancipation. This has given rise to the controversy over whether in this case one can speak at all about Marxism or neo-Marxism, especially because the theory of this school was eclectic.

Some people speak about the Marxism or neo-Marxism of the Frankfurt school, while others consider it to have been outright anti-Marxist. Both opinions seem oversimplified.[36] On the one hand, the historical significance and influence of the school were due to its application of Marxist theory (especially in the version offered by Korsch and Lukács) to problems, including sociological and extrasociological ones, that were not taken up on any large scale by vulgarized official Marxism. On the other hand, there is no doubt that in many cases the Marxism of the Frankfurt school was of a most dubious quality, as it was strongly seasoned with Hegelianism, psychoanalysis, and elements of many other doctrines.

The Frankfurt school is the popular term used for a group of German scholars gathered in the Institut für Sozialforschung ("Institute of Social Research"), founded in Frankfurt in 1923. It functioned there until its members had to leave Germany for France and, later, France for the United States. The institute returned from New York to Frankfurt in 1950. It had its first director in Carl Grünberg (1861-1940), usually considered to be an Austro-Marxist, who was a renowned historian of socialism and of the worker movement. Under his guidance the institute took up a number of valuable studies, but its proper intellectual history began in 1931, when it came to be headed by Max Horkheimer (1895-1973), a philosopher and the author of so-called critical theory; together with Theodor Wiesengrund Adorno (1903-1969) he was the real initiator of most research projects undertaken by the institute. Other well-known coworkers were Friedrich Pollock (1894-1970), Herbert Marcuse (1898-), Erich Fromm (1900-), Leo Lowenthal (1900-), and Walter Benjamin (1892-1940). The principal works of that group were published in the *Zeitschrift für Sozialforschung* (1932-1941).

Not all of the authors mentioned above were connected with the institute equally closely and for an equally long period. Furthermore, all of them were strong personalities, and so it would be risky to reconstruct any comprehensive set of opinions accepted by all of them from the beginning to the end of their scholarly careers. They shared the dislike of system construction and preferred denouncing existing systems to formulating a system of their own. As N. McInnes wrote,

what began in Marx as the critique of political economy . . . becomes in Critical Theory the rejection of all the social sciences as mere instances of reification and domination. There is nothing in society that is not man-made and man-dependent; so anything natural (repetitive, law-abiding) discovered there by a social science would be a fair target for the revolutionary dialectics, which would soon reabsorb its usurped *Being* back into eternal *Becoming* of man's activity.[37]

The most systematic exposition of the programmatic assumptions of the Frankfurt school (undermined on many points, however, in his later writings) is to be found in Horkheimer's papers of the 1930s, collected in the two volumes of *Kritische Theorie* (1968).

The Frankfurt school was not a school of sociology, and many studies in the history of sociology do not mention it at all. The advocates of critical theory (it is only recently that the term *critical sociology* came to be applied to it) stood for a *sui generis* return to social philosophy and to philosophy pure and simple. They criticized representatives of specialized social disciplines (including sociologists) for imagining that it would be possible to acquire the knowledge of social facts through a simple accumulation of data by specialized positive disciplines. Horkheimer claimed that "the 'given' is not . . . something that exists generally and independently of theory. Rather, it is mediated through the conceptual whole in which such statements function."[38] This directly refers to Lukács. Yet the attitude of the Frankfurt school toward sociology was far from being unambiguously negative, which is proved by the empirical studies conducted by that school,[39] and also by the positive assessment of such works as *Middletown* by the Lynds. The problem, rather, was finding a good definition of the mutual relationships between philosophy and sociology. Once the leading role of philosophy was ensured, the possibility of constructing one's own sociology remained an open issue, with the proviso that the autonomy of such a sociological system would be relative.

The scope of social interests of the Frankfurt school fairly coincided with the traditional subject matter of historical materialism, extended to cover empirical sociology and social psychology. But the problems of historical materialism, as interpreted by that school, came to be modified significantly. As P. Connerton wrote, "from the beginning there is a switch from the infrastructure to the superstructure. Then the critique of political economy is replaced by the critique of instrumental rationality. Next, the system of needs is re-interpreted through an assimilation of Freud. And finally Marx's philosophical anthropology is revised by drawing on the tradition of Hermeneutics."[40]

These modifications were due, first, to the reference to a definite tradition within Marxism itself (Lukács and the recently discovered writings of the young Marx) and, second, to the intense and many-sided search for non-Marxist sources of inspiration that would strengthen the original antipositivist stand of the school. Thus, the members of the school assimilated elements of the German humanities as developed at the turn of the nineteenth century, together with their characteristic stress on the essential difference between the sciences of culture and the natural sciences. Next, the loss of hope for the emancipation of man, owing to the mechanisms of economic development, resulted in increased attention for ideological and psychological problems. In this way a reinterpretation of Marx's views often proved to be a critique of his ideas. This tendency intensified over the course of time and was reflected both in the conceptions advanced by the school and in the phraseology used, in which the share of the traditional Marxist terms was dwindling. This, obviously, does not alter the fact that, under the specifically American conditions, some members of the Frankfurt school could pass for propagators of Marxism.

Especially characteristic of this tendency of moving away from Marxism was the shifting of the focus of attention from the socioeconomic analysis of the capitalist system to the analysis of its typical forms of consciousness, particularly so-called instrumental rationality, which reduces all social issues to problems of technical effectiveness. Representatives of critical theory, in fact, replaced the critique of society by that of its consciousness. Not only they did not consider that consciousness to be something epiphenomenal, but they ascribed to it outright the decisive role in maintaining the relations based on domination and coercion. Their vision of social development in the Western societies emphasized superseding the ideal of good life by an eagerness for maximum accumulation of goods and stepping up production at all costs. To make matters worse, instrumental rationality in those societies, at first confined to the field of technology, gradually conquered all spheres of life, including human relations and politics. The autonomy of the individual was thus threatened totally. Man was seen by another man merely as an instrument used in performing technical tasks. Advances in science and technology contributed to the enslavement of man, who can be manipulated by and subordinated to forces beyond his control. Thus, in the Frankfurt school the critique of capitalism changed into the critique of industrial civilization, and the individual was seen as imperiled by economic development, which in the opinion of the other Marxists was interpreted as a promise of a better future. The only hope was in a reform of consciousness, carried out against the objective conditions and without any guarantee of success.

Psychoanalysis was, after the critique of instrumental rationality, another important element in the conception advanced by the Frankfurt school.

Its members claimed that in order to explain human behavior, one has to take into account psychological elements, too, and not only ideological ones. A limitation of the Marxist theory consists, among other things, of belittling the role of psychological elements. Horkheimer wrote in the first issue of the *Zeitschrift für Sozialforschung:*

As long as theory has not recognised how structural changes in economic life are transformed, via the psychic constitution of the various social groups at a given moment in time, into changes in the expression of their life as a whole, then the theory of the dependence of the one on the other contains a dogmatic element which seriously restricts this theory's hypothetical value in the explanation of the present."[41]

These problems absorbed representatives of the Frankfurt school and especially Erich Fromm, who in his many works, of which *Escape from Freedom* (1941) was the most important, tried to adapt Freudian ideas to the needs of the antinaturalistic conception of society. There was no question of taking over the Freudian theory lock, stock, and barrel. Fromm was opposed to explanations both in terms of economics (characteristic of many Marxists) and in terms of psychology (characteristic of orthodox Freudians): "In contrast to these explanations, we have assumed that ideologies and culture in general are rooted in the social character; and the social character itself is moulded by the mode of existence of a given society; and in their turn the dominant character traits become productive forces shaping the social process."[42]

Fromm tried to bring into harmony two kinds of determinism—the Marxian and the Freudian—which in their original formulations contradicted one another. In his interpretation the social character, understood by Kardiner as "the nucleus of the character structure which is shared by most members of the same culture,"[43] is "the intermediary between the socio-economic structure and the ideas and ideals prevalent in a society. It is the intermediary in both directions, from the economic basis to the ideas and from ideas to economic basis."[44]

The adoption of this standpoint—intended to dismiss the simplified ways of interpreting the relation between the base and the superstructure—required a re-interpretation of both historical materialism and psychoanalysis. In the case of the former, Fromm tried to bring out, in the writings of Karl Marx, the problems of elementary human needs, independent of changing historical conditions; that is, he opposed an overly literal interpretation of the aphorism about man as "the totality of social relations." In the case of the latter, Fromm opposed the tendency toward a biological interpretation of human behavior by suggesting that "the instinct structure, namely the libidinal, the largely unconscious attitude of the group" be understood "in terms of its socioeconomic structure."[45] By introducing the concept of "total life experience" *(Lebensschicksal)*, Fromm turned psychoanalysis into an instrument of the study of the social man.

Psychoanalysis, as modified by Fromm and other representatives of the Frankfurt school, found application above all in the numerous interpretations of fascism. In these interpretations, emphasis was put jointly on definite mental traits of individuals, on their social conditionings, and on those traits of ideologies whereby they could satisfy the psychical needs shaped under given socioeconomic conditions. Fundamental in that field was a collective work edited by T. W. Adorno and Else Frenkel-Brunswick, *The Authoritarian Personality* (1950), about which L. Bramson wrote that it "represents a landmark in the attempt to correlate psychological characteristics and political predispositions."[46] Tentative descriptions of the social character that developed under bourgeois society were also significant contributions of representatives of the Frankfurt school, especially of Fromm and Marcuse. This school also gave rise to the humanistic Utopia that was propagated by those authors and was to play an important role in the radical movement in the late 1960s.

The impact of the Frankfurt school is still difficult to assess, for "if Critical Theory was a creation of the early thirties, it was also a discovery of the late sixties. In the invervening period the work of the Institute had become difficult to access."[47] In the United States, where the Institute of Social Research had to work for a large period of its existence, there was no good soil for the reception of critical theory as a whole: it was deeply rooted in the Hegelian and Marxian tradition, alien to the Americans and openly opposed to the main trends in American sociology. As a result, only the psychoanalytic ideas and those elements of social criticism in which one could find an analysis of mass culture met with comprehension by the Americans. In its home country the Frankfurt school could return to work only in the 1950s, when it had already dispersed as a school and had lost much of its original intellectual drive. It has, nevertheless, perceptibly influenced West German sociology, to which both Horkheimer and Adorno have contributed. But the greatest credit for that must be ascribed to Jürgen Habermas (1929-), their talented disciple, who seems to be one of the most prominent personalities in present-day sociology.[48]

MARXISM AND KARL MANNHEIM'S SOCIOLOGY OF KNOWLEDGE

The scholarly production of Karl Mannheim (1893-1947) also testifies to the popularity of Marxism in the 1920s, which reached far beyond the party ranks of communists and social democrats. Mannheim, an eminent sociologist and professor at Frankfurt University and later, as an émigré, at the London School of Economics, certainly cannot be called a Marxist, nor did he ever pretend to be one. Yet it is striking to see how much the key issues in his principal works, especially *Ideologie und Utopie* (1929) and *Man and Society in an Age of Reconstruction* (1935), were determined by Marxism. This applies primarily to his sociology of knowledge, which—to paraphrase Max Weber—is a positive criticism of the Marxian theory of ideologies, developed under the influence of *History and Class Consciousness* by G. Lukács, with whom Mannheim was on friendly terms in his youth.

Manneheim's views—like those of Lukács—were a result of a *sui generis* combination of the new German humanities (he had studied under Rickert and Simmel) and Marxism. In the latter, however, he looked only for theoretical inspirations, not for a political revelation. Mannheim was a programatically academic thinker, though he was aware that an entanglement in social antagonisms and ideologies is the essential element of sociological cognition. His contribution to the humanities is the idea that

knowledge is from the very beginning a co-operative process of group life, in which everyone unfolds his knowledge within the framework of a common fate, a common activity, and the overcoming of common difficulties (in which, however, each has a different share). Accordingly the products of the cognitive process are already, at least in part, differentiated because not every possible aspect of the world comes within the purview of the members of a group, but only those out of which difficulties and problems for the group arise. And even this common world (not shared by any outside groups in the same way) appears differently to the subordinate groups within the larger group. It appears differently because the subordinate groups and strata in a functionally differentiated society have a different experiential approach to the common contents of the objects of their world.[49]

Mannheim's point of departure was absolute historicism and its emphasis on the unity of cognitive, emotional, and volitional acts (an analysis of *Weltanschauung* instead of an analysis of scientific knowledge), resulting from the inevitable participation of the cognizing subject in the social reality about which he acquires his knowledge. At first, Mannheim reflected on the need and the possibility of formulating a new "dynamic" theory of cognition, but later he abandoned epistemological issues and focused his attention on the functioning of ideas in social life. He was, however, invariably interested in thinking as an expression and instrument of collective action and not as the province of pure ideas, isolated from human history. "Life" and even "History" seemed to him too indefinite to be the context of ideas, and the attractiveness of Marxism lay in its ability to make that context more concrete by taking into account the class division of society, the relations of domination and subordination, intergroup conflicts, and so on. This resembled Dilthey's *Weltanschauungslehre* combined with Marx's conception of ideology and consciousness (less essential in this regard is the

fact that Mannheim was interested not only in class determinants of thinking, even though he argued with the Marxists over this point). This combination gave rise to Mannheim's sociology of knowledge.

While noting the theoretical attainments of Marx (and Lukács, too),
Mannheim raised an essential objection to his conception. In Mannheim's
opinion the Marxian theory of ideology consisted not of explaining the
social conditionings of all social knowledge, but of unmasking definite
systems of knowledge as conscious or subconscious deformations of facts,
dictated by group interests. There are, he claimed, two essentially different
conceptions of ideologies: the particular and the total. According to the
former, the ideological nature of human thinking lies in the concealing or
deforming by some people of the truths that are equally accessible to all.
According to the latter, the very access to the truth is differentiated socially,
regardless of the good or bad intentions of the members of various groups.
The former conception tends to assign false consciousness only to one's
opponents, whereas the latter requires the assumption that one's own views
are somehow deformed, too. Mannheim ascribed the former interpretation
of ideologies to Marx and his followers; the latter, to himself. Obviously,
his polemic with the particular conception of ideologies must have resulted
in his questioning the Marxian thesis on the cognitively privileged position
of the proletariat. In Mannheim's opinion, "with the emergence of the
general formulation of the total conception of ideology, the simple theory
of ideology develops into the sociology of knowledge. What was once the
intellectual armament of a party is transformed into a method of research
in social and intellectual history generally."[50]

In his sociology of knowledge, Mannheim stood for the idea that social
facts are inevitably viewed from definite angles, determined by the position
of the cognizing subject in the social structure. This was very instructive for
the study of the history of social thought. A good example of the latter is
Mannheim's well-known study of conservatism, in which he analyzes the
specific style of thought of the aristocratic opponents of the bourgeois
revolution at the turn of the eighteenth century. *Ideologie und Utopie*, too,
is very inspiring for the historian of social thought. On the other hand, the
epistemological consequences of Mannheim's position give rise to grave
doubts. "Such a standpoint," Schaff wrote, "means relativism, and a
consistent application of that doctrine to the social sciences . . . must result
in the destruction of these disciplines. For if scientific truth depends on a
system of reference, this eliminates the possibility of arriving at an objective
truth that would be binding intersubjectively, and this annihilates scientific
cognition."[51]

Mannheim himself realized the dangers of relativism and tried to avoid
them, but with little success. Without going into the details of his analysis,
which were an interesting continuation of Weber's search for the guarantees

of objectivity, we shall only mention that Mannheim ultimately resorted to that which he criticized in Marx and Lukács: He introduced the concept of a group that is privileged in its cognitive possibilities. In his opinion, such a group consists of socially unattached intellectuals, who come from all strata of the population, but are linked to none of them and hold a supraclass position. Owing to their special situation within society, they are in a position to rise above the particular perspectives of the various groups and to produce social knowledge that has supragroup validity. Thus Mannheim failed to escape a particularism *sui generis*, that of an academic thinker.

MARXISM AND SOCIOLOGY: CONCLUDING REMARKS

The controversy over the interrelationships between historical materialism and sociology, which at certain periods aroused lively interest in Marxist circles, was a function of relationships between various interpretations of historical materialism and various orientations in sociology, which agreed or, much more often, disagreed with those interpretations. In fact, the controversy consisted of two other ones: what historical materialism should be like, and what sociology really is. As long as Marxists failed to speak out on these two issues, the controversy over the interrelationship between historical materialism and sociology transformed itself easily into a purely verbal dispute, dominated by mutual prejudices due to isolation, ignorance, and ideological conflicts. Such prejudices reached their peak in the 1930s through the 1950s, when the tendency toward theoretical self-sufficiency triumphed in Marxist circles, and bourgeois sociology came to be dominated by the empirical approach, which shunned the great problems that marked sociology in the nineteenth century and attracted the attention of historical materialism, even though the latter failed to cope with them. This merely strengthened the isolation, especially since the almost total lack of Marxist empirical studies precluded the possibility of discussing even purely technical issues. To make matters worse, in those countries in which the Marxist doctrine had prevailed, sociology as a discipline was banned.

This situation, which began to change in the late 1950s, was certainly not a result of any simple misunderstanding. Nor can it fully be explained by the natural dislike by monopolistic organizations of the pluralist conceptions of social life, which were characteristic of sociology and shaped under free ideological competition. The conflict between Marxism and sociology had begun much earlier and was due to the fact that Marxism was programmatically a party doctrine, whereas sociology cherished the ideal of a science free from valuations; Marxism strove to shape a revolutionary world view, whereas sociology aspired to the role of a specialized discipline; Marxism wanted to change the world, whereas sociology wanted above all to explain it. All this proved decisive: Marxism did not become a school of academic sociology, nor could it become one without losing its identity.

Of course, this does not bar (although it often did) dialogue and interaction between Marxism and the various schools of academic sociology. We have already witnessed the assimilation by Marxists of certain achievements of sociology and the assimilation by sociologists of certain elements of the Marxist theory.

NOTES

1. Lucien Goldmann, *Recherches dialectiques* (Paris: Gallimard, 1959), p. 289.
2. Cf. T. B. Bottomore, Introduction to Karl Marx, *Selected Writings in Sociology and Social Philosophy*, ed. T. B. Bottomore and M. Rubel; Tom Bottomore, *Marxist Sociology* (London: Macmillan, 1975).
3. Antonio Gramsci, "The Study of Philosophy and of Historical Materialism," in Gramsci, *The Modern Prince and Other Writings* (London: Lawrence and Wishart, 1957), pp. 69-70, 75.
4. Karl Korsch, *Marxism and Philosophy* (New York: Modern Reader, 1970), p. 62.
5. Herbert Marcuse, *Reason and Revolution: Hegel and the Rise of Social Theory*, 2d ed. (New York: Humanities Press, 1954), p. 400.
6. Cf. Peter Gay, *The Dilemma of Democratic Socialism: Eduard Bernstein's Challenge to Marx* (New York: Collier Books, 1962), p. 158.
7. See Lucio Colletti, *From Rousseau to Lenin* (London: NLB, 1976), p. 73.
8. Tadeusz Kowalik, "Filozofia spoleczna Ludwika Krzywickiego," in Barbara Skarga, ed., *Polska myśl filozoficzna i spoleczna* (Warsaw: KiW, 1975), 2:427.
9. Ibid., p. 426.
10. Ludwik Krzywicki, "Idea a zycie," in Krzywicki, *Wybór pism* (Warsaw: PWN, 1978), pp. 893-94.
11. Ludwik Krzywicki, "Rozwój spoleczny wśród zwierzat i u rodzaju ludzkiego", in ibid., p. 352.
12. Georg Lukács, *Lenin: A Study on the Unity of His Thought* (Cambridge, Mass.: MIT Press, 1971), p. 9.
13. S. Kozyr-Kowalski, "Lenin: socjolog nie odkryty w pelni" (O sposobach badania socjologii leninowskiej), *Studia socjologiczne* (1970): 73.
14. Perry Anderson, *Considerations on Western Marxism* (London: NLB, 1976), p. 9.
15. V. I. Lenin, "What the 'Friends of the People' Are and How They Fight against the Social-Democrats," in Lenin, *Selected Works in Two Volumes* (Moscow: Foreign Languages Publishing House, 1952), vol. 1, pp. 111-13, 132.
16. Ibid., pp. 132, 163.
17. V. I. Lenin, *Collected Works* [in Russian], 5th ed. (Moscow: Gospolitizdat, 1958), 1:444-45.
18. Cf. Leszek Kolakowski, *Glówne nurty marksizmu* (Paris: Instytut Literacki, 1977), 2:385.
19. Lenin, *Collected Works*, 1:436.
20. Ibid., p. 418.
21. Goldmann, *Recherches dialectiques,* p. 293.
22. G. Lukács, *History and Class Consciousness: Studies in Marxist Dialectics* (Cambridge, Mass.: MIT Press, 1972), p. 7.
23. Ibid., pp. 10-11.
24. Ibid., p. 27.
25. Ibid., pp. 50-51.
26. Ibid., p. 149.
27. Antonio Gramsci, "The Modern Prince," in Gramsci, *The Modern Prince and Other Writings*, p. 182.

28. Antonio Gramsci, "Critical Notes on an Attempt at a Popular Presentation of Marxism by Bukharin," in ibid., p. 101.

29. Ibid., p. 93.

30. Gramsci, "Modern Prince," p. 181.

31. Gramsci, "Critical Notes," p. 101.

32. Gramsci, "Modern Prince," p. 166.

33. Gramsci, "Critical Notes," p. 90.

34. Cf. B. A. Cagin, *Ocerk istorii socjologiceskoj mysli v SSSR, 1917-1969* (Leningrad: "Nauka," 1971).

35. Julian Hochfeld, *Studia o marksowskiej teorii spoleczeństwa* (Warsaw: PWN, 1963), pp. 63-64.

36. Cf. Phil Slater, *Origin and Significance of the Frankfurt School: A Marxist Perspective* (London: RKP, 1977), pp. xiii-xiv.

37. Neil McInnes, *The Western Marxists* (London: Alcove Press, 1972), p. 177.

38. See Slater, *Origin and Significance*, p. 51.

39. Cf. Susanne P. Schad, *Empirical Social Research in Weimar-Germany* (The Hague: Mouton, 1972), pp. 76-96.

40. Paul Connerton, ed., *Critical Sociology* (Harmondsworth: Penguin Books, 1976), p. 23.

41. See Slater, *Origin and Significance*, p. 94.

42. Erich Fromm, *The Fear of Freedom* (London: RKP, 1960), p. 252.

43. See Zbigniew Wieczorek, *Neopsychoanaliza i marksizm* (Warsaw: WP, 1973), p. 117.

44. Ibid., p. 118.

45. See Martin Birnbach, *Neo-Freudian Social Philosophy* (Stanford: Stanford University Press, 1961), p. 79.

46. Leon Bramson, *The Political Context of Sociology* (Princeton: Princeton University Press, 1961), p. 127.

47. Connerton, *Critical Sociology*, p. 12.

48. Cf. his *Theorie und Praxis* (1963), *Erkenntnis und Interesse* (1968), *Legitimationprobleme in Spätkapitalismus* (1973).

49. Karl Mannheim, *Ideology and Utopia: An Introduction to the Sociology of Knowledge* (London: RKP, 1954), p. 26.

50. Ibid., p. 69.

51. Adam Schaff, *Historia i prawda* (Warsaw: KiW, 1970), p. 151.

14

SOCIAL PRAGMATISM: DEWEY, COOLEY, THOMAS, AND MEAD

The antinaturalistic revolution did not affect American sociology. Max Weber came to be known in the United States as a methodologist and a sociologist about a quarter of century after his death (he had been noticed there much earlier as an economic historian). Some American sociologists had at an earlier time accommodated the ideas of Simmel, but these were interpreted one-sidedly, their philosophical aspect being unnoticed. Robert E. Park, who had initiated the orientation representing standard sociology in the United States throughout the period between the world wars and who was an American disciple of Windelbandt and Simmel, continued the ideas of Comte and Spencer rather than those of the German humanities. By the early twentieth century, American sociology was in full swing, which would ensure it the leading position in the world for some time and would result in sociology's being labeled an American science.

Of course, that vigorous expansion of American sociology was to a large extent conditioned by nonscientific factors: In the United States, for the first time in its history, sociology won a sound institutional basis and financial resources. But the prolific growth of American sociology would have been inconceivable if it had not been accompanied by an intellectual revolution that resulted in liberation from the various nineteenth-century doctrines and in something more than the adaptation of European ideas, to which the work of Sumner, Ward, Ross, and Small ultimately shrank. Those scholars had certainly paved the way for the advance in American sociology by popularizing the new discipline and adapting it to the local tradition, strongly tinged with individualism and voluntarism, but they were not the founders of that sociology. In its most original features it was a result (next to the so-called new history and new psychology) of the intellectual revolution in American life that was marked by pragmatism.

Certain features of that philosophy, which make it akin with positivism, make it difficult for a European observer to notice the depth and scope of the revolution. As compared with what was achieved in European thought by neo-Hegelianism, neo-Kantianism, Bergsonism, and other trends in the antipositivist revolution, the controversy between the pragmatists and nineteenth-century positivism may seem to be a family quarrel. But if we consider all the effects of this controversy, then it turns out that it should not be underestimated. The revolution had special importance to psychology, connected with pragmatist philosophy, and to the formation of the sociological orientation known today as symbolic interactionism and believed by many authors to have been the most original American contribution to social theory.

PRAGMATISM VERSUS SOCIAL THOUGHT

An analysis of pragmatism as such does not seem to be relevant here. It is necessary, however, to realize what were its main effects in social science, particularly in sociology, where the "idea of an open universe in which uncertainty, choice, hypotheses, novelties and possibilities are naturalized"[1] (Dewey's expression), associated with the name of William James (1842-1910), probably had the strongest response. By adopting that idea, pragmatism effected a total destruction of Spencerianism (which was exceptionally strong in early American sociology) and created the idea of man as the actor and not merely as an object subjected to the laws of nature and, at best, a watcher of processes that are independent of him. At the same time, however, pragmatism promised both the right to retain the standard of a science, which had been popularized by Spencerianism, and also the possibility of experimental science.

In American thought, the boundary between pragmatism and Spencerianism was one between epochs. As Hofstadter wrote,

Spencer's outlook had been the congenial expression of a period that looked to automatic progress and *laissez-faire* for its salvation; pragmatism was absorbed into the national culture when men were thinking of manipulation and control. Spencerianism had been the philosophy of inevitability; pragmatism became the philosophy of possibility. . . . The pragmatists' most vital contribution to the general background of social thought was to encourage a belief in the effectiveness of ideas and the possibility of novelties. . . . As Spencer had stood for determinism and the control of man by the environment, the pragmatists stood for freedom and the control of the environment by man.[2]

The conception of man as suggested by the pragmatists was of key importance. It did not leave any room either for the idea of man as a readymade product of nature (as did instinctivism) or for the idea of a *tabula rasa* that passively lends itself to the impact of the natural or social environment. Man becomes what he is through interaction with the environment, of which other active organisms are, of course, also parts. Acquiring the knowledge of the world is part of that process. The cognizing subject, as James wrote, "is not simply a mirror floating with no foothold anywhere and passively reflecting an order that he comes upon and finds simply existing. The knower is an actor, and coefficient of the truth on one side, whilst on the other he registers the truth which he helps to create."[3]

Pragmatism, especially in James's version, was an individualistic philosophy. It meant individualism in the sense of its adherents' rejecting the possibility of interpreting society as other than a collection of interacting individuals. But, except for such interaction, an individual was for them an abstraction, a metaphysical fiction whom they criticized in Spencer, Ward, and Kidd. "Society," John Dewey wrote,

is the process of associating in such ways that experiences, ideas, emotions, values are transmitted and made common. To this active process, both the individual and the institutionally organized may truly be said to be subordinate. The individual is subordinate because except in and through communication of experience from and to others, he remains dumb, merely sentient, a brute animal. . . . Organization . . . is also subordinate because it becomes static, rigid, institutionalized whenever it is not employed to facilitate and enrich the contacts of human beings with one another.[4]

It is the process of social interaction that turns its participants into human beings by transforming and restraining the biological instincts. Even if the pragmatists' attention is focused on the individual, that individual is *social* by definition.

Finally, from the point of view of its impact on social thought, an important feature of pragmatism must be seen in its programmatic antidualism, which abolishes the traditional opposition between soul and body, consciousness and life, thought and action, organism and environment, individual and society. The focal concept was that of *process*, which was to some extent due to both Darwinian and Hegelian tradition, the latter being particularly strong during the period when Dewey's views were being shaped.

THE PSYCHOLOGY OF WILLIAM JAMES AND ITS RELEVANCE TO SOCIOLOGY

The main ideas of social pragmatism are found in their nuclear form in *The Principles of Psychology* (1890) by William James, even though James himself was not very interested in the theory of society. If we may speak at all about the *social* psychology of the founder of pragmatism (the term *sociology* here would not make any sense whatsoever), than it is only, to use F. B. Karpf's formulation, in the sense of a "by-product of his discussion of such relevant topics as 'habit,' 'instinct,' the 'stream of thought' and, more specifically, the 'social self.'"⁵ James did not produce any sociological theory.

Nevertheless, owing to James, some sociologists came to realize that the individual, in Dewey's words, is "a blanket term for immense variety of specific reactions, habits, dispositions and powers of human nature that are evoked and confirmed under the influence of associated life"⁶ and not a label for a molecule that bears the same relation to other molecules as a physical body does to other physical bodies. James discovered, or at least supplied data for the discovery, that the study of social processes must at the same time be the study of the process of the emergence of the human individual, who acquires his basic properties only in the course of that interaction. That, in fact, was the novel element of James's individualism, because the earlier individualistic conceptions as a rule made given properties of the individual the condition and the starting point of interactions, and society was supposed to satisfy existing needs rather than to create them. Further, James provided concepts that proved of key significance for the study of that process: above all, the concept of *social self.*

The sociological aspects of James's psychology can most clearly be seen in his analysis of social self. In this analysis he assumed that there does not exist any substantial consciousness, but only an unbroken process in man of the formation of his sense of individual identity through interaction with other men. In the process of acquiring the knowledge of the world, man is both the cognizing subject (the Cartesian "pure ego," *I*) and the object of cognition (the "empirical ego," *me*). The empirical ego includes everything that an individual calls his and that can be a source of certain emotions (self-feeling) and an inspiration to certain actions (self-seeking and self-preservation); hence, it covers "not only his body and his psychic powers, but his clothes and his house, his wife and children, his ancestors and friends, his reputation and works, his land and horses, and yacht and bank-account."⁷ James further distinguishes "material self" (one's body, clothes, house, and family, the things that one has, especially those acquired as a result of one's work), "social self," and "spiritual self." When discussing social self, James made a penetrating analysis of the process by which the sense of individual identity emerges when a man imagines how he is assessed by others and what he is expected to do or achieve by those whose opinion he considers important. Since the individual usually is a member of many groups, there is the problem of the plurality of social selves, each of which is to some extent different from the others: To different men, one shows one's different aspects by playing, as it were, different roles. Thus, as Coser writes,

by dissolving the unitary Cartesian subject into a multiplicity of selves, all of which come into being through a variety of transactions with the outside world, and by stressing that these plural selves, no less than the external world, may be seen as objects, James laid the foundation for both Cooley and Mead's social psychology and . . . for much later sociological and social psychological role theory.[8]

DEWEY AS THE FOUNDER OF SOCIAL PRAGMATISM

John Dewey (1859-1952) played the decisive role in the rise of social pragmatism, although this role has not yet been fully examined.[9] To historians of philosophy, Dewey's social theory is of secondary importance; and to historians of sociology, Dewey is mostly a philosopher, a psychologist, and an educator. He contributed to advances in sociology and social psychology not only with his works concerned directly with those disciplines, but also with works on philosophy, ethics, education, and politics. He was a creative theorist in the field of sociology and social psychology, but—probably more important still—he was one of the principal contributors to that intellectual atmosphere in which other American theorists were active. His direct influence on Cooley, Thomas, and Mead—those authors who are usually considered to be the originators of symbolic interactionism—is still to be established. Dewey's social theory is to be sought not only in such works as *Human Nature and Conduct* (1922) and *The Public and Its Problems* (1927), but also in his works on education, such as *The School and Society* (1915) and *Democracy and Education* (1916); on philosophy, such as *Essays in Experimental Logic* (1916), *Experience and Nature* (1925), *The Quest for Certainty* (1929), and *Logic: The Theory of Inquiry* (1938); on psychology; and on public issues.

Unlike James's pragmatism, Dewey's instrumentalism was *par excellence* a social philosophy, and sociological elements are almost omnipresent in it.

Dewey was first active in psychology, his field being far from social psychology, and it was only his paper "The Need for Social Psychology" (1917) and his book *Human Nature and Conduct* (1922) that marked an essential change in that respect. The point, however, was that American social psychology probably would have followed the psychologistic course indicated by Ross and McDougall had it not been for the revolution in interpreting the foundations of psychology, achieved by Dewey together with Angell, Moore, Mead, and other pragmatists of the Chicago school. That revolution took the form of functionalism, which was originally called behaviorism and was first formulated in Dewey's well-known paper entitled "The Reflex Arc Concept in Psychology" (1897).

It will serve our purpo e to sum up that psychological orientation in three points. First, it recommended the study of the activity of the organism as an integrated process (for Dewey did not have any doubts about psychology's being concerned with activity and not with mental life that is dissociated from action). Breaking this process up into elements must inevitably result in a deformed description of human behavior. Second, it assumed that mental processes could not be satisfactorily explained as long as they are taken independently of the functioning of the organism as a whole and independently of the interaction between the organism and the environment, since all those processes take place under given circumstances. And third, it recommended the study of human experience and behavior from the point of view of the functions that the various responses of the organism perform in the process of its adaptation to and control of the environment.[10]

Dewey himself was not interested, at the outset, in the sociological implications of his standpoint in psychology. With the lapse of time, he concentrated on the interpretation of social life, but this was never an autonomous task for him and it remained subordinated to his quest for the scientific basis of a reform of ethics, education, and even society as a whole. Sociological investigations also played for him an ancillary role in solving philosophical problems, such as those of meaning, universals, language, and the like.

Evolution of Dewey's interest in psychology left untouched his basic conception of interaction between the organism and the environment; but the concepts of both organism and environment were given a precision that resulted in their being *socialized*. When speaking about the environment, Dewey used to emphasize that he meant the "natural and social environment," and he drew attention to the fact that the natural environment is not merely given to human beings, but is to some extent a result of their own activity, which is necessarily social in character.[11] On the other hand, the concept of a human nature that interacts with the environment also became socialized. For Dewey, it was not a biological concept, although he remained an opponent of those anthropological theories that contrast man with the rest of nature. Contrary to assumptions of individualistic psychology, no property that is an attribute of the human individual as such can explain the behavior of that individual in society, and it is only such a social individual who is accessible to our observation. The traditional dispute—whether the individual or society is "primary"—is absurd, but it is true that every indivudal is preceded by some society, some form of interaction between him and individuals or customs or institutions that are older than himself. The problem is to find out *how* these "systems of interaction" shape individuals and *how* individuals, in turn, transform these systems.[12]

Dewey's social psychology was thus set on finding the golden mean. The task was not to oppose man to nature, but to discover the specifically human way of living in the natural environment; to retain the nominalistic viewpoint of naturalistic psychology and sociology, but also to show the dominant influence of society on the individual; to bring out man's dependence on the natural and the social environment, but also to demonstrate that adaptation is two-sided; to show both man's determination by his external conditions and his freedom, his dependence on the past and his ability to shape the future. Dewey's point was to find a concept that would serve to mediate between determinism and voluntarism, between dependence on received customs and creativity, between biological impulses and abstract reason.

The concept of habit, which Dewey came to consider the "key to social psychology," served that purpose excellently. Dewey deliberately imposed a new meaning on the old term by stating that "we need a word to express that kind of human activity which is influenced by prior activity and in that sense acquired; which contains within itself a certain ordering or systematization of minor elements of action; which is projective, dynamic in quality, ready for overt manifestation, and which is operative in some subdued subordinated form even when not obviously dominating activity."[13]

This concept of habit had little in common with that employed by James. To the latter, habit was primarily a preserving force that enables society to exist by keeping everything in its own place: Social difference were interpreted by him as being not innate, but nevertheless stable. Dewey stressed not only that habit is learned, but also that it is plastic and subject to change and that it determines the general direction of behavior rather than its detailed forms. Dewey's concept of habit comes closest to that of attitude, which was introduced at the same time by other American authors.

The essential point seems to be that habit is a property not of the organism as such, but of the individual who interacts with others: "Some activity proceeds from a man; then it sets up reactions in the surroundings. . . . Conduct is always shared; this is the difference between it and a physiological processes."[14]

The environment for Dewey is not any rigid system of social relations or readymade norms to which the individual has to adjust his behavior. The environment is a naturally fluid situation to which the individual responds at first habitually; if he encounters obstacles, then he gradually modifies his behavior until he brings about a desirable change. An individual's behavior, whether habitual or not, always is a response to a situation and not to any single stimulus.

Since individual behavior is shaped in the process of interaction between that individual and other individuals who are component parts of successive situations, it cannot be explained without taking up the problem of human *communication*, by which human behavior can be shared. Everything points to the fact that Dewey was the first to draw attention to the sociological importance of that problem. Retaining its key significance in all of Dewey's works, the problem of communication came to be most completely exposed in *Democracy and Education* and *Experience and Nature*. In the former book Dewey wrote that

society not only continues to exist *by* transmission, *by* communication, but it may fairly be said to exist *in* transmission, *in* communication. There is more than a verbal tie between the words common, community, communication. Men live in a community in virtue of the things which they have in common; and communication is the way in which they come to possess things in common. What they must have in common in order to form a community or society are aims, beliefs, aspirations, knowledge—a common understanding—like-mindedness, as the sociologists say. Such things cannot be passed physically from one to another like bricks; they cannot be shared as persons would share a pie by dividing it into physical pieces.[15]

The vision of society as a community of thoughts and feelings is, of course, as old as social thought itself, and most sociologists, from Comte on, attached immense significance to it. Dewey's (and also Cooley's and Mead's) originality consisted of shifting the center of gravity from reflections on consensus as an attribute of society to reflections on the *process* of emergence of a community of thoughts and emotions through interaction by human individuals. Comte and Durkheim—and the later functionalists as well—were interested in the community as something given, whereas Dewey was interested in it as something emerging or being produced. It is not society that shapes individuals, but individuals shape themselves through interactions, owing to which society exists. One of the important consequences of that change in perspective was the adoption of a radically pluralistic idea of society. Individuals enter into manifold relations with one another, which accordingly produce a plurality of associations and not any homogeneous organization.

COOLEY'S SOCIAL PHILOSOPHY

Charles Horton Cooley (1864-1929) was professor of sociology at the University of Michigan at Ann Arbor. His sociological and psychological ideas, arrived at mainly on his own, reveal numerous affinities with those of Dewey and Mead. He occupies a special place in the history of American sociology by being probably the most eminent representative of what is called the second generation of American sociologists, which followed that of Ward and Sumner and preceded the third one, consisting of scholars oriented toward empirical studies.[16] Of course, that succession of generations is conceptual rather than historical, because, for example, Giddings, Cooley, and Park were practically coevals. The point is that Cooley, the author of *Human Nature and Social Order* (1902), *Social Organization* (1909), and *Social Process* (1918), started the process of overcoming the heritage of the great sociological systems born in the nineteenth century, but continued to be determined by the terminology and the subject matter characteristic of these systems. From that point of view, the concepts of evolution and organism, typical of the first generation of sociologists, played a specific role in his work. He gave them new meanings and used them to destroy the systems from which he had drawn them.

Like the representatives of the first generation, Cooley was an armchair scholar. He never conducted any research, nor did he follow carefully the empirical studies conducted in his lifetime by other sociologists. He was probably one of the few sociologists who did not aspire to make sociology scientific. On the contrary, he considered the separation of sociology from literature and philosophy to be a fatal error, and he wanted sociology to be a form of art.[17]

World Without Oppositions. The organic view of social life was the prime idea in Cooley's sociology and an element of a more comprehensive philosophical syndrome. The adoption of this philosophy was decisive for Cooley's critical attitude toward the heritage of nineteenth-century sociology and for his dismissal of many of the dilemmas that had haunted the founders of that discipline. Most problems were for him just ill posed. In social life, everything is an "aspect" or a "phase" of a more comprehensive, "organic" whole; hence we must say *and* rather than *or:* the individual and the group, man and society, egoism and altruism, freedom and necessity, conflict and cooperation, struggle and mutual aid, innovation and tradition, heredity and environment, imitation and creativity, spirit and matter, humanistic culture and technology, free will and determinism, science and art.

The organic view was thus leveled against all "particularism" or, to use Cooley's and Thomas's terminology, against the opinion that a single phase of a process can be interpreted as the cause of all other phases, the latter being considered only as results of the former. Whatever kind of particularism is represented by assent—biologism, psychologism, economism, and so on—it always results in a deformation of the image of a given process and, hence, of life as a whole. Every aspect of that whole plays an essential role, but no one role is more essential than any other. Thus, when speaking about organic relations, Cooley reverted to its romantic interpretation rather than continuing any sociological conceptions.

The organic view was in fact opposed to organicist sociology; likewise, Cooley's "evolutionary point of view" proved largely to be opposed to sociological evolutionism, as a result of the enthusiasm with which he stressed the specific nature of social life, which—because of evolution—becomes absolutely irreducible to organic life. Evolution was for him an infinite process of adaptation of the various phases of the evolving whole. When describing that process, Cooley did not formulate any laws, nor did he mark any stages, an activity that was a passion of the evolutionists. He also gave quite a different sense to the concept of prediction, which in his opinion could succeed as cosentient participation, and not as the knowledge of mechanisms that are independent of consciousness.

Individual and Society. These assumptions were applied by Cooley in his reflections on a traditional issue: the relations between individual and society. While he was critical of individualism, deeply rooted in the American mind, he was equally firmly opposed to collectivism and sociological realism. Like Dewey, Thomas, and Mead, he found the problem not to be admitting the absolute primacy of the individual or of society, but examining how the individual exists in the group and how the group exists in the individual.

In agreement with his holistic *Weltanschauung*, Cooley assumed that "a separate individual is an abstraction unknown to experience, and so likewise is society when regarded as something apart from individuals. The real thing is Human Life, which may be considered either in an individual aspect or in a social, that is to say a general, aspect."[18]

Yet it was not this formulation, repeated by Cooley in many versions, that was decisive for his role in the history of sociology, even though it certainly concluded the epoch of extreme atomistic individualism, which survived the longest in the United States. It seems more important that he initiated a new epoch, marked—not only in American thought—by the question of what that interaction, or interpenetration, is like.

Cooley paid most attention to the refutation of instinctivism. While he was far from denying the role of heredity, he claimed—anticipating Dewey's conception of habits—that "the distinctively human heredity is not an inborn tendency to do definite things, but an inborn aptitude to learn to do whatever things the situation may call for."[19]

The only way of learning is communicating with other human beings. The concept of communication—introduced by Cooley in his youthful work, *The Theory of Transportation*—seems to be the most important idea in his sociological system. By communication he meant "the mechanism through which human relations exist and develop—all the symbols of mind, together with the means of conveying them through space and preserving them in time. It includes the expression of the face, attitude and gesture, the tones of voice, words, writing, printing, railways, telegraphs, telephones, and whatever else may be the latest achievement in the conquest of space and time."[20]

Development of Personality. Personality develops through a child's communication with his mother, the other members of his family, his coevals, and other members of the local community. As he grows older, the individual broadens his contacts, participates in various groups, and, owing to the printed word, establishes contacts with the whole world. The means of communication are extremely different, but the mechanism of the shaping of human personality is fairly homogeneous. Its basic element is the phenomenon that Cooley termed *looking-glass self.* Man comes to have his own ego by imagining how he is seen by others.

Focusing attention on this phenomenon made Cooley inclined to see social interaction, above all, as the play of imagination and to dematerialize society completely, which alarmed Mead, among others.[21] "The immediate social reality" consisted for Cooley of mental facts alone. "Our real environment," he wrote, "consists of those images which are most present to our thoughts."[22] Only that which is imagined is socially real. Society is immediately given to us as *a relation among personal ideas.*"[23] Hence arose Cooley's belief that introspection plays a great role in sociology and that "a true sociology is systematic biography."[24]

Cooley's "solipsism" (as Mead called it) was certainly a feature of his system alone, but some of its elements came to be continued in works by Thomas and Znaniecki.

Primary Groups and the Development of Forms of Socialization. Mental differences between human beings can be explained not by biological heredity, but by differences in systems of communication within which people live. The same explanation applies to those mental similarities that are traditionally referred to as human nature.

Cooley did not elaborate any detailed classification or typologies of such systems (although he marginally referred to "social types"), nor did he define any stages of their evolution. This is why we have to be very cautious when comparing his ideas with the numerous typologies of societies worked out by other sociologists. Cooley's conception consists of two elements, of which only the second—in fact, the less essential of the two—is comparable to the conceptions of Tönnies and Durkheim. The first element is the concept of primary groups, which is an endeavor to solve the age-old problem of human nature. The other element, loosely connected with the former, is the conception of changes in the forms of socialization. The former is Cooley's original contribution; the latter, one of the countless variations on the same theme.

By stating that certain human ideals—faithfulness, loyalty, brotherhood, charity, and the like—are universal and, at the same time, by rejecting the possibility of any extrasocial explanation of this fact, Cooley had to point to forms of communication that would be as universal as those ideals are. This seems to explain the origin of the concept of primary group. The term itself was drawn from *An Introduction to the Study of Society* by Small and Vincent (1894). The idea had earlier emerged in the numerous American publications on social problems, which had been alerted by a crisis in family and neighborhood relations in that industrializing and urbanizing country.[25] The primary groups in which the individual participates in everyday life— that is, the family, the play group of children, the neighborhood or community group—were considered by Cooley to be "the nursery of human nature" and the main centers of socialization of individuals: "By primary group I mean those characterized by intimate face-to-face association and co-operation. They are primary in several senses, but chiefly in that they are fundamental in forming the social nature and ideals of the individual.''[26]

Cooley wrote only a few pages on primary groups, but they were pages of exceptional impact on sociology. They contributed, more than the studies by Le Play and Simmel, to the introduction into sociology of the problems of small groups, which had previously been almost the exclusive hunting ground of philanthropists and social reformers.

By engaging in a sociological explanation of universal human nature, Cooley was also interested in changes as a result of which the influence of primary groups on the individual ceases to be as overwhelming as it used to be, and so other kinds of associations emerge, too.[27] In Cooley's description of those changes we can find traces of certain ideas of Spencer (from militarism to industrialism) and Maine (from status to contract). But Quandt is right in claiming that the image outlined by Cooley was closely connected with the realities of American life.[28]

The main feature of the evolution observed by Cooley was that human relations were becoming depersonalized while at the same time, owing to advances in communication techniques, they were expanding and multiplying. Depersonalization meant that the individual did not participate in most groups as a full person, but entered into them "with a trained and specialized part of himself"[29]—with a "role," as Park would say later. The more developed the society, the lesser the role played in an individual's life by exclusive and integral participation in any single social group. The individual thus can be seen as "the point of intersection of an indefinite number of circles representing social groups."[30] Cooley was confident that in these new conditions it would be possible to reconstruct, over the course of time, the system of the values prevailing in the primary group—that "Utopia of society" (as he called the family).

Social Organization. Cooley's social psychology is undoubtedly his most important contribution, but his conception of social institutions should not be neglected.

The author of *Social Organization* thought that impersonal phenomena play a very significant part in social life, especially in modern societies, and that "many forms of life . . . cannot be understood, can hardly be seen at all, by one who will interest himself only in persons. They exist in the human mind, but to perceive them you must study this from an impersonal standpoint."[31] Such phenomena—for example, language, myths, tradition, ideologies, public opinion, institutions—have their own respective life histories. However, they do not form any ontologically distinct reality, because they are secondary aspects of the same whole of which relations among persons are primary aspects. Social organization was all objectifying (or interpersonalizing) of human ideas, ideals, and aspirations, which results in their consolidation beyond the limits of individual life and their interconnection as an impersonal system that is able to evolve further without any participation by its founders.

The basic concepts used by him in the analysis of that set of facts were public opinion ("a co-operative activity of many minds"), institution ("a definite and established phase" of such opinion—the church, law, custom, educational system), class (a group with a specific function within society, which usually has an analogue in a specific state of public opinion and a distinct system of pattern and traditions), and, of course, communication, on which the type and scope of a given organization always depends.

Without elaborating on those issues, let us pay some attention to the problem of social classes, as Cooley's discussion of them sheds more light on the problem of social change. Classes are the fundamental elements of the structure of all societies except the most primitive ones, namely, those in which the division of labor has not yet emerged. He called a class "any persistent social group, other than the family, existing within a larger group."[32] All societies are differentiated in one way or another, and their differentiation increases; hence, their division into classes is both inevitable and functional. The point is that classes can be either open classes or castes. In the former case, they are formed as a result of the individual usefulness of members of society in specified functions; in the latter, as a result of inheritance of social position. An open class develops its own specific consciousness, but is not opposed to other classes, with which it shares some of its ideals. A caste develops a consciousness that is not only specific to it, but actually totally distinct from those of other classes: Specialization in this case means separation. The difference is due partly to the fact that an individual can simultaneously be a member of many different classes, but of only one caste. The main factors determining whether a class is open or closed are the composition of the population, the pace of social change, and the state of communication and education, whose improvement transforms castes into open classes.

Following the intensification of the communication processes, stratification gradually changes from caste-based into open-class-based: It is not the status acquired by birth, but the function performed, with the various rewards attached to it, that becomes decisive. Thus, class struggle gradually becomes a controversy in which there are common rules of the game.

Cooley's introduction of the problem of the state as an organ of public opinion and as the arbiter in controversies between classes marked a peculiarity of his sociology against the background of the American tradition. Yet he complied with the American political tradition and his own organic philosophy in not opposing the state to society and in seeing in the development of the state an aspect of the expansion of public opinion, the other aspects being the development of voluntary associations, trade unions, corporations, clubs, phratries, and the like.

Cooley's Method. Cooley was not particularly concerned with methodological issues, due to his fear of methodological dogmatism and his tendency to associate methodology with the establishment of strict rules, which can have no application in the humanities.

The basic assumptions of Cooley's method were the result of his views of the social process. If that process is an organic unity, then it is not legitimate to split it into parts, even for research purposes. The surest way of acquiring knowledge of the whole is to grasp it as such. That whole is mainly the consciousness, and if its "phases" are the ideas that individuals have, which are given to us as the immediate reality, then we must strive above all for *understanding* those individuals. This can be achieved only by imagination and sympathetic introspection—that is, from inside, and not from outside, the social process. The social sciences are exceptional, because those who engage in social studies "are a conscious part of the process. We can know it by sympathetic participation, in a manner impossible in the study of plant or animal life. . . . This involves unique methods which must be worked out independently. The sooner we cease circumscribing and testing ourselves by the canons of physical and physiological science the better."[33]

It is evident that such statements were leveled against the naturalistic tradition. Of much greater interest is Cooley's attitude toward the "third generation," in which methodological dogmatism was much less frequent and (if we disregard Watson) much less aggressive. Cooley seemingly was cooperative when it came to the new trends in psychology and sociology and in the 1920s even called himself a behaviorist (as Thomas and Mead did). But his behaviorism was to be *social,* because "records of behavior without introspective interpretation are like a library of books in a strange language."[34] For the same reason, Cooley criticized the first symptoms of fascination with statistical methods, for he thought that they could play only an auxiliary role, as was the case in Durkheim's study, *La Suicide:* "On its affirmative side the quantitative ideal—Measure everything you can—is admirable; on its negative side—Deal with nothing you cannot measure—I believe it to be obstructive."[35] It seems that the monographs by the Chicago school were the maximum that he could accept in the new sociology; only these monographs complied with his principles of case study, the aim of which was to grasp the whole of the social process.

Cooley did not leave any disciples, because the type of sociology that he represented could hardly be taught; above all, it requires imagination, sensitivity, and intuition. Cooley's influence on American sociology was mainly indirect: dismissing a number of traditional problems and posing new ones (those concerning small groups and the process of socialization). Cooley contributed to American sociological imagination, but not to research methods and techniques.

THE SOCIOLOGY OF W. I. THOMAS

William Isaac Thomas (1863-1947) was Cooley's coeval, and it was nearly at the same time that he decided to specialize in sociology. However, in the development of that discipline in the United States, he represented another stage by being not an armchair thinker, but a researcher. Social psychology was for him "a research technique" and not merely "a point of view and basis of criticism of traditional social and psychological thought."[36] He did not attach much importance to expounding his theoretical standpoint. Yet in his writings we can note certain permanent guiding ideas that allow us to speak about his theoretical orientation, not just about loosely connected ideas of an exceptionally bright empirical researcher.

The Discovery of Social Psychology. Thomas began with psychologism that referred to *Völkerpsychologie* and was used in the study of primitive societies; he rather quickly came to the conclusion that human behavior must be explained in terms of history and social life, rather than in terms of biology. While he never became a radical anti-instinctivist, he followed the tracks of Cooley, Dewey, and Mead and postulated, as early as 1904, that social psychology was the discipline that would investigate individual mental processes only insofar as they were conditioned by society and social processes only insofar as they were conditioned by states of consciousness. The characteristic of that new field of study, as he saw it, was its close connection with history, social anthropology, and sociology. It was to be not a new discipline, but a new approach to the problem in which these three disciplines were interested. This approach was first applied in his *Source Book for Social Origins* (1907). While *Source Book* was of no consequence whatever in the history of anthropology, its importance lay in its including a theory of human behavior that could he applied in the analysis of all social change.

This theory contained in embryo all the leading ideas of Thomas's sociology, in particular the beliefs that (1) social change is the most important problem; (2) social change takes places through crises that disturb the operation of habits and force people to seek new forms of adaptation; and (3) explanation of a change requires simultaneous consideration of objective conditions and conscious human actions, the social and the individual aspects of the process, or—to use the terminology that would develop later —values and attitudes, culture and personality.

Thomas's sociological ideas were shaped, however, not by the study of primitive societies, but by that of modern ones, on which he focused his research for the next twenty-five years. He was convinced that he lived in a world so new that one could not learn much about it by studying the past. It was only toward the close of his life that he reverted to social anthropology, when preparing his *Primitive Behavior* (1937). His turn toward his own times meant a change in the subject of research, but not in the viewpoint. Thomas began his investigation of modern society, concentrating at first on immigration problems, about 1908, when he obtained financial means for his work. Having gained a new type of data and new research experience, he broadened the set of his theoretical concepts and also engaged in a more detailed examination of the data that offer insight into the subjective aspect of social processes. In 1912 he first formulated the recommendation that private letters, diaries, court and church records, sermons, and school curricula should be used as data, which, as it were, announced the opus about Polish peasants that he was to write jointly with Florian Znaniecki.[37]

The Study of Polish Emigrants. The Polish Peasant in Europe and America (1918-1920) marked a turning point in sociology primarily by being a combination of social theory and empirical studies. While it was novelty in each of these two domains, it did not mark the beginning of either, for in the United States there had been a tradition of both armchair sociology (of which Cooley was the last eminent representative) and social surveys. Yet, construction of theories and empirical studies had so far been two separate activities, largely independent of each other. Thomas and Znaniecki combined them into a single whole and, in their *Methodological Note*, formulated the manifesto of the new social science, which questioned the inveterate habits in thinking about social problems. They criticized the common-sense sociology that pretended to offer reliable knowledge without any methodical studies; the restriction of research to fragmentary observations made with a view to an immediate practical goal; the examination of social facts outside the integrating context of social life; and, finally, the belief that people always respond in the same manner to the same environmental stimuli, regardless of the differences in their respective experience.

In their positive program Thomas and Znaniecki maintained that the social science should (1) be based on methodically conducted research; (2) be guided by a specified conception of the social process as a whole; (3) investigate all facts as connected with other facts, with culture as a whole; and (4) adopt the assumption that both the influence of external conditions on individuals and that of individuals on external conditions require examination, since there is certainly no simple relationship, but a complex process of interaction. But first of all, Thomas and Znaniecki formulated the requirement that sociology be turned into a science that offers causal explanations of social facts and discovers "laws of social becoming,"[38] for only such a sociology can be an effective instrument of control over the social process.

This ambitious program was put into effect only in part. *The Polish Peasant* was an enormous stride forward: It was based on a comprehensive and methodically designed corpus of sources. In its study Thomas and Znaniecki used a set of theoretical hypotheses that will be discussed briefly below.

The most doubtful point is the degree to which they succeeded in making the social science a discipline that provides causal explanations and discovers laws. It is characteristic enough that Thomas would soon abandon that requirement, although neither he nor Znaniecki would drop the idea of sociology as an inductive science bearing certain analogies to natural science.

If we disregard their novel approach to the choice of sources, their most durable achievements seems to have been their grasp of the interaction of objective and subjective factors, culture and personality, social values and individual attitudes. That interaction is the focal issue throughout *The Polish Peasant,* especially when the authors analyze the traditional social organization in the Polish rural areas, organization based on primary groups, and when they discuss social disorganization and reorganization in Poland and America and, *a fortiori*, the formation of the social personality of the emigrants. To do so, they used a set of theoretical concepts that must be discussed separately, because it was the starting point for further research to be undertaken, single-handedly, by each author. We must take into consideration the concepts of attitude and value, social personality, and organization, disorganization, and reorganization, which together provide an interpretation of the process of social change. In commenting on them, we shall refer to Thomas's other works, especially *The Unadjusted Girl* (1923).

Attitudes and Values. The conception of attitudes and values would help to solve the traditional problem of the interrelationship between the individual and the social group. Values are "the objective cultural elements of social life," while attitudes are "the subjective characteristics of the members of the social group."[39]

The Polish Peasant does not contain precise definitions of these two key concepts. In both cases we are dealing with comprehensive terms that cover the vast sphere of problems of culture and personality. When Thomas and Znaniecki spoke about attitudes, they intended not to explain their nature and their place in psychical life, but rather to point to an aspect of social life that had been underestimated by those orientations in sociology which studied objective processes separately from their correlates in human consciousness. Thomas's and Znaniecki's theory was not so much a theory of attitudes as one of the social process. The important point was not to explain what an attitude is, but to stress that the social process always includes a psychological variable that modifies the effect of the objective factors. Social processes have as their participants human beings, who in one way or another respond to environmental stimuli. *Attitude* is a blanket term covering all of the elements of their psychical life that affect the type, direction, and intensity of those responses. The theoretical schema will not change if we stress those of other elements of psychical life and define attitude in one way or another. No element of psychical life is an attitude by itself, but it becomes such by being oriented toward a social value.

The same applies to the problem of value, as discussed in *The Polish Peasant.* In it one should not seek an expanded theory of culture or even the philosophy of value earlier formulated by Znaniecki. We find there merely a theory of social process based on the assumption that this process cannot be explained by reference to the characteristics of individuals only, because it always includes a sociological variable called social values. The interpretation of those values remains an open issue. Thomas and Znaniecki were mainly interested in distinguishing the two fundamental variables inherent in the social process and in formulating general assumptions concerning their interrelationship.

The first assumption was that this relationship is one of cause and effect. The other defined the relation between cause and effect in the social process in greater detail: "The cause of a social or individual phenomenon is never another social or individual phenomenon alone, but always a combination of a social and an individual phenomenon. Or, in more exact terms: a cause of a value or of an attitude is never an attitude or a value alone, but always a combination of an attitude and a value."[40] These two assumptions were formulated in a very general manner, and the second had an underlying polemic intention. It was leveled, on the one hand, against all forms of sociological determinism (in the version quoted above it seems to be leveled directly against *The Rules of Sociological Method* by Durkheim, according to whom a social phenomenon can have its cause only in another social phenomenon) and, on the other, against all forms of psychologism, which deduced social facts from human individuals taken in isolation. In the domain of practical activity, adopting this assumption meant abrogating the age-old question: Are we to change conditions *or* human beings?

The greatest weakness of the positive program contained in *The Polish Peasant* lay in the fact that at the very outset they excluded the possibility of isolating the two variables between which the sociologist must determine causal relationships. A value does not exist without attitudes, for it is attitudes that impart to a thing the meaning that turns it into a value, and a value can be defined only by reference to attitudes.[41] This being so, we are concerned not with two orders of facts, but with two aspects of a single whole. Those aspects can be isolated analytically, but any possibility of discovering laws that govern the relationships between them seems dubious.

This leaves merely a very general recommendation for which explanations are to be avoided and which part of social reality one should examine to find the appropriate explanations. In other words, the worth of the conceptions of attitudes and values, as formulated in *The Polish Peasant*, lay not so much in their being a valid theory of "social becoming" as in their paving the way for the study of important problems, that had been neglected by all sociological orientations before that time. The work of Thomas and Znaniecki protested against the limitations imposed by both sociologism and psychologism.

Development of Social Personality. The study of attitudes makes one face the problem of social personality, which is their configuration, and the study of values leads to the problem of social organization. "The human personality," Thomas and Znaniecki wrote, "is both a continually producing factor and a continually produced result of social evolution. . . . When viewed as a factor of social evolution the human personality is a ground of a causal explanation of social happenings; when viewed as a product of social evolution it is causally explicable by social happenings."[42]

But how are we to pass from facts given in autobiographical data to "nomothetic generalizations"? For that purpose "a theory of human individuals as social personalities" is necessary.[43] Such a theory is arrived at when numerous biographies are studied comparatively. Each of them is something unique and unrepeatable, but biographies of many individuals reveal tangible similarities that make it possible to determine specified personality types. They reduce to the three basic types: the philistine, the bohemian, and the creative man. In the first, all aspirations of the individual are dominated by the desire for security; in the second, by the desire for new experience. In the third, there is relative balance between the desire for new experience and the striving for the necessary minimum of stability.

The three basic types of personality differ in the chances of the occurrence of new attitudes: They are very high for the bohemians, very slight for the philistines, and somewhere in the middle of the scale for the creative men.

Personality types are not to be understood as ready-made structures that determine individual behavior. In *The Polish Peasant* we read: "the fundamental problems of the synthesis of human personalities are not problems of personal *status*, but problems of personal *becoming* . . . the ultimate question is not what temperaments and characters there are but what are the ways in which a definite character is developed out of a definite temperament."[44] Thomas, like Mead, was interested in personality not in a definitively shaped structure, but in a process that never terminates.

The development of personality has a definite biological substratum, to which Thomas ascribed a varying importance (decreasing, on the whole). He was, however, mainly interested in how the working of biologically determined dispositions and impulses is restrained and modified in human society. Some of his formulations resemble Durkheim's opinions on the suppression of biological impulses under the impact of life in a group. But the difference is strongly marked: Thomas, like Mead, does not point to the process by which the individual is forced to behave in a manner sanctioned by the group. Rather, he stresses the process of the more or less conscious adjustment by the individual to the requirements of his social environment.

Socialization consists above all of the individual's developing his ability to conscious adaptation to existing conditions. The process, accordingly, results in the individual's realization in the schemata of situations, which enable him to behave in accordance with the rules adopted in a given society, rather than by the development of habits (as understood by Dewey). Consciousness plays in immense role in this process: The individual interprets situations and finds the appropriate solutions.

This largely conscious nature of the individual's socialization, which continues throughout his lifetime, requires special methods of study, because the behaviorist methods of investigating habits prove useless. Human behavior "must be interpreted in terms of intentions, desires, emotions, etc. . . . We cannot neglect the meanings, the suggestions which objects have for the conscious individual, because it is these meanings which determine the individual's behavior."[45] The methods of behaviorist observation fail also because the individual is not only an organism that responds to the stimuli coming from the environment, but also an agent who works upon that environment.

Social Organization. While most attitudes are expressed only in individual actions, some of them become objectified and find an indirect expression in "more or less explicit and formal *rules* of behavior by which the group tends to maintain, to regulate, and to make more general and frequent the corresponding type of actions among its members."[46] Such rules—customs and rites, moral and legal norms, and the like—can be considered manifestations of attitudes of these individuals who observe them, and nothing more. But such a radically nominalistic viewpoint does not suffice, as it merely takes into account the origin of such rules and disregards the influence that they exert on human beings. Those rules are not only manifestations of attitudes, but also a factor that affects formation of attitudes. Social rules form internally interconnected systems called institutions, the totality of which constitutes the social organization of a given group. This is the other pole of interactions between the individual and society, with which sociology is concerned, unlike social psychology, which is concerned with the study of attitudes.

It must be emphasized that for Thomas sociology is the science of social values and, hence, is not concerned with all that which was described as social facts by Marx, Spencer, Durkheim, and other authors. Sociology is interested exclusively in the aspects of social facts that at a given moment and in a given group acquire importance because of human attitudes referring to them. Other aspects of social reality are the subject matter of other disciplines. What sociologists are concerned with is only that reality which exists for men (that is, which is assumed by them to exist). "If men define situations as real, they are real in their consequences," Thomas will write later.[47]

As in the case of personality, Thomas was interested in social organization not from the point of view of structure, but from that of process. For Thomas and Znaniecki, sociological theory was not so much a theory of social organization as one of social change. In their *Methodological Note* the interest in change became a mark of a scientific orientation: "A method which permits us to determine only cases of stereotyped activity and leaves us helpless in face of changed conditions is not a scientific method at all, and becomes even less and less practically useful with the continual increase of fluidity in modern social life."[48]

Thomas was most interested in the mechanism of change, not in its direction. The main question was how it is that the dominant system of norms is destroyed and a new one is born; that is, how do *disorganization* and *reorganization* take place? Social disorganization was defined by Thomas and Znaniecki as "decrease of the influence of existing social rules of behavior upon individual members of the group."[49] A certain degree of disorganization is, of course, to be found in all societies. Thomas rejected the fiction of primitive society and peasant community in which there would be perfect agreement between individual behavior and group norms. Every social group has at its disposal the means of opposing disorganization; but under certain conditions such means prove ineffective, and disorganization begins to threaten the very existence of the group.

Such conditions are created predominantly by the emergence on a mass scale of new attitudes, which the group is no longer in a position to control and which are incompatible with the rules binding until then. The emergence of the new attitudes is, in turn, linked to an increasing number of contacts with the outside world. Counteracting the disorganization of the group by suppressing the new attitudes can be effective only as long as such contacts are relatively restricted. When a certain limit is passed, preserving the former social organization in its unchanged form becomes impossible. "The problem is . . . no longer how to suppress the new attitudes, but how to find for them institutional expression, how to utilize them for socially productive purposes."[50]

That new problem is one of social reorganization—namely, how "to create new schemes of behavior . . . which will supplant or modify the old schemes and correspond better to the changed attitudes."[51] Unlike disorganization, and also unlike protection of the old organization through suppression of the new attitudes, reorganization is not and cannot be a spontaneous process.

This schema of social change was a schema of change in institutions only. Thomas and Znaniecki claimed that there is no strict correspondence between that change and change in human personalities, for instance. That fact, by the way, makes a later reorganization possible. This point seems to mark the difference between the conception of Thomas and Znaniecki and Durkheim's conception of anomie, which it resembles in many respects. The difference is due primarily to the fact that for the authors of *The Polish Peasant* the individual is a sovereign subject who makes a *sui generis* selection of the stimuli received from society. This is, of course, not to say that the two series of phenomena—social disorganization and demoralization of individuals—are totally independent of one another.

Situational Analysis. Thomas's role in sociology is usually associated with *The Polish Peasant*, yet Volkart is right when he calls situational analysis, fully developed by Thomas only in the 1920s, the core of Thomas' social theory. The concept of situation, one of the many points on which Thomas's theory bordered on pragmatism, can be found in his works very early, even though the term itself was introduced only in *The Polish Peasant*. In the *Methodological Note* there is the formulation that all concrete activity means finding a way out of a situation. The term occurs in many places in *The Polish Peasant* and in *The Unadjusted Girl*, as "definition of the situation" is often used instead of "schemes of behavior," "rules of behavior," and so forth. To Thomas its value lay in its enabling him to stress that he meant agents who consciously choose their behavior and do not just succumb to binding rules. In Thomas's successive works the role of the concept of situation, which was accompanied by its other modifications, became more and more important. They consisted of (1) discarding the requirement that relationships between causes and effects be discovered and replacing the *why* by the *how*; and (2) ridding oneself of all relics of instinctivism, namely, the concepts of inborn wishes and temperaments, which were assumed in his earlier works.

In his later years Thomas was influenced by behaviorists (Pavlov, Watson, and Thorndike), from whom he adopted the requirement of the experimental method. This yielding to the behaviorist school, was, however, more apparent than real, for Thomas did not abandon his humanistic approach. He merely tried to save social behaviorism as he considered classical behaviorism to be a nonsociological conception, which disregarded "reactions of the individual to other persons or groups of persons." Accordingly, he wanted to introduce into an experimental situation not a responding organism, but a conscious subject, for whom "the most important content of situations is the attitudes and values of other persons with which his own come into conflict and co-operation."[52] Hence, the reactions of the individual to others cease to be reactions to what they do or say and become reactions to whatever significance the individual ascribes to their actions and words.

Thomas's situational analysis was, thus, an endeavor to bridge the gap between the experimental method, as developed by the behaviorists, and social psychology as reflected in *The Polish Peasant* and *The Unadjusted Girl*. It was to combine the precision of laboratory experiments with the consideration of the peculiarities of the human world, which never ceased to be a world of meanings for Thomas. Obviously, putting these two things together could only be apparent, especially as Thomas interpreted *situation* very broadly, making that term cover phenomena that escape all control.

This opinion is corroborated by the text of *Primitive Behavior: An Introduction to the Social Sciences* (1937), a new version of *Source Book for Social Origins*, written thirty years earlier. Various chapters reveal reflections of new items on Thomas's reading list on psychology, but the most important change is in his consideration of new anthropological studies and interpretation of culture in terms of the definition of situation.

MEAD'S SOCIAL PSYCHOLOGY

George Herbert Mead (1863-1931) was—unlike Cooley and Thomas— directly connected with the pragmatist trend in philosophy; and even though he lectured in Chicago on social psychology for nearly forty years, he considered himself to be primarily a philosopher. His starting point was philosophical issues: How is it that in the course of evolution men developed specifically human traits, such as abstract thinking, self-knowledge, and morality? He assumed, like Dewey, that these traits could have developed only through language and social interaction. Therefore, solution of philosophical problems required research in the field of the social sciences, and these could find the answer only if thoroughly reformed. In this way Mead started his career as sociologist, as a result of which, many years after his death, he came to be one of those authors who are frequently quoted by (mainly American) sociologists and much less often mentioned by philosophers and historians of philosophy.

One of the peculiarities of his career was that it began very late. While Mead was coeval with Cooley and Thomas, his influence began when those two were passing into oblivion. This was partly due to the fact that Mead did not publish a single book during his lifetime, and his works, in the form in which they are accessible today, are largely reconstructions of his university lectures. This is not to say that he did not exert any influence earlier, but his influence had been confined to philosophical pragmatists and graduates from the University of Chicago (his later ardent adherents mostly belonged

to the latter group). It was Herbert Blumer (1900-   ) who turned the author
of *Mind, Self and Society* into a *sui generis* classic of contemporary sociology; he did so by revealing the sociological implications of Mead's philosophy and by formulating the postulates and the name of the orientation
(symbolic interactionism) that is the present-day continuation of Mead's
ideas. After World War II the symbolic interactionists became, next to the
functionalists, the largest school in American sociology, and Mead's writings
came to be known outside the United States—in France, Germany, and
Poland.

The Idea of Social Behaviorism. The term *social behaviorism*, used
already by Thomas and Cooley, was much more precisely defined in Mead's
system of social philosophy. It was for that reason that he criticized Cooley
for solipsism—focusing attention on what takes place in the individual's
mind. He also rejected introspection as a method to be used in the science
of man. These differences of approach were due mainly to the fact that
Cooley assumed consciousness as something given, while Mead was also
interested in the birth of consciousness at the level of primary communication between animals and between human beings, a problem with which
Cooley had not been concerned at all. Hence, Mead was much more closely
connected with Darwin, Wundt and the naturalistic tradition, and Watson's
behaviorism. Mead started from four assumptions.

First, he rejected the possibility of ascribing any mental qualities whatsoever to human individuals in isolation. Mental processes simply do not take
place outside the process of communication. Language does not serve to
express something that had previously existed—namely, mental states (as
is claimed by Darwin in *Expression of the Emotions in Man and Animals*)—
nor is it a medium through which individuals establish contact between one
another when they already have something to communicate. On the contrary, social relationship is primary with respect to all forms of consciousness. Mead's anthropology was Aristotelian in nature: The group is logically primary with respect to the individual. It was Hegelian, too: The whole
is concrete, and the part is abstract. Like other pragmatists, Mead totally
denied that tradition in European thought which originated with Hobbes.
At the beginning there was the social act, not human individuals.

Second, Mead opposed all dualism that assumed consciousness to exist
as part of some order other than that of physical facts. He wrote, "We
don't want two languages: one of certain physical facts and one of certain
conscious facts."[53] There is no entity called consciousness, and psychology
is not the science of consciousness, considered as something qualitatively
different from the rest of the organic world. Psychology is concerned with
facts that are objectively observable: behavior of organisms under definite
environmental conditions (in the case of social psychology, under social

conditions). Mead rejected the existence of consciousness as a *sui generis* substance, but accepted its existence as a function of the organism. He recommended that human behavior be studied from the outside, but stated that it includes important elements that such observation does not reveal, although the behavior in question cannot be explained if such elements are disregarded. This seems self-contradictory at first. It would certainly be so if Mead had not introduced into his idea the concept of act; by this, he strove to overcome dualism not by eliminating consciousness and inner experience, but by incorporating them into the same order of phenomena that includes behavior that is observable externally. In Mead's approach, inner experience proves to be part of a more comprehensive whole, an act, another "phase" of which is the "external act," observable from the outside. By defining "internal acts" in this way, we are in position to construct a naturalistic theory of introspection that would be compatible with the requirements of behaviorism.

Third, Mead opposed the mechanistic model of interaction between individuals. Human actions and reactions differ from collisions of billiard balls because man is not merely a passive receiver of stimuli. He selects and interprets them; by referring to his earlier experience, he chooses one of the various possible responses. Moreover, every organism seeks certain stimuli and does not merely receive them. Blumer is right in pointing out that Mead was opposed to all conceptions dominant in the social sciences, because he did not explain human behavior by the effect of the independent factors (biological, psychological, and social) on the human subject but concentrated instead on the activity of that human subject himself. Mead rejected the idea of the social world given to the individual just as he rejected the idea of psychical traits given to that individual. He was interested above all in what is taking place between the individual and his social environment.

And fourth, Mead was convinced that science, like practical experience in everyday life, always deals with *processes* and never with states. For him, like Thomas, problems of the structure of society and of personality were nonexistent. All was incessantly becoming. Hence his fascination with Darwin's idea of evolution and with Hegel's philosophy, in which he saw phases of one and the same intellectual trend; hence also his interest in Bergson.

Gestures and Significant Symbols. In Mead's opinion, the simplest cooperation between organisms has a purely biological substratum. All living organisms, he wrote, "are bound up in a general social environment or situation, in a complex of social interrelations and interactions upon which their continued existence depends," and human society "is in a sense merely an extension and ramification of those simple and basic socio-physiological relations among its individual members."[54]

In Mead's analysis, the fundamental role in those elementary forms of social interaction was played by the concept of gesture (taken from Wundt). Every moment of the organism that evokes an adaptive response on the part of other organisms is a gesture. That response is instinctive—spontaneous, unreasoned, and unconscious—like the behavior that evokes it. A gesture is made without any intention to evoke a definite reaction: The organism is not conscious of its meaning. Consciousness emerges only if a gesture is accompanied by an intention of evoking a definite response and if organism A is able to respond to its own gesture in the same way as organism B, to which that gesture is addressed. It is as that level that the replacement of a gesture by a significant symbol becomes possible. The emergence of symbolic interaction indicates the emergence of social relations in the full sense of the term. This transition from gesture to symbol, from social relations based on a purely biological substratum to those based on symbolic communication, was the main subject of Mead's philosophy.

He considered that transition to have been a complex process that had four dimensions, none of which, however, can be separated from the remaining ones or is considered to be more important than any other. The first dimension is the shaping of *language*, owing to which meanings are not only realized by the participants in a social act, but are also communicated. This gives rise to a community of human beings, which cannot emerge in the animal world. The second dimension is the emergence of abstract *thought* the mind's entering what Mead calls "the world of discourse." The third dimension, most completely worked out by Mead, is the acting subject's becoming an object for himself, achieving the ability to respond to his own stimuli, conversing with himself, acting toward himself in the role of other human beings, interpreting his own acts, reflections, and so on. This process is the emergence of *self*. The fourth dimension, least clearly outlined by Mead and disregarded by some of his commentators, is the formation of social *institutions*, for communication is not possible without a fairly stable framework.

The Conception of Self. Man's individuation within the animal kingdom meant, according to Mead, acquiring, over the course of evolution, the ability to use significant symbols (language), to think, to reflect on his own actions, to guide his actions in full consciousness, and, finally, to live within the framework of social organization. Mead paid most attention to the development of self, which concept was missing in the classical behavioristic theory, in his opinion.

Man can be defined, in Mead's philosophy, as the organism that has a self, the organism that can perceive itself, has definite opinions about itself, regulates its own actions by reflection, or a dialogue with itself that results in changes in its own attitudes. Man is merely an organism that is capable of internalizing the social act. The relation "stimulus from organism A leads to adaptive response by organism B" is internalized within man himself, because man responds to his own stimulus just as others would if his attitude had been externalized. But his point was not in the definition of man or in the complete list of the characteristics of self. Mead was interested above all in the formation and the functioning of that which he had termed *self*.

First of all, he assumed that "the body is not a self, as such; it becomes a self only when it has developed a mind within the context of social experience."[55] The self has a social origin, because it is constituted by a dialogue. All thinking is "inner conversation"; hence, in order to learn how to converse with oneself, one must first converse with others. The individual discovers an interlocutor in himself owing to his social experience. It is other people who are first given to him in experience, and in a sense it is only from them that he learns about his own existence. It is in this sense, and in this sense only, that the social whole is primary with respect to the individual. Mead states unambiguously that the process he describes should not be imagined as something that exists objectively. The problem with which he is concerned is not that of ready-made norms (standards or patterns of behavior) assimilated by the individual, but the development by that individual of the ability to assess independently his own behavior.

The individual thus appears to himself in the role of others. He thinks about what they would say about his own behavior, poses himself the question of how they would respond to him, and knows how to imagine their response. He incessantly plays his part to an imaginary audience: He resembles an actor who studies his facial expressions in the mirror and thinks about how the audience would respond to his acting. Here we have found, in fact, a slightly different version of Cooley's looking-glass self. Mead defined that as role taking.

Mead's analysis, however, goes further than Cooley's, for the latter confined himself to a very general characterization of the looking-glass self. Mead singled out two phases in the development of self, phases that differ from one another by the manner of role taking. In the earlier one, the individual takes the role of other individuals with whom he participates in social acts; in the later one, it is the social group as a whole that becomes "others": Attitudes of other individuals are generalized and appear to the individual as all people, society, nation, morality, or God. The former might be termed the phase of play; the latter, the phase of game. In the former, one acts the parts of specified persons (Dad, Mom, the postman, and so on) and imitates their behavior; in the latter, one acts in accordance with certain general rules and adjusts one's own behavior to that of the group as a whole. In the game phase the attitudes of others are generalized, and "the generalized other" emerges.[56]

Reading certain passages of Mead's works may result in associating the generalized other with Durkheim's "collective representations" and the process of role taking with the learning of social conformism, but the similarity is rather limited. What has been said so far about the development of self, as interpreted by Mead, applies only to the "collectivistic" aspect of self, which Mead called *me*. But there is also the other, "individualistic," aspect of self, *I*, and the full description of the development of self requires that the latter be taken into account on an equal footing with the former.

The "me" is a conventional, habitual individual. It is always there. It has to have those habits, those responses which everybody has; otherwise the individual could not be a member of the community. . . . The "I" is the response of the organism to the attitudes of the others; the "me" is the organized set of attitudes of others which one himself assumes. The attitudes of the others constitute the organized "me", and then one reacts toward that as an "I."[57]

It could be said that human personality (self) is the process of an incessant interaction between me and I, which is an analogue of the interaction between the organism and the environment; it is also an analogue of conscience and free will in Christian theological doctrines.

The idea of I as something incalculable, creative, and unpredictable was important in Mead's criticism of sociological determinism or, as Wrong will later put it, of the "oversocialized conception of Man."[58] The individual is shaped under the influence of the group, but he always remain a monad *sui generis*, something exceptional and unique. From the theoretical point of view, that was closely linked to the assumption, fundamental in Mead's system, of an active attitude by the individual toward his social environment. From the ideological point of view, it was an endeavor (like that made by Thomas) to describe a creative individual, in whom the striving for conformist security is in harmony with the striving for new experience. The individual is to participate in social life as a sovereign and conscious subject who assimilates social norms, but is also able to question them and thereby able to save the community from the stagnation that it would face if the shaping of personality consisted only of the assimilation of habits. It is interesting to note that I has a social origin, in Mead's opinion. For this reason, the reader is warned against the temptation of comparing Mead with Freud, me with superego, and I with id.

Society. Mead did not attempt to be a sociologist and was concerned with sociological issues only when they seemed indispensable because of the psychological and philosophical conceptions that he was working out. Even his most ardent followers do not try to find any clearly formulated sociological theory in his writings and look at most for some sociological implications. We have already discussed the most important ones. A sociology based on Mead's assumptions would have to be humanist, interactionist, and indeterminist. It would have to be humanist because, according to Mead, there is no social reality that is not a correlate of conscious actions of human subjects; it would have to interactionist because the entities called individuals and society do not exist outside the process of interaction; it would have to be indeterminist because the human individuals who interact with one another are largely autonomous and capable of creative activity. It is personality (self) that is the foundation of any specifically human society. The main concepts in Mead's sociology are control, institution, communication, and social objects.

Mead speaks about three kinds of control: the individual's control of himself, society's control of its own development, and society's control of its natural environment. The mechanism of the individual's control of his own behavior—that is, social control—is set in operation at the moment that he becomes an object for himself.

Self-consciousness means incessant self-criticism, and the development of reflection is accompanied by the development of conscious conformism. Not only does the development of the individual's self not weaken his bonds with the community, but, on the contrary, it strengthens them, because the individual seeks the definitions of situations (to use Thomas's terminology) that are binding in his group. Mead's analogue of that term was the concept of institution or "institutionalized attitudes," which he never defined with any considerable precision. The salient characteristic of Mead's thought was the identification of social control with self-control and the total disregard of the problems of power. These problems simply cannot be confined within Mead's theoretical schema, for it requires assuming that the individuals are equal to one another and cooperate voluntarily.

The second kind of control that makes human society differ from animal society is the ability, potential at least, to control its own development. Mead was one of the last believers in the idea of progress: Human intelligence has a boundless ability to solve the problems that mankind has to face. Crises and obstacles are the motive power of progress.

The third kind of control is that of the natural environment. This idea is implicit in Mead's interpretation of adaptation, but it is repeated in his works explicitly as well. Mead's important hypothesis on the role of the hand in human evolution (and, hence, man's ability to manipulate things) is linked exactly to these problems.

The term *society* was applied by Mead to all those situations in which there is interaction among individuals. Since human interaction is mainly symbolic, the limits of society are marked by the limits of communication and, therefore, by the taking of roles of those individuals who are not within one's closest environment. In the future the world of discourse would cover all mankind. Society is cemented by the existence of social objects. In agreement with his general philosophical assumptions, Mead claimed that social objects do not exist by themselves, but only in connection with the organisms that experience them. Their nature, as Blumer writes, is constituted by the significance that they have for those individuals to whom they are social objects. This being so, every community can be characterized by an indication of those social objects which are significant to it.[59] The set of those objects changes incessantly; nevertheless, at every moment there are things that evoke fairly homogeneous behavioral responses in the members of a given group. Social objects are those to which the aforementioned institutionalized attitudes of individuals refer. Here we come across a concept that is a fairly exact analogue of the concept of value worked out by Thomas and Znaniecki.

Apparently, the most important feature of Mead's sociology was the relinquishment of all problems that could not be presented in terms of social psychology. According to Blumer, Mead's interpretation

sees human society not as an established structure but as people meeting their conditions of life; . . . it sees society not as a system, whether in the form of a static, moving, or whatever kind of equilibrium, but as a vast number of occurring joint actions, many closely linked, many not linked at all, many prefigured and repetitious, other being carved out in new directions, and all being pursued to serve the purpose of the participants and not the requirements of a system.[60]

It was these features of Mead's thought that were decisive for its attractiveness to many American sociologists when his writings were made public.

THE COMMON FEATURES OF SOCIAL PRAGMATISM

When pointing to certain similarities of the writers whose works are discussed above, we have not considered them to be representatives of any uniform theoretical standpoint. They differed in interests, ways of doing research, assumptions, and terminologies. It is, however, beyond all doubt that the social theories of Dewey, Cooley, Thomas, and Mead can be classed together.[61]

The historical significance of those authors rests primarily in their having taken up new problems, namely, those of social personality, in opposition to both sociologism and psychologism. As A. Boskoff wrote, the sociology of "the old masters" did without the concept of personality and concentrated its attention on social structure and social process as such.[62] That sociology, of course, resorted excessively to psychological explanations, which were even pushed to the forefront by psychologism dominant in the late nineteenth century. But those psychological explanations consisted as a rule of ascribing to individuals or groups certain permanent mental properties that were then used to explain phenomena in collective life. For all the advances in psychology, that way of thinking still savored of Hobbes's social philosophy. On the other hand, these thinkers, realizing that human nature is subject to change, brought out the role of social influence and claimed that the individual owes all his mental features to the influence of his social environment or to education, in the broad sense of the term. According to them, the individual is such as he has been made by society.

In both cases the mechanism of the influence of the mental makeup on society, or vice versa, remained a puzzle. The situation was not changed much by the introduction (for instance, by Simmel) of the interactionist viewpoint, because the individual involved in such interaction was considered at first to be an atom endowed with certain permanent properties and not analyzable in any further way. Progress allowed the human individual to be seen as a problem in himself. That was done by Freud and Durkheim: The former analyzed human personality in terms of id, superego, and ego, and the latter adopted the hypothesis of *homo duplex*, whose animal instincts are gradually restrained by social norms. Max Weber approached the problem from another side, but he ultimately focused his attention on other issues.[63] The comprehensive formulation of the problem was the work of the American social pragmatists.

They realized that such statements as "human individuals are the basic factors of the social process" and "man is shaped by the social conditions he lives in" are only very preliminary formulations of the problem whose solution remains almost completely unknown as long as we abstain from systematically investigating the mechanisms of interactions that shape both society and the individual. Social pragmatists focused their interests on these two mechanisms. As it usually happens, the choice of a new field of research resulted in a drastic limitation of interest in other topics examined by sociology, such as the social system, social structure, or social development. Beside the problems of the formation of social personality, room was left only for the study of institutionalization processes and social change, and the latter was a concern only insofar as it is linked to changes in personality. On the other hand, social pragmatists (except for Thomas) revealed little interest in the biological determinants of human behavior, coming back in a sense to the idea of *tabula rasa*, which in turn made them very critical of psychoanalysis.

It seems to be beyond doubt that, as has been stressed by many commentators, the one-sidedness of social pragmatism was due not only to the desire to explore neglected fields of social theory, but also to the specifically American *Weltanschauung* of its founders.[64] Dedicated to the ideals of democracy and convinced of its durability, they were inclined to underestimate rigid social structures, the hierarchy of wealth and power, violence, and class struggle. Society was to them almost by definition a society of equals, who by mutual role taking gradually adjust themselves to one another, develop values that are common to all, and establish a definite institutional order that is susceptible to change whenever, and only if, individuals need that. Optimism, the belief in the need and possibility of constant improvements, favored the dislike of all varieties of biologism that make people think that the fortune of every individual is predetermined by heredity. Social pragmatism thus seems to have been a philosophical presentation of the democratic way of life, a presentation disregarding almost everything that changed reality into myth at that time.

It was typical of social pragmatism to strive for a maximally objective description of human behavior; however, it was combined with the belief that the fundamental issue is to penetrate the sphere of subjective experiences of the participants in social interaction. This is why they gave preference to those research techniques (if research was undertaken) that intended to acquire the appropriate data (personal documents, participant observation, and so on); moreover, these data had to be such that would allow them to acquire the knowledge of the individual as the acting subject, as a complete social self, in a natural social situation.

Putting all these things together, we can consider social pragmatism to have been the American variety (developed quite independently of the European ones) of *humanistic sociology*, although in Mead we find strongly marked elements of naturalism. Mead's idea was, in fact, an endeavor to bridge the gap between the heritage of Darwinian evolutionism and the more recent antinaturalistic trends in the humanities. Mead's humanistic sociology was not intended to be antinaturalistic. Its fundamental problem, however, was the specific character of the human world and its distinctiveness from the rest of the animal world.

The theoretical heritage of social pragmatism has been taken over in its most important elements by contemporary symbolic interactionism. The problems of social personality and the idea of finding the golden mean between sociologism and psychologism have largely become the common property of all present-day sociology.

NOTES

1. R. Hofstadter, *Social Darwinism in American Thought* (Boston: Beacon Press, 1959), p. 123.

2. Ibid., p. 123-24.

3. W. James, *Collected Essays and Reviews* (New York: Longman, 1920), p. 67.

4. J. Dewey, *Reconstruction in Philosophy* (Boston: Beacon Press, New York: Mentor 1957), p. 161.

5. F. B. Karpf, *American Social Psychology* (New York: McGraw-Hill, 1932), p. 251.

6. Dewey, *Reconstruction*, p. 156.

7. W. James, *The Principles of Psychology* (New York: Holt, 1890), 1:291.

8. Lewis A. Coser, *Masters of Sociological Thought* (New York: Harcourt Brace Jovanovich, 1971), p. 321.

9. Cf. John W. Petras, "John Dewey and the Rise of Interactionism in American Social Theory," *Journal of the History of Behavioral Sciences* 4 (1968): 18-27.

10. J. Dewey, "New Psychology," in Dewey, *Philosophy, Psychology and Social Practice* (New York, 1963), pp. 57-58.

11. J. Dewey, *Democracy and Education: An Introduction to the Philosophy of Education* (New York: Macmillan, 1948), pp. 56-57.

12. J. Dewey, *Human Nature and Conduct: An Introduction to Social Psychology* (New York: Modern Library, 1930), pp. 89-94.

13. Ibid., pp. 40-41.

14. Ibid., pp. 16-17, 58.

15. J. Dewey, *Democracy and Education*, pp. 5-6.

16. C. H. Cooley, "Now and Then," in Cooley, *Sociological Theory and Practice* (New York: Holt, 1930), pp. 281-85.

17. Edward C. Jandy, *Charles Horton Cooley: His Life and His Social Theory* (New York: Octagon, 1969), pp. 230-60.

18. C. H. Cooley, *Human Nature and Social Order* (New York: Scribner's, 1902), pp. 36-37.

19. C. H. Cooley, *Social Process* (Carbondale: Southern Illinois University Press, 1966), p. 200; Cooley, *Human Nature*, pp. 3-31.

20. C. H. Cooley, *Social Organization* (New York: Scribner's 1909), p. 61.

21. G. H. Mead, *Mind, Self and Society* (Chicago: University of Chicago Press, 1972), p. 224.

22. Cooley, *Human Nature*, p. 301.

23. Ibid., pp. 118-119, 95.

24. Jandy, *Charles Horton Cooley*, p. 233.

25. Jean B. Quandt, *From the Small Town to the Great Community* (New Brunswick, N.J.: Rutgers University Press, 1970), pt. 1, pp. 23-78.

26. Cooley, *Social Organization*, p. 23.

27. The term *secondary group* is purposely avoided here, though it is commonly ascribed to this author. It was Park who started to use the term systematically.

28. Quandt, *From the Small Town*, p. 18.

29. Cooley, *Social Organization*, p. 319; "Personal Competition," in Cooley, *Sociological Theory*, pp. 185-86.

30. Cooley, *Human Nature*, p. 148.

31. Cooley, *Social Process*, pp. 4-5, 28.

32. Cooley, *Social Organization*, p. 209. Cooley's conception of social classes is discussed in detail by Charles Hunt Page, *Class and American Sociology* (New York: Schocken Books, 1969).

33. Cooley, *Social Process*, pp. 396-97.

34. Cooley, "The Roots of Social Knowledge," in *Sociological Theory*, pp. 299-300.

35. Cooley "The Life-Study Method . . .," in ibid., p. 332.

36. Karpf, *American Social Psychology*, p. 351. The evolution of Thomas's views is discussed by Morris Janowitz in the introduction to the book that he edited: Thomas, *On Social Organization and Social Personality* (Chicago: University of Chicago Press, 1966) and by Kimball Young in "Contributions of W. I. Thomas to Sociology," *Sociology and Social Research* 47 (1962-63): 3-24, 123-37, 251-72, 381-97.

37. It is practically impossible to evaluate exactly the contribution of either coauthor. But in brief, the main ideas and hypotheses, as well as the very concept of *The Polish Peasant*, belong mostly to Thomas, since they are to be found in his earlier publications and are absent in the earlier works by Znaniecki (except the concept of value). Znaniecki's role in formulating

Thomas's hypotheses remains unclear. According to oral tradition, the consecutive parts of the work were discussed in detail, while Thomas preferred to leave the formulation of the standpoints to Znaniecki, once they agreed. It seems, therefore, that *The Polish Peasant* is a result of cooperation in the fullest meaning of this word. It is also known that the *Methodological Note* was Znaniecki's initiative.

38. W. I. Thomas and F. Znaniecki, *The Polish Peasant in Europe and America* (Boston: Richard Bedger, 1918-20). See Robert Bierstedt, ed., *Florian Znaniecki on Humanistic Sociology* (Chicago: University of Chicago Press, 1969), p. 82.

39. Ibid., pp. 69-71.

40. Ibid., p. 89.

41. H. Blumer, *An Appraisal of Thomas and Znaniecki's "The Polish Peasant in Europe and America"* (New York: Social Science Research Council, 1939), pp. 25-26.

42. Thomas and Znaniecki, *Polish Peasant*, 2:1831, 1834.

43. Ibid., pp. 1835-36.

44. Ibid., p. 1843.

45. Ibid., p. 1849.

46. Ibid., 1:32.

47. W. I. Thomas with D. S. Thomas, *The Child in America* (New York: Knopf, 1928), p. 572.

48. Thomas and Znaniecki, *Polish Peasant*, 1:43.

49. Ibid., 2:1128.

50. Ibid., p. 1121.

51. Ibid., p. 1303.

52. Thomas, "Situational Analysis: The Behavior Pattern and the Situation," *On Social Organization and Social Personality*, pp. 155-56.

53. Mead, *Mind, Self and Society*, p. 40.

54. Ibid., pp. 228-29.

55. Ibid., p. 50.

56. Ibid., pp. 154-55.

57. Ibid., pp. 197-98, 175.

58. Dennis H. Wrong, "The Oversocialized Conception of Man in Modern Sociology," in Lewis A. Coser and Bernard Rosenberg, eds., *Sociological Theory: A Book of Readings* (New York: Macmillan, 1964), pp. 11-22.

59. H. Blumer, "Sociological Implications of the Thought of George Herbert Mead," in Blumer, *Symbolic Interactionism: Perspectives and Method* (Englewood Cliffs, N.J.: Prentice-Hall, 1969), pp. 74-75.

60. Ibid., p. 74.

61. Don Martindale includes Ernst Cassirer and Jean Piaget in the same category; *The Nature and Types of Sociological Theory* (Boston: Houghton Mifflin, 1960), pp. 359-69.

62. Alvin Boskoff, *Theory in American Sociology* (New York: Crowell, 1969), p. 39.

63. T. Parsons, "Cooley and the Problem of Internalization," in Albert J. Reiss, Jr., ed., *Cooley and Social Analysis* (Ann Arbor: University of Michigan Press, 1968), pp. 49-67.

64. L. Shaskolsky, "The Development of Sociological Theory in America: A Sociology of Knowledge Interpretation," in Larry T. Reynolds and Janice M. Reynolds, eds., *The Sociology of Sociology* (New York: McKay, 1970), pp. 17-20.

15

THEORETICAL HORIZONS OF AMERICAN DESCRIPTIVE SOCIOLOGY

THE DISCOVERY OF THE COMMUNITY

Social pragmatism had a strong impact on social science in America, but American sociology between the world wars was also influenced by other traditions, primarily those of social surveys and muckraking journalism at the turn of the nineteenth century. Some role was also played by other inspirations, such as ecology (Galpin, the Chicago school, and Warner), Simmel's formal sociology (Park), the social anthropology of Boas and his disciples (Park and Lynd), that of Radcliffe-Brown (Warner), and Durkheimism (Mayo and Warner). As a matter of fact, American sociology was eclectic in its theoretical assumptions, tended to avail itself of anything that seemed to be useful instrument of research, and was open to all theoretical novelties.

Sociology without Theory? American sociology between the world wars can be characterized by specifying its typical topics and research procedures better than by listing its assumptions. Over the course of time it gained the status of an atheoretical discipline, socio*graphy* rather than socio*logy*. The main task of this sociology, which was pursued primarily in Chicago or by scholars trained there, was not the construction of new theoretical systems. As Faris wrote, the fashion dictating that every sociologist be a founder of a new school of sociology was over.[1] Questions traditional in sociology remained topical only as long as they were connected with techniques and procedures used by the field worker. Traditional answers, still fairly well known to that generation of empirical researchers, were considered useful only insofar as they could be adjusted to the needs of the new style of sociological research. And that style consisted on a growing scale (as was also the case in social anthropology) in looking at the social world through one's own eyes and in avoiding—to the point of exaggeration—all apriority. Like all other sciences, sociology would gradually transform itself into an "experimental" discipline.[2] This reorientation was, of course, due not only to an increased interest in empirical studies of social reality, but also to the fact that the sociologist was more and more often a teacher and a leader of a research team; as such, he had to offer his students and co-workers something more than general views of society and social development.

For all that, the opinion that American sociology between the world wars was basically atheoretically oriented seems untenable, and in some cases —Park and Warner, for example—it is simply untrue. It will be to the point to reconstruct the theoretical assumptions that lay at the foundation of sociographic research procedures and quite often happened to be stated explicitly. Lynd was right in saying that research without a viewpoint is impossible; if science were photography, it would have to stop, burdened by a mass of undifferentiated details; science is thus dependent on a sensitive and coherent approach to reality, and the researcher's *Weltanschauung* affects the choice and formulation of the questions that he considers important enough to pose.[3] Sociographic studies were always based on some theory, even if it was invisible to those who undertook them. This theory did not comply with the now current standards of theoretical activity, but it was a fairly adequate expression of an important stage in the development of sociology.

When trying to understand what that theory consisted of, we have to take two things into account: its close links with empirical research (in that respect, Thomas was the predecessor of the authors to be discussed in this chapter) and its concentration on the problems of community.

While social pragmatism took up the issue of social personality, at that time a novel one, descriptive sociology took up the issue of community and turned it into the pivotal subject matter of sociology. Its novelty was certainly relative, because—beginning with the conservatives in the early nineteenth century—thinkers often concerned themselves with communities, which are parts of every society. However, the representatives of descriptive sociology considered these communities to be the best place for the study of all social processes. They started from the assumption that,

in a sense, the community is the meeting place of the individual and the larger society and culture. It is in his own locality, characteristically, that, through most of mankind's history and to a very great extent today, the individual confronts his society's institutions, its manner of religious expression, its ways of regulating behavior, its ways of family living, its ways of socializing the young, its ways of providing sustenance, its ways of esthetic expression.[4]

As compared with the earlier social theories, which as a rule were macro-sociological rather than microsociological, these researchers had not only a subject matter of their own, but specific methods and theories as well.

The Subject Matter. What Is a Local Community? The term *community* often has two distinct meanings: first, a territorial group and, second, something shared in common. The difficulty lies in the fact that students of the local community in most cases did not always distinguish between the two.

Hillery, who managed to review the immense literature of the subject in search of a definition of the term *community*, claims that an overwhelming majority of researchers ascribed to local community the following basic attributes: (1) territory, (2) social interaction, and (3) a durable bond among its members. Few authors emphasized either the common territory alone or the relations among human beings alone.[5] The concept constructed in this way has to be ambiguous; and according to the researcher's orientation, stress was laid either on the objective determinants of the community or on definite attitudes, convictions, and beliefs of its members—on their consciousness—which was not only described, but evaluated as well. As J. Bernard says, interests were focused either on *the community* or on *Community*,[6] while many authors deliberately accepted such an ambivalence and endowed the term *community* with both geographical and mental or moral connotations.

The concept of community borders, on the one hand, on an ecological population, a territorial group analogous to gatherings of plants and animals, and, on the other, on a moral order, such as that in the Greek *polis* or that ascribed by Tönnies to *Gemeinschaft*, understood as an ideal type. The ambiguity seems to stem from the fact that the interest of social thinkers in problems of community was born as they watched the dissolution of certain kinds of bonds following the advances of capitalism, urbanization, and industrialization. All kinds of primary groups came to be studied when it was found that they were in a state of profound crisis and that much effort would be required either to restore them or to find some new institutions that could perform similar functions.[7]

The notorious ambiguity of the term was closely connected with incessant oscillation between description and norm, fact and ideal, scholarly objectivism and reforming passion, so that even those authors who, like Park, strove to clarify the term *community* were not consistent in that respect.

It would be erroneous to see all the works concerned with communities as having abandoned studies of great sociological problems. The point is that in the United States such problems were for a long time not those of the state, of classes and class conflicts, of bureaucratic organizations working on the national scale, but those of self-governed and largely self-sufficient communities. This applied especially to those small towns about which Thorstein Veblen wrote: "The country town is one of the great American institutions, perhaps the greatest, in the sense that it has had and continues to have a greater part than any other in shaping public sentiment and giving character to American culture."[8]

American sociology between the world wars rang the death knell of the spirit of Middletown and also posed the question, sometimes dramatically, about the future of the values that had their traditional habitat in the former community. That sociology was marked by fascination with the new urban and industrial world, combined with the yearning for the vanishing world of the community.

The Method. In the opinion of some authors, the most characteristic feature of the studies of communities was not so much their subject matter as their method, which could be used for the study of many various social processes, such as urbanization, industrialization, and stratification. From that point of view, a community served as a kind of laboratory in which almost everything could be studied. This, of course, required the assumption that the community was a microcosm and that the phenomena and processes observable in it were more or less universal. This assumption—that a community is "a complete way of life and the system of institutions that makes it possible"[9]—was of key significance for the sociological orientation now under consideration. Although this statement could be questioned more and more as localism was weakening and each community was becoming increasingly dependent on the national political, social, economic, and cultural system, it did play an enormous role and, in its less radical version, happens to be asserted even now. It was this statement that had determined the research perspective and method typical of the students of communities.

Arensberg and Kimball summed that method up in the following way:

In community study, indeed, the three main problems in executing a research design are *sui generis*. . . . First is the construction of a model of the whole . . . from data gathered in with the widest possible net. Second comes comparison, at least implicit comparison, with other similar wholes. Third is the fitting of any particular problem or other object of study . . . into its proper niche within the model.[10]

The same authors emphasize that studies of local communities are "multifactoral" by their very nature, which means that the researcher "must treat his people, the members of the community, as full animal and human beings . . . , he must deal with all facets of their lives."[11]

The adoption of this viewpoint and this research strategy meant bringing the description closer to the pattern of anthropological monographs. In Steward's opinion, community studies were the application of "a cultural or ethnographic method to contemporary society."[12] That anthropological pattern was in many cases adopted deliberately. Park called for availing oneself of the examples of Boas and Lowie in the studies of contemporary society.[13] The Lynds prepared *Middletown* as an anthropological monograph and referred directly to Wissler and Rivers. Warner, a disciple of Radcliffe-Brown, was an anthropologist by training and started working on *Yankee City*, following his studies of Australian aborigines, in the belief that he continued the same research project. Whither, the author of *Plainville*, who used the pen name of James West, was an anthropologist, too. The work of Robert Redfield also was in the border area between sociology and social anthropology, as it was an endeavor to bridge, in the sphere of theory, the research on urbanization and urbanism that had been conducted by the Chicago school and the ethnological studies of primitive and peasant communities.

The anthropological pattern was attractive primarily by making people hope that an empirically minded observer could discover relationships among all spheres of social life, all aspects of individual behavior, and all social institutions. But the relationship between sociography and social anthropology is fairly complex, and the formula that the latter be merely "applied" to the former simplifies matters too much. The point was that in the 1920s American anthropology still concentrated its interest on the relics of the old ways of life rather than on the new forces that worked on traditional communities. It provided, at best, the pattern for treating the local community as a living whole, but not any pattern for studying how that community was changing.

As a result, the whole life of a community was only apparently whole, because the various researchers shifted the subject matter of their studies in various ways. The question "How does a community function?" was gradually changed into "How do such and such processes take place in a community?" The pattern of the anthropological monograph was thus becoming more and more remote. Among the community studies, Steward singled out, "monographic studies" and "social relations studies."[14] The latter group formed a large majority: Except for *Middletown* by the Lynds and the *Yankee City Series* by Warner and his coworkers, it would be difficult to find studies that could unreservedly be included in the former category. That specialization did not, however, exclude the study of a community "as if it were a primitive tribe—that is, as if it were a self-contained structural and functional whole which could be understood in terms of itself alone."[15]

The perspective adopted determined, to a great extent, the choice of the research techniques to be used. Since interest was focused on a natural social whole, a given human community, those techniques which require creating artificial situations and taking individuals out of the context of their everyday life were excluded. The researcher's long stay on the spot was a sine qua non. Of course, there was, and could be, no uniform canon of sources. The principle of "the more, the better" prevailed. The following formula given by Steward makes the point: "The field work in community studies must begin with the old and proven ethnographic techniques: participant observation; long, frequent and directed interviews with informants qualified to give information of special kinds; consultation of archives, records and documents, recording of case histories, and use of any other sources of information that become available."[16] Students of communities seem to have been marked by restraint in using statistical techniques, which was due to the belief that the primary task was to discover the integrated pattern of culture of a given community, and, as Steward notes, culture patterns cannot be shown in mathematical terms.[17] As compared with *The Polish Peasant*, the students of communities significantly broadened the repertory of techniques used, but they did not change their nature in any essential manner. Among Chicago sociologists the work of Thomas and Znaniecki retained the status of a model in many respects, even though it was neither directly continued nor imitated.

Main Theoretical Orientations. As has been said, American descriptive sociology was eclectic in the sphere of theory. It is doubtful that any community research conducted in the United States before World War II was marked by a consistent application of a definite general sociological theory. On the other hand, we can notice certain theoretical trends connected with the endeavors to explain the processes that were the immediate subject of observation. We can distinguish three basic orientations: typological, ecological, and structural-functional.[18]

The peculiarity of the typological orientation was its considering the communities studied to be representations of a broader category of relations or groups. This was usually combined with locating them on the scale whose limiting points were country and town, primary and secondary group, localism and cosmopolitanism, community and society, and so on. We have here many variations on the theme of Tönnies's dichotomy of *Gemeinschaft* versus *Gesellschaft*, with the proviso that it required considerable modifications because the United States lacked social realities that the German sociologist used in defining the term *Gemeinschaft*. Inspired as they were by Tönnies's work, American sociologists had to work out their own set of concepts that would be better adapted to an analysis of life in preindustrial and nonurbanized America, which, on the whole, had not known rural life in the European sense of the word. Such, for instance, was the conception of Carle C. Zimmerman, the prominent student of American rural areas, who made the distinction between "localistic" and "cosmopolitan" communities, and also the conception of Robert Redfield (1897-1958), who introduced the popular "folk-urban continuum."[19]

The peculiarity of the ecological orientation—initiated by Charles J. Galpin, the founder of American rural sociology, and developed especially by the Chicago school—was the privileged position assigned within the community studies to the influence exerted on their structure and evolution by the natural environment. Ecologically oriented researchers assumed that in the evolution of human communities there are definite regularities and that various areas are settled after repeatable patterns determined by environmental conditions. They also assumed that it is possible to make a distinction between two kinds of interaction among human beings: "ecological interaction" and "social interaction" (Quinn), or "community" and "society" (Park); the first of each pair is unconscious, spontaneous and largely beyond human control, and it can be studied in the same way in which natural phenomena are. Those students also tended to draw analogies between human ecology and animal and plant ecology. The ecological orientation found most application in the studies of great cities, where social interaction seemed much less intense than in traditional communities. Ecology offered maximum objectivity in the approach to a community as a phenomenon that develops on a natural basis. Yet, it had its consistent advocates in exceptional cases only, and even the Chicago school could not be considered purely ecologically oriented. This seems understandable, because it was concern about the future of social interaction that lay at the foundation of the studies of communities.

Finally, the peculiarity of the structural-functional orientation was the emphasis on treating a community as an internally connected system. This tendency marked all community research, but in some cases presenting those communities as systems was the principal goal of research. Such was the task that Warner set for himself. It gained in popularity following the advances of functionalism and its penetration from social anthropology into sociology. The spreading of this orientation changed essentially the nature of community studies, because of the connenctions between such research and the general sociological theory, and because of the fact that the disintegration of traditional communities ceased to be the focus of interest.

Singling out these three orientations does not, of course, fully explain the complexity of studies of local communities. For instance, some studies primarily tended to reveal the social stratification of communities or the community power structure. These studies are interesting as a testimony of the rediscovery of *homo politicus* by American sociologists. Yet, it is not always clear whether in such cases we are finding new conceptions of community or new choices of research problems within the same or similar conceptions. On the one hand, the privileged position assigned by Warner and his coworkers to problems of class stratification did not contradict their structural-functional orientation, because of the specific interpretation of classes adopted by them. On the other hand, in *Middletown in Transition*, written by the Lynds after the Great Depression, we find the concept of class that resulted in Robert Lynd's going far beyond the standpoints discussed here and, in fact, abandoning the viewpoint of the local community.

THE CHICAGO SCHOOL:
STUDIES IN URBANIZATION AND URBANISM

The role of the Chicago school was that it ennobled field work by making it a fully legitimate academic undertaking and the very foundation of sociology as such. Field work ceased to be a quasi-scientific appendage to social work or a marginal element of the proper activity of an armchair sociologist, who draws conclusions from data accumulated by others. Chicago sociologists wanted to see the social world with their own eyes, and they turned registering such observations into their principal calling.

The researchers gathered at the University of Chicago were mainly concerned with urbanization and its multifarious social consequences, not with small and relatively closed communities. In this sense one might say that the members of the Chicago school did not produce any "ethnographic monographs." And yet there are serious reasons to consider the activity of the Chicago school in connection with the community studies. First, in the United States the school lay the foundations of the tradition of field work, indispensable for such studies; second, it worked out the principles of social ecology, which could be applied in those studies; third, it produced a number of monographs of urban subcommunities; fourth, its interest was largely focused on the same problem of community (*society*, in Park's terminology) with which most community students were concerned.

The Chicago School Defined. The opening, in 1892, of the Department of Sociology and Anthropology at the newly founded University of Chicago was an important event in the history of American sociology. The discipline thus gained a solid institutional foundation, which sociology did not have even in those European countries in which sociological theory was more advanced. If the way of pursuing sociological research adopted by the majority of Chicago sociologists became the standard between the world wars, that was mainly due to the achievements that were possible owing to the new organizational facilities in Chicago.[20]

The department itself, however, was not a scientific school, as it included scholars of different orientations who managed to cooperate harmoniously within the university and other institutions (such as the Social Science Research Council, founded in 1923, and the American Sociological Society), but did not stand for any unity of views. They were united, at most, by the common tendency to do away with the heritage of speculative social philosophy, to free sociology from servitude on behalf of social work, and to turn it into a professional discipline that requires special training. The Chicago school was a group of researchers gathered around Robert Ezra Park (1864-1944). It may be assumed that it became active in 1915 (the publication date of Park's programmatic paper, *The City: Suggestions for the Investigation of Human Behavior in the Urban Environment*) and ceased to exist in the mid-1930s, even though many of its members remained active longer and continued the same type of research. The later date marks Park's retirement, yet that was not the main cause of the decline of the school's inventiveness. The causes of its crisis are to be sought rather in external facts: Chicago sociologists studied the natural history of the city in the epoch of free-competition capitalism, which in the United States came to an end with the Great Depression.[21] During those twenty years Park's coworkers developed an atmosphere of genuine teamwork, owing to which they outlined research programs, produced a number of valuable monographs, and acquired almost a monopoly status in American sociology.[22]

Urban Area as a Laboratory. The salient characteristic of the Chicago school was the very subject matter of its studies, which was the city, and in particular Chicago, which to this day has probably remained the best-described city in the world. But if we say that the sociology pursued by that school was urban sociology, we mean the way of approaching sociological problems in general, rather than the special discipline within sociology that was to emerge. The school was interested not only in problems of urban sociology as it is understood today, but also in those of the sociology of vocations, social stratification, political movements, the press, the family, national and racial relations, religion, delinquency, and the general problems of social psychology and social change. Focusing attention on the studies of cities affected the formulation rather than the choice of problems. We should speak about the sociology of urbanism instead of urban sociology, for the Chicago school considered the city and urbanism to be the principal social phenomena in the present-day world.

The practical importance of these phenomena lay in the fact that, as Park put it, "the social problem is fundamentally a city problem. It is the problem of achieving in the freedom of the city a social order and a social control equivalent to that which grew up naturally in the family, the clan, and the tribe."[23] Their theoretical importance was due to the fact that, as was claimed by L. Wirth, "almost every significant proposition that can be advanced about contemporary society contains urbanism as one of its causal forms. . . . The attempt to understand the city inevitably leads to the major facets of civilization."[24] Hence the idea of the city as the laboratory or the clinic in which the most important facts of human nature and social life can be studied.

The discovery of the city as the subject of scientific investigations or, *a fortiori*, as a social phenomenon of great significance does not, of course, go to the credit of the Chicago sociologists. Without going too far into the past, we can list at least four lines of tradition to which they could refer: (1) reflections of such thinkers as Oswald Spengler and Georg Simmel, as the study *Die Grossstädte und des Geistes Leben* (1903) by the latter author was well known to them; (2) studies in historical demography; (3) muckraking journalism like *The Shame of the Cities* (1904) by Lincoln Steffens, whom Park valued very much; and (4) numerous social surveys made both in Europe and in the United States, including Chicago. Yet the principal source of inspiration was the avalanchelike process of urbanization in the United States. Characteristically, many Chicago sociologists had had some kind of practical experience in that field. On the other hand, their theoretical knowledge was strong enough to make them understand the limited value of superficial data, collected for practical purposes only. Earlier students of urban life strove primarily to disclose the evil and to point to the necessity of reforms, not to acquire the knowledge of urban life in its totality. They did much to show the disorganization that typifies big cities, but little to make one understand their organization and the reorganization that was, nevertheless, taking place. The Chicago school strove to acquire such knowledge of the cities that would be most closely connected with empirical data (and, indirectly, with practical activity as well), but would at the same time comply fully with the standards of scientific work.

A handbook of field work, which was a kind of codification of the procedures used by the school, states that a "sociological" survey differs essentially from a "social" one by its striving to discover how human society functions, not merely to reveal pathological facts and to indicate the ways of putting an end to them. A sociological survey has the knowledge of "social laws" in view, while a social one merely aims at immediate practical effects. A social worker is interested solely in given situations, whereas a sociologist selects given communities for his investigations. The latter is interested in comparing a number of communities and focuses on certain social patterns and processes for further examination, rather than just acquiring the knowledge of any single community.

Chicago sociologists succeeded in formulating and quite consistently carrying out their program of research in urban sociology, which also attracted representatives of other disciplines. The existence of this program created a new situation in American sociology: From that moment on, all study of human behavior under the conditions existing in big cities had to refer in some way to the paradigm formulated by the Chicago school.

Theory and Empirical Studies. Chicago sociologists wanted to be more empirically minded than the armchair sociologists and more theoretically minded than social surveyors. But the relation between theory and empirical study in their scholarly activity has been rather complicated. On the one hand, we have Park's theoretical system, complemented and amplified by other authors (Burgess, McKenzie, and Wirth), and, on the other hand, a series of monographs written by members of his seminar, which to varying extents were results of application of his theoretical conceptions. Those monographs were descriptions of selected fragments of reality in terms of

Park's theory rather than verifications of his hypotheses. Regardless of Park's sweeping theoretical ideas, his seminar was primarily a school of observation and description, not a school of theoretical thinking. *Introduction to the Science of Sociology* by Park and Burgess (1921) states plainly that the student must learn to collect data and not to formulate opinions.[25] There are also no indications that those monographs, excellent as they were in many respects, helped Park himself to modify his theoretical system. The low degree of standardization of the research techniques used by members of the school rendered accumulation of results difficult. Most monographs produced by the Chicago school could probably have been written without the acceptance of Park's theoretical system.

The only exception from that loose connection between empirical studies and theory was a set of fairly general ecological hypotheses expounded primarily in *The City* (1925).

Those hypotheses can be summed up thus:

1. The "natural history"[26] of human communities shows a definite and repeatable pattern of distribution of population.
2. The various "zones" form "natural areas" that are distinct from one another not only by their respective positions in space, but also by specified social characteristics of their respective populations—income, occupation, ethnic membership, religion, manners, tradition, mentality, and, in some cases language.
3. Those characteristics are consequences both of the place occupied by a given zone within the urban organism (division of labor) and of the tradition represented by the people who settled in it.
4. Change is the "natural" state of the city and of the urban population, there being a correspondence between spatial and social change.
5. The principal processes taking place in the urban space are concentration, centralization, segregation, invasion, and succession.[27]
6. The fundamental social processes taking place in the cities can be assigned to definite points in the urban space and shown by maps and diagrams.

Yet, the Chicago school monographs must be given credit not for their theoretical or methodological refinement, but primarily for a systematic accumulation of data, in a manner that was maximally objective and critical of the sources of information. These monographs started the unbroken tradition of empirical studies, without which present-day sociology would be unthinkable and which even a philosophizing theorist could not disregard without detriment to his scholarly reputation.

The most important monographs turned out by the Chicago school were *The Hobo: The Sociology of the Homeless Man* (1923) by Nels Anderson, *The Gang* (1927) by Frederic M. Thrasher, *The Ghetto* (1928) by Louis Wirth, *A Study of a Secular Institution: Chicago Real Estate Board* (1928) by Everett C. Hughes, *Suicide* (1928) by Ruth S. Cavan, *The Neighborhood*

(1928) by R. D. McKenzie, *The Gold Coast and the Slum* (1929) by Harvey W. Zorbough, *Delinquency Areas* (1929) by Clifford R. Shaw and Henry D. McKay, *The Jack-Roller* (1930) and *The Natural History of a Delinquent Career* (1931) by C. G. Shaw, *The Negro Family in Chicago* (1933) by Walter C. Reckless, and *The Marginal Man* (1937) by Everett V. Stonequist.[28]

These studies were written by the application of various research techniques, none of which had been invented in Park's seminar, even though they were used here with greater care for the reader's ability to check the sources and the procedures used.[29] Chicago sociologists were not particularly attached to any single research technique, but they considered the case study method to be the best for their purposes.[30]

PARK'S THEORETICAL CONCEPTIONS

Park was incomparable in inspiring empirical research, but on the whole he did not engage in it personally. There is also a striking disproportion between the range of the statements formulated by him and that of the empirical data on which they were based. His theoretical statements often originated from everyday observations, press news, unverified generalizations made by other scholars. The intention of the main coauthor of *Introduction to the Science of Sociology*[31] was not to formulate one more system of social knowledge, but to summarize that which was known about social life and which could be most useful in augmenting that knowledge. Park's works were primarily tentative codifications of sociological terminology and systematizations of problems. Their nature was certainly due to Park's role as a teacher of a group of field workers.

The main feature of Park's conception is the dualism of community versus society, the biotic versus the cultural level of relationships among human beings, the ecological base versus the moral superstructure.

Community versus Society. Park strove to overcome the opposition between two conceptions of society, which had been formulated first (and, in any case, most comprehensively) by Spencer and Comte. As Park wrote, human societies have two aspects:

They are composed of individuals who act independently of one another, who compete and struggle with one another for mere existence, and treat one another, as far as possible, as utilities. On the other hand, it is quite as true that men and women are bound together by affections and common purposes; they do cherish traditions, ambitions, and ideals that are not all their own, and they maintain, in spite of natural impulses to the contrary, a discipline and a moral order that enables them to transcend what we ordinarily call nature and through their collective action "recreate" the world in the image of their collective aspirations and their common will.[32]

The first of these two dimensions of social life was called by him *community*; and the other, *society*. Social evolution consists of developing the specifically human ability to create moral order, which, however, in each period in human history has its own physical base.[33]

That base is not specifically human and can be seen in the entire organic world. When describing community, Park drew amply from works by biologists, physiologists, and ecologists. He also willingly referred to Darwin and Darwinism. However, his point of departure was not what has been established by natural science, but the earlier tradition of social thought that included Hobbes and Adam Smith, the latter in his capacity as the theorist who interpreted competition as a natural phenomenon.[34] The aspect of relations among human beings that comes closest to nature was treated by Park as that which can be handled by rigorous scientific methods, and that is why sociology should start from it.

This is not to say that the knowledge provided by natural science can be used directly in the social sciences. Within society, natural or ecological relations always coexist with social and moral relations. Park's intention, accordingly, was not to explain social facts by including them in a broader and better-known category, as nineteenth-century naturalists had done, but to single out the kind of facts to which knowledge provided by natural science could be applied. Even though he did not always realize it, his singling out the community referred to the concept of ideal types: In the human world, there is no community in its pure form, but every society has some of its attributes. The most important of these attributes is a definite territory, the peculiarities of which have their societal consequences. Community as an ideal type consists of individuals who strive only for satisfaction of their egoistic needs. There is no social contact, no communication, and no understanding among individuals, but only struggle for existence and sharp competition. If there happens to be cooperation among individuals, it is competitive and transient in nature, and more important still, it develops spontaneously, like symbiosis in the world of plants and animals. It is not quite clear what is, according to Park, the relationship between symbiosis and the division of labor or that between the human ecological population and the economy based on free competition, but it seems that he was inclined to consider economic life as a phenomenon on the asocial or presocial level and, in any case, as that which comes closest to the biotic level of relations among human beings.

Society, as Park understood it, is in opposition to community in almost every respect, although the basic ecological processes do not cease to be at work in it and merely occur in less hostile forms. Park wrote, "The existence of a society presupposes a certain amount of solidarity, consensus, and common purpose."[35] Comte's term *consensus* is perhaps not the most fortunate choice here, because what calls society into existence is not the state of sympathy, but two processes; one makes sympathy possible, and the other results from it: communication and collective action. On that point, Park referred directly to social pragmatism, as he also did in his social psychology. Collective action requires not only communication among individuals, but social control as well, the latter being the third essential attribute of society that distinguishes it from community. To put it briefly, society means consensus (communication), social control (which fixes the effects of communication), and the resulting collective action, because society exists for action and in action. When describing society, Park says that it consists not of individuals, but of persons—that is, such individuals who not only occupy a definite place in space, but also have their moral place, the status assigned to them by other persons in accordance with the norms accepted by all of them. Unlike ecological processes, social processes are more or less conscious in nature.

Processes of Interaction. Although Park emphasized that society is not only an aggregate of individuals, he consistently maintained that the explanation of sociological facts does not require adopting the fiction of society as a kind of person. An appropriate analysis can reveal the set of elementary processes whose participants are individual persons or, more precisely, the attitudes of those persons. Park's *Introduction* is mostly a treatise on processes of interaction. In his system the key position is held by four processes: competition, conflict, accommodation, and assimilation.

The concept of competition refers primarily to the struggle for existence that is described by biologists, but covers also economic competition, studied by Smith and Bastiat. The demarcation line between competition and the higher forms of interaction is also the demarcation line of consciousness, that is, social contact. When that line is crossed, competition becomes conflict, and the individuals who struggle with one another come to realize that they are rivals or enemies. The object of the struggle changes, too: "Competition determines the position of the individual in the community; conflict fixes his place in society. Location, position, ecological interdependence—these are characteristics of the community. Status, subordination and superordination, control—these are distinctive marks of a society."[36]

In Park's opinion, conflict is the most common process of social interaction. This is decisive for the importance of accommodation, which, being the social counterpart of biological adaptation, consists of the mutual adjustment of antagonistic elements and their achievement of an unstable equilibrium that continues as long as the system of forces remains unchanged. In a new situation (and we should note that change is the natural state of society) the process of accommodation begins anew. While accommodation is only a temporary suspension of conflict, assimilation means its cessation, for the latter is "a process of interpenetration and fusion in which persons and groups acquire the memories, sentiments, and attitudes of other persons or groups."[37] It is only that process which produces society in the full sense of the term, even though it does not eliminate the possibility of new conflicts or the necessity of new processes of accommodation.

Owing to all these processes, "community assumes the form of a society."[38] Competition yields a symbiotic economic equilibrium; conflict yields social order; accommodation yields social conformism and social organization; assimilation yields common culture and the corresponding features of personality.

Social Psychology: The Individual versus the Person. Transition from ecological community to society means transformation of the individual into the person. We come here across the strongest manifestation of Park's dualism: On the one hand, there is the "natural" man, whose instincts must be restrained by social order; on the other hand, we find the social man, whose "human nature" is a product of social relations.[39] The former is a member of a community; and the latter, of a society. Insofar as Park is concerned with the society, his views converge with those of social pragmatists, to whom he also explicitly referred. Park's sociology was not opposed to social pragmatism, but it covered a much broader range of facts (the sphere of ecology, common to the whole organic world, and its effect on social life, in the strict sense of the term). Some interpretations reduce Park's social theory to his ecology, but his theory included social psychology as an integral part in accordance with Park's belief that "all the problems of social life are . . . problems of the individual; and all problems of the individual are at the same time problems of the group."[40] In the manner of posing those problems Park followed Dewey, Thomas, Cooley, and Mead.

But he is original on some points, which is probably due to the urban perspective of his sociology. Thus, the primary group loses for him the particular role in producing social personality that it had for Cooley, because its proximity to the biotic level makes it less social than the secondary groups (it was Park who introduced that term to the vocabulary of sociology). The individual becomes the person by entering the sphere of "civilization," "adventure," plurality and variety of contacts. This was related to Park's concept of "marginal man," who lives in two social worlds at the same time (as did Jews in Europe, mulattoes in America, and Simmel's "strangers") and hence "becomes . . . the individual with the wider horizon, the keener intelligence, the more detached and rational viewpoint. The marginal man is always relatively the more civilized human being."[41]

One of the peculiarities of Park's social psychology was the linking of the conception of social personality to the concept of social role, which was later to be elaborated by Linton and Znaniecki. A given man's idea of himself is connected with the role that he tries to play in society and the recognition and status that society assigns to the various roles. Park's other contribution to social psychology was the search for spatial correlates of the feelings of strangeness and hostility between members of different social groups (such as classes and ethnic groups), which led to the conception of measurable social distance; this idea was not fully used until Bogardus, who constructed his well-known scale of such distance. Park also helped to popularize the concept of attitudes, which he held to be the basic units of social interaction. Only attitudes are given empirically, because "being tendencies to act, they are expressive and communicable. They present us human motives in the only form in which we can know them objectively, namely, as behavior."[42]

Social Psychology: Collective Behavior. One of the issues on which Park focused his interest was collective behavior; this meant that he continued the tradition of Edward Allsworth Ross (1866-1951) and European social psychologists. He defined collective behavior as "the behavior of individuals under the influence of an impulse that is common and collective, an impulse, in other words, that is the result of social interaction."[43] Such facts provided the subject of most works written by Park himself (beginning with his journal articles and his doctoral thesis on the crowd and the public) and a large part of those which he inspired, the most notable ones being *The Natural History of Revolution* (1927) by Lyford P. Edwards, *The Strike as Group Behavior* (1924) by Ernest T. Miller, and *Rural Unrest* (1929) by Thomas C. McCormick.

Park created an expanded system of concepts that made it possible to analyze various forms of collective behavior, from social unrest to institutionalized forms of social movements. The system included the concepts of crowd and the public, sects and institutions, mental epidemics, propaganda, mass movements, fashion, reforms, and revolution. The concept of circular reaction was pivotal in Park's conception of collective behavior: in such an interaction, an individual's response reproduces the stimulation that came from another and sends it back, thus reinforcing the latter's stimulation. Such interstimulation becomes circular, and the individuals involved mutually reflect their emotional states, thereby increasing their intensity.

Park's Theoretical Conceptions versus Empirical Studies. It cannot be said with certainty that Park's endeavor to integrate the theoretical achievements of sociology and to adjust them to the requirements of empirical studies was successful. Park did provide researchers from the Chicago school with a terminology and with stimulating hypotheses, and he also opened their eyes to the wealth of the social world, especially that of a big city. Yet, there is a disproportion between the range of Park's theoretical ideas and that of the interests revealed by the school. The reasons are to be seen primarily in Park's system itself, which, being a system of concepts and classifications, could not be verified by researchers. They treated the city mostly as an organization that is both moral and physical, both community and society, as an "organism," as Park himself was fond of calling it. When concerned with facts, he would blunt his dichotomy and would even endow the term *community* with meanings opposed to the ecological one. The distinctions made in theory were blurred in practice. While the ecological conception retained its significance, it did so mainly as a recommendation to take the spatial aspects of social life into account. It was must less often used to explain social facts.

Park's theoretical dualism had its analogue in his methodological eclecticism. On the one hand, he recommended maximum precision of the methods used, as he started from the assumption that spatial relations can fully be measured and can also serve as indicators of social relations. As an ecologist, Park was an advocate of the statistical method and its application. On the other hand, as a student of society and a social psychologist, Park was enthusiastic about qualitative methods, because sociology "is not concerned with individuals as such, but with a special type of relation, not fundamentally physical, existing between individuals, and which constitutes them persons."[44] Statistics is not useful in the study of such relations and of human attitudes. What is recommended instead is an analysis of autobiographical data, which offers an insight into the motives and experiences of persons. True, sociology is a natural discipline that discovers laws, but it needs support from idiographic history, which teaches one to understand human beings and events. Still another aspect of Park's dualism is the acceptance of the free-competition struggle for existence as a natural phenomenon, opposed to a reformer's dream of a society in which morality would triumph over animal instincts and would give that struggle ever more sublimated forms.

The nature of Park's sociology was responsible, it seems, for the disintegration of the school that he had created. While he had many disciples in American sociology, none would try to develop his views as a whole. Some of his disciples continued specialized empirical research in Chicago and in other urban centers; others focused their attention on expanding the theory of social ecology; and still others (Blumer, for example) concentrated on social psychology, thereby coming close to symbolic interactionism in its pure form. There were also those who continued Park's conceptual formalism (Howard Becker), thus referring to more recent works by L. von Wiese; those who tried to improve the statistical method (Samuel A. Stouffer); and even those who turned to ideas that had been completely alien to the founder of the school (psychoanalysis in the case of Harold Lasswell;

the theory of social actions in the case of Edward Shils). Even Louis
Wirth—next to Burgess, the most loyal of Park's coworkers, endeavored in
the 1930s to familiarize American sociologists with recent achievements of
German theoretical thought (Mannheim's sociology of knowledge).

But even the empirical research represented by the Chicago school came
to lose its dominant position to studies that were closer to the pattern of
ethnographic monograph, represented in sociology by *Middletown* and the
Yankee City Series. Warner, who held the achievements of the Chicago
school in great esteem, wrote about the need of coming to know a small
community more fully and in greater detail than it was possible in the case
of a big city,[45] which as a subject of study is too vast and too varied. American empirical sociology of the 1930s returned to those small towns about
which Veblen used to write, as it saw them to be much better laboratories
of social science than Chicago was.

THE SOCIAL WORLD OF THE SMALL TOWN: THE LYNDS' MIDDLETOWN

The perspective adopted by Robert Staughton Lynd (1892-1970) and his
coworkers (the most important of whom was Helen Lynd, his wife) was not
chosen intentionally. That choice was not a manifestation of opposition
to Chicago sociologists, but simply a consequence of the fact that when
starting his research, Lynd knew very little about sociology and planned
his work on the basis of studies made by social anthropolgists: *Man and
Culture in America* (1923) by Clark Wissler and *Social Organization* (1924)
by W. H. R. Rivers. Lynd's point of departure was thoroughly practical:
A graduate of a theological seminary and a would-be Presbyterian minister,
he became interested in the scope and determinants of religious practices
in an average American town. Influenced by the principles of social anthropology, he decided to analyze religious attitudes and practices in the context
of the life of a local community in its entirety, which yielded one of the
most comprehensive monographs of such a community; the original subject
matter became merely one of many issues. As Wissler wrote in his preface to
Middletown, Lynd's experiment initiated "the social anthropology of contemporary life."[46] In collecting and classifying his data, Lynd adopted the
six-point schema of classification of human actions suggested by Rivers in
Social Organization: earning a living, making a home, training the young,
spending leisure time, engaging in religious practices, and engaging in community activities. The town of Muncie, Indiana, the subject of his study,
was considered to be an average American town (hence the code name
Middletown). There the Lynds engaged in intensive field work for eighteen
months in 1924 and 1925—before the appearance of most studies produced
by the Chicago school.

Middletown (1929). Muncie was chosen for two essential reasons: It met the Lynds' requirements of being a representative town, and it was small and homogeneous enough to be described as a whole. It was probably during their field work that the authors noted what would be the principal subject of their monograph: the impact of industrialization on the life of a traditional American town. Following the discovery in Muncie of natural gas deposits, the town changed from a very small place with 6,000 inhabitants in 1885 into a town of 37,000 in 1920 (and 47,000 in 1935). This was why the Lynds considered it necessary to contrast the conditions in 1924-1925 with those which preceded the rapid expansion of the town. Even though they had not written a history of the town, but merely compared the conditions prevailing in it at two selected moments, they succeeded in picturing the process of industrialization and its varied consequences. The picture was even clearer because the relative homogeneity of the population (there was a negligible percentage of immigrants and Negroes) left the image unobscured by other processes.

There is also a striking difference from the studies by the Chicago school: The Lynds did not try to grasp the full wealth and variety of the social processes provoked by rapid industrialization in the United States, but interpreted the popular metaphor of laboratory more literally. This made *Middletown* come closer to a scholarly monograph, whereas works produced by Chicago sociologists bordered on journalism. The Lynds were also the first sociologists to describe systematically the methods that they had used; they did so in a special supplement to their book.

One characteristic of *Middletown*, as compared with other early community studies, was its use of the concept of social class.[47] That concept was later to become increasingly important both in the works of Lynd himself and in other community studies (especially those by Warner). The concept of class used by the Lynds in their first monograph was extremely simple: They divided the population of Middletown into two large groups, the working class and the business class, the criterion thus being the main source of income. The novelty lay not in formulating any remarkable conception of class and class structure, but rather in giving rise to thinking about local communities in terms of class divisions. This viewpoint was very rare in American sociology in the 1920s, when the subject of study was the traditional American community of white Anglo-Saxon protestants and not the human mosaic of a big city, whose social differentiation could be explained by differences in the Americanization of the various groups of immigrant population. In Lynd's later works his conception of class structure became more complex.

Middletown in Transition. Lynd's second work—*Middletown in Transition: A Study in Cultural Conflicts* (1937)—was a result of field work conducted in the same town some ten years later. The idea of a repeated study was excellent in itself. But the importance of that undertaking was primarily due to the fact that the intervening decade was marked by the Great Depression, which affected both Muncie (Lynd himself referred to "the experimental situation") and the world view of the researchers. This time Lynd decided to find out what had been the effect of the depression on the life of an average American town. Most interesting, however, were not his conclusions on that matter, but the fact that under the impact of his new experience he came to view the facts that he had learned earlier from a different angle.

Middletown had been written from the position of a social anthropologist who tried to look at his own society from the outside, as if observing a primitive tribe. In *Middletown in Transition* Lynd deliberately abandoned that viewpoint and engaged in a controversy with his own society, which had understood so little of its latest history. In effect, the book was a sociological manifesto of the New Deal, and it provides one of the best testimonies to the radicalization of American university circles in the 1930s. At that time Lynd also discovered Marx—something quite extraordinary in American sociology of that period—and showed much interest in the results of the Soviet social experiment.

Middletown in Transition is primarily a journalist's treatise on the end of frontier America, the America of free, equal, and enterprising pioneers. The opinions upheld by the inhabitants of Middletown seem to Lynd to be anachronistic and at variance with facts. This can best be observed when he takes up anew the problems of class structure in Muncie. The class structure described in *Middletown* was, in fact, not hierarchical. The position of an independent businessman was attractive to all, but—in accordance with the American myth—it was also accessible to all. In *Middletown in Transition* the class structure is seen as a multilevel hierarchy, and, moreover, Lynd discovers in Middletown a family that seems to control exclusively many spheres of life in the town. The division of the community into classes came to be associated by Lynd with inequality in the participation in power; in this, he anticipated a distinct trend in the community studies, a trend that became very strong after World War II. The class structure discovered by Lynd—unlike Warner's school—is objective in nature: It is a significant fact in the life of the community even if its members, sticking to ideas from another epoch, fail to notice it.

The Calling of Social Science. Lynd's journalistic temper was given fullest vent in *Knowledge for What?* (1939), consisting of his lectures at Princeton in 1938. Lynd abandoned completely the role of a dispassionate chronicler of American provinces and assumed that of an advocate, discussing the issues of American society as a whole and teaching his colleagues what, thanks to Mills, we have called "the sociological imagination." In fact, it was Lynd who initiated in the United States that trend of critical sociology which was later to be followed by the author of *White Collar* and his disciples in the 1960s. The link between the two roles in which Lynd came to be known—that of a chronicler and that of an advocate—was his conviction that myths must be constantly confronted with facts and that sociology plays an important educational role. *Knowledge for What?* is a classical work concerned with the search for the proper calling of sociology and also provides an interesting testimony of the ideological and theoretical crisis in American sociology in the late 1930s that resulted in the rejection of the paradigm of the Chicago school.

He saw several causes of the intensifying crisis of the social sciences. First of all, these sciences proved incapable of facing the burning social issues and of opposing the prevailing opinions. They failed to influence effectively the decisions made by politicians and to change those current folk assumptions that were glaringly at variance with the realities of changing America. Fascinated by the model of natural science, the social sciences tended to accept as natural all that exists and is subject to observation, as they assumed the existence of a hidden order that the scholar has to discover. "We social scientists," Lynd wrote, "tend to begin by accepting our contemporary institutions as the datum of social science; we then go on to view them as a 'system'; this, in turn, endows the system, by definition, with its laws, and then we seek to discover these laws as the laws of social science."[48] If one can speak about the order of culture, then it is only on the condition that we consider it not to be something given, like a natural phenomenon, but to be something *created* by men. The task of the social sciences is not to discover that order, but to build it into the social reality.

According to Lynd, another cause of the weakness of the social sciences was their excessive specialization, dispersion of interests, and loss of any common system of reference. Despite all their declarations that everything is linked to a broader context, representatives of the various social disciplines behaved as if they thought that there were separate social, economic, and political facts. In truth, all those facts belong in a single whole that "is nothing less than the entire culture."[49] This idea is not worked out theoretically in *Knowledge for What?* although we find there an interesting description of American culture as a whole, which proves the attractiveness of the patterns created by psychoculturally minded anthropologists.

While turning toward a kind of holism, Lynd warned against "cultural determinism, viewing culture as self-contained force, operating by inner laws of its own to coerce and to shape people to its ends."[50] Lynd also blamed the social sciences for having lost the ability to see persons and having left that task to the psychologists. What was needed was interpreting institutions as parts of total culture and "viewing culture as living in and operating as the learned habits and impulses of persons."[51] Such a social science would be, in Lynd's opinion, a synthesis of Marxism and Freudianism, free from the one-sidedness of either.

Lynd's theoretical reflections in *Knowledge for What?* would not by themselves deserve any special attention. Their significance is due to the fact that they were largely a self-criticism by a representative of descriptive sociology, who had come to realize that by studying fragments, one thereby accepted the existing system, occupied a position inside that system, and approved "definitions of situation" that disagreed with the conscience and the calling of a scholar. Lynd sought a way out by suggesting a social science that would cover the entire range of human behavior.

YANKEE CITY *AND WARNER'S FUNCTIONALISM*

The third great undertaking in American descriptive sociology was the research conducted by W. Lloyd Warner (1898-1970) and his coworkers, particularly the detailed study of Newburyport, a small town in Massachusetts, that is summed up in the six volumes of the *Yankee City Series* (1941-1959).

Warner is best known as the initiator of the popular, although often criticized, method of investigating the class stratification of society. As Tumin wrote, "More than anyone else, Warner has been responsible for the emphasis in American studies of stratification on reputation and prestige."[52] Warner was not a theorist, and in his works elements of theory are usually hidden beneath the numbers of descriptive data. Nevertheless, his main theoretical ideas—even though sometimes bordering on banalities—were on the main track of the development of American theoretical thought in sociology in the 1940s, and they were also one of the major announcements of the coming triumph of functionalism. Warner himself thought that he represented in sociography a standpoint that was theoretically more refined than that of the Chicago school.[53]

Roots of Warner's Functionalism. Warner's sociology had two roots. First, it was social anthropology, in which he had engaged at the beginning of his field work (for instance, in 1937 he published *A Black Civilization: A Study of an Australian Tribe*). Second, it was a reflection of Elton Mayo (1880-1949), stimulated by the unrest caused by the development of industrial civilization and by the experience of the earliest studies and experiments in industrial sociology.[54]

These two sources of inspiration were far less different from one another than they might seem to be at first. Social anthropology pursued in the spirit of Radcliffe-Brown made one think that "most, if not all, societies have a fundamental structure or structures which integrate and give characteristic form to the rest of society."[55] On the other hand, industrial research revealed that "although [a worker's] relations with fellow workers and with management are of very great importance, they are but part of the total number of interrelations which make up the worker's behavior and tie him not only to the factory but to the total community."[56]

Mayo, whom Warner met shortly after his return to the United States, was one of the first American sociologists to discover Durkheim and an advocate of making industrial research cover a broader social context of human work. And it was probably he who initiated cooperation between students of industry and anthropologists and encouraged Warner to use his Australian experience in the study of American society.

In any case, Warner did not have to change radically the viewpoint that he had developed in his research on tribal communities: He had to face the same problem of social integration and interrelationships among the various spheres of social life. The introduction to the first volume of the *Yankee City Series* says that, "Yankee City, we assumed, was a 'working whole' in which each part has definite functions which had to be performed, or substitutes acquired, if the whole society were to maintain itself. The problem faced by the research was a structural one."[57]

Research Strategy. This tendency to view the community as a working whole predetermined the choice of the subject matter and the set of concepts to be used. Warner deliberately abandoned the aspiration to grasp the almost infinite wealth of the social world of a big city, with which the Chicago school concerned itself (he held the Chicago school in great esteem, and, in contrast, there is not a single reference to the Lynds in his works). Hence the choice of the community to be studied, which was extremely characteristic of Warner:

We sought above all a well-integrated community, where the various parts of the society were functioning with comparative ease. We did not want a city where the ordinary daily relations of the inhabitants were in confusion or in conflict. . . . We wanted a group which had not undergone such rapid social change that the disruptive factors would be more important than those which maintained a balanced grouping of the members of the society.[58]

This choice of the sociological laboratory marked the difference between Warner, on the one hand, and the members of the Chicago school and the Lynds, on the other, for the latter were fascinated by the disruptive factors that were operating in American society more and more strongly. Warner remained a sociologist of social integration and stabilization and came to be appreciated fully only when the unrest caused by the Great Depression had abated.

Hence arose Warner's interest in the common values upheld by the members of the community that he studied. Hence also arose his truly Durkheimist interest in "symbol systems which function to integrate the people into total community activities."[59] This interest reached its peak in the last volume of the *Yankee City Series*, entitled *The Living and the Dead* (1959), which carries a comprehensive analysis of the beliefs and symbols linking Americans together.

Warner's Conception of Class Structure. It is merely an apparent paradox that Warner became one of the leading students of class and class structure in American sociology.[60] The point is that the conception of social classes advanced by the students of Yankee City was almost a total denial of all those conceptions (not popular in the United States) that covered the problems of class conflict and class struggle. The peculiarity of Warner's conception also lay in the rejection of the economic concept of class and in the focus on the study of social stratification from the point of view of prestige. This does not mean that Warner rejected all other dimensions of social stratification, but he thought them of secondary rank. By classes he meant groups of people who "are believed to be, and are accordingly ranked by the members of the community, in socially superior and inferior positions."[61] Such an interpretation of social classes required the assumption that the community in question has a common system of values. Thus, we can construct a uniform social hierarchy if we refer to the assessment of social positions made by the members of that community. This approach to class structure not only did not infringe on the solidaristic conception of society, but even reinforced it. It may be said in conclusion that Warner's conceptions were based both on definite ideological options (different from those which marked the Lynds) and on certain habits developed during his research on primitive societies.

SOCIOGRAPHY AND THE DEVELOPMENT OF SOCIOLOGICAL THOUGHT

We have focused attention on selected achievements of American sociography between the world wars. We have disregarded sociography in other countries, although it was developing vigorously and was better and better appreciated by theoretically minded sociologists. This omission, however, seems justified for two reasons. First, it was in the United States that descriptive sociology became, with few exceptions, *the* sociology. Second, in the United States it moved further away from the pattern of earlier social surveys than it did elsewhere, and it moved beyond the study of specified social issues that required immediate practical solutions. American descriptive sociology was an endeavor to bridge the gap between a sociology with scholarly and scientific aspirations and an unassuming striving to disclose burning social issues. It had to comply with the standards of academic science without losing sensitivity to the dramas of contemporary society and without abandoning the hope of effective actions.

While one must appreciate the intention of this endeavor, one can hardly consider its result to be a success. In practice, American descriptive sociology was marked either by fascination with details, which eliminated all general social theory, or by superficial theorizing that was intended exclusively to provide researchers with good instruments of describing and ordering a mass of empirical findings. This theorizing was rather eclectic and did not offer any satisfactory point of departure for formulation of genuine syntheses, which Lynd came to realize so clearly in *Knowledge for What?* Moreover, that inability to produce syntheses made people doubt whether sociology pursued in that way could prove equal to the great social tasks that it had undertaken deliberately.

NOTES

1. Robert E. L. Faris, "American Sociology," in Georges Gurvitch and Wilbert E. Moore, eds., *Twentieth Century Sociology* (New York: Philosophical Library, 1946), p. 546.

2. Robert E. Park and Ernest W. Burgess, *Introduction to the Science of Sociology* (Chicago: University of Chicago Press, 1921), p. 45.

3. Robert S. Lynd and Helen M. Lynd, *Middletown in Transition* (New York: Harcourt, Brace, 1937), p. xviii.

4. Roland L. Warren, *The Community in America*, 2d ed. (Chicago: Rand McNally, 1972), p. 21.

5. George A. Hillery, Jr., "Definitions of Community: Areas of Agreement," *Rural Sociology* 20 (1955); 111-19.

6. J. Bernard, *The Sociology of Community* (Glenview, Ill.; Scott, Foresman, 1973), pp. 3-5.

7. Cf. especially Robert A. Nisbet, *The Quest for Community* (London: Oxford University Press, 1953) and *The Sociological Tradition* (London: Heinemann, 1967).

8. See D. W. Minar and S. Greer, eds., *The Concept of Community: Readings with Interpretations* (Chicago: Aldine, 1969), p. 91.

9. Don Martindale, *American Social Structure: Historical Antecedents and Contemporary Analysis* (New York: Appleton, 1960), p. ix.

10. C. M. Arensberg and S. T. Kimball, *Culture and Community* (New York: Harcourt, Brace, 1965), p. 34.

11. Ibid., p. 31.

12. Cf. Julian H. Steward, *Area Research: Theory and Practice*, Social Science Research Council, Bulletin no. 63 (New York: Social Science Research Council, 1950), p. 21.

13. Robert E. Park, Ernest W. Burgess, and Roderick D. McKenzie, *The City* (Chicago: University of Chicago Press, 1925), p. 3.

14. Steward, *Area Research*, p. 29.

15. Ibid., p. 22.

16. Ibid., p. 45.

17. Ibid.

18. See Bernard, *Sociology of Community*, and Dennis E. Poplin, *Communities: A Survey of Theories and Methods of Research* (New York: Macmillan, 1972).

19. Robert Redfield, *The Little Community: Viewpoints for the Study of a Human Whole* (Chicago: University of Chicago Press, 1955).

20. E. Shils, "Tradition, Ecology, and Institutionalization in the History of Sociology," *Daedalus* (Fall 1970); 792-93; Anthony Oberschall, "The Institutionalization of American Sociology," in Oberschall, ed., *The Establishment of Empirical Sociology: Studies in Continuity, Discontinuity and Institutionalization* (New York: Harper and Row, 1972), pp. 187-251.

21. Bernard, *Sociology of Community*, p. 41.

22. Henrika Kuklick, "A 'Scientific Revolution': Sociological Theory in the United States, 1930-1945," *Sociological Inquiry* 43 (1973):3-22.

23. R. E. Park, "The City as a Social Laboratory," in T. V. Smith and L. D. White, eds., *Chicago: An Experiment in Social Science Research* (Chicago: University of Chicago Press, 1929), p. 2.

24. L. Wirth, "The Urban Sociology and Civilization," in Wirth, ed., *Eleven Twenty Six: A Decade of Social Science Research* (Chicago: University of Chicago Press, 1940), p. 52.

25. Park and Burgess, *Introduction*, p. vi.

26. The concepts of "nature" and "natural history" are among the key concepts of Chicago sociology. To them "natural" meant unplanned, unintentional, uncontrolled, independent of one's will, and yet governed by laws and predictable. Milla A. Alihan, *Social Ecology: A Critical Analysis* (New York: Columbia University Press, 1938), pp. 50-52.

27. Ibid., pp. 143-81.

28. This enumeration is not claimed to be complete. Moreover, it does not include later works written by the same authors outside the scope of the school, although there are among them outstanding studies, such as Hughes's works. *The Social Fabric of the Metropolis: Contributions of the Chicago School of Urban Sociology* (Chicago: University of Chicago Press, 1971), edited by James F. Short, Jr., is a very useful anthology of the Chicago school's studies.

29. John Madge, *The Origins of Scientific Sociology* (London: Tavistock, 1963), pp. 114-25.

30. Vivien M. Palmer, *Field Studies in Sociology: A Student Manual* (Chicago: University of Chicago Press, 1928), p. 19-20.

31. Ernest W. Burgess (1886-1956) was the younger coauthor of this handbook of sociology, which was both a reader and a treatise and went through a number of editions.

32. R. E. Park, "Sociology," in Wilson Gee, ed., *Research in the Social Sciences: Its Fundamental Methods and Objectives* (New York: Macmillan, 1929), pp. 6-7.

33. Alihan, *Social Ecology*, pp. 13-14, 26, 69-70.

34. Ibid., pp. 92.

35. Park, "Sociology," p. 7.

36. Park and Burgess, *Introduction*, pp. 574-75.

37. Ibid., p. 735.

38. Ibid., p. 785.

39. Park, *The City*, p. 43; Park and Burgess, *Introduction*, pp.20, 46-47, 161.

40. Park and Burgess, *Introduction*, p. 57. See E. W. Burgess, ed. *The Personality* (Chicago: University of Chicago Press, 1929).

41. See Ralph H. Turner, ed., *Robert E. Park on Social Control and Collective Behavior* (Chicago: University of Chicago Press, 1967), p. xv.

42. Park and Burgess, *Introduction*, p. 438.

43. Ibid., p. 865.

44. Park, "Sociology," p. 5.

45. W. L. Warner and P. S. Lunt, *The Social Life of Modern Community* (New Haven: Yale University Press, 1941), p. 4.

46. Robert S. Lynd and Helen M. Lynd, *Middletown* (New York: Harcourt, Brace, 1929), p. vi.

47. See Milton M. Gordon, *Social Class in American Sociology* (New York: McGraw-Hill, 1950), chap. 3.

48. Robert S. Lynd, *Knowledge for What? The Place of Social Science in American Culture* (Princeton: Princeton University Press, 1939), p. 1.

49. Ibid., pp. 18-19.

50. Ibid., p. 22.

51. Ibid., p. 24.

52. Melvin M. Tumin, *Social Stratification: The Forms and Functions of Inequality* (Englewood Cliffs, N.J.: Prentice-Hall, 1967), p. 8.

53. Warner and Lunt, *Social Life*, p. 12.

54. Madge, *Origins*, chap. 6.

55. Warner and Lunt, *Social Life*, p. 36.

56. Ibid., p. 1.

57. Ibid., p. 14.

58. Ibid., p. 38.

59. Ibid., p. 63.

60. Gordon, *Social Class*, chap. 4.

61. Warner and Lunt, *Social Life*, p. 82.

16

CULTURE, SOCIETY, AND PERSONALITY: THE NEW VISTAS OF ANTHROPOLOGY

ANTHROPOLOGY VERSUS SOCIOLOGY

As the specialization and institutionalization of the social sciences intensified, anthropology and sociology moved farther and farther apart, the process already being marked in the late nineteenth century. The process was caused by advances in the division of intellectual labor, which began in the epoch of evolutionism, and at least two other factors. One was the aggravating crisis of the theories of social evolution, theories that naturally required the union of sociology and anthropology as the science of the earliest stages of the development of mankind. The other was the anthropologists' turn toward field work, dating from the 1890s, which favored their taking up issues about which sociologists had less and less to say. Thus, each of the two disciplines began to develop its own domains of interests, theories, terminology, and research techniques. It is true that the situation was not the same in all countries: In some—for instance, in France and England—the links between anthropology and sociology remained practically unimpaired.

Nevertheless, we are inclined to maintain that the basic theoretical dilemmas of sociology and anthropology have been the same, regardless of the institutional relationships between these disciplines. This is why we think it necessary to pay some attention to the development of anthropological conceptions. This seems advisable also for the following reasons.

First, those theoretical and methodological discussions which are essential for sociology have their analogues in anthropology (and not only in social anthropology, but in cultural anthropology and ethnology as well). On the other hand, the various anthropological conceptions had a noticeable effect on sociological orientations. In many cases anthropologists were more advanced in theory building than sociologists and in some situations (Britain between the world wars) merely replaced them in formulating sociological theory.

Second, counter to the simplified opinion, anthropologists were not necessarily interested exclusively in primitive societies and preliterate cultures, but often believed themselves to be competent to make statements about modern society and society in general. Many of them were inclined to think that what characterizes them is a certain attitude rather than the subject matter of investigations. Primitive societies were usually believed to provide a *sui generis* laboratory that allowed scholars to discover truths that have wider applications. Note also that twentieth-century anthropology has dealt less and less with isolated traditional societies and more and more with their decomposition, modernization, cross-cultural contacts, and the like; as a result, it inevitably has met with sociology. The opposition between traditional and modern, primitive and civilized societies, so popular not long ago, has been losing its importance.

And third, it was in anthropology that the modern concept of culture was formed, a concept without which—despite all its ambiguity—no social science can do today.

It is, however, not our intention to present the unquestionable contribution of anthropology to the modern social sciences. Our point is rather to show the changes that it has undergone and the new vistas that have opened before it as the heritage of the nineteenth century was being overcome. We shall discuss diffusionism, historicism, functionalism, and the so-called culture and personality approach. Evolutionistic anthropology, of course, continued to develop, but we shall not be concerned with it any longer and shall pay only brief attention to the beginnings of neo-evolutionism.

Anthropology did not witness the emergence of any theories that would be analogues of Max Weber's interpretative sociology or other trends of humanistic sociology. In anthropology, the influence of naturalism proved more persistent; nevertheless, that discipline undersent a deep transformation similar to the antipositivist revolt in the humanities as a whole. The significance of this revolt was enhanced by the fact that theoretical reflections of anthropologists were accompanied by a thorough reconstruction of their research methods, following which anthropology became an empirical discipline earlier than sociology did. The first generation of anthropologists worked in their offices and in libraries; the second moved to museums; and the third made it their absolute duty to do field work without abandoning ambitions to contribute to the theory of their discipline.

DIFFUSIONISM

The first stage of postevolutionistic anthropology (or, rather, ethnology in this case) was represented by scholars who, because of their particular interest in the problems of the diffusion of culture, came to be known as "diffusionists" even though they did not use that term themselves. Diffusionism was rather poor in its theoretical aspect, and it is its research strategy that deserves attention: Historical reconstructions came to replace evolutionistic constructions. Diffusionists were, in fact, much more anti-organicistically minded than antievolutionistically minded, as they exerted themselves much more to refute the conception of culture as a spontaneous-ly developing whole than to overcome the very idea of development. The main difference between diffusionists and evolutionists lay in the former's having shifted the focus of their attention from the development of social wholes to the fortunes of their various elements without, however, having freedom themselves from the dangers of the comparative method and the inclination to construct arbitrarily long sequences of evolutionary stages based on unreliable and heterogeneous data. Lévi-Strauss is right in stating that diffusionists and evolutionists had a similar attitude toward history: They all revealed little comprehension of historical individualities and were concerned primarily with making combinations of more or less universal elements,[1] even though they had different ends in view and based their theories on different principles. Where the evolutionist sought laws, the diffusionist tried to find causal and chronological relationships.

It seems, however, that the perspective adopted by the diffusionists was more conducive to the study of the actual development of culture, and that was why they were the eminent field workers of their times, a type that could not be found among the evolutionists. The diffusionists enriched the body of anthropological data, even though those data were often not only wrongly interpreted, but also marked by a characteristic one-sidedness: The diffusionists were almost exclusively concerned with material civiliza-tion and had little to say on social organization.

Variations of Diffusionism. Diffusionists did not form any uniform school, and the term *diffusionism* is used as a general label with respect to many different conceptions. Even if we disregard their later continuations and also their less original and influential varieties, we can list several of them.

First, it is Friedrich Ratzel (1844-1904), the author of *Völkerkunde* (1885-1895) and *Anthropogeographie* (1899), who is correctly held to have originated, though not founded, diffusionism as a trend of research. He is also believed to be a founding father of geographical determinism in sociol-ogy. His role consisted mainly of bringing out the differentiating influence of the geographical environment on culture (but not of the latter being one-sidedly determined by the former) and, hence, of shifting attention from universal processes to those specific to the various regions. He also empha-sized the significance of migrations and cross-cultural contacts for the development and stagnation of societies.

Ratzel's work was continued by Leo Frobenius (1873-1938), the eminent German student of African cultures and author of *Die Weltanschauung der Naturvölker* (1898), *Problem der Kultur* (1900), and *Paideuma* (1921). He is known in the history of diffusionism by having taken up not only the problem of separate elements of culture, but also the problem of sets of such elements. His example was the best refutation of the stereotype, spread by the functionalists, of the diffusionist as the student of culture who saw everything in isolation from the rest.

Diffusionistic methodology had its most representative spokesman in Fritz Graebner (1877-1934), who, as the author of *Methode der Ethnologie* (1911) originated the concept of culture circle *(Kulturkreis)*. The key concept in the diffusionist theory, it was to become the identification mark of German and Austrian ethnology for a long time, and it had its analogue in the American term *culture area*. Graebner is also to be credited with his endeavors to define precisely those criteria which make it possible to single out the cases in which similarities between cultures can be ascribed to diffusion.

Graebner's ideas were developed most systematically by Wilhelm Schmidt (1868-1954), Roman Catholic priest, originator of what is called the Vienna school or the cultural history school, founder (in 1906) of the valuable periodical *Anthropos*, and author of many works, the best known of which are *Der Ursprung der Gottesidee* (twelve volumes, 1926-1955) and *Handbuch der Methode der kulturhistorischen Ethnologie* (1937). Schmidt elaborated the conception of humanity, seen in its various manifestations as a result of the spreading and intercrossing of a limited number of basic circles.

In Britain the ideas of diffusionism found a radical manifestation in the works of Grafton Elliot Smith (1871-1937), who developed the monogenetic theory of culture, which claims that all human culture originated in ancient Egypt. This was probably the purest form of the tendency, characteristic of the majority of diffusionists, to interpret changes in cultures as transfer and transformation, rather than invention and creation.

Finally, the so-called American school, which includes F. Boas, Clark Wissler, Alfred L. Kroeber, and others, is often also classed as diffusionistic, although its members certainly represented diffusionism in its most moderate form. There are, however, reasons for which neither Boas nor Kroeber should be crammed into the framework of diffusionism.

The Basic Assumptions of Diffusionism. Since we deal with scholars who differed so much from one another, it would be a vain task to try to list the statements that were asserted by all of them. We can at most point to certain very general options that seem typical of that orientation.

Diffusionism assumes a specific anthropology, according to which man has a limited ability to discover new things and usually rests satisfied with imitating that which is known and tested. While the evolutionists assumed man's unlimited ability to make inventions necessitated by circumstances, the diffusionists believed inventions to be exceptional and thought that culture developed mostly through replication of rarely invented patterns. That was why they claimed the development of culture to be determined mainly by the intensity of cross-cultural contacts: Isolated cultures were doomed to stagnation.

Since imitation is so important for the development of culture, the student of culture must be mainly concerned with migrations of elements of culture in time and space: He has to find out how mutual connections develop even between cultures that are extremely distant from one another. Like the evolutionists, the diffusionists were fascinated by similarities among cultures, but in such similarities they saw the proof of frequent contacts and influences not of the universality of the laws of evolution.

Being concerned with migrations of elements of culture, the diffusionists tended to understand culture as a set of elements and not as an organic whole nor an internally interconnected system. This was why they later came to be vehemently criticized by the functionalists, who blamed them for treating culture "as a thing which can be . . . transported across oceans and continents, mechanically taken to pieces and recompounded."[2] But the functionalists were mistaken. The diffusionists used to speak about *Kulturkomplexen*, and a culture circle for them was not a conglomerate of disconnected elements of culture. Such coherence was not a research problem for them. They were interested, rather, in the elements of a cultural whole that proved capable of independent life. Nor did they ask how a culture assimilated a borrowed element: They were satisfied with stating that such assimilation took place.

Unlike the evolutionists, the diffusionists were interested in culture as a property of collectivities determined in time and in space and differentiated from one another exactly by their respective cultures; they did not think of culture as an attribute of all human communities that distinguishes them from the animal world. Their problem was not the fact that every society has its culture, but the fact that each society has a different culture, that difference not being dependent on its advancement toward civilization. Differences among cultures are qualitative, not quantitative. Culture circles were mainly interpreted as rival centers located at various points of the globe and radiating toward the peoples who lived between them.

Finally, in anthropology, diffusionism was the most radical refutation of the naturalistic conception of social science and a specific implementation of the requirement that the social sciences should be concerned not with discovering universal laws, but with acquiring the knowledge of concrete processes and events. Many diffusionists referred directly to the results of the antipositivist revolution in the humanities, thus striving for ethnology as an idiographic humanistic discipline and not a nomothetic natural one.

An assessment of diffusionism in the history of the social sciences is rather difficult to make. On the one hand, it was a school whose influence did not extend far beyond ethnology and whose radical formulations encountered early and sharp criticism. On the other hand, the crucial interests of that school have not been abandoned and can be found even in present-day neo-evolutionists. Diffusionism proved to be a poor theory, but it took up essential research problems that had not been paid sufficient attention by the evolutionists.

HISTORICISM: BOAS AND HIS SCHOOL

When speaking about historicism in anthropology, we mean the production of Franz Boas (1858-1942), who is believed by many authors, especially the Americans, to have originated anthropology as a science. Boas in fact revolutionized the research methods of anthropology by imposing on its representatives the duty of conducting field work (he himself became known as a student of the life of the Eskimos and North American Indians) and—even more extraordinary at that time—of acquiring the knowledge of the language of the studied community (Boas himself was an eminent linguist). His role was also to popularize the requirement of a critical approach to sources and to observe the rigor of induction, disregarded by generations of anthropologists who were fascinated by the prospects of an all-embracing synthesis.

Boas wrote much, but his publications—except such books as *The Mind of Primitive Man* (1911), *Primitive Art* (1927), and *Anthropology and Modern Life* (1928)—were either reviews and polemic items, outlines of ideas that he would abandon before they were fully developed, or reports on research work, written in the style of official records. The only fairly complete review of his activity of more than fifty years is his collected papers and reports, a book entitled *Race, Language and Culture* (1940).

Boas, nevertheless, deserves attention not only because he was a master of accumulating factual data, but also because his ascetic approach to theory was due to an overconsciousness and not to naivete. He was marked by an exceptionally vast philosophical knowledge and profound theoretical interests. The point was that any theory, even at a fairly low level, immediately revealed its one-sidedness to him.

Intellectual Background. Franz Boas was born in Germany, where he took his Ph.D. in physics. Having behind him, as geographer, field work on Baffin Island and showing a growing interest in ethnology, he began his scientific career by becoming a junior researcher in the Museum für Völkerkunde, headed by A. Bastian, and later by qualifying as a docent at Berlin University. He decided to settle in the United States when he was nearing thirty and had been fully formed intellectually in the milieu of German scientists and scholars. In his young age his masters included Rudolf Virchow, Adolf Bastian, Theodor Fischer, Friedrich Ratzel, and—particularly interesting in this company—Dilthey and the neo-Kantians.[3] In the American world of science, Boas was an outsider who had not been influenced by the heritage of Anglo-Saxon evolutionism and also a man who both had a good training in natural science and was acquainted with the methodological discussions that began in Germany at that time. In the course of his intellectual evolution Boas modified his whole idea of science. He largely retained the standards of what is scientific, taken over from natural science, but he made room for history (in natural science, too) and tried to grasp the peculiarities of the world of culture as the subject of research.

Controversy with the Evolutionist Heritage. Boas enjoyed the well-deserved renown as the most consistent critic of evolutionism in the history of the social sciences. He questioned the evolutionist orientation *in toto* and shifted the focus of interest from a uniform process of evolution to the peculiarities of the various cultures; in doing so, he replaced the ordering of cultures along the higher-lower axis by the proclamation of their equal rights.

Boas's critique of evolutionism followed two lines. First, he maintained that theories like those constructed by the evolutionists were premature in the social sciences; second, he claimed that such theories can never be truly scientific because of the exceptional complexity of the social sciences' subject matter.

The former line of criticism consisted of proving that the discovery of such laws would be possible only after the various cultures have been investigated. "We must," Boas wrote, "so far as we can, reconstruct the actual history of mankind, before we can hope to discover the laws underlying that history."[4] If one does not observe that principle, one inevitably takes appearances for reality and sees regularities where there are merely superficial similarities. When talking about laws that govern society or culture, the evolutionists assumed that which, at best, can be concluded. To their method Boas opposed the historical method, which consisted of studying cultural facts not as parts of a hypothetical evolutionary process, but as given elements of a given culture of a given people that lives in a given geographical region and interacts with other peoples—a culture that has a certain past and forms a whole within which all parts have multiple interconnections. From that point of view, the questions posed by the evolutionists remained valid to a large extent, and it was mainly the evolutionist procedure of finding the answers that had to be rejected.

But in Boas's writings we can trace the other line of antievolutionist argumentation, gradually gaining in strength and leveled against the very conception of science as the activity intended to discover laws. Boas's conviction that the world of culture is infinitely complex led him to the conclusion that anthropology is a historical discipline; that is, it is concerned only with individual or historical units, namely, the various cultures, each of which has its own unique history. This is why "we may be able to *understand* social phenomena. I do not believe that we shall ever be able to *explain* them by reducing one and all of them to social law."[5] This is not an empiricist who rebels against speculations, but a follower of the neo-Kantian philosophy of the humanities who rejects the positivist ideal of social science.[6]

In Boas's opinion, the error of the evolutionists was not confined to the striving for the inaccessible goal of discovering the laws of the development of culture. Their generalizations were wrong, as they forced other cultures to fit the schema abstracted from their own culture, considering this schema to be the universal standard. This is the grossest blunder that the anthropologist can make. Every culture must be studied on its own basis—from the inside, as it were—and one must try to grasp its specific psychological, environmental, and historical conditions without assessing it by criteria alien to its "genius." This was Boas's renowned principle of cultural relativism, which was an effective weapon against ethnocentrism and lack of toleration, which were then deeply rooted in current thinking and in many social doctrines.

The conviction that the world of culture is extremely complex and varied made Boas turn also against all conceptions that strove to explain it in a uniform manner by referring to a single, decisive factor. He wrote: "Every attempt to deduce cultural forms from a single cause is doomed to failure, for the various expressions of culture are closely interrelated and one cannot be altered without having an effect upon all the others."[7] Since in culture everything affects everything, nothing entitles us to assume that a given cause always has the same effect and that the presence of a given phenomenon must be preceded by a given cause. In culture, similar causes may produce different effects, and similar effects may have different causes.

The Search for a New Theory of Culture. Boas's program of research remained clear and consistent as long as it was leveled against evolutionism. Matters became complicated when people started seeking in that program the nuclei of a theory that, while being in agreement with facts, could replace evolutionism and help to integrate the rapidly accumulating knowledge of human cultures.

Boas is sometimes considered to be merely an American representative of diffusionism. Arguments in favor of that claim could certainly be found in some of his studies, in which he enumerated the various elements of culture and investigated their distribution over the various regions. His concept of culture area, used in the studies of diffusion of cultures, would point to certain affinities with the concept of culture circle, used by German diffusionists.

However, Boas paid much attention to how an alien element is "adopted [by a given culture] and changed in form according to the genius of the people who borrowed it."[8] Boas was convinced that every culture always forms a *sui generis* spiritual unity. Thus, his approach to culture was both atomizing and integrating, diffusionist and functionalist. He himself called it the *historical* approach, as he strove to reconstruct the actual development of a given culture as a unique phenomenon. This is why classing Boas as a diffusionist would certainly be misleading, especially as he did engage in the criticism of diffusionism.

Boas sought a kind of a third path, which he called the actual history of culture and which, in his opinion, was missing in both evolutionism and diffusionism. That actual history was supposed to consist not only of studying given cultures, determined spatially and temporally, as more or less integrated wholes, but also in finding answers to the questions about the emergence and formation of such cultures.

Yet, in the case of Indian cultures that he investigated, this requirement could not be met. Lévi-Strauss pertinently wrote in this regard about the Boas paradox, which made Boas seek scholarly salvation in history, whereas, in fact, the subject matter of his research was such that in most cases its history was beyond reach.[9] Boas himself realized the difficulty.

While Boas never renounced considering anthropology to be a historical discipline, his reservations concerning historical reconstructions show him to have been *sui generis* functionalist. His functionalism can also be seen in the emphasis that he laid on the integration of every culture.

But even with respect to his functionalism, Boas also raised doubts and reservations; this is comprehensible since the Indian cultures that he studied —unlike the cultures investigated by Malinowski and Radcliffe-Brown— were marked by a fairly high degree of disintegration. For the same reason he was a student of culture rather than of social structure. While suggesting that interrelations between the various aspects of culture be brought out and complying with that requirement in his own work, he used to say that it was groundless to believe that

the whole culture must be a compact unit, that contradictions within a culture are impossible, and that all features must be parts of a system. We should rather ask in how far so-called primitive cultures possess a unity that covers all aspects of cultural life. Have we not reason to expect that here as well as in more complicated cultures, sex, generation, age, individuality, and social organization will give rise to the most manifold contradictions?[10]

Thus Boas, a supposed functionalist or quasi-functionalist, was a forerunner of the critics of functionalism, who most often pointed to the functionalist tendency to see all cultural facts as elements of a coherent system.

After the peculiarities of the cultures that he investigated, the cause of Boas's antifunctionalism seems to have been mainly his individualism, which was common in American sociology of his times. He came up against the evolutionist laws of development that abolish the variety of cultures and also against the functionalist laws of a system that level down personal individualities. The anthropologist ought to be interested not in culture alone, but also in the responses of the individuals who are under its influence.[11]

Again anticipating the later critics of functionalism (such as Wrong), Boas complained that the data used in the social sciences were overstandardized:

It is given to us as a list of inventions, institutions, and ideas, but we learn little or nothing about the way in which the individual lives under these institutions and with those inventions and ideas, nor do we know how his activities affect the cultural groups of which he is a member. Information on these points is sorely needed, for the dynamics of social life can be understood only on the basis of the reactions of the individual to the culture in which he lives and of his influence upon society.[12]

Or, "the causal conditions of cultural happenings lie always in the interactions between individual and society."[13]

By taking up these issues, Boas opened one more vista for modern anthropology, especially significant in American anthropological studies: the culture and personality approach.

Summing up Boas's ideas is thus extremely difficult, for, as Kardiner and Preble wrote, he can be connected "with almost every major theoretical and methodological doctrine in modern anthropology. He worked always to keep anthropology free from 'speculative theory,' and held to any theory himself only so long as it served the purpose of destroying or weakening the current dogma."[14] Yet, we do not always fully realize that in the field of theory Boas was a great inspirer, too, although his attempts at theory construction revealed in his thought co-occurence of elements whose combination was not possible. There has never been and never could be a "Boasism" in the same meaning as, for instance, there is Durkheimism, but few scholars can equal Boas in his impact on the theoretical development of his discipline. There is no path in American anthropology that does not start from Boas. His heritage, however, consisted of questions and problems, rather than solutions and unambiguous answers.

The Dilemmas of Boas's School: Kroeber versus Sapir. Boas's school includes such prominent personalities as Clark Wissler (1870-1947), Alfred L. Kroeber (1876-1960), Alexander Goldenweiser (1880-1942), Robert H. Lowie (1883-1957), Edward Sapir (1884-1939), Ruth F. Benedict (1887-1949), and Melvile J. Herskovits (1895-1963). That school is to be credited with the unprecedented advancement of anthropology in the United States: From a discipline that performed ancillary functions in the work of museums, anthropology turned gradually into one of the leading social sciences.

The term *school* is used loosely here, because it was not characterized by any profound theoretical unity. Nevertheless, to use the language of the members of that school themselves, it represented a common way of pursuing anthropological research, marked by the following principal features.

First, it was typified by total rejection of the assumptions adopted in evolutionistic anthropology, which continued to be criticized in the 1920s, although evolutionism in the United States was then almost completely dead (its revival, originated by White, began only after World War II). The criticism of evolutionism was leveled in particular against the belief that anthropology is a law-discovering discipline.

Second, the school shared the assumption, interpreted in various ways, but repeated by all in similar formulations, that anthropology is or ought to be a historical science; its concern is with definite cultures and does not claim to establish anything that would be universally valid. The anthropologist deals with certain universal phenomena, but these are biological or psychological, and not cultural, in nature.

Third, the historical approach in anthropology does not in the least imply focusing attention on historical reconstructions. Kroeber says outright that "the time factor . . . is not the most essential criterion of the historic approach. Space relations can and sometimes must take its place."[15]

Fourth, the historicist anthropology of Boas's school was, like Boas himself, marked by two trends that oppose one another: the diffusionist and the functionalist. On the one hand, culture is considered to be a set of separate traits, and advances in anthropology are seen in their registration and description. On the other hand, there is a very strong tendency (its best-known manifestation being *Patterns of Culture* by Ruth Benedict) to assert that the character of a given culture is determined not by separate elements, but by the context in which they function in a given case. Of course, the term *organism*, linked to the evolutionist tradition, became anathema, but a number of other terms, drawn from linguistics, the history of art, and the like, came to be used in order to refer to the integration of culture: *configuration*, *pattern*, and *style*. Kroeber defined culture patterns as "those arrangements or systems of internal relationship which give to any culture its coherence or plan, and keep it from being a mere accumulation of random bits."[16]

Fifth, American anthropologists were marked by a fairly consistent sociological nominalism (if we disregard some formulations by Kroeber, modified in his later works): Society is a number of interacting individuals, and culture does not exist outside its individual carriers. For all the ontological agreement on the issue, this question gave rise to the most important controversy within the school.

Sixth, Boas's disciples, like their master, were marked by radical cultural relativism. That attitude, best expounded in the concluding chapter of *Patterns of Culture*, consists of the refusal to adopt any single culture as the standard form and to assess any culture by criteria drawn from the outside.

Seventh, unlike their British colleagues, American anthropologists were *cultural*, and not social, anthropologists. This is not merely a point of terminology, but constitutes a rather essential difference, because the definitions of culture had evolved considerably since the time of Tylor, and in the 1920s and 1930s many of them did not cover the problems of social structure, the crucial problems for social anthropologists. While no uniform definition of culture was obligatory in Boas's circles, there was a clear tendency to eliminate from the extension of that concept both social structure and what is called material culture or, at least, to assign them a subordinate place in comparison to ideas, values, and attitudes. Spengler's distinction between culture and civilization enjoyed some popularity in that group, as did Kroeber's distinction between "value culture" and "reality culture." Interest was focused on the former, that is, on what Boas metaphorically called "the genius of the people." It is worth noting here that the concept of configuration referred to a different kind of integration of culture than did the concept of organism, and it was also applied to a different class of phenomena.

Eighth, in the period now under consideration, American anthropologists tended to link anthropology to other disciplines, particularly linguistics, psychology, and history. Their view of the latter two were differentiated and changed occasionally, but even the staunchest antipsychologist among them—Kroeber—was permanently fascinated by psychology. The connection with linguistics was of a special significance, not only because Boas, Kroeber, and Sapir worked as linguists, but mainly because they discovered a methodological affinity between the science of culture and the science of language. Kroeber wrote that "their most fertile procedure is essentially the same."[17] The science of language contributed the concept of pattern, the assumption that every configuration is unique, the supposition that the most important phenomena of culture are unconscious, and the analogy between the individual's relation to culture and his relation to language.[18]

Ninth, all the cultural anthropologists mentioned above were field workers of the highest rank, especially expert in the study of cultures of North American Indians, the survival of which cultures provided a strong impetus for the development of anthropology in the United States. A large part of their field work was diffusionist in nature, the principal theoretical concept being that of culture areas.

Finally, note also that the belief in the social mission of anthropology was an essential feature of the Boas circle: Anthropology was to shape the attitudes of ordinary people by spreading the comprehension and toleration of other cultures. In some cases, it in fact did so; the total printing of *Patterns of Culture*—in its original English-language versions only—exceeded 1.6 million copies. It was also expected to help in shaping enlightened cultural policies.

When formulating this characteristic of the school, we have made several references to its not being unanimous in opinions. It is worthwhile to discuss, as an example, one of the fundamental dilemmas that resulted in the differentiation of standpoints, namely, the cultural versus the psychological approach to the key problem of integration of culture. All agreed that every culture forms a definite configuration or has its specific pattern or style (the vagueness of these terms justifies, to some extent, their being used alternately). But at least two different aspects of integration of culture are possible. Both of them can be found, for instance, in the works of Ruth Benedict, who implicitly makes a distinction between two orders or levels of such integration: the level of culture traits and that of attitudes and emotions.[19]

Kroeber and Sapir represented these two standpoints in almost pure forms: The former was interested in culture configurations regardless of individuals; the other tried to discover them in individuals and considered supraindividual culture to be an abstraction.

In his much-publicized book *The Superorganic* (1917), which was received rather critically in Boas's circle, Kroeber formulated his view of culture. Many associated it with Durkheim's sociologism, as it refuses "to deal with either individuality or individual as such"[20] and suggests that phenomena of culture be explained exclusively by reference to other phenomena of culture. The paper was leveled primarily against biologism and did not expound any anti-Boas heresy, but it referred to culture as a superorganic entity (the term itself coming from Spencer) with an unveiled allusion that a *sui generis* reality is meant. In his later works Kroeber was inclined to soften some of his most radical formulations, but he did stick to his opinion that all reductionism is disastrous for the study of culture. Thus, in 1948 he wrote that "now while persons undoubtedly make and produce the cultural *forms*, our knowledge of persons—and very largely also our knowledge of societies of persons—has failed conspicuously to explain the cultural *forms*; it has failed to derive specific cultural effects from specific psychic or social causes. In fact, psychological and social concepts or mechanisms are not even much good at *describing* cultural forms."[21] This opinion placed Kroeber in marked opposition to the culture and personality approach. Yet, an analogy with Durkheim seems misleading: Kroeber did not claim that the personality of the individual is derivative with respect to culture; what he did claim was that one may, and should, study culture without studying the individual's personality.

In Boas's circle, Kroeber's standpoint did not have many adherents, even though he was not alone in his culturalism. Much more common was the opinion that culture is in fact an abstraction, and that which can be observed directly is only human individuals who behave in such and such way. There were also definitions of culture stating that this term merely denotes learned behavior of individuals. While culture was a configuration of objectified forms to Kroeber, other theorists considered it to be a set of common traits of individual attitudes, a set that cannot be described in abstraction from individuals. It was a controversy not over the choice between cultural and psychological determinism, but rather over the strategy of research. Edward Sapir was the first theorist to suggest a strategy opposed to that of Kroeber.[22]

In a series of papers started in the early 1920s, Sapir outlined the idea of cultural anthropology as an essentially psychological discipline. In "The Emergence of the Concept of Personality in a Study of Culture" (1934) that

there is no reason why the culturalist should be afraid of the concept of personality, which must not, however, be thought of . . . as a mysterious entity resisting the historically given culture but rather [it should be considered] as a distinctive configuration of experience which tends always to form a psychologically significant unit and which, as it accretes more and more symbols to itself, creates finally that cultural microcosm of which official "culture" is little more than a metaphorically and mechanically expanded copy.[23]

Culture subsists in human personalities and in them alone in the same way that language subsists only in individual acts of speech. It is only in the works of Sapir that we must look for the nuclei of the culture and personality approach, or *psychoculturalism* (as that orientation will be called later in this book).

But before we proceed to discuss in greater detail that orientation which took shape in the 1930s, we have to analyze at some length another anthropological orientation that took up the same issue of the integration of culture: functionalism.

FUNCTIONALISM

Functionalist social anthropology developed in Great Britain as a result of the activity of Alfred R. Radcliffe-Brown (1881-1955) and Bronislaw Malinowski (1884-1942). It differed essentially from American cultural anthropology in many respects, and none of the infrequent endeavors to bridge the gap between the two has fully succeeded. Neither party appreciated the novel approach of the other, and each ascribed to itself the merit for having brought about a scientific revolution in anthropology. The two orientations are linked almost exclusively by the tendency to see culture as a more or less integrated whole and the belief that field work must be the point of departure for every anthropologist.

The Position of Functionalism in Anthropological Thought. "The term 'functionalism,'" Hatch wrote, "remained imprecise enough to cover a number of forms of interpretation which actually had little in common."[24] Even if we disregard the complications due to the later sociological functionalism, the term has at least three different meanings: (1) a theory of society and culture that gives preference to a certain kind of explanation; (2) a conceptual schema that makes a coherent description of facts possible; and (3) a research method that happened to be applied without a clearly formulated theory and that made use of a traditional language.[25] To make matters worse, in each of these three fields the various authors represented so widely divergent views that one of them found it possible to write thus: "I have been described on more than one occasion as belonging to something called the 'Functional School of Social Anthropology' and even as being its leader, or one of its leaders. This Functional School does not exist; it is a myth invented by Professor Malinowski."[26]

When we speak about British functionalism, it is worthwhile to start with the statement that it was a *sociological* orientation from its very inception, unlike other orientations in anthropology. Unlike the American cultural anthropologists and the German ethnologists, the British social anthropologists usually considered themselves sociologists or, at least, representatives of a branch of sociology. They called themselves *social* anthropologists in order to point out that they represented "a distinctive discipline in which theoretical problems of general sociology are investigated by research in primitive societies."[27] Radcliffe-Brown even abandoned Tylor's formula of a "science of culture" and focused his interest on social structure and social system. Malinowski would construct "a scientific theory of culture," but he would retain the belief that it is a way of engaging in comparative sociology. The British functionalists remained faithful to their evolutionistically minded masters, who had always considered anthropology to be a branch of sociology. The lack in Britain of any other form of sociological research (except for sociography, which did not show theoretical aspirations) gave sociologically oriented anthropology a special status.[28]

The functionalists are usually considered to have been the critics and the gravediggers of evolutionism. They have deserved that reputation because of their shift in the focus of interest. Malinowski defined functionalism as "a method which consists above all in the analysis of primitive institutions as they work at present, rather than in the reconstruction of a hypothetical past."[29]

It seems, however, that the opposition of functionalism to evolutionism has been exaggerated, to the detriment of a clear comprehension of both orientations. Neither Radcliffe-Brown nor Malinowski waged a holy war against the evolutionists (who remained active at British universities),[30] and their first books, essential for the new orientation—*The Andaman Islanders* by Radcliffe-Brown and *Argonauts of the Western Pacific* by Malinowski, both appearing in 1922—were far from being hailed as announcements of a scientific revolution.

Functionalism can be defined as a return to the idea of social anthropology as a natural science, which is supposed to discover laws. According to Evans-Pritchard, Malinowski's unfaithful disciple, it was "doctrinaire positivism at its worst."[31] Radcliffe-Brown formulated his reservations concerning historicism from the position of the naturalistic conception of science: "Now while ethnology with its strictly historical method can only tell us that certain things have happened, or have probably or possibly happened, social anthropology with its inductive generalizations can tell us how and why things happen, i.e., according to what laws."[32]

No less salient was the functionalists' attachment to organicist analogies, so typical of evolutionist sociology. Radcliffe-Brown, in particular, used such analogies in abundance. Thus he wrote, for instance, that "the concept of function applied to human societies is based on an analogy between social life and organic life."[33]

Functionalism was a kind of evolutionism without the idea of evolution: It rejected the evolutionist fascination with the problems of the origin and development of social life, but retained the evolutionist image of society as an organism in which every organ works to keep the whole alive. The image of evolution was discarded, but this did not have to imply—theoretically at least—that the problems of evolution were considered to be unimportant. It was just assumed that under existing conditions (there being only a scanty amount of information about the past of the primitive societies) the best strategy would be to seek the laws of co-occurrence and not those of sequence. Hence, the functionalists questioned in evolutionism almost the same points that they did in diffusionism and disregarded the otherwise essential differences between those two trends. Radcliffe-Brown wrote, for example:

> There are at present two different and opposing tendencies in the study of culture. One view, by far the most popular, regards culture purely from the historical point of view and attempts, in the absence of any historical records, to multiply and elaborate hypothetical reconstructions of an unknown past. . . . The other tendency, best represented in England by Malinowski, is to treat each culture as a functionally interrelated system and to endeavour to discover the general laws of function for human society as a whole.[34]

The link between functionalism and evolutionism was Durkheim's work, but no version of functionalism was a simple continuation of Durkheimism. British anthropologists, Radcliffe-Brown being the first, availed themselves of its inspiration and drew from it a number of concepts and hypotheses that they found useful. They never appeared as Durkheim's disciples, however, and it would be in vain to seek in them many ideas typical of the author of *The Elementary Forms of the Religious Life.*

The relation between functionalism and American cultural anthropology, led by Boas, may seem the most complex of all, at least insofar as the latter attached essential importance to the problem of the integration of culture (for which reason some followers of Boas were even called functionalists).

The Theoretical Specificity of Functionalism. The reduction of functionalism to a simple "integrational approach" (to use Hatch's terminology) resulted in blurring its difference from other theoretical trends in social anthropology and sociology. As Buckley has noted, "If the label [functionalism] means only that social systems are seen as integrated to some extent and can be analyzed into certain elements that may be related to other elements and to the operation of the system as a whole—then . . . we are all functionalists."[35]

Integrationism was an important component of functionalism. It could be said that it was a necessary, but not a sufficient, condition. It was certainly of primary significance in field work, which—whatever its subject matter—was intended by the functionalists to grasp the manifold connections between the various phenomena in the life of a given community. As Malinowski wrote in his first monograph, "One of the first conditions of acceptable ethnographic work certainly is that it should deal with the totality of all social, cultural, and psychological aspects of the community, for they are so interwoven that not one can be understood without taking into consideration all the others."[36]

But functionalism was also marked, again in Hatch's terms, by a *sui generis* utilitarianism,[37] which was particularly clear when its representatives proceeded from description to explanation. In their theorizing, functionalists were concerned not so much with interrelations between elements of culture, but with the question of how those elements "served," "contributed to," or "enabled" the survival of the whole of which they are parts. From the integrational point of view, the term *function* was needed only to describe the changes in the system resulting from transformation or elimination of one or more of its elements. From the utilitarian point of view, that term meant something more, namely, the specific contribution of a given element to the functioning of the system as a whole.

Robert K. Merton wrote about three interconnected assumptions of early functionalism (that is, anthropological functionalism as distinct from the later sociological functionalism): (1) functional unity of society; (2) universal functionalism; and (3) functional indispensability.[38] According to the first assumption, every component of a system contributes to its survival as a whole. According to the second, every part of a social system performs a vital function in it. According to the third, every part of a system is absolutely indispensable to it. Note that these three assumptions were often explicitly formulated by functionalists themselves.

These assumptions reveal both the strong and the weak points of functionalism. Its strength consisted above all of releasing inquisitiveness in research, formerly fettered by the evolutionist formula of survivals and even more by the collector's mentality of ethnographers, which resulted in the accumulation of data without any theoretical guiding idea. Its weaknesses were many, and so functionalism early became a target of criticism that continues to this day, despite the corrections that the functionalists have introduced into their theoretical conceptions.

The main lines of that criticism were as follows. First, functionalism was blamed for supporting holistic metaphysics and for assuming as given that which should be proved. What was assumed, in fact, was the functional unity of society. This was especially blameworthy, because the concept of system used by early functionalists was not a theoretical fiction, but applied directly to empirical facts. Second, it was blamed for teleology, which consisted in the tendency to explain a given social phenomenon by pointing to its usefulness for the maintenance of a given social system. Third, it was also blamed for being unable to explain social change or even to pose that problem correctly without abandoning its fundamental theoretical assumptions.[39] Finally, it was pointed out that the functionalist social theory had conservative political implications: If everything is functional, then every change may be considered to be a threat to the system.

It is to be noted that the more strongly functionalism aspired to the status of a general theory of society, the more it exposed itself to justified criticism, losing thereby part of that immense credibility that it had acquired through its representatives' monographic studies.

Functionalism as Sociologism: Radcliffe-Brown. All historical analysis of functionalism requires taking into account its different varieties. The structural variety, which probably came closest to the later sociological functionalism, was represented by Alfred Reginald Radcliffe-Brown (1881-1955). He conducted field work in the Andaman Islands (1906-1908) and in Australia (1910-1912). He did not write much, but his influence as a teacher of social anthropology was enormous. The formulation of his principal theoretical ideas came rather late, and they are to be found mainly in *A Natural Science of Society* (1937), *Structure and Function in Primitive Society* (1952), and *Method in Social Anthropology* (1958).

Radcliffe-Brown singled out the three basic aspects of every social system: (1) "the social structure"; (2) "the totality of all social usages"; and (3) "the special modes of thinking and feeling which we can infer or assume (from behavior or speech) to be related with the social usages and the social relations that make up the structure."[40] He also stated explicitly that the first of these aspects is the most important of all, and he assessed the functionality of the various beliefs and practices according to whether, or how far, they help to consolidate a given structure. Such was his interpretation of magic, religion, and economic phenomena. This emphasis on the problems of social structure resulted in his refusal, unique among the anthropologists,, to treat culture as an autonomous subject of study: He was interested in culture only as a secondary aspect of the social system, subordinated within that system to a definite structure and instrumental with respect to the supreme need of "co-adaptation," that is, the mutual adaptation of members of society to each other.[41] It was also for the same reason that he, unlike Malinowski, thought psychology to be unimportant for a social anthropologist.

In his earliest works Radcliffe-Brown defined social structure as an arrangement of groups or sections of society, as Durkheim had done. The works written by him in the later period, marked by a more theoretical approach, reveal a significant shift: The term *structure* came to be used mainly with reference to relationships among individuals. To put it more precisely, he meant relationships not so much among individuals as among persons—that is, in accordance with the distinction made by Park, among individuals who play specified social roles. One of his numerous formulas was that social structure is "an arrangement of persons in institutionalised roles and relationships."[42] In any case, the fundamental problem of social structure was reduced to the regulation of relationships among individuals and the elimination of conflicts among them—in Durkheim's terminology, to the maintenance of social solidarity. Radcliffe-Brown himself gave preference to other terms, such as *unity*, *harmony*, and *consistency*.

The concept of organization was for Radcliffe-Brown an analogue of the concept of structure; while the latter referred to a given arrangement of persons, the former referred to a given arrangement of activities. "Social organization," he wrote, "is the arrangement of activities of two or more persons which are adjusted to give a united combined activity."[43] Institution was another important concept in his theory, because "in any of the relationships of which the social structure consists there is an expectation that a person will conform to certain rules or patterns of behavior. The term *institution* is used to refer to this, an institution being an established or socially recognised system of norms or patterns of conduct referring to some aspect of social life."[44] It is to be noted that to Radcliffe-Brown these terms were names of concrete, directly observable facts in social life. This can clearly be seen in his letter to Lévi-Strauss: "I use the term 'social structure' in a sense so different from yours as to make discussion so difficult as to be unlikely to be profitable. While for you, social structure has nothing to do with reality, but with models that are built up, I regard the social structure as reality."[45]

Briefly, Radcliffe-Brown's approach to the problem of social structure was still very remote from what is common in present-day anthropology and sociology. Naive realism was, however, quite understandable in the case of this researcher, who had only just begun the construction of a theory based on empirical data and was, above all, keen on avoiding any return to the practice of earlier social anthropology, which had started from theoretical concepts rather than from facts.

Functionalism as Psychologism: Malinowski. Malinowski was interested mainly in the needs of biological organisms and not in those of a social system. While Radcliffe-Brown asked how social order was consolidated, Malinowski's question was how social order satisfied natural needs of human beings. Note also that while Radcliffe-Brown subordinated culture to social structure, Malinowski, like the American cultural anthropologists, subordinated social structure to culture. The latter became the focal concept in his theory of society.

Malinowski's unquestionable position in the history of anthropology is due primarily to his monographs—*Argonauts of the Western Pacific* (1922), *The Sexual Life of Savages in North Western Melanesia* (1929), and *Coral Gardens and their Magic* (1935)—which were a result of his thorough field work in the Trobriand Islands (1914-1918). Their undisputed values are (1) rare versatility, resulting from Malinowski's assumption that no element of culture can be explained in isolation from its other elements; (2) rigorous criticism of sources of information, due to his conviction that a strict distinction must be made between what people say about their actions and what these actions really are; and (3) the tendency to discover a specific logic in the thoughts and actions of the "savages," due to his firm belief that all cultures must be put on equal footing.

Malinowski's merits as a teacher are also beyond dispute. His seminar at the London School of Economics, with which he was connected for almost all his life, trained a host of prominent anthropologists and sociologists, both British and non-British. That seminar was the main center of functional thought for nearly the whole period between the two world wars.

There has been much less agreement about such works as *Crime and Custom in Savage Society* (1926), *Sex and Repression in Savage Society* (1927), *A Scientific Theory of Culture* (1944), and *The Dynamics of Culture Change* (1945), which rest on a sound base of factual data, but are intended to solve universal problems rather than to describe specified societies or communities. While recognizing Malinowski's achievements—such as undermining the Freudian belief that the Oedipus complex is universal in nature—many commentators consider him to have been a poor theorist. Lévi-Strauss claims that his works are marked by "a strange mixture of dogmatism and empiricism,"[46] and other authors, including some of his disciples, blame him for obscurities, unsubstantiated generalizations, and even plain errors and contradictions.

The starting point of his theory was a biological organism endowed with a set of permanent needs or, as he called it, "human nature." "The theory of culture," he wrote, "must take its stand on biological fact."[47] Malinowski's theory of culture implied a definite conception of man. In accordance with the instinctivist theories, he assumed that man has a number of innate predispositions, "fundamental human impulses," or "basic needs," which, Hatch wrote, "are at the basis of a good deal of cultural behavior."[48] Culture, in the last analysis, is nothing other than an immense apparatus for satisfaction of needs, a set of responses to those needs, and instruments indispensable for meeting them. To describe a culture means to describe the conditions that must be satisfied if the community is to survive. Interpreted in this way, functionalism is "the theory of transformation of organic—that is, individual—needs into derived cultural necessities and imperatives."[49]

In the case of the human species, which differs from the animal world, the process of satisfying these basic biological needs produces a new category of needs, which Malinowski termed instrumental. He listed four such needs:

1. The cultural apparatus of implements and consumers' goods must be *produced*, used, maintained, and replaced by new production. 2. Human behaviour, as regards its technical, customary, legal, or moral prescription, must be codified, regulated in action and sanction. 3. The *human material* by which every institution must be renewed, formed, drilled, and provided with full knowledge of tribal tradition. 4. Authority within each institution must be defined, equipped with power, and endowed with means of forceful execution of its orders.[50]

These needs have their instrumental imperatives in the form of economics, social control, education, and political organization, respectively.

Finally, Malinowski spoke about the other kind of derived needs, in addition to the instrumental ones; namely, the integrative needs, which have as their respective analogues the following integrative imperatives of culture: science, magic, myth, religion, and art.

Malinowski emphasized very strongly that at all these levels of the analysis of culture we are "never to forget the living, palpitating flesh and blood organism of man which remains somewhere at the heart of every institution."[51] It would, however, be erroneous to conclude that Malinowski's standpoint was that of biological or psychological reductionism. On the contrary, he expressed numerous reservations against such an interpretation of his theory of culture. And he claimed that where there is culture, simple physiological impulses cannot exist, because in culture we do not deal with individuals as biological organisms, but with individuals who are socially organized and whose satisfaction of even the most elementary physiological needs is subject to culture-based regulation (taboos, imperatives, prohibitions, and the like). It is institutions that constitute the basic form of that organization. As Malinowski wrote, "We can define an institution as: a group of people united for the pursuit of a simple or complex activity, always in possession of a material endowment and a technical outfit; organized on a definite legal or customary charter, linguistically formulated in myth, legend rule, and maxim; and trained or prepared for the carrying out of its task."[52]

As a result of social organization, culture "steps beyond instinctive endowment,"[53] and while it cannot be explained without reference to the latter, it also cannot be reduced to it. Malinowski even claims that the social heritage is the key concept in social anthropology.

For Malinowski, culture was not an abstract concept whose adoption would facilitate the description and comprehension of how human instincts work. On the contrary, it was rather the instincts that were abstract concepts adopted by the theory in order to understand the regularities observable in human culture, the wealth of which evades reduction to any single and simple formula. In other words, in the case of Malinowski's functionalism, we find a conflict between a theorist who, like other British functionalists, sought a single principle of explanation of human behavior and a researcher who was fascinated by the plurality and variety of human institutions. Malinowski's endeavors to find a solution softened his psychologism, but inevitably affected the coherence of his theory.

The Move beyond the Functionalist's Naturalism: Evans-Pritchard. The history of British anthropology includes, first, intensive continuation of field work after Malinowski's pattern and, second, revision and more precise formulation of the theoretical schemata left by the two founders of functionalism. The prevailing opinion is that the chief contribution of the British anthropologists was an improved knowledge of specific cultures (especially in Africa) and a definition of the problems that were neglected in the monographs of the founders of functionalism (primitive political systems). Increased interest in social change, reflected in Malinowski's late book, *The Dynamics of Culture Change*, also deserves mention. Among the disciples of Malinowski and Radcliffe-Brown we have to list Audrey I. Richards (1899-   ), Raymond Firth (1901-   ), E. E. Evans-Pritchard (1902-1973), S. F. Nadel (1903-1956), Isaac Schapera (1905-   ), Meyer Fortes (1906-   ), and Edmund Leach (1910-   ). The monographs produced by the second generation of functionalists, excellent as they were, did not abound in new theoretical ideas that would be even indirectly important for the sociologists. Except for Arensberg and Warner, whose novel ideas consisted of applying the anthropological viewpoint to the study of advanced societies, and Leach, whose originality as a theorist has become known only recently, it is the production of Evans-Pritchard that deserves attention. That author, one of the first disciples of Malinowski, moved farther and farther away from his master in his own work (he became professor at Oxford in 1937). He seems to have been one of the most interesting social anthropologists in the twentieth century, even though in the eyes of the many he has been third best, the best being Malinowski and Radcliffe-Brown.

The scholarly renown of Evans-Pritchard rests on the solid foundation of his two classic monographs that followed many years of research work in the Sudan: *Witchcraft, Oracles and Magic Among the Azande* (1937) and *The Nuer: A Description of the Modes of Livelihood and Political Institutions of a Nilotic People* (1940). These monographs seemingly do not differ essentially from the standard monographs by members of the functional school. But when read in the light of his other works, especially his *Social Anthropology* (1951) and *Essays in Social Anthropology* (1962), they reveal the specific interests of that scholar, who finally came to the conclusion, surprising for a functionalist, that social anthropology is a humanistic and historical discipline. One should also note that Evans-Pritchard had an exceptionally well-developed methodological consciousness and was not attracted by description for description's sake, if it were not accompanied by a defined theoretical objective. He wrote, "We tell our anthropological students to study problems and not peoples."[54]

Many a time did Evans-Pritchard voice his dissatisfaction with the state of social anthropology and question Malinowski's and, to a lesser extent, Radcliffe-Brown's anthropological theory and practice.

Evans-Pritchard took up the problem of *abstraction*, which is of extraordinary importance for a functionalist. If an anthropologist proceeds to describe a given society and if he assumes that all facts are interconnected, as Malinowski did, then he inevitably faces the necessity of being concerned with everything and thus deprives himself of the possibility of explaining anything. He must, therefore, choose either the single-problem kind of study or an analysis of a given social system at a higher level of abstraction, a level at which the concept of social system does not apply to relationships among specified actions and events, persons and groups, but refers to the very nature of such relationships.

Evans-Pritchard criticized the inclination, which marked Malinowski and his disciples, to formulate generalizations on social life on the basis of facts taken from one isolated society. He was an advocate of the method that he called "experimental" and that consisted of testing the conclusions drawn from the study of one society by comparing them with the findings obtained in the study of other societies; the goal was to reach the "final stage," that is, "a comparison of all types of societies in order to discover general tendencies and functional relationships that are common to human societies as a whole.''⁵⁵ We see here a return to Durkheim's program of comparative studies, for which the early functionalists had little understanding.

Evans-Pritchard focused his interest on the problem of "subjective culture," which was refused autonomous existence by both Radcliffe-Brown and Malinowski. The former was interested in it only insofar as it contributes to consolidation of a given social structure; and the latter saw in it mainly a means of relieving individual anxieties. For Evans-Pritchard, human ideas and beliefs had an independent value; as Hatch claims, "it seems that to him the phenomenal features of culture and society are manifestations of subjective factors. People do things willfully—at least within limits—and are not automatons whose thoughts and actions are governed by the laws regulating some larger social system.''⁵⁶ This interest in consciousness, combined with a dislike of all determinism, distinguished Evans-Pritchard from Malinowski, with whom, however, he shared the conviction that the anthropologist should never lose sight of the acting human individual. The research task that Evans-Pritchard set himself was, above all, a reconstruction of social consciousness (subjective culture) as an integrated whole, a reconstruction to be achieved by analyzing consciousness itself, by revealing its inner coherence and its "idiom" typical of a given society. The essential point was the inner logic of magic or religion, not its purpose. This had at least two important consequences. First, it resulted in abandoning the utilitarian approach to the interpretation of the functions served by beliefs and rites. Second, it led to adopting the procedure of understanding such beliefs and rites in the broader "idiomatic" whole, understanding "from the inside," as Evans-Pritchard says. This procedure has more in common with Ruth Benedict's reflections on patterns of culture than with the explanations of culture offered by the functionalists who strove to discover its laws.

Evans-Pritchard drew theoretical conclusions from his research experience and came to interpret social anthropology as a humanistic discipline—again in opposition to the founder of functionalism. Thus, he wrote, for instance, "The thesis I have put before you, that social anthropology is a kind of historiography, and therefore ultimately of philosophy or art, . . . that it is interested in design rather than in process, and that it therefore seeks patterns and not scientific laws, and interprets rather than explains.''⁵⁷ As can be seen, he opposed ultimately not only definite solutions provided by functional anthropology, but also some of its basic assumptions.

PSYCHOCULTURALISM

When we discussed Boas's school, we saw that its fundamental problem, as in the case of the British functionalists, was integration of culture. Boas's work offered many suggestions on the issue, but not a single consistent solution. The proposals of British functionalists proved inacceptable to the Americans. These proposals evoked some interest and a better understanding in the United States by the late 1930s (Radcliffe-Brown lectured at the University of Chicago from 1931 to 1937). The main barrier to the reception of functionalism—and Durkheimism—in the United States is probably to be seen in voluntaristic nominalism, which prevailed in the American social sciences. It consisted of the assumptions that "the structure of all social groups is the consequence of the aggregate of its separate component individuals and that social phenomena ultimately derive from the motivations of these knowing, feeling and willing individuals."[58] From the point of view of voluntaristic nominalism, the problem of integration of culture or of society could be solved only as the problem of agreement between attitudes and behavior of conscious human individuals and in no case as the problem of depersonalized requirements of the social system or even the problem of the basic biological needs.

Beginnings of American Psychoculturalism. When discussing the opinions of Boas and his school, we pointed to the theoretical possibility, first articulated by Sapir, of basing the problem of the unity of culture on the study of social personality considered to be a *sui generis* microcosm. This was an analogue of the views gaining acceptance in social psychology and sociology.[59]

Patterns of Culture by Ruth Benedict (1934) was the first outstanding anthropological work that offered a tentative psychological characterization of culture. As Kardiner and Preble write, Benedict in that book "exposed the weakness of the functionalist orientation as signally stated by Durkheim: that institutions are things, are related to each other, and can only be explained in terms of other institutions. She stepped out of this circle by invoking the analogy of institutional clusters with human character types."[60] She thus posed clearly the question, How can culture be studied as a whole without being considered a *sui generis* reality? Unfortunately, she did not have any adequate psychological theory at her disposal, but merely an aggregate of rather general psychological ideas, drawn mainly from German philosophy of culture. Hence, psychology in *Patterns of Culture* consisted of the use of psychological terminology in descriptions of cultures and of rather unfounded assurances that there always exists correspondence between the type of culture and the dominant type of personality. But the problem of how the personality that is typical of a given culture is shaped remained unsolved.

It was Margaret Mead, in her monographs *Coming of Age in Samoa* (1928), *Growing Up in New Guinea* (1930), and *Sex and Temperament in Three Primitive Societies* (1935), who came, perhaps, much closer to the solution of this problem, and that is so because she started collecting the descriptive data that is indispensable for this purpose. Yet that researcher, eminent as she was, had little to offer in the field of theory, nor did she venture, in her monographs, to seek patterns of culture as a whole.

All this explains the increased popularity of psychoanalysis among American anthropologists, which was noticeable in the 1930s. Psychoanalysis promised a psychological theory of the development of personality, and without such a theory psychoculturalism could not survive in the long run.

Reception of Psychoanalysis by American Anthropologists: Kardiner. In this chapter we have so far disregarded psychoanalysis because, first, there is no necessary connection between the study of personality in culture and the acceptance of any variety of Freudianism, and, second, Freud's doctrine did not necessarily yield any program of study of culture and even included elements rendering the formulation of any such program difficult. The doctrine had to undergo many modifications in order to be taken as the basis for a psychological anthropology of culture.

Those elements were as follows.

1. Classical Freudianism was marked by instinctivism, very unpopular in the social sciences in America in the 1920s and 1930s and varied from the general trend of interest in personality in culture.
2. Freud tended to interpret culture as a force that is basically repressive with respect to individual aspirations, and he thus in fact supported the traditional dichotomy of the individual versus society, rejected by American thinkers who focused their attention on the interpenetration of individual and social factors.
3. Freud's perspective was universalistic: He strove to explain the mechanism of human psychology as such and not to grasp the psychological peculiarities of various societies, which was a crucial problem for anthropologists.
4. Freud's anthropological views seemed glaringly anachronistic to the anthropologists of the Boas school, because they were both speculative and based on evolutionist assumptions.

Briefly, Freud was not acceptable to the American cultural anthropologists. They needed a Freud who did not yet exist at the time when interest in personality and culture was born. Such a Freud was created only by the earliest representatives of neo-psychoanalysis: Karen Horney (1885-1952), Harry Stack Sullivan (1892-1949), and Erich Fromm (1900-   ).[61]

Yet it was the work of Abram Kardiner (1881-   ) that was of special importance for the anthropological theory of society and culture. He carried out a revision of Freudianism. But, more important still, he initiated —together with anthropologists who attended his seminar (Ralph Linton,

Cora Du Bois, Charles Wagley, Carl Withers, writing under the assumed name of James West, and others)—a genuine study of how personality is shaped in culture and he developed semiliterary descriptions of culture in psychological terms. He was not satisfied with the statement about an "isomorphism" of personality and culture, but strove to disclose the mechanisms of interaction between them. Kardiner and his group, whose most important achievements were *The Individual and His Society* (1939) and *The Psychological Frontiers of Society* (1945), were guided by a set of fairly precise theoretical assumptions. Another novelty was the use of psychological techniques (including the Rorschach test and TAT).

Kardiner's theoretical assumptions were formulated following a radical revision of classical Freudianism. It consisted of eliminating from that doctrine the elements of instinctivism, universalism, and evolutionism and also of rejecting the idea of culture as being mainly repressive. In his denial of instinctivism, Kardiner proved as radical as American social psychologists from the school of social pragmatism. He wrote, for instance, "We must be extremely careful what factors we attribute to 'human nature' because there is no such thing: we know only specific types of 'human nature' under specific environmental and social conditions."[62] Kardiner put exclusive emphasis on the "adaptive" aspect of Freud's theory: The basic characteristics of the human psyche emerge in the process of the individual's adaptation to the conditions and requirements of the social environment. But in his conception of that environment he did not move toward sociologism: The relationship between culture and personality is interaction, and the personality of the individual as a whole is not determined by society.

Kardiner's fundamental assumption referred to the existence, within every society integrated by a common culture, of a basic personality structure that is common to all, or at least to the majority, of its members and is in harmony with its institutions. This idea is seemingly very close to that expounded by Ruth Benedict in *Patterns of Culture*, but the difference is that in Kardiner's interpretation this basic personality is a substructure, a deep and hidden layer, on which each individual personality is molded. Acquiring knowledge of basic personality necessitates going beyond the standard anthropological research techniques, so that "the social scientist needs the psychologist. . . . The observer must be trained to look beneath the surface of social institutions, and attempt to discern the relationships that exist between social pressures and the integration of the individual."[63] Modified Freudian psychoanalysis can serve this purpose.

In his striving for a psychodynamic interpretation of personality in culture, Kardiner made an analytic distinction between two levels of every culture: that of "primary" institutions and that of "secondary" institutions. The distinction was based on the type of hypothetical relationships between either of these levels and the traits of basic personality. Primary institutions include, above all, the practices connected with the socialization of the younger generation; they are primary in the sense of determining the basic mental characteristics of the individuals who are subjected to them. Since those institutions are fairly homogeneous within every culture, they produce the uniform basic personality that is decisive for the psychological distinctiveness of every culture. On the contrary, the secondary institutions—religion, ideologies, ways of thinking, rites, and so forth—are secondary in the sense of being produced by basic personality through "projection" and "rationalization" (in the classical Freudian sense of these terms). The concept of primary institutions refers to the impact of society on the individual; that of secondary institutions, to the impact of individuals on society. This is a concise description of Kardiner's "dialectical causality" (a term coined by Linton), which was supposed to enable one to go beyond the enigmatic formula of isomorphism of personality and culture. Shown here in a very simplified form, this conception was an endeavor to answer two fundamental questions: why do participants in a given culture reveal certain psychological similarities? And why is every culture internally coherent?

Kardiner's idea, like those of other neo-Freudians, proved fairly influential in American cultural anthropology and sociology, even though it was frequently criticized and practically no one followed it firmly. Kardiner indicated the general trend of investigations. In any case, all progress in the study of personality in culture required what he had started: to bridge the gap between anthropology and psychology, to produce explanatory concepts, to formulate hypotheses, and to verify them in research. The result was an imposing activity in the field of research (not always directly inspired by Kardiner's theory) that yielded such works as *The People of Alor: A Social-Psychological Study of an East Indian Island* (1944) by Cora Du Bois, *Balinese Character* (1942) by G. Bateson and Margaret Mead, *And Keep Your Powder Dry: An Anthropologist Looks at America* (1942) by Margaret Mead, *The Cultural Background of Personality* (1945) by R. Linton, *Plainville, USA* (1945) by James West, *The American People* (1948) and *Exploring English Character* (1955) by Geoffrey Gorer, *The People of Great Russia* (1949) by Gorer and John Rickman, *The Chrysanthemum and the Sword* (1946) by Ruth Benedict, *Childhood and Society* (1950) by Erik Erikson, and *The Lonely Crowd: The Study of the Changing American Character* (1955) by David Riesman.[64]

It is worth noting, as the very list of titles shows, that psychocultural studies were on an increasing scale covering modern complex societies and not only primitive ones, which for long was the main field of interest of anthropologists. This meant bringing cultural anthropology closer to sociology and at the same time gave rise to many problems with which the theorists had to cope.

Critique of Psychoculturalism. Before we come to discuss these new problems, we must realize that the study of interrelationships between personality and culture encountered profound criticism, which followed the lines listed below.

Some authors pointed to the fact that psychoculturalism was distinguished by a new phraseology rather than a really new set of problems studied or new theorems. Attention was also drawn to the fact that the psychoculturalists' generalizations were made not as a result of psychological research, but as a result of analysis of such data as folklore, religious beliefs and practices, organization of the family, ways of raising children, ideological systems, and so on. They drew conclusions about the psychological traits of members of society from observation of collective behavior. Critics noted that such conclusions are not legitimate, at least until we are able to substantiate the assumption that in every society culture is fully internalized. Otherwise, statements about the personality of individuals, based on such data, are merely reformulations of statements about culture that were made long ago by anthropologists.

To make matters worse, using traditional anthropological data as the point of departure not only rendered it impossible to take up really new issues, but also resulted in apparent explanations. From observations of a given culture they deduced statements about the type of personality that is characteristic of that culture. The traits of that culture were, in turn, explained by the domination in it of the deduced type of personality.[65] In criticizing the work of Ruth Benedict, Aberle noted that such an approach "destroys the field of culture and personality by providing it with nothing to relate to anything else. To the degree that culture and personality are identical, there is no interaction between them."[66]

Further, the critics claimed that the notoriously obscure relationships between psychological and cultural variables were closely connected with the difficulty of drawing a demarcation line between these two groups of variables. When the demarcation line was drawn, this was sometimes accompanied by causal explanations, but most often there were only references to reciprocal influences. The only way out consisted of assigning a privileged position to socialization practices, a solution originated by Kardiner and later supported by Erikson, Gorer, and other neo-Freudians.

The psychoculturalist tendency to see culture as a homogeneous whole, with a corresponding uniform type of personality, was often criticized, too. That inclination can partly be explained by the fact that at that time anthropological studies were mainly concerned with primitive societies, and the cultural anthropology of American society (represented by Lynd, Warner, and James West) was still in its nascent stage. This, however, is a poor justification, for no society has a fully homogeneous culture, in which all its members participate to the same degree regardless of sex, age, social status, and so on.

The assumption that socialization was the main factor of both social stabilization and social change also raised critical remarks. The critics stressed the necessity of asking why stabilization and change took given forms in various cultures and emphasized that an answer to this question requires reference to social structure and other variables of this kind.

Finally, critical remarks concerned the tendency, clearly noticeable in some psychoculturalists, to confuse their own theoretical constructions with facts and to reify such concepts as the "basic personality structure," "patterns of culture," "national character," and the like. Kaplan and Manners wrote that representative of that orientation "did not even question the *existence* of group personality, assuming instead that each culture exhibits a dominant personality type. Thus, rather than asking *whether* a society could be characterized in terms of a basic or modal personality type, they were led to ask *what* is the nature of its basic or modal personality."[67]

Psychoculturalism and the Problem of Social Differentiation. In the discussion on psychoculturalism the key issue was the possibility its recognizing social differentiations in all—and especially contemporary—societies. "But as soon as one moves into a more complex and differentiated society," Riesman was to write many years later, "what is basic for one group may not be basic for another, and groups may struggle to define what is to be regarded as 'basic' for the society as a whole."[68] Note that some representatives of psychoculturalism postulated not only the study of personality in culture, but also the study of personality in *subcultures.* This interest was inspired, on the one hand, by researches into American society (by the Lynds, Warner, John Dollard, and others[69]), which revealed its profound inner differentiation and, on the other hand, by theories, which were popular in the Chicago school and with others (Park, Znaniecki, and Linton), of the plurality of social statuses and roles. The influence of Marxism, however, was negligible, even though Lynd suggested combining Freud with Marx in reflections on culture and personality.

This resulted in a specific branch of psychoculturalism that might be termed *sociological*, because its representatives focused their attention on the problems of social structure. It is well exemplified by the views of Ralph Linton (1893-1953), Boas's successor at Columbia University in 1937-1946, who, however, is one of the few American anthropologists of that generation who cannot be included in the Boas school. Linton began his scholarly activity as a field worker (see *The Tanala, A Hill Tribe of Madagascar* [1933]), but later concentrated on theory and wrote such books as *The Study of Man* (1936), *The Cultural Background of Personality* (1945), and *The Tree of Culture* (1955). For some time he was in touch with Radcliffe-Brown, and later he had fairly close links with Kardiner. His interest in sociology was shaped under the influence of the Chicago school. When he began cooperation with Kardiner his interest, he wrote, pertained mainly to "the relation of culture to personality content and . . . the adaptation of individuals to particular positions within the social system."[70]

Linton assimilated the important elements of Kardiner's ideas and helped to popularize the basic postulates of psychoculturalism, especially through *The Cultural Background of Personality*. However, he modified Kardiner's conception considerably, by abandoning the myth of homogeneity of culture and by introducing the ideas of class subculture and status personality.

In his discussions with Kardiner, he claimed that no individual knows, or can know, the whole of the culture in which he participates and no individual reveals in his behavior all patterns of that culture. Every society, beginning with the most primitive ones, divides its members into different categories, and each category has corresponding "sectors of culture." The individual's participation in culture is conditioned by his place in the social structure—that is, by his status.

This viewpoint was decisive for establishing Linton's originality within psychoculturalism. Most important for him were not the patterns of culture typical of a given society in general, but the patterns associated with the different positions in the social structure. He was interested mainly in status personality and not in basic personality. According to him, the impact of the community on the individual was connected not only with the existence of a common culture, but also with the difference in the expectations addressed to the various members of society according to their respective statuses. The functioning of society as an integrated whole depends both on the existence of basic personality, shaped by early socialization, and especially on the adaptation of individuals to the respective positions assigned to them in the social structure.

Another original element in Linton's ideas was the introduction of the concept of modal personality, which had, or at least could have had, far-reaching theoretical and methodological consequences.

Unfortunately, Linton failed to make use of his ideas in his research work, and hence they are primarily an illustration of the difficulties that psychoculturalism had to face and an announcement of its approaching crisis. In fact, that orientation, extremely popular at one time, does not have any major importance today.

EVOLUTIONISM ONCE MORE

All the orientations in anthropology discussed up to here were anti-evolutionist. This does not mean that the heritage of evolutionist anthropology was doomed to oblivion once and for all. Not only did it survive in Soviet ethnography, but in the late 1930s it also began to win advocates among those representatives of Anglo-Saxon anthropology who were not satisfied with the prevailing interpretations of culture. To the theories that analyzed culture (or cultures) as a property of specific societies, they opposed the idea of culture as a property of human species and made the universal processes of the cumulative growth of culture, its laws and direction, the subject of their study again. This approach, first presented by Leslie A. White (1900-   ), returned to evolutionism and the idea of progress. However, the advocates of that approach cannot just be called evolutionists, because they did take into account the critique of classical evolutionism that had been carried out by twentieth-century anthropologists. Their point was not so much to revive the theories of Morgan, Tylor, and Spencer as to restore the legitimacy of some problems posed by them. Those scholars are now usually called neo-evolutionists.

Leslie A. White's Neo-Evolutionistic Theory of Culture. White, who began his work with a standard monograph of Pueblo Indians, took up the issues of the general theory of culture in the 1930s under the influence of Morgan and of Marxist authors. This resulted in *The Science of Culture: A Study of Man and Civilization* (1949) and *The Evolution of Culture: The Development of Civilization to the Fall of Rome* (1959). In these works he presented the theory of culture, which was something extraordinary in the social sciences, as pursued in America. At that time the latter were marked by a strong dislike of the heritage of the social thought of the nineteenth century and also by ignorance of that heritag   His works include also a fundamental criticism of the orientation prevailing in American cultural anthropology in the first half of the twentieth century, especially of historicism and psychoculturalism.

White's point of departure was Spencerian. He maintained that there are three category of phenomena: physical, biological, and cultural (in Spencer, they are inorganic, organic, and superorganic). The last-named group is connected with the species *Homo sapiens*, whose special feature is the ability to use symbols.[71] The use of symbols makes it possible to accumulate and to transmit experience, extrasomatic inheritance, and—hence—culture, which endows the human species with the unique ability of adaptation to the environment. Culture is an instrument by which man copes with the external world and expands his domination over it. This interpretation of culture had its strict analogue in White's image of its evolution as a gradual increase in the amount of energy utilized by man: Cultures of food gatherers and hunters, based solely on the use of the energy of the human body, were followed by those which availed themselves of the energy of animals, wind, and water (agriculture) and then by those which were based on artificially produced, nonorganic energy (the industrial revolution).

A system of culture has a definite inner structure, and its changes follow a determined order. White singled out four basic components or aspects of culture: technological, social, ideological, and psychological; he assigned the key importance to the first of them. In his description of the evolution of culture this factor most frequently occurs as an independent variable: "Social systems are therefore determined by technological systems; and philosophies and the arts express experience as it is defined by technology and refracted by social systems."[72] In White's theory, technology holds the place that in the theories of Radcliffe-Brown and Malinowski was held, respectively, by the social structure and human needs: The whole system of culture is functional relative to technology.

Radical antivoluntarism and anti-individualism are the salient characteristics of White's theory of culture. White claimed that "we add nothing to an explanation of this culture process by including man in our calculation."[73] He also claimed that "it is . . . culture that determines the behavior of man, not man who controls culture. And culture changes and develops in accordance with laws of its own, not in obedience to man's desire or will."[74] This recognition of the supraindividual character of culture placed White in opposition to two important orientations in anthropology: psychoculturalism and functionalism in Malinowski's version. His dislike of psychoculturalism is quite obvious: Human personality is an epiphenomenon of the development of culture as a reality *sui generis,* and hence such anthropology, focused on personality, inevitably disregards the most important issues. White differed from Malinowski by the conviction that biology is not important in cultural anthropology, because "culture exerts a powerful and overriding influence upon the biological organisms of Homo sapiens, submerging the neurological, anatomical, sensory, glandular, muscular, etc., differences among them to the point of insignificance."[75]

His idea of culture as a universal human phenomenon and his interest in objectified elements of culture were decisive for his dislike of cultural relativism of the Boas school and also for his opposition to the demand that culture should be understood or examined from the inside. White identified Boas's relativism with capitulation to the reactionary social forces in the twentieth century, which were rising against the idea of progress.

Cultural Ecology and Neo-Evolutionism: Steward. White's neo-evolutionism was relatively close to nineteenth-century evolutionism, especially Morgan's theory. White's specific feature was his link with Marxism (mainly in Bukharin's version). But neo-evolutionism in the form given to it by

Julian H. Steward (1902-1972) was different in many respects. Steward, an outstanding expert on the life of South American Indians, was Kroeber's disciple and the author of *Theory of Culture Change: The Methodology of Multilinear Evolution* (1955).

Like White, Steward saw in culture primarily a complex of means of adaptation to the requirements of the natural environment, developed by the human species. Culture ensures that "man enters the ecological scene . . . not merely as another organism which is related to other organisms in terms of his physical characteristics. He introduces the super-organic factor of culture. . . ."[76] The relationship between that factor and the properties of the natural environment was the focus of Steward's theory of culture. He did not deny the importance of other problems, nor did he underestimate— as White did—the achievements of cultural anthropologists in that field. He merely stated that those problems, which had been the most popular so far, interested him rather little.

Steward, again like White, distinguished levels or strata of culture, linked more or less directly, more or less necessarily with the environment. He also ordered institutions according to whether they were "core" or "peripheral." All of this resulted in distinguishing within culture the following systems: technological and economic, sociopolitical, and ideological, the last consisting of the most peripheral institutions.

This distinction was based on the assumption that different levels of culture are not determined to the same degree by the natural environment. The more peripheral an institution, the less determined its form is and the more varieties it has. Hence the fairly small variety of technological and economic systems and an almost infinite number of ideological systems. Steward did not doubt that every culture is an internally interconnected system, and he considered a study of the strength and type of interconnections found in specific cultures to be an urgent task.

In general, Steward was empirically oriented; this accounted for his caution in formulating general laws of the evolution of culture and also for numerous discussions with White.

Steward sought, in effect, an intermediate solution that would stand midway between White's evolutionism and Boas's historicism: He wanted to discover general laws of the evolution of culture without abandoning the knowledge of specific cultures and the construction of historical generalizations based on this knowledge. His program is best summed up in the statement that "cultures, societies, and areas have distinctive traditions or histories and unique patterns, no two being alike in their totality. At the same time, it is possible to identify certain institutions and modes of behavior which are similar in different areas. . . . The problem, then, is one of specifying the particular conditions under which similar behavior patterns may be produced."[77]

According to Steward, who called himself an evolutionist from 1952 on, evolution is multilinear. A modern anthropologist who is evolutionistically minded "simply seeks cross-cultural regularities and explanations, but presupposes no universal schemes. According to this view, there may be many kinds of evolution and many unlike factors involved."[78]

Steward's viewpoint has affected present-day neo-evolutionism, which came to refer both to White and to him. He can probably be crédited with the idea of "specific" evolution, treated as a matter of study on equal footing with "general" evolution. According to Sahlins, "general cultural evolution . . . is passage from less to greater energy transformation, lower to higher levels of integration, and less to greater all-round adaptability. Specific evolution is the phylogenetic, ramifying, historic passage of culture along its many lines, the adaptative modification of particular cultures."[79]

CONCLUSION

In the first half of the twentieth century, social and cultural anthropology advanced considerably: It fundamentally remade its research methods and techniques by working out standards of field work that have not been surpassed to this day; it produced a number of new theories that did away with the relics of traditional evolutionism; it made notable progress in its organization by establishing a network of academic and nonacademic institutions concerned with teaching and promotion of study of alien cultures; it won high prestige among other social sciences by arousing interest of historians, sociologists, linguists, and so on; it left the ethnographic museums in order to voice its opinion on the important issues of modern society; it began to strive for becoming an applied discipline. More important, it had a notable impact on current thinking and contributed to the spread of the principles of cultural relativism and the idea of the equal rights of, and respect for, all cultures. To sum up, the balance sheet of anthropology seems to be very strong and almost unprecedented in the history of other social sciences with such a short record. Even sociology, for which the first half of the twentieth century was also a period of immense advancement, could envy anthropology. Sociology was incessantly availing itself of anthropology's achievements, using data accumulated by anthropology, and taking advantages of its theoretical conceptions (mainly in the study of culture and personality and in the functional interpretation of social systems) and methodological patterns.

The essential weakness of social anthropology (and of sociology as well) has been its inability to integrate achievements of its various orientations within a single theory. There was, of course, an intense exchange of ideas among those orientations, and their various representatives assimilated ideas and conceptions developed outside their respective schools. Nevertheless, differences in interests and research methods easily turned into controversies over the nature of the reality under investigation. In the case of the anthropologists, the controversy was primarily over what culture really is. Since that concept was, as a rule, used in a very broad sense, the controversy often was over the basic problems of social life and the methods of its investigation.

NOTES

1. C. Lévi-Strauss, *Anthropologie structurale* (Paris: Plon 1958), p. 8.
2. B. Malinowski, *A Scientific Theory of Culture and Other Essays* (New York: Galaxy Books, 1960), p. 32.
3. George W. Stocking, Jr., *Race, Culture, and Evolution: Essays in the History of Anthropology* (New York: Free Press, 1968), pp. 152-55.
4. See E. Hatch, *Theories of Man and Culture* (New York: Columbia University Press, 1973), p. 44.
5. F. Boas, *Anthropology and Modern Life* (New York: Norton, 1962), pp. 215-16.
6. Marvin Harris, *The Rise of Anthropological Theory* (New York: Crowell, 1968), pp. 268-69.
7. F. Boas, "The Aims of Anthropological Research", in Boas, *Race, Language and Culture* (New York: Macmillan, 1940), p. 256.
8. Stocking, *Race, Culture, and Evolution*, p. 214.
9. Lévi-Strauss, *Anthropologie structurale*, pp. 12-13.
10. See Bernhard J. Stern, *Historical Sociology* (New York: Citadel Press, 1959), p. 231.
11. Boas, *Race, Language, and Culture*, pp. 258-59.
12. Ibid., p. 268.
13. Ibid., p. 257.
14. A. Kardiner and E. Preble, *They Studied Man* (Cleveland and New York: World Publishing, 1961), p. 153.
15. Alfred L. Kroeber, *The Nature of Culture* (Chicago: University of Chicago Press, 1952), p. 64.
16. Hatch, *Theories of Culture*, p. 95.
17. Kroeber, *Nature of Culture*, p. 115.
18. David F. Aberle, "The Influence of Linguistics on Early Culture and Personality Theory," in Robert A. Manners and David Kaplan, eds., *Theory in Anthropology: A Sourcebook* (Chicago: Aldine-Atherton, 1968), pp. 303-17.
19. Hatch, *Theories of Culture*, pp. 76-82.
20. Kroeber, *Nature of Culture*, p. 115.
21. Ibid., p. 114.
22. The most important of Sapir's papers have been edited by G. D. Mandelbaum, *Selected Writings of Edward Sapir in Language, Culture and Personality* (Berkeley and Los Angeles: University of California Press, 1949).
23. Edward Sapir, *Culture, Language and Personality: Selected Essays* (Berkeley and Los Angeles: University of California Press, 1970), p. 203.
24. Hatch, *Theories of Culture*, p. 314.
25. Piotr Sztompka, *Metoda funkcjonalna w socjologii in antropologii* (Wroclaw: Ossolineum, 1971), pp. 16-31.
26. A. R. Radcliffe-Brown, *Structure and Function in Primitive Society* (London: Oxford University Press, 1952), pp. 188-89.
27. E. E. Evans-Pritchard, *Social Anthropology* (London: RKP, 1972), p. 56.

28. Cf. Alvin W. Gouldner, *The Coming Crisis of Western Sociology* (New York: Equinox Books, 1971), pp. 125-34.

29. See J. Goody, "British Functionalism," in R. Naroll and F. Naroll, eds., *Main Currents in Cultural Anthropology* (Englewood Cliffs, N.J.: Prentice-Hall, 1973), p. 188.

30. Harris, *Rise of Anthropological Theory*, p. 525.

31. Evans-Pritchard, *Social Anthropology*, p. 57.

32. A. R. Radcliffe-Brown, *Method in Social Anthropology* (Chicago: University of Chicago Press, 1958), p. 29.

33. See Don Martindale, *The Nature and Types of Sociological Theory* (Boston: Houghton Mifflin, 1960), p. 456.

34. See J. Goody, "British Functionalism," p. 187.

35. Cf. A. Pierce, "Durkheim and Functionalism," in Kurt H. Wolff, ed., *Emile Durkheim, 1858-1917* (Columbus, Ohio: Ohio State University Press, 1960), p. 154.

36. B. Malinowski, *Argonauts of the Western Pacific* (New York: Dutton, 1922), p. xvi.

37. Hatch, *Theories of Culture*, pp. 319-20.

38. Robert K. Merton, *Social Theory and Social Structure* (Glencoe, Ill.: Free Press, 1957), pp. 25-35.

39. Radcliffe-Brown wrote, "In such an analysis we are dealing with a system as it exists at a certain time, abstracting as far as possible from any change that it may be undergoing." Quoted in Harris, *Rise of Anthropological Theory*, p. 516.

40. See Hatch, *Theories of Culture*, p. 224n.

41. Adam Kuper, *Anthropologists and Anthropology: The British School, 1922-1972* (Harmondsworth: Penguin Books, 1975), p. 72.

42. Radcliffe-Brown, *Method*, p. 176.

43. Ibid., p. 169.

44. Ibid., p. 174.

45. See Kuper, *Anthropologists and Anthropology*, p. 70.

46. Lévi-Strauss, *Anthropologie structurale*, pp. 20-21.

47. Malinowski, *Scientific Theory of Culture*, p. 36.

48. Hatch, *Theories of Culture*, p. 283.

49. Cf. Kardiner and Preble, *They Studied Man*, p. 174.

50. Malinowski, *Scientific Theory of Culture*, p. 125.

51. Hatch, *Theories of Culture*, p. 276.

52. Bronislaw Malinowski, *The Dynamics of Culture Change* (New Haven: Yale University Press, 1945), p. 50.

53. Hatch, *Theories of Culture*, p. 289.

54. Evans-Pritchard, *Social Anthropology*, p. 87.

55. Kuper, *Anthropologists and Anthropology*, p. 108.

56. Hatch, *Theories of Culture*, p. 245.

57. See Kuper, *Anthropologists and Anthropology*, p. 162.

58. Roscoe C. Hinkle, Jr., and Gisela J. Hinkle, *The Development of Modern Sociology: Its Nature and Growth in the United States* (Garden City, N.Y.: Doubleday, 1954), p. vii.

59. Robert E. Park and Ernest W. Burgess, *Introduction to the Science of Sociology* (Chicago: University of Chicago Press, 1921), p. 57.

60. Kardiner and Preble, *They Studied Man*, p. 213.

61. Martin Birnbach, *Neo-Freudian Social Philosophy* (Stanford: Stanford University Press, 1961).

62. See ibid., p. 71.

63. Kardiner and Preble, *They Studied Man*, pp. 248-49.

64. See Milton Singer, "A Survey of Culture and Personality Theory and Research," in Bert Kaplan, ed., *Studying Personality Cross-Culturally* (Evanston, Ill.: Row, Peterson, 1961), pp. 9-92.

65. David Kaplan and Robert A. Manners, *Culture Theory* (Englewood Cliffs, N.J.: Prentice-Hall, 1972), p. 136.

66. Aberle, "Influence of Linguistics", p. 315.

67. Kaplan and Manners, *Culture Theory*, p. 146.

68. D. Riesman and N. Glazer, "The Lonely Crowd: A Reconsideration in 1960," in S. M. Lipset and L. Lowenthal, eds., *Culture and Social Character* (Glencoe, Ill.: Free Press, 1967), p. 426.

69. Nicolas Herpin, *Les Sociologues américains et le siècle* (Paris: P.U.F., 1973), pp. 32-36.

70. See A. Linton and C. Wagley, *Ralph Linton* (New York: Columbia University Press, 1971), p. 58.

71. Leslie A. White, *The Science of Culture: A Study of Man and Civilization* (New York: Grove Press, 1949), p. 35.

72. Leslie A. White, *The Evolution of Culture: The Development of Civilization to the Fall of Rome* (New York: McGraw-Hill, 1959), pp. 390-91.

73. Hatch, *Theories of Culture*, p. 142.

74. Ibid., p. 136.

75. Ibid., p. 138.

76. Julian H. Steward, *Theory of Culture Change: The Methodology of Multilinear Evolution* (Urbana: University of Illinois Press, 1955), p. 31.

77. See Hatch, *Theories of Culture*, p. 124.

78. Ibid., p. 117.

79. Marshall D. Sahlins and Elman R. Service, eds., *Evolution and Culture* (Ann Arbor: University of Michigan Press, 1960), p. 38.

SOCIOLOGICAL FUNCTIONALISM AND ITS CRITICS

Sociological functionalism[1] is an original, perhaps epoch-making orientation, despite the fact that its influence has almost never reached beyond the American universities. Its originality certainly did not mean inventiveness, for the various ideas advanced by functionalism had been known long before, and many of them had been sociological platitudes from their very inception. Possibly, functionalism owed its brilliant career to these very platitudes. It succeeded in bringing together the various theoretical ideas and acted as the heir, legitimate or not, of all sociological tradition (except Marxism), which had previously been split into rival orientations or schools.

It is simply astounding how functionalism, especially in its version advanced by Talcott Parsons, proved able to assimilate ideas of diverse provenance. Functionalism was a theoretical superstructure erected on the solid, institutionalized, academic sociology; it was reconciled to the existing social order at a time when the United States was not witnessing any major ideological confrontations and the social world seemed perfectly stabilized. Functionalism was also probably the first orientation in sociology that constructed its sociological theory, seemingly at least, without any extra-sociological inspirations. It aspired above all to settle sociological practice with the help of an expanded system of concepts, the elements of which had been known to sociologists before the emergence of functionalism.

FUNCTIONALISM AS A SPECIFIC SOCIOLOGICAL ORIENTATION

One characteristic of many representatives of functionalism (also known as structural functionalism or functional structuralism) was their tendency to blur its distinctive features and to present themselves as advocates of the sociological "normal science." Thus, for instance, Kingsley Davis in a lecture symptomatically entitled "The Myth of Functional Analysis as a

Special Method in Sociology and Anthropology" and delivered in 1959 said that "functionalism is most commonly said to do two things: to relate the parts to the whole and to relate one part to another. . . . It strikes me that . . . [these] simply describe what any science does. If there is a functional method, it is simply the method of sociological analysis."[2] The critics of functionalism resemble its advocates in one respect: They are inclined to believe that the influence of that orientation has been overwhelming.

This exaggeration of the importance of functionalism is primarily due to the fact that whenever one either refers to society as a system or points to the necessity of studying the "functions" of an institution, he is considered to be a functionalist. Such functionalists are in fact very numerous, because, as A. Inkeles notes, "there are very few socologists who would argue that there is no order or system in social life."[3] However, if we try to describe functionalism in greater detail by seeking its really distinctive characteristics, then it turns out that it is not identical with sociology and actually encounters firm resistance on the part of many sociologists. This resistance is a result of functionalism's inclination: Rather than standing for sociological common sense, it advocates a specific *Weltanschauung*, which can be questioned on both theoretical and ideological grounds.

When reconstructing functionalism as a *sui generis* sociological orientation, we must bear in mind at least four things. First, there are many varieties of functionalism, and this is why one cannot present any long list of statements accepted by all sociologists who are commonly considered to be functionalists. Second, functionalist theoretical reflection is situated at different levels of generality, and in many cases it concerns only particular problems of sociological subdisciplines that are remote from fundamental macrosociological issues. Third, contrary to the deeply rooted stereotype, it is not legitimate to identity functionalism with the views of Talcott Parsons. As G. Rocher writes, "it is a great oversimplification to see Parsons' sociology as the prototype of all functionalism, and equally so to reduce the whole of Parsonian theory to functionalism."[4] Fourth, there are profound differences between sociological functionalism and the functionalism developed earlier within social anthropology. The similarities between the two are confined to terminology and few general assumptions.

The most important assumptions of sociological functionalism, adopted explicitly or implicitly, merit brief discussion.

Holism. Radcliffe-Brown wrote, "If functionalism means something at all, it does mean the attempt to see the social life of a people as a whole, as a functional unity."[5] The belief that all forms of human activity and all human institutions are interconnected favored the reference by functionalists to the organicist tradition and to biological terminology. While the traces of organicism can clearly be seen in present-day functionalism, it does not resort to the primitive analogies whereby nineteenth-century organicists, and even Radcliffe-Brown himself, tried to describe society as an internally connected whole. The concept of organism came to be replaced by that of system, and the latter in turn underwent a generalization and a relativization.

According to P. Sztompka,

Generalization proceeds by means of isolating those fundamental structural properties which may characterize any system, and then selecting a particular set of those fundamental properties which lend themselves to characterizing social reality. . . . *Relativization* is the double expansion of the domain to which the notion of a system is applied. . . . One trend of relativization may be considered as realistic, in the philosophical sense of the term. The system is construed as a real whole, existing "out there," but it is exemplified not only by global societies, but also by less inclusive social wholes such as social groups, communities, etc. . . . The second trend of relativization . . . represents some assumptions of nominalistic (or even conventionalistic) philosophy. It construes a system as a useful tool for identifying certain important complexes or networks of social relations—economy, polity, culture, society, and social personality.[6]

This change has had two main sources. First, modern sociological functionalism has been interested in providing theoretical foundations to different sociological subdisciplines and not only in reconstructing theoretical macrosociology. Second, it could on an increasing scale avail itself of the achievements of the general systems theory. An essential novelty lies also in the acceptance of the opinion that the integration of a system has various degrees and that defining that degree in a given system is the important task of a student.

Functionalist Explanation. Holism is a necessary, but not a sufficient, condition of functionalism. The reference to the concept of system, and even to that of function, also does not suffice to distinguish functionalism from other theoretical orientations. The distinctive characteristic of functionalism is a specific method of analyzing the social facts included in a given system. It consists, first, of assuming that the fact in question performs a definite function in that system (that is, that it has a noticeable influence on its survival), and, second, of supposing that the identification of that function means the explanation of the fact itself: "to functionally explain a particular phenomenon means to deduce it (or more precisely: a statement about it) from an assertion about the functions which it fulfills."[7] To explain a fact, the functionalist asks about its effects rather than its causes.

The specific feature of functionalism qua theory has perhaps been most clearly formulated by Homans, who claimed that "to say that an item of behavior has consequences and that a sociologist ought to look for them is not the same thing as saying that the item exists *because* its consequences are of a particular sort. Only when the latter kind of statement is made does the functional analysis begin to become functional theory, that is, functional explanation."[8] One may thus say that functionalist explanations are more or less teleological in nature. In the early anthropological functionalism, there was a tendency to apply this schema of explanation to all elements of culture (the postulate of universal functionalism)—that is, to accept in a modified form the old principle that whatever exists is reasonable. Contemporary sociological functionalism assumes that every system also includes dysfunctional elements that tend to burst it from the inside and that cannot be explained by the needs of the system as a whole.[9]

The Functional Prerequisites of a Society. Since explaining a given social fact requires referring it to a social system and analyzing it in the light of the functions that it performs within that whole, it is natural for the functionalist to ask whether there are constant needs that unconditionally require satisfaction and that every social system has. This was also a problem in classifying the functions performed by the various elements of a given system, and it gave rise to the concept of functional prerequisites of a society. In anthropological functionalism one very often came across the assumption that every component of the social whole was indispensable. As Malinowski wrote, it was believed that "in every type of civilization, every custom, material object, idea and belief fulfils some vital function, has some task to accomplish, represents an indispensable part within a working whole."[10] In the modified functionalism (in its sociological version) the statement about the indispensability of every element of culture has been replaced by the statement that the only thing that is indispensable is that certain functions be performed; one and the same function, however, can be performed by different elements and, conversely, one and the same element can, under different conditions, perform different functions.

The formulation of the functional prerequisites of a society was thus one of the aspects of the generalization of the concept of social system. From Malinowski to Parsons, many catalogues of such prerequisites were made, with a considerable degree of agreement, assuming that, as Aberle and others have written, "functional prerequisites refer broadly to the things that must get done in any society if it is to continue as a going concern, i.e., the generalized conditions necessary for the maintenance of the system concerned."[11] An example is provided by the catalogue of functional prerequisites, made by these authors, which includes the following nine items:

(1) provision for adequate relationship to the environment and for sexual recruitment; (2) role differentiation and role assignment; (3) communication; (4) shared

cognitive orientation; (5) a shared, articulated set of goals; (6) the normative regulation of means; (7) the regulation of affective expression; (8) socialization; (9) the
effective control of disruptive forms of behavior.[12]

The conception of functional prerequisites involves grave theoretical
problems (mostly because its assumptions can be verified only when those
prerequisites are not satisfied, which is excluded by definition); nevertheless,
it has been fairly commonly accepted by the functionalists. One of its best-
known applications is the functional theory of stratification, which has
been debated on more than one occasion. The theory is based on the assumption that "as a functioning mechanism a society must somehow dis-
tribute its members in social positions and induce them to perform the duties
of these positions."[13]

Social Order as Sociology's Focus of Interest. Contrary to what some
of its critics claim, functionalism does not in the least eliminate unrest
and change from its picture of the social world; instead, it merely does
not focus its attention on them. The functionalist model of society shows
it in a state of order, equilibrium, or homeostasis. Pierre L. van den Berghe
presents the functionalist point of view:

Although integration is never perfect, social systems are fundamentally in a state of
dynamic equilibrium, i.e., adjustive responses to outside changes tend to minimize
the final amount of change within the system. The dominant tendency is thus towards
stability and inertia, as maintained through built-in mechanisms of adjustment
and social control. . . . Disfunctions, tensions and "deviance" do exist and can
persist for a long time, but they tend to restore themselves or to be "institutionalized"
in the long run. In other words, while perfect equilibrium or integration is never
reached, it is the limit towards which social systems tend.[14]

Functionalism is thus a sociology of social order, which strives above all
to define the mechanisms and conditions of that order.

Methodological Sociologism. Interest in a social system as a whole does
not make functionalists the representatives of sociologism, claiming—after
Durkheim—that society is a reality *sui generis.* Such an approach would
simply be impossible, in view of the relativization of the concept of social
system. But they stand for methodological sociologism: trying to single out
a specific category of social facts and subordinating the analysis of individual behavior to the study of social facts. "The subject-matter of functionalism is not individuals *per se.*"[15] Functional analysis is focused, Merton says, on social roles, institutional patterns, social processes, cultural
patterns, culturally patterned emotions, social norms, group organization,
social structure, and devices for social control.[16] To use D. Wrong's for-

mulation, we may say that functionalism resorts to "the oversocialized conception of man"[17] and thus breaks with the individualist tradition, which has been strong in American sociology.

Ahistoricism. Finally, ahistoricism, or formalism, seems to be characteristic of functionalism. The theoretical schemata constructed by functionalists were, by assumption, applicable universally.

Functionalism was exceptionally strongly rooted in sociological tradition. In American sociology, it represented a return (in many cases deliberate) to problems that had been *the* problems of European sociology in the early twentieth century, but were later renounced by empirical sociology and social psychology. Functionalism is also to be credited with the reception in the United States of many European theorists, especially Pareto, Durkheim, and Max Weber. This link to the tradition certainly strengthens the functionalists' belief that their sociological standpoint is "natural." Of course, as in the case of all original trends, the attitude of the functionalists toward tradition has been highly selective, best illustrated by the reinterpretation of that tradition by Talcott Parsons. It seems that sociological functionalism was, next to the ideas of British anthropological functionalists, greatly influenced by the new reading of Vilfredo Pareto, who interpreted as the theorist of social system. This new interpretation was mainly attributable to Harvard physiologist Lawrence Joseph Henderson (1878-1942), who in 1932-1934 gathered around him a small group of students of Pareto's works, including Parsons and Homans, who were later to become very influential as sociologists.

The principal representatives of sociological functionalism are Talcott Parsons and Robert K. Merton (1910-   ), author of *Social Theory and Social Structure* (1949), a renowned collection of papers. Functionalism probably owes the most to the latter when it comes to precisely defining the basic concepts and to bringing the theory, which was extremely abstract in Parsons's version, to the practical needs of empirically minded researchers. But present-day functionalism is a product of a group that includes such scholars as Kingsley Davis, Marion Levy, Wilbert E. Moore, Kaspar Naegele, Edward A. Shils, and Neil J. Smelser.

SOCIOLOGICAL THEORIES OF TALCOTT PARSONS

Talcott Parsons (1902-1979), author of *The Structure of Social Action* (1937), *Essays in Sociological Theory Pure and Applied* (1949), *The Social System* (1951), *Working Papers in the Theory of Action* (1953) with Robert F. Bales and Edward A. Shils, *Economy and Society* (1956) with Neil J. Smelser, *Structure and Personality* (1964), *Societies: Evolutionary and Comparative Perspective* (1966), *Sociological Theory and Modern Society*

(1967), and *The System of Modern Societies* (1971), deserves to be discussed here separately. However we assess his work, there is no doubt that it results from one of the most ambitious theoretical undertakings in twentieth-century sociology. It has also largely outlined the horizon of present-day sociology, which is proved by the criticism so frequently leveled against him, especially after 1960. One can, and probably should, engage in socio-logical theorizing against Parsons, but one cannot behave as if Parsons had never existed.

The Significance of Parsons's Theory. Parsons's exceptional role in American sociology (and in sociology in general, because the experience of America's "incurable theorist" will probably also count in those countries in which he has found no followers) consists of his having taken up the task, unprecedented in the mid-twentieth century, of constructing an all-embrac-ing theoretical system. During the time marked by triumphs of empirical sociology, Parsons was bold enough to claim that what sociology needs most is a theory and to demonstrate, counter to deeply rooted prejudices, that a theory does not emerge by itself as a result of accumulation of data, because data themselves are, in a sense, derivatives of a theory. Parsons approvingly quotes Henderson: "A fact is a statement about experience in terms of a conceptual scheme."[18] He is convinced more firmly than any other sociologist of his generation that if a scientist is to work effectively, he must have appropriate theoretical concepts at his disposal. This is why he was sometimes linked to the Kantian tradition. In his opinion, facts are not just given to the researcher; "sociology is not a tabula rasa upon which things called 'facts' inscribe their determinate and essential paths and shapes."[19] Sociology must not only lead to a theory (which is, in fact, claimed by all), but it must begin with a theory as well.

The theoretical system that Parsons has been laboriously constructing for nearly fifty years is extraordinary for at least three reasons. First, it is, by assumption, a system not of sociology alone, although it has evoked a lively response only from sociologists and political scientists. Rather, it is a system of the social sciences in general, a system in which each social discipline is assigned its own place and is situated with respect to sociology. Second, the system is extremely abstract, which led P. Sorokin to comment dryly that "the meshes of the abstract nets are so large that practically all the empirical fish slip through, leaving nothing in the hands of the fisherman-researcher."[20] Parsons has never bothered about the sufficient empirical base for his con-structions, for he does not consider a theory to be a generalization of empir-ical data. Except in a few of his papers, he did not aspire to write about the real world. He would never take any particular problem as his point of departure. He has constructed a *general* theory, leaving others to worry whether that theory can serve any purpose other than its own self-improvement. We see the difference on this point between Parsons and Merton, the other prominent functionalist. Being concerned about the empirical nature of theories, Merton suggested that sociologists should confine themselves for the time being to "theories of the middle range." He stated:

the search for a total system of sociological theory . . . has the same large challenge and the same small promise as those all-encompassing philosophical systems which have fallen into deserved disuse. There are some who talk as though they expect, here and now, formulation of *the* sociological theory adequate to encompass vast ranges of precisely observed details of social behavior and fruitful enough to direct the attention of thousands of research workers to pertinent problems of empirical research. This I take to be a premature and apocalyptic belief. We are not ready. The preparatory work has not yet been done."[21]

Parsons did not have any doubts on that matter, although it seems that his opinion on what that general theory should be was not fully formed. He used to call it alternately a "conceptual scheme" and a "general sociological theory."[22] But he was certainly one of the main initiators of the discussion about what a modern sociological theory should be.

Parsons's theoretical system was oriented toward synthesizing all valuable ideas in the social sciences. An important part of his undertaking consisted in reading anew the history of sociology (especially since Weber, Pareto, and Durkheim) in order to discover in it a single theory instead of many. Parsons's works are marked almost obsessively by the idea of the convergence of sociological theories. This was also the leading idea of a monumental anthology, *Theories of Society* (1961), prepared by Parsons jointly with Edward Shils, Kaspar D. Naegele, and Jesse R. Pitts. In modern sociology, Parsons initiated a new approach to the heritage left by the classics of sociology: It no longer consists of recording innumerable schools, nor of assimilating the attainments of some authors and ignoring the achievements of others. Parsons's attitude toward that heritage was marked by the ever renewed effort to articulate the truly common output of the discipline as a whole. Thus, he assimilated the essential elements of the work of such authors as Weber and Durkheim, Pareto and Freud, Tönnies and Cooley, Spencer and Malinowski. The list was continually expanded. Parsons proved to be least kind to Marx, although he tried to make Marxian ideas, too, topical from the viewpoint of functionalism.

Whether or not he interpreted all those thinkers correctly, he has done the important endeavor to integrate the theoretical achievements of sociology and to cancel the majority of traditional dilemmas and oppositions of sociological thought. What has usually been taken for elements of theoretical alternatives Parsons takes for aspects of one general theory. Voluntarism with determinism, antinaturalism with naturalism, individualism with holism, psychologism with sociologism, statics with dynamics—all are combined in one theoretical system. This is why one sometimes speaks about Parsons's eclecticism and stresses the astounding ease with which he dismisses controversies. But it is this eclecticism alone that allowed an interesting experiment and enabled us to answer the question of whether present-day sociology can produce a uniform general theory. True, the result of that experiment seems to be negative. As a matter of fact, Parsons has even failed in turning out a uniform conceptual schema, even though he has made great efforts to put sociological terminology in order, which caused him to be blamed for verbalism and scholasticism. Parsons's set of concepts has remained largely his own property, and acceptance of his system as a whole has proved to be even more difficult.

Social Action. A concise presentation of Parsons's theory is almost impossible for two reasons. First, it has been worked out by him in great detail and is encyclopedic by assumption. Second, over time it was often complemented and transformed, so that the problem of the continuity and change in Parsons's ideas has become a subject matter in itself. In the literature of the subject there are two rival opinions. According to one, the views of the author of *The Structure of Social Action* changed radically, and Parsons, originally a social behaviorist, became, as the author of *The Social System*, a macrofunctionalist.[23] According to the other, Parsons has been fairly consistent in all his work, shifting stress rather than changing his basic theoretical options. Counter to appearances, these two opinions are not incompatible with one another: Before World War II Parsons was not yet a functionalist, and as a functionalist he did not abandon the basic assumptions of his earlier theory of social action. As a result, it is easier to point to the new elements in his opinions than to indicate the opinions that he has abandoned for good. However it may be, the point of departure (both historical and systemic) of his theory is the concept of social action. Parsons's conception of social action excludes the possibility of explaining human actions both in purely individual terms (a critique of utilitarianism) and without reference to individuals' freedom of choice and consciousness. Further, Parsons reveals unchanging interest in the question, How is social order possible?

As interpreted by Parsons, social action is not to be identified with behavior. If we are to speak about action, it does not suffice to say that an organism reacts in a definite manner to the environment, because we are interested in a relation not between an organism and its environment, but between actor and situation. As seen by Parsons (and also by the earlier theorists of humanistic sociology), social action is purposeful by definition, as it has a subjective meaning and a motivation. Whoever engages in social action must have some knowledge of the conditions in which he will try to

attain his goal and of the objects with which he will be concerned; he must
have the need of attaining his goal connected with his other needs, and he
must respond to that goal emotionally; finally, he must have criteria with
which to assess both the goal itself and the means by which he is to attain it.
Accordingly, Parsons speaks about three modes of motivational orientation
—cognitive, cathectic, and evaluative—and about three modes of value
orientation—cognitive, appreciative, and moral—and he tries to show that
social action is determined not only by the orientation of the actor himself,
but also by the expectations addressed to him by others. Hence, in his value
orientation the actor is guided by the criteria by which all his doings will be
assessed. Parsons puts the stress not on one's individual needs, but rather
on the social norms with which he must comply when satisfying them.

The problem of norms and values gains in importance when Parsons
proceeds from analyzing the simplest relation, namely, that between actor
and situation (this subject of interest is common to sociology and psychology), to analyzing interactions among many actors (which constitute the
specific subject matter of sociology). A situation—the totality of elements
of the environment that are essential from the actor's point of view—has
as its components "social objects"—other actors, individual or collective,
who strive for definite goals. Their every action inevitably becomes interaction, because another man's action is an essential element of the conditions under which one accomplishes one's goals. The sociological question
is, How does interaction become fixed? As a matter of fact, Parsons reverts
here to the problem formulated by Hobbes and discussed over centuries by
social thinkers who tried to answer the questions of how social order came
to be established and why its principles have been observed by all. In Parsons's opinion, the issue must have remained unsolved as long as vulgar
utilitarian psychology was dominant, since it considered all human actions
to be simply striving to satisfy individual interests. He claims that the great
discovery of the social sciences at the turn of the nineteenth century was
noting the role of social norms and values in shaping human behavior; these
norms and values make up the normative order of human relations, which
emerges in the course of interaction and fixes it in turn.

This is why Parsons became particularly interested in Durkheim's conception of collective ideas and, much later, in Freud's conception of superego.
Durkheim and Freud had pointed to two social processes of fundamental
importance, namely, institutionalization and internalization. The former
is the assimilation of a pattern of action by the collectivity; and the latter,
its assimilation by the individual. These two processes complement and
condition one another. Parson's originality as a theorist of social action lies
in that double perspective: combining the analysis of social order at the
individual level (the theory of social action) with the analysis of social order
at the collective level (the theory of social system). Over time Parsons has

become more and more interested in the latter, problems that could not be solved at the individual level, as they emerged only at a certain level of organizational complexity.

Social System. The concept of system was present in Parsons's theory almost from the very beginning. Since in human actions there is always a certain regularity resulting from their being subordinated to social norms, one has to seek their defined structure. "Social structure is a system of patterned relationships of actors in their capacity as a playing roles relative to one another. Role is a concept which links the subsystem of the actor as a 'psychological' behaving entity to the distinctively *social* structure."[24] Social system exists only where there exists a differentiation of social roles and positions, together with the acceptance of respective differentiations of rights and duties and the existence of commonly shared norms and values. All these conditions emerge—at least in embryo—together with integration, the normative aspects of which are strongly stressed by Parsons. A social system is not, however, identical with the totality of interactions. Parsons introduces that concept with a clear intention to articulate the problems, which cannot be articulated at the level of an analysis of interactions. In his opinion, a system has properties that are not reducible to the properties of its component elements. Hence, by taking up a system analysis, he changes essentially the main subject of his interest, if not his philosophy: The actors whose interactions form a definite configuration are replaced by the configuration itself. One might say that he moves away from Max Weber's interactionism toward Durkheim's sociologism, with the proviso that Parsons's concept of system is not connected with any idea of a concrete social entity. It is merely an instrument of analysis, whose use does not require one to declare which side one takes in the old controversy over the nature of social reality.

His analysis of the system qua system, which disregards its origin, suggests to Parsons problem of two kinds: those of the relations between the system and its environment (the most important part of the latter being other systems of action or nonaction) and those of the relations within the system itself. Further, a system can be viewed either from its goals or its means. By combining these two distinctions, we obtain four "dimensions" of "functions" of the system. This is Parsons's own formulation of the problem of "functional prerequisites." For a system of social action to keep functioning, it must be capable of adaptation, goal attainment, integration, and latency (abbreviated as AGIL), or pattern maintenance and tension management.

This schema of the basic functions of a system of social action indicates also the conditions of its equilibrium, the inevitable specialization within it, and its division into the four analytically separable subsystems: organism, personality, social system, and culture. It is also the point of departure of Parsons's reflections on the interconnections between the various functions of a system and on the contributions of each subsystem to the survival of the whole.

In analyzing the interrelations among the four subsystems of action—and between these systems and the environments of action—it is essential to keep in mind the phenomena of *interpenetration.* Perhaps the best-known case of interpenetration is the *internalization* of social objects and cultural norms into the personality of the individual. Learned content of experience, organized and stored in the memory apparatus of the organism, is another example, as is the *institutionalization* of normative components of cultural systems as constitutive structures of social systems. . . . It is by virtue of the zones of interpenetration that process of interchange among systems can take place.[25]

Processes of this kind produce a state of dynamic equilibrium among the various dimensions of a system of social action.

The network of concepts was constructed by Parsons with extraordinary tenacity and consistency. He aimed at a set of sociological concepts for all possible occasions. We do not want to take up the almost impossible task of its full reconstruction, but we shall present one of its elements, the conception of "pattern variables," which is considered to be one of Parsons's key ideas and which is a bridge between the *voluntaristic* and the *systemic* components of Parsons's theoretical system.

Pattern variables are used both for the analysis of the choices that every actor must make and for the analysis of systems. As H. Strasser notes, these variables

should be applicable to all societies and thus permit comparisons between groups as well as across cultures. They must be action-oriented variables in that they follow from the action frame of reference. In other words, "when applied to particular actors they should yield a classification of types of orientations, when applied to social systems they should serve to classify role expectations, and when applied to cultural systems they should deal with types of normative patterns."[26]

The significance of this conception, which is probably the best and most original of Parsons's ideas, is due to the fact that in his theory the problem of social order is, ultimately, one of the correspondence between individual motivations and cultural patterns (social expectations).

Parsons's idea of pattern variables originated from Tönnies's distinction between two types of social relations: *Gemeinschaft* and *Gesellschaft.* Parsons, however, gave to it a new form and thus made it more precise, multidimensional, and applicable to all levels of sociological analysis. In Parsons's theory, this distinction took on the form of four or five basic dilemmas, which have been inevitably inherent in every social action and also in the world of values.

The first dilemma—affectivity versus affective neutrality—is whether action is to provide affective gratification by itself or is to be a means of attaining other goals. The second dilemma—specificity versus diffuseness—is whether action is to be oriented toward another person qua performer of a specified role or qua person—toward a selected aspect of the object with which one deals or toward such an object as a whole. The third dilemma—universalism versus particularism—is whether action is to be directed toward an object because of its properties that can be attributes of many other objects or only because of those properties which are its attributes alone. The fourth dilemma—quality versus performance—is whether another person is to be treated according to what he is, regardless of his actions, or according to what his personal merits are. The fifth dilemma—self-orientation versus collective orientation—was later abandoned by Parsons in his exposition of the theory; it concerns whether action is egoistically oriented or aimed at collective advantage.

As has been said, pattern variables are applicable in the analysis of all systems and subsystems of social action. Parsons also deduced from them a specific typology of societies, to be used in comparative studies.

Despite their complexity, Parsons's ideas were certainly a step forward in adapting the concept of system, which has occurred in sociological thought from Comte on, to the needs of sociological analysis. Parsons took that concept for an ideal type and extended its scope beyond the social organism as a whole. His most important contribution was generalization and relativization of the concept of system. Modern sociological functionalism would not be possible without these ideas.

Parsons as Theorist of Social Evolution. Parsons has often been criticized for focusing on social order, equilibrium, norms and values that keep social systems together, and the like and for neglecting social change and development. In his later works, however, Parsons becomes a *sui generis* social evolutionist. In the third stage of his scholarly activity the problem of evolution is for him no less crucial than the voluntaristic theory of action was in the first stage and the problem of system was in the second. Even Parsons's attitude toward Spencer has changed. Yet, Parsons did not consider his evolutionism to be a renunciation of the functionalist assumptions. He tries to put his "idea of social evolution in the context of the major theoretical and empirical advances that have accumulated since the earlier evolutionists wrote,"[27] in the context of the theory of action and the theory of system. Contrary to his critics' opinion Parsons himself has never thought that he dismissed problems of social change and social development by undertaking functional analysis. He merely maintained that, like in biology, one had to begin with studying structures in order to be able to study processes.

Parsons's reflections on social change cover four groups of problems: social equilibrium, structural change, structural differentiation, and social evolution. He goes step by step from problems of changes within a system to the problem of change of the system. The last problem is the most original one, especially since functionalism emerged as an orientation whose representatives disregarded the change of the system. Evolution, as seen by Parsons (who in this respect does not go far beyond classical evolutionism), consists of the "enhancement of adaptative capacity" of society. This is achieved by two processes, described already by Spencer: differentiation and integration. The former consists of the emergence every now and again of new functions with their corresponding new roles and groups within society. This creates problems of coordination that must be solved by the creation of new systems of values adapted to the new, more complex conditions. The growing complexity of social structure requires cultural patterns to become more and more general. Integration consists precisely in the emergence of adequate means of social control. Parsons's interest in social evolution is concentrated on changes of culture because culture ensures control.

Parsons singles out three stages of evolution, according to the criteria of differences in adaptive capacity and forms of social control. Three types of society—primitive, intermediate, and modern—correspond to these stages. The historical fact that marked the end of primitive society was literacy. Owing to it, culture could be objectified and stabilized, made less dependent on chance, and formed as a separate system of action. The next turning point in human history was the birth of law and related institutions, in which Parsons sees a further step toward the consolidation of culture. As G. Rocher wrote, "Thus for Parsons social evolution takes the form of the progressive strengthening of culture in human social life."[28] In Parsons's studies of evolution, nearly all of the concepts worked out in his theory of action and theory of system found their application. Theory of evolution crowns Parsons's theoretical system. It is intended to bring that system closer to empirical data and also to be the foundation of comparative studies.

THE CONTROVERSY OVER FUNCTIONALISM IN PRESENT-DAY SOCIOLOGY

Functionalism, especially in the version advanced by Parsons, has become the subject matter of innumerable discussions. There has never been an orientation in sociological thought that has been criticized so often or from so many standpoints as functionalism has. This is true not only because the functionalists have raised really important sociological issues, but also because they have presented their theory at the time of a far-reaching institutionalization of sociology, when the authors of new conceptions would not rest satisfied with having adherents grouped in a self-sufficient school, but would address all representatives of the discipline. The claims that functionalism *is* sociology pure and simple, and also the prestige that it has gained in American sociology must have evoked an opposition, especially as functionalism has left many obscurities and failed to keep all its promises. Now and again the criticism of functionalism was vehement, because it was viewed as an ideology and not just as an innocent academic doctrine.

There are three kinds of objections against functionalism.[29] First, it does not comply with the standards of scientific theory; second, it is a one-sided theory and hence is misleading; and third, it is a conservative theory in view of its practical implications. Often these objections are put forward together.

Functionalism as a Poor Theory. When maintaining that functionalism does not comply with the standards of scientific theory, its critics point to the obscurities inherent in it, to the nonverifiability of many of its statements, and to its inclination to teleological explanations, as it sees the *raison d'être* of social institutions in the effects that they produce. Some critics also claim that functionalism is not a theory at all, but merely a conceptual scheme. Homans wrote:

No science can proceed without its system of categories, or conceptual scheme, but this in itself is not enough to give it explanatory power. A conceptual scheme is not a theory. The science also needs a set of general propositions about the relations between the categories, for without such propositions explanation is impossible. No explanation without propositions! But much modern sociological theory seems quite satisfied with itself when it has set up its conceptual scheme.[30]

Functionalism as a One-Sided Theory. Most often, functionalism has been criticized for focusing attention on social order and thus imposing on sociologists a one-sided and, thus, distorted view of social facts. It was claimed that it is typical of the functionalist perspective to see social stability, but not social change; consensus, but not conflict; conformism, but not creativity; the binding force of the norms, but not the mechanisms whereby norms are established or replaced by new ones. Dahrendorf's "Out of Utopia: Toward a Reorientation of Sociological Analysis" (1958) is certainly the best example of this kind of criticism. The functionalist image of the social world is compared there to that image characteristic of Utopians of all times: The world does not have a history and exists, as it were, outside the flow of time; there is universal harmony in it, so all values and institutions are in perfect agreement with one another; internal sources of conflict do not exist; society is isolated from other societies; and so on.[31] From a similar standpoint Parsons has been attacked by C. Wright Mills in the latter's well-known book entitled *The Sociological Imagination* (1959) and by Alvin W. Gouldner in *The Coming Crisis of Western Sociology* (1970). In the decade between two books, there has been a large number of studies concerned with these defects of functionalism.

These studies do not lack misunderstandings. First, they often disregard the fact that functionalism, while focusing its attention on social order and stability, does not prevent an analysis of other problems. Merton has even introduced into functionalism the concept of dysfunction and thus has demonstrated that from the functionalist point of view not everything contributes to the equilibrium of the system. Nor is it true that functionalism totally precludes the possibility of studying social change. Second, they do not take into account the fact that modern sociological functionalism treats order as a problem, rather than a fact.[32] In other words, functionalists do not try to demonstrate that all societies are in a state of equilibrium and harmony and, therefore, that whatever occurs is rational. Instead, they try to find the conditions of equilibrium and harmony. Functionalists do not claim, either, that every individual is a conformist; they merely try to show that a modicum of conformism is necessary for the preservation of social order. Thus, their specific interest in social order is not identical with a social philosophy, which is ascribed to them. The objection of one-sidedness is, however, still justified; as Dahrendorf wrote, "the models with which we work, apart from being useful tools, determine to no small extent our general perspectives, our selection of problems, and the emphasis in our explanation."[33] Making use of the functionalist model of society favors the image of society as a well-integrated and balanced whole and overlooks the facts that vary from that image.

Functionalism as a Conservative Theory. Blaming functionalism for one-sidedness usually goes together with the opinion that this orientation is a conservative one. It is claimed that functionalism shows how institutions contribute to the survival of society and thus legitimates the status quo ideologically. If one's attention is focused on what makes society a harmonious system, then he is less inclined to criticize that society and to sympathize with demands for its radical reconstruction. This opinion has never referred to the personal political leanings of the founders of functionalism, for these happened to cover a very wide range, but it points to the allegedly inevitable implications of their theoretical views. It is true that some formulations found in the functionalist theory seemed to imply conservative political attitudes. Such was, for instance, the case when it was demonstrated that an element of culture "represents an indispensable part

within a working whole,'' without explanation of what is indispensable:
performance of a definite function or its performance by that element only.
The introduction of the concept of functional alternatives,[34] that is, the
admission that a given functional prerequisite can be satisfied in many different ways, has markedly weakened the arguments of the political critics of
functionalism.

The principal objection being advanced now is that the functionalists are
unable to take up, within their theory, the major problems of present-day
societies, which abound in conflicts and need essential reforms. The functionalists in general are blamed for indifference to actual social problems
and for inclination to theorize in abstract terms when the condition of
society requires from sociologists the moral concern that marked the founding fathers of their discipline. Ideological arguments play a rather important role in discussions concerned with functionalism. Characteristically
enough, the endeavors to explain the popularity of functionalism in post-
1945 American sociology by pointing to the new political and socioeconomic
situation in the United States and to the ideological needs of groups interested in consolidating that situation have had a very wide scope. In the
history of sociology the functionalists are the first group of thinkers who
completely lack aspirations to be social reformers.

Discussions of functionalism have contributed but little to its better
understanding and did not signally affect the orientation itself, although
they perhaps accelerated the formulation of the functionalist theory of
change. However, reference to those discussions is necessary if we are to
comprehend some of the new theories that have emerged as a result of the
polemics with the functionalists. This applies in particular to conflict
theory and exchange theory, which Walter L. Wallace counts with functionalism among *structuralist* theories (not to be confused with structuralism
in social anthropology)—that is, theories that strive to explain the social
world by investigating the relations between its various elements.[35]

CONFLICT THEORY VERSUS FUNCTIONALISM

It is more appropriate, perhaps, to speak about conflict theories than
about conflict theory. Furthermore, it is far from certain whether in the
case of conflict theory we have come across a distinct sociological orientation or merely an attempt to articulate the problems that functionalism has
driven into the background in recent sociology, although in earlier sociology
(even at the time of the domination of the Chicago school) and in historical
materialism as well they held an important place. In any case, during the
last twenty-five years we have seen increased interest in social conflict. The
functionalists concentrated on agreement, accommodation, and cooperation; the conflict theorists, on conflict and strife. The functionalists studied

the adjustment of one element to another; the conflict theorists, the degree of their maladjustment. The former considered the equilibrium of the social system to be the crucial concept; for the latter a change of that system was crucial. To use functionalist language, one may say that theorists of conflict replaced the study of the eufunctions of social institutions by the study of their dysfunctions. Some of them even deliberately refer to this concept introduced by Merton. For instance, Dahrendorf writes: "In every science, residual categories are a fruitful departure for new developments. It seems to me that a careful analysis of problems which the term 'dysfunction' hides in the structural-functional theory automatically puts us on the trace of a meaningful sociological theory of conflict."[36]

This change in the focus of interests has not resulted in the emergence of any uniform orientation. Even the attitudes of conflict theorists toward functionalism varied greatly. Some considered their own undertaking to be a *sui generis* complement of functionalism; others, to be a part of a future general theory; still others, to be a nucleus of an independent theory that would rival functionalism in every respect. The typical representatives of these three groups were, respectively, Lewis A. Coser (1913-), Ralf Dahrendorf (1929-   ), and C. Wright Mills (1916-1962).

The Moderate Version of Conflict Theory. Lewis A. Coser, author of *The Functions of Social Conflict* (1956) and *Continuities in the Study of Social Conflict* (1967), is one of those sociologists who have contributed most to popularizing the problems of social conflict anew. He has been concerned

mainly with the functions, rather than the dysfunctions, of social conflict, that is to say, with those consequences of social conflict which make for an increase rather than a decrease in the adaptation or adjustment of particular social relationships or groups. Far from being only a "negative" factor which "tears apart," social conflict may fulfil a number of determinate functions in groups and other interpersonal relations: it may, for example, contribute to the maintenance of group boundaries and prevent the withdrawal of members from the group.[37]

Coser, in effect, wanted to accustom his contemporaneous sociologists to the idea that conflicts play an important role in social life, and to achieve this he demonstrated that conflicts contribute to social integration. This was a "rehabilitation" of conflict, without abandoning the functionalist frame of reference. It was also characteristic of Coser that he sought sources of conflicts in individual aspirations rather than in the properties of social structure. He was interested in the effects of social conflicts on social structure rather than the opposite. Although social structure determines the forms of manifestation and solution of conflicts, the sources of conflicts are to be sought elsewhere. Coser does not attach much importance to the concept of antagonistic group interests, which has always played an important role in theories of social conflict. In analyzing conflict as a form of interaction among individuals Coser has a predecessor in Simmel, but not in Marx nor in Gumplowicz.

Equal Footing of Conflict Theory and Social Order Theory. When speaking about the critics of functionalism, we have mentioned a paper by Ralf Dahrendorf, author of *Soziale Klassen und Klassenkonflikt in der industriellen Gesellschaft* (1957) and *Essays in the Theory of Society* (1968), in which he vehemently attacked the functionalist Utopia of equilibrium and integration. In that paper Dahrendorf claimed a place in sociology for a "conflict model of society" and wrote that "a Galilean turn of thought is required which makes us realize that all units of social organization are continuously changing, unless some force intervenes to arrest this change."[38] What is extraordinary in social life is not change, but rest and equilibrium.

Some of his formulations might indicate that he wanted to replace the functionalist model by a conflict model. But his intention is to ensure an equal footing for both rival models: "Society has two faces of equal reality: one of stability, harmony, and consensus and one of change, conflict, and constraint."[39] Recent sociology has been primarily concerned with the former, and so the point is to undertake the investigation of the latter and to formulate a theory of social conflict that is indispensable for the explanation of change. It is characteristic of Dahrendorf, and of many other representatives of that orientation, that he links conflict very closely with social change.

Dahrendorf's model of society is based on four assumptions, which are diametrically opposed to those on which functionalism rests: "(1) Every society is subjected at every moment to change: social change is ubiquitous; (2) Every society experiences at every moment social conflict; social conflict is ubiquitous; (3) Every element in a society contributes to its change; (4) Every society rests on constraint of some of its members by others."[40] Dahrendorf does not claim that this model is in itself better or more valid than the functionalist one. He criticizes the latter not for being useless, but for distorting the picture of social reality if it is used as the only and universal one. He imposes the same constraints on his own theory as on the theory that he criticizes. He is inclined to believe that what is needed is not a choice between the two rival models, but the formulation in the future—once conflict theory is developed—of a single theory that would take into consideration both aspects of society, both consensus and conflict, at a higher level of generality. Dahrendorf thus tends to restrict the applicability of the functionalist theory of social order and to formulate a conflict theory, symmetrical to the former. He also says that both theories could largely avail themselves of the same concepts, although they have to emphasize different aspects of the social world.

Functionalism shows the social system in a state of equilibrium. Conflict theory is to answer the question of what disturbs that equilibrium and brings about a change of the system, with the proviso that the causes of that change are to be found within the system itself. Hence,

it must develop a model which makes understandable the structural origin of social conflict. This seems possible only if we understand conflicts as struggles among social groups. . . . Under this supposition three questions come especially to the forefront, which conflict theory must answer: (1) How do conflicting groups arise from the structure of society? (2) What forms can the struggles among such groups assume? (3) How does the conflict among such groups affect a change in the social structure?[41]

Dahrendorf seeks answers to these questions. First, he states that relations of dependence are omnipresent in social relations. All social organizations are based on the distinction between higher and lower positions; "every position in an imperatively co-ordinated group can be recognized as belonging to one who dominates or one who is dominated."[42] The interests of those who wield power and those who are deprived of it are incompatible: The former are interested in maintaining the status quo; the latter, in its abolition. Yet the conflict does not burst out immediately, because at first those interests are latent. Their carriers still do not form groups in the full sense of the term, but merely constitute quasi-groups, which become groups when the interests become manifest, or come to be realized by group members. The transformation of latent interests into manifest ones, and of quasi-groups into groups, means the outbreak of the conflict, which in turns means a rapid or slow change in the status quo. Dahrendorf also concerns himself in detail with the various conditions of that process and attaches importance to the possibility of its empirical investigation.

At first glance, this schema resembles the Marxian conception of the transformation of a class in itself into a class for itself, and this is why Dahrendorf is sometimes called a neo-Marxist. The similarity between Dahrendorf and Marx, however, is superficial. Dahrendorf assumes an absolute primacy of power relations and applies this dichotomous schema not to society as a whole, but to each group or aggregate within society, so that a given individual who holds a subordinated position in one group may wield power in another group. The only Marxian element in Dahrendorf's theory is accepting conflict as one of the principal issues in the science of society.

Conflict Theory as Weltanschauung. Functionalism was frontally attacked by C. Wright Mills (1916-1962), author of *The New Men of Power: America's Labor Leaders* (1948), *Character and Social Structure* (1953) with Hans H. Gerth, *White Collar: The American Middle Classes* (1953), *The Power Elite* (1956), *The Sociological Imagination* (1959), *The Marxists* (1962), and so on. He may correctly be called "the prime catalytic agent in the reintroduction of the 'conflict' posture within sociology."[43] Although he is one of the most widely known and most willingly read sociologists, he is certainly underestimated as a theorist. This might have been due to the journalistic style of most of his programmatic formulations and to a lack of disciples who would order and expand his ideas. This is to be regretted, because Mills offered a very interesting proposal, which could have started an intellectual, and not merely political, ferment.

From the very beginning, Mills was fascinated by the problems of power and its uneven distribution in society. He saw, on the one side, the mighty elites that accumulate power, prestige, and wealth and, on the other, the masses of people in the street (whom he described, for example, in *White Collar*), deprived of all influence on public affairs, totally dependent on forces beyond their control, lost in the alien world of big organizations, and incapable of gaining a consciousness of their place in society.

While he did not share most diagnoses advanced by Marx, Mills did share with him the inclination to macrosociological interpretation of social conflicts and the view of society as split into two antagonistic parts with incompatible interests. Mills contrasted Marx's approach to the approaches dominant in the recent social sciences.

The social scientists study the details of small-scale milieus; Marx studied such details, too, but always within the structure of a total society. The social scientists, knowing little history, study at most short-run trends; Marx, using historical materials with superb mastery, takes as his unit of study entire epochs. The values of the social scientists generally lead them to accept their society pretty much as it is; the values of Marx lead him to condemn his society—root, stock and branch. The social scientists see society's problems as matters only of "disorganization"; Marx sees problems as inherent contradictions in the existing structure. The social scientists see their society as continuing in an evolutionary way without qualitative breaks in its structure; Marx sees in the future of this society a qualitative break: a new form of society—in fact a new epoch—is going to come about by means of revolution.[44]

In all these matters, Mills was coming closer and closer to Marx. Moreover, he imitated him in admitting that the calling of the social scientist was not just to produce information, but to help ordinary people in finding an orientation in their world, in finding their paths in "the welter of their daily experience." This change in social scientists' attitudes was supposed to overcome the crisis that, in Mills's opinion, marked the social sciences.

While accepting the Marxian view of social science as an instrument of emancipation, Mills was far from declaring himself in favor of Marxism, especially the Marxism of his time, which he sometimes sharply criticized. He did not declare himself to be historical materialist. His sociological views had been much more deeply influenced by Max Weber, from whom he adopted, among other things, the multidimensional approach to social structure. He was strongly affected by social pragmatism (not only as the coauthor of *Character and Social Structure*) and also by Lynd, the author of *Knowledge for What?* Mills's original ideas developed at the crossing of these various intellectual traditions: He strove "to grasp the interplay of man and society, of biography and history, of self and world."[45]

Mills made sociology face three groups of questions:

(1) What is the structure of this particular society as a whole? What are its essential components, and how are they related to one another? How does it differ from other varieties of social order? Within it, what is the meaning of any particular feature for its continuance and for its change?

(2) Where does this society stand in human history? What are the mechanics by which it is changing? What is its place within and its meaning for the development of humanity as a whole? What does any particular feature we are examining affect, and how is it affected by, the historical period in which it moves? And this period—what are its essential features? How does it differ from other periods? What are its characteristic ways of history-making?

(3) What varieties of men and women now prevail in this society and in this period? And what varieties are coming to prevail? In what ways are they selected and formed, liberated and repressed, made sensitive and blunted? What kinds of "human nature" are revealed in the conduct and character we observe in this society in this period? And what is the meaning for "human nature" of each and every feature of the society we are examining?[46]

As can be seen, Mills's sociology had far-reaching aspirations. In fact, it was an endeavor to make topical the great questions posed by sociological systems in the nineteenth century and brought back enthusiastically by Mills in the anthology entitled *Images of Man* (1960). His point was not only to recall the problems ignored by the orientations dominant in sociology in the mid-twentieth century, to shift accents, or to complete the dominant paradigm. He was convinced that sociology should be given a quite different perspective. The new perspective could be achieved not by opposing the sociology of conflict and change to that of order and stabilization, but by focusing on man in history. (Or, in Mills's words, on the connections between biography and history.) Mills's originality in Western sociology rested largely in his rehabilitating the idea of historical sociology, the denial of which reached its peak in sociological functionalism. In Mills's opinion, sociology can be either historical or poor in quality, incapable of grasping the most important problems. The adoption of this viewpoint resulted in numerous methodological consequences, including an escape from standard sociological data. It also accounted for Mills's dislike of all abstraction: He was interested in given people in a given place and time, whom he wanted to understand as such and to teach an active attitude toward the world. He questioned the possibility of discovering any general sociological laws. He claimed that such suprahistorical laws must be either empty abstractions or tautologous statements.[47]

While Mills's conception has remained undeveloped, it was at the time of its birth the only alternative of functionalism—next to Marxism—that counted in macrosociology. The range of the possible opposition between Mills's perspective and the functionalist perspective was best shown by John Horton, who compared the assumptions on man and society, human nature, sets of values, ways of analyzing social facts, and possible applications in research inherent in the two approaches.[48] Conflict theory in Mills's version came closest to an all-embracing theory of social life.

EXCHANGE THEORY

Exchange theory, developed by George Caspar Homans (1910-) and Peter Blau (1918-), certainly rose to a high level of theoretical articulation. The former author formulated it most comprehensively in *Social Behavior: Its Elementary Forms* (1961); the latter, in *Exchange and Power in Social Life* (1964). Like conflict theory, exchange theory developed as a reaction to functionalism, of which it was both a complementation and a refutation.

The reasoning that resulted in the formulation of exchange theory goes as follows. Functionalism focused its attention on the effect that fact A has on a broader system B. Exchange theorists do not underestimate the importance of questions about functions (Homans himself was first a functionalist), but consider them of secondary significance, because knowledge of functions does not allow one to explain why fact A occurs, or why individuals behave in a given way. The concept of norms or patterns, to which individuals subordinate themselves, also does not explain anything, because we do not know what induces individuals to observe the norms and how the norms develop. If we want to explain fact A, we have to assume that the individual behavior of which A consists is somehow rewarded by the system B, which in this way reinforces that behavior. There must be a relation of reciprocity between the two. Thus, "the relationship between functional structuralism and exchange structuralism may be summed up in the following manner: whereas functional structuralism typically focusses on one side of a given social transaction, exchange structuralism attends to both sides."[49] The distinctive feature of exchange theory is its interest not only in how a given action consolidates the system, but also in why that action is undertaken, repeated, and fixed.

Seemingly, the point is to complement functionalism or to return from Radcliffe-Brown's sociologically oriented functionalism to Malinowski's psychologically oriented one (Homans often refers to Malinowski), the latter being interested in individual needs rather than in the needs of a system as such. In fact, the functionalism of exchange theorists proves to be very dubious. In their striving for explanation of human behavior, they merely reversed the perspective: Instead of asking about the way in which society functions, they fix their minds on how society is able to function at all. The image of man as a member of society is replaced by them by the image of man as a member of a biological species, who must create society in order to satisfy his natural needs. Exchange theorists have thus become critics of functionalism.

First, they claim that functionalists do not study real behavior of human individuals, but only norms of such behavior; that they do not study the development of forms of association, but only their existing and petrified structures. Second, they maintain that functionalists lose sight of man and are concerned primarily with a hypostasis of the system. "But," Homans says,

an institution is functional for society only because it is functional for men. There is no functional prerequisite for the survival of a society except that the society provide sufficient rewards for its individual members to keep them contributing activities to its maintenance, and that it reward them not just as members of that society but as men. . . . The secret of society is that it was made by men, and there is nothing in society but what men put there.[50]

Sociology's "most interesting theoretical task will remain that of showing how structures, relative enduring relationships between men, are created and maintained by individual human choices, choices constrained by the choices of others, but still choices."[51]

Homans's critique of the social sciences goes in the direction opposite to Mills's since the latter blamed them for ahistoricism. Homans reproaches those disciplines for being too fascinated with the specific features of the various societies and cultures and for losing sight of that which is common to all men: human nature, which "is the only true 'cultural universal.'"[52] Regardless of the degree of civilization's development, human nature remains changeless, and hence social knowledge is superficial and unsound as long as it fails to ensure a foundation in the form of the science of behavior of men qua men and not only qua members of society. Hence the tendency, observable in exchange theorists and especially in Homans, to study elementary phenomena and to construct very general statements on the basis of the data provided by sociology and social anthropology. Hence also the fascination with psychology, specifically, that psychology which disregards social and cultural determinants (Skinner's behaviorism). "The general propositions of all the social sciences are the same, and all are psychological."[53]

Statements of behaviorist psychology serve Homans as the basis for his sociological theory, whose principal idea is that "social behavior is an exchange of goods, material goods but also non-material ones, such as the symbols of approval and prestige. Persons that give much to others try to get much from them, and persons that get much from others are under pressure to give much to them. This process of influence tends to work out at equilibrium to a balance in the exchanges."[54] Homans draws additional inspiration from economics, and he uses such concepts as costs, profits, supply, and demand.

Exchange theory has evoked considerable interest for two quite different reasons. On the one hand, it could be attractive as a promise of a really general theory that would pave the way for a genuine unity of the behavioral sciences and would provide them with a system of interconnected theorems resembling those used by more mature disciplines. On the other hand, it could prove enticing by shifting the center of interests to the process whereby social relations are formed and by considering individuals to be the founders of social order and not merely those who adjust themselves to that social order which is given. Some authors even saw in this radically naturalistic conception certain similarities to contemporary humanistic sociology.

Exchange theory met with criticism: It was blamed for a lack of originality (in fact, that theory can be deduced from rationalistic materialism and utilitarianism), for the obscurity or tautologous nature of many of its formulations, for its incapability of going beyond the study of small groups (P. Blau tried to remedy this), and for an illegitimate extension of exchange relations to all social relations and a disregard for the role of coercion, to which so much attention has been paid by conflict theorists.

FUNCTIONALISM AS SEEN BY THE SOCIOLOGY OF EVERYDAY LIFE

The third important trend in the theoretical critique of functionalism recently took the shape of a new humanistic sociology, which—in view of one of its slogans—we call here the sociology of everyday life. As a matter of fact, we call it a trend only with great reservations, because so far we have come across only a small number of vaguely formulated assumptions, their common feature being a dislike of conventional sociology and an intention to see the principal subject matter of sociology not in social facts, analyzed as something given, but in the very process of their emergence over the course of interaction among individuals.

This is a protest against the sociological conceptions that, to quote Herbert Blumer,

in treating society or groups as "social systems," regard group action as an expression of a system, either in a state of balance or seeking to achieve balance. Or group action is conceived as an expression of the "functions" of a society or of a group. Or group action is regarded as the outward expression of elements lodged in society or the group, such as cultural demands, societal purposes, social values, or institutional stresses. These typical conceptions ignore or blot out a view of group life or a group action as consisting of the collective or concerted actions of individuals seeking to meet their life situations.[55]

Protests against such conceptions (hence, principally against functionalism) are to bring about an essential reorientation of sociological thinking by turning it from analyzing social reality as something given toward analyzing the mechanisms of encounters among human beings, encounters by which that reality is continually constructed anew by conscious participants. According to these critics, functionalist sociology has sinned by "misplaced concreteness": It has taken for the real thing the system that it has constructed and not the directly given actions of individuals.

Such a critique of functionalism tends to belittle the elements of a voluntaristic theory of action that are inherent in it. In this interpretation, functionalism appears as a kind of neosociologism, which reduces the range of human options to conformity with, or deviance from, the fixed norms and/or values. Its adherents are also blamed for leaving social order beyond discussion by taking it just as a fact.

David Walsh wrote thus:

What is lacking in Parsons' model is a satisfactory account of how actors come to recognize roles and perform them accordingly. Like all functionalists, he treats norms and values as formal rules of interaction which measure fixed amounts of consensual agreement between actors upon substantive issues. But this idea of consensual agreement assumes precisely that which is to be explained. At the very most, norms and values represent only idealized and generalized rules, expectations, and definitions of the situations (that is, social meanings). What is problematic is the manner of their enactment. How do actors depict rules and invest them with meaning; in other words, how do actors recognize rules? How do actors recognize which rules apply in what situations? How do actors recognize when an action conforms to a rule? . . . None of these questions is either handled or can be handled by an approach that focuses upon the determinate character of social rules within the context of a social system and yet they are crucial to an understanding of the character of social action and social order. Rather, the systems framework treats social order as the taken-for-granted background to social action in terms of institutionalized norms and values and their internalization by actors.[56]

It remains to be seen what theoretical orientation will ultimately emerge from this criticism and these demands—especially as various inspirations and tendencies are at work. Among them we have to mention in particular symbolic interactionism in the modified version offered by H. Blumer (1900-   ) and his disciples (especially Erving Goffman) and philosophical phenomenology, adjusted to some extent to the needs of sociological theory by Alfred Schutz (1899-1959). Interpenetration and overlapping of the various ideas is characteristic of present-day humanistic sociology. This is best seen in such programmatic publications as *Understanding Everyday Life* (1970), edited by J. Douglas, and *New Directions in Sociological Theory* (1972) by P. Filmer, M. Phillipson, D. Silverman, and D. Walsh. An essential role is played also by ethnomethodology, initiated by Harold Garfinkel (1917-   ) in *Studies in Ethnomethodology* (1967). We shall not even try to list all those numerous varieties of present-day humanistic sociology that have won some popularity in the discussions on the crisis in sociology and during the intensive search for remedies for that discipline. What is remarkable is the vitality of that trend, which proves that the functionalists' claims to represent *the* sociology were certainly premature.

At first glance, it might seem that the new humanistic sociology is not an alternative to functionalism, but merely takes up special problems—primarily microsociological ones—in which functionalists have not been seriously interested. But, in fact, we find here a different image of the social world and a different conception of how the sociologist should work: He should change from a theorist of the social system into a careful watcher of everyday life, from a researcher who approaches social reality with ready-made principles of ordering and explaining it into a person who strives to discover in that social reality the order that continually emerges anew and that has its role legitimated in the consciousness of its participants.

NOTES

1. The adjective *sociological* is necessary here to distinguish this approach from functionalism in anthropology, discussed earlier in this book.

2. K. Davis, "The Myth of Functional Analysis as a Special Method in Sociology and Anthropology," *American Sociological Review* 25 (1959): 760.

3. A. Inkeles, *What Is Sociology?* (Englewood Cliffs, N.J.: Prentice-Hall, 1964), p. 37.

4. Guy Rocher, *Talcott Parsons and American Sociology* (London: Nelson, 1974), p. 155.

5. Radcliffe-Brown's statement is cited by Piotr Sztompka in *System and Function: Toward a Theory of Society* (New York: Academic Press, 1974), p. 47.

6. Sztompka, *System and Function*, pp. 53-54. Cf. Don Martindale, *The Nature and Types of Sociological Theory* (Boston: Houghton Mifflin, 1960), pp. 449-50.

7. P. Sztompka, "The Logic of Functional Analysis in Sociology and Social Anthropology," in *Quality and Quantity* 5 (December 1971): 382-83.

8. G. C. Homans, "Contemporary Theory in Sociology," in Robert E. L. Faris, ed., *Handbook of Modern Sociology* (Chicago: University of Chicago Press, 1964), p. 963.

9. Robert K. Merton, *Social Theory and Social Structure* (Glencoe, Ill.: Free Press, 1957), p. 53.

10. See ibid., p. 32.

11. See Sztompka, *System and Function*, p. 101.

12. Ibid., p. 105.

13. K. Davis and W. Moore, "Some Principles of Stratification," in Lewis A. Coser and Bernard Rosenberg, eds., *Sociological Theory: A Book of Readings* (New York: Macmillan, 1964), p. 414. Cf. George A. Huaco, "The Functionalist Theory of Stratification: Two Decades of Controversy," *Inquiry* 9 (1966): 215-40.

14. Pierre L. van den Berghe, "Dialectic and Functionalism: Toward a Theoretic Synthesis," in Walter L. Wallace, ed., *Sociological Theory* (Chicago: Aldine-Atherton, 1969), p. 202.

15. William Skidmore, *Theoretical Thinking in Sociology* (Cambridge: Cambridge University Press, 1975), p. 127.

16. Merton, *Social Theory*, p. 50.

17. Dennis H. Wrong, "The Oversocialized Conception of Man in Modern Sociology," in Coser and Rosenberg, *Sociological Theory*, pp. 112-22.

18. T. Parsons, "On Building Social System Theory: A Personal History," *Daedalus* 99 (Fall 1970): 830.

19. See Sztompka, *System and Function*, p. 28.

20. See Theodore Abel, *The Foundation of Sociological Theory* (New York: Random House, 1970), p. 165.

21. Merton, *Social Theory*, p. 6.

22. Irving M. Zeitlin, *Rethinking Sociology: A Critique of Contemporary Theory* (Englewood Cliffs, N.J.: Prentice-Hall, 1973), p. 20.

23. Don Martindale, *Prominent Sociologists Since World War II* (Columbus, Ohio: Merrill, 1975), pp. 89-90. John Finley Scott, "The Changing Foundations of the Parsonian Action Scheme," in Wallace, *Sociological Theory*, pp. 246-67.

24. T. Parsons, *Essays in Sociological Theory*, rev. ed. (New York: Free Press, 1964), p. 230.

25. T. Parsons, *The System of Modern Societies* (Englewood Cliffs, N.J.: Prentice-Hall, 1971), pp. 5-6.

26. Hermann Strasser, *The Normative Structure of Sociology* (London: RKP, 1976), pp. 132-33.

27. T. Parsons, *Societies: Evolutionary and Comparative Perspectives* (Englewood Cliffs, N.J.: Prentice-Hall, 1966), p. 109.

28. Rocher, *Talcott Parsons*, p. 72.

29. Percy S. Cohen, *Modern Social Theory* (New York: Basic Books, 1968), pp. 47-64.

30. G. C. Homans, *Social Behavior: Its Elementary Forms* (New York: Harcourt Brace and World, 1961), pp. 10-11.

31. R. Dahrendorf, "Out of Utopia: Toward a Reorientation of Sociological Analysis," in Coser and Rosenberg, *Sociological Theory*, pp. 209-27.

32. Rocher, *Talcott Parsons*, p. 33.

33. Dahrendorf, "Out of Utopia," p. 222.

34. Merton, *Social Theory*, pp. 33-36.

35. Walter L. Wallace, "Overview of Contemporary Sociological Theory," in Wallace, *Sociological Theory*, pp. 24-25.

36. R. Dahrendorf, "Toward a Theory of Social Conflict," in *The Journal of Conflict Resolution*, vol. 2 (1958); see Wallace, *Sociological Theory*, p. 216.

37. Lewis Coser, *The Functions of Social Conflict* (New York: Free Press, 1964), p. 8.

38. Dahrendorf, "Out of Utopia," p. 223.

39. Ibid., p. 225.

40. Dahrendorf, "Toward a Theory," p. 217.

41. Ibid., p. 218.

42. Ibid., p. 219.

43. Robert W. Friedrichs, *A Sociology of Sociology* (New York: Free Press, 1972), p. 48.

44. C. Wright Mills, *The Marxists* (New York: Dell, 1962), pp. 10-11.

45. C. Wright Mills, *The Sociological Imagination* (New York: Oxford University Press, 1959), p. 4.

46. Ibid., pp. 6-7.

47. Ibid., pp. 149-50.

48. John Horton, "Order and Conflict Theories of Social Problems as Competing Ideologies," in Larry T. Reynolds and Janice M. Reynolds, eds., *The Sociology of Sociology* (New York: McKay, 1970), pp. 152-71.

49. Wallace, "Overview of Contemporary Sociological Theory," p. 28.

50. G. C. Homans, *Social Behavior*, pp. 384-85.

51. G. C. Homans, "A Life of Synthesis," in J. L. Horowitz, ed., *Sociological Self-Images: A Collective Portrait* (Oxford: Pergamon Press, 1970), p. 27.

52. Homans, *Social Behavior*, p. 384.

53. Homans, "Life of Synthesis," p. 27.

54. See Calvin J. Larsen, *Major Themes in Sociological Theory* (New York: McKay, 1973), p. 158.

55. Herbert Blumer, "Society as Symbolic Interaction," in Arnold Rose, ed., *Human Behavior and Social Processes* (Boston: Houghton Mifflin, 1962), p. 186.

56. David Walsh, "Functionalism and Systems Theory," in Paul Filmer et al., *New Directions in Sociological Theory* (London: Collier-Macmillan, 1973), p. 64.

BIBLIOGRAPHY

GENERAL

Abel, Theodore. *The Foundation of Sociological Theory.* New York: Random House, 1970.

Abraham, J. H. *The Origins and Growth of Sociology.* Harmondsworth: Penguin Books, 1973.

Abrams, Philip, ed. *The Origins of British Sociology.* Chicago: University of Chicago Press, 1968.

Aron, Raymond. *Les Etapes de la pensée sociologique.* Paris: Gallimard, 1967.

———. *Main Currents in Sociological Thought.* Harmondsworth: Penguin Books, 1970.

———. *La Sociologie allemande contemporaine.* Paris: P.U.F., 1950.

Barbano, F. *Lineamenti di storia del pensiero sociologico.* Torino: Giappichelli, 1970.

Barnes, Harry Elmer, ed. *An Introduction to the History of Sociology.* Chicago: University of Chicago Press, 1948.

Beach, Walter Greenwood. *The Growth of Social Thought.* New York: Scribner's, 1939.

Becker, Ernest. *The Lost Science of Man.* New York: Braziller, 1971.

Becker, Howard, and H. E. Barnes. *Social Thought from Lore to Science.* 3 vols., 3d ed. New York: Dover, 1961.

Benton, Ted. *Philosophical Foundations of the Three Sociologies.* London: RKP, 1977.

Bernal, J. D. *Science in History.* London: Watts, 1956.

Bernsdorf, Wilhelm ed. *Internationales Soziologen Lexikon* (Stuttgart: F. Enke, 1959).

Bogardus, Emory S. *The Development of Social Thought.* New York: Longman, 1940.

Bouthoul, Gaston. *Histoire de la sociologie.* Paris: P.U.F., 1956.

Braunleuther, Kurt. *Probleme der Geschichte der burgerlichen Soziologie.* Berlin: Akademie Verlag, 1975.

Brett, George Sidney. *History of Psychology.* Edited and abridged by R. S. Peters. London: Allen and Unwin, 1952.

Brunschvicg, Léon. *Le Progrès de la conscience dans la philosophie occidentale.* 2 vols. 2d ed. Paris: P.U.F., 1953.

Bryant, Christopher G. A. *Sociology in Action: A Critique of Selected Conceptions of the Social Role of the Sociologists.* London: Allen and Unwin, 1976.

Catton, William R., Jr. "The Development of Sociological Thought." In Robert E. L. Faris, ed., *Handbook of Modern Sociology.* Chicago: Rand McNally, 1964.

Cazeneuve, Jean, and David Victoroff. *La Sociologie: Les idées, les oeuvres, les hommes.* Paris: P.U.F., 1970.

Chambliss, Rollin, ed. *Social Thought from Hammurabi to Comte.* New York: Dryden Press, 1954.

Châtelet, François, ed. *L'Histoire des idéologies.* 3 vols. Paris: Hachette, 1977.

Collins, Randall, and Michael Makowsky. *The Discovery of Society.* New York: Random House, 1972.

Coser, Lewis A. *Masters of Sociological Thought: Ideas in Historical and Social Context.* New York: Harcourt Brace Jovanovich, 1971.

Cuvillier, Armand. *Manuel de sociologie.* 2 vols. Paris: P.U.F., 1954.

Cuzzort, Raymond Paul. *Humanity and Modern Sociological Thought.* New York: Holt, Rinehart and Winston, 1969.

Easthope, Gary. *History of Social Research Methods.* London; Longman, 1974.

Eisenstadt, S. N., with M. Curelaru. *The Form of Sociology: Paradigms and Crises.* New York: Wiley, 1976.

Ellwood, Charles Abram. *The Story of Social Philosophy.* Englewood Cliffs, N.J.: Prentice-Hall, 1938.

Fay, Brian. *Social Theory and Political Practice.* London: Allen and Unwin, 1975.

Ferrarotti, F. *Il pensiero sociologico da Auguste Compte a Max Horkheimer.* Milano: Mondadori, 1974.

Fletcher, Ronald. *The Making of Sociology: A Study of Sociological Theory.* Vol. 1, *Beginnings and Foundations*; vol. 2, *Developments.* London: Nelson, 1972.

Freund, Julien, *Les Théories des sciences humaines.* Paris: P.U.F., 1973.

Furfey, Paul H. *A History of Social Thought.* New York: Macmillan, 1942.

Gella, Aleksander, Sue Curry Jansen, and Donald F. Sabo, Jr. *Humanism in Sociology: Its Historical Roots and Contemporary Problems.* Washington, D.C.: University Press of America, 1978.

Gide, Charles, and Charles Rist. *Histoire des doctrines économiques depuis les physiocrates jusqu'à nos jours.* Paris: Librairie du Recueil Sivey, 1929.

Goldmann, Lucien. *Sciences humaines et philosophie.* Paris: P.U.F., 1952.

Goudsblom, Johan. *Sociology in the Balance: A Critical Essay.* Oxford: Blackwell, 1977.

Gough, J. W. *The Social Contract: The Critical Study of Its Development.* 2d ed. Oxford: Clarendon Press, 1957.

Gouldner, Alvin W. *The Coming Crisis of Western Sociology.* New York: Equinox Books, 1971.

Gurvitch, Georges. *La Vocation actuelle de la sociologie.* 2 vols. Paris: P.U.F., 1963.

———, ed. *Traité de sociologie.* Vol. 1, sec. 1. Paris: P.U.F., 1958.

Gurvitch, Georges, and Wilbert E. Moore, eds. *Twentieth Century Sociology.* New York: Philosophical Library, 1946.

Habermas, Jürgen. *Knowledge and Human Interests.* Boston: Beacon Press, 1972.

Harris, Marvin, *The Rise of Anthropological Theory: A History of Theories of Culture.* New York: Crowell, 1968.

Hawthorn, Geoffrey. *Enlightenment and Despair: A History of Sociology.* Cambridge: Cambridge University Press, 1976.

Herpin, Nicolas. *Les Sociologues américains et le siècle.* Paris: P.U.F., 1973.

Hinkle, Roscoe C., Jr., and Gisela J. Hinkle. *The Development of Modern Sociology: Its Nature and Growth in the United States.* Garden City, N.Y.: Doubleday, 1954.

Horowitz, Irving K. *Professing Sociology: Studies in the Life Cycle of Social Sciences.* Chicago: Aldine, 1968.

House, Floyd Nelson. *The Development of Sociology.* Westport, Conn.: Greenwood Press, 1970.

Israel, Joachim. *Alienation: from Marx to Modern Sociology: A Macrosociological Analysis.* Boston: Allyn and Bacon, 1971.

Janet, Paul. *Histoire de la science politique dans ses rapports avec la morale.* 2 vols. Paris: Librairie philosophique de Ladrange, 1872.

Jarvie, J. C. *The Story of Social Anthropology.* New York: McGraw-Hill, 1971.

Jonas, Friedrich. *Geschichte der Soziologie.* 4 vols. Munich: Rewohlt, 1969.

Keat, Russell, and John Urry. *Social Theory as Science.* London: RKP, 1975.

Kinloch, Graham C. *Sociological Theory: Its Development and Major Paradigms.* New York: McGraw-Hill, 1977.

Kiss, Gabor. *Einführung in die Soziologischen Theorien.* 2 vols. 3d ed. Opladen: Westdeutscher Verlag, 1977.

Kuhn, Thomas S. *The Structure of Scientific Revolutions.* 2d ed. Chicago: University of Chicago Press, 1970.

Lengermann, Patricia H. *Definitions of Sociology: A Historical Approach.* Columbus, Ohio: Merrill, 1974.

Lerner, Daniel, ed. *The Human Meaning of the Social Sciences.* New York: Meridian Books, 1959.

Lichtenberger, J. P. *Development of Social Theory.* New York: Century, 1923.

Lowie, Robert H. *The History of Ethnological Theory* New York: Holt, Rinehart and Winston, 1937.

Madge, John. *The Origins of Scientific Sociology.* London: Tavistock, 1963.

Martindale, Don. *The Nature and Types of Sociological Theory.* Boston: Houghton Mifflin, 1960.

―――. *Sociological Theory and the Problem of Values.* Columbus, Ohio: Merrill, 1974.

Maus, Heinz. *A Short History of Sociology.* New York: Citadel Press, 1966.

Mercier, Paul. *Histoire de l'anthropologie.* Paris: P.U.F., 1971.

Merton, Robert K. "On the History and Systematics of Sociological Theory." In Merton, *On Theoretical Sociology: Five Essays, Old and New.* New York: Free Press, 1967.

Mihanovich, C. S., ed. *Social Theorists.* Milwaukee: Bruce Publishing, 1953.

Mills, C. Wright. *The Sociological Imagination.* New York: Oxford University Press, 1959.

―――, ed. *Images of Man: The Classic Tradition in Sociological Thinking.* New York: Braziller, 1960.

Mitchell, G. Duncan. *A Hundred Years of Sociology.* Chicago: Aldine, 1968.

Mongardini, Carlo. *L'epoca, della societá: Saggi di storia della sociologia.* Rome: M. Bulzoni, 1970.

Murphy, Gardner. *An Historical Introduction to Modern Psychology.* 2d ed. London: Kegan Paul, Trench, Trubner, 1930.

Naroll, Raoul, and Frada Naroll, eds. *Main Currents in Cultural Anthropology.* Englewood Cliffs, N.J.: Prentice-Hall, 1973.

Nisbet, Robert A. *Social Change and History: Aspects of the Western Theory of Development.* New York: Oxford University Press, 1969.

―――. *The Social Philosophers: Community and Conflict in Western Thought.* New York: Crowell, 1973.

―――. *The Sociological Tradition.* London: Heinemann, 1967.

―――. *Sociology as an Art Form.* London: Heinemann, 1976.

Oberschall, Anthony, ed. *Establishment of Empirical Sociology: Studies in Continuity, Discontinuity, and Institutionalization.* New York: Harper and Row, 1972.

Odum, H. W. *American Sociology: The Story of Sociology in the United States through 1950* New York: Longmans, Green, 1951.

Ossowski, Stanislaw. *O osobliwościach nauk społecznych. Dzieta,* vol. 4. Warsaw: PWN, 1967.

Parsons, Talcott. *The Structure of Social Action: A Study in Social Theory with Special Reference to a Group of Recent European Writers.* 2 vols. New York: Free Press, 1968.

Penniman, T. K. *A Hundred Years of Anthropology.* 3d ed. London: Duckworth, 1965.

Phillips, D. C. *Holistic Thought in Social Science.* London: Macmillan, 1976.

Plamenatz, John. *Man and Society: A Critical Examination of Some Important Social and Political Theories from Machiavelli to Marx.* London: Longman, 1969.

Poirrier, Jean. *Histoire de l'ethnologie.* Paris: P.U.F., 1969.

Raison, Timothy, ed. *The Founding Fathers of Social Science.* Harmondsworth: Penguin Books, 1969.

Reynolds, Larry T., and Janice M. Reynolds, eds. *The Sociology of Sociology.* New York: McKay, 1970.

Ritzer, George. *Sociology: A Multiple Paradigm Science.* Boston: Allyn and Bacon, 1975.

Rossides, Daniel. *The History and Nature of Sociological Theory.* Boston: Houghton Mifflin, 1978.

Runciman, W. G. *Sociology in Its Place and Other Essays.* Cambridge: Cambridge University Press, 1970.

Russell, Bertrand. *History of Western Philosophy and Its Connections with Political and Social Circumstances from the Earliest Times to the Present Day.* London: Allen and Unwin, 1946.

Sabine, George H. *A History of Political Theory.* 3d ed. London: George G. Harrap, 1951.

Sahay, Arun. *Sociological Analysis.* London: RKP, 1972.

Salomon, Albert. *The Tyranny of Progress: Reflections on the Origins of Sociology.* New York: Noonday Press, 1955.

Schilling, Kurt. *Histoire des idées sociales: Individu—Communauté—Société.* Paris: Payot, 1962.

Schoeck, Helmut. *Soziologie: Geschichte ihrer Probleme.* Munich: K. Alber, 1952.

Schumpeter, Joseph A. *History of Economic Analysis.* London: Allen and Unwin, 1972.

Shils, Edward. "Tradition, Ecology, and Institutionalization in the History of Sociology." *Daedalus* 99 (Fall 1970):760-825.

Sills, David L., ed. *International Encyclopedia of the Social Sciences.* 17 vols. New York: Macmillan, 1968.

Sklair, Leslie. *The Sociology of Progress.* London: RKP, 1970.

Small, Albion W. *Origins of Sociology.* Chicago: University of Chicago Press, 1924.

Sorokin, Pitirim A. *Contemporary Sociological Theories.* New York: Harper and Row, 1928.

———. *Sociological Theories of Today.* New York: Harper and Row, 1966.

Stark, Werner, *The Fundamental Forms of Social Thought.* London: RKP, 1962.

———. *Social Theory and Christian Thought: A Study of Some Points of Contact.* London: RKP, 1959.

Stern, Fritz, ed. *The Varieties of History from Voltaire to the Present.* New York: Meridian Books, 1956.

Strasser, Hermann. *The Normative Structure of Sociology: Conservative and Emancipatory Themes in Social Thought.* London: RKP, 1976.

Suchodolski, Bogdan. *Narodziny nowozytnej filozofii czlowieka.* Warsaw: PWN, 1963.

———. *Rozwój nowozytnej filozofii czlowieka.* Warsaw: PWN, 1967.

Szczepański, Jan. *Socjologia: Rozwój problematyki i metod.* 3d. ed. Warsaw: PWN, 1969.

Thompson, J. W. *A History of Historical Writing.* 2 vols. New York: Macmillan, 1958.

Timasheff, Nicholas S. *Sociological Theory: Its Nature and Growth.* 3d ed. New York: Random House, 1967.

Tiryakian, Edward A., ed. *The Phenomenon of Sociology.* New York: Appleton-Century-Crofts, 1971.

Truzzi, Marcello, ed. *Sociology: The Classic Statements.* New York: Random House, 1971.

Vaughan, C. E. *Studies in the History of Political Philosophy before and after Rousseau.* 2 vols. Manchester: Manchester University Press, 1939.

Voget, Fred W. "A History of Cultural Anthropology." In John J. Honigmann, ed. *Handbook of Social and Cultural Anthropology.* Chicago: Rand MacNally, 1973.

Wagner, Donald O. *Social Reformers: Adam Smith to John Dewey.* New York: Macmillan, 1934.

Walicki, Andrzej. *Rosyjska filozofia i myśl spoleczna od Oświecenia do marksizmu.* Warsaw: Wiedza Powszechna, 1973.

Widgery, Alban G. *Interpretations of History.* London: Allen and Unwin, 1961.

Wiener, Philip P., ed. *Dictionary of the History of Ideas: Studies of Selected Pivotal Ideas.* 5 vols. New York: Scribner's, 1973.

Wiese, Leopold von. *Soziologie: Geschichte und Hauptprobleme.* 6th ed. Berlin: Walter de Gruyter, 1960.

Wolin, Sheldon S. *Politics and Vision: Continuity and Innovation in Western Political Thought.* London: Allen and Unwin, 1961.

Zeitlin, Irwing M. *Ideology and the Development of Sociological Theory.* Englewood Cliffs, N.J.: Prentice-Hall, 1968.

Znaniecki, Florian. *Cultural Sciences: Their Origin and Development.* Urbana: University of Illinois Press, 1952.

CHAPTER 1.
FROM THE CITY-STATE TO MODERN CIVIL SOCIETY

Aristotle. *The Works.* Tr. into English under the Editorship of W. D. Ross, 12 vols. Oxford: Clarendon Press, 1910-1937.

Augustine, Saint. *The City of God,* tr. M. Dods. Edinburgh: T. & T. Clark, 1872.

Barker, Ernest. *Greek Political Theory: Plato and His Predecessors.* London: Methuen, 1957.

———. *The Political Thought of Plato and Aristotle.* New York: Russel, 1959.

Baszkiewicz, Jan. *Myśl polityczna wieków średnich.* Warsaw: Wiedza Powszechna, 1970.

Bergin, T. G., and M. H. Fisch, eds. *The New Science of Giambattista Vico.* Ithaca, N.Y.: Cornell University Press, 1968.

Bloch, Marc. *La Société féodale: La Formation des liens de dépendance: Les Classes et le gouvernement des hommes.* 2 vols. Paris: A. Michel, 1939-40.

Bodin, Jean. *Six Books of the Commonwealth,* tr. M. J. Tooley. Oxford: Blackwell, n.d.

Borkenau, Franz. *Der Übergang vom feudalen zum bürgelichen Weltbild.* Paris: F. Alcan, 1934.

Burckhardt, Jacob. *The Civilisation of the Renaissance in Italy.* 2d ed. London: Allen and Unwin, 1944.

Carlyle, A. J. Sir Robert Warrand, and Alexander James. *History of Mediaeval Political Theory in the West.* 6 vols. Edinburgh: Blackwood, 1903-36.

Châtelet, François. *La Naissance de l'histoire.* Paris: Editions de Minuit, 1962.

———. *Plato.* Paris: Gallimard, 1965.

Cochraine, Charles Norris. *Christianity and Classical Culture: A Study of Thought and Action from Augustus to Augustine.* New York: Oxford University Press, 1957.

Crombie, A. C. *Augustine to Galileo: Medieval and Early Modern Science.* 2 vols. London: Mercury Books, 1961.

Dunn, John. *The Political Thought of J. Locke.* Cambridge: Cambridge University Press, 1969.

Dunning, William A. *A History of Political Theories Ancient and Medieval.* New York: Macmillan, 1902.

Edelstein, Ludwig. *The Idea of Progress in Classical Antiquity.* Baltimore: Johns Hopkins University Press, 1967.

Farrington, Benjamin. *Greek Science: Its Meaning for Us: Thales to Aristotle.* Harmondsworth: Penguin Books, 1944.

Finley, Moses J. *The Ancient Greeks.* London: Chatto and Windus, 1963.

———, ed. *The Greek Historians: The Essence of Herodotus, Thucydides, Xenophon and Polybius.* London: Chatto and Windus, 1959.

Fromm, Erich. *Escape from Freedom*. London: RKP, 1941.

Gierke, Otto. *Natural Law and the Theory of Society, 1500 to 1800*. Boston: Beacon Press, 1957.

―――. *Political Theories of the Middle Ages*. Boston: Beacon Press, 1958.

Gilson Etienne. *The Christian Philosophy of St. Thomas Aquinas*. New York: Random House, 1956.

―――. *History of Christian Philosophy in the Middle Ages*. London: Sheed and Ward, 1955.

―――. *Introduction à l'étude de Saint-Augustin*. Paris: J. Urin, 1929.

―――. *The Spirit of Medieval Philosophy*. New York: Scribner's, 1936.

Gitler, Joseph B. *Social Thought among the Early Greeks*. Athens: University of Georgia Press, 1941.

Glotz, Gustave. *The Greek City and Its Institutions*. New York: Knopf, 1951.

Goldsmith, Maurice M. *Hobbes' Science of Politics*. New York: Columbia University Press, 1966.

Gouldner, Alvin W. *Enter Plato: Classical Greece and the Origins of Social Theory*. New York: Harper and Row, 1971.

Guriewicz, Aron. *Kategorie kultury średniowiecznej*. Warsaw: PIW, 1976.

Hearnshaw, F. J. C., ed. *The Social and Political Ideas of Some English Thinkers of the Augustian Age, A.D. 1650-1750*. London: Dawsons of Pall Mall, 1967.

―――, ed. *The Social and Political Ideas of Some Great Mediaeval Thinkers*. London: Dawsons of Pall Mall, 1967.

―――, ed. *The Social and Political Ideas of Some Great Thinkers of the Sixteenth and Seventeenth Centuries*. London: Dawsons of Pall Mall, 1967.

Hearnshaw, F. J. C., and Ernest Barker, eds. *The Social and Political Ideas of Some Great Thinkers of the Renaissance and the Reformation*. London: Dawsons of Pall Mall, 1967.

Hertzler, J. O. *The Social Thought of the Ancient Civilizations*. New York: McGraw-Hill, 1936.

Hobbes, Thomas. *Leviathan*. In *Great Books of the Western World*, vol. 23. Chicago: Encyclopaedia Britannica, 1952.

Hodgen, Margaret T. *Early Anthropology in the Sixteenth and Seventeenth Centuries*. Philadelphia: University of Pennsylvania Press, 1964.

Horkheimer, Max. *Anfänge der bürgelichen Geschichtsphilosophie*. Frankfurt: Fischer, 1971.

Huizinga, Johan. *The Waning of the Middle Ages*. Garden City, N.Y.: Doubleday, 1956.

Jaeger, Werner. *Paideia: The Ideals of Greek Culture*. 3 vols. Oxford: Blackwell, 1939-45.

Jarrett, Bede. *Social Theories of the Middle Ages, 1200-1500*. London: E. Benn, 1969.

Kitch, M. J., ed. *Capitalism and the Reformation*. London: Longman, 1967.

Kolakowski, Leszek. *Jednostka i nieskończoność: Wolność i antynomie wolności w filozofii Spinozy*. Warsaw: PWN, 1958.

Krieger, Leonard. *The Politics of Discretion: Puffendorf and the Acceptance of Natural Law*. Chicago: University of Chicago Press, 1966.

Kuksewicz, Zdzisław. *Filozofia średniowieczna jako ideologia*. Warsaw: WP, 1973.

Lacoste, Yves. *Ibn Khaldun: Naissance de l'histoire passé du tiers monde*. Paris: Maspero, 1962.

LeGoff, Jacques. *La Civilisation de l'Occident médiéval*. Paris: Arthaud, 1965.

Lifsic, M. A., ed. *Istorija filosofii i voprosy kultury*. Moscow: "Nauka," 1975.

Locke, John. *On Politics, Religion and Education*. Edited by Maurice Cranston. New York: Collier Books, 1965.

―――. *An Essay Concerning Human Understanding*, 2 vols. Oxford: Clarendon Press, 1894.

―――. *Two Tracts on Government*. Cambridge: Cambridge University Press, 1967.

Losev, A. F. *Antichnaja filosofija istorii*. Moscow: "Nauka," 1977.

Machiavelli, N. *Chief Works and Others*. 3 vols. Durham, N.C.: Duke University Press, 1965.

―――. *The Prince*. Tr. W. K. Marriott. London: J. M. Dent, New York. E. P. Dutton.

Macpherson, Crawford Brough. *The Political Theory of Possessive Individualism: Hobbes to Locke.* London: Oxford University Press, 1962.

Martin, Alfred. *Sociology of the Renaissance.* New York: Oxford University Press, 1944.

Meinecke, Fredrich. *Machiavellism, the Doctrine of Raison d'Etat and Its Place in Modern History.* New York, Praeger 1962.

Mesnard, Pierre. *L'Essor de la philosophie politique au XVIIᵉ siècle.* Paris, J. Vrin, 1951.

Ogonowski, Zbigniew. *Locke.* Warsaw: Ksiazka i Wiedza, 1972.

Plato. *The Dialogues.* In *Great Books of the Western World*, vol. 7. Chicago: Encyclopaedia Britannica, 1952.

————. *The Republic.* Trans. A. D. Lindsay. London: J. M. Dent/New York: E. P. Dutton, 1937.

Popper, Karl R. *The Open Society and Its Enemies.* Vol. 1, *The Spell of Plato.* Princeton: Princeton University Press, 1971.

Rybicki, Pawel. *Arystoteles: Początki i podstawy nauki o społeczeństwie.* Wroclaw: Ossolineum, 1963.

Stark, Werner. *Social Theory and Christian Thought: A Study of Some Points of Contact.* London: RKP, 1959.

Strauss, Leo. *Thoughts on Machiavelli.* Glencoe, Ill.: Free Press, 1958.

Tagliacozzo, G., ed. *Giambattista Vico: An International Symposium.* Baltimore: Johns Hopkins University Press, 1969.

Tawney, R. H. *Religion and the Rise of Capitalism.* London: Murray, 1927.

Thomson, George D. *The First Philosophers.* London: Lawrence and Wishart, 1955.

Tönnies, Ferdinand. *On Social Ideas and Ideologies.* New York: Harper and Row, 1974.

Troeltsch, Ernst. *The Social Teaching of the Christian Churches.* New York: Harper Torchbooks, 1960.

Vernant, Jean Pierre. *Les Origines de la pensée grecque.* Paris, P.U.F., 1962.

Voisé, Waldemar. *La Réflexion présociologique d'Erasme à Montesquieu.* Wroclaw: Ossolineum, 1977.

Watkins, J. W. N. *Hobbes' System of Ideas: A Study in the Political Significance of Philosophical Theories.* New York: Hutchison, 1968.

Weber, Max. *The Protestant Ethic and the Spirit of Capitalism.* London: Unwin University Books, 1930.

Windolph, Fr. L. *Leviathan and Natural Law.* Princeton: Princeton University Press, 1973.

CHAPTER 2.
THE ADVENT OF MODERN SOCIETY:
SOCIAL PHILOSOPHY IN THE ENLIGHTENMENT

Althusser, Louis. *Politics and History: Montesquieu, Rousseau, Hegel and Marx.* London: NLB, 1972.

Baczko, Bronislaw. *Rousseau: Samotność i wspólnota.* Warsaw: PWN, 1964.

Barker, Ernest, ed. *Social Contract: Essays by Locke, Hume, and Rousseau.* London: Oxford University Press, 1971.

Barnard, F. M. *Herder's Social and Political Thought from Enlightenment to Nationalism.* Oxford: Clarendon Press, 1965.

————, ed. *Herder on Social and Political Culture.* Cambridge: Cambridge University Press, 1969.

Baumgarten, Arthur. *Grundposizionen der Französischen Aufklärung.* Berlin: Rütten und Loening, 1955.

Becker, Carl. *The Heavenly City of the 18th Century Philosophers.* New Haven: Yale University Press, 1932.

Berlin, Isaiah. *Vico and Herder: Two Studies in the History of Ideas.* London: The Hogarth Press, 1976.

Blumfitt, John H. *Voltaire: Historian.* London: Oxford University Press, 1958.

Bongie, Lawrence, L. *David Hume: Prophet of the Counter-Revolution.* Oxford: Clarendon Press, 1965.

Bredvold, Louis, J. *The Brave New World of the Enlightenment.* Ann Arbor: University of Michigan Press, 1961.

Bryson, Gladys. *Man and Society: The Scottish Inquiry of Eighteenth Century.* New York: Kelley, 1968.

Carcassonne, Ely. *Montesquieu et le problème de la constitution française au XVIIIeme siècle.* Paris: P.U.F., 1927.

Cassirer, Ernst. *The Philosophy of the Enlightenment.* Princeton: Princeton University Press, 1951.

Chitnis, Anand. *The Scottish Enlightenment.* London: Croom Helm, 1977.

Clark, Robert T., Jr. *Herder: His Life and Thought.* Berkeley and Los Angeles: University of California Press, 1955.

Cobban, Alfred. *In Search of Humanity: The Role of the Enlightenment in Modern History.* London: Cape, 1960.

―――. *Rousseau and the Modern State.* London: Allen and Unwin, 1934.

Colletti, Lucio. *From Rousseau to Lenin: Studies in Ideology and Society.* London: NLB, 1976.

Cotta, Sergio. *Montesquieu et la scienza della societa.* Turin: Ed. Ramella, 1953.

Cragg, Gerald R. *Reason and Authority in the Eighteenth Century.* Cambridge: Cambridge University Press, 1964.

Cumming, Jan. *Helvetius: His Life and Place in the History of Education.* London: RKP, 1955.

Dagon, Jean. *L'Histoire de l'esprit humain dans la pensée française de Fontenelle á Condorcet.* Paris: Librairie Klincksieck, 1977.

Delvaille, Jules. *Essai sur l'histoire de l'idée de progrès jusqu'á la fin du 18e siècle.* Paris: F. Alcan, 1910.

Derathé, Robert. *Jean Jacques Rousseau et la science politique de son temps.* Paris: P.U.F., 1950.

Duchet,‚ Michèle. *Anthropologie et histcire au siècle des lumières: Buffon, Voltaire, Rousseau, Helvétius, Diderot.* Paris: Maspero, 1971.

Durkheim, Emile. *Montesquieu et Rousseau: Précurseurs de la sociologie.* Paris: Rivière, 1953.

Ergang, Robert. *Herder and the Formation of German Nationalism.* Columbia University Studies in History, Economics and Public Law, no. 341. New York: Columbia University, 1931.

Fairchild, H. N. *The Noble Savage: A Study in Romantic Naturalism.* New York: Columbia University Press, 1928.

Ferguson, Adam. *An Essay on the History of Civil Society.* Edinburgh: Edinburgh University Press, 1966.

Foley, Vernard. *The Social Physics of Adam Smith.* West Lafayette, Ind.: Purdue University Press, 1976.

Forbes, Duncan. *Hume's Philosophical Politics.* Cambridge: Cambridge University Press, 1975.

Frankel, Charles. *The Faith of Reason: The Idea of Progress in the French Enlightenment.* New York: King's Crown Press, 1948.

Galston, William A. *Kant and the Problem of History.* Chicago: University of Chicago Press, 1975.

Gay, Peter. *The Enlightenment: An Interpretation.* 2 vols. London: Weidenfeld and Nicolson, 1967-70.

Goldmann, Lucien. *La Communauté humaine et l'univers chez Kant.* Paris: P.U.F., 1948.

Granger, Gilles Gaston. *La Mathematique sociale du marquis de Condorcet.* Paris: P.U.F., 1956.

Groethuysen, Bernard, *Les Origines de l'esprit bourgeois en France.* Paris: Gallimard, 1927.

———. *Philosophie de la Révolution française précédé de Montesquieu.* Paris: Gallimard, 1956.

Gusdorf, Georges. *Les Sciences humaines et la pensée occidentale.* 2 vols. Paris: Payot, 1966.

Halévy, Elie. *The Growth of Philosophic Radicalism.* London: Faber and Faber, 1972.

Hazard, Paul. *The European Mind, 1680-1715.* London: Hollis and Carter, 1953.

———. *European Thought in the 18th Century from Montesquieu to Lessing.* London: Hollis and Carter, 1954.

Hubert, Réné. *Les Sciences sociales dans l'Encyclopédie.* Paris: F. Alcan, 1923.

Hume, David. *Essays Moral, Political and Literary.* London: Oxford University Press, 1963.

———. *A Treatise of Human Nature.* 2 vols. London: Longmans, Green, 1898.

Jogland, Herta. *Ursprünge und Grundlagen der Soziologie bei Adam Ferguson.* Berlin: Duncker und Humblot, 1959.

Kettler David. *The Social and Political Thought of Adam Ferguson.* Columbus, Ohio: Ohio State University Press, 1965.

Lechartier, Georges. *David Hume, moraliste et sociologue.* Paris: F. Alcan, 1900.

Lehmann, William, C. *Adam Ferguson and the Beginnings of Modern Sociology.* Columbia University Studies in History, Economics and Public Law, no. 328. New York: Columbia University, 1930.

———. *John Millar of Glasgow (1735-1801): His Life and Thought and His Contributions to Sociological Analysis.* Glasgow University, Sociological and Economical Studies, no. 4. Cambridge: Cambridge University Press, 1960.

Leroy, Maxime. *Histoire des idées sociales en France: De Montesquieu à Robespierre.* Paris: Gallimard, 1947.

Lichtenberger, André. *Le Socialisme au XVIIIème siècle.* Paris: F. Alcan, 1895.

Lovejoy, Arthur O., et al. *Documentary History of Primitivism.* Baltimore: Johns Hopkins University Press, 1935.

Manuel, Frank E. *The Eighteenth Century Confronts the Gods.* Cambridge, Mass.: Harvard University Press, 1959.

———. *The Prophets of Paris.* Cambridge, Mass.: Harvard University Press, 1962.

Martin, Basil Kingsley. *French Liberal Thought in the 18th Century: A Study of Political Ideas from Bayle to Condorcet.* London: Turnstile Press, 1954.

Meek, Ronald L. *Social Science and the Ignoble Savage.* Cambridge: Cambridge University Press, 1976.

———, ed. *Turgot on Progress, Sociology and Economics.* Cambridge: Cambridge University Press: 1973.

Meinecke, Friedrich. *Historism: The Rise of a New Historical Outlook.* London: RKP, 1972.

Montesquieu. *The Spirit of Laws.* In *Great Books of the Western World*, vol. 38. Chicago: Encyclopaedia Britannica, 1952.

Mornet, Daniel. *Les Origines intellectuelles de la Révolution française, 1715-1787.* Paris: A. Colin, 1953.

Ossowska, Maria. *Myśl moralna Oświecenia angielskiego.* Warsaw: PWN, 1966.

Plekhanov, G. V. *Essays in the History of Materialism.* London: J. Lane, 1934.

Pollard, Sidney. *The Idea of Progress: History and Society.* Harmondsworth: Penguin Books, 1968.

Proust, Jacques. *Encyclopédie.* Paris: A. Colin, 1965.

Reiss, Hans, ed. *Kant's Political Writings.* Cambridge: Cambridge University Press, 1970.

Rihs, Charles. *Voltaire: Recherches sur les origines du materialisme historique.* Geneva: Droz, 1962.

Rousseau, J. J. *On the Origin of Inequality, On Political Economy—The Social Contract.* In

Great Books of Western World, vol. 38. Chicago: Encyclopaedia Britannica, 1952.

Sampson, R. V. *Progress in the Age of Reason*. London: Heinemann, 1965.

Schneider, Louis, ed. *The Scottish Moralists on Human Nature and Society*. Chicago: University of Chicago Press, 1967.

Skinner, Andrew S., and Thomas Wilson, eds. *Essays on Adam Smith*. London: Oxford University Press, 1976.

Slotkin, James Sydney, ed. *Readings in Early Anthropology*. Viking Fund Publications in Anthropology, no. 40. New York: Wennergreen Foundation for Anthropological Research, 1965.

Small, Albion. *Adam Smith and Modern Sociology*. Chicago: University of Chicago Press, 1907.

Smith, Adam. *Theory of Moral Sentiments*. London: Oxford University Press, 1976.

Stephen, Leslie. *History of English Thought in the Eighteenth Century*. 2 vols. London: Murray, 1927.

Stewart, John B. *The Moral and Political Philosophy of David Hume*. New York: Columbia University Press, 1963.

Szacka, Barbara. *Teoria i utopia Stanislawa Staszica*. Warsaw: PWN, 1965.

Talmon, J. L. *The Origins of Totalitarian Democracy*. London: Secker and Warburg, 1952.

Van de Pitte, Frederick. *Kant as Philosophical Anthropologist*. The Hague: M. Nijhoff, 1971.

Venturi, Franco. *Utopia and Reform in the Enlightenment*. Cambridge: Cambridge University Press, 1971.

Volgin, W. P. *Razvitije obscestvennoj mysli vo Francii v XVIII veke*. Moscow: Izd. Akademii Nauk SSSR, 1958.

———, ed. *Voltaire*. Moscow-Leningrad: Izd. Akademii Nauk SSSR, 1948.

Voltaire. *Essai sur les moeurs et l'esprit des nations*. Paris: Editions Sociales, 1962.

Vyverberg, Henry. *Historical Pessimism in the French Enlightenment*. Cambridge, Mass.: Harvard University Press, 1958.

Waddicor, Mark H. *Montesquieu and the Philosophy of Natural Law*. The Hague: M. Nijhoff, 1970.

Wade, Ira O. *The Intellectual Development of Voltaire*. Princeton: Princeton University Press, 1969.

———. *The Intellectual Origins of the French Enlightenment*. Princeton: Princeton University Press, 1971.

Wasserman, Earl R. *Aspects of the Eighteenth Century*. Baltimore: Johns Hopkins University Press, 1965.

Wells, G. A. *Herder and After: A Study in the Development of Sociology*. The Hague: Mouton, 1959.

Zirmunski, W. M. *Jagann Gotfrid Gerder*. Moscow-Leningrad, 1959.

CHAPTER 3.
POSTREVOLUTIONARY SOCIOPOLITICAL THOUGHT AS A SOURCE OF SOCIAL THEORY

Ansart, Pierre. *Marx et anarchisme: Essai sur les sociologies de Saint-Simon, Proudhon et Marx*. Paris: P.U.F., 1969.

———. *Saint-Simon*. Paris: P.U.F., 1969.

———. *Sociologie de Proudhon*. Paris; P.U.F., 1969.

Assorodobraj, Nina. "Elementy świadomości klasowej mieszczaństwa," *Przeglad Socjologiczny* 10:139-190 (1949).

Bagge, Dominique. *Les Idées politiques en France sous la Restauration*. Paris: P.U.F., 1952.

Barth, Hans. *The Idea of Order*. Dordrecht: Reidel, 1960.

Baxa, Jakob, ed. *Gesellschaft und Staat im Spiegel deutscher Romantik*. Jena: Fischer, 1924.

Bayle, Francis. *Les Idées politiques de Joseph de Maistre*. Paris: Donat-Montchrétien, 1945.

Beik, Paul H. *French Revolution Seen from the Right*. American Philosophical Society Transactions, new series, vol. 46, pt. 1. Philadelphia: American Philosophical Society, 1956.

Boas, George. *French Philosophers of the Romantic Period*. Baltimore: Johns Hopkins University Press, 1925.

Bouglé, Celestin. *La Sociologie de Proudhon*. Paris: A. Colin, 1911.

Bravo, Gian Mario, ed. *Les socialistes avant Marx*, 3 vol. Paris: Maspero, 1970.

———. *Storia de socialismo, 1789-1848: Il Pensiero socialista prima di Marx*. Rome: Ed. Riuniti, 1971.

Bredvold, Louis I., and Ralph G. Ross, eds. *The Philosophy of Edmund Burke*. Ann Arbor: University of Michigan Press, 1960.

Cobban, Alred. *Burke and the Revolt against the Eighteenth Century: A Study of the Political and Social Thinking of Burke, Wordsworth, Coleridge and Southey*. London: Allen and Unwin, 1934.

Coker, F. W. *Organismic Theories of the State: 19th Century Interpretations of the State as Organism or as a Person*. New York: Columbia University Press: 1910.

Cole, G. D. H. *A History of Socialist Thought*. Volume 1, *The Forerunners, 1789-1850*. London: Macmillan, 1955.

Cuvillier, Armand. *P. J. B. Buchez et les origines du socialisme chrétien*. Paris: P.U.F., 1948.

———. *Proudhon*. Paris: Edition Sociales Internationales, 1937.

Desroche, Henri. *Socialisme et sociologie religieuse*. Paris: Cujas, 1965.

Droz, Jacques, ed. *Le Romantisme politique en Allemagne: Textes choisis*. Paris: A. Colin, 1963.

Duprat, Jeanne. *Proudhon sociologue et moraliste*. Paris: F. Alcan, 1929.

Durkheim, Emile. *Le Socialisme: Sa définition, ses débuts: La Doctrine saint-simonienne*. Paris: F. Alcan, 1928.

Duroselle, Jean-Baptiste. *Les Débuts du catholicisme sociale en France*. Paris: P.U.F., 1951.

Engels, Friedrich. *Socialism Utopian and Scientific*. New York: International Publishers, 1945.

Epstein, Klaus. *The Genesis of German Conservatism*. Princeton: Princeton University Press, 1966.

Evans, D. O. *Social Romanticism in France*. Oxford: Clarendon Press, 1951.

Fehlbaum Rolf Peter. *Saint-Simon und die Saint Simonisten: Vom Laissez-Faire zur Wirtschaftsplannung*. Basel: Kyklos-Verlag, 1970.

Fennessey, R. R. *Burke, Paine and the Rights of Man: A Difference of Political Opinion*. The Hague: M. Nijhoff, 1963.

Garewicz, Jan. *Miedzy marzeniem a wiedza. Poczatki myśli socjalistycznej w Niemczech*. Warsaw: Ksiazka i Wiedza, 1975.

Gerstenberger, Heide. *Der revolutionäre Konservatismus: Ein Beitrag zur Analysis des Liberalismus*. Berlin: Duncker und Humblot, 1969.

Gouhier, Henri. *La Jeunesse d'Auguste Comte et la formation du positivisme*. 3 vols. Paris: J. Vrin, 1933-41.

Gurvitch, Georges. *Proudhon: Sa vie, son oeuvre avec un exposé de sa philosophie*. Paris: P.U.F., 1965.

Halévy, Elis. *Histoire de socialisme européen*. Paris: Gallimard, 1948.

Harvey, R. H. *Robert Owen: Social Idealist*. University of California Publications in History, vol. 38. Berkeley and Los Angeles: University of California, 1949.

Hearnshaw, F. J. C., ed. *The Social and Political Ideas of Some Representative Thinkers of the Age of Reaction and Reconstruction, 1815-1865*. London: Dawsons of Pall Mall, 1967.

Iggers, G. G. *The Cult of Authority, the Political Philosophy of the Saint-Simonians: A Chapter in the Intellectual History of Totalitarianism*. The Hague: M. Nijhoff, 1958.

Isambert, François-André. *Politique, religion et science de l'homme chez Ph. Buchez, 1796-1865*. Paris: Cujas, 1965.

Jackson, J. H. *Marx, Proudhon and European Socialism*. London: English University Press, 1957.

Jaurès, Jean. *Les Origines du socialisme allemand*. Paris: Maspero, 1960.

Kirk, Russell. *The Conservative Mind from Burke to Santayana*. London: Faber and Faber, 1954.

Kucerenko, G. S. *Sen-simonizm v obscestvennoj mysli XIX veka*. Moscow: "Nauka," 1975.

Landauer, Carl. *European Socialism: A History of Ideas and Movements*. Berkeley and Los Angeles: University of California Press, 1959.

Lansac, Maurice. *Les Conceptions méthodologiques et sociales de Charles Fourier*. Paris: J. Vrin, 1926.

Laski, Harold J. *Authority in the Modern State*. New Haven: Yale University Press, 1919.

―――. *The Rise of European Liberalism*. London: Allen and Unwin, 1936.

Leroy, Maxime. *Histoire des idées sociales en France*. Vol. 2, *De Babeuf à Proudhon*. Paris: Gallimard, 1950.

―――. *Histoire des idées sociales en France*. Vol. 3, *D'Auguste Comte à P. J. Proudhon*. Paris: Gallimard, 1954.

Lichtenberger, André. *Le Socialisme utopique*. Paris, 1898.

Lichtheim, George. *The Origins of Socialism*. New York: Praeger, 1969.

Mannheim, Karl. "Conservative Thought," In Mannheim, *Essays on Sociology and Social Psychology*. London: RKP, 1953.

Manuel, Frank E. *The New World of Henri de Saint-Simon*. Cambridge, Mass.: Harvard University Press, 1956.

―――. *The Prophets of Paris*. Cambridge, Mass.: Harvard University Press, 1962.

Markham, Felix M. H., ed. *Henri Comte de Saint-Simon: Social Organization, the Science of Man and Other Writings*. New York: Harper and Row, 1964.

Minoque, Kenneth. *The Liberal Mind*. London: Methuen, 1964.

Mougin, Henri. *Pierre Leroux*. Paris: Editions Sociales Internationales, 1938.

Nisbet, Robert A. *The Quest for Community*. London: Oxford University Press, 1953.

―――. *Tradition and Revolt: Historical and Sociological Essays*. New York: Random House, 1968.

Oechslin, J. J. *Le Mouvement ultra-royaliste sous la Restauration: Son Idéologie et son action politique, 1814-1830*. Paris: Pichon et Durand-Aurias, 1960.

O'Gorman, Frank. *Edmund Burke: His Political Philosophy*. London: Allen and Unwin, 1973.

Osborn, A. *Rousseau and Burke*. New York: Oxford University Press, 1940.

Pareto, Vilfredo. *Les Systèmes socialistes*. 2 vols. Paris, Droz, 1926.

Parkin, Charles. *The Moral Basis of Burke's Political Thought*. Cambridge: Cambridge University Press, 1956.

Petitfils, Jean-Christian. *Les Socialismes utopiques*. Paris: P.U.F., 1977.

Ramm, Thilo. *Die grossen Sozialisten als Rechts und Sozialphilosophen*. 2 vols. Stuttgart: Fischer, 1955.

Riasanovsky, Nicholas V. *The Teaching of Charles Fourier*. Berkeley and Los Angeles: University of California Press, 1969.

Saint-Simon, Henri de. *Oeuvres complètes, 1760-1825.*. 6 vols. Paris: Anthropos, 1966.

Sombart, Werner. *Sozialismus und soziale Bewegung*. Bern: Steiger, 1897.

Spaemann, R. *Der Ursprung der Soziologie aus dem Geist der Restauration*. Munich: Kosel, 1959.

Stanlis, Peter J. *Edmund Burke and the Natural Law*. Ann Arbor: University of Michigan Press, 1958.

Szacki, Jerzy. *Kontrrewolucyjne paradoksy: Wizje świata francuskich antagonistów Wielkiej Rewolucji, 1789-1815.* Warsaw: PWN, 1965.

Tönnies, Ferdinand. *Die Entwicklung der sozialen Frage.* Berlin: Goeschen, 1907.

Volgin, V. P. *Francuzskij utopiceskij kommunizm.* Moscow: Izdatelstvo Akademii Nauk SSSR, 1960.

Walicki, Andrzej. *The Slavophile Controversy: History of a Conservative Utopia in Nineteenth Century Russian Thought.* London: Oxford University Press, 1975.

Watkins, Frederick. *The Political Tradition of the West: A Study in the Development of Modern Liberalism.* Cambridge, Mass.: Harvard University Press, 1948.

Wilkins, B. T. *The Problem of Burke's Political Philosophy.* Oxford: Clarendon Press, 1967.

CHAPTER 4.
HISTORIOGRAPHY AS THE STUDY OF
THE "SOCIAL CONDITION"

Birnbaum, Pierre. *Sociologie de Tocqueville.* Paris: P.U.F., 1970.

Fabian, Bernhard. *Alexis de Tocqueville Amerikabild.* Heidelberg: Carl Winter, 1957.

Febvre, Lucien. *Pour une histoire à part entière.* Paris: S.E.V.P.E.N., 1962.

Guizot, François. *Histoire de la civilisation en France depuis la chûte de l'empire romain.* 2d ed. 4 vols. Paris: Didier, 1840.

———. *Histoire générale de la civilisation en Europe depuis la chûte de l'empire romain jusqu' à la Révolution française.* 3d ed. Paris: Didier, 1840.

Herr, Richard. *Tocqueville and the Old Regime.* Princeton: Princeton University Press, 1962.

Lelewel, Joachim. *Dziela* vol. 2, *Pisma metodologiczne* in two volumes ed. by Nina Assorodobraj. Warsaw: PWN, 1964.

Lively, Jack. *The Social and Political Thought of Alexis de Tocqueville.* Oxford: Clarendon Press, 1962.

Mayer, J. P. *Alexis de Tocqueville.* Paris: Gallimard, 1948.

Mellon, Stanley. *The Political Uses of History: A Study of Historians in the French Restoration.* Stanford: Stanford University Press, 1958.

Nantet, Jacques. *Tocqueville.* Paris: Seghers, 1971.

Plekhanov, G. *The Development of the Monist View of History.* Moscow: Foreign Languages Publishing House, 1956.

Poggi, Gianfranco. *Images of Society: Essays on the Sociological Theories of Tocqueville, Marx and Durkheim.* Stanford: Stanford University Press, 1972.

Pouthas, Charles H. *Guizot pendant la Restauration: Préparation de l'homme d'état, 1814-1830.* Paris: Plon, 1923.

———. *La Jeunesse de Guizot, 1787-1814.* Paris: F. Alcan, 1936.

Reizov, B. G. *Francuzskaja romanticeskaja istoriografia.* Leningrad: Izdatelstvo Leningradskovo Universiteta, 1956.

Small, Albion W. *Origins of Sociology.* Chicago: University of Chicago Press, 1924.

Stern, Fritz, ed. *The Varieties of History from Voltaire to Present.* New York: Meridian Books, 1956.

Tocqueville, Alexis de. *Democracy in America.* 2 vols. New York: Schocken Books, 1961.

———. *Oeuvres complètes.* Vol. 1, *De la démocratie en Amérique.* Paris: Gallimard, 1961.

———. *Oeuvres complètes.* Vol. 2, *L'Ancien Régime et la révolution.* Paris: Gallimard, 1953.

Weintraub, Karl J. *Visions of Culture.* Chicago: University of Chicago Press, 1966.

Zetterbaum, Marvin. *Tocqueville and the Problem of Democracy.* Stanford: Stanford University Press, 1970.

CHAPTER 5.
PHILOSOPHY AS A SOCIAL THEORY: HEGEL

Avineri, Shlomo. *Hegel's Theory of the Modern State.* Cambridge: Cambridge University Press, 1972.
Barion, Jakob. *Hegel und die marxistische Staatslehre.* Bonn: Bouvier, 1970.
Colleti, Lucio. *Marxism and Hegel.* London: NLB, 1977.
Fleischmann, Eugène. *La Philosophie politique de Hegel: Sous la forme d'un commentaire des "Fondements de la philosophie du droit."* Paris: Plon, 1964.
Gulian, C. J. *Hegel ou la philosophie de la crise.* Paris: Payot, 1970.
Hegel, G. W. F. *Hegel's Political Writings.* Translated by T. M. Knox with an Introductory Essay by Z. A. Pelczyński. Oxford: Oxford University Press, 1964.
———. *The Philosophy of Right; The Philosophy of History.* In *Great Books of the Western World,* vol. 46. Chicago: Encyclopaedia Britannica, 1952.
Hondt, Jacques d'. *Hegel: Philosophie de l'histoire vivante.* Paris: P.U.F., 1966.
Kainz, Howard P. *Hegel's "Philosophy of Right" with Marx's Commentary: A Handbook for Students.* The Hague: M. Nijhoff, 1974.
Kelly, George Armstrong. *Idealism, Politics and History: Sources of Hegelian Thought.* Cambridge: Cambridge University Press, 1969.
Kroński, Tadeusz. *Rozwazania wokól Hegla.* Warsaw: PWN, 1960.
Löwith, Karl. *From Hegel to Nietzsche: The Revolution in Nineteenth-Century Thought.* Garden City, N.Y.: Doubleday, 1967.
Marcuse, Herbert. *Reason and Revolution: Hegel and the Rise of Social Theory.* 2d ed. New York: Humanities Press, 1954.
Negt, Oskar. *Strukturbeziehungen zwischen den Gesellschaftslehren Comtes und Hegels.* Frankfurt: Europäische Verlag, 1964.
O'Brien, George D., ed. *Hegel on Reason and History.* Chicago: University of Chicago Press, 1975.
Ottmann, Henning. *Individuum und Gemeinschaft bei Hegel.* Berlin: Walter de Gruyter, 1977.
Pelczyński, Z. A., ed. *Hegel's Political Philosophy: Problems and Perspectives: A Collection of New Essays.* Cambridge: Cambridge University Press, 1971.
Popper, Karl R. *The Open Society and Its Enemies.* Vol. 2. Princeton: Princeton University Press, 1971.
Riedel, Manfred. *Bürgerliche Gesellschaft und Staat: Grundproblem und Struktur der Hegelschen Rechtsphilosophie.* Neuwied: Luchterhand, 1970.
Shklar, Judith N. *Freedom and Independence: A Study of the Political Ideas of Hegel's "Phenomenology of Mind."* Cambridge: Cambridge University Press, 1976.
Taylor, Charles. *Hegel.* Cambridge: Cambridge University Press, 1975.
Vogel, Paul. *Hegels Gesellschaftsbegriff und seine geschichtliche Fortbildung durch Lorenz Stein, Marx, Engels und Lassalle.* Berlin: R. Heise, 1925.
Wilkins, B. T. *Hegel's Philosophy of History.* Ithaca, N.Y.: Cornell University Press, 1974.

CHAPTER 6.
HISTORICAL MATERIALISM: MARX AND ENGELS

Adler, Max. *Soziologie der Marxismus.* 3 vols. Vienna: Europa-Verlag, 1964.
———. *Der soziologische Sinn der Lehre von Karl Marx.* Leipzig: Hirzhfeld, 1914.
Althusser, Louis. *Pour Marx.* Paris: Maspero, 1967.
Althusser, Louis, and Etienne Balibar. *Reading Capital.* London: NLB, 1970.
Althusser, Louis, et al. *Lire le Capital.* 2 vols. Paris: Maspero, 1967.
Amsterdamski, Stefan. *Engels.* Warsaw: WP, 1964.

Asmus, V. F. "Marks i burzaznyj istorizm." In Asmus: *Izbrannyje filosofskije trudy*, vol. 2. Moscow: Moskovskij Universitet, 1971.

Avineri, Shlomo. *The Social and Political Thought of Karl Marx.* Cambridge: Cambridge University Press, 1968.

Berlin, Isaiah. *Karl Marx: His Life and Environment.* New York: Oxford University Press, 1948.

Bloch, Ernst. *On Karl Marx.* New York: Herder and Herder, 1971.

Bottomore, Tom. *Marxist Sociology.* London: Macmillan, 1975.

Cole, G. D. H. *A History of Socialist Thought.* Vol. 2, *Marxism and Anarchism, 1850-1890.* London: Macmillan, 1964.

Cornu, Auguste. *Karl Marx und Friedrich Engels: Leben und Werk.* 2 Vols. Berlin: Aufbau-Verlag, 1954.

———. *The Origins of Marxian Thought.* Springfield, Ill.: Charles C Thomas, 1957.

Croce, Benedetto. *Historical Materialism and the Economics of Karl Marx.* London: Cass, 1966.

Duncan, Graeme. *Marx and Mill: Two Views of Social Conflict and Social Harmony.* Cambridge: Cambridge University Press, 1973.

Fleischer, Helmut. *Marxism and History.* London: Allen Lane, 1973.

Fromm, Erich. *Marx's Concept of Man.* New York: Frederick Ungar, 1963.

Giddens, Anthony. *Capitalism and Modern Social Theory: An Analysis of the Writings of Marx, Durkheim and Max Weber.* Cambridge: Cambridge University Press, 1971.

Goldmann, Lucien. *The Human Sciences and Philosophy.* London: Cape, 1969.

———. *Recherches dialectiques.* Paris: Gallimard, 1959.

Gurvitch, Georges. *Etudes sur les classes sociales: L'Idée de classe sociale de Marx à nos jours.* Paris: Gonthier, 1971.

Habermas, Jürgen. *Theory and Practice.* Boston: Beacon Press, 1973.

Henderson, W. O. *The Life of Friedrich Engels.* 2 vols. London: Cass, 1976.

Hochfeld, Julian. *Studia o marksowskiej teorii spoleczenstwa.* Warsaw: PWN, 1963.

Hook, Sidney. *From Hegel to Marx: Studies in the Intellectual Development of Karl Marx.* Ann Arbor: University of Michigan Press, 1952.

Jordan, Z. A., ed. *Karl Marx: Economy, Class and Social Revolution.* London: Michael Joseph, 1971.

Kolakowski, Leszek. *Glówne nurty marksizmu: Powstanie—rozwój—rozklad.* Vol. 1. Paris: Instytut Literacki, 1976.

Korsch, Karl. *Karl Marx.* London: Chapman and Hall, 1938.

Kozyr-Kowalski, Stanislaw. *Max Weber a Karol Marks: Socjologia Maxa Webera jako "pozytywna krytyka materializmu historycznego."* Warsaw: KiW, 1967.

Krader, Laurence. *The Asiatic Mode of Production: Sources, Development and Critique in the Writings of Karl Marx.* Assen: Van Gorcum, 1975.

Lange, Oskar. *Political Economy.* Vol. 1. Pergamon Press and Polish Scientific Publishers, 1963.

Lefebvre, Henri. *The Sociology of Marx.* London: Allen Lane, 1969.

Lichtheim, George. *Marxism: An Historical and Critical Study.* New York: Praeger, 1962.

McLellan, David, *Karl Marx: His Life and Thought.* London: Macmillan, 1973.

———. *The Thought of Karl Marx: An Introduction.* London: Macmillan, 1971.

———. *The Young Hegelians and Karl Marx.* London: Macmillan, 1969.

Marx, Karl, *Selected Writings.* Edited by David McLellan. London: Oxford University Press, 1977.

———. *Selected Writings in Sociology and Social Philosophy.* Edited by T. B. Bottomore and M. Rubel. London: Watts, 1961.

Marx, K., and F. Engels. *Basic Writings on Politics and Philosophy.* Edited by Lewis S. Feuer. Garden City, N.Y.: Doubleday, 1959.

————. *Collected Works*. London: Lawrence and Wishart, 1974-

Mehring, F. *Karl Marx: The Story of His Life*. London: Allen and Unwin, 1948.

Meszáros, Istvan. *Marx's Theory of Alienation*. London: Merlin Press, 1970.

Michel, Henri. *Marx*. 2 vols. Paris: Gallimard, 1976.

Mills, C. Wright. *The Marxists*. New York: Dell, 1962.

Naville, Pierre. *Le Nouveau Léviathan*. Vol. 1. *De L'aliénation à la jouissance: La Genèse de la sociologie chez Marx et chez Engels*. Paris: Anthropos, 1970.

Nowak, Leszek. *U podstaw marksowskiej metodologii nauk*. Warsaw: PWN, 1971.

Ollman, Bartell. *Alienation: Marx's Conception of Man in Capitalist Society*. Cambridge: Cambridge University Press, 1971.

Ossowski, Stanislaw. *Class Structure in the Class Consciousness*. London: RKP, 1963.

Plamenatz, John. *Marx's Conception of Man*. Oxford: Clarendon Press, 1975.

Rossi, Mario. *De Hegel à Marx*. 2 vols. Milan: Feltrinelli, 1970.

Rubel, Maximilien. *Karl Marx: Essai de biographie intellectuelle*. Paris: Rivière, 1957.

Schmidt, Alfred. *Der Begriff der Natur in der Lehre von Marx*. Frankfurt: Europäische Verlag, 1962.

Schwan, Gesine. *Die Gesellschaftskritik von Karl Marx*. Stuttgart: W. Kohlhammer, 1974.

Shaw, William H. *Marx's Theory of History*. Stanford: Stanford University Press, 1978.

Terray, Emmanuel. *Le Marxisme devant les sociétés primitives*. Paris: Maspero, 1970.

Therbom, Göran. *Science, Class and Society: On the Formation of Sociology and Historical Materialism*. London: NLB, 1976.

Tucker, Robert C. *Philosophy and Myth in Karl Marx*. Cambridge: Cambridge University Press, 1961.

Vranickij, Predrag. *Geschichte des Marxismus*. 2 vols. Tübingen: Suhrkamp, 1972-74.

Vygodskij, V. S. *The Story of Great Discovery: How Karl Marx Wrote "Capital"* Berlin: Die Wirtschaft, 1973.

Witt-Hansen, J. *Historical Materialism*. Copenhagen: Munksgaard, 1960.

Zelubovskaja, E. A., et al. *Marks-istorik*. Moscow: "Nauka," 1968.

CHAPTER 7.

EARLY POSITIVISM AND THE BEGINNINGS OF SOCIOLOGY:
COMTE, MILL, AND QUÉTELET

Arbousse-Bastide, Paul. *Auguste Comte*. Paris: P.U.F., 1968.

Arnaud, Pierre. *Le "Nouveau Dieu": Introduction à la politique positive*. Paris: J. Vrin, 1973.

————. *La Pensée d'Auguste Comte*. Editions Bordas, 1969.

————. *Sociologie de Comte*. Paris: A Colin, 1969.

————, ed. *Politique d'Auguste Comte*. Paris: A. Colin, 1965.

Böhme, Monika. *Die Moralstatistik: Ein Beitrag zur Geschichte der Quantifizierung in der Soziologie, darstellt an den Werken Adolphe Quetelets und Alexander von Oettingens*. Marburg: Lahn, 1969.

Borchert, Heinrich. *Der Begriff des Kulturzeitalters bei Comte*. Halle: John, 1927.

Charlton, Donald G. *Positivist Thought in France during the Second Empire, 1852-1870*. Oxford: Clarendon Press, 1957.

Comte, Auguste. *A General View of Positivism*. New York: Speller, 1957.

————. *Oeuvres*. Paris: Anthropos, 1968-71.

————. *Sociologie: Textes choisis par J. Laubier*. Paris: P.U.F., 1957.

————. *System of Positive Policy*. 4 vols. London: Longman, 1875-77.

Cowling, Maurice. *Mill and Liberalism*. Cambridge: Cambridge University Press, 1963.

Durkheim, Emile. *The Rules of Sociological Method*. New York: Free Press, 1962.

Fletcher, Ronald, ed. *John Stuart Mill: A Logical Critique of Sociology.* London: Nelson, 1971.

Giddens, Anthony, ed. *Positivism and Sociology.* London: Heinemann, 1975.

Gouhier, Henri. *La Jeunesse d'Auguste Comte.* 3 vols. Paris: J. Vrin, 1933-41.

Grunicke, Lucia. *Der Begriff der Tatsache in der positivistischen Philosophie des 19 Jahrhunderts.* Halle: M. Niemeyer, 1930.

Gurvitch, Georges. *Auguste Comte, Karl Marx et Herbert Spencer.* Paris: C.D.U., 1957.

Habermas, Jürgen. *Knowledge and Human Interests.* Boston: Beacon Press, 1972.

Halbwachs, Maurice. *Statique et dynamique sociale chez Auguste Comte.* Paris: F. Alcan, 1943.

———. *La Théorie de l'homme moyen: Essai sur Quételet et la statistique morale.* Paris: F. Alcan, 1913.

Hankins, Frank. *Adolphe Quételet as Statistician.* New York: Longman, 1908.

Hawkins, Richard L. *Auguste Comte and the United States.* Cambridge, Mass.: Harvard University Press, 1936.

Kellermann, P. *Organizistische Vorstellungen in soziologischen Konzeptionen bei Comte, Spencer und Parsons.* Munich: C. Schön, 1969.

Kolakowski, Leszek. *Positivist Philosophy: From Hume to the Vienna Circle.* Harmondsworth: Penguin Books, 1972.

Kon, I. S. *Pozitivizm v socjologii.* Leningrad: Izdatelstvo Leningradskovo Universiteta, 1964.

Kremer-Marietti, Angèle. *Auguste Comte et la théorie sociale du positivisme.* Paris: Seghers, 1970.

Lacroix, Jean. *La Sociologie d'Auguste Comte.* 2d ed. Paris: P.U.F., 1956.

Lazarsfeld, Paul F. "Notes on the History of Quantification in Sociology: Trends, Sources and Problems." *Isis* 52 (1961):227-333.

Lévy-Bruhl, L. *The Philosophy of Auguste Comte.* New York: Putman, 1900.

Littré, Emile. *Auguste Comte et la philosophie positive.* Paris: Hachette, 1863.

Lottin, Joseph. *Quételet: Statisticien et sociologue.* Louvain: Bibl. de l'Institut Supérieur de Philosophie, 1912.

Marcuse, Alexander. *Die Geschichtsphilosophie Auguste Comtes.* Berlin: Cotta, 1932.

Martineau, H. *The Positive Philosophy of Auguste Comte.* London: Bell and Sons, 1913.

Marvin, F. S. *Comte: The Founder of Sociology.* London: Chapman and Hall, 1936.

Mill, John Stuart, *Collected Works.* Vol. 4, *Essays on Economics and Society.* Toronto: University of Toronto Press, London: RKP 1967.

———. *Collected Works.* Vol. 10, *Essays on Ethics, Religion and Society.* Toronto: University of Toronto Press, London: RKP, 1969.

———. *Lettres inédites de . . . à Auguste Comte.* Paris: F. Alcan, 1899.

———. *Principles of Political Economy with Some of Their Applications to Social Philosophy.* London: Longmans, Green, 1923.

———. *A System of Logic, Ratiocinative and Inductive.* 2 vols., 6th ed. London: Longmans, Green, 1856.

Mueller, J. W. *John Stuart Mill and French Thought.* Urbana: University of Illinois Press, 1956.

Negt, Oskar. *Strukturbeziehungen zwischen den Gesellschaftslehren Comtes und Hegels.* Frankfurt: Europäische Verlag, 1964.

Quételet, Adolphe. *Du Système social et les lois qui le régissent.* Paris: Guillaumin, 1848.

———. *Physique sociale, ou Essai sur le développement des facultés de l'homme.* 2 vols. Brussels: J. Issakoff, 1869.

Robson, John M. *The Improvement of Mankind: The Social and Political Thought of John Stuart Mill.* Toronto: University of Toronto Press, 1968.

Ryan, A. *John Stuart Mill.* London: RKP, 1974.

Simon, W. M. *European Positivism in the Nineteenth Century: An Essay in Intellectual History.* Ithaca, N.Y.: Cornell University Press, 1963.

Skarga, Barbara. *Comte.* Warsaw: WP, 1966.

Stephen, Leslie. *The English Utilitarians.* 3 vols. London: Duckworth, 1900.

Utkina, H. F. *Pozitivizm, antropologiceskij materializm i nauka v Rossii.* Moscow: "Nauka," 1975.

Vaysset-Boutbien, R. *John Stuart Mill et la sociologie française contemporaine.* Paris: P.U.F., 1940.

Varrier, René. *Roberty: Le Positivisme russe et la fondation de la sociologie.* Paris: F. Alcan, 1931.

CHAPTER 8.
THE EVOLUTIONIST SOCIOLOGY

Andreski, Stanislav, ed. *Herbert Spencer: Structure, Function and Evolution.* London: Michael Joseph, 1971.

Banton, Michael, ed. *Darwinism and the Study of Society: A Centenary Symposium.* London: Tavistock, 1961.

Barnett, S. A., ed. *A Century of Darwin.* London: Mercury Books, 1962.

Bee, Robert L. *Patterns and Processes: An Introduction to Anthropological Strategies for the Study of Sociocultural Changes.* New York: Free Press, 1974.

Bock, Kenneth E. *The Acceptance of Histories. Toward a Perspective for Social Sciences.* University of California Publications in Sociology and Social Institutions, vol. 3, no. 1. Berkeley: University of California, 1956.

Buckle, H. T. *History of Civilization in England.* New York: Appleton, 1874.

Burrow, J. W. *Evolution and Society: A Study in Victorian Social Theory.* Cambridge: Cambridge University Press, 1970.

Carneiro, Robert L., "Classical Evolution." In Raoul Naroll and Trada Naroll, eds., *Main Currents in Cultural Anthropology.* Englewood Cliffs, N.J.: Prentice-Hall, 1973.

———, ed. *The Evolution of Society: Selections from Herbert Spencer's "Principles of Sociology."* Chicago: University of Chicago Press, 1967.

Colson, E. *Tradition and Contract: The Problem of Order.* Rochester: New York University L. H. Morgan Lectures, 1973.

Downie, Robert A. *James George Frazer and the Golden Bough.* New York: Humanities Press, 1970.

Duncan, D. ed. *The Life and Letters of Herbert Spencer.* New York: Appleton, 1908.

Engels, Friedrich. *Origin of the Family, Private Property, and the State.* Moscow: Foreign Languages Publishing House, 1954.

Evans-Pritchard, E. E. *Social Anthropology.* London: RKP, 1951.

Feaver, G. A. *From Status to Contract: A Biography of Sir Henry Maine, 1822-1888.* London: Longman, 1969.

Fortes, Meyer. *Kingship and the Social Order: The Legacy of L. H. Morgan.* London: RKP, 1969.

Gella, Aleksander. *Ewolucjonizm a poczatki socjologii: L. Gumplowicz i L. F. Ward.* Wroclaw: Ossolineum, 1966.

Himmelfarb, Gertrude. *Darwin and the Darwinian Revolution.* London: Chatto and Windus, 1959.

Hirst, Paul Q. *Social Evolution and Social Categories.* London: Allen and Unwin, 1976.

Hodgen, T. M. *The Doctrine of Survivals.* London: Allenson, 1936.

Hofstadter, Richard. *Social Darwinism in American Thought.* Boston: Beacon Press, 1972.

Kimball, Elsa P. *Sociology and Education: An Analysis of the Theories of Spencer and Ward.* New York: Columbia University Press, 1932.

Lubbock, J. *The Origin of Civilization and the Primitive Condition of Man: Mental and Social Condition of Savages.* London: Longmans, Green, 1870.

Lutyński, Jan. *Ewolucjonizm w etnologii anglosaskiej a etnografia radziecka.* Lodz: Lódzkie Towarzystwo Naukowe, 1956.

McLennan, J. F. *Studies in Ancient History,* first series. London: B. Quaritch, 1976.

———. *Studies in Ancient History,* second series. London: Macmillan, 1896.

MacRae, Donald G. *Ideology and Society: Papers in Sociology and Politics.* London: Heinemann, 1961.

———, ed. *Spencer: The Man Versus the State.* Harmondsworth: Penguin Books, 1969.

Maine, Henry S. *Ancient Law.* London: Murray, 1861.

———. *Dissertations on Early Law and Customs.* London: Murray, 1883.

———. *Lectures on the Early History of Institutions.* New York: Holt, 1888.

Marret, Robert R. *Tylor.* New York: Wiley, 1936.

Morgan, L. H. *Ancient Society.* New York: Holt, 1877.

Peel, J. D. Y., ed. *Herbert Spencer on Social Evolution.* Chicago: University of Chicago Press, 1972.

———. *Herbert Spencer: The Evolution of a Sociologist.* London: Heinemann, 1971.

Resek, Karl. *Lewis Henry Morgan: American Scholar.* Chicago: University of Chicago Press, 1960.

Rumney, J. *Herbert Spencer's Sociology.* London: Williams and Norgate, 1934.

Spencer, Herbert. *An Autobiography.* New York: Appleton, 1900.

———. *Descriptive Sociology.* 16 vols. London: Williams and Norgate, 1873-1934.

———. *Education: Intellectual, Moral and Physical.* New York: Appleton, 1881.

———. *Essays: Scientific, Political and Speculative.* 2 vols. London: Williams and Norgate, 1891.

———. *First Principles.* London: Williams and Norgate, 1863.

———. *The Principles of Biology.* 2 vols. London: Williams and Norgate, 1864-67.

———. *The Principles of Psychology.* 2 vols. London: Williams and Norgate, 1870-67.

———. *The Principles of Sociology.* 3 vols. London: Williams and Norgate, 1876-96.

———. *Social Statics.* London: J. Chapman, 1851.

———. *The Study of Sociology.* London: C. Kegan Paul, 1880.

Stocking George W. Jr. *Race, Culture and Evolution: Essays in the History of Anthropology.* New York: Free Press, 1968.

Szczurkiewicz, Tadeusz. *Studia socjologiczne.* Warsaw: PWN, 1969.

Tylor, E. B. *Primitive Culture: Researches into the Development of Mythology, Philosophy, Religion, Language, Art and Custom.* 2 vols. London: Murray, 1871.

Wilshire, David. *The Social and Political Thought of Herbert Spencer.* New York: Oxford University Press, 1978.

CHAPTER 9.
PSYCHOLOGISM: PSYCHOSOCIOLOGY AND THE RISE OF SOCIAL PSYCHOLOGY

Bastide, Roger. *Sociologie et psychoanalyse.* Paris: P.U.F., 1950.

Bocock, Robert, ed. *Freud and Modern Society: An Outline and Analysis of Freud's Sociology.* London: Nelson, 1976.

Borkenau, Franz. *Pareto.* London: Chapman and Hall, 1936.

Bousquet, Georges H. *The Work of Vilfredo Pareto.* Minneapolis: Sociological Press, 1928.

Busino, Giovanni. *Introduction à une histoire de la sociologie de Pareto.* Geneva: Droz, 1967.

Cioffi, Frank, ed. *Freud: Modern Judgements.* London: Macmillan, 1973.

Clark, Terry N., ed. *Gabriel Tarde on Communication and Social Influence.* Chicago: University of Chicago Press, 1969.

Davis, Michael M., Jr. *Psychological Interpretations of Society.* New York: Longman, 1906.

Ellwood, Charles A. *An Introduction to Social Psychology.* New York: Appleton, 1921.

Essertier, Daniel. *Psychologie et sociologie.* Paris: F. Alcan, 1927.

Finer, S. E., ed. *Vilfredo Pareto's Sociological Writings.* New York: Praeger, 1966.

Freud, Sigmund. *Character and Culture.* New York: Collier Books, 1963.

———. *Civilization and Its Discontents.* New York: Norton, 1962.

———. *The Major Works.* In *Great Books of the Western World*, vol. 54. Chicago: Encyclopaedia Britannica, 1952.

Freund, Julien. *Pareto: La Théorie de l'équilibre.* Paris: Seghers, 1974.

Friedlander, Saul. *Histoire et psychoanalyse* Paris: Seuil, 1927.

Fromm, Erich. *Sigmund Freud's Mission.* New York: Harper and Brothers, 1959.

Galdston, Iago, ed. *Freud and Contemporary Culture.* New York: International Universities Press, 1957.

Gedo, John E., and George H. Pollock, eds. *Freud: The Fusion of Science and Humanism: The Intellectual History of Psychoanalysis.* New York: International Universities Press, 1976.

Henderson, Lawrence J. *Pareto's General Sociology.* Cambridge, Mass.: Harvard University Press, 1935.

Homans, George C., and Charles P. Curtis, Jr. *An Introduction to Pareto: His Sociology.* New York: Knopf, 1934.

Johnston, Thomas. *Freud and Political Thought.* New York: Citadel Press, 1965.

Jones, Ernest. *The Life and Work of Sigmund Freud.* 3 vols. New York: Basic Books, 1953-57.

Karpf, F. *American Social Psychology: Its Origins, Development and European Background.* New York: McGraw-Hill, 1932.

Le Bon, Gustave. *The Crowd: A Study of the Popular Mind.* London: T. Fischer Unwin, 1909.

Leenhardt, J., ed. *Psychanalyse et sociologie.* Brussels, 1973.

Lopreato, J. *Vilfredo Pareto.* New York: Crowell, 1965.

McDougall, William. *The Group Mind.* Cambridge: Cambridge University Press, 1927.

———. *Introduction to Social Psychology.* 26th ed. London: Methuen, 1945.

Marcuse, Herbert. *Eros and Civilization: A Philosophical Inquiry into Freud.* Boston: Beacon Press, 1955.

Marcuse, Ludwig. *Sigmund Freud: Sein Bild vom Menschen.* Hamburg: Rewohlt, 1956.

Masserman, H., ed. *Psychoanalysis and Social Process.* New York: Grune and Stratton, 1961.

Matagrin, Amédée. *La Psychologie sociale de Gabriel Tarde.* Paris: F. Alcan, 1910.

Mazlish, Bruce, ed. *Psychoanalysis and History.* New York: Grosset and Dunlap, 1971.

Meisel, James H., ed. *Pareto and Mosca.* Englewood Cliffs, N.J.: Prentice-Hall, 1965.

Milet, J. *Gabriel Tarde et la philosophie de l'histoire.* Paris: J. Vrin, 1970.

Moscovici, Serge. *La Psychanalyse, son image et son publique.* 2d ed. Paris: P.U.F., 1976.

Muensterberger, W., ed. *Man and His Culture: Psychoanalytic Anthropology after "Totem and Taboo."* London: 1969.

Muensterberger, W., et al., eds. *Psychoanalytic Study of Society.* 6 vols. New York: International Universities Press, 1960.

Mullahy, Patrick. *Oedipus: Myth and Complex: A Review of Psychoanalytic Theory.* New York: Grove Press, 1955.

Nolte, Helmut. *Psychoanalyse und Soziologie: Die Systemtheorien Sigmund Freuds und Talcott Parsons.* Bern-Stuttgart-Vienna: H. Huber, 1970.

Pareto, Vilfredo. *The Mind and Society: A Treatise on General Sociology.* New York: Dover, 1963.

———. *Oeuvres complètes publiées sous la direction de G. Busino.* 15 vols. Geneva: Droz, 1964-71.

Parsons, Talcott. *Social Structure and Personality.* New York: Free Press, 1965.

Perrin, G. *Sociologie de Pareto.* Paris: P.U.F., 1966.

Rieff, Philip. *Freud: The Mind of the Moralist.* New York: Viking Press, 1959.

Roazen, Paul. *Freud: Political and Social Thought.* New York: Vintage Books, 1970.

Róheim, Géza, *Psychoanalysis and Anthropology: Culture, Personality and the Consciousness.* New York: International Universities Press, 1950.

Róheim, Géza, Werner Muensterberger, and Sidney Axelrad, eds. *Psychoanalysis and the Social Sciences.* 4 vols. New York: International Universities Press, 1947-58.

Ross, Edward A. *Social Psychology.* New York: Macmillan, 1908.

Ruitenbeek, Hendrik M., ed. *Psychoanalysis and Social Science.* New York: Dutton, 1962.

Samuels, Warren, J. *Pareto on Policy.* New York: Elsevier, 1974.

Schneider, Louis. *The Freudian Psychology and Veblen's Social Theory.* New York: King's Crown Press, 1948.

Schoene, W. *Über die Psychoanalyse in der Ethnologie.* Dortmund: Ruhfus, 1966.

Sutherland, John D., ed. *Psychoanalysis and Contemporary Thought.* New York: Grove Press, 1959.

Tarde, Gabriel. *Essais et mélanges sociologiques.* Lyon: Storck, 1895.

———. *Etudes de psychologie sociale.* Paris: Gierd et Brière, 1898.

———. *The Laws of Imitation.* New York: Holt, 1903.

———. *La Logique sociale.* Paris: F. Alcan, 1893.

———. *Les Lois de l'imitation.* Paris: F. Alcan, 1890.

———. *Les Lois sociales.* Paris: F. Alcan, 1898.

———. *L'Opinion et la foule.* Paris: F. Alcan, 1901.

———. *L'Opposition universelle.* Paris: F. Alcan, 1897.

———. *Psychologie économique.* 2 vols. Paris: F. Alcan, 1902.

———. *Social Laws.* New York: Macmillan, 1907.

Thompson, Clara. *Psychoanalysis: Evolution and Development.* New York: Grove Press, 1975.

Trilling, Lionel. *Freud and the Crisis of Our Culture.* Boston: Beacon Press, 1955.

Watson, John B. *The Ways of Behaviorism.* New York: Harper and Brothers, 1928.

Weinstein, Fred, and Gerald M. Platt. *Psychoanalytic Sociology: An Essay on the Interpretation of Historical Data and the Phenomena of Collective Behavior.* Baltimore: Johns Hopkins University Press, 1973.

Whyte, L. L. *The Unconscious before Freud.* New York: Basic Books, 1960.

Wundt, Wilhelm. *Elements of Folk Psychology: Outlines of a Psychological History of the Development of Mankind.* New York: Macmillan, 1916.

———. *Logik: Eine Untersuchung des Prinzipien der Erkenntnis und der Methoden wissenschaftlicher Forschung.* Vol. 3, *Logik der Gesteswissenschaften.* 3d. ed. Stuttgart: F. Enke, 1908.

Wyss, Dieter. *Marx und Freud: Ihr Verhältnis zur modernen Anthropologie.* Göttingen: Vundenhoeck und Zuprecht, 1969.

CHAPTER 10.
SOCIOLOGISM: SOCIOLOGY AS THE FUNDAMENTAL SOCIAL SCIENCE

Aimard, Guy. *Durkheim et la science économique.* Paris: P.U.F., 1962.

Alpert, Harry. *Emile Durkheim and His Sociology.* New York: Columbia University Press, 1939.

Bellah, R. N., ed. *Emile Durkheim on Morality and Society.* Chicago: University of Chicago Press, 1973.

Bierstedt, Robert. *Emile Durkheim*. London: Weidenfeld and Nicolson, 1966.

Bouglé, Celestin. *Bilan de la sociologie française contemporaine*. Paris: F. Alcan, 1935.

————. *The Evolution of Values*. New York: Macmillan, 1926.

————. *Qu'est-ce que la sociologie?* Paris: F. Alcan, 1907.

Cazeneuve, J. *Sociologie de Marcel Mauss*. Paris: P.U.F., 1968.

Clark, Terry Nichols. *Prophets and Patrons: The French University and the Emergence of Social Sciences*. Cambridge, Mass.: Harvard University Press, 1973.

Cuvillier, Armand. *Où va la sociologie française? Avec une étude d'Emile Durkheim sur la sociologie formaliste*. Paris: Rivière, 1953.

Czarnowski, Stefan. *Dziela*. 5 vols. Warsaw: PWN, 1956.

————. *Le Culte des héros et ses conditions sociales: Saint Patrick, héros national de l'Irlande*. Paris: F. Alcan, 1919.

Davy, Georges. *Durkheim: Choix de textes avec étude du système sociologique*. Paris: L. Michaud, 1924.

————. *Sociologues d'hier et d'aujourd'hui*. Paris: F. Alcan, 1931.

Douglas, Jack D. *The Social Meanings of Suicide*. Princeton: Princeton University Press, 1967.

Durkheim, Emile. *The Division of Labor in Society*. New York: Free Press, 1969.

————. *L'Education morale*. Paris: F. Alcan, 1925.

————. *The Elementary Forms of the Religious Life*. London: Allen and Unwin, 1976.

————. *Journal sociologique*. Paris: P.U.F., 1969.

————. *Leçons de sociologie: Physique de moeurs et du droit*. Paris: P.U.F., 1950.

————. *Montesquieu et Rousseau: Précurseurs de la sociologie*. Paris: Rivière, 1953.

————. *Pragmatisme et sociologie*. Paris: J. Vrin, 1955.

————. *The Rules of Sociological Method*. New York: Free Press, 1958.

————. *La Science sociale et l'action*. Paris: P.U.F., 1970.

————. *Socialism and Saint-Simon*. Kent, Ohio: Kent State University Press, 1958.

————. *Sociology and Philosophy*. New York: Free Press, 1974.

Duvignaud, J., ed. *Durkheim: Sa Vie, son oeuvre, avec un exposé de sa philosophie*. Paris: P.U.F., 1965.

Gehlke, C. E. *Emile Durkheim's Contributions to Sociological Theory*. New York: Columbia University Press, 1915.

Gella, Aleksander. *Ewolucjonizm a poczatki socjologii: L. Gumplowicz i L. F. Ward*. Wroclaw: Ossolineum, 1966.

Giddens, Anthony. *Capitalism and Modern Social Theory: An Analysis of the Writings of Marx, Durkheim and Max Weber*. Cambridge: Cambridge University Press, 1971.

————, ed. *Emile Durkheim: Selected Writings*. Cambridge: Cambridge University Press, 1972.

Guitton, J. *Regards sur la pensée française, 1870-1940*. Paris, 1968.

Gumplowicz, Ludwig. *Ausgewählte werke*. 4 vols. Innsbruck: Wagner, 1883-1905.

————. *Outlines of Sociology*. Edited with an introduction and notes by Irving L. Horowitz. New York: Paine-Whitman Publishers, 1963.

————. *System socjologii*. Warsaw: Spólka Nakladowa, 1887.

Güntzel, K. *Die gesellschaftliche Wirklichkeit: Eine Studie der Emile Durkheims Soziologie*. Eschenhage: Ohlau und Schl., 1934.

Gurvitch, Georges. *La Vocation actuelle de la sociologie*. 2 vols. Paris: P.U.F., 1963.

Halbwachs, Maurice. *Les Cadres sociaux de la mémoire*. Paris: F. Alcan, 1925.

————. *Les Causes du suicide*. Paris: F. Alcan, 1930.

————. *La Classe ouvrière et les niveaux de la vie*. Paris: F. Alcan, 1913.

————. *L'Evolution des besoins dans les classes ouvrières*. Paris: F. Alcan, 1933.

————. *La Mémoire collective*. Paris: P.U.F., 1959.

————. *Les Origines du sentiment religieux d'après Durkheim*. Paris: Stock, 1925.

————. *Population and Society: Introduction to Social Morphology*. Glencoe, Ill.: Free Press, 1960.

————. *The Psychology of Social Classes*. London: Heinemann, 1958.

Hirst, P. Q. *Durkheim, Bernard and Epistemology*. London: RKP, 1975.

LaCapra, D. *Emile Durkheim: Sociologist and Philosopher*. Ithaca, N.Y.: Cornell University Press, 1972.

Lacombe, Roger. *La Méthode sociologique d'Emile Durkheim: Etude critique*. Paris: F. Alcan, 1926.

La Fontaine, A. P. *La Philosophie d'Emile Durkheim: Sociologie générale*. Paris: J. Vrin, 1926.

Lévy-Bruhl, Lucien. *L'Ame primitive*. Paris: F. Alcan, 1927.

————. *Les Fonctions mentales dans les sociétés inférieures*. Paris: F. Alcan, 1910.

————. *La Mentalité primitive*. Paris: F. Alcan, 1922.

————. *La Morale et la science des moeurs*. Paris: F. Alcan, 1903.

Lukes, Steven. *Emile Durkheim: His Life and Work: A Historical and Critical Study*. Harmondsworth: Penguin Books, 1975.

Mariça, Georg M. *Emile Durkheim: Soziologie und Soziologismus*. Jena: Fischer, 1932.

Mauss, Marcel. *Oeuvres*. 3 vols. Paris: Editions de Minuit, 1968-69.

————. *Sociologie et anthropologie*. Paris: P.U.F., 1960.

Mirek, F. *System socjologiczny Ludwika Gumplowicza: Studium krytyczne*. Poznan: I. Zamecznik, 1930.

Monnerot, J. *Les Faits sociaux ne sont pas les choses*. Paris: Gallimard, 1946.

Nandan, Yash. *The Durkheimian School. A Systematic and Comprehensive Bibliography*. Westport, Conn.: Greenwood Press, 1977.

Nisbet, Robert, A., ed. *Emile Durkheim*. Englewood Cliffs, N.J.: Prentice-Hall, 1965.

————. *The Sociology of Emile Durkheim*. London: Heinemann, 1975.

Osipova, E. V. *Socjologia Emila Durkheima*. Moscow: "Nauka." 1977.

Parsons, Talcott. *The Structure of Social Action*. New York: Free Press, 1968.

Pickering, W. S. F., ed. *Durkheim on Religion: A Selection of Readings with Bibliographies*. London: RKP, 1975.

Poggi, Gianfranco. *Images of Society: Essays on the Sociological Theories of Tocqueville, Marx and Durkheim*. Stanford: Stanford University Press, 1972.

Pope, Whitney. *Durkheim's Suicide*. Chicago: University of Chicago Press, 1978.

Proto, Mario. *Durkheim e il marxismo: Dalla scienza sociale all'ideologia cooporativa*. Manduria: Lacaita, 1973.

Seger, Imogen. *Durkheim and His Critics on the Sociology of Religion*. New York: Bureau of Applied Social Research, Columbia University, 1957.

Simiand, F. *La Méthode positive en science économique*. Paris: F. Alcan, 1912.

Simpson, G., ed. *Emile Durkheim*. New York: Crowell, 1963.

Szacki, Jerzy. *Durkheim*. Warsaw: WP, 1964.

Tarkowska, Elzbieta. *Ciagłość i zmiana socjologii francuskiej: Durkheim, Mauss, Lévi-Strauss*. Warsaw: PWN, 1974.

Tiryakian, Edward A. *Sociologism and Existentialism: Two Perspectives on the Individual and Society*. Englewood Cliffs, N.J.: Prentice-Hall, 1962.

Wallwork, E. *Durkheim: Morality and Milieu*. Cambridge, Mass.: Harvard University Press, 1972.

Wolff, Kurt H., ed. *Emile Durkheim, 1858-1917: A Collection of Essays with Translations and a Bibliography*. Columbus, Ohio: Ohio State University Press, 1960.

CHAPTER 11.
ABSOLUTE HISTORICISM:
THE ANTIPOSITIVIST TURN IN SOCIOLOGY

Antoni, Carlo. *From History to Sociology: The Transition in German Historical Thinking.* London: Merlin Press, 1962.

Aron, Raymond. *La Philosophie critique de l'histoire.* Paris: J. Vrin, 1969.

Bischoff, Dietrich W. *Wilhelm Diltheys geschichtliche Lebensphilosophie.* Leipzig: B. G. Teubner, 1935.

Bollnow, Otto Friedrich. *Dilthey: Eine Einführung in seine Philosophie.* Stuttgart: Kohlhammer, 1935.

Bravo, Benedetto. *Philosophie, histoire, philosophie de l'histoire: Etude sur J. G. Droysen, historien de l'antiquité.* Wroclaw: Ossolineum, 1968.

Dilthey, Wilhelm. *Gesammelte Schriften.* Vol. 1, *Einleitung in die Geisteswissenschaften: Versuch einer Grundlegung für das Studium der Gesellschaft und die Geschichte.* Leipzig: B. G. Teubner, 1933.

————. *Gesammelte Schriften.* Vol. 7, *Der Aufbau der geschichlichen Welt in den Geisteswissenschaften.* Leipzig: B. G. Teubner, 1933.

————. *Pattern and Meaning in History: Thoughts on History and Society.* Edited with an introduction by H. P. Rickman. New York: Harper and Row, 1962.

————. *Selected Writings.* Edited by H. P. Rickman. Cambridge: Cambridge University Press, 1976.

Diwald, Helmut. *Wilhelm Dilthey: Erkenntnistheorie und Philosophie der Geschichte.* Göttingen: Musterschmidt, 1963.

Gerhard, Wilfred. *Ernst Troeltsch als Soziologe.* Cologne: W. Kleinkamp, 1975.

Gorsen, Peter. *Zur Phänomenologie des Bewusstseinsstroms: Bergson, Dilthey, Husserl, Simmel und die Lebensphilosophischen Antinomien.* Bonn: H. Bouvier, 1966.

Habermas, Jürgen. *Knowledge and Human Interests.* Boston: Beacon Press, 1971.

Hodges, Herbert A. *The Philosophy of Wilhelm Dilthey.* London: RKP, 1952.

————. *Wilhelm Dilthey: An Introduction.* 2d ed. London: RKP, 1949.

Kluback, William. *Wilhelm Dilthey's Philosophy of History.* New York: Columbia University Press, 1956.

Kremer-Marietti, A. *Wilhelm Dilthey et anthropologie historique.* Paris: Seghers, 1971.

Kuderowicz, Zbigniew. *Dilthey.* Warsaw: WP, 1967.

————. *Światopoglad i zycie u Dilthey'a.* Warsaw: PWN, 1966.

Makkreel, Rudolf A. *Dilthey: Philosopher of the Human Studies.* Princeton: Princeton University Press, 1975.

Mandelbaum, Maurice. *The Problem of Historical Knowledge: An Answer to Relativism.* New York: Liveright, 1938.

Meinecke, Friedrich. *Historism: The Rise of a New Historical Outlook.* London: RKP, 1972.

Mokrzycki, Edmund. *Zalozenia socjologii humanistycznej.* Warsaw: PWN, 1971.

Outhwaite, William. *Understanding Social Life: The Method Called Verstehen.* London: Allen Unwin, 1975.

Palmer, Richard E. *Hermeneutics: Interpretation Theory in Schleiermacher, Dilthey, Heidegger and Gadamer.* Evanston, Ill.: Northwestern University Press, 1965.

Rickert, Heinrich. *Science and History: A Critique of Positivist Epistemology.* Princeton: Van Nostrand, 1962.

Rickman, H. P. *Understanding and the Human Studies.* London: Heinemann, 1967.

Salov, V. I. *Istorism i sovremennaja burzuaznaja istoriografija.* Moscow: "Mysl," 1977.

Stein, Arthur. *Begriff des Verstehen bei Wilhelm Dilthey.* Tübingen: J. C. B. Mohr, 1926.

Suter, Jean-*François*. *Philosophie et histoire chez Dilthey*. Basel: Verlag für Recht und Gesellschaft, 1960.

Truzzi, Marcello, ed. *Verstehen: Subjective Understanding in the Social Sciences*. Reading, Mass.: Addison-Wesley, 1974.

Tuttle, Howard N. *Wilhelm Dilthey's Philosophy of Historical Understanding: A Critical Analysis*. Leiden: E. J. Brill, 1969.

Zöckler, Christofer. *Dilthey und die Hermeneutik*. Stuttgart: J. B. Metzler, 1975.

CHAPTER 12.
THE FIRST SYSTEMS OF HUMANISTIC SOCIOLOGY:
TÖNNIES, SIMMEL, AND WEBER

Abel, Theodore. *Systematic Sociology in Germany: A Critical Analysis of Some Attempts to Establish Sociology as an Independent Science*. New York: Columbia University Press, 1929.

Abramowski, Günther. *Das Geschichtsbild Max Webers*. Stuttgart: Klett, 1966.

Adler, Max. *Georg Simmels Bedeutung für die Geistesgeschichte*. Vienna and Leipzig: Anzengruber-Verlag, 1919.

Antoni, Carlo. *From History to Sociology: The Transition in German Historical Thinking*. London: Merlin Press, 1962.

Aron, Raymond. *La Philosophie critique de l'histoire*. Paris: J. Vrin, 1969.

———. *La Sociologie allemande contemporaine*. Paris: P.U.F., 1950.

Bacher, H. J. *Georg Simmel: Die Grundlagen seiner Soziologie*. Stuttgart, 1971.

Baumgarten, Eduard, ed. *Max Weber: Werk und der Person: Dokumente*. Tübingen: J. C. B. Mohr, 1964.

Becker, Howard. *Systematic Sociology on the Basis of the Beziehungslehre and Gebildeslehre of Leopold von Wiese*. New York: Wiley, 1932.

Beetham, David. *Max Weber and the Theory of Modern Politics*. London: Allen and Unwin, 1974.

Bellebaum, A. *Das soziologische System von Ferdinand Tönnies unter besonderer Berichsichtigung seiner soziographischen Untersuchungen*. Meisenheim: A. Hain, 1966.

Bendix, R. *Max Weber: An Intellectual Portrait*. Garden City, N.Y.: Doubleday, 1962.

Bendix, R. and G. Roth. *Scholarship and Partisanship: Essays on Max Weber*. Berkeley and Los Angeles: University of California Press, 1971.

Bennion, L. L. *Max Weber's Methodology*. Paris: Les Presses modernes, 1933.

Boesse, Franz. *Geschichte des Vereins für Sozialpolitik, 1872-1932*. Berlin: Duncker und Humblot, 1939.

Bosse, H. *Marx-Weber-Troeltsch: Religionssoziologie und marxistische Ideologiekritik*. Munich: Kaiser and Grünewald, 1970.

Bruun, H. H. *Science, Values and Politics in Max Weber's Methodology*. Copenhagen: Munksgaard, 1972.

Burger, Thomas. *Max Weber's Theory of Concept Formation*. Durham, N.C.: Duke University Press, 1976.

Cahnman, Werner J., ed. *Ferdinand Tönnies: A New Evaluation: Essays and Documents*. Leiden: E. J. Brill, 1973.

Cahman, Werner J., and Rudolf Heberle, eds. *Ferdinand Tönnies on Sociology: Pure, Applied and Empirical*. Chicago: University of Chicago Press, 1971.

Coser, Lewis A., ed. *Georg Simmel*. Englewood Cliffs, N.J.: Prentice-Hall, 1965.

Dronberger, Ilse. *The Political Thought of Max Weber: In Quest of Statesmanship.* New York: Appleton-Century-Crofts, 1971.

Eisenstadt, S. N., ed. *Max Weber on Charisma and Institution Building.* Chicago: University of Chicago Press, 1968.

————. *The Protestant Ethic and Modernization: A Comparative View.* New York: Basic Books, 1968.

Eldridge, J. E. T., ed. *Max Weber: The Interpretation of Social Reality.* London: Michael Joseph, 1971.

Freund, Julien. *Max Weber.* Paris: P.U.F., 1969.

————. *The Sociology of Max Weber.* New York: Vintage Books, 1969.

Gassen, K., and M. Landmann, eds. *Buch des Denkens an Georg Simmel: Briefe, Erinnerungen, Bibliographie.* Berlin: Duncker und Humblot, 1958.

Giddens, Anthony. *Capitalism and Modern Social Theory: An Analysis of the Writings of Marx, Durkheim and Weber.* Cambridge: Cambridge University Press, 1971.

————. *Politics and Sociology in the Thought of Max Weber.* London: Macmillan, 1972.

Grab, H. J. *Der Begriff des Rationalen in der Soziologie Max Webers.* Karlsrue: G. Braun, 1927.

Green, R. W., ed. *Protestantism, Capitalism, and Social Science: The Weberian Thesis Controversy.* Lexington, Mass.: Heath, 1973.

Hennen, Manfred. *Krise der Rationalität: Dilemma der Soziologie: Zur kritischen Rezeption Max Webers.* Stuttgart: F. Enke, 1976.

Henrich, Dieter. *Die Einheit der Wissenschaftslehre Max Webers.* Tübingen: Mohr-Siebeck, 1952.

Honigsheim, Paul. *On Max Weber.* New York: Free Press, 1968.

Hughes, H. Stuart. *Consciousness and Society: The Reorientation of European Social Thought, 1890-1930.* New York: Vintage Books, 1958.

Jacoby, E. Georg. *Die moderne Gesellschaft im sozialwissenschaftlichen Denken von Ferdinand Tönnies.* Stuttgart: F. Enke, 1971.

Janoska-Bendl, Judit. *Methodologische Aspekte des Idealtypus: Max Weber und die Soziologie der Geschichte.* Berlin: Duncker und Humblot, 1965.

Jurkat, Ernst, ed. *Reine und angewandte Soziologie: Eine Festgabe für Ferdinand Tönnies zu seinem achtzigsten Geburstag am 26 Juli 1935.* Liepzig: H. Buske, 1936.

Kozyr-Kowalski, Stanislaw. *Max Weber a Karol Marks: Socjologia Maksa Webera jako "pozytywna krytyka materializmu historycznego."* Warsaw: K:W, 1967.

————. *Miejsce wartości w poznaniu humanistycznym w ujeciu Maksa Webera i Karola Marksa: Studium z socjologii wiedzy.* Torun: Uniwersytet im. M. Kopernika, 1968.

Lachmann, Ludwig M. *The Legacy of Max Weber: Three Essays.* London: Heinemann, 1970.

Lawrence, Peter, ed. *Georg Simmel: Sociologist and European.* London: Nelson, 1976.

Leemans, Victor. *Ferdinand Tönnies et la sociologie contemporaine en Allemagne.* Paris: F. Alcan, 1933.

Leif, J. *La Sociologie de Toennies.* Paris: P.U.F., 1946.

Levine, Donald N., ed. *Georg Simmel on Individuality and Social Forms.* Chicago: University of Chicago Press, 1971.

Lewis, John. *Max Weber and Value-Free Sociology: A Marxist Critique.* London: Beekman Publishers, 1975.

Loos, Fritz. *Zur Wert- und Rechtslehre Max Webers.* Tübingen: Mohr-Siebeck, 1970.

Löwenstein, Karl. *Max Webers staatspolitische Auffassungen in der Sicht unserer Zeit.* Frankfurt and Bonn: Athenäum, 1965.

MacRae, Donald G. *Weber.* London: Fontana/Collins, 1974.

Mamelet, Albert. *Le Relativisme philosophique chez Georg Simmel.* Paris: F. Alcan, 1914.

Marcuse, Herbert. *Negations: Essays in Critical Theory.* Boston: Beacon Press, 1969.

Mayer, Jacob. *Max Weber and German Politics*. London: Faber and Faber, 1943.

Menger, Carl. *Problems of Economics and Sociology*. Urbana: University of Illinois Press, 1963.

Miller, S. M., ed. *Max Weber: Selections*. New York: Crowell, 1963.

Mills, C. Wright, and H. Gerth, eds. *From Max Weber*. London: RKP, 1961.

Mitzman, Arthur. *The Iron Cage: An Historical Interpretation of Max Weber*. New York: Knopf, 1970.

Mommsen, Wolfgang J. *The Age of Bureaucracy: Perspectives on the Political Sociology of Max Weber*. New York: Harper and Row, 1974.

Muhlmann, W. E. *Max Weber und die rationelle Soziologie*. Tübingen: J. C. B. Mohr, 1966.

Oberschall, Anthony. *Empirical Social Research in Germany, 1848-1914*. New York: Basic Books, 1965.

Pappenheim, Fritz. *The Alienation of Modern Man: An Interpretation based on Marx and Tönnies*. New York: Monthly Review Press, 1959.

Parsons, Talcott. *The Structure of Social Action*. New York: Free Press, 1968.

Ringer, Fritz. *The Decline of the German Mandarins: The German Academic Community, 1890-1933*. Cambridge, Mass.: Harvard University Press, 1969.

Rogers, Rolf E. *Max Weber's Ideal Type Theory*. New York: Philosophical Library, 1969.

Runciman, W. G. *A Critique of Max Weber's Philosophy of Social Science*. Cambridge: Cambridge University Press, 1972.

Sahay, Arun, ed. *Max Weber and Modern Sociology*. London: RKP, 1971.

Seyfarth, C., and G. Schmidt. *Max Weber Bibliographie: Eine Dokumentation der Sekundärliteratur*. Stuttgart: F. Enke, 1977.

Simmel, Georg. *Conflict and the Web of Group-Affiliations*. Glencoe, Ill.: Free Press, 1955.

———. *Grundfragen der Soziologie*. Berlin: Walter de Gruyter, 1917.

———. *Philosophie des Geldes*. Leipzig: Duncker und Humblot, 1892.

———. *Die Probleme des Geschichtsphilosophie*. Leipzig: Duncker und Humbolt, 1892.

———. *Soziologie: Untersuchungen über die Formen der Vergesellschaftung*. Leipzig: Duncker und Humblot, 1890.

Sombart, Werner. *Nationalökonomie und Soziologie*. Jena: Fischer, 1930.

———. *Sozialismus und soziale Bewegung im 19 Jahrhundert*. Vienna: Europa-Verlag, 1966.

———. *Soziologie*. Berlin: R. Heise, 1924.

Spykman, Nicholas J. *The Social Theory of George Simmel*. Chicago: University of Chicago Press, 1925.

Stammer, Otto, ed. *Max Weber and Sociology Today*. Oxford: Blackwell, 1971.

Strauss, Leo. *Natural Right and History*. Chicago: University of Chicago Press, 1953.

Tönnies, Ferdinand. *Community and Society [Gemeinschaft und Gesellschaft]*. New York: Harper and Row, 1963.

———. *Custom: An Essay on Social Codes*. Chicago: Henry Regnery, 1971.

———. *Einführung in die Soziologie*. Stuttgart: F. Enke, 1931.

———. *Fortschritt und soziale Entwicklung*. Karlsrue: G. Braun, 1926.

——— *Kritik der öffentlichen Meinung*. Berlin: Springer, 1922.

——— *Marx: Leben und Lehre*. Jena: E. Lichtenstein, 1921.

———. *On Social Ideas and Ideologies*. New York: Harper and Row, 1974.

———. *Der Selbstmord in Schleswig-Holstein: Eine statistischsoziologische Studie*. Breslau: Hirt, 1927.

———. *Soziologische Studien und Kritiken*. 3 vols. Jena: Fischer, 1925-29.

———. *Thomas Hobbes: Leben und Lehre*. Stuttgart: Frommann, 1896.

Weber, Marianne. *Max Weber: A Biography*. New York: Wiley, 1975.

Weber, Max. *Economy and Society: An Outline of Interpretative Sociology*. 3 vols. New York: Bedminster Press, 1968.

——. *Gesammelte Aufsätze zur Religionssoziologie.* 3 vols. Tübingen: J. C. B. Mohr, 1920-21.

——. *Gesammelte Aufsätze zur Sozial- und Wirtschaftsgeschichte.* Tübingen: J. C. B. Mohr, 1924.

——. *Gesammelte Aufsätze zur Wissenschaftslehre.* Tübingen: J. C. B. Mohr, 1922.

——. *Gesammelte politische Schriften.* Munich: Drei Masken Verlag, 1921.

——. *The Methodology of the Social Science.* New York: Free Press, 1949.

——. *The Protestant Ethic and the Spirit of Capitalism.* London: Unwin University Books, 1965.

——. *Roscher and Knies: The Logical Problems of Historical Economics.* New York: Free Press, 1975.

Weinreich, M. *Max Weber: L'Homme et le savant.* Paris: J. Vrin, 1938.

Weiss, Johannes. *Max Webers Grundlagen der Soziologie.* Munich: Verlag Documentation, 1975.

Weyembergh, M. *Le Volontarisme rationnel de Max Weber.* Brussels: Académie Royal de Belgique, 1972.

Wiese, Leopold von. *Allgemeine Soziologie.* 2 vols. Munich: Duncker und Humblot, 1924-29.

Williame, R. *Les Fondements phénomenologique de la sociologie compréhensive: Alred Schutz et Max Weber.* The Hague: N. Nijhoff, 1973.

Wrong, Dennis, ed. *Max Weber.* Englewood Cliffs, N.J.: Prentice-Hall, 1970.

CHAPTER 13.
HISTORICAL MATERIALISM AFTER MARX VERSUS SOCIOLOGY

Adler, Max. *Kausalität und Teleologie im Streite um die Wissenschaft.* Vienna: Brand, 1904.

——. *Lehrbuch der materialistischen Geschichtsauffasung.* Berlin: E. Laubsch, 1930.

——. *Marxistische Probleme.* Stuttgart: Dietz, 1913.

——. *Natur und Gesellschaft.* Vienna: Europa-Verlag, 1964.

Adorno, Theodor Wiesengrund, and Max Horkheimer. *Dialectic of Enlightenment.* London: Allen Lane, 1972.

——. *Gesellschaftstheorie und Kulturkritik.* Frankfurt: Suhrkamp, 1975.

Althusser, Louis. *Lenin and Philosophy and Other Essays.* New York: Monthly Review Press, 1972.

Anderson, Perry. *Considerations on Western Marxism.* London: NLB, 1976.

Baron, Samuel H. *Plekhanov: The Father of Russian Marxism.* Stanford: Stanford University Press, 1963.

Bauer, Otto. *Die Nazionalitätfrage und die Sozialdemokratie.* Vienna: Brand, 1907.

Bernstein, Eduard. *Evolutionary Socialism: A Criticism and Affirmation.* New York: Schocken Books, 1963.

Bessonov, B. N.; I. S. Narskij; and M. V. Jakovlew, eds. *Socjalnaja filozofia frankfurtskoj skoly.* Moscow: Progress, 1975.

Bockarev, N. I. *V. I. Lenin i burzuaznaja socjologia v Rossii.* Moscow: Izdatelstvo Moskovskovo Universiteta, 1973.

Bottomore, Tom, ed. *Austro-Marxism.* New York: Oxford University Press, 1978.

Bottomore, Tom. *Marxist Sociology.* London: Macmillan, 1975.

——, ed. *Austro-Marxism.* New York: Oxford University Press, 1978.

Bourdet, Y. *Otto Bauer et la révolution.* Paris: Maspero, 1968.

Bukharin, N. *Historical Materialism: A System of Sociology.* Ann Arbor: University of Michigan Press, 1969.

Cagin, B. A., *Ocerk istorii socjologiceskoj mysli w SSSR, 1917-1969.* Leningrad: "Nauka," 1971.

————. *Razrabotka G. V. Plekhanovym obscesocjologiceskoj teorii marksizma.* Leningrad: "Nauka," 1977.

Cagin, B. A., and V. I. Klusin. *Borba za istoriceskij materialism v SSSR v 20- gody.* Leningrad: "Nauka," 1975.

Cammet, John M. *Antonio Gramsci and the Origins of Italian Communism.* Stanford: Stanford University Press, 1967.

Choron, Jacques, *La Doctrine bolcheviste, Philosophie, Economie politique, Sociologie D'après les oeuvres de Lénine.* Paris: M. Rivière, 1935.

Cohen, Alain J. *Marcuse: Le Scénario freudo-marxien.* Paris: Ed. Universitaires, 1974.

Cole, G. D. H. *A History of Socialist Thought.* Vol. 3. London: Macmillan, 1956.

Colletti, Lucio. *From Rousseau to Lenin: Studies in Ideology and Society.* London: NLB, 1976.

Connerton, Paul, ed. *Critical Sociology: Selected Readings.* Harmondsworth: Penguin Books, 1976.

Conquest, Robert. *Lenin.* London: Fontana/Collins, 1972.

Davidson, Alastair. *Antonio Gramsci: Towards an Intellectual Biography.* London: Merlin Press, 1972.

Drachkovitch, Milorad M., ed. *Marxism in the Modern World.* Stanford: Stanford University Press, 1965.

Eissenstat, Bernard W., ed. *Lenin and Leninism: State, Law and Society.* Lexington, Mass.: Heath, 1971.

Fiori, Giuseppe. *Antonio Gramsci.* London: NLB, 1970.

Frankfurt Institute of Social Research. *Aspects of Sociology.* London: Heinemann, 1972.

Fröhlich, Paul. *Rosa Luxemburg: Sa Vie et son oeuvre.* Paris: Maspero, 1965.

Fromm, Erich. *The Fear of Freedom.* London: RKP, 1960.

Galasso, Giuseppe. *Croce, Gramsci e eltri storici.* Milan: A Montadori, 1969.

Gay, Peter. *The Dilemma of Democratic Socialism: Eduard Bernstein's Challenge to Marx.* New York: Collier Books, 1962.

Geras, Norman. *The Legacy of Rosa Luxemburg.* London: NLB, 1976.

Goldmann, Lucien. *Recherches dialectiques.* Paris: Gallimard, 1959.

Gramsci, Antonio. *The Modern Prince and Other Writings.* London: Lawrence and Wishart, 1957.

Haimson, Leopold. *The Russian Marxists and the Origins of Bolshevism.* Cambridge, Mass.: Harvard University Press, 1955.

Heiseler, Johannes Heinrich von, et al., eds. *Die "Frankfurter Schule" im Lichte des Marxismus: Zur Kritik der Philosophie und Soziologie von Horkheimer, Adorno, Marcuse, Habermas.* Frankfurt: Verlag Marxistische Blätter, 1970.

Haveši, M. A. *Iz istorii kiritiki filosofskich dogm II Internacjonala.* Moscow: "Nauka," 1977.

Hochfeld, Julian. *Studia o marksowskiej teorii spoleczeństwa.* Warsaw: PWN, 1963.

Holda-Róziewicz, Henryka. *Ludwik Krzywicki jako teoretyk spoleczeństw pierwotnych.* Wroclaw: Zaklad Narodowy im. Ossolińskich, 1976.

Hook, Sidney, ed. *Marx and the Marxists.* Princeton: Van Nostrand, 1955.

Horkheimer, Max. *Critical Theory: Selected Essays.* New York: Herder and Herder, 1972.

Howard, Dick, ed. *Selected Writings of Rosa Luxemburg.* New York: Monthly Review Press, 1971.

Howard, Dick, and Karl E. Klave. *The Unknown Dimension: European Marxism Since Lenin.* New York: Basic Books, 1972.

Jay, Martin. *The Dialectical Imagination: A History of the Frankfurt School and the Institute of Social Research, 1923-1950.* Boston: Little, Brown, 1973.

Kautsky, Karl. *Materialistische Geschichtsauffassung.* Berlin: Dietz, 1929.

Kern, Walter. *Hegel, Marx und die Frankfurter Schule.* Munich: Herder, 1970.

Kolakowski, Leszek. *Główne nurty marksizmu: Powstanie—rozwój—rozklad.* Vols. 2-3. Paris: Instytut Literacki, 1977-78.

Korsch, Karl. *Marxism and Philosophy.* New York: Modern Reader, 1970.

———. *Three Essays on Marxism.* New York: Modern Reader, 1971.

Kowalik, Tadeusz. *Krzywicki.* Warsaw: WP, 1965.

Krzeczkowski, Konstanty, et. al. *Ludwik Krzywicki: Praca zbiorowa poświecona jego zyciu i twórczości.* Warsaw: Instytut Gospodarstwa Spolecznego, 1938.

Krzemień-Ojak, Slaw. *Benedetto Croce i marksizm.* Warsaw: PWN, 1975.

Krzywicki, Ludwik. *Wybór pism.* Warsaw: PWN, 1978.

Lefebvre, Henri. *La pensée de Lenine.* Paris: Editions Bordas, 1957.

Lenin, V. I. *Materialism and Empirio-Criticism: Critical Comments on a Reactionary Philosophy.* Moscow: Foreign Languages Publishing House, 1952.

———. *Selected Works in Two Volumes.* Moscow: Foreign Languages Publishing House, 1952.

Lichtheim, George. *From Marx to Hegel and Other Essays.* New York: Herder and Herder, 1971.

———. *Lukács.* London: Fontana/Collins, 1970.

Lipshires, Sidney. *Herbert Marcuse: From Marx to Freud and Beyond.* Cambridge, Mass.: Schenkman, 1974.

Lowy, Michel. *L'Evolution politique de Lukács, 1909-1929: Contribution à une sociologie de l'intelligentsia révolutionnaire.* Lille: Université de Lille, 1975.

Lukács, Georg. *History and Class Consciousness: Studies in Marxist Dialectics.* Cambridge, Mass.: MIT Press, 1972.

———. *Lenin: A Study on the Unity of His Thought.* Cambridge, Mass.: MIT Press, 1971.

———. *Political Writings, 1919-1929.* London: NLB, 1972.

McInnes, Neil. *The Western Marxists.* London: Alcove Press, 1972.

Mannheim, Karl. *Diagnosis of Our Time.* New York: Oxford University Press, 1944.

———. *Essays on Sociology and Sociology Psychology.* London: RKP, 1953.

———. *Essays on the Sociology of Culture.* London: RKP, 1956.

———. *Essays on the Sociology of Knowledge.* London: RKP, 1952.

———. *Ideology and Utopia: An Introduction to the Sociology of Knowledge.* London: RKP, 1954.

———. *Man and Society in an Age of Reconstruction.* New York: Harcourt, Brace, 1940.

Marcuse, Herbert. *Eros and Civilisation: A Philosophical Inquiry into Freud.* London: Sphere, 1969.

———. *Negations: Essays in Critical Theory.* Boston: Beacon Press, 1968.

———. *Soviet Marxism: A Critical Analysis.* Harmondsworth: Penguin Books, 1971.

Mészáros, Istvan. *Lukács' Concept of Dialectics with Biography, Bibliography and Documents.* London: Merlin Press, 1972.

Mills, C. Wright. *The Marxists.* New York: Dell, 1962.

Portelli, Hughes. *Gramsci et le bloc historique.* Paris: P.U.F., 1972.

Rainko, Stanislaw. *Marksizm i jego krytycy.* Warsaw: KiW, 1976.

Riechers, Christian. *Antonio Gramsci: Marxismus in Italien.* Frankfurt, 1970.

Rozental, M. M., ed. *Lenin kak filozof.* Moscow: Izdatelstvo Politiceskoj Literatury, 1969.

Rudziński, Roman. *Ideal moralny a proces dziejowy w marksizmie i neokantyzmie.* Warsaw: KiW, 1975.

Schaff, Adam. *Historia i prawda.* Warsaw: KiW, 1970.

Schmidt, Alfred. *Die kritische Theorie als Geschichtsphilosophie.* Munich: C. Hauser, 1976.

Schroyer, Trent. *The Critique of Domination: The Origins and Development of Critical Theory.* New York: Braziller, 1973.

Slater, Phil. *Origin and Significance of the Frankfurt School: A Marxist Perspective.* London: RKP, 1977.

Spiewak, Pawel. *Gramsci.* Warsaw: WP, 1977.

Topolski, Jerzy. *Marksizm i historia.* Warsaw: PIW, 1977.

Tucker, Robert C., ed. *Stalinism: Essays in Historical Interpretation.* New York: Norton, 1977.

Waldenberg, Marek. *Kautsky.* Warsaw: WP, 1976.

Wellmer, Albrecht. *Critical Theory of Society.* New York: Herder and Herder, 1971.

Wolff, Kurt H., ed. *From Karl Mannheim.* New York: Oxford University Press, 1971.

Zitta, Victor. *Georg Lucács' Marxism: Alienation, Dialectics, Revolution: A Study in Utopia and Ideology.* The Hague: M. Nijhoff, 1964.

CHAPTER 14.
SOCIAL PRAGMATISM: DEWEY, COOLEY, THOMAS, AND MEAD

Baldwin, J. M. *The Individual and Society, or Psychology and Sociology.* New York: Macmillan, 1911.

―――. *Mental Development in the Child and the Race.* New York: Macmillan, 1895.

―――. *Social and Ethical Interpretations in Mental Development.* New York: Macmillan, 1897.

Bernard, L. L. *Instincts: A Study in Social Psychology.* New York, 1924.

Bierstedt, Robert, ed. *Florian Znaniecki on Humanistic Sociology.* Chicago: University of Chicago Press, 1969.

Blewett, John, ed. *John Dewey: His Thought and Influence.* New York: Fordham University Press, 1960.

Blumer, H. *An Appraisal of Thomas and Znaniecki's "The Polish Peasant in Europe and America."* New York: Social Science Research Council, 1939.

―――. "Social Psychology." In E. P. Schmidt, ed., *Man and Society: A Substantive Introduction to the Social Sciences.* New York: Prentice-Hall, 1937.

―――. *Symbolic Interactionism: Perspectives and Method.* Englewood Cliffs, N.J.: Prentice-Hall, 1969.

Boskoff, Alvin. *Theory in American Sociology.* New York: Crowell, 1969.

Commager, H. S. *The American Mind: An Interpretation of American Thought and Character Since 1880's.* New Haven: Yale University Press, 1950.

Cooley, C. H. *Human Nature and Social Order.* New York: Scribner's, 1902.

―――. *Life of the Student: Roadside Notes on Human Nature, Society and Letters.* New York: Knopf, 1927.

―――. *Social Organization.* New York: Scribner's, 1909.

―――. *Social Process.* Carbondale: Southern Illinois University Press, 1966.

―――. *Sociological Theory and Practice.* Edited by R. C. Angell. New York: Holt, 1930.

Corti, W. R. *The Philosophy of George Herbert Mead.* Wintethur, Switzerland: Amrisweiler Bücherei. 1973.

Dewey, J. *Democracy and Education: An Introduction to the Philosophy of Education.* New York: Macmillan, 1948.

―――. *Experience and Nature.* London: Allen and Unwin, 1929.

―――. *Human Nature and Conduct: An Introduction to Social Psychology.* New York: Modern Library, 1930.

―――. *The Influence of Darwin on Philosophy and Other Essays in Contemporary Thought.* New York: Holt, 1910.

―――. *Logic: The Theory and Inquiry.* New York: Holt, 1938.

―――. *Philosophy and Civilization.* New York: Dover, 1958.

―――. *The Philosophy of John Dewey.* Edited by Paul A. Shilpp. New York: Tudor, 1951.

―――. *Philosophy, Psychology and Social Practice.* New York: Putnam, 1963.

―――. *Psychology.* New York: Harper and Brothers, 1887.

―――. *Reconstruction in Philosophy.* Boston: Beacon Press, 1957.

Duncan, H. D. *Symbols and Social Theory.* New York: Oxford University Press, 1969.

Faris, E. *Nature of Human Nature.* New York: McGraw-Hill, 1937.

Hansen, D. A. *An Invitation to Critical Sociology.* New York: Free Press, 1976.

Hofstadter, R. *Social Darwinism in American Thought.* Boston: Beacon Press, 1959.

James W. *The Principles of Psychology.* 2 vols. New York: Holt, 1890.

Jandy, Edward C. *Charles Horton Cooley: His Life and His Social Theory.* New York: Octagon, 1969.

Karpf, F. B. *American Social Psychology: Its Origins, Development, and European Background.* New York: McGraw-Hill, 1932.

Lee, G. C. *G. H. Mead: Philosopher of the Social Individual.* New York: King's Crown Press, 1945.

Manis, J. G., and B. N. Meltzer, eds. *Symbolic Interaction: A Reader in Social Psychology.* 2d ed. Boston: Allyn and Bacon, 1972.

Mead, G. H. *G. H. Mead: Essays on His Social Philosophy.* Edited by J. W. Petras. New York: Teachers College, 1968.

———. *Mind, Self and Society from the Standpoint of a Social Behaviorist.* Chicago: University of Chicago Press, 1972.

———. *Movements of Thought in the Nineteenth Century.* Chicago: University of Chicago Press, 1936.

———. *On Social Psychology.* Edited by A. Strauss. Chicago: University of Chicago Press, 1964.

———. *The Philosophy of the Act.* Chicago: University of Chicago Press, 1938.

———. *The Philosophy of the Present.* Chicago: Open Court Publishing, 1934.

———. *Selected Writings.* Edited by A. Reck. Indianapolis: Bobbs-Merrill, 1964.

Meltzer, B. N.; J. W. Petras; and L. T. Reynolds. *Symbolic Interactionism: Genesis, Varieties and Criticism.* London: RKP, 1975.

Miller, D. L. *G. H. Mead: Self, Language and the World.* Austin: University of Texas Press, 1973.

Mills, C. W. *Sociology and Pragmatism: The Higher Learning in America.* New York: Oxford University Press, 1964.

Natanson, M. *The Social Dynamics of G. H. Mead.* Washington, D.C.: Public Affairs Press, 1956.

Noble, D. W. *The Paradox of Progressive Thought.* Minneapolis: University of Minnesota Press, 1958.

Pfuetze, P. E. *Self, Society, Existence.* New York: Harper and Brothers, 1954.

Quandt, Jean B. *From the Small Town to the Great Community.* New Brunswick, N.J.: Rutgers University Press, 1970.

Reck, A. J. *Recent American Philosophers: Studies of Ten Representative Thinkers.* New York: Pantheon Books, 1964.

Reiss, Albert J., Jr., ed. *Cooley and Social Analysis.* Ann Arbor: University of Michigan Press, 1968.

Rucker, D. *The Chicago Pragmatists.* Minneapolis: University of Minnesota Press, 1969.

Sewny, V. D. *The Social Theory of J. M. Baldwin.* New York: Kelley, 1945.

Stone, G. P., and H. A. Farberman, eds. *Social Psychology through Symbolic Interaction.* Waltham, Mass.: Xerox College Publishing, 1970.

Thayer, H. S. *Meaning and Action: A Critical History of Pragmatism.* Indianapolis: Bobbs-Merrill, 1968.

Thomas, W. I., (with D. S. Thomas). *The Child in America: Behavior Problems and Programs.* New York: Knopf, 1928.

———. *On Social Organization and Social Personality.* Edited and with an introduction by M. Janowitz. Chicago: University of Chicago Press, 1966.

——— (with F. Znaniecki). *The Polish Peasant in Europe and America.* 5 vols. Boston: Richard Bedger, 1918-20.

————. *Primitive Behavior. An Introduction to the Social Sciences.* New York: McGraw-Hill, 1937.

————. *Sex and Society: Studies in the Social Psychology of Sex.* Chicago: University of Chicago Press, 1907.

————. *Social Behavior and Personality.* Edited by E. H. Volkart. New York: Social Science Research Council, 1951.

————. *Source Book for Social Origins: Ethnological Materials, Psychological Standpoint, Classified and Annotated Bibliography for the Interpretation of Savage Society.* Chicago: University of Chicago Press, 1909.

————. *The Unadjusted Girl.* Boston: Little, Brown, 1923.

Victoroff, D. *G. H. Mead: Sociologue et philosophe.* Paris: P.U.F., 1953.

White, Morton. *Pragmatism and the American Mind.* New York: Oxford University Press, 1973.

————. *Science and Sentiment in America.* New York: Oxford University Press, 1972.

————. *Social Thought in America: The Revolt against Formalism.* Boston: Beacon Press, 1963.

Young, K. "Contributions of W. I. Thomas to Sociology," *Sociology and Social Research* 47 (1962-63).

CHAPTER 15.

THEORETICAL HORIZONS OF AMERICAN DESCRIPTIVE SOCIOLOGY

Abrams, Mark. *Social Surveys and Social Action.* London: Heinemann, 1951.

Alihan, Milla A. *Social Ecology: A Critical Analysis.* New York: Columbia University Press, 1938.

Arensberg, C. M., and S. T. Kimball. *Culture and Community.* New York: Harcourt, Brace, 1965.

Bernard, J. *The Sociology of Community.* Glenview, Ill., : Scott, Foresman, 1973.

Burgess, E. W., and Donald J. Bogue, eds. *Contributions to Urban Sociology.* Chicago: University of Chicago Press, 1964.

Carey, James T. *Sociology and Public Affairs: The Chicago School.* Beverly Hills, Calif.: Sage Publications, 1976.

Easthope, Gary. *History of Social Research Methods.* London: Longman, 1974.

Faris, Robert E. L. *Chicago Sociology, 1920-1932.* Chicago: University of Chicago Press, 1967.

Gee, Wilson, ed. *Research in the Social Sciences: Its Fundamental Methods and Objectives.* New York: Macmillan, 1929.

Gordon, Milton M. *Social Class in American Sociology.* New York: McGraw-Hill, 1950.

Gottschalk, L.; C. Kluckhohn; and R. Angell. *The Use of Personal Documents in History, Anthropology and Sociology.* New York: Social Science Research Council, 1951.

Gusfield, J. R. *Community: A Critical Response.* Oxford: Blackwell, 1975.

Hawley, Amos H., ed. *R. D. McKenzie on Human Ecology.* Chicago: University of Chicago Press, 1968.

Herpin, Nicolas. *Les Sociologues américains et le siècle.* Paris: P.U.F., 1973.

Hillery, George A., Jr. "Definitions of Community: Areas of Agreement." *Rural Sociology* 20(1955): 111-19.

Jahoda, Marie; Paul F. Lazarsfeld; and Hans Zeisel. *Marientahl: The Sociography of an Unemployed Community.* Chicago: Aldine-Atherton, 1972.

Janickij, O. N. *Urbanizacja i socjalnyje protivorecija kapitalizma.* Moscow: "Nauka," 1975.

König, René. *The Community.* New York: Schocken Books, 1968.

Lynd, Robert S. *Knowledge for What? The Place of Social Science in American Culture.* Princeton: Princeton University Press, 1939.

Lynd, Robert S., and Helen M. Lynd. *Middletown: A Study in Contemporary American Culture.* New York: Harcourt, Brace, 1929.

―――. *Middletown in Transition: A Study in Cultural Conflict.* New York: Harcourt, Brace, 1937.

Martindale, Don. *American Social Structure: Historical Antecedents and Contemporary Analysis.* New York: Appleton, 1960.

Mayo, Elton. *The Human Problems of Industrial Civilization.* Cambridge, Mass.: Harvard University Press, 1946.

Minar, D. W., and S. Greer, eds. *The Concept of Community: Readings with Interpretations.* Chicago: Aldine, 1969.

Nelson, Lowry. *Rural Sociology: Its Origin and Growth in the United States.* Minneapolis: University of Minnesota Press, 1969.

Nisbet, Robert A. *The Quest for Community.* London: Oxford University Press, 1953.

Palmer, Vivien M. *Field Studies in Sociology: A Student Manual.* Chicago: University of Chicago Press, 1928.

Park Robert E. *The Collected Papers.* Edited by Everett C. Hughes et al. 3 vols. Glencoe, Ill.: Free Press, 1950-55.

Park, Robert E., and Ernest W. Burgess. *Introduction to the Science of Sociology.* Chicago: University of Chicago Press, 1921.

Park, Robert E., Ernest W. Burgess, and Roderick D. McKenzie. *The City.* Chicago: University of Chicago Press, 1925.

Poplin, Dennis E. *Communities: A Survey of Theories and Methods of Research.* New York: Macmillan, 1972.

Redfield, Robert. *The Little Community: Viewpoints for the Study of a Human Whole.* Chicago: University of Chicago Press, 1955.

Reiss, Albert, ed. *Louis Wirth on Cities and Social Life.* Chicago: University of Chicago Press, 1964.

Shils, Edward, *The Present State of American Sociology.* Glencoe, Ill.: Free Press, 1948.

Short, James F., Jr., ed. *The Social Fabric of the Metropolis: Contributions of the Chicago School of Urban Sociology.* Chicago: University of Chicago Press, 1971.

Smith, T. V., and L. D. White, eds. *Chicago: An Experiment in Social Science Research.* Chicago: University of Chicago Press, 1929.

Stein, M. R. *The Eclipse of Community: An Interpretation of American Studies.* Princeton: Princeton University Press, 1960.

Steward, Julian H. *Area Research: Theory and Practice.* Social Science Research Council, Bulletin no. 63. New York: Social Science Research Council, 1950.

Turner, Ralph H., ed. *Robert E. Park on Social Control and Collective Behavior.* Chicago: University of Chicago Press, 1967.

Vidich, A. J.; J. Bensman; and M. R. Stein, eds. *Reflections on Community Studies.* New York: Wiley, 1964.

Warner, W. L., and P. S. Lunt. *The Social Life of Modern Community (Yankee City Series I).* New Haven: Yale University Press, 1941.

―――. *The Status System of Modern Community (Yankee City Series II).* New Haven: Yale University Press, 1942.

Warner, W. L., and L. Srole. *The Social System of American Ethnic Group (Yankee City Series III).* New Haven: Yale University Press, 1945.

―――, and J. O. Low *The Social System of Modern Factory (Yankee City Series IV).* New Haven: Yale University Press, 1947.

―――. *The Living and the Dead (Yankee City Series V).* New Haven: Yale University Press, 1959.

Warren, Roland L. *The Community in America.* 2d ed. Chicago: Rand McNally, 1972.

White, L. D., ed. *The State of Social Research.* Chicago: University of Chicago Press, 1956.

Wilson, R. J. *In Quest of Community: Social Philosophy in the United States, 1860-1920.* New York: Oxford University Press, 1970.

Wirth, L., ed. *Eleven Twenty Six: A Decade of Social Science Research.* Chicago: University of Chicago Press, 1940.

CHAPTER 16.
CULTURE, SOCIETY, AND PERSONALITY:
THE NEW VISTAS OF ANTHROPOLOGY

Bauman, Zygmunt. *Kultura i spoleczeństwo: Preliminaria.* Warsaw: PWN, 1966.

Benedict, Ruth. *The Chrysanthemum and the Sword.* Boston: Houghton Mifflin, 1946.

———. *Patterns of Culture.* New York: Mentor Books, 1959.

Birnbach, Martin. *Neo-Freudian Social Philosophy.* Stanford: Stanford University Press, 1961.

Boas, Franz. *Anthropology and Modern Life.* New York: Norton, 1936.

———. *The Mind of Primitive Man.* New York: Macmillan, 1911.

———. *Primitive Art.* Cambridge, Mass.: Harvard University Press, 1927.

———. *Race, Language and Culture.* New York: Macmillan, 1940.

Brew, J. O., ed. *One Hundred Years of Anthropology.* Cambridge, Mass.: Harvard University Press, 1968.

Bromlej, J. W., ed. *Koncepcii zarubeznoj etnologii: Kriticeskije etiudy.* Moscow: "Nauka," 1976.

Duvignaud, Jean. *Le Langage perdu: Essai sur la différence anthropologique.* Paris: P.U.F., 1973.

Eggan, Fred, ed. *Social Anthropology of North American Tribes.* Chicago: University of Chicago Press, 1955.

Epstein, A. L., ed. *The Craft of Social Anthropology.* London: Tavistock, 1967.

Evans-Pritchard, E. E. *Essays in Social Anthropology.* London: RKP, 1962.

———. *The Nuer.* Oxford: Clarendon Press, 1940.

———. *Social Anthropology.* London: RKP, 1972.

———. *Theories of Primitive Religion.* Oxford: Clarendon Press, 1965.

———. *Witchcraft, Oracles and Magic among the Azande.* Oxford: Clarendon Press, 1937.

Firth, Raymond, ed. *Man and Culture: An Evaluation of the Work of Bronislaw Malinowski.* London: RKP, 1957.

Gluckman, Max. *The Sociological Theories of Malinowski.* In *Rhodes-Livingstone Papers.* No. 16. London: Oxford University Press, 1949.

Goldschmidt, Walter, ed. *The Anthropology of Franz Boas: Essays on the Centennial of His Birth. Memoirs of the American Anthropological Association,* no. 89. 1959.

Hatch, Elvin. *Theories of Man and Culture.* New York: Columbia University Press, 1973.

Herskovits, Melville. *Franz Boas: The Science of Man in the Making.* New York: Scribner's, 1953.

Inkeles, Alex, and Daniel J. Levinson. "National Character: A Study of Modal Personality and Sociocultural Systems." In Gardner Lindzey, ed., *Handbook of Social Psychology.* Reading, Mass.: Addison-Wesley, 1954.

Kaplan, David, and Robert A. Manners. *Culture Theory.* Englewood Cliffs, N.J.: Prentice-Hall, 1972.

Kardiner, Abram, ed. *The Individual and His Society.* New York: Columbia University Press, 1939.

Kardiner, Abram, with the collaboration of Ralph Linton, Cora Du Bois, and James West. *The Psychological Frontiers of Society.* New York: Columbia University Press, 1945.

Kroeber, Alfred L. *An Anthropologist Looks at History.* Berkeley and Los Angeles: University of California Press, 1963.

————. *Anthropology.* Chicago: University of Chicago Press, 1953.

———— *Configurations of Culture Growth.* Berkeley and Los Angeles: University of California Press, 1944.

————. *The Nature of Culture.* Chicago: University of Chicago Press, 1952.

————. *Style and Civilization.* Ithaca, N.Y.: Cornell University Press, 1957.

Kuper, Adam. *Anthropologists and Anthropology: The British School, 1922-72.* Harmondsworth: Penguin Books, 1975.

————, ed. *The Social Anthropology of Radcliffe-Brown.* London: RKP, 1977.

Leach, Edmund R. *Rethinking Anthropology.* London: Athalone Press, 1966.

Lévi-Strauss, C. *Anthropologie structurale.* Paris: Plon, 1958.

Lewis, I. *Social Anthropology in Perspective.* Harmondsworth: Penguin Books, 1976.

Linton, A., and C. Wagley. *Ralph Linton.* New York: Columbia University Press, 1971.

Linton, Ralph. *The Cultural Background of Personality.* New York: Appleton-Century, 1945.

————. *The Study of Man: An Introduction.* New York: Appleton-Century, 1936.

————. *The Tree of Culture.* New York: Knopf, 1955.

Malinowski, Bronislaw. *Argonauts of the Western Pacific.* New York: Dutton, 1922.

————. *Crime and Custome in Savage Society.* London: Kegan Paul, Trench, Trubner, 1926.

————. *A Diary in the Strict Sense of the Term.* New York: Harcourt, Brace, 1967.

————. *The Dynamics of Culture Change: An Inquiry into Race Relations in Africa.* New Haven: Yale University Press, 1945.

————. *Freedom and Civilization.* London: Allen and Unwin, 1947.

————. *Magic, Science and Religion and Other Essays.* Garden City, N.Y.: Anchor Books, 1948.

————. *A Scientific Theory of Culture and Other Essays.* New York: Galaxy Books, 1960.

————. *Sex and Repression in Savage Society.* London: RKP, 1927.

————. *Sex, Culture and Myth.* New York: Harcourt, Brace, 1962.

————. *The Sexual Life of Savages in Northwestern Melanesia.* London: G. Routledge, 1929.

Manners, Robert A., and David Kaplan, eds. *Theory in Anthropology: A Sourcebook.* Chicago: Aldine-Atherton, 1968.

Mead, Margaret. *Ruth Benedict.* New York: Columbia University Press, 1974.

————, *An Anthropologist at Work: Writings of Ruth Benedict.* Boston: Houghton Mifflin, 1959.

Murphy, Robert F. *Robert H. Lowie.* New York: Columbia University Press, 1972.

Paluch, Andrzej K. *Konflikt, modernizacja i zmiana społeczna: Analiza i krytyka teorii funkcjonalnej.* Warsaw: PWN, 1976.

Panoff, Michel. *Malinowski.* Paris: Payot, 1972.

Radcliffe-Brown, A. R. *The Andaman Islanders.* Cambridge: Cambridge University Press, 1922.

————. *Method in Social Anthropology.* University of Chicago Press, 1958.

————. *A Natural Science of Society.* New York: Free Press, 1948.

————. *Structure and Function in Primitive Society.* London: Oxford University Press, 1952.

Róheim, Géza. *Psychoanalysis and Anthropology.* New York: International Universities Press, 1950.

Sahlins, Marshall D., and Elman R. Service, eds. *Evolution and Culture.* Ann Arbor: University of Michigan Press, 1960.

Sapir, Edward. *Culture, Language and Personality. Selected Essays.* Berkeley and Los Angeles: University of California Press, 1970.

————. *Selected Writings of Edward Sapir in Language, Culture and Personality.* Berkeley and Los Angeles: University of California Press, 1949.

Sargent, S. S., and M. W. Smith, eds. *Culture and Personality.* New York: Viking Fund, 1949.

Schneider, Louis, and Charles Bonjean, eds. *The Idea of Culture in the Social Science.* Cambridge: Cambridge University Press, 1973.

Singer, Milton. "A Survey of Culture and Personality Theory and Research." In Bert Kaplan, ed., *Studying Personality Cross-Culturally*. Evanston, Ill.: Row, Peterson, 1961.

Stern, Bernhard J. *Historical Sociology*. New York: Citadel Press, 1959.

Steward, Julian H. *Alfred Kroeber*. New York: Columbia University Press, 1973.

———. *Theory of Culture Change: The Methodology of Multilinear Evolution*. Urbana: University of Illinois Press, 1955.

Stocking, George W., Jr. *Race, Culture, and Evolution: Essays in the History of Anthropology*. New York: Free Press, 1968.

———, ed. *The Shaping of American Anthropology*. New York: Basic Books, 1974.

Veselkin, E. A. *Krizis britanskoj socjalnoj antropologii*. Moscow: "Nauka," 1977.

Waligórski, Andrzej. *Antropologiczna koncepcja czlowieka*. Warsaw: PWN, 1973.

White, Leslie A. *The Evolution of Culture: The Development of Civilization to the Fall of Rome*. New York: McGraw-Hill, 1959.

———. *The Science of Culture: A Study of Man and Civilization*. New York: Grove Press, 1949.

CHAPTER 17.
SOCIOLOGICAL FUNCTIONALISM AND ITS CRITICS

Abrahamson, Mark. *Functionalism*. Englewood Cliffs, N.J.: Prentice-Hall, 1978.

Atkinson, Dick. *Orthodox Consensus and Radical Alternative: A Study in Sociological Theory*. London: Heinemann, 1971.

Bauman, Zygmunt. *Wizje ludzkiego świata*. Warsaw: KiW, 1964.

Black, Max, ed. *The Social Theories of Talcott Parsons*. Englewood Cliffs, N.J.: Prentice-Hall, 1961.

Blau, Peter. *Exchange and Power in Social Life*. New York: Wiley, 1967.

Bourricaud, F., *L'individualisme institutionnel. Essai sur la sociologie de T. Parsons*. Paris: P.U.F., 1977.

Buckley, W. *Sociology and Modern Systems Theory*. Englewood Cliffs, N.J.: Prentice-Hall, 1967.

Chadwick-Jones, J. K. *Social Exchange Theory: Its Structure and Influence in Social Psychology*. New York: Academic Press, 1976.

Cohen, Percy S. *Modern Social Theory*. New York: Basic Books, 1968.

Coser, Lewis. *The Functions of Social Conflict*. New York: Free Press, 1964.

Dahrendorf, Ralf. *Class and Conflict in Industrial Society*. Stanford: Stanford University Press, 1959.

———. *Essays in the Theory of Society*. Stanford: Stanford University Press, 1968.

Demerath, Neil S., and Richard A. Peterson, eds. *System, Change and Conflict*. New York: Free Press, 1967.

Douglas, Jack, ed. *Understanding Everyday Life*. Chicago: Aldine, 1971.

Eteh, Peter. *Social Exchange Theory*. London: Heinemann, 1974.

Filmer, Paul, et al. *New Directions in Sociological Theory*. London: Collier-Macmillan, 1973.

Friedrichs, Robert W. *A Sociology of Sociology*. New York: Free Press, 1972.

Garfinkel, Harold. *Studies in Ethnomethodology*. Englewood Cliffs, N.J.: Prentice-Hall, 1976.

Giddens, Anthony. *New Rules of Sociological Method*. London: Hutchinson, 1976.

Gouldner, Alvin W. *The Coming Crisis of Western Sociology*. New York: Equinox Books, 1971.

Homans, George C. *Social Behavior: Its Elementary Forms*. New York: Harcourt, Brace, 1961.

Isajiw, Wsewolod W. *Causation and Functionalism in Sociology*. New York: Schocken Books, 1968.

Johnson, Benton. *Functionalism in Modern Sociology*. Morristown, N.J.: General Learning Press, 1975.

Levy, Marion J. *The Structure of Society*. Chicago: University of Chicago Press, 1952.

Loomis, Charles P. *Modern Social Theories: Selected American Writers*. Princeton: Van Nostrand, 1961.

Martindale, Don. *Prominent Sociologists Since World War II*. Columbus, Ohio: Merrill, 1975.

Menzies, Ken. *Talcott Parsons and the Social Image of Man*. London: RKP, 1977.

Merton, Robert K. *Social Theory and Social Structure*. Glencoe, Ill.: Free Press, 1957.

Mills, C. Wright. *The Marxists*. New York: Dell, 1962.

————. *Power, Politics, and People: The Collected Essays of C. Wright Mills*. New York: Oxford University Press, 1963.

————. *The Sociological Imagination*. New York: Oxford University Press, 1959.

Mitchell, William. *Sociological Analysis and Politics: The Theories of Talcott Parsons*. Englewood Cliffs, N.J.: Prentice-hall, 1967.

Mulkay, M. J. *Functionalism, Exchange and Theoretical Strategy*. London: RKP, 1975.

Mullins, Nicholas C. *Theories and Theory Groups In Contemporary American Sociology*. New York: Harper and Row, 1973.

Parsons, Talcott. *Essays in Sociological Theory*. Rev. ed. New York: Free Press, 1964.

————. *Social Structure and Personality*. New York: Free Press, 1964.

————. *The Social System*. Glencoe, Ill.: Free Press, 1951.

————. *Societies: Evolutionary and Comparative Perspectives*. Englewood Cliffs, N.J.: Prentice-Hall, 1966.

————. *Sociological Theory and Modern Society*. New York: Free Press, 1967.

————. *The Structure of Social Action*. New York: Free Press, 1968.

————. *The System of Modern Societies*. Englewood Cliffs, N.J.: Prentice-Hall, 1971.

Parsons, Talcott, and Edward A Shils, eds. *Toward a General Theory of Action*. Cambridge, Mass.: Harvard University Press, 1951.

Parsons, Talcott, with Robert F. Bales and Edward A. Shils. *Working Papers in the Theory of Action*. Glencoe, Ill.: Free Press, 1953.

Rex, John. *Key Problems of Sociological Theory*. London: RKP, 1961.

Rocher, Guy. *Talcott Parsons and American Sociology*. London: Nelson, 1974.

Ruschemeyer, D., ed. *Talcott Parsons: Beiträge zur soziologischen Theorie*. Neuwied-Berlin: 1964.

Skidmore, William. *Theoretical Thinking in Sociology*. Cambridge: Cambridge University Press, 1975.

Smith, Anthony D. *The Concept of Social Change: A Critique of the Functionalist Theory of Social Change*. London: RKP, 1971.

Strasser, Hermann. *Functionalism and Social Change*. Vienna: Inst. für Hohere Studien, 1977.

Sztompka, Piotr. *System and Function: Toward a Theory of Society*. New York: Academic Press, 1974.

Turner, Jonathan H. *The Structure of Sociological Theory*. 2d ed. Homewood, Ill.: Dorsey Press, 1978.

Wallace, Walter L., ed. *Sociological Theory: An Introduction*. Chicago: Aldine-Atherton, 1969.

Warschay, Leon H. *The Current State of Sociological Theory. A Critical Interpretation*. New York: McKay, 1975.

Zeitlin, Irving M. *Rethinking Sociology: A Critique of Contemporary Theory*. Englewood Cliffs, N.J.: Prentice-Hall, 1973.

INDEX

Page numbers in italics indicate the main discussion of an individual's ideas.

About the Author

JERZY SZACKI, one of Eastern Europe's most respected sociologists, is professor of sociology at the University of Warsaw. His books include *Durkheim, Tradition: A Survey of Problems,* and *Utopias.*